ASHGATE
RESEARCH
COMPANION

THE ASHGATE RESEARCH COMPANION
TO PLANNING THEORY

ASHGATE
RESEARCH
COMPANION

The *Ashgate Research Companions* are designed to offer scholars and graduate students a comprehensive and authoritative state-of-the-art review of current research in a particular area. The companions' editors bring together a team of respected and experienced experts to write chapters on the key issues in their speciality, providing a comprehensive reference to the field.

The Ashgate Research Companion to Planning Theory

Conceptual Challenges for Spatial Planning

Edited by

JEAN HILLIER
University of Newcastle Upon Tyne, UK

PATSY HEALEY
University of Newcastle Upon Tyne, UK

ASHGATE

Published by
Ashgate Publishing Limited
Wey Court East
Union Road
Farnham
Surrey GU9 7PT
England

Ashgate Publishing Company
Suite 420
101 Cherry Street
Burlington,
VT 05401-4405
USA

www.ashgate.com

British Library Cataloguing in Publication Data
The Ashgate research companion to planning theory :
   conceptual challenges for spatial planning.
   1. City planning. 2. Regional planning.
   I. Research companion to planning theory II. Hillier, Jean.
   III. Healey, Patsy.
   307.1'2-dc22

Library of Congress Cataloging-in-Publication Data
The Ashgate research companion to planning theory : conceptual challenges for spatial planning / [edited] by Jean Hillier and Patsy Healey.
    p. cm.
 Includes bibliographical references and index.
 ISBN 978-0-7546-7254-8 (hardback)
1. City planning. 2. Re███████████████████████████ley, Patsy.

 T166.A823 2010
 7.1'216--dc22

2009045791

)78 0 7546 7254 8

Mixed Sources
Product group from well-managed
forests and other controlled sources
www.fsc.org Cert no. SA-COC-1565
© 1996 Forest Stewardship Council

Printed and bound in Great Britain by
MPG Books Group, UK

Contents

List of Figures, Tables and Boxes

Figures

Tables

Box

Acknowledgements

We would like to acknowledge the enormous contribution to this project of Val Rose, our Commissioning Editor from Ashgate. It was Val's original idea for a Companion collection to the *Critical Essays in Planning Theory* (Ashgate, 2008) and her invitation to us which has evolved into this volume. Val has shown enormous faith in, and patience with, us and our authors as we have grappled with *Conceptual Challenges for Planning Theory*. Thank you, Val.

The editors also thank Professor Phil Powrie, Research Dean of Newcastle University's Faculty of Humanities and Social Science (HASS) who kindly funded a mini-conference in Newcastle in January 2008 from the NIASSH budget allocation for Research Groups – FRSG (£2,494.15). The funding permitted drafts of several of the papers to be presented to an audience of peer academics and Newcastle University HASS Early Career Researchers.

We also wish to thank everyone who participated in lively debate at the mini-conference and who gave feedback on the papers. We especially thank those who took the time to review written papers and make valuable comments. In particular, our thanks to Carolyn A. Fahey, John Forester, Andrew Law, Diana MacCallum, Abid Mehmood, John Sturzaker, Joris Van Wezemael.

Thanks to Theo van Looij for his patience with translating everyone's different chapter formats into something resembling the required Ashgate house style.

The chapter by Tore Sager is a modified version of his paper, Sager, T. (2009) 'Planners' role: torn between dialogical ideals and neo-liberal realities' *European Planning Studies* 17: 65–84. Thanks to Taylor and Francis for copyright permission.

The chapter by Manuel DeLanda (Chapter 8), *Cities and Nations,* is reproduced from Chapter 5 of DeLanda, M. (2006) *A New Philosophy of Society*. Continuum: London and New York (pages 94–119 plus notes pages 137–42) by kind permission of Continuum International Publishing Group.

The chapter by J.K. Gibson-Graham and Jenny Cameron (Chapter 10), *Community Enterprises: Imagining and Enacting Alternatives to Capitalism,* is reproduced from J.K. Gibson-Graham and J. Cameron (2007) *Social Alternatives*, Volume: 26(1), Special Issue on Counter Alternatives: pages 20–25 by kind permission of the Social Alternatives Collective, Queensland, Australia.

Julie Graham sadly passed away on 4th April 2010. We acknowledge the enormous contribution which Julie has made – and which her work will continue to make – to the disciplines of planning and geography in particular. We are honoured to be able to publish a co-authored chapter by Julie in this volume.

List of Contributors

Louis Albrechts is Emeritus Professor of Planning at the Department of Architecture, Urbanism and Planning of the University of Leuven. He was responsible for the Structure Plan Flanders (1992–1997) and scientific coordinator for the Transport Plan for Flanders (1999–2000). His recent research interests are in strategic spatial planning with regard to its implementation and its relation to political decision-making and power; creativity and diversity as a process; and sustainability.

Luca Bertolini is Professor of Urban and Regional Planning in the Department of Geography, Planning and International Development Studies at the Faculty of Social and Behavioural Sciences of the University of Amsterdam. His research and teaching focus on the integration of transport and land use planning, on methods for supporting the option-generation phase of the planning process, on concepts for coping with uncertainty in planning, and on ways of enhancing theory-practice interaction. Main publication topics include the redevelopment of station areas, planning for sustainable accessibility in urban regions, conceptualizing urbanism in the network society, and the application of evolutionary theories to planning. He is actively involved in a variety of international and national research and policy networks. He co-chairs the 'Transport Planning and Policy' thematic group of AESOP (the Association of European Schools of Planning), and is member of the editorial team of the journal *Planning Theory and Practice*. He leads the national research programs DESSUS (designing sustainable accessibility), KEI (development of station areas in a corridor context: economic significance and institutional incentives) and OBBRI (design and assessment of regional spatial and infrastructure plans).

Jenny Cameron is Associate Professor in the Discipline of Geography and Environmental Studies at the University of Newcastle, Australia. Along with J.K. Gibson-Graham, Jenny is a founding member of the Community Economies Collective (<www.communityeconomies.org>). She has conducted participatory action research working with marginalized groups to develop community economic projects. She has also collaborated with the Queensland Department of Local Government and Planning to evaluate, through action research, public participation in regional planning. Her most recent work has been with grassroots community enterprises, documenting the issues faced by these enterprises. She has published articles in journals that include *Geoforum*; *Gender, Place and Culture*; *Rethinking*

Marxism; and *Urban Policy and Research*. She is also committed to communicating research outcomes to a general audience and has produced a documentary on asset based community economic development and several resource kits.

Manuel DeLanda is the author of five philosophy books: *War in the Age of Intelligent Machines* (1991), *A Thousand Years of Nonlinear History* (1997), *Intensive Science and Virtual Philosophy* (2002), *A New Philosophy of Society* (2006), and *Philosophy, Emergence, and Simulation* (2009). He teaches two seminars at the University of Pennsylvania, Department of Architecture: 'Philosophy of History: Theories of Self-Organization and Urban Dynamics', and 'Philosophy of Science: Thinking about Structures and Material'.

J.K. Gibson-Graham is the pen-name of Julie Graham (Professor of Geography, University of Massachusetts Amherst) and Katherine Gibson (Professorial Fellow, Centre for Citizenship and Public Policy, University of Western Sydney). In 1992 Katherine and Julie adopted a joint name to honor and enliven their longstanding collaboration. Their 1996 book *The End of Capitalism (As We Knew It): A Feminist Critique of Political Economy* was republished in 2006 by Minnesota Press along with its sequel *A Postcapitalist Politics*. They have co-edited collections with Stephen Resnick and Richard Wolff: *Class and Its Others* (2000) and *Re/Presenting Class* (2001).

Professor Dr Enrico Gualini was appointed Professor for Planning Theory and History at the Institute for Urban and Regional Planning of the Technische Universität Berlin in 2006. His academic career developed through experiences in research and teaching conducted at the Politecnico di Milano, the University of Dortmund, the University of Amsterdam, as well as through research experiences in other countries. His major interests are the policy dimension of spatial development processes, the 'social construction of space', emergent governance practices and their challenges for politics and institutions, and related planning-theoretical issues. His publications include '"Territorial cohesion" as a category of agency: the missing dimension in the EU spatial policy debate' *European Journal of Spatial Development*, March 2008(28); *Framing Strategic Urban Projects: Learning from Current Experiences in European Urban Regions* (co-edited with W.G.M. Salet, 2007).

Maarten Hajer has been a Professor of Political Science and Public Policy at the University of Amsterdam since 1998. He is a Member of the Amsterdam School for Social Science Research (ASSR) and of AMIDSt (Amsterdam Institute of Metropolitan and International Development Studies), and one of the founders of the Amsterdam Centre for Conflict Studies (ACS). Among his publications are *The Politics of Environmental Discourse* (1995); *Living with Nature* (1999; edited together with Frank Fischer); *Deliberative Policy Analysis – Understanding Governance in the Network Society* (2003, edited together with Henk Wagenaar) and *Authoritative Governance: Policy Making in the Age of Mediatization* (2009). In October 2008 he was appointed Director of the Dutch 'Planbureau voor de Leefomgeving', the Cabinet's assessment and policy analysis agency on environment, nature conservation and land use planning, while continuing his professorship at the UvA part time.

Patsy Healey is Emeritus Professor in the School of Architecture, Planning and Landscape at Newcastle University, UK. She is a specialist in planning theory and the practice of planning and urban regeneration policies. She has undertaken research on how planning strategies work out in practice and on partnership forms of neighbourhood regeneration experiences. Recent books include *Collaborative Planning: Shaping Places in Fragmented Societies* (1997, 2nd edn 2006) and *Urban Complexity and Spatial Strategies* (2007). She was Senior Editor of the journal *Planning Theory and Practice* until 2009. Her new book, *Making Better Places* will be published by Palgrave Macmillan in 2010.

Jean Hillier is Professor of Town and Country Planning at Newcastle University, UK, where she teaches planning theory and professional ethics. Her research interests lie in developing Deleuzean-inspired planning theory and a methodology for strategic practice in conditions of uncertainty. She is also interested in narrative complexity theories and draws inspiration from Deleuze, Guattari, Foucault and Latour, et al. in analyzing planning decisions and processes. She is Managing Editor of the international journal *Planning Theory*. Recent publications include the three volumes, edited with Patsy Healey, *Critical Essays in Planning Theory* (2008) to which this book is the Companion; *Stretching Beyond the Horizon: On Governance, Space and Time* (2007); 'Interplanary practice: towards a Deleuzean-inspired methodology for creative experimentation in strategic spatial planning', in van den Broeck J. et al. *Empowering the Planning Fields: Ethics, Creativity and Action* (2008); 'Do we know what a body can do? Emergent subjectivities in Another Place' *Rhizomes*, Issue 17(winter); 'Assemblages of Justice: the "ghost ships" of Graythorp' *IJURR* (2009).

Richie Howitt is Professor of Human Geography, Department of Environment and Geography, Macquarie University, Sydney. He teaches in the planning, environmental and geography programmes and has contributed to major social impact studies in Queensland and the Northern Territory. He leads Macquarie's postgraduate SIA programme. His research deals with the social impacts of mining on indigenous peoples and local communities, and generally is concerned with the interplay across scales of social and environmental justice, particularly in relation to Indigenous rights. He received the Australian Award for University Teaching (Social Science) in 1999 and became Fellow of the Institute of Australian Geographers in 2004.

Margo Huxley is currently a Visiting Research Fellow in Geography at Queen Mary, University of London. Previously, she has been Senior Lecturer in the Department of Town and Regional Planning, University of Sheffield, and before that at RMIT University, Melbourne, the University of Melbourne, and the University of New England, NSW, teaching in urban studies, public policy and urban planning. Her academic background is in English and History, Urban Planning and Geography and she has worked as, among other things, a freelance music journalist, and in government and private planning practice. Her research interests include historical examinations of spatial planning and land use control as forms of Foucauldian governmentality and technologies of subjectification; gender and the built environment; community activism, residential protest groups and resistance to urban development projects.

Nikos Karadimitriou is a Lecturer in Planning and Property Development and Programme Director of the MSc in Urban Regeneration at the Bartlett School of Planning, UCL. He is a founding member of the 'AESOP Complexity and Planning' Thematic Group. His latest research focuses on the way complexity theory can transform our understanding of spatial planning as well as the implications of the application of complexity theory to planning practice. In his recently published work he draws on ideas from complexity theory to examine how space, place and heritage are socially constructed in regeneration areas in Manchester and London. Currently he is involved in a project comparing regeneration practices in the UK, the Netherlands and France with a view to developing a better understanding of the links between social policy, regeneration and housing provision. Nikos' past projects have been funded by the ESRC, the HBF, the NHBC and the British Council-France.

Gaim James Lunkapis is a Lecturer in the School of Social Sciences, Universiti Malaysia Sabah and is currently completing his Ph.D. at Macquarie University. He was trained as a Physical Geographer with a B.Sc. in Geography, MA in Urban and Regional Planning and an MSc in Remote Sensing and GIS. His career commenced as State Town Planner. He was Project Manager and Research Officer for the DANCED-Malaysian sponsored projects, the Integrated Coastal Zone Management (ICZM) and the Environmental Local Plan (ELP) for Sabah. It was in these roles that he had the opportunity to work with local and international researchers to look at land use and natural resources governance from different perspectives. This influenced his research outlook for his post-graduate studies. He had unique opportunities to sharpen his research skills through several collaborative research initiatives and later developed a keen interest in applying Social Impact Assessment and Community Mapping as a tool for participatory planning in the spirit of coexistence and sustainability.

David Pinder is Reader in Geography at Queen Mary, University of London. His research focuses on urbanism and city cultures, and he has written about the utopian visions of modernist and avant-garde movements in twentieth-century Western Europe, especially the situationists; and about artistic practices, urban interventions and the politics of space. He is the author of *Visions of the City: Utopianism, Power and Politics in Twentieth Century Urbanism* (2005), and a co-editor of *Cultural Geography in Practice* (2003). He is also reviews editor of *Cultural Geographies*, and guest edited a theme issue of that journal on 'Arts of urban exploration' (2005).

John Pløger is Associate Professor at ENSPAC (the Department of Environmental, Social and Spatial Change) at Roskilde University, Denmark. His work includes published and forthcoming articles on 'agonism and strife', 'contested urbanism', 'the eventalization of city space', 'fluid urban planning' and 'urban design'. His research fields and interests also include neo-pragmatism, architecture and social space, strategic urban planning, and (first and last) the meaningful city, Michel Foucault and Georg Simmel.

Ananya Roy is Professor of City and Regional Planning at the University of California, Berkeley, where she also serves as Co-Director of the Global Metropolitan Studies Center and Education Director of the Blum Center for Developing Economies. Roy's research has been concerned with the political economy and politics of urban development in the cities of the global South, with a particular emphasis on socio-spatial formations of inequality. She is the author of *City Requiem, Calcutta: Gender and the Politics of Poverty* (2003) and co-editor of *Urban Informality: Transnational Perspectives from the Middle East, South Asia, and Latin America* (2004). Her most recent work studies issues of poverty and development at a global scale and will be published in the forthcoming book, *Poverty Capital: Microfinance and the Frontiers of Millennial Development* (2010).

Tore Sager is Professor in the Department of Civil and Transport Engineering at the Norwegian University of Science and Technology, Trondheim, Norway. His research is mostly directed at the interfaces between institutional economics, decision processes in transport, and communicative planning theory (CPT). Sager has published on communicative planning theory in a dozen international academic journals. His main publications in English are *Communicative Planning Theory* (1994) and *Democratic Planning and Social Choice Dilemmas* (2002), and he is currently researching the moral responsibilities of planning theorists and the tensions between CPT and neo-liberalism. Sager recently directed an interdisciplinary project on mobility, resulting in two edited books: *Spaces of Mobility* (2008) and *The Ethics of Mobilities* (2008).

Erik Swyngedouw is Professor of Geography at Manchester University. He was Professor of Geography at Oxford University and Fellow of St Peter's College until 2006. He holds a Ph.D. in Geography and Environmental Engineering from the Johns Hopkins University and a Masters in Urban Planning and in Agricultural Engineering from the University of Leuven, Belgium. He has held visiting professorships at the Universities of Seville, Spain, the Aristotle University of Thessaloniki, Greece, the Catholic University of Leuven, Belgium, the University of Washington, Seattle, and York University, Toronto. His research interests include political-ecology, urban governance, democracy and political power, water and water resources, the political-economy of capitalist societies, the dynamics of urban and regional change, and the politics of globalization. He has published over 50 papers on these themes. Recent books include *Urbanising Globalisation* (co-edited, 2003), *Social Power and the Urbanization of Water – Flows of Power* (2004) and *In the Nature of Cities* (co-edited, 2006).

Joris E. Van Wezemael is an Associate Professor at the Geography Unit of the University of Freiburg, Switzerland. Before this, he was a Lecturer at the Economic Geography Division (University of Zurich), Visiting Scholar at the Global Urban Research Unit (Newcastle University, UK) and Director of the Centre for Research on Architecture, Society and the Built Environment (ETH Zurich). His teaching and research interests are focused on economic and political geography and on planning. Currently he guides several projects which conceptualize processes of collective decision-making in urban governance and planning, design, and housing policy on the basis of post-structural approaches to social complexity. The role of the material and technology in decision-making, the places of the political and the creation of knowledge in experimental practice define some key interests of his work.

Niraj Verma is Professor and Chair in the Department of Urban and Regional Planning at the University at Buffalo (The State University of New York). His work focuses on the role of rationality in planning and particularly on how sentiments and reasons can be integrated. This has taken him to American pragmatism and the philosophy of William James and led to concepts such as 'pragmatic rationality' and 'similarity' as ingredients of planning and management. Verma is the author of *Similarities, Connections, Systems* (1998) and editor of *Institutions and Planning* (2007) as well as many other articles, chapters, and papers. Some of his work has been translated into Italian, German, and Korean.

Wytske Versteeg is a researcher at the Department of Political Science of the University of Amsterdam. Her research interests include qualitative methods of public policy analysis, practices of conflict resolution and governance, environmental and social policy. She has contributed to Hajer's *Authoritative Governance: Policy Making in the Age of Mediatization* (2009) and several other volumes. She has published on visions of homelessness (in Dutch: *Dit is geen dakloze*), and is currently working on a book about trauma, political violence and art.

Introduction

Jean Hillier

Planning at yet Another Crossroads?

Planning theory for what? (Friedmann 2008: 248)

In 1973, the year in which I first studied a module in urban planning (with Derek Diamond at the London School of Economics), David Eversley[1] wrote *The Planner in Society: The Changing Role of a Profession*.[2] Eversley began his book by announcing that British town planning faced a crossroads, repeating the metaphor invoked by Lewis Keeble in 1961. Eversley described a crossroads at which planners had a choice of paths:

> *Straight ahead, perhaps, he (sic) can plod on with what he has been doing, and probably doing conscientiously enough: administering the law of the land. To one side: an abyss, a total disgrace, an abdication from social responsibility, the planner at the bottom of the heap and the scapegoat for all the evils of society. But in other directions, the road points to the possibility that the planner may be on the brink of greatness: a long, hard climb, not to a height where his judgment is unassailable, and not so far removed from the realities of the urban scene that he need no longer communicate. (1973: 304)*

Besides there being far more women planners and those from minority ethnic backgrounds than in Eversley's day, can we tell which path planners have taken since 1973? Clearly, many have chosen to 'plod on'; a few may have fallen into the abyss (as authors such as Jon Gower Davis (1974) and Peter Hall (1982) describe); and a few may have achieved Eversley's 'greatness' (such as Pierre Clavel and

---

1   David Eversley was Chief Strategic Planner at the new Greater London Council from 1969–1972.

2   I admit to not having read Eversley's book at the time, being far more influenced by another text published that same year: David Harvey's *Social Justice and the City*.

Norman Krumholz in the US).[3] But this is to exclude other definitions of 'greatness', non-Western planning and planners and, in particular, the role of planning theory.

Almost 40 years later, 'planning' in Britain has become more than the town and country planning of Eversley's time,[4] as the Overall Introduction to *Critical Essays in Planning Theory* (Hillier and Healey 2008a) and the readings in the three volumes clearly indicate. The 'planning idea' (Hillier and Healey 2008a: ixv), at the beginning of the twenty-first century, is committed to a focus on the relations between theory and practice; to an increasing internationalization of knowledge of planning as theorized and practised; to an openness to intellectual ideas from other disciplines; and to a recognition of the importance of power and politics (Hillier and Healey 2008a).

Theorists and practitioners have always been faced with uncertainty, though positivists might not have admitted it in public! Such theorists and practitioners in the past sought robust laws and principles grounded in well-tested scientific propositions, which dealt with uncertainty by reducing its dimensions to those which could be managed, or rendered certain. Today, however, at a time of potentially radical changes in the ways in which humans interact with their environments – changes brought about through financial crises and resulting lack of investment and development in property; changes brought about through environmental crises of floods, droughts and global warming – the *raison d'être* of spatial planning faces substantial conceptual and empirical challenges. If one accepts the broad mission of spatial planning as being stewardship of the future wellbeing of the planet – comprising humans, non-humans and their natural and constructed environments – then planning is faced with challenges posed by both the potential and the limitations of that mission. Whilst I would not argue that planning is at yet another crossroads, I do suggest that the planning field, and planning theorists in particular, should be aware of some of the conceptual challenges which lie in wait. Attempts have been made for the past 25 years to live and plan with uncertainty, rather than to reduce it, but much more work still needs to be done.

This volume, the *Ashgate Research Companion to Planning Theory*, is Companion to the three volumes, *Critical Essays in Planning Theory (CEPT)* (Hillier and Healey 2008a). This consists of a series of papers and excerpts from books which, as editors, Patsy Healey and I regarded as being influential in the development of planning theory. The *Companion* does not, therefore, historically trace the field of planning theory. Rather, it seeks to interrogate planning theory in more complex ways, considering a wide range of conceptual challenges which the chapter authors regard as important for theorists of planning to engage with in the early twenty-first century. The chapters thus focus on important current and likely future conceptual challenges for spatial planning theory and practice.

As Nigel Taylor (2003: 93) indicates, concepts are fundamental to both planning theory and planning practice, 'for they specify what, in its actions, town planning is trying to *do*' (emphasis in original). As Taylor argues, debate is inevitable over

---

3   See Clavel, et al. (1980); Clavel (1986); Krumholz and Forester (1990); Krumholz and Clavel (1994).
4   In 1960s US, planning was already much more than 'town and country planning'.

which concepts are more relevant and/or important; over which interpretations of the same concept (such as informality, economy, sustainability and so on) are more 'sound', and indeed over the meaning of 'concept'. The chapters in this volume engage planning theory and practice from a variety of perspectives, offering both contemporary analyses of planning itself – of 'planning ideas and planning practices' – and critical commentaries on several key issues with which planning practice and planners interact.

The authors focus on important conceptual challenges for planning theory, including new approaches to substantive (concerned with the substance of what the planning field deals with) and procedural (concerned with the processes of planning) questions; new and re-theorisations of uncertainty, conflict and political complexities. A key question for the early twenty-first century is, perhaps, not so much what planning theory is, but what can planning theory do?

Before I continue, it is important to clarify my usage of the terms 'spatial planning' and 'planning practice'. 'Spatial planning' is a predominantly European term which refers to the processes used by agencies (in both public and private sectors) in deliberate attempts to influence the spatial distributions of humans and non-humans and of various land-using activities. As such, spatial planning includes urban planning, regional planning, producing and implementing national spatial plans and also (in the EU) transnational plans. During the twentieth century, the domain of urban planning expanded to include economic development planning, community social planning and environmental planning issues. The EU Torremolinos Charter (1983) definition of spatial planning is: '[r]egional/spatial planning gives geographical expression to the economic, social, cultural and ecological policies of society. It is at the same time a scientific discipline, an administrative technique and a policy developed as an interdisciplinary and comprehensive approach directed towards a balanced regional development and the physical organisation of space according to an overall strategy.' (CEMAT 1983: 5)

Land-use planning (also 'planning' or 'zoning') involves the 'scientific, aesthetic and orderly disposition of land, resources, facilities and services with a view to securing the physical, economic, social and environmental efficiency, health and well-being of urban and rural communities' (CEMAT 2007: 17).

I regard 'planning practice' as an activity of spatial planning undertaken in different parts of the world by professionals trained in disciplines including planning, architecture, engineering, surveying, public administration and technical drafting, all of whom I loosely label as 'planners'.

Conceptual challenges for spatial planning practice include, 'what might it mean to plan in circumstances of complexity?' and 'what issues could planning theorists think about to help practices of planning and governance?'

In *CEPT* we argued that most 'theories' are actually associations of ideas, discussions and debates which are 'in conversation' with each other (Healey and Hillier 2008). They offer perspectives for viewing aspects of the world; a reasonable definition since the classical Greek origins of *theōria* meant 'visual sight' (as explained below). John Forester (2004) takes this further with his analogy of planning theory as a telescope through which we can look at an issue. Our ability to see that issue clearly depends on the equipment we use – in this case, the theoretical frame we use for the questions we ask and how we understand the answers to those questions. As Forester suggests, when our theoretical telescope is good, it lets us see and understand more about the issue, its context and what we might be able to do about it. When that telescope is bad, we put it to the wrong eye, we use it backwards or forget to take the cover off the lens, it can give us a headache, eyestrain and a very confused picture.

Debates about planning ideas and theories are not conducted amongst a closed elite of dedicated academics, even though it may sometimes seem like it. Planning theory discussions are situated in the contexts of the intellectual environments, lived experiences and values of the time they are written. As a result, planning theories demonstrate many different philosophical and other referents and styles of argumentation. Readers may be tempted to conclude, after reading the various contributions to this volume, that planning theory is too slippery a term to be of much significance. As this Introduction and the chapter authors illustrate, there is a very wide range of theoretical approaches available. It is not our aim as editors to choose between approaches; to 'recommend' one over another; to fix the meaning of 'planning theory' or its vocabulary, but to open up different perspectives to provoke and stimulate readers to further investigate relationships between planning theories and perspectives from other disciplines and also relationships between planning theories and their roles in relation to planning practice. As Taylor (1998: 167) points out, there are different kinds of theories, posing and answering different kinds of questions in situations where more than one theory is often of relevance.

As editors, we believe that engaging in critical debate in and around planning theory 'is essential to the vitality and continued relevance of planning as a profession' (Friedmann, 2003: 9) and moreover, that there is a huge difference between treating theory as a dogmatic credo and as a guide to understanding action. We argue that planning theories should ask fundamental questions about a world which is never fully knowable and about the role of planning in such an unknowable world. We recognize the differing natures of 'planning' as a group of practices, including spatial planning, economic development planning, regional planning, transport planning and often urban regeneration, each of which may have referents in specialist theories and approaches. We have no space to include what would be a long list of conceptual challenges for all the specialized areas of planning. Our approach must inevitably lie in a broad engagement with the entangled terrains of planning as a disciplinary multiplicity, which, for our purposes, we term 'spatial planning': a perspective which draws out the spatial dimensions of how to think about deliberate efforts to manage and develop place qualities and to pay attention to spatial connectivities.

I find it helpful to focus on the interrelation of praxis between spatial planning theory and practice. The concept of praxis was one of Aristotle's three basic activities of free men in the *Nicomachean Ethics* (*c*.350BC). Praxis was also important to Marxist thinking, exemplified by Karl Marx's famous comment, in the 11th *Thesis on Feuerbach*, that 'philosophers have only interpreted the world in various ways; the point is to change it' (cited in Bernstein, 1971: 13), while Paulo Friere (1970) regarded praxis as a synthesis of theory and practice in which each informs the other. Adopting the above connotations of praxis I ask, what might be the role of planning theories as a field of debate about the purpose and nature of spatial planning? Should they reflect or critique planning practice? Should they inform planning practice? Should they theorize understanding and explanation of what exists? Should they theorize what can be?, what might be?, what ought to be? Should they challenge and/or liberate ways of thinking about planning, about societies, and so on?

John Friedmann (2008) suggests that an important role for theorists is to translate knowledge and ideas generated in other fields into that of planning. For this volume, we have invited contributions from authors who have a particular interest in issues of spatiality and who have strong theoretical foundations for their work. We have especially invited authors from beyond what is often narrowly defined as the 'planning' field because we find their perspectives on space particularly stimulating and relevant. We have also aimed for a range of authorial ages and experiences, geographical spread and insights (although we recognize that we have tended to favour the global North-West).

The authors theorize the conceptual challenges which spatial planning might face in contexts of uncertainty, diversity and incommensurability.[5] The very nature of a conceptual challenge is that it questions traditional assumptions and ways of being, knowing and doing. Such challenges act as catalysts to help us to see spatial planning in a different way: to learn from different ontologies, to reflect on what planning practitioners are doing and even to reconsider reflexively the nature and purpose of planning itself.

From their different disciplinary traditions and theoretical frames, the authors explore different ways of understanding the field of spatial planning, networks, complexity and so on, through different ontological and epistemological lenses. Such 'free-thinking' offers a potentially rich collection of material. We have encouraged authors to go beyond the current boundaries of reading and understanding spatial planning theory and practice. We hope that this encourages readers to do similarly. Free-thinking, then, begins with a critical response to a particular concept, issue or text. It considers what else might be thought; what other options might there be, and how might such options perform – by including or excluding certain elements. It offers an evolving conversation with planning theory and practice about their meanings and values.

By involving scholars from disciplines other than that of spatial planning, we invite problematization of the planning project from the outside as well as the inside. A widely-held 'inside' view is that 'planning theory and practice are posited upon (largely unquestioned and overgeneralized) suppositions – often exported from the UK to the rest of the world – that space and environment have causal effects on individuals and citizens, populations and territories; and that spatial planning

---

5   Abstract values, such as equality and liberty, may be regarded as incommensurable in the sense that they are irreducible to a common comparative measure. Scientific incommensurability involves similar comparative irreducibility between rival theories or paradigms (see Feyerabend 1978; Kuhn 1983).

systems, and planners as individuals, are (potentially) capable of bringing about significant positive social, economic and environmental outcomes' (Huxley 2007a: 156). It follows, therefore, that with better understandings of situations and contexts, more evidence-based policies and more able practitioners, spatial planning can become both more efficient in its shaping of places and more responsive to local needs (Huxley 2007a: 158). Such comments, however, fail to recognize what is, in several international administrations, a large and important gap between planning 'systems' as legislated and planning activities as performed.

I cite Huw Thomas (2007: 333): 'much of what is written as planning theory explicitly or implicitly takes as its focus the planning system broadly as it is'. If we really are looking for radical changes in our societies and economies, Thomas (2007: 334) suggests that we need to lose a concern with 'planning systems and institutions for their own sakes' in order to free up possibilities of thinking about radical transformation. As Thomas continues, '[w]ithin such an analysis the planning system may sometimes emerge as relatively unimportant, or a potential diversion from more promising areas of struggle', or thinking about social or economic processes (such as patriarchy, racism, capitalism and so on). One of the conceptual challenges for spatial planning praxis is, therefore, to 'require planning thinkers not to take the usefulness of planning as a given and ... cause them to challenge ... its very existence' (Yiftachel 2001: 7, cited in Thomas 2007: 333).

By inviting contributions from the outside of planning we aim both to make visible the limits of traditional planning theories – developing, in particular, from Volume 3 of *CEPT* – and to illustrate how, by thinking about new issues, or by regarding issues in different ways, through different theoretical lenses, we might begin a 'counter-discourse' (Law-Yone 2007: 321) which 'liberates us to think about the nature of the social changes we are struggling for, the complex ways and many fronts on which such a struggle needs to be waged (in general terms) and the particular opportunities offered in specific circumstances' (Thomas 2007: 334).

This is a book for planning practitioners interested in a theory-informed practice and for graduate students and academics interested in thinking about some of the conceptual challenges which are relevant to issues of spatiality, spatial planning and governance. Patsy Healey and I offer this book as a volume in which different theoretical frames approach and encounter each other, in a spirit of experiment and innovation, folding lines of the outside with those of more 'mainstream' spatial planning. In our Introductions to the three Parts of the book, Patsy (Part 1) and I (Parts 2 and 3) outline the purpose of the particular Part, key debates and current understandings relating to issues discussed and the conceptual challenges raised.

In the remainder of this Overall Introduction, I locate this Companion volume in a chronological trajectory of volumes which have debated the state-of-the-art of planning theory, including the *Critical Essays in Planning Theory* (Hillier and Healey 2008a) which this volume accompanies. I then discuss some definitions of planning, which themselves form a conceptual challenge for the field, before flagging some of the challenges which are addressed in various contributions. I outline the structure of the volume before concluding that whilst planning theory might not be at a crossroads as such, it does need to engage with several important conceptual challenges.

A Trajectory of Companions: Context Matters

[T]he need for different kinds of theories shifts as societies change. (Sandercock, 1998: 104)

Planning practice is concerned with 'imagining the future' (Healey and Hillier 2008). Such planning work involves 'taking risks, the consequences of which can be thought about, but cannot be known' (Healey 2008: 28). The forces impacting transformation of the planet have changed and are continuing to change dramatically, yet spatial planning 'systems' across the world appear to have changed little (UN-HABITAT 2009). If planning practices are to be relevant in dynamic circumstances, there is a need to develop and/or to reference theories which will help practitioners to understand and cope with the messiness of uncertainty. On this point, context matters. 'One cannot do anything, least of all speak, without determining (in a manner that is not only theoretical, but practical and performative) a context' (Derrida 1988: 136).

Our Introductions to the three volumes of *Critical Essays (CEPT)* offer a chronologically-based overview of the contexts in which the approaches contained in the 'essays' were theorized. Several of the approaches have themselves formed intellectual contexts for current theorizations, either as re-recognition (such as Jamesian or Deweyan pragmatism), development (such as systems theories and complexity theories) or opposition (poststructuralism in opposition to structuralism, posthumanism to humanism and so on). 'Boundaries' between some theories may become blurred or destabilized and claims may be made for the value of metatheoretical perspectives (see, for example, the review by Del Casino Jr et al. 2000).

This volume adds to a growing series of 'companions' to the debates and conversations which comprise planning theory. There are clear differences between conceptualizations of planning and its 'worlds' evident in the various collections and conversations. For instance, the views associated with the 1970s and early 1980s that 'planning' was a spatially Euclidian, fixed, self-contained, unique entity, were increasingly rejected and replaced with the conceptual challenge of places as 'relationally constituted, polyvalent processes embedded in broader sets of social relations' (Jessop et al. 2008: 390). More recently, space is often regarded as an actor (or actant)[6] entangled in meshworks or rhizomes of relations of potentially unbounded connectivities (see, for example, Massey 2005; Hillier 2007). Space, therefore, is one among several factors influencing outcomes, rather than the sole determinant of outcomes, which some early twentieth-century planning writers used to think (see Huxley 2007a).

In 1978, Robert W. Burchell and George Sternlieb's *Planning Theory in the 1980s: A Search for Future Directions*, consisted of 25 contributions by 29 authors, all of

---

6   An actant, after Greimas (1966), implies either a human or non-human entity. In actor-network theory, after Latour (1996), the term actant also avoids the problem of restricting actors to acting and systems to behaving, by conjoining both agent and agency.

whom were based in the USA and all bar two were male. The aim of the volume was to 'attempt to provide insight to future directions for planning theory of the next decade' (Burchell and Hughes 1978: xvii). The main themes running through the papers reflect the major concerns at the time; some of which seem rather dated 30 years later, whilst others retain their relevance. For instance, 'the gap between the planner's capacities to deliver and the nominal goal structure' (Sternlieb 1978: xi) still exists – though for different reasons to the 1970s – but the 'long-range perspective' (Sternlieb 1978: xii) has become far less specific and rigid than was typical at that time.

There was a belief that 'the environment and its preservation through correct use is the prime basis of planning' and that 'rationality, a systems orientation, and non-biased, apolitical perspectives' (both quotations Burchell and Hughes 1978: xxiv and xxv) should dominate the tenets of environmental planning. Compare these assertions with the far more contingency-based, relational view of nature in this present volume. Similarly, in 1978, Burchell and Hughes could state, without fear of challenge, that 'the "commonsense" of planning rests on maximum utilisation of resources and perfect equilibrium of economics' (p. xxxi); a continuation of the post-World War II 'American Dream' of an upward trajectory of material and moral progress achievable through rational scientific management. (See Hillier and Healey 2008b, Part III.)

At about the same time in the UK, a conference was held, which resulted in the text, *Planning Theory: Prospects for the 1980s* (1982), edited by Patsy Healey, Glen McDougall and Michael J. Thomas. There were 18 authors, of whom 5 were women, and an overlapping 5 from outside the UK (Denmark, Netherlands, Israel, South Africa). In contrast to the 1978 anthology edited by Burchell and Sternlieb, with its emphasis on a rational social choice of development trajectories, a key objective of the 1982 collection was to find ways to have a debate between what was identified as a plurality of positions in planning theory.

The editors' position paper (Healey et al. 1982) recognized the critiques of the rationalist and traditional physical design conceptions of the planning project, the rise of neo-Marxist political economy critique and the entry of Habermasian critical theory into the discussion of planning issues in an Anglo-Saxon context. Where the editors found a certain amount of confusion between theories and a 'general ignorance' among theorists of others' points of view (Healey et al. 1982: 2), there today seems to be a more general acceptance that our plural world calls for a multiple approach to planning which lends itself to theoretical diversity.

By 1996, and Seymour Mandelbaum, Luigi Mazza and Robert W. Burchell's *Explorations in Planning Theory*, the 'cast' of 31 authors included 13 from countries other than the USA and 8 women. The legitimate existence of multiple planning theories – or what Mandelbaum (1996: xiii) referred to as 'a capacious rhetorical form' – was recognized, as was the importance of the as-yet-incipient 'communicative turn' (Innes 1995) in planning theory, based, as several chapters illustrate, on the authors' empirical research experience.

Recurring themes in the 1996 papers included what was known as 'the structure/agency debate', a debate about the dominance of structures (especially the capitalist system) or agents and what might accordingly be possible for planners and planning. A second major theme was that of plurality (not yet termed 'multiplicity'). A plurality of lifeworlds, of intentions and expectations was recognized, as was the potential of Habermasian-influenced consensus-building as a way forward in the theorization and practical design of planning processes. The theory-practice relation had also taken a different 'turn' by 1996. Several of the theories expounded in the volume were grounded in empirical research or experience of practice, notably in discursive forms; of talk, ritual, protocol, routine and so on.

The 1997 collection, *Town Planning into the 21st Century*, edited by Andrew Blowers and Bob Evans, presents a set of planning-related responses[7] to the dominant 'Thatcherite' period of governance in the UK from 1989–97.[8] Cliff Hague predicted that town planning in the twenty-first century would become 'an exercise in managing change rather than imposing comprehensive designs' (1997: 139) under the three market-economy-rooted influences of recession, resources and plurality. Hague (1997: 140–1) envisaged the central state continuing to facilitate the operation of a relatively free market, with planning practitioners in correspondingly weak bargaining positions in times of recession; a prediction which appears to have come true in 2009. Similarly, Hague's (1997: 149–50) anticipation that planning 'will become more broad-based, promotional and flexible', requiring 'imaginative thinking' and 'a vision of new possibilities' also holds.

Planning Futures: New Directions for Planning Theory (2002) edited by Philip Allmendinger and Mark Tewdwr-Jones, continues this practice-based, communicative theoretical vein. 'Intentionally' taking collaborative planning theory as a focus (see *CEPT*, Volume 3, Part 1), the aim of the collection was to 'review' the then-current 'state of planning theory'[9] combined with 'critiques of the practical concerns of professional planning discussed within a strong theoretical context' (Allmendinger and Tewdwr-Jones 2002: xi). The theory-practice relation remains a strong focus in this 'post-positivist' collection.

The set of *Critical Essays in Planning Theory* (*CEPT*) (Hillier and Healey 2008a) – this volume's Companion – demonstrated how planning theories have been open to the intellectual waves and political movements which have swept across the social (and more recently, the physical) sciences since the mid-twentieth century, from the management-science influenced thinking of the US Chicago School, through cybernetic systems thinking in the 1960s, to structuralist political economy in the 1970s, to the post-modernist and other 'posts' of the 1980s and 1990s, the 'cultural turn' and post-structuralism in the 1990s and the interest in 'complexity' in the 2000s. As we wrote, '[t]his openness creates huge challenges in 'reading'

---

7   Presented originally at a conference in 1992.

8   Thatcherite neo-economic liberalism, inspired by Friedrich Hayek, was replicated in the 1980s and 1990s in various countries as, for example, Reaganism (after Ronald Reagan, President of the USA), Rogernomics (after Roger Douglas, Finance Minister in New Zealand) and Howardism (after John Howard, Prime Minister of Australia).

9   The volume is predominantly UK-related with 8 of the 12 authors working in British universities at the time.

planning theory contributions, as authors rarely have space to explain adequately how their ideas and vocabularies derive from these 'waves', and there are all kinds of time-lag effects, as foundational ideas of one group of authors are rediscovered and given a different colouring by a later group' (Healey and Hillier 2008: xiii). The 'porosity' of the field, its very openness, gives planning theory a capaciousness which helps to create a sensitivity to the multiple dimensions of the manifestations of planning as a practical activity.

In the final volume of the *CEPT* set, we offered some recent inspirations in order to give a sense of how ideas about the nature and purposes of planning theory and planning practices might evolve. In the twenty-first century planning theorists and practitioners are increasingly engaging issues and 'problems' which severely challenge many of their traditional assumptions. Planning theory and practice have to cope with uncertainty, insurgence, complexity and wildness through imagination and experimentation in attempts to understand events and to shape futures. Meaning and action, set in a context of extensive, often contested, relations, perform in complex and unanticipated ways. Meanings, and planning theories, are not fixed, static entities, but are likely to change as new interpretations emerge.

In introducing discussion of the latest debates and developments in planning theory in Volume 3 of *CEPT*, we stated that '[w]e have no crystal ball to predict which of the several different theoretical strands will 'travel' into the future to form new paradigms' (Hillier and Healey 2008c: 405). In this present volume, we have asked authors to identify and engage with what might be some of the main conceptual ontological and epistemological challenges, with regard to social, political, economic and environmental issues with which planning theorists and practitioners could engage.

Some Definitions and Questions for Planning Theory and Practice

> *Theoretical does not, of course, mean abstract. From my point of view, it means reflexive. (Roland Barthes, cited in Young 1981: 1, emphasis in original)*

Spatial planning theory and practice attempt to cope with complexity and uncertainty through imagination and experimentation in what is increasingly recognized as 'a world of continuous variation, becoming and chance' (Doel 1996: 421) rather than of stability and predictability. If the world comprises multiple fluxes and flows, how might spatial planners seek to affect and 'manage' environments in undecidable situations? Can we develop theories and practices which rely less on closure and more on discovery and provisionality, which reveal potentialities and opportunities and which open up difficult ambiguities (such as of conflict or agonism) and so on?

As the essays in Volume 1 of *CEPT* (Hillier and Healey 2008b) indicate, spatial planning practice was traditionally considered either without recourse to theory or as an application of theory. In the everyday world of spatial planning practice, planners are more likely to rely on intuition or practical wisdom (phronesis) than explicitly on planning theory (Sanyal 2002). Yet, as Campbell and Fainstein (2003: 2) point out, this intuition may actually be assimilated theory or 'cumulative professional knowledge'. One of the key roles of theory, therefore, is to stimulate critical reflection and constructive reflexivity in practitioners – and academics.

But can 'theory' be easily defined? The online *Etymology Dictionary* (Harper 2001) defines 'theory' as 'conception, mental scheme, contemplation, speculation, a looking at', from the Greek *theōria*, as mentioned above. Someone who practised *theōria* was a *theōros*: a 'spectator'.[10] If theory entails looking at something and proposing or conceiving a mental scheme about it which unconceals it (see, for example, Gadamer 1999), I suggest that it involves speculation. To speculate may be defined as 'to use the powers of the mind, as in conceiving ideas, drawing inference and making judgments' (Hillier 2007: 76), all of which are incorporated in theorizing planning.

A theory, typically, was not regarded as 'a theory at all, until it has been used ['tested'] in practice over a considerable period of time' (Reade 1987: 156). More recently, recognition of the innovative, experimental practices engaged by some spatial planners has led to practice inspiring theory, as indicated in *CEPT* Volume 3 in particular. I agree with Deleuze's view that 'practice is a set of relays from one theoretical point to another, and theory is a relay from one practice to another. No theory can develop without eventually encountering a wall, and practice is necessary for piercing this wall' (in Foucault and Deleuze 1972: 3).

Rather than viewing spatial planning as simply a process or collection of policies, for instance, I have found it helpful to regard planning as a complex, performative multiplicity of practices, knowledges, human and non-human actants. Along with Patsy Healey, I am committed to an interactive relation between theory and practice. This relation often appears to be under challenge, however. It sometimes seems that the gap between theorists and practitioners resembles a yawning abyss, with neither group really understanding the other. Moreover, what actually *is* planning practice? Is it the planning of societal development, or the development and delivery of any public policy programme, or is it the planning of neighbourhoods, of cities and regions? What is the contribution of planning? Does it lie in an approach to government – perhaps a process idea of 'good governance' in general, or of transparent, inclusive, democratic, policy-driven government? Does it lie in the values about society which planning promotes, in considerations of social justice or cohesion, of environmental quality and sustainability, of economic vitality and 'competitiveness'? Or does the *raison d'être* of planning lie in how these sets of values are combined? And what happens when such planning ideas are

---

10   Rausch (1982, cited in McNeill, 1999: 263) suggests that *theōros* can have several different, though related, meanings of relevance to spatial planning: someone seeking advice from an oracle; an envoy; someone announcing a festival or event; an official with a local authority who oversees and enforces the observance of laws; a beholder.

promoted in situations where these values are themselves marginalized? How then might planning perform?

A major conceptual challenge is thus the definition of planning itself. In the Introduction to Part 1 of this volume, Patsy Healey describes planning as 'about dreaming alternate futures about place qualities, their potentials and possibilities'. But, as she continues, 'it is also about actively shaping futures and the practices, now and in the future, which might bring more desirable futures into being'.

John Friedmann (1987) emphasizes the wide range of conceptual definitions of planning; from operational definitions, identifying what lies at the core of planning practice, to formal conceptualizations involving action, processes of societal guidance and/or societal transformation. I offer a few general definitions of spatial planning below, in chronological order of publication. The definitions range from those which regard planning practice as having power to achieve futures to those which are more uncertain, but all embrace an orientation towards the future:

> *a forward-looking activity that selects from the past those elements that are useful in analysing existing conditions from a vantage point of the future – the changes that are thought to be desirable and how they might be brought about (John Friedmann 1987: 11);*

> *the exercise of deliberate forethought (Ernest Alexander 1992: 13, cited in Connell 2009: 86);*

> *the specification of a proposed future coupled with systematic intervention and/or regulation in order to achieve that future (David Byrne 2003: 174);*

> *a form of persuasive storytelling about the future (Jim Throgmorton 2003: 146);*

> *self-conscious collective efforts to re-imagine a city, urban region or wider territory and to translate the result into priorities for area investment, conservation measures, strategic infrastructure investments and principles of land use regulation. The term 'spatial' brings into focus the 'where of things', whether static or in movement; the protection of special 'places' and sites; the interrelations between different activities and networks in an area; and significant intersections and nodes in an area which are physically co-located (Patsy Healey 2004: 46, cited in Healey 2007: 3);*

> *the investigation of 'virtualities' unseen in the present; the speculation about what may yet happen; the temporary inquiry into what at a given time and place we might yet think or do and how this might influence socially and environmentally just spatial form (Jean Hillier 2007: 225);*

> *spatial planning is one of the few disciplines within social sciences that is preoccupied by not just understanding possible urban futures, but also*

finding ways of changing them in the pursuit of collectively agreed preferable futures (Simin Davoudi 2008: 230);

collective place-shaping efforts aimed to improve the qualities and connectivities of places into the future for the benefit of present and future publics and their potential values (Patsy Healey 2008: 3);

the objective of cultivating particular place qualities and encouraging the emergence of particular development trajectories (Patsy Healey 2008: 8).

This volume is concerned with conceptual challenges for planning theory – including concepts such as contingency, complexity, subjectivity, schemes of signification, creativity, etc. and the challenge of reconceptualizing or retheorizing planning practice – and for planning practice and its key concepts such as sustainability, multiculturalism and so on. We call for advances in both conceptual and empirical knowledges, which address theoretical and practical issues, if the future wellbeing of the planet and its inhabitants is to stand a chance of becoming more achievable.

Conceptual Challenges for Spatial Planning

Specific conceptual challenges for spatial planning are discussed by the various chapter authors throughout this volume. In what follows here, I highlight several, more general, conceptual challenges for readers to bear in mind. These challenges include problematizing planning itself, the values which underpin planning, theory-practice relations and planning ethics.

Conceptually Challenging the Paradox of Planning

Bernard Tschumi (1994) suggests that architecture is haunted by a 'strange paradox', which, I suggest, similarly haunts planning. This paradox is, in Tschumi's words, 'the impossibility of simultaneously questioning the nature of space and, at the same time, making or experiencing real space' (1994: 67). Can planners 'experience' real places and 'make ' real plans at the same time as they reflexively question the nature of space and the nature of planning as a practice which aims to manipulate space? I argue, following Tschumi (1994: 69), that planning constitutes the reality of subjective experience whilst this reality gets in the way of the overall concept of planning. Or, as Patsy Healey paraphrases, planners are always thinking about and making plans for possible futures while continually being dragged back to the messiness of 'going on in the world'. As a means of coping, planners, therefore, choose not to reflexively question either the nature of space or of planning practice. Planning is thus always incomplete. As such, does planning miss both the concept and the reality? Where is the junction between ideal planning and planning in reality?

I believe in the importance of planning theorists and practitioners attempting to confront the unthought of planning; that which definitively 'cannot be thought and yet must be thought' (Deleuze and Guattari 1994: 60, cited in Casarino 2002: xix). We can only grasp this paradox if planning, as a practice, is understood as constantly being influenced by the pressures of outside forces – whether in the form of the forces of capitalist exploitation (see Huxley and Gibson-Graham and Cameron, this volume), of colonialism (see Howitt and Lunkapis, this volume) or other forces.

Lost in the energy of action, practitioners may fail to ask what is the action for and why is it structured the way it is. How, then, does planning practice 'think itself' as practice? Casarino (2002: xxiii) suggests that there is a fissure of 'immanent interference' at the very heart of a practice; a zone of indiscernability between two distinct modalities: between a practice and its relation to itself as a practice. There is generally, to adapt Deleuze and Guattari's (1994: 1) words, too much desire to *do* planning to wonder what it *is*.

I advocate what Casarino (2002: xxv) terms 'the silent double questioning' of planning; a double questioning which is both a questioning of itself as a practice and of its practitioners and also a questioning of all the other practices and practitioners which come into active contact with planning. The problematization of planning practice and what it is, what it stands for (see below), would become an unavoidable problem, which should cause planning practice to reach beyond itself, to reflexively (Schön 1983) experiment with unthought possibilities.

Conceptually Challenging Planning Values

Spatial planning, wherever practised, is driven by a set of values which underpin its normative aims: what planning should be attempting to achieve. Such aims might include social justice, environmental protection or facilitation of economic markets and city 'competitiveness'. The task for planning practitioners would then be to provide the technical means (such as land use zoning, development management) to achieve these aims. It has traditionally not been regarded as the task of planning practitioners to debate the aims themselves (see Taylor 1998). Practice, in such a reading, often entails working within, rather than challenging, given social categories and, thereby, working with the social relations of power that produce/d those categories (see Dixon and Jones III 1998). One of the key contributions of planning theory (as demonstrated in *CEPT*) is/has been to pursue critical debates about just these issues.

Planning practice has been informed by progressive ideas (see the Introduction to Part 1, this volume; also Forester 1989; Fainstein 2000), typically about how to make people's lived environments better, especially the poor. As Pierre Clavel (1986) explained, progressive political leaders and planners have formulated redistributive policies, in which the design and implementation of planning activity is shared with grassroots organisations. Clavel regarded planning as a profession 'dedicated to visions and models that could be validated by catching the popular imagination' (1986: 18), rather than by marketing. Progressive planning is planning 'in the interests of the present populations' (Clavel 1986: 9) rather than 'business-backed managerialism' (p. 10) in support of the 'growth-oriented' programmes of developers, property investors and hoped-for, more affluent future populations. This is a statement which appears to directly contradict many recent urban regeneration programmes inspired by advocates of global competitiveness, such as Richard Florida (2000, 2002, 2004). Is much of today's, neo-economic influenced, urban regeneration, then, not 'progressive', or has the definition of 'progressive' changed? Moreover, as Huxley (2007a) indicates, planning, by itself, cannot effect permanent improvements in people's lives due to its inability to address the fundamental contradictions of capitalism.

A conceptual challenge for planning theorists and practitioners, therefore, is to problematize the assumptions which underlie key planning axioms. Very specifically, for instance, Le Corbusier's modulor, which has had a major influence on architecture, interior architecture and design, street design and furniture and so on, is a representation of an able-bodied, six-foot tall, Anglo-Saxon male (Estatopia, nd). The modulor is typical of the many universalizing assumptions about normality which planners make in both theory and practice.[11]

A second, generally unproblematized assumption underlying planning practice, is that planning is a 'good thing', which provides a better future, as in several of the definitions of planning above. Yet as Eisenschitz (2008) points out in detail, despite aims of social justice, such a 'better future' has not been associated with social reform, which is difficult to achieve through technical, physically-oriented means relating to land use. Eisenschitz (2008: 137) cites Peter Hall's 1972 assessment of some 25 years of town and country planning in England as 'the main distributive effect was to keep the poor, or a high proportion of them, poor' (Hall 1972: 267). The drivers behind such an outcome may well include some of the following forces as developed in many contexts:

- planning practice reduces economic impulses to spatial ones which are then given technical 'solutions' (Eisenschitz 2008: 139);
- planning practice reduces, or even evacuates, political impulses in its search for practical, technical outcomes (Blowers 1984; Swyngedouw 2005, 2007, this volume).

Back in 1844, Friedrich Engels identified the urban form of Manchester, with its segregation of rich and poor residential areas, as a product of private property ownership and political economic influences (2009: 86–7). Hunt argues that little has changed. In Manchester (and other cities of the global North West) gentrification programmes demolish working class neighbourhoods and privatize informal urban

---

11   See Gunder and Hillier (2009) for in-depth problematization of ten common planning universals, including 'sustainability', 'smart growth', 'multiculturalism' and so on.

spaces in the name of regeneration. 'While Manchester's city centre glistens amidst a revitalized historic core, glitzy bars and restaurants, high-rise hotels and buy-to-let penthouses, critics complain that the communities of Moss Side and Gorton have failed to benefit' (Hunt 2009: 27). One could probably substitute any number of Western cities for Manchester in this quotation and suburbs for Moss Side and Gorton. In the global South East, however, as authors such as Hunt (2009), Davis (2006) and Lee (2007) point out, Engels' critique of urban form resonates still.

The above discussion raises the question of whether spatial planning practice can possibly impinge on, or alter the logic of, capitalism in the absence of strong funding for public sector development or strong political will (see the Introduction to Part 2 of this volume). A conceptual (let alone practical) challenge is to destabilize hegemonic interpretations of 'the economy' and 'economic' and to legitimize new meanings and forms (see the chapters by Roy and byGibson-Graham and Cameron, this volume).

It is also important to recognize that there is no universal culture of planning. If we adopt Sanyal's (2005: xxi) understanding of planning culture as 'the collective ethos and dominant attitudes of planners regarding the appropriate role of the state, market forces, and civil society in influencing social outcomes', it is inevitable that planning cultures will differ significantly around the world, between and within states. In many countries of the global North and West, a progressive 'people-centred' culture exists, although in Western Australia (see Hillier 2007: 15) several influential senior strategic planners continue to enact a culture of expertise, in which planners 'know best' and local people do not know what is good for them such that 'a process must be put in place to enlighten people' (Duc, 2005: 2). As one senior planner wrote, even though it may be 'empowering to pretend' that a plan responds to a community's wishes, 'a clear view of the plan's outcome [from the start] gives those preparing the plan a sound basis to say NO to those who seek to have their issues included' (McRae 2005: 10, cited in Hillier 2007: 15). In other jurisdictions, planning may be equated with development and, thereby, with economic growth and 'progress'. This may be particularly so for post-colonial states (Sanyal 2005), but is also experienced around the world, especially in times of economic recession.

Different social and philosophical traditions may also be reflected in planning cultures. In countries such as China and Japan, for example, communication may be indirect and symbolic rather than descriptive or rationally analytical, reflecting a correlative way of thinking very different to Western emphases on linear-thinking and its verbal and conceptual expression (Abe, 1990). The Japanese philosopher, Kitarō Nishida's conceptualizations of pure or lived experience and *Ba* as a place or epistemological platform for advancing individual and collective knowledge (Chia, 2003) – a shared physical, mental or virtual space of emerging relationships – may offer a more deeply-rooted metaphysical orientation to new Western ideas. Such an orientation would be relational, oriented towards experimental and ethical action which would reject the idea of an ultimate end-point in favour of continuous innovation and improvement; something which, I believe, is highly relevant to planning in uncertainty. In addition to Robert Chia's work on organizational analysis (1995, 1998, 1999; Chia and Tsoukas 1999, 2003), which I relate to spatial planning and governance elsewhere (Hillier 2007: 73–5), the concept of *Ba* has been applied to transport planning by Ullrich Zeitler (2008) and to knowledge creation in urban planning by Joris Van Wezemael (2008). Ellen Shoshkes (2004) has also examined Japanese/Western influences on urban planning.

As Sanyal (2005) points out, even though a planning culture may appear to stabilize for some time, it is actually dynamic, affected by political change, technological innovation, economic crises, social traditions and so on. It is such forces, rather than a planning culture, in itself, which influence planning practitioners in different situations.

Conceptually Challenging Theory-Practice Relations

In Campbell's (2000: 125) words, 'a thinking, learning planning profession should be both practically astute and theoretically informed'. Moreover, good theory offers a 'way of understanding action, or what a planner does' (Forester, 1987: 203). Hubert Law-Yone (2007: 318) makes a distinction between planning practice as technical and professional power, ('an applied science of social control located within a hegemonic space/time disciplinary framework'), and planning praxis as practical, social power – an application of knowledge/theory to action and planning theory. Is there an issue here? Do we need to worry about 'blending' or separating practice and theory?

A distinctive feature of this Companion (and also of *CEPT* more generally) is what Hudson (1979: 396) termed 'reciprocal feedback between theory and practice, knowledge and action, conceptual models and the real world'. We reproduced Hudson's article in Volume 1 of the *Critical Essays* (Hillier and Healey 2008a), in which we demonstrate a commitment to focus on the relation between theory and practice. That commitment is continued in this Companion volume, as most authors illustrate. However, I suggest that it is also important to conceptually challenge a relation in which failures of planning practice are sometimes blamed on attempts to implement impossibly abstract or Utopian theory, or in which practice-based discreditation of theoretical 'norms' is blamed on empirical 'freak occurrences' or 'grubby practice' (see Huxley, this volume) in unbridgeable gulfs between 'ivory towers and concrete cities' (Hall 2002: 372).

Unthinking, rigid application of theoretical concepts may be as environmentally and socially damaging as ignoring theories completely. For instance, the Stockholm Resilience Centre (2007) reveals that dogmatic application of theories of environmental management based on linear dynamics – which suggest the existence of optimal solutions to problems – has led to a loss of ecological support functions and a reduction in socio-ecological capacity to deal with change, resulting in an increase in system vulnerability.

Moreover, as Eyal Weizman (2006) illustrates, the Israeli army's application of the work of Deleuze and Guattari, Clifford Geertz and John Forester has redefined the practice of urban warfare. The extent to which Deleuze's or Forester's ideas influence military tactics raises questions about the relation between theory and practice. The authors' theories have been used to develop and 'even justify ideas that emerged independently within disparate fields of knowledge and with quite different ethical bases' (Weizman 2006: 20). The idea of planning theory as an intimidating weapon of 'shock and awe' takes planning's 'dark side' to new extremes.

Whilst Kurt Lewin (1951: 169) might claim that 'there's nothing so practical as a good theory', perhaps practitioners might learn sometime to expect less from theory? (Richardson 2005). Theories cannot give definitive answers or solutions to what is right or wrong. They do not provide templates as to exactly how planning should be practised. As John Forester (1993: 1) perspicaciously wrote, 'theories do not provide answers to problems: people do'. As Forester continued, 'but a theory can provide a framework of analysis' for attempting to make some sense of the messiness of real world situations and to cultivate critical reflexivity.

Conceptual Challenges to Power

Michel Foucault's conceptualization of power as a capillary process, and its potential spatial ramifications are well-known to planning theorists through discussions of governmentality,[12] of discourse and discourse-analysis of planning-related issues.[13] The Foucauldian-derived methodology of actor-network theory is also well known.[14] I leave interested readers to seek out these challenges for themselves. The interesting questions are where are those scholars working with these ideas in the planning field now taking them and what new conceptual challenges they might pose.

Several chapters in this volume contain conceptual challenges to the issue of power. It is important not to dismiss the significance of power-laden conflict in planning decision making. Practitioners' managerialist attempts to evacuate the political in favour of gaining easy, weak, consensual decisions, as described by Swyngedouw (2005, 2007) may temporarily put a sticking plaster over what may be deep-rooted underlying conflicts, but they will not make the conflicts disappear.

John Forester (1989, 1999, 2006, 2009) uses practice-based accounts to conceptually challenge notions of intractable conflict. He advocates mediation, rather than moderation, if deliberation is not to be swamped by the power-plays of vocal interests. Mediation centres on cultivation of socially-shared norms of moral standing; recognition of and respect for the histories and claims of others. It allows the political a place. For me, this is about turning antagonism into agonism: a positive channelling of conflict which does not seek to eliminate 'the other', but to confront and discuss differences with respect and concern for those holding different views (see Nietzsche, 1954; Arendt, 1968, Mouffe, 1992, 1993, 1996, 1999; Connolly, 1998; Hillier, 2002).

---

12 See, for example, Flyvbjerg 1998; Dean 1999; Raco and Imrie 2000; Flyvbjerg and Richardson 2002; Elden 2007; Huxley 2007b; Murakami Wood 2007.
13 See Richardson, 1996, 2002; Flyvbjerg 1998; Hastings 1999; Hajer 1995; Flyvbjerg and Richardson 2002; Hajer and Versteeg 2005; Jacobs 2006.
14 See Marsden et al. 1993; Thrift 1996; Murdoch 1998; Hetherington and Law 2000; Hillier 2007; Ruming 2008.

Conceptual Challenges to Planning Ethics

Following discussions of values and power above, it is pertinent to raise questions about differences between doing good and doing right; what might be 'better'? How might 'better' actualize? Better for whom? Some will always lose: who should it be? What does responsibility mean in a globalized world of interconnected environmental, economic and social flows? As Campbell and Marshall (1998: 117) comment, 'moral judgments and ethical questions pervade the daily practice of planning'.

These are not new challenges, as the trajectory of work on ethics and planning indicates (see, for example, Marcuse 1976; Howe and Kaufman 1979, 1981; Wachs 1982, 1985; Howe 1990, 1992, 1994; Hendler 1994, 1995, 1996, 2005; Campbell and Marshall 2000, 2002; Campbell 2006). Gunder and Hillier (2007) note, however, the dominance of work from North America and, to a lesser extent, the UK. There is little, to date, easily available from the global South. The emphasis in the work cited above is on the micro-scale ethics of planning practice.[15] Most published material does not problematize the ontology of ethics as such, which constitutes the very meaning of the concept in relation to planning.

What is considered ethical practice is, of course, a social construct. Examples of 'unethical' practice, then, are not criticisms of planning in itself, but of the way in which the institutions and practices of planning may be manipulated and their ideals subverted by various interests (see Healey 2010; Kirkman 2004, 2009). This is a veritable 'dark side' of planning (Yiftachel 1998), brilliantly exemplified by Weizman's (2007) stories from Israel where the architects and planners of urban form are often the military and politicians, rather than design professionals. Weizman demonstrates how the architectural and planning methods of Israeli construction in the Occupied Territories have negatively impacted on the lives of Palestinians. 'Both in their form and their location, settlements were designed to bisect a Palestinian traffic artery, at others to surround a village; to overlook a major city or a strategic crossroad' (2007: 262). Weizman calls on architects and planners to incorporate the 'ethical motivations' and the 'methodological capacities' to 'bear professional witness to those crimes conducted through the transformation of the built environment' (2007: 260).

Other Conceptual Challenges

I cannot provide an exhaustive list of conceptual challenges for planning theory and practice in the early twenty-first century as it is impossible to predict what might eventuate. Nevertheless, a rapid scan of disciplines outside spatial planning suggests a few challenges which could be influential on its future theoretical and practical evolution. For instance:

---

15   I retain a narrow definition of ethics at this point which does not include work on the
     wider aspects of values in planning or on professionalism.

- As poststructuralist views are increasingly accepted into planning, I envisage debates taking place concerning the degree of influence of structures, such as capital, legal and institutional structures.
- Issues of whether institutions – here and above in the sociological sense as used by Patsy Healey (2007) and others[16] – perform as structures, agencies, or both. As Healey (2007: 14–15) clearly explains, institutionalization involves the 'fixing' (albeit temporarily) of certain ways of thinking and doing as accepted practices. The family is an institution, with parents having more 'power' than children. Certain policy discourses and practices may be institutionalized in local planning authorities. Debates may take place about how these discourses and practices might be challenged and changed.
- Futures-thinking. As the limitations of 'visioning' and 'scenarios' are appreciated, how might futures be imagined more helpfully? Can we anticipate futures?
- How is place conceptualized? Are there differences between conceptions of space and place? What is 'spatiality'? How might 'spacing' perform? What is 'development'? What are place qualities? How are they expressed? What makes them important?
- Judgement and decision making – is there a role for provisionality? For temporary spaces or 'temporary' decisions, perhaps with sunset clauses?
- Contingency and the aleatory – chance occurrences and their role in planning theory and practice.

Within the messy, contentious field of spatial planning, I believe that consideration of the above concepts could help planning praxes to address current issues and to understand their deeper roots and potential trajectories, by framing strategies, mobilizing actants and generating transformative forces. This volume is composed of 'directions in motion' (Deleuze and Guattari 1987: 21); a speculation on what directions theorizations of spatial planning and spatial planning practice might take. The papers in this collection cannot offer definitive answers to any of these questions, but they do engage critical debates.

A Tangled Assemblage

tangled beings … rhizomes and networks. (Latour 2004: 24)

As John Friedmann (2008: 254) writes: '[p]lanners' work has mostly to do with urban and sometimes regional issues and their dynamics that cannot be properly understood except in a way that cuts across disciplines'. The disciplinary fields which contribute to enlarging the imagination of 'planning' theory include geography,

---

16   Institution is *not*, therefore, to be confused with organization. See Hall and Taylor (1996).

sociology, political studies, philosophy, anthropology, history, cultural studies, economics, mathematics, physics, engineering, architecture, design, aesthetics and so on. It would seem clear that the issues with which planning is concerned are far too complex to be theorized through any single discipline.[17]

I regard this volume as an assemblage of papers. It is a multiplicity, reflecting the necessarily open and contested theoretical object of planning (Friedmann 1998: 3) and our invitation as editors to the authors for 'free-thinking'. We have asked authors to think across the frontiers of their subject. As such, the authors write from a range of ontological and epistemological positions. We have endeavoured to make the various elements of the book (the pages, chapters and so on) perform together, to constitute an open whole which creates new thoughts and ideas and which allows the encounter and connection of non-predetermined relations between elements. We have advocated a creative multiplicity of organisation, based on – often chance – encounter and connection, rather than a controlled pluralist structure based on a theoretical frame.

Following the principle that heterogeneity triggers the emergence of new ideas and prevents theories and processes solidifying or getting 'locked in', Joris Van Wezemael (2009) suggests that every setting gives rise to a space of potential becoming (to what it can 'do'), which emerges on the basis of the connections of component parts. I regard this volume as a 'setting' in this manner: a product of the connections between its component chapters; encounters between manifold relations. I offer no hierarchy of chapters or ideas, but envisage this volume as a mesh or rhizome, comprised of a multiplicity of threads of thought and disciplinary genres, which, hopefully, reveal some of the many possible ways to assemble theorists in always-impossible processes of theorization. In my view, the individual chapters perform 'lines' which transgress the boundaries between disciplinary traditions, between theory and practice, making connections between papers, becoming intertwined in readers' minds to provoke new modes of thought. My rhizome, or what Deleuze and Guattari would call a 'book-machine' (1987: 4), connects and assembles in movement. In this book-rhizome, international authors from several disciplines connect with texts from around the world, in hard copy and electronic form, in various languages. They also connect with each other.

This tangled assemblage is incomplete, however. Despite our attempts to involve scholars from around the world, there is a distinct North-Western emphasis in the contributors' locations. We lack contributions especially from non-Anglophone scholars in the global South (including South America, Africa and Asia) who are directly able to engage with and theorize the framing realities facing spatial planning decision making and implementation. Our hope is that, by the time that

---

17   See also the paper by Phelps and Tewdwr-Jones (2008) which identifies similarities in the conceptual constructs informing writing in both geography and planning disciplines and Hajer and Wagenaar (2003) which brings together policy analysts and planners.

the next 'companion' to planning theory is published, this current lack will be rectified.[18]

On Naming of Parts

Despite our insistence on the interrelations between theory and practice, we have decided to group chapters in three Parts: conceptual challenges from perspectives on spatial planning practice (Part 1); conceptual challenges for spatial planning theory (Part 2); and conceptual challenges for spatial planning in complexity (Part 3). The Parts correspond broadly to:

- Part 1, issues from practice to which planning theorists should give attention;
- Part 2, key concepts in current theorizing from mainly poststructuralist perspectives;
- Part 3, what discussion on complexity may offer planning theory and practice.

We recognize the inevitably reductionist nature of this (or indeed any) categorization. The Parts are an artificial heuristic device to facilitate reading. Many contributions cross-cut two or even three Parts, as they emphasize ideas, directions or re-directions which affect how planning is and may be theorized and practised. More detailed discussion is found in the Introductions to individual Parts.

Part 1: Conceptual Challenges from Perspectives on Spatial Planning Practice

This Part includes seven contributions which address different ways to understand and advance how planning activity is and should be practised. They all reflect an appreciation that planning activity is situated in a wider context of governance dynamics, but they seek a much more nuanced and detailed grasp of the diversity of contexts and the contingencies of practices. This reflects the distaste for the 'grand, totalising narratives' of the mid-twentieth century, whether of the managerial variety or that of Marxist structural analysis. Several of the authors explore ways of moving beyond the inheritance of the 'heavy' states of Western European democracies in which many formal planning systems are embedded. They examine the potential of governance energy 'beyond the (formal) state', and the extent to which 'insurgent practices' have the possibility to challenge and limit the unravelling of formal government practices promoted by the so-called 'neo-

---

18   The volume edited by Healey and Upton (2010), on the international exchange of planning ideas, has promise in this respect.

liberal' project. In this way, they hope to identify more clearly the dynamics of who gets access to such arenas, who controls their practice dynamics and which future dreams may live on to shape future action.

Part 2: Conceptual Challenges for Spatial Planning Theory

For Aristotle, in the *Nicomachean Ethics* (1985), *theōria* is the highest form of praxis. Conceptual challenges for planning theory link to philosophical questions of ontology and epistemology. If, as defined above, spatial planning is concerned with 'dreaming alternative futures', 'understanding possible urban futures', 'deliberate forethought', 'the specification of a proposed future' and 'storytelling about the future', the authors in Part 2 indicate the complexity and contingency of the relations through which futures may actualize and the inevitable uncertainty of planning in shaping futures. As Marcus (1994: 567) suggests, it is all too-easy to assimilate 'the phenomenon of interest by given analytic, ready-made concepts'. The authors resist such temptation.

Part 3: Conceptual Challenges for Spatial Planning in Complexity

Practitioners and academics in spatial planning have traditionally singularized 'town', 'country' and 'governance'. In texts, images and plans, 'they have fashioned an ordered and unifiable whole out of what is often a disordered, spontaneous, even intractable multiplicity of places, practices and people' (Robbins 1998: 37). There are well-known, but less well-accepted, contradictions between the assumptions and expectations of spatial planning and the complex realities of the 'systems' through which planning and governance take place. Karen Christensen (1999: 5) wrote that 'planning aims at ensuring future certainty in a complex, dynamic intergovernmental system that is rife with turbulence and uncertainty'.

Planning theory has moved on a long way from the positivist tradition outlined in *CEPT*, Volume 1 (Hillier and Healey 2008b). The time has passed for making 'accurate predictions' of spatial equilibria, based on positivist, logical empiricist epistemology (Plummer and Sheppard 2006). As theorists and practitioners are becoming more aware of the many, multiple and dynamic interrelations between entities, issues, places and so on, references to complexity theories in planning-related literature are increasing exponentially. In the final Part, the authors attempt to locate diagonals or transversals between various elements in earlier chapters and to identify possibilities that these connections might open up. Some attempt to 'map' future theoretical performativities. We have asked authors to identify connections and potentialities; to pay attention to affect and to trajectories of potential emergence; to think or speculate experimentally across boundaries.

Conclusions

Theory is something to do, not simply to read. (Calhoun et al. 2007: 20)

Returning to Eversley's (1973) metaphor with which I commenced this Introduction, I do not consider planning theory to be at a crossroads as such. There are, however, always choices to be made: between forms of theory and practice which support either the collective good or the individual over the collective in which the idea of 'public interest' loses meaning; between efficiency and equity; between distribution and redistribution in favour of the poor; between linear and non-linear understandings; between path-dependent rigidity and experimentation.

In 1998, John Friedmann predicted that 'we will keep writing planning theory, because it's fun' (p. 5). In this spirit, Patsy Healey and I hope that the chapters in this assemblage will generate, not only critical reflection, but also creative ideas about some of the conceptual challenges with which planning theory and practice might engage. We hope that the authors' encounters and conversations with ideas and theories from both within and outside the field of spatial planning will stimulate readers to do likewise in ongoing conversations, discussions and debates. If the chapters appear speculative and provisional, this is because they form only one aspect of a wider, turbulent process which also includes empirical enquiry, close textual analysis and further theorization.

We thus offer this book as an event of thought. For Jacques Derrida (1977), an event constitutes 'the emergence of a disparate multiplicity' (cited in Tschumi, 1994: 257). For Michel Foucault, an event is not simply a sequence of words (or chapters), but the moment of questioning or problematizing the very assumptions of the setting in which the problematization takes place and which occasions the possibility of another, different setting (Rajchman 1991: viii; Tschumi 1994: 256). An event embraces the productive potential of the forces from which it developed (Deleuze 1990); a field of new possibilities which causes its readers/participants no longer to think about certain things in the same manner.

Conceptual research is in continual evolution, growing in its multiplicity, yet requiring some stability and temporary fixity through writing and publication. It is a constructive process of positive ontologies; a process of interconnection and movement between ideas, generating a multiplicity of configurations of possibilities from the interconnections. We regard the different conceptual frames in the book, not as competing, but as a multidimensional unfolding narrative of often complementary theories and challenges. The different authorial standpoints are indicative of the range of conceptualizations of planning and the spatial, the social, the political, the economic and so on. The various chapters may be read as mapping different ways of conceptualizing planning and the challenges it faces in the early twenty-first century. We gave authors no predetermined paths or destinations. We believe that theory is not oriented to apprehension of (a single) truth, but we regard theory as 'a practical means of going on' (Thrift, 1996: 304) which recognizes and transgresses its own contextual limitations.

We offer the papers in this volume as 'a glint of lights in the fog' and, like Marco Polo in Italo Calvino's *Invisible Cities*, 'if [we] tell you that the city toward which [our] journey tends is discontinuous in space and time, now scattered, now more condensed, you must not believe the search for it can stop' (1997: 164).

> *You do not go back to a theory, you make others and there are always more to be made. (Deleuze, 1972, cited in Ramonet, 2006: 1)*

Acknowledgements

My thanks to Patsy Healey for maintaining my focus with invaluable comments through the various iterations of this Introduction.

References

Abe, M. (1990) 'Introduction', in Nishida, K. [1921] *An Inquiry into the Good* (trans. Abe, M.). New Haven: Yale University Press.

Alexander, E.R. (1992) *Approaches to Planning: Introducing Current Planning Theories, Concepts and Issues*. Amsterdam: Gordon and Breach.

Allmendinger, P. (2002) *Planning Theory*. Basingstoke: Palgrave.

Allmendinger, P. and Tewdwr-Jones, M. (2002) 'Preface' in Allmendinger, P. and Tewdwr-Jones, M. (eds) *Planning Futures: New Directions for Planning Theory*. London: Routledge, xi–xii.

Arendt, H. (1968) *Between Past and Future*, New York: Viking Press.

Aristotle (1985) [c.350BC] *Nicomachean Ethics* (ed. Rackham, D.). Harvard University Press/Perseus Digital Library, <http://perseus.mpiwg-berlin.mpg.de/> [accessed January 2004].

Ballantyne, A. (2007) *Deleuze and Guattari for Architects*. London: Routledge.

Bernstein, R. (1971) *Praxis and Action*. Pittsburgh, PN: University of Pennsylvania Press.

Blowers, A. (1984) *Something in the Air: Corporate Power and the Environment*. London: Harper & Row.

Blowers, A. and Evans B. (eds) (1997) *Town Planning into the 21st Century*. London: Routledge.

Burchell, R.W. and Hughes, J. (1978) 'Introduction: Planning Theory in the 1980s: a search for future directions', in Burchell, R.W. and Sternlieb, G. (eds) (1978) *Planning Theory in the 1980s: A Search for Future Directions*. New Brunswick, NJ: Center for Urban Policy Research, Rutgers University, xvii–liii.

Burchell, R.W. and Sternlieb, G. (eds) (1978) *Planning Theory in the 1980s: A Search for Future Directions*. New Brunswick, NJ: Center for Urban Policy Research, Rutgers University.

Byrne D. (2003) 'Complexity theory and planning theory: a necessary encounter' *Planning Theory* 2(3): 171–8.

Calhoun, C., Gerleis, J., Moody, J., Pfaff, S. and Virk, I. (2007) 'General introduction', in Calhoun, C., Gerleis, J., Moody, J., Pfaff, S. and Virk, I. (eds), *Contemporary Sociological Theory* (second edition). Malden, MA: Blackwell, 1–22.

Calvino, I. (1997) [1972] *Invisible Cities* (trans. Weaver W.). London: Vintage.

Campbell, H. (2000) 'Interface: theory and practice should mix' *Planning Theory and Practice* 1(1): 125.

Campbell, H. (2006) 'Just planning: the art of situated ethical judgment' *Journal of Planning Education and Research* 25: 1–15.

Campbell, H. and Marshall, R. (1998) 'Acting on principle: dilemmas in planning practice' *Planning Practice and Research* 13: 117–28.

Campbell, H. and Marshall, R. (2000) 'Moral obligations and the public interest: a commentary on current British practice' *Environment and Planning B* 27(2): 297–312.

Campbell, H. and Marshall, R. (2002) 'Utilitarianism's bad breath? A re-evaluation of the public interest justification for planning' *Planning Theory* 1(2): 163–87.

Campbell, S. and Fainstein, S. (2003) 'Introduction: the structure and debates of planning theory', in Campbell, S. and Fainstein, S. (eds), *Readings in Planning Theory* (second edition). Malden, MA: Blackwell, 1–16.

Casarino, C. (2002) *Modernity at Sea: Melville, Marx, Conrad in Crisis.* Minneapolis, MN: University of Minnesota Press.

CEMAT (European Conference of Ministers Responsible for Regional/Spatial Planning) (1983) *Chartre Européenne de l'Amenagement du Territoire (Chartre de Torremolinos)*, adopted 20/05/1983, Strasbourg: Council of Europe. <http://www.siseministeerium.ee/public/terr.harta.ingrtf.rtf> [accessed 09/07/2009].

CEMAT (European Conference of Ministers Responsible for Regional/Spatial Planning) (2007) *Spatial Development Glossary. Territory and Landscape, No. 2.* Strasbourg: Council of Europe.

Chia, R. (1995) 'From modern to postmodern organisational analysis' *Organisation Studies* 16(4): 579–605.

Chia, R. (1998) 'From complexity science to complex thinking: organisation as simple location' *Organization* 5(3): 341–69.

Chia, R. (1999) 'A "rhizomic" model of organisational change and transformation: perspective from a metaphysics of change' *British Journal of Management* 10: 209–27.

Chia, R. (2003) 'From knowledge-creation to the perfecting of action: Tao, Basho and pure experience as the ultimate ground of knowing' *Human Relations* 56(8): 953–81.

Chia, R. and Tsoukas, H. (1999) *On Organisational Becoming: Rethinking Organisational Change*, WP No. 99/12. Colchester: Dept. of Accounting, Finance and Management, University of Essex.

Chia, R. and Tsoukas, H. (2003) 'Everything flows and nothing abides: towards a "rhizomic" model of organisational change, transformation and action' *Process Studies*, 32(2): 196–24.

Christensen, K. (1999) *Cities and Complexity*. Thousand Oaks, CA: Sage.

Cilliers, P. (2005) 'Complexity, deconstruction and relativism' *Theory, Culture and Society* 22(5): 255–67.

Clavel, P. (1986) *The Progressive City: Planning and Participation 1969-1984*. New Brunswick, NJ: Rutgers University Press.,

Clavel, P., Forester, J., and Goldsmith, W. (eds) (1980) *Urban and Regional Planning in an Age of Austerity*. Oxford: Pergamon Press.

Connell, D. (2009) 'Planning and its orientation to the future' *International Planning Studies* 14(1): 85–98.

Connolly, W. (1998) 'Beyond good and evil: the ethical sensibility of Michel Foucault', in Moss, J. (ed.) *The Later Foucault*. London: Sage, 108–28.

Davis, M. (2006) *Planet of Slums*. London: Verso.

Davoudi, S. (2008) 'Key issues for planning futures and the way forward: Introduction' *21st Century Society* 3(3): 229–32.

Dean, M. (1999) *Governmentality: Power and Rule in Modern Society*. London: Sage.

del Casino Jnr, V., Grimes, A., Hanna, S. and Jones III, J.P. (2000) 'Methodological frameworks for the geography of organisations' *Geoforum* 31: 523–38.

Deleuze, G. (1972) 'Les intellectuels et le pouvoir' *Arc* 49 (May), Aix-en-Provence.

Deleuze, G. (1990) [1969] *The Logic of Sense* (trans. Lester, M. and Stivale, C.). London: Athlone Press.

Deleuze, G. and Guattari, F. (1987) [1980] *A Thousand Plateaus: Capitalism and Schizophrenia* (trans. Massumi, B.) London: Athlone Press.

Deleuze, G. and Guattari, F. (1994) [1991] *What is Philosophy?* (trans. Tomlinson H. and Burchill, G.). London: Verso.

Derrida, J. (1988) [1977] *Limited Inc.* (trans. Weber, S. and Mehlman, J.). Evanston, IL: Northwestern University Press.

Derrida, J. and Eisenman, P. (1997) *Chora L Works*, (ed. Kipnis, J. and Leeser, T.). New York: Monacelli Press.

Dixon, D. and Jones III J.P. (1998) 'My dinner with Derrida, *or* spatial analysis and poststructuralism do lunch' *Environment and Planning A* 30: 247–60.

Doel, M. (1996) 'A hundred thousand lines of flight: a machinic introduction to the nomad thought and scrumpled geography of Gilles Deleuze and Félix Guattari' *Environment and Planning D, Society and Space* 14: 421–39.

Duc, E. (2005) 'Urban design – future or past' *Urban Design Forum* No. 70 (June): 2.

Eversley, D. (1973) *The Planner in Society: The Changing Role of a Profession*. London: Faber & Faber.

Eisenschitz, A. (2008) 'Town planning, planning theory and social reform' *International Planning Studies* 13(2): 133–49.

Elden, S. (2007) 'Governmentality, calculation, territory' *Environment and Planning D, Society and Space* 25(3): 562–80.

Engels, F. (2009) [1845] *The Condition of the Working Class in England*. London: Penguin.

Estatopia (nd) *Inch Perfect: Le Corbusier's 'Modulor'*, <http://www.users.zetnet.co.uk/ estatopia/inch3.htm#lecorb> [accessed 18/06/2009].

Fainstein, S. (2000) 'New directions in planning theory' *Urban Affairs Review* 34: 451–78.

Feyerabend, P. (1978) *Science in a Free Society*. London: New Left Books.

Florida, R. (2000) *Competing in the Age of Talent*. Pittsburgh, PA: Mellon Foundation.

Florida, R. (2002) 'The economic geography of talent', *Annals of the Association of American Geographers* 92(4): 743–55.

Florida, R. (2004) *Cities and the Creative Class*. London: Routledge.

Flyvbjerg, B. (1998) *Rationality and Power*. Chicago, IL: University of Chicago Press.

Flyvbjerg, B. and Richardson, T. (2002) 'Planning and Foucault: in search of the dark side of planning theory', in Allmendinger, P. and Tewdwr-Jones, M. (eds) *Planning Futures*. London: Routledge, 44–62.

Forester, J. (1987) 'Critical theory and planning practice', in Forester, J. (ed.) *Critical Theory and Public Life*. Cambridge, MA: MIT Press, 202–30.

Forester, J. (1989) *Planning in the Face of Power*. Berkeley, CA: University of California Press.

Forester, J. (1993) *Critical Theory, Public Policy and Planning Practice: Toward a Critical Pragmatism*. Albany, NY: SUNY Press.

Forester, J. (1999) *The Deliberative Practitioner*. Cambridge, MA: MIT Press.

Forester, J. (2000) 'Epistemology, reductive ethics, far too narrow politics: some clarifications in response to Yiftachel and Huxley' *IJURR* 24(4): 914–16.

Forester, J. (2004) 'Reflections on trying to teach planning theory' *Planning Theory and Practice* 5(2): 242–51.

Forester, J. (2006) 'Making participation work when interests conflict: moving from facilitating dialogue and moderating debate to mediating negotiations' *Journal of the American Planning Association* 72: 447–56.

Forester, J. (2009) *Dealing with Differences: Dramas of Mediating Public Disputes*. Oxford: Oxford University Press.

Foucault, M. (1982) 'On the genealogy of ethics', in Dreyfus, H. and Rabinow, P. (eds) *Michel Foucault*. Chicago, IL: University of Chicago Press.

Foucault, M. and Deleuze, G. (1972) 'Intellectuals and power: a conversation between Michel Foucault and Gilles Deleuze' *L'Arc*, 49: 3–10. <http://libcom.org/library/intellectuals-power-a-conversation-between-Michel-Foucault-and-Gilles-Deleuze> [accessed 27/03/2008].

Freire, P. (1970) [1968] *Pedagogy of the Oppressed* (trans. Ramos, M.R.). New York: Continuum.

Friedmann, J. (1987) *Planning in the Public Domain: From Knowledge to Action*. Princeton, NJ: Princeton University Press.

Friedmann, J. (1998) 'Planning theory revisited' *European Planning Studies* 6(3): 245–54.

Friedmann, J. (2003) 'Why do Planning Theory?' *Planning Theory* 2(1): 7–10.

Friedmann, J. (2008) 'The uses of planning theory: a bibliographic essay' *Journal of Planning Education and Research* 28: 247–57.

Gadamer, H-G. (1999) 'In praise of theory', in *Praise of Theory: Speeches and Essays* (trans. Dawson, C.). New Haven: Yale University Press.

Goodwin, B. (1997) 'Community, creativity and society' *Soundings* 5: 111–23.

Gower Davies, J. (1974) *Evangelistic Bureaucrat: Study of a Planning Exercise in Newcastle-upon-Tyne*. London: Tavistock Publications.

Greimas, A.J. (1966) *Sémantique Structurale*. Paris : PUF.

Gunder, M. and Hillier, J. (2007) 'Problematising responsibility in planning theory and practice: on seeing the middle of the string?' *Progress in Planning* 68: 57–96.

Gunder, M. and Hillier, J. (2009) *Planning in Ten Words or Less*. Farnham: Ashgate.

Hague, C. (1997) 'Town planning into the 21st century: diverse worlds and common themes', in Blowers, A. and Evans, B. (eds) (1997) *Town Planning into the 21st Century*. London: Routledge, 137–51.

Hajer, M. (1995) *The Politics of Environmental Discourse*. Oxford: Clarendon Press.

Hajer, M. and Versteeg, W. (2005) 'A decade of discourse analysis of environmental politics: achievements, challenges, perspectives' *Journal of Environmental Policy and Planning* 7(3): 175–84.

Hajer, M. and Wagenaar, H. (eds) (2003) *Deliberative Policy Analysis: Understanding Governance in the Network Society*. Cambridge: Cambridge University Press.

Hall, P. (1972) 'Planning and the environment', in Townsend, P. and Bosanquet, N. (eds) *Labour and Equality*. London: Fabian Society, 262–75.

Hall, P. (1982) *Great Planning Disasters*. Berkeley, CA: University of California Press.

Hall, P. (2002) *Cities of Tomorrow* (3rd edn). Oxford: Wiley-Blackwell.

Hall, P. and Taylor, R. (1996) 'Political science and the three institutionalisms' *Political Studies* XLIV: 936–57.

Harper, D. (2001) *Online Etymology Dictionary* <http://dictionary.reference.com>

Harvey, D. (1973) *Social Justice and the City*. London: Edward Arnold.

Hastings, A. (1999) 'Analysing power relations in partnerships: is there a role for discourse analysis?' *Urban Studies* 36(1): 91–106.

Healey, P. (2004) 'The treatment of space and place in the new strategic spatial planning in Europe' *International Journal of Urban and Regional Research* 28: 45–67.

Healey, P. (2006) *Collaborative Planning* (2nd edn). Basingstoke: Palgrave Macmillan.

Healey, P. (2007) *Urban Complexity and Spatial Strategies: Towards a Relational Planning for our Times*. Abingdon: Routledge.

Healey, P. (2008) 'Making choices that matter: the practical art of situated strategic judgement in spatial strategy-making', in van den Broeck, J., Moulaert, F. and Oosterlynck, S. (eds) *Empowering the Planning Fields: Ethics, Creativity and Action*. Leuven: Acco, 23–41.

Healey, P. (2010) *Making Better Places: The Planning Project in the 21st Century*. Basingstoke: Palgrave Macmillan.

Healey, P. and Hillier, J. (2008) 'Introduction', in Hillier, J. and Healey, P. (eds) (2008) *Critical Essays in Planning Theory, Volume 1, Foundations of the Planning Enterprise*. Aldershot: Ashgate, ix–xxvii.

Healey, P. and Upton, R. (2010) *Crossing Borders: International Exchange and Planning Practices*. London: Routledge.

Healey, P., McDougall, G. and Thomas, M. (eds) (1982) *Planning Theory: Prospects for the 1980s: Selected Papers from a Conference Held in Oxford, 2–4 April 1981*. New York: Pergamon.

Healey, P., McDougall, G. and Thomas, M.J. (1982) 'Theoretical debates in planning: towards a coherent dialogue', in Healey, P., McDougall, G. and Thomas, M.J. (eds), *Planning Theory: Prospects for the 1980s*. Oxford: Pergamon Press, 5–22.

Hendler, S. (1994) 'Feminist planning ethics', *Journal of Planning Literature* 9(2): 115–27.

Hendler, S. (ed.) (1995) *Planning Ethics: A Reader in Planning Theory, Practice and Education*. New Brunswick, NJ: Centre for Urban Policy Research.

Hendler, S. (1996) 'On the use of models in planning ethics', in Mandelbaum, S., Mazza, L. and Burchell, R. (eds), *Explorations in Planning Theory*. New Brunswick, NJ: Centre for Urban Policy Research, 400–13.

Hendler, S. (2005) 'Towards a feminist code of planning ethics' *Planning Theory and Practice* 6(1): 53–69.

Hetherington, K. and Law, J. (eds) (2000) Special issue on actor-network-theory and spatiality, *Environment and Planning D, Society and Space* 18(2): 127–55.

Hillier, J. (2002) *Shadows of Power: An Allegory of Prudence in Land-use Planning*. London: Routledge.

Hillier, J. (2007) *Stretching Beyond the Horizon: A Multiplanar Theory of Spatial Planning and Governance*. Aldershot: Ashgate.

Hillier, J. and Healey, P. (eds) (2008a) *Critical Essays in Planning Theory*. Aldershot: Ashgate.

Hillier, J. and Healey, P. (eds) (2008b) *Critical Essays in Planning Theory, Volume 1, Foundations of the Planning Enterprise*. Aldershot: Ashgate.

Hillier, J. and Healey, P. (2008c) 'Introduction: the complexity 'turn' – hope, critique and postmodernism', in Healey, P. and Hillier, J. (eds) *Critical Essays in Planning Theory, Volume 3, Contemporary Movements in Planning Theory*. Aldershot: Ashgate.

Howe, E. (1990) 'Normative ethics in planning' *Journal of Planning Literature* 5(2): 123–50.

Howe, E. (1992) 'Professional roles and the public interest in planning' *Journal of Planning Literature* 6(3): 230–48.

Howe, E. (1994) *Acting on Ethics in City Planning*. New Brunswick, NJ: Rutgers University Press.

Howe, E. and Kaufman, J. (1979) 'The ethics of contemporary American planners' *Journal of the American Planning Association* 45(3): 243–55.

Howe, E. and Kaufman, J. (1981) 'The values of contemporary American planners' *Journal of the American Planning Association* 47(3): 266–78.

Hudson, B. (1979) 'Comparison of current planning theories: counterparts and contradictions' *APA Journal* 45: 387–98.

Hunt, T. (2009) 'Introduction', in Engels F., *The Condition of the Working Class in England*. London: Penguin, 1–31.

Huxley, M. (2007a) 'Planning, space and government', in Cox K. (ed.) *Handbook of Political Geography*. London: Sage, 153–74.

Huxley, M. (2007b) 'Geographies of governmentality', in Crampton, J. and Elden, S. (eds) *Space, Knowledge and Power: Foucault and Geography*. Aldershot: Ashgate, 186–204.

Ingold, T. (1990) 'An anthropologist looks at biology' *Man* (NS) 25: 208–29.

Innes, J. (1995) 'Planning theory's emerging paradigm: communicative action and interactive practice' *Journal of Planning Education and Research* 14: 183–9.

Jacobs, K. (2006) 'Discourse analysis and its utility for urban policy research' *Urban Policy and Research* 24(1): 39–52.

Jessop, B., Brenner, N. and Jones, M. (2008) 'Theorizing sociospatial relations' *Environment and Planning D, Society and Space* 26: 389–401.

Keeble, L. (1961) *Town Planning at the Crossroads*. London: Estates Gazette.

Kirkman, R. (2004) 'The ethics of metropolitan growth: a framework' *Philosophy and Geography* 7(2): 201–18.

Kirkman, R. (2009) 'At home in the seamless web: agency, obduracy and the ethics of metropolitan growth' *Science, Technology and Human Values* 34(2): 234–58.

Krumholz, N. and Clavel, P. (1994) *Reinventing Cities: Equity Planners Tell their Stories*. Philadelphia, PA: Temple University Press.

Krumholz, N. and Forester, J. (1990) *Making Equity Planning Work: Leadership in the Public Sector*. Philadelphia, PA: Temple University Press.

Kuhn, T. (1983) 'Commensurability, comparability, communicability', in Asquith P. and Nickles, T. (eds) *PSA 198: Proceedings of the 1982 Biennial Meeting of the Philosophy of Science Association*. East Lansing, MI: Philosophy of Science Association, 670–73.

Latour, B. (1996) 'On actor-network-theory: a few clarifications' *Soziale Welt* 47: 369–82.

Latour, B. (2004) *Politics of Nature*. Cambridge, MA: Harvard University Press.

Law, J. (2004) 'And if the global were small and noncoherent? Method, complexity and the baroque' *Environment and Planning D, Society and Space* 22: 13–26.

Law-Yone, H. (2007) 'Another planning theory? Rewriting the meta-narrative' *Planning Theory* 6(3): 315–26.

Lee, C.K (2007) *Against the Law: Labour Protests in China's Rustbelt and Sunbelt*. Berkeley: University of California Press.

Lewin, K. (1951) *Field Theory in Social Science*. New York: Harper.

Mandelbaum, S. (1996) 'Introduction: the talk of the community', in Mandelbaum, S., Mazza, L. and Burchell, R.W. (eds) *Explorations in Planning Theory*, New Brunswick, NJ: Center for Urban Policy Research, Rutgers University, xi–xix.

Mandelbaum, S., Mazza, L. and Burchell, R.W. (eds) (1996) *Explorations in Planning Theory*. New Brunswick, NJ: Center for Urban Policy Research, Rutgers University.

Marcus, G. (1994) 'What comes (just) after "post"? The case of ethnography', in Denzin, N. and Lincoln, Y. (eds) *Handbook of Qualitative Research. Thousand Oaks*, CA: Sage, 563–74.

Marcuse, P. (1976) 'Professional ethics and beyond: values in planning' *Journal of the American Institute of Planners* 42(3): 264–74.

Marsden, T., Murdoch, J., Lowe, P., Munton, R. and Flynn, A. (1993) *Constructing the Countryside*. London: UCL Press.

Massey, D. (2005) *For Space*. London: Sage.

McNeill, W. (1999) *The Glance of the Eye: Heidegger, Aristotle and the Ends of Theory*. Albany, NY: SUNY Press.

McRae, I. (2005) 'How strategic planning is really done' *Western Planner* 24(10): 8–11.

More, T. (1965) [1516] *Utopia*. Harmondsworth: Penguin.

Mouffe, C. (1992) *Dimensions of Radical Democracy: pluralism, citizenship and community*. London: Verso.

Mouffe, C. (1993) *The Return of the Political*. London: Verso.

Mouffe, C. (1996) 'Deconstruction, pragmatism and the politics of democracy', in Mouffe, C. (ed.) *Deconstruction and Pragmatism*. London: Routledge, 1–12.

Mouffe, C. (1999) 'Deliberative democracy or agonistic pluralism?' *Social Research* 66(3): 745–58.

Murakami Wood, D. (2007) 'Beyond the Panopticon? Foucault and surveillance studies', in Crampton, J. and Elden, S. (eds) *Space, Knowledge and Power: Foucault and Geography*. Aldershot: Ashgate, 245–63.

Murdoch, J. (1998) 'The spaces of actor-network-theory' *Geoforum* 29(4): 357–74.

Nietzsche, F. (1954) *Twlilight of the Idols*. New York: Penguin.

Phelps, N. and Tewdwr-Jones, M. (2008) 'If geography is anything, maybe it's planning's alter-ego? Reflections on policy relevance in two disciplines concerned with place and space', *Transactions of the Institute of British Geographers* NS 33: 566–584.

Plato (1992) [c.387-380 BC] *The Republic*. Indianapolis, IN: Hackett.

Plummer, P. and Sheppard, E. (2006) 'Geography matters: agency, structures and dynamics at the intersection of economics and geography' *Journal of Economic Geography* 6: 619–37.

Raco, M. and Imrie, R. (2000) 'Governmentality and rights and responsibilities in urban policy' *Environment and Planning A* 32(12): 2187–204.

Rajchman, J. (1991) *Philosophical Events: Essays of the 80s*. New York: Columbia University Press.

Ramonet, I. (2006) 'Silent thought' *Le Monde Diplomatique* (May), 1.

Rausch, H. (1982) *Theoria: von ihren Sakralen zur Philosopischen Bedeutung*. Munich: Fink.

Reade, E. (1987) *British Town and Country Planning*. Milton Keynes: Open University Press.

Richardson, K. and Cilliers, P. (2001) 'What is complexity science? A view from different directions' *Emergence* 3(1): 5–23.

Richardson, T. (1996) 'Foucauldian discourse: power and truth in urban and regional policy making' *European Planning Studies* 4(3): 279–92.

Richardson, T. (2002) 'Freedom and control in planning: using discourse in the pursuit of reflexive practice' *Planning Theory and Practice* 3(3): 353–61.

Richardson, T. (2005) 'Environmental assessment and planning theory: four short stories about power, multiple rationality, and ethics' *Environmental Assessment Review* 25(4): 341–65.

Robbins, E. (1998) 'Thinking the city multiple' *Harvard Architecture Review* 10: 36–45.

Ruming, K. (2008) Negotiating Development Control: Using Actor-network-theory to Explore the Creation of Residential Building Policy. City Futures Research Centre, UNSW, Sydney. <http://www.fbe.unsw.edu.au/cf/publications/othercfresearch/attachments/negotiatingdevelopmentcontrol.pdf> [accessed 19/09/2008]

Sandercock, L. (1998) *Towards Cosmopolis*. New York: Wiley.

Sanyal, B. (2002) 'Globalization, ethical compromise and planning theory' *Planning Theory* 1(2): 116–23.

Sanyal, B. (2005) 'Preface', in Sanyal, B. (ed.), *Comparative Planning Cultures*, New York: Routledge, xix–xxiv.

Sanyal, B. (2007) 'Déjà-vu' *Planning Theory* 6(3): 327–31.

Schön, D. (1983) *The Reflective Practitioner: How Professionals Think in Action*. New York: Free Press.

Shoshkes, E. (2004) 'East-West: interactions between the US and Japan and their effect on utopian realism' *Journal of Planning History* 3(3): 215–40.

Sternlieb, G. (1978) 'Preface' in Burchell, R.W. and Sternlieb, G. (eds) (1978) *Planning Theory in the 1980s: A Search for Future Directions*. New Brunswick, NJ: Center for Urban Policy Research, Rutgers University, xi–xiii.

Stockholm Resilience Centre (2007) *Complex Adaptive Systems*. <http://www.stockholmresilience.org/research/researchbackground/researchframework/complexadaptivesystems.4.aeea46911a3127427980006772.html> [accessed 05/02/2009].

Swyngedouw, E. (2005) 'Governance innovation and the citizen: the Janus face of governance-beyond-the-State' *Urban Studies* 42(11): 1991–2006.

Swyngedouw, E. (2007) 'Impossible "sustainability" and the postpolitical condition', in Krueger, R. and Gibbs, D. (eds) *The Sustainable Development Paradox*. New York: Guilford Press, 13–40.

Taylor, N. (1998) *Urban Planning Theory since 1945*. London: Sage.

Taylor, N. (2003) 'More or less meaningful concepts in planning theory (and how to make them more meaningful): a plea for conceptual analysis and precision' *Planning Theory* 2(2): 91–100.

Thomas, H. (2007) 'From radicalism to reformism' *Planning Theory* 6(3): 332–35.

Thrift, N. (1996) *Spatial Formations*. London: Sage.

Thrift, N. (1999) 'The place of complexity' *Theory, Culture and Society* 16(3): 31–69.

Throgmorton, J. (2003) 'Planning as persuasive storytelling in a global-scale web of relationships' *Planning Theory* 2(2): 125–51.

Tschumi, B. (1994) *Architecture and Disjunction*. Cambridge, MA: MIT Press.

UN-HABITAT (2009) *Global Report on Human Settlements: Planning Sustainable Cities*. London: Earthscan.

Urry, J. (2005) 'The complexity turn' *Theory, Culture and Society* 22(5): 1–14.

Van Wezemael, J. (2008) 'Knowledge creation in urban and knowledge environment', in Yigitcanlar, T., Velibeyoglu, K. and Baum S. (eds) *Knowledge-based Urban Development*. Hershey, PA: IGI Global, 1–20.

Van Wezemael, J. (2009) 'Housing studies between romantic and baroque complexity' *Housing, Theory and Society* 26(2): 81–121.

Wachs, M. (1982) 'Ethical dilemmas in forecasting for public policy' *Public Administration Review* 42(6): 562–7.

Wachs, M. (1985) 'Introduction', in Wachs, M. (ed.) *Ethics in Planning*. New Brunswick, NJ: Centre for Urban Policy Research, xiii–xxi.

Weizman, E. (2006) 'The art of war: Deleuze, Guattari, and Debord and the Israeli Defense Force'. <http://info.interactivist.net/node/5324> [accessed 11/05/2009].

Weizman, E. (2007) *Hollow Land: Israel's Architecture of Occupation*. London: Verso.

Yiftachel, O. (1998) 'Planning and social control: exploring the dark side' *Journal of Planning Literature* 12: 395–406.

Yiftachel, O. (2001) 'Introduction: outlining the power of planning', in Yiftachel, O., Little, J., Hedgcock, D. and Alexander, I. (eds) *The Power of Planning*. Amsterdam: Kluwer Academic, 1–20.

Young, R. (1981) *Untying the Text: A Post-structuralist Reader*. London: Routledge and Kegan Paul.

Zeitler, U. (2008) 'The ontology of mobility, morality and transport planning', in Bergmann, S. and Sager, T. (eds) *The Ethics of Mobilities*. Aldershot: Ashgate, 233–40.

PART ONE
CONCEPTUAL CHALLENGES
FROM PERSPECTIVES
ON SPATIAL PLANNING
PRACTICE

Introduction to Part One[1]

Patsy Healey

The Planning Idea and its Contexts

As outlined in Jean Hillier's Overall Introduction, the planning idea focuses on dreaming alternative futures abut place qualities, their potentials and possibilities. It is these days infused with a commitment to seeking futures which offer better and more sustainable opportunities than those at present available for many people, and which pay more attention to the environmental systems within which we humans live our lives. But the planning idea is not just about dreaming. It is also about actively shaping practices, now and in the future, which might bring more desirable worlds into being. The focus of 'planning theory' is therefore on ideas and practices, and how these interact in an active project of bringing futures into being, in a 'project of becoming' (Hillier 2007). Following Friedmann (1987), it is about how ideas, knowledge and ways of thinking get to shape action, and how action in turn shapes the development of ideas, knowledge and imaginations.[2]

A major lesson from the experience of the planning field in the twentieth century (see Hillier and Healey 2008a) is that this relationship is not linear. John Friedmann's influential thinking grew from his experiences in promoting regional economic development in Latin America (1973, 2010). John Forester evolved his conceptual apparatus for understanding the micro-practices of planning activity as he discussed with planners how they did their work (Forester 1989, 1999). My own approach to understanding what was involved in doing planning work grew from empirical study of how the formal instrument of a British 'development plan' was being used in practice (Healey 1983, 1988, 1997). Contributions such as these helped to dislodge the dominant planning imaginations of the mid-twentieth century. In these perspectives the method of planning work was understood as

---

[1]   My thanks to Jean Hillier and Margo Huxley for comments on earlier drafts of this chapter.

[2]   Many terms are being used these days to describe ways of thinking and organizing knowledge and experience, from 'viewpoint' and 'perspective', to 'conceptualizations' and 'mentalities'. I use 'imagination' here, to capture the creative and 'dreaming' quality of thinking about possibilities.

articulating a design for a city (a 'theory' as it was then called), using this as a building programme, or as a process for arriving at an appropriate policy solution for 'steering the city', and then 'implementing' the policy arrived at.

An interactive understanding of the theory/practice relationship and the policy/ action relationship moves from privileging attention to the articulation of theory and policy. It centres instead on how action is accomplished, and how policy ideas are created and made manifest in practices. This shift demands much more attention to the socio-economic, cultural and political-administrative dimensions which get to shape the practices through which communities and societies think about what places mean to them and devote energy to developing place qualities. The planning 'function' becomes 'one among many' forces shaping place qualities, instead of being the 'grand designer' of place evolution. It is only rarely that planning experts can attach themselves to a political leader who embodies a clear place development agenda in an uncontested way. The examples where this has happened tend to come from colonial situations of extreme inequality or from imperial or enthusiastic post-colonial 'modernisers'.[3] Elsewhere, planning experts have either to act as advocates, as the early twentieth century planners often did, or to work out how to insert a contribution to shaping place quality futures into a complex institutional context. This means affecting how others think about future possibilities and about how they use their resources – material, legal and socio-political – to shape how futures might evolve. Planning ideas in this way move from being embodied in the imagination of individual 'planning experts' to being expressed through policies and strategies. They become part of the cultures, governance systems and arenas of practice developed for collective action purposes, for the governance of political communities. This shift to understanding the planning theory/practice relationship in an interactive way thus results in recognizing that planning ideas and planning activity are intimately connected with the cultures and practices of politics and administration, with the practices of formal government and the governance processes of a polity.

Two key challenges for planning theory arise from this shift. The first is an analytical one. This challenge centres on how to conceptualize the relationships between government, wider governance processes and cultures, and the ideas and practices which evolve and could evolve to promote future-oriented thinking and acting about developing place qualities. The second challenge is a normative one. It centres on disentangling how governance activity informed by 'progressive' dreams about the future (see the Overall Introduction) can be distinguished from that which promotes narrowly-focused, elite-dominated and environmentally-damaging future options. The planning field is full of narratives about how good planning ideas were subverted to oppressive and exploitive purposes, or linked to the interests of self-regarding elites. Howitt and Lunkapis, in Chapter 3, illustrate an extreme version of such subversion in their accounts of the way in which the planning practices of colonizing powers in Australia and Malaysia continue to

---

3   See Nasr and Volait (2003), Banerjee (2009), Vidyarthi (2010), as well as Boyer (1983) and Madanipour (2007).

neglect the very different philosophies and approaches of Indigenous peoples to imagining and dwelling within places. Some planning ideas have themselves been criticized as narrowly-based around bourgeois aspirations.[4] The design ideas associated with the 'new urbanism' movement (Grant 2006) provide a contemporary example.

One response to the tensions between taking a critical analytical approach and promoting a normative agenda for planning activity is to treat them as rigorously separate arenas. But no analysis is free of normative concerns, however implicit, and those who propose ways forward draw on some kind of analysis to ground their propositions. This means that it is important to probe for both concerns when considering a contribution to the planning theory literature and to make clear how they relate. The intention of normative and analytical concerns becomes clearer when accounts of planning activity are located in some wider understanding of the societal processes which generate them. Gualini in Chapter 1 does this through a discussion of tendencies in contemporary governance. Roy in Chapter 2 suggests a focus on the processes of urbanization through which huge urban conglomerations around the world are currently being created.

This Part includes seven contributions, all very different, which address alternative ways to understand and advance how planning activity is and should be practised. They all reflect an appreciation that planning activity is situated in a wider context of governance dynamics. They also seek a nuanced and detailed grasp of the diversity of contexts and the contingencies of practices. This reflects a distaste for the 'grand, totalizing narratives' of the mid-twentieth century, whether of the managerial variety or that of structural Marxist analysis. They explore ways of moving beyond the inheritance of the 'heavy' states of Western European democracies in which many formal planning systems are embedded (see the contributions from Gualini in Chapter 1 and Albrechts in Chapter 7). They examine the potential of governance energy 'beyond the (formal) state', and the extent to which 'insurgent practices' have the possibility to challenge and limit the unravelling of formal government practices promoted by the so-called 'neo-liberal' project (see the contributions from Roy (Chapter 2), Howitt and Lunkapis (Chapter 3) and Sager (Chapter 6), see also Sandercock 1998, Briggs 2008). Versteeg and Hajer in Chapter 5 emphasize the importance of looking at the arenas where governance practices are performed, and at the struggles over their 'staging, setting and scripting'. In this way, they hope to identify more clearly the dynamics of who gets access to such arenas, who controls their practice dynamics and which future dreams live on to shape future action.

In the rest of this Introduction, I look first at the different intellectual perspectives which the authors draw upon to develop their contributions. I then summarize what emerge, in my reading of their work, as key messages for debates in planning

---

4   In the US in the 1960s, sociologists criticized planners for promoting middle class ideas about what a neighbourhood should be like, rather than recognizing the diversity of neighbourhood qualities represented in a vibrant city. See Gans (1969), Jacobs (1963), and also Pløger in Chapter 12.

theory, centred around two issues. The first relates to how contextual dynamics are understood. The second relates to the significance of micro-practices. I then make a small conclusion of my own.

Multiple Perspectives

The Chapters in this Part reflect both the diversity of intellectual perspectives through which the relation between planning activity and its contexts are being imagined and analyzed, and the contemporary political debates between them. Strands of Foucauldian thinking (the use of concepts such as disciplining and governmentality, and the methods of discourse analysis and genealogy) interplay with ideas from regulation theory, particularly Jessop's 'strategic regulation' approach, and socio-technical systems ideas with their emphasis on actors and networks. Global political economy ideas challenge what is seen as the preoccupation in planning theory debates with the qualities of policy processes. Among those who look at policy processes, ideas drawn from debates about modes and arrangements of governance activity interact with more pragmatic and interpretive analyses of how governance work is actually done, and how planners think it should be done.

Most of the contributions acknowledge a relational focus, in that they focus on the dynamics of the social relations through which governance activity is shaped and performed. There is also a recognition of the complex nature of urban dynamics and governance processes, though the chapters make less use of the post-structural and complexity analyses which are to be found in Parts II and III of this Volume. There are, however, two 'foils' which help to identify the authors' normative and analytical commitments. The first is the 'neo-liberal' political project. This is understood as a hegemonic political project with global reach, which portrays formal government as inefficient, bureaucratic and liable to corruption, in contrast to market forms of allocating resources and generating material wealth. For those involved in the planning field and promoting 'progressive' agendas, this is far too limited a way of advancing human flourishing in sustainable ways. It also leads to outcomes which increase inequalities within and between political communities. In any case, the financial collapse and subsequent economic crisis of the late 2000s has dramatically exposed the limits of this project, and brought 'the state' back into play as an important actor in safeguarding future possibilities. The struggle for a wider agenda, as Sager (Chapter 6) stresses, demands a view of the human condition and of development that has the breadth to include an expansive grasp of the way we humans live with and relate to our planet, rather than a narrow focus on material 'wealth' measured in monetary terms.

The second foil is communicative planning theory, which has become a strong strand of mainstream planning theory since the 1990s (see Hillier and Healey 2008c).[5]

---

5   By 'mainstream', I mean as taught in many planning programmes. Such programmes typically expose students to a range of theories and debates. The three volumes of

Some of the contributions challenge its conceptions, following well-established lines of critique developed in the past decade, drawing on either Foucauldian or Marxist political economy (see the contributions in Hillier and Healey 2008b). Others seek to build on and expand its concepts and methods.[6] Only Sager makes a link to the discussion of rational choice theory, as developed in relation to planning in the work of Webster and Lai (2003) and Pennington (2000), despite its significance in underpinning the policy implications of the neo-liberal project and creating micro-practices with which many planners have to engage these days.

Gualini's contribution provides a very helpful review of the genealogy of the concept of 'governance', carefully distinguishing its normative and analytical usages. Intellectually, he draws on a German and British literature, and emphasizes the value of Jessop's state-theoretical perspective on governance as a mode of regulation. This views the development of the political as a mode of governance, to accompany the economic shift to a mode of accumulation based on developing financial and entrepreneurial capacity – that is, the neo-liberal project. The result of this largely structural analysis is a shift from politics 'as the pursuit of a social utility function, defined within the political system ... (of) ... representative democracy, to the centrality of policy as the institutional framing of issue-related voluntary exchange and private market initiative' (p. 66). Governance activity then becomes fragmented, in a 'polycentric' regulatory environment, which is often expected somehow to be 'self-regulatory'. In this conception, the 'local' is seen as an important institutional site where exogenous pressures to appear economically attractive ('competitive') meet endogenous pressures to promote social integration. This leads Gualini to emphasize the importance of understanding the micro-practices of these encounters, and how they relate to the 'dynamics of hegemony formation' and its wider effects on 'governmentality' within the context of the re-configuration of political life. Grounded in this analysis, Gualini then argues that the project of planning theory should be about developing the critical tools to empower alternative practices which challenge prevailing emerging narrow hegemonies. To do this, he argues, requires more attention among the planning theory community, firstly to the substantive and process dimensions of the new policy spaces emerging in the above re-configurations. Secondly, more attention is needed to the tension between advocacy of the potential for experimentation and innovation in policy practices (see Part II) and the ease with which such activity can be co-opted by hegemonic forces without careful attention to questions of legitimacy and accountability. In other words, these micro-practices must be analyzed as sites of struggle over future possibilities, not just for the particular place in question, but for the quality of the political realm more generally.

Hillier and Healey (2008a, b, and c) provide a useful overview of the likely content of such programmes.

6   For recent reviews of the body of work associated with communicative planning theory, see Fischer (2009), which assesses its contribution to social justice, and Healey (2008) for a history of the ideas.

Roy explores these structural shifts in political economy from an analysis of so-called 'informal' urban development processes. She argues that planning theorists need to pay much more attention to the massive urbanization which has occurred very rapidly across the world in the later twentieth century and what this means for the struggle for quality of life in the cities of the burgeoning metropolises of Asia, Africa, Latin America and the Middle East. In such contexts, informal land and development processes are a major form of spatially differentiated modes of the production and management of urban life. She argues that the concept of 'informality' should be used to describe a pervasive phenomenon. But attention to 'informal' practices is also advocated within two different perspectives, or 'ensembles' of ideas. Within a neo-liberal ensemble, informal processes are often celebrated as evidence of a lively civil society, nimble in self-regulation, and full of innovative energy. This leads to policies which centre on 'formalizing' practices. As Roy argues, this in effect means commodifying such practices. Such a romantic presentation of the informal, however, neglects the lived experience of marginality, which is often violent, oppressive and exhausting. Roy notes that a more radical view of informality was promoted by Castells, in his advocacy of grassroots struggles for citizenship (Castells 1983). This suggests that what those living in such informal situations need are stronger rights, a theme which is also taken up by Howitt and Lunkapis (in Chapter 3). This, of course, brings the state back in, as the institutional site where formal rights are defined. Roy's analysis leads to an argument about the focus of planning theory which parallels that of Gualini. Planning theory should give much more attention to understanding 'informal' processes as a mode of production in late capitalism. This implies focusing on the production of space and the politics of space, and to forms of 'governmentality', in which informal processes emerge as important sites of experimentation and struggle for urban futures. Such understanding should encourage those doing planning work to position themselves knowledgeably and carefully if they are to avoid merely becoming handmaidens of a neo-liberal hegemonic agenda.

Howitt and Lunkapis help to fill out this demand, through a discussion of cultural clashes over how people's relation to land and natural resources are imagined. The challenge they take up is how to address the coexistence of peoples with very different understandings of each other and of place. In Australia and Malaysia, planning systems have developed which are located in Western notions of individualized land and property rights, a central development both in the evolution of modern capitalism and in justifying the spatial ordering of newly-colonized territories. But these notions were quite different to those held by the people who already lived there. As Howitt and Lunkapis argue, such peoples and their own notions were erased, literally rendered 'out of place'.[7] In such

---

7   There is a critical debate around the concept of 'Indigenous peoples'. In Australia, of
       course, the clash between peoples present on the continent for well over 40,000 years
       and the western colonizers was and remains extreme. In the Americas, 'native' peoples
       are more recent colonizers and had themselves been competing with each other for
       territorial control. In Europe and Asia, there are all kinds of clashes between groups

situations, it is hardly sufficient to ask members of such 'erased' communities to discuss with those who have taken land from them about how to 'coexist' with each other through consensus-building practices. Slowly, the uneasy conscience of the inheritors of these colonial regimes has led to attempts to redress such gross inequities by the allocation of rights. This has allowed Indigenous peoples to use the law of their colonizers to redress grievances. But they still have to use an alien language of rights to reclaim what they had previously understood was available to their communities as a common resource through links to an ancestral past.[8] In Malaysia, there are further problems due to conflicts of rights between different legal instruments. The authors argue that the value of the use of formal law is in the added power it gives to formerly marginalized people. This moves struggles for coexistence beyond consensus-building initiatives, which are likely to be dominated by the culture of the dominant groups, to a much stronger basis for negotiating coexistence.[9] Howitt and Lunkapis therefore argue for more attention in planning theory to issues of recognition and rights, as opposed to concerns about building social integration and cohesion.

Huxley focuses her critical attention on the 'planning histories' which those writing about the planning field construct as a foundation for the ideas they put forward about future possibilities. She argues that these origin myths often look back in time in ways which erase the power struggles through which planning systems and practices have been produced. She suggests that more attention is needed to careful investigative histories which question these myths. She underlines, in parallel with Gualini and Roy, that accounts of the emergence of planning activity need to be located in a wider appreciation of the complex intersections of different conceptions of problems through which the legislation, procedures and practices of planning systems get produced. She argues that it is important to apprehend the specificities of such intersections by suspending the idea of 'planning' in order to interrogate it through careful use of Foucault's 'genealogical' approach to historical analysis. She then draws out the relevance of this kind of analysis to addressing some of the contemporary preoccupations of those proposing critical and progressive initiatives in the planning field. She concludes that it is not helpful to prescribe overly generalized principles for reducing inequalities and repressions in a specific situation. Instead, those seeking to contribute to such a project need to offer their critical capacities as tools for those engaged in struggle – even *against* the idea of planning – the outcomes of which cannot be determined or predicted.

---

who have lived in an area for a very long time and new claimants, which lead to clashes between cultures, which have political and legal implications. Examples from Northern Europe include the experience of the Sami, pushed to the fringes of Northern Scandinavia, and that of the Highland crofters in Scotland brutally 'cleared' from their ancestral lands, both long histories which still affect disputes over land, territory and modes of governance.

8   Note that the way a 'common resource' is conceived is likely to vary between cultures. This affects legal systems, see Glenn (2007).

9   See also Forester (2006) on the negotiation/consensus-building distinction.

The next three Chapters return to a European context as their practice referent. In different ways, they pick up the theme of the significance of micro-practices as sites of struggle over place qualities and place development trajectories in which planning ideas and initiatives are implicated. Versteeg and Hajer argue that this demands more, and more methodologically-informed, empirical analysis of the micro-political practices emerging in the new governance spaces identified by Gualini. They seek to develop the insights of communicative planning theory and the claims of deliberative forms of democracy by looking at material practices as well as analyzing the formation and transmission of discursive frames. Their concern is primarily analytical – to assess why some policy narratives about place qualities in some contexts get to have persuasive power and expand their reach, while others fail to survive for long. Drawing on March and Olsen (1989), they underline the importance of examining the 'performance' of governance micro-practices, through an analysis of their staging, setting and scripting. From the field of socio-technical systems, they emphasize the significance of the way artefacts, such as designs and maps, are constructed in specific practices, and how these may then have significant material effects. They are particularly interested in the way such work helps to construct 'publics' around particular issues and policy ideas, echoing Dewey's conception of how 'publics' are formed (Dewey 1927/1991). They argue that an analysis of micro-practices as performances provides a rich tool for examining how politics and power dynamics play out in the institutional sites of the emerging networked forms of governance, so long as attention is maintained to how such practices are shaped by, and in turn shape, the wider governance 'cultures' and systems in which micro-practices are situated. Their argument, by implication, suggests that planning theory needs to pay much more attention to the empirical examination of practices.

Sager's concern is with the moral tensions which planners in public administrations face when they have to resolve the conflicting demands of a management regime informed by concepts which have evolved to promote a more neo-liberal conception of how government should be performed, and the concepts of communicative action and deliberative democracy which they have absorbed through their professional education and commitments. Challenging some analysts who have claimed that communicative planning theory and ideas abut deliberative democracy are themselves a way of realizing the neo-liberal political project because they too challenge the more paternalist and top-down practices of twentieth-century welfare states,[10] Sager presents a careful contrast between communicative planning theory and the new public management. He notes that the two approaches share some similar concerns. Both are concerned with improving the quality of public services and with being responsive to users. But they are otherwise deeply different. The communicative approach treats users as citizens, with broad and diverse concerns, who build practices of collective problem-solving as particular issues are addressed. The new public management treats users as consumers, with little concern for anything other than their particular,

---

10   Sager is referring in particular to a Scandinavian discussion, see his references to comments by Christer Bengs in the *European Journal of Spatial Development*.

individualized economic interests. He uses various studies to highlight planners' experience of role tensions resulting from these conflicting expectations. He argues that planning theorists need to engage much more with the dilemmas of planning practitioners in such situations and advocates the promotion of an alternative ethic of public service with which to challenge the economic reductionism of the new public management. This echoes other calls for a more positive reconsideration of the role of the 'bureaucrat' in contemporary states (see du Gay 2000).

Albrechts speaks with the voice of a committed strategic planning practitioner. He draws on his long experience of both planning practice and of reading and writing on strategic planning in a Western European context. He argues that there is an urgent need in the present period for a strategic approach to how cities and regions could develop, with a broad social and environmental perspective rather than a narrow economic preoccupation merely with 'competitiveness'. He believes that this requires a transformation of traditional politics and planning practices. Rather than an emphasis on service delivery and responsiveness to users, which Sager identifies as driving new approaches to how governance activity is performed, he stresses the development of a proactive capacity to envision, analyze, debate and implement new visions of future possibilities. Along with the advocates of deliberative democracy, he is supportive of efforts to involve many people, including citizens generally, in discussions about shaping and implementing visions of alternative futures. But he argues that professionally-trained planners too have an important role to play, beyond merely facilitating such multi-actor discussions. For what is needed, he suggests, is the cultivation of informed and creative ways of thinking about future alternatives, which planners should have developed through their training, knowledge and experience. Drawing on futures thinking from the late 1960s, as well as more recent discussions of strategic planning as a transformative process, his contribution emphasizes that planning theory should not let an overly critical stance to planners and their practices disable planning practitioners from making strong contributions towards creating practices with progressive transformative energy.

Key Messages

All the papers recognize that the present period is one where old certainties are breaking down, while new projects are attempting to gain hegemonic status, but are themselves undermined by contradictions. These breakdowns and uncertainties in turn create opportunities for alternative, more progressive strategies to emerge. Planning activity, planning in practice, is caught up in these processes of re-configuration, experimentation and struggle over which alternatives will emerge and endure to shape future place qualities. The authors therefore demand more attention from planning theory to understanding how these struggles are being played out, to the potential for alternatives, in terms of both content and process (substance and procedure), and to how transformative change comes about. Parts

II and III of the present volume offer some resources for this enterprise, but the authors in this Part argue strongly that such contributions need to be grounded in a good, empirically-informed and historically-grounded understanding of contemporary developments in urban dynamics and governance processes. Two inter-related themes emerge from these chapters.

Understanding Contextual Dynamics

For some time now, there have been calls to give more attention to 'situating' planning concepts and analyses of planning practices (Watson 2008). Recent analyses of the development of planning systems and practices have been advancing such 'situated' understanding through careful research on the historical development of planning ideas and practices in particular countries or specific contexts.[11] Huxley, in Chapter 4, calls for more such work. Communicative planning theory has underlined the need for attention to the specific contingencies of planning activity as practised (see Hillier and Healey 2008c, Part 1). But, as Watson argues, the challenges are not just about situating planning activity in a specific institutional environment. They are also about clashes between systems and 'mentalities' or cultures. Planning practice, as Howitt and Lunkapis underline, is often at the sharp end of such clashes. For Roy, the clashes are about different modes of production of the city. For Howitt and Lunkapis, they are about cultures and philosophies. For Huxley, they are about tensions between planning histories that take 'planning' for granted and seek lessons for improvement, and genealogies that unsettle the taken-for-granted status of 'planning' and its history, in order to foster thinking differently. For Sager, they are about different attitudes to public service and the formation of the public realm. For Albrechts, the clashes are in the minds of people doing 'planning work', between old inertias and new commitments to a creative, transformative energy.

Empirically, this means that analyses of planning practices need to pay more attention not just to descriptions of organizations and actors, the practices through which some get privileged and some marginalized, and the modes of production through which cities are produced. It involves attention to systemic biases. In a period of institutional re-configuration on a global scale, such systemic clashes are particularly evident, and particularly likely to be missed by 'grand narrative' accounts of structural change. Accounts of systemic, or structural, shifts need to be nuanced by attention to how such shifts are experienced in many different kinds of practice context. The recognition of systemic biases also requires careful attention to the extent to which such phenomena as formal planning systems, the practices which build up around these and the advocacy of ideas about place qualities and governance processes are linked to specific institutional contexts, or instead have the capacity to be 'transplanted' into different contexts without

---

11   See for example, Sorensen's work on Japanese urban planning (Sorensen 2002), the special edition edited by Birch and Silver (2009) on 20th Century US planning, see also Huxley (2006) and work in the planning history field.

losing a progressive innovation potential.[12] Cultures and systems are not static and pre-given, but are themselves evolving phenomena.[13] Planning ideas and practices are inherently part of these evolutions. One important role for planning theory is to enhance appreciation of the contribution that such ideas and practices have made, make and could make to such evolutions. With a more practice focus, such attention to systemic biases is also an important consideration for those who get involved in designing and re-designing 'planning systems'. Designing 'planning systems' is itself an attempt to consciously mobilize a systemic bias in how practices subsequently evolve.

Such a recognition raises the long-standing question in planning theory about the relation between planning activity, power and politics. In the 1970s, critical urban political economists argued that planning systems and practices were a tool of the state, which was itself an arm of hegemonic capitalism. This enlarged the claim of the critical sociologists of the 1960s that planning ideas about city design reflected a narrow bourgeois view of a desirable urban way of life. Power lay with economic elites who shaped what policy systems and practices were able to achieve. The ambition of many post-1960s planners to limit capitalist economic excesses by promoting social welfare and environmental protection in their strategies, projects and designs was often, from this perspective, denigrated as naïve and utopian (see Hillier and Healey 2008b).

Since then, such a crude characterization of the state has given way to a more fractured and fragmented understanding of the relation between economy, state and society. The understanding of power dynamics has in turn been influenced by a Foucauldian recognition that power is generative as well as authoritative. It lies embedded in cultures and practices, in 'mentalities' and modes of acting, as much as in formal institutions. Some analysts stay with this idea, analyzing the 'governmentalities' of particular institutional configurations in which planning activity is to be found (see, for example, Huxley 2002, Raco 2003). Huxley, in Chapter 4, emphasizes the richness of this approach and the way it can uncover the production and regulation of practice (see also Huxley 2007). But, within the planning field, our concern is not just with analysis, important though that is, but with transformative possibilities, with identifying and using moments of opportunity to change the way things go on. It is with understanding contexts in order to see how to 'make a difference' in the policies and practices of place development. For a progressive agenda in the planning field, it involves confronting an economics which reduces human life to materially-self-interested individuals and a politics which centres on a singular model of the 'good society'.[14] This sets up a specific

12   The term 'institutions' is here used to refer to the norms and ways of acting which have built up through time, and often get to be 'taken-for-granted' as the 'natural' way of doing things.

13   See Healey (2004) for how I have thought about such issues, which Versteeg and Hajer take up in Chapter 5.

14   See Connolly (2005) for arguments about contrasts between a pluralist and a monist polity.

reason for understanding the power dynamics of particular contexts, but renders this particularly difficult. As Gualini and Versteeg and Hajer argue, in the present period of multiple re-configurations, power and politics have migrated from the arenas of formal representative democracy to all kinds of other institutional sites. This creates opportunities for progressive innovation and experimentation, through which material improvements and new governance cultures or 'mentalities' may evolve. It also means that initiatives to take such opportunities are always open to contestation and capture by other forces.

This suggests that more attention is needed, in the intellectual resources available within planning theory, to the generative power of the way planning activity is performed and expressed in planning 'systems' and practices. In many instances where planners are heavily criticized, particularly in some of the newly-urbanizing parts of the world (see UN-HABITAT 2009), planning activity does little more than advance the ambitions of modernizing and post-colonial elites. But there are many other examples where those informed by the planning project have helped to carry forward social movement initiatives which have not only instantiated significant shifts in the promotion of liveability and environmental sustainability, but have helped to enhance the 'intelligence' of the polities in which they are situated.[15] In other words, in some situations, planning activity not only expresses cultures and philosophies. It helps to transform and create the imagination and philosophy of the culture of a polity. It is here that the 'hope' carried by the progressive potential within planning ideas may get some practical leverage.

The Significance of Micro-practices

All the chapters in this Part recognize that attention to the micro-practices in which planning activity takes place is important. Through enriching the empirical referents which theorists draw on, they challenge tendencies in the social science literature on planning activity to overgeneralize, essentialize 'planning' and populate accounts with stereotypes of 'the planner'. But they do not imply an endless stream of narratives of practice experiences. They call instead for more attention to ways of analyzing them. Huxley finds methodological inspiration from the Foucauldian tradition. Versteeg and Hajer argue that meso-level tools for analyzing practice experiences need to be better developed. They supplement and extend those already in use in interpretive institutionalist analyses of governance practices, such as the analysis of framing discourses, the formation of arenas and networks, and the significance of policy communities and communities of practice in shaping micro-practices.[16] Others have looked to the field of policy analysis generally, and in particular to the way problems and solutions encounter and interact with each other, as in Kingdon's work on policy streams (Kingdon 2003).

---

15   See examples of Vancouver (Punter 2003), Portland, Oregon (Abbott 2001), Amsterdam (Fainstein 2005), and also Briggs (2008), Healey (2010).
16   See Hajer and Wagenaar (2003), Fischer (2003), Yanow (1996).

Another methodological inspiration, which Versteeg and Hajer also draw on, has been the work in the socio-technical systems field on how technologies and artefacts travel from one arena to another, carrying ideas and ways of practising embodied within their materialities (Murdoch and Abram 2002, Murdoch 2006, Callon et al. 2009). This could contribute to analyzing some of the issues which arise in the inter-cultural clashes which Howitt and Lunkapis are concerned with, especially with respect to technologies of mapping, measuring and categorizing, or the way planning officials and consultants get to use legally-required tools like Strategic Environmental Assessment in their practices. The chapters in Parts II and III provide further methodological possibilities based in poststructuralist modes of analysis.

But methods of analysis are not independent of intellectual perspectives. It would be helpful to have much more attention in the planning theory field to the different approaches being developed to analyze micro-practices, the methodologies that are used in each, and their value in addressing the questions being explored. What difference does it make if we analyze an instance of planning practice using the concept of 'governmentality' and methods of Foucauldian genealogy, compared to the 'sociological institutionalist' analysis of policy arenas, policy communities, policy discourses and governance cultures,[17] or the socio-technical systems ideas about actors, networks, translation and inscription? More attention, too, would be useful to the normative considerations which underlie why the analyses are being undertaken, and the social problems to which they are, often implicitly, addressed. All this underlines the value, not just of careful attention to analytical methods, but to the need for producing empirical work through well-grounded historical work (see Huxley in Chapter 4) and 'thick' narrative accounts, as advocated in recent work on the methods of interpretive policy analysis (see Yanow and Schwartz-Shea 2006). Good 'science', as Latour (2000) argues, proceeds by allowing the 'recalcitrant' nature of the objects being studied to 'strike back' at scientists' attempts to generalize about them. Attention to the dynamics of micro-practices helps to make sure that, within the planning field, our generalizations are continually bombarded with experiences which do not fit. This helps to cultivate attentiveness to the contingencies of time and place.

The authors in this Part also emphasize that attention to micro-practices does not mean a neglect of structuring dynamics and systemic biases. They draw on different ways of relating micro-practices to macro-dynamics, and the relation between structuring dynamics and agency energy. But they do not present particular practice experiences as capable of transforming local place qualities independently of the wider context. Instead, they emphasize how different relations, with variable systemic properties and dynamics, encounter each other in specific situations. They explore how these play out, not just in particular places, but have effects in the wider relations in which those active in a locality are situated. They avoid typologies of regimes of governance or manifestations of planning practices. Instead, they focus

---

17   Such institutionalist work is associated with that of Hajer (1995) and also my own work (Healey 2007).

on how the interplay of different forces interacts in the construction of practices and contexts. What is important in analyzing micro-practices, they suggest, is to explore how the micro-dynamics through which, in some places and at some times, the energy is generated to create a transformative power which not only produces specific benefits at the micro-scale, but also spreads more widely, to provide a base for more systemic structural transformations, in urban dynamics and in the formation of governance cultures or 'governmentalities' (see Briggs 2008).

Greater conceptual and methodological sophistication in analyzing micro-practices would help to enrich the resources available to those engaged in 'doing planning work' by enhancing their 'intelligence' when confronting the particularities of the situations they face, and seeking ways to challenge forces which head in a regressive direction. For practitioners exist in a world of micro-practices, as Latour (1993) has pointed out. Officials designing changes to planning laws, analysts undertaking the 'spatial analysis' of urban complexes, consultants advising on the design of new settlements, facilitators mediating disputes or orchestrating a consensus-building process, planning officials doing development regulation work, are all involved in the messy work of creating what becomes their 'advice'. It is only if and when such 'advice' becomes consolidated, usually through many interactions with other 'micro-practices', into a policy statement, a law, a technique or a design imagination, that it gets to have more systemic properties. As John Forester has long urged us to recognize, it is therefore important within the planning theory field to maintain attention to what it takes to 'do' planning work. This is not just a matter of the skills and knowledge which planners have and/or should have, although, as Albrechts argues in Chapter 7, these need a critical re-think in the present period. It relates also to the general perceptual apparatus, moral commitments, empathies and emotive sensibilities and capabilities for shrewd political and institutional judgement which people doing planning work mobilize (Hoch 2007). Sager tells us that planners face acute moral dilemmas in Western Europe as they struggle through conflicting 'moral imperatives'. This underlines the need for continuing work on the ethical demands placed on those who get involved in planning practices (see Campbell and Marshall 2000, Campbell 2006). Perhaps it would be helpful to have more biographies from planning practitioners, to provide greater understanding of how the development of their knowledge interacted with their various experiences and exposure to different kinds of ideas, and how this in turn affected what they came to 'advise' and do in various situations in their evolving careers.

Some Neglected Issues

The general message from the Chapters in this Part is that planning theory needs to engage in greater conceptual and empirical depth with practice experiences, both of the past and the present. This would have the advantage of reinforcing the substantive dimension of understanding the planning project, probing in particular the way in which particular techniques which get to be used in practice – of evaluation and assessment, of design and costing, of management and measurement, etc. –

embody particular values and perspectives, and how alternative techniques could be designed to promote alternative values. The analytical methods used in the field of socio-technical systems are particularly useful in this regard. But it would also be helpful if the planning theory field were to engage more with the debates in the environmental policy field on how scientific, technical and experiential knowledge are interconnected in policy debates (Owens et al. 2004, 2006; Fischer 2000; Callon et al. 2009). More generally, Roy's challenge to the 'planning theory community' to vigorously engage with the dynamic evolution of urban complexes outside Europe and North America surely opens up an array of issues which are likely to recast planning ideas and planning practices in the coming decades.

The need to overcome cultural introversion and naïve encounters with unfamiliar practices has long been obvious (see Sanyal 2005, Healey and Upton 2010). This is particularly important with respect to the concern with process issues in planning theory. Many across the world may want the material assets available in Western contexts, such as reliable water and energy supplies to the home. They may also seek formal government capacities which are more effective and less elite-dominated and corrupt than their present institutions. But they do not necessarily want the particular forms of governance process which those educated in Western planning contexts may promote. Working out how to make use of exogenous concepts and expertise, while developing locally specific governance processes and planning practices, is a major field of creative invention which deserves more attention in the planning theory field.

Finally, it would be helpful to give careful, critical attention to the broad field of 'institutionalist' analyses to be found in economics and political science. The focus of this work is inspired by the search for ways of giving greater recognition to the specificities of institutional contexts, which prove very 'recalcitrant' to attempts to generalize about them. The field is inhabited by different trajectories of analysis, and divided by very different philosophical assumptions about ontology and epistemology. But, as the chapters by Versteeg and Hajer in this Part and by Bertolini in Part III indicate, there are rich resources here with which those in the planning field could usefully engage (see Moulaert and Sekia 2003, Moulaert and Mehmood 2007, Sorensen and Torfing 2007, Verma 2007).

Into the Future

In summary, the contributions to planning theory emphasized in this Part centre on developing a better understanding of contemporary urban development processes, expanding an analysis of the role which planning activity has and could play in shaping and transforming governance processes, and providing the resources to identify and challenge narrow neo-liberal hegemonies. They imply an important role for planning theory discussion in developing intellectual resources with which to critique established and evolving practices of managing place development. But they also suggest that such discussion must do more than this. It needs to provide resources to help empower those engaged in the practices of progressive place development with more knowledgeable practical sensitivities through which to grasp the dimensions of the situations they are in.

This implies that planning practices get to be understood not as pieces of governance infrastructure which somehow are inappropriate and need to be transformed to realize the innovative potential proposed in a particular theory. Instead, planning practices need to be appreciated as important empirical sites where struggles are being played out over what and whose material conditions and which governance mentalities/cultures will get privileged in emerging urban futures. This demands that theorists do not treat practices in the language of stereotypes and broad generalisations.[18] Instead, they should be encouraged to see them as a myriad of institutional sites, with particular histories and geographies, specific power dynamics and variable capacities to promote progressive futures. Grasping the variability and complexity of the multiple worlds of planning practices itself demands innovative and imaginative conceptualizations. If the relationship between planning theory and planning practice is interactive, theorists need to learn from practices. For examining practices, particularly through methodologically careful and 'thick' accounts, teaches theory as well as tests it. It creates theoretical insights as well as illustrates them.

References

Abbott, C. (2001) *Greater Portland: Urban Life and Landscape in the Pacific Northwest.* Philadelphia: University of Pennsylvania Press.

Banerjee, T. (2009) 'US planning expeditions to postcolonial India: from ideology to innovation in technical assistance' *Journal of the American Planning Association* 75: 193–208.

Birch, E.L. and Silver, C. (2009) 'One hundred years of city planning's enduring and evolving connections' *Journal of the American Planning Association* 75: 113–22 and special issue.

Boyer, C. (1983) *Dreaming the Rational City.* Cambridge, MA: MIT Press.

Briggs, X.d.S. (2008) *Democracy as Problem-solving.* Boston, MA: MIT Press.

Callon, M., Lascoumes, P. and Barthe, Y. (2009) *Acting in an Uncertain World: An Essay on Technical Democracy.* Cambridge, MA: MIT Press.

Campbell, H. (2006) 'Just planning: the art of situated ethical judgement' *Journal of Planning Education and Research* 26: 92–106.

Campbell, H. and Marshall, R. (2000) 'Moral obligation, planning and the public interest: a commentary on current British practice' *Environment and Planning B: Planning and Design* 27: 297–312.

---

18   This caveat should of course also apply to our characterizations of planning theories and ideological positions. My thanks to M.H. for highlighting this.

Castells, M. (1983) *The City and the Grassroots*. Berkeley, CA: University of California Press.

Connolly, W.E. (2005) *Pluralism*. Durham, NC: Duke University Press.

Dewey, J. (1927/1991) *The Public and its Problems*. Athens, OH: Swallow Press/Ohio University Press.

du Gay, P. (2000) *In Praise of Bureaucracy*. London: Sage.

Fainstein, S. (2005) 'Cities and diversity: should we plan for it? Can we plan for it?' *Urban Affairs Review* 41: 3–19.

Fischer, F. (2000) *Citizens, Experts and the Environment: The Politics of Local Knowledge*. Durham, NC and London: Duke University Press.

Fischer, F. (2003) *Reframing Public Policy: Discursive politics and Deliberative Practices*. Oxford: Oxford University Press.

Fischer, F. (2009) 'Discursive planning: social justice as a discourse' in Marcuse, P. (ed.) *Searching for the Just City: Debates in Urban Theory and Practice*. London: Routledge, pp. 52–71.

Forester, J. (1989) *Planning in the Face of Power*. Berkeley: University of California Press.

Forester, J. (1999) *The Deliberative Practitioner: Encouraging Participatory Planning Processes*. London: MIT Press.

Forester, J. (2006) 'Making participation work when interests conflict: moving from facilitating dialogue and moderating debate to mediating negotiations' *Journal of the American Planning Association* 72: 447–56.

Friedmann, J. (1973) *Re-tracking America: A Theory of Transactive Planning*. New York: Anchor Press.

Friedmann, J. (1987) *Planning in the Public Domain*. Princeton, NJ: Princeton University Press.

Friedmann, J. (2010) 'Crossing borders: do planning ideas travel?' in Healey, P. and Upton, R. (eds), *Crossing Borders: International Exchange and Planning Practices*. London: Routledge, pp. 313–27.

Gans, H. (1969) 'Planning for people not buildings' *Environment and Planning A* 1: 33–46.

Glenn, H.P. (2000/2007) *Legal Traditions of the World*. Oxford: Oxford University Press.

Grant, J. (2006) *Planning the Good Community: New Urbanism in Theory and Practice*. London: Routledge.

Hajer, M. (1995) *The Politics of Environmental Discourse*. Oxford: Oxford University Press.

Hajer, M. and Wagenaar, H. (eds) (2003) *Deliberative Policy Analysis: Understanding Governance in the Network Society*. Cambridge: Cambridge University Press.

Healey, P. (1983) *Local Plans in British Land Use Planning*. Oxford: Pergamon.

Healey, P. (1988) 'The British planning system and managing the urban environment' *Town Planning Review* 59: 397–417.

Healey, P. (1997/2006) *Collaborative Planning: Shaping Places in Fragmented Societies*. London: Macmillan.

Healey, P. (2004) 'Creativity and urban governance' *Policy Studies* 25: 87–102.

Healey, P. (2007) *Urban Complexity and Spatial Strategies: Towards a Relational Planning for our Times*. London: Routledge.

Healey, P. (2010) *Making Better Places: The Planning Project in the Twenty-first Century*. London: Palgrave Macmillan.

Healey, P. (2008) 'The idea of "communicative" planning: practices, concepts and rhetorics; talk to MIT series on the "History of Planning Ideas", Boston. 2nd draft 10 April 2008. To be published in forthcoming volume, *History of Planning Ideas*. Editors: Sanyal, B., Vale, L. and Rosan, C.

Healey, P. and Upton, R. (eds) (2010) *Crossing Borders: International Exchange and Planning Practices*. London: Routledge.

Hillier, J. and Healey, P. (eds) (2008a) *Foundations of the Planning Enterprise: Critical Readings in Planning Theory, Volume I*. Aldershot: Ashgate.

Hillier, J. and Healey, P. (eds) (2008b) *Political Economy, Diversity and Pragmatism: Critical Readings in Planning Theory, Vol II*. Aldershot: Ashgate.

Hillier, J. and Healey, P. (eds) (2008c) *Contemporary Movements in Planning Theory: Critical Readings in Planning Theory, Volume III*. Aldershot: Ashgate.

Hoch, C. (2007) 'Pragmatic communicative action theory' *Journal of Planning Education and Research* 26: 272–83.

Huxley, M. (2002) 'Governmentality, gender, planning: A Foucauldian perspective', in Allmendinger, P. and Tewdwr-Jones, M. (eds) *Planning Futures: New Directions for Planning Theory*. London: Routledge, pp. 136–53.

Huxley, M. (2006) 'Spatial rationalities: order, environment, evolution and government' *Social and Cultural Geography* 7(5): 771–87.

Huxley, M. (2007) 'Geographies of governmentality', in Crampton, J. and Elden, S. (eds) *Space, Knowledge and Power*. Aldershot: Ashgate, pp. 185–204.

Jacobs, J. (1963) *The Death and Life of Great American Cities*. New York: Vintage.

Kingdon, J.W. (2003) *Agendas, Alternatives, and Public Policies*. New York: Longman.

Latour, B. (1993) *We Have Never Been Modern*. London: Harvester Wheatsheaf.

Latour, B. (2000) 'When things strike back: a possible contribution of "science studies" to the social sciences' *British Journal of Sociology* 51: 107–23.

Madanipour, A. (2007) *Designing the City of Reason: Foundations and Frameworks*. London: Routledge.

March, J.G. and Olsen, J.P. (1989) *Rediscovering Institutions: The Organizational Basis of Politics*. New York: Free Press.

Moulaert, F. and Mehmood, A. (2007) 'Analysing regional development: from territorial innovation to path dependent geography', in Dolfsma, W. and Davis, J. (eds) *The Elgar Handbook of Socio-Economics*. Cheltenham: Edward Elgar, 607–31.

Moulaert, F. and Sekia, F. (2003) 'Territorial innovation models: a critical survey' *Regional Studies* 37: 289–302.

Murdoch, J. (2006) *Post-structuralist Geography*. London: Sage.

Murdoch, J. and Abram, S. (2002) *Rationalities of Planning: Development versus environment in Planning for Housing*. Aldershot: Ashgate.

Nasr, J. and Volait, M. (eds) (2003) *Urbanism: Imported or Exported? Native Aspirations and Foreign Plans*. London: Wiley-Academy.

Owens, S., Petts, J. and Bulkeley, H. (2006) 'Boundary work: knowledge, policy and the urban environment' (theme issue: 'Knowledge and policy in the context of urban environments: introduction') *Environment and Planning C: Government and Policy* 24: 633–43.

Owens, S., Rayner, T. and Bina, O. (2004) 'New agendas for appraisal: reflections on theory, practice and research' *Environment and Planning A* 36: 1943–59.

Pennington, M. (2000) *Planning and the Political Market: Public Choice and the Politics of Government Failure*. London: Athlone Press.

Punter, J. (2003) *The Vancouver Achievement*. Vancouver, BC: UBC Press.

Raco, M. (2003) 'Governmentality, subject-building, and the discourses and practices of devolution in the UK' *Transactions of the Institute of British Geographers* 28: 75–95.

Sandercock, L. (Ed.) (1998) *Making the Invisible Visible: A Multicultural Planning History*. Berkeley, CA: University of Berkeley Press.

Sanyal, B. (ed.) (2005) *Comparative Planning Cultures*. London: Routledge.

Sorensen, A. (2002) *The Making of Urban Japan*. New York: Routledge.

Sorensen, E. and Torfing, J. (eds) (2007) *Theories of Democratic Network Governance*. London: Palgrave Macmillan.

UN-HABITAT (2009) *Planning Sustainable Cities: Global Report on Human Settlements 2009*. London: Earthscan.

Verma, N. (ed.) (2007) *Planning and Institutions*. Oxford: Elsevier.

Vidyarthi, S. (2010) 'Exploring the travel of the American neighbourhood unit to India', in Healey, P. and Upton, R. (eds) *Crossing Borders: International Exchange and Planning Practices*. London: Routledge, pp. 73–93.

Watson, V. (2008) 'Down to earth: linking planning theory and practice to the "metropole" and beyond' *International Planning Studies* 13: 223–37.

Webster, C. and Lai, L.W.-C. (2003) *Property Rights, Planning and Markets: Managing Spontaneous Cities*. Cheltenham: Edward Elgar.

Yanow, D. (1996) *How Does a Policy Mean?* Washington, DC: Georgetown University Press.

Yanow, D. and Schwartz-Shea, P. (eds) (2006) *Interpretation and Method: Empirical Research Methods and the Interpretive Turn*. New York: ME Sharpe.

Governance, Space and Politics: Exploring the Governmentality of Planning

Enrico Gualini

Introduction

Moving from the conviction that reflecting on 'governance' has (still) something to say to planning theory, this chapter presents an attempt at focusing on three key critical implications of governance discourse and practices: the redefinition of the spatiality of planning practices; the redefinition of the political dimension of planning; and the redefinition of the public and of civil society as a domain of social struggles. The aim is to highlight some possibly undervalued consequences of governance research for planning theory, to indicate possible elements for re-framing its heuristics, and to address new terrains for trans-disciplinary inquiry.

'Governance' – whether viewed as an analytical-descriptive, theoretical, or policy-oriented concept – is a difficult, possibly not very rewarding subject. As a summary term for the evolution of forms of public action in late capitalism, it has gained wide currency in both research and policy. Its diffusion, however, goes hand in hand with difficulties in translation and with a broad amenability to interpretation. Not surprisingly, this is among the reasons for its very success. 'Governance' has come to signify, in Rhodes' words, either 'a change in the meaning of government, referring to a *new* process of governing; or a *changed* condition or ordered rule; or the *new* method by which society is governed' (1996: 652–3), or even much else besides. Its sensitizing power makes it easy to appropriate as well as liable to ambiguity and manipulation. Discomfort with the use and misuse of the notion is therefore widespread among scholars in general and among planning theorists in particular. This is, in my view, understandable, but also revelatory of a dual difficulty in dealing with it: the difficulty of clearly distinguishing between governance as an epistemic and discursive construct, on the one hand, and governance as a set of concrete practices, on the other hand; and the difficulty of assuming a reflective attitude towards governance discourses and practices while being constitutively involved in their very construction.

It is precisely by pointing at the traps that lie along its path that reflecting on 'governance' still has something to say to planning theory. This is true in at least three fundamental ways. In the first place, attempts at conceptualizing policies and planning practices in terms of 'governance' are not a mere fashion, but stem from an interest in emergent phenomena 'which make ... new conceptualizations necessary' (Le Galès 1998: 495). Secondly, despite the inflationary diffusion of the term, an analytically grounded understanding of historical-concrete processes of governance is needed, and will be a research task for years to come. Thirdly, the planning enterprise needs to deal reflectively with the implications of governance discourse and practices, as these are constitutively linked to its cognitive frames as well as to its material possibilities.

This chapter tries therefore to highlight what can be seen as key implications of governance for planning theory and its further development. In doing so, it will draw attention to two important aspects: the need to consider both the discursive and material dimension of governance practices, as their complex and often ambiguous intertwinement is part and parcel of their legitimating construct; and the need not to avoid making interpretive choices with regard to the political meaning and scope of this construct. Only on the basis of a critical interpretation – rather than on received understandings – can a reflection on 'governance' contribute to a progressive planning-theoretical inquiry. One key implication, as we shall see, is the need to reject any unreflective normative assumption of the term, and rather to deconstruct it, questioning what conception of politics lies behind it.

The argument develops in three steps. First, a discussion is presented of the genealogy, domains of meanings, and theoretical contributions which make the notion of 'governance' relevant for planning theory. Then, the focus turns to key implications of governance discourse and practices for understanding the nature of policy objects and spaces and of the relationship between politics and spatiality. Finally, some possible consequences are drawn for framing a critical perspective within planning theory.

Genealogy and Domains of Meaning of 'Governance'

'Governance': Semantic Shifts and Interpretive Options

The term 'governance' is not so much new, as it is novel in its currently prevailing meaning. This novelty can be traced back to a dual development: a shift in understanding of the nature of state steering, from central delivery to decentralized regulation – a shift which is sometimes referred to in the literature by a distinction between 'old' and 'new' governance discourse; and a shift in the object of analysis, from institutional structures and political regimes to policies and processes and to actors and networks. As a joint result of these conceptual developments, the term governance has come to be increasingly referred to actual, emergent policy practices rather than to formal 'regimes', intended as stable, institutionalized patterns of distribution of authority.

Secondly, since about the early 1980s, as a result of changes in state-society relationships in Western welfare democracies, 'governance' emphatically expresses a re-assessment – and often a more or less ideologically biased critique – of the effectiveness of public action and of the role and functioning of governments. Reference to 'governance' conveys attention towards practices and abilities of achieving governing effects as the complex but ordered combination of a variety of inputs from different societal domains. A convergence has therefore emerged on understanding governance as – in principle – an 'inclusive' mode of decision-making, whereby public and private interests converge via negotiation and/or deliberation towards integrative problem-solving. It denotes a mode of policy-making that is constitutively multi-actor and multi-level, stressing interconnected (strategic, ad-hoc) rather than hierarchical ('nested', authority-based) patterns of relations. Governance settings are thus seen as defining emergent relationships between policy actors in situations where a 'logic of command' is no longer viable or desired, and where structural dispersion of resources requires coordination as an exercise of mutual adjustment 'among peers'.

Thirdly, this conception expresses a shift in focus from state-centered rationales of public policy towards collective modes of problem-solving situated along a continuum between 'government' and society. While it would be incorrect to infer from this some sort of theoretical consistency, it is hence fair to say that, in an analytical perspective, 'the various approaches to governance share a rejection of the conceptual trinity of market-state-civil society which has tended to dominate mainstream analyses of modern societies' (Jessop 1995: 310). At their basis stands a dissatisfaction with top-down explanations of the exercise of power as well as an interest for inquiry into forms of socio-political coordination which broaden the field of traditional relations between the public and the private, constituting new forms of interdependencies in the public sphere: hence their emphasis on the shift from a restricted conception of 'government' to an enlarged conception of 'governance' as governing activity, characterized by the demise of the presumption – typical of classical political theory – of public action being grounded on an exercise of authority and on decision-making mechanisms anchored in national-state sovereignty. This suggests that 'governance' is a useful analytical framework particularly for inquiring into change in policy processes as are taking place within emergent, non-conventional, extended policy arenas, and across hierarchy, market and self-governance mechanisms, passing through forms of co-decision and co-management. As I will point out, however, a commonsensical, unreflective assumption of these features also bears the potential for mystification of what 'governance' is about.

Finally, it is important to bear in mind that the fortune of 'governance' as a material and discursive practice is strictly related to a paradigmatic change in public policies introduced since the 1980s along with references to 'reinventing government' and to 'new public management' models (Osborne and Gaebler 1993). It conveys therefore a distinctive, if often implicit, normative meaning, in as far as it stems from a critical assessment of a model of public intervention that has dominated post-war economic reconstruction and has come to be increasingly seen as ineffective, calling for change in public policy rationales and forms of intervention. This has also generated distinctive normative interpretations of 'governance' as a concept amenable to policy transfer and exportation, as is most notably the case in the politics of international organizations, such as the World Bank, or in initiatives for enhancing 'performance management' in the public sector, such as the OECD programme on 'Public Management and Governance'.

As a result, reference to 'governance' is at risk of appearing not only theoretically undetermined, but also normatively overdetermined, and this makes attempts at balancing between analytical and normative attitudes often ambiguous. This ambiguity can also produce a fertile critical tension, obviously. But even if acknowledging that this line may be sometimes dangerously thin, it is important to distinguish 'governance' as an analytical-theoretical concept from its understanding as a normative policy concept. This is a necessary, if not sufficient condition for countering ideological instrumentalizations of governance discourse. There is a difference, in other words, between assuming 'governance' as a conceptual framework for critical inquiry into state change, and assuming it as an ideological 'anti-statist' recipe.

'Governance': Discursive Tropes and Theoretical Propositions

Despite a variety of conceptual underpinnings, comprehensive theorizations of governance are rare. Only a few attempts have been made at meta-theoretical generalizations of the concept or at embedding it in distinctive theoretical perspectives. Under such conditions, proposed definitions often bear a 'stipulative' character, meant to confer on the notion a specific, if 'local', heuristic or explanatory role, circumscribed to defined objects of analysis (Rhodes 1996).

Despite the lack of a consistent, let alone dominant, 'governance theory', significant constants may be recognized in its domain of reference: recurrent structuring elements, or 'tropes', of governance discourse. First and foremost – and possibly key to its fortune – is the distinction between 'governance' and 'government'. Governance, intended as a complex of activities implied in governing, relying on, but not exhausting structures and forms of action of statutory governmental authorities, is assumed to express some kind of autonomy in relation to government. Contrary to traditional state-theoretical assumptions of political steering theory, governance discourse puts emphasis on the centrality of agency, on the background of a redefinition of institutional rationales framed by a conception of the 'cooperative state' as the basis of legitimacy for governmental action. Non-institutional actors, as an integral part of the policy-making process, if not as its initiators, are seen as filling in a void in action and steering capacity by governmental institutions.

Along this line, a divide can be identified between two different positions: one that emphasizes a dichotomy between 'government' as state-centered governmental activity and 'governance' as an alternative mode of governing, implying a 'retreat' or 'withdrawal' of the state; and one that points to 'governance' as the emergence of new modes of public policy-making lying at the very core of the state. The former position, which emphasizes a government-governance dualism or even advocates it – in terms of a (neo-)liberal model of the 'minimal state' – is mostly represented by normative definitions of 'governance' and is, as such, particularly liable to political instrumentalization. The latter position, conversely, emphasizes the (re-)articulation of the dual relationships between government and society and is found in research grounded on the analysis of late-capitalist societies – in institutional economics, political economy, economic sociology, policy analysis and other disciplines – with a particular emphasis on state change. In this sense, while rejecting methodologically state-centric assumptions, 'governance' intended in the latter sense does not imply either a-priori assumptions on the 'hollowing out' of the state or 'the neo-liberal rhetoric of delegitimizing governments and politics' (Le Galès 2001: 172) that characterizes some of the more ideological approaches: rather, it is concerned with local, context- and situation-specific processes of reconstruction of policy-making in fragmented, competitive, multi-actor and multi-level policy environments which challenge and transform the rationale and meaning of state action.

A further remarkable trope focuses on governance as a new mode of public action in the pursuit of collective problem-solving. 'Governance' is seen as a form of exercise of power and authority no longer identifiable with forms of action and with guidance-and-control functions of governmental institutions alone. Accordingly, the management of public issues is seen as being premised upon an extended but loose framework of interdependencies between governmental and non-governmental actors. In this sense, 'governance' can be defined as a public activity 'concerned with the resolution of (para-)political problems (in the sense of problems of collective goal-attainment or the realisation of collective purposes)' under new emergent configurations of actors, organizations and institutions (Jessop 1995: 317) that structurally involve decentralized non-state actions and initiatives stemming from the field of economic and social activities.

A particular consequence of such understanding resides in dissolving distinctions between the state, market(s) and civil society as distinct spheres of agency. Particularly where an understanding of governance as the emergent outcome of complex interactions in the public sphere is emphasized, a dual relationship is posited between politics and society, between governmental institutions and 'civicness'. Such a perspective questions an idea of civil society as either the expression par excellence of bourgeois-individualism or the residual place of expression of communitarian ties, in an implied dualism with the sphere of the state. In a governance perspective, ideal-typically, '[t]he state becomes a collection of interorganisational networks made up of governmental and societal actors with no sovereign actor able to steer or regulate' (Rhodes 1996: 666). The challenge of government and administrative action thus becomes one of co-production, of the pursuit of public aims through the joint activity of social actors.

In this perspective, a key question for research concerns the extent to which potentials for collective action and for democratic and emancipatory social practices are actually introduced through new modes of governance. On the one hand, in the domain of governance practices, problem-solving becomes a central motivation and source of legitimation for public action. By the same token, on the other hand, governance practices redefine arenas for addressing public problems in terms that are less dependent on state structures and on their rationales of authority, control and accountability. Governance arenas are characterized as multi-actor environments, with complex implications in terms of blurring divisions among societal sub-sectors, increasing mutual dependence, and redistribution of responsibilities. Through governance practices, public action becomes thus less dependent on abstract and generalized state-centered welfare imperatives, and more dependent on concrete but contingent and situated constellations of actors and interest. Meanwhile, the sites for public accountability become decentralized and less clearly defined. This obviously bears profound implications for the effectiveness and legitimacy of public action (Stoker 1998; Swyngedouw 2005).

This introduces a further divide among approaches to understanding 'governance'. A significant strand of governance research features a convergence of theoretical and normative attitudes with regard to change in rationales of public action. This is most evident in socio-cybernetic approaches that view governance as the outcome of interactive socio-political forms of governing. 'Governance' is intended here as more than a mere theoretical alternative to competing analytical-interpretive models of public policy, like pluralism and corporatism. 'Modern governance' (Kooiman 1993a) is rather explicitly seen as a way out of an effectiveness crisis of governing activity – characterized by decreasing returns, sub-optimal outcomes, and implementation constraints – and as an alternative to classic liberal models of the 'minimal state' as well as corporatist or neo-liberal models of 'lean' government based on privatization of governing tasks. Rather than between 'government' and 'governance', a distinction is emphasized between 'governing activity' as the complex of governmental interventions directed to scope, and 'governance' as the coevolutive outcome of this activity, as the result or sum of the effects of interventions and interactions of a socio-political-administrative nature which are implied in governing and which contribute to its eventual prospects of effectiveness. Accordingly, if '[g]overning in contemporary society is mainly a process of coordination, steering, influencing and "balancing"' of interactions between public and private actors, governance 'can be seen as the pattern or structure that emerges in a social-political system as "common" result or outcome of the interacting intervention efforts of all involved actors. This pattern cannot be reduced to one actor or group of actors in particular ... This emerging pattern forms the "rules of the game" within a particular system or, in other words, the medium through which actors can act and try to use these rules in accordance with their own objectives and interests' (Kooiman 1993b: 255, 258). Governance, while system- and context-dependent, is thus above all an interactional outcome. According to the idea of a 'duality of structure' (Giddens 1984) 'in which a pattern of governance is not only the unintended outcome of social (inter)action but also the mechanism through which actors have the capability to act and govern, ... governing and governance are subjected to a permanent process of mutual interaction. Actors who govern, or try to govern, also influence the governance structure of a subsystem. Some (more powerful) actors have the possibility to rewrite some "rules of the game" but no one has complete control. There is always some intended and unintended change, which creates manoeuvring space for actors willing to change the existing pattern' (Kooiman 1993b: 258). In this interaction, the possibility is given for an open balance between creativity and order, innovation and control.

Despite its important emphasis on the co-evolutionary character of governance practices and outcomes, the critical scope of this interpretation is limited. Others point more explicitly to the potential democratic deficit of governance practices. A notable example is Rhodes' understanding of 'governance' as a complex of governmentally promoted practices challenging democratic politics. According to his 'stipulative definition' of governance as the 'public management of networks' – embedded in analysis of the neo-liberal turn in 1980s British politics – governance refers to 'self-organising, inter-organisational networks' (Rhodes 1996: 660) complementary to markets and hierarchies in allocating resources and in exercising coordination and control. The public management of inter-organizational relations thus operates in a field which extends beyond the traditional boundaries of the public, the private and the 'third' sector, constituting an alternative for public action rather than a hybrid between given forms of market-based or hierarchical regulation. On the other hand, however, the networks in question feature important and diffuse elements of self-coordination and self-governing capacity. This turns them into organizational and operational forms capable of creating their own action environment, and tendentially resilient to external guidance by democratically legitimated public authorities.

These interpretations are consistent with an assumption of governance as pertaining to – and not distinct from – governing practices of the state. While pointing at the role of the state in developing governance practices, they imply relations between state and non-state practices not defined in terms of opposition, but rather of a government-governance continuum. By this, however, they also lend themselves to 'exogenist' explanations. According to these, governance is seen as the result of transformations allegedly exogenous to classical 'government', typically referring to phenomena such as market-driven economic neo-liberalism, 'globalization', 'Europeanization', and the like, to which governments respond with an 'extension' of their governmental rationales to structurally include non-governmental practices.

A further important theoretical divide emerges here: that between an understanding of 'governance' as a mere extension of the paradigm of political steering, and an understanding of 'governance' as implying a paradigmatic change in the conception of public policy. In the latter perspective, analysis of change in the nature and provision of public goods leads to understanding governance discourse and practices, in their own right, as an expression of a substantive rather than merely procedural change in public policy: as an expression, that is, of an endogenous change in normative frameworks concerning the aims and forms of public intervention and state agency. This aspect bears important interpretive implications, and is therefore worth a more detailed discussion.

'Governance' and Political Steering

It has been in particular Renate Mayntz (2005) who has recently raised the question whether attempts at theorizing on governance simply represent an extension or a further stage in established theories of political steering. The question, as she argues, is of relevance despite the fact that attempts at translation – like with the German *Steuerung* and with similar terms from other languages – often equal 'governance' to current notions of 'steering', suggesting that only a fashionable but unreflective Anglicism may be at hand. Her answer, however, is not unambiguous, and hints at a crucial interpretive alternative. In this section, I will review related arguments, putting the basis for further analysis and for finally advancing my own interpretation.

'Governance': Extending or Challenging Political Steering Theories?

The genealogy of the notion of 'steering' in sociology and political science highlights two distinct lines of ascendancy: on the one hand, a system-theoretical and cybernetic paradigm of societal control – strongly influenced by Parsons – in which 'steering' is seen as a function of social systems relatively independent from the agency of concrete actors; on the other hand, an increasingly actor-centered orientation of political analysis, which can be related to developments in empirical research in organizational sociology and policy analysis since the late 1960s. In this latter tradition, the notion of 'steering' specifies an understanding of politics as the expression of a normative orientation of the state towards the achievement of collective welfare goals. In this perspective, the meanings of 'governance' and 'steering' converge upon a rationale of 'active politics', expressed by the centrality of the state's steering function in the context of a dramatic extension of its welfare tasks. The rise of this 'old governance' discourse, as Mayntz (2005) argues, represents a change in normative framework in as far as it stems from recognition of the failure of a liberal-democratic tradition of public policy, assuming exchange among individuals as autonomously capable of defining a socially acceptable aggregate of preferences, and markets operating under conditions of 'perfect competition' as the ideal-typical mechanism for the social allocation of values and resources.

Problems with this 'zero option' of public intervention obviously arise when these exchange mechanisms 'fail': in the face of natural monopolies, structural asymmetries, negative externalities, and the specific dilemmas posed by the delivery of goods characterized by non-rivalry and non-excludability from access and consumption. Against this background, public intervention is seen as necessary in order to guarantee optimal supply and equal distribution of public goods, according to the definition of a social utility function. This in turn provides the *ratio* for an institutional design of public policies in which the production and allocation of public goods are politically regulated and publicly administered.

'Governance' as steering, in this sense, relates to an institutional framework of public policy as defined in a classic, Eastonian model of the political system, in which the state takes an active and direct role in the production of public goods. It conveys an understanding of political steering embedded in a holistic conception of the steering capacity of the state – an important expression of it being the 'rational-comprehensive' planning ideal. Political steering is a notion grounded on an understanding of the state as a structured form of agency in pursuit of the 'public interest', as the democratically legitimated welfare-theoretical vehicle for realizing a 'just' society. As state-centred and mainly concerned with the forms, means and processes of goal-oriented state intervention, political steering theory thus conceived implies a systematic distinction between the subject and the object of steering: between the 'steering capacity' (*Steuerungsfähigkeit*) of state actors, and the 'amenability to steering' (*Steuerbarkeit*) of existing social sub-systems, the relatively autonomous path and dynamic of development of which is the object of purposive (and legitimate) political agency as performed by the state (Mayntz 1987).

Belief in the legitimacy and effectiveness of state steering remains dominant in political science as long as it is not empirically questioned. As welfare-state societies enter their late-modernization stage, however, such a conception of the 'steerability' of society is challenged on both empirical and theoretical grounds. The 'producer state' as agent of the central delivery of public goods faces increasing dilemmas. Theories of democratic choice (Downs 1957; Arrow 1963) and of collective action (Olson 1965) undermine beliefs in the viability of a social utility function in directing public choices. Policy analysis highlights the involvement of non-state actors in their definition, and thus unsuspected potentials for heterodirection and manipulation. Implementation research draws attention to the behaviour of the addressees of public policy (societal and political actors and related sub-systems), pointing to their relative autonomy as a challenge to purposive state agency (Pressman and Wildavsky 1973; Bardach 1977; Barrett and Fudge 1981). Questions about the effectiveness of the central planning and delivery of goods and services arise, as a reality of goal displacement (Selznick 1949) and unintended effects (Boudon 1977) undermines the legitimacy of the pursuit of a 'social optimum' and reference to the 'public interest'. Similarly, planning theoretical reflection points to the increasing divide between authoritarian state practices, based on expert knowledge hegemony, and grassroots civic movements. Overall, public policy appears as the outcome of complex mechanisms of delegation and co-production, the expression of polycentric patterns of power rather than of a centralized authority. Through the development of neo-corporatist structures, networks and 'private governments', significant degrees of self-regulation are functionally embedded into the sphere of public policy (Streeck and Schmitter 1985). Further research explores mechanisms that make the emergence of governing effects possible. In political economy, redefining the role of the state goes hand in hand with defining alternatives to neoclassical postulates. New institutional economics addresses the role of coordination through private firm institutions as a regulatory input to markets (Williamson 1975, 1985; North 1981, 1990). Mechanisms of market-based self-regulation are set by new institutional economics on the background of the historically contingent systems of institutionalized rules and routines in which they are embedded. Forms of 'corporate governance' and alternative coordination approaches in business relations – such as relational contracting, organized markets in group enterprises, clans, networks, trade associations and strategic firm alliances – point to non-state modes of regulating complex markets. Mechanisms for regulating issues of public interest extend beyond the agency of state structures but are institutionally embedded and co-determined (Hollingsworth and Boyer 1997). The 'governance of the economy' is therefore conceived as defined by the constitution and functioning of institutional regimes that are interdependent with state regulation in an enlarged 'public sphere'.

All this bears an impact on views of public steering and on normative models of public policy. At the same time, it introduces a distinction from traditional political steering theory. Political steering is no longer identifiable with state action as expressed by its political-administrative structures, but is rather the result of interactions between different forms of regulation that converge towards a new, 'cooperative' definition of the 'public interest'. 'Governance' now refers to the effect of variable combinations of different forms of state and non-state regulation in the functioning of complex economic sub-systems.

As a response to the perceived failure of political decision-making and centralized planning, the 'new governance' represents a shift from a centrality of politics as the pursuit of a social utility function, defined within the political system through the mechanisms of voting and representative democracy, to the centrality of policy as the institutional framing of issue-related voluntary exchange and private market initiative.

Key to this development is a dual shift in the state's role in supplying public goods: from direct state intervention to market-based regulation, and from their substantial delivery to the regulation of their institutional features. In order to re-establish individual choices and voluntary market exchange as a mechanism of regulation, the 'new governance' requires redefining and distributing property rights over public goods, and decentralizing responsibilities in their delivery. Key mechanisms for this are privatization and delegation. Privatization, as a measure of conferring property rights over public goods, is the condition for circumventing their non-excludability and for inserting them into market regulation. Delegation, as the transfer of political rights and responsibilities to private instances and independent agencies, is the condition for realizing the separation between the regulation and the production-delivery of public goods.

This, however, also changes the locus of regulation. While implementation is privatized, public control is exercised on the basis of effectiveness criteria. In its role as a principal, the state exercises direction and control on social agents in a way that is primarily output-oriented. The ideal-typical rationale pursued is that of 'contract steering', defined by the delivery rules specified by the contract of delegation with third-party suppliers.

Thus, the 'new governance' conveys a substantial change in the way of viewing and producing public policies. In an 'active' or 'producer state', public intervention is meant to prevent failures of voluntary (market) exchange by directly addressing the production and delivery of public goods. The state's role in securing them is grounded on a public utility norm which, as a substitute for market exchange rules, is legitimated on two grounds: politically, by its underlying mechanisms of representative democracy; and technically, by being operated within a distinct, 'rational' and allegedly 'apolitical' administrative space, situated at the core of the state apparatus. In the 'new governance', conversely, public intervention is primarily meant to counteract the negative effects of voluntary market exchange.

Accordingly, this introduces significant changes in key functions of public policy. Direct public intervention loses the function of direct delivery of state supplied and administered public goods and services, which is increasingly decentralized and delegated. The state primarily devises the institutional rules for the functional delegation of political authority to the semi-autonomous entities endowed with their delivery. Regulation loses its juridical rationale of legitimate command, and takes the form of negotiating and private contracting practices to ensure conformance with desired objectives. Incentives and subsidies progressively lose their redistributive function of unconditional compensation for socio-economic disparities, to become selective instruments for promoting actions targeted at desired objectives. Similarly, policy discourse becomes increasingly 'strategic', targeted at directing and shaping actors' preferences in order to promote distinctive behaviours, seen as conforming to desired objectives.

The consequences are crucial. Given its output-orientation, public policy becomes increasingly reliant on private sector supply and, by this, increasingly dependent on preferences expressed within the market sphere and outside the political system. As a result of delegation mechanisms, moreover, relevant decisions are dispersed among multiple decentralized actors. The range of actors involved, however, is selective if pluralistic, and access to related arenas is only formally open. An increasing asymmetry and imbalance arises therefore in favour of outcomes and of their producers. This obviously impacts on conceptions of what are politically viable public aims and on their legitimation. The legitimacy of public policy no longer resides in the way collective preferences are aggregated, but in the way expressed demands are satisfied. Legitimacy shifts from a primarily input-oriented to a primarily output-oriented emphasis, and policy effectiveness is measured by achieved results. Potential gains in effectiveness through enhanced responsiveness to expressed preferences are traded against a shift towards markets in their definition and towards contractual modes of regulation in their delivery. This makes public goals basically dependent on tradable criteria.

In this perspective, governance does not represent a simple 'extension' of traditional policy-making arenas, but rather a paradigmatic change in the normative orientation of public policy. Rather than an 'exogenous' factor of change, fragmentation of decision-making is endogenous to public policy, as the composition of preferences is emphatically externalized from the conventional arenas of the political system, and decisions on the allocation of resources (public and private) are increasingly made to rely on end-users and consumers and, accordingly, on expressed market preferences.

While it is hence true that governance discourse reflects a 'problem-solving bias', as noted by Mayntz (2005), what makes this observation relevant is the fact that the definition of collective problems is tendentially 'exogenized' from political discourse. No longer identifiable with a social utility function, for which direct political responsibility must be born, it depends on the aggregate of voluntary (market) exchanges seen as hetero-directed, and in relation to which political responsibility is restrained to the steering of contingent, 'local' conditions of regulation.

The nature of governance practices appears hence in several respects as Janus-faced (Swyngedouw 2005). 'New governance' emphasizes less state coercion and more reliance on individual and collective choices. As such, it bears potentials for the autonomy and empowerment of society. It does so, however, in the framework of a new paradigmatic understanding of the 'public' that heavily relies on market-conforming performance rather than on the political expression of collective preferences. The implications are crucial for the definition of both discursive contexts and substantive objects of public policy. Altogether, they introduce potentials for subtle forms of manipulation of preferences (material and symbolic) and for a surreptitious naturalization and de-politicization of potentially contentious public choices.

'Governance' and the Challenges to 'Bounded' State Territoriality

A particular implication of this shift in public policy is that governance practices largely define their own policy spaces. 'Governance' comes to be understood as a mix of different forms of regulation, both state and non-state based, in a polycentric regulatory environment. State sovereignty, and territoriality as one of its key expressions, is increasingly relativized, and requires to be reinvented, in order to be effective, as a new form of negotiated and 'pooled' sovereignty. Accordingly, governance practices are increasingly delegated from national states to other instances, their relationship to which is defined by strategic dependence and mutual adjustment, but also by relative political autonomy.

The state-theoretical relevance of this aspect is highlighted by the emergence of phenomena that increasingly exceed the scope and influence of state territoriality. In the wake of the revival and 'theoretical radicalization' of neo-liberal economic theory (Mayntz and Sharpf 2005), the rise of global governance structures at the service of open market transactions increasingly restrains the steering capacity of the national state. In international relations, supra- or trans-national, 'global', regulatory practices thus take the form of self-regulated organizations endowed with effective authority – even in the absence of formal political legitimation – that may be interpreted as performing 'governance without government' (Rosenau and Czempiel 1992).

To a certain extent, the post-national institutional experiment represented by the EU and its policies is a paradigmatic embodiment of such developments. Reference to 'multi-level governance' as an emergent feature of EU policy processes highlights the need for interpretations alternative to state-centric assumptions on European integration (Hooghe and Marks 2001). It points to the new position gained by both sub-national and supra-national policy-making vis-à-vis the national state, in what is seen as an upward and downwards redefinition of the nature of power and influence in the EU. By extension, it also points at the development of new policy spaces besides, if not 'beyond', formal-statutory government institutions, in what is seen as a 'sideways' movement away from 'bounded' territorial domains of public policy-making (Hooghe and Marks 2003). Governance practices in a multi-level environment are seen as generative of new 'opportunity structures' for actors to engage in European politics at different levels. The development of forms of self-organization and self-regulation in networking in non-hierarchical settings is highlighted as a specific dimension of European politics (Kohler-Koch and Eising 1999; Héritier 2002). The EU appears accordingly as an in-progress construct defined by specific governance practices as well as by its sui-generis institutional features, and European 'integration' comes to be understood as a 'polity creating process' (Hooghe and Marks 2001: 124) that challenges given articulations of authority within the nested articulation of the national state.

The implications of new governance practices in terms of emergent patterns of spatiality can be found throughout different administrative levels and spatial scales. It is at the regional-local level, however, where their potential contradictions become more tangible. In regional and local policies, governance practices – by moving away from a territorial towards a functional and issue-related rationale – offer potentials for expressing 'local' forms of identity and involvement. By this, however, they also detach policy processes from practices of territorially-based political representation. While institutional redundancy threatens to emerge from the proliferation of ad-hoc governance arrangements and forms of 'delegated government', an institutional void threatens to emerge in terms of legitimate political representation. The spatiality of governance practices must hence be considered as a constitutive dimension of their underlying, and often implicit, political project. It needs therefore to be further discussed in the following sections.

'Governance' and the Constitution of New 'Policy Spaces': Implications for Spatial Practices

Governance bears a peculiar duality of meaning. It is about processes of governing that are situated at the core of the state, but that increasingly affect the rationale of its action. It conveys 'ideas of leading, steering and directing', but without the primacy accorded to the sovereign state' (Le Galès 1998: 494–5). The notion of 'governance', in this sense, combines an engagement in questions of institutional design – in a primarily meso-political and inter-organizational perspective – with an acknowledgement of the emergent and contingent character of socio-political regulation. This requires the discussion of three key aspects: the way governance redefines the nature of policy objects, of policy spaces, and of relationships between politics and spatiality.

Governance and the Constitution of Policy Objects

In reflecting on change in modes of political steering, Mayntz and Scharpf (1995) adopt a translation of 'governance' as 'regulation' (*Regelung*) that hints at implications exceeding the centrality of a political will expressed by the purposive and legitimate political agency of the state, as posited in the dominant theoretical paradigm of political steering. Similar implications are crucial in the approach of the 'French school' of regulation theory, centred on the notion of the embeddedness of economic processes in socially constructed organizational and institutional contexts. Social relations as objects of regulation concern 'not only the articulation of the technical and social division of labour within the circuits of capital but also the articulation between its economic and extra-economic moments', including 'the direct and indirect extra-economic conditions of accumulation as well as the handling of the various repercussions of commodification and accumulation on the wider society' (Jessop 2000: 325). Far from being primarily a voluntarist activity, regulation is seen as a 'process without a subject', in which 'specific modes of regulation are always emergent, evolutionary effects of a multiplicity of actions in specific, strategically selective contexts' (Jessop 1995: 329).

Understanding 'governance' as a mix of different forms of regulation leads therefore to recognizing a common interest of governance and regulation theories 'in the path-dependent, constitutive relationship between modes of governance/ regulation and objects of governance/regulation. Neither regulation theory nor theories of governance can be seen as teleological in character or as committed to ex post functionalist arguments: for they imply that it is in and through governance (or regulation) that the elementary objects of their attention are transformed through complex articulation into specific moments within a given mode of governance (or regulation)' (Jessop 1995: 326).

This has implications for understanding the nature of the objects of governance/ regulation. At stake in governance/regulation processes is the constitution of their very objects. While regulation theory implies that the objects of regulation do not fully pre-exist the process of regulation, theories of governance underline that the objects of governance may be recognized as such only through efforts in governing them, through governance activity itself. Thus, 'the very processes of regulation or governance constitute the objects which come to be regulated or governed in and through a form of self-referential self-organisation'. In this sense, 'just as there is neither regulation in general nor general regulation, there is no governance in general nor general governance. Instead, there is only particular regulation and the totality of regulation, only particular governance and the totality of governance ... In the real world there are only definite objects of regulation that are shaped in and through definite modes of regulation; and definite objects of governance that are shaped in and through definite modes of governance' (Jessop 1995: 315).

A further implication can be seen in a common neo-institutionalist horizon of governance research, as it refers to 'the complex totality of co-existent forms of collective regulation of societal relations' (Mayntz 2004: 66, my translation). In a neo-institutionalist perspective, the outcomes of governance/regulation are seen as relatively stabilized systems of relations. Accordingly, governance and regulation concur to modes of institutionalization of an essentially emergent, co-evolutive nature. Again Jessop (1995: 322) underlines that '[n]ew governance mechanisms, like new structural forms, emerge from a trial-and-error search process which operates through evolutionary variation, selection and retention. It is in this context that issues of strategic selectivity and strategic capacities are so crucial and that attention must be paid to the material and discursive appropriateness of proposed responses'.

In a political economy perspective, this neo-institutionalist attitude extends well beyond the domain of institutional economics, and leads to rethinking the role of the state in its interplay with non-state forms in realizing regulation effects. 'Governance' appears not as 'other' than 'government', but as the situationally determined principle by which forms of regulation are re-articulated – and forms of institutional agency and policy-making redefined – in contexts that exceed formal-hierarchical arenas. Focusing on the emergent, evolutive and situated nature of modes of regulation implies a pluralist view on sites of governance. As political regulation trespasses the boundaries of hierarchical settings, relying on interaction among institutional and social, state and non-state actors, the emergence of systems of governance appears as a process of re-articulation of different modes of regulation across different social sub-sectors (Le Galès 1998). Their institutional embeddedness as well as their dynamics of institutionalization appear dependent on the specific and contextual nature of their integration and on its specific spatio-temporal dimension.

Governance and the Constitution of Policy Spaces

The new 'political economy of governance', as understood above, has profound implications for the spatiality of state authority and power. Its key effects are a spatio-temporal relativization of geographical scale and a change in the nature of state territoriality.

The constitution of territorial scales as domains of relative structural coherence between the political-administrative, the institutional and the economic sphere – the local, as the expression of the geographical range of daily reproduction, the regional, as the expression of the geographical coherence of distinct production systems, and the national, as their territorial 'container' and principle of sovereignty – has developed within modern processes of state formation as a function of the regulation of capital accumulation. National states embodied political-institutional compromises that defined national systems of production and reproduction as distinct 'laws of value' (Smith 1995/2003: 229) legitimized through national social-cultural identities (Anderson 1991). As a neo-liberal intensification of exchanges is actively pursued among as well as within sovereign territorial entities, however, the de-nationalization, the increase in scale, and the transnationalization of economic processes redefine spatial conditions for capital accumulation in ways that increasingly challenge given territorial orderings. The relative scalar fixity of the territorial state appears thus as a contingent historical outcome of the constitution of national-state structures as gatekeepers of national economies: '[f]ar from neutral and fixed, ... geographical scales are the product of economic, political and social activities and relationships: as such, they are as changeable as those relationships themselves' (Smith 1995/2003: 60).

State responses to these processes emerge as necessary. But what challenges their territorial features and makes their geographical dimension contradictory is the fact that, while 'the necessity of discrete scales and of their internal differentiation is fixed' (Smith 1984: 147, in Marston 2000: 230), the scales themselves are not fixed, but change along with the development of capitalism. They are a systemic condition for capital accumulation processes, but also a co-evolving, contextually contingent outcome. Processes of the reconstruction of 'spatio-temporal fixes' around the economic and extra-economic elements of a capital accumulation regime are defined by 'a general tension between neoliberal demands to accelerate the flow of abstract (money) capital through an increasingly disembedded space and the need for the more concrete forms of capital to be "fixed" in time and place as well as embedded in specific social relations as a condition for their valorization' (Jessop 2000: 346). This tension accounts for the variety of forms taken by spatio-temporal fixes – and the institutional compromises to which they are associated – in various territorial contexts; it furthermore accounts for their experimental, unstable and contingent patterns (Peck and Tickell 1995; Jones 1997; Swyngedouw 1997). New 'modes of regulation' may only emerge from concrete regulation 'processes' (Goodwin 2001) redefining their scale-specific territorial and institutional rationales.

From a state-theoretical perspective on regulation, the 'political economy of governance' and its spatial implications appear as a response to the need for the state to redefine its role as a key site of regulation. Emergent governance processes reflect change in the forms of agency by which the state attempts to provide conditions for the regularization of economic processes under the pressure of changing accumulation regimes. Accordingly, phenomena of relativization and reconfiguration of scale express a struggle for the reconfiguration of the spatial dimension of state agency that questions the territorial relationship between local, regional and national levels of government.

This leads to a variety of state-promoted forms of 'scale differentiation' into which governance practices take form as a response to scale relativization. Their spatial nature increasingly diverges from traditional principles of territoriality. New governance practices redefine their own spatiality. Rather than being the outcome of hierarchical modes of state coordination and control embedded in 'bounded' territorial entities and in 'nested' territorial systems, they express spatially specific forms of social organization and mobilization, involving variable actors' arenas and constellations. As such, they often bear an unstable, provisional and weakly institutionalized character. However, state territoriality and territory, place- and scale-specific modes of governance are non-mutually exclusive dimensions. A constant tension exists between them, as extant territorial structures persist next to emergent ones. As they exceed 'bounded' territorial arenas and their formal-institutional jurisdictions, governance practices contribute to the 'de-territorialization' of modes of socio-political regulation. As they are stabilized in new policy rationales, they contribute to their spatial reconfiguration or 're-territorialization'.

Rather than being sidelined, the state plays an active role in promoting de- and re-territorialization. Inquiry into these phenomena requires therefore rejecting 'methodological territorialism' and relaxing assumptions of state centrality, but also focusing on the specific role of the state in promoting (re-)scaling processes. 'The state' cannot be assumed in this respect as a given, independent unit of analysis. Rather, viewing the state in an 'integral sense' (Jessop 1995), as a construct articulating relations between the economic and extra-economic in a dynamic and strategically selective way, directs attention to the co-evolution between policy rationales and territorial features of state agency. Acting on scale organization, state policies attempt at redefining a 'spatial fix' (Harvey 1985) as a new condition for exerting its role as an instance of regulation. By this, however, their spatial boundaries are 'discursively constituted, institutionally materialized, structurally coupled to other institutional boundaries, essentially contested and liable to change' (Jessop 2002: 37). (Re-)scaling processes by which the state promotes the enactment of governance practices are a constitutive part of a process of change in its nature. What defines a 'politics of scale' is hence a struggle involving, on the one hand, a potential opening to new forms and arenas of collective action and, on the other hand, a potentially radical redefinition of the rationale and purpose of state agency.

This has important interpretive consequences for understanding 'glocalization' processes as an expression of the political construction of spatiality. Unlike a 'mono-directional implosion of global forces into sub-global realms' (Brenner 1997: 159), or 'a unitary causal mechanism', globalization 'should be understood as the complex, emergent product of many different forces operating on many scales' (Jessop 2002: 114). It implies change in the rationales of state agency, rather than merely causing it. In globalized capitalism, the state contributes to organizing the spatio-temporal conditions for the operation of economic systems at all levels: world-economy formation and the rescaling of state territorial power are hence two dimensions of the same process. Accordingly, transnationalization and the production of new 'policy spaces' are interrelated phenomena. On the one hand, locality is (re-)constructed within the context of 'broader' capitalist relations that exceed the national domain of political-economic and social relations. On the other hand, its 'institutionalization' increasingly relies on 'global' relations of capitalist accumulation as well as on their discursive appropriation. As such, it involves mobilizing new discursive and symbolic frames of identification (Appadurai 1996; Paasi 2001). Significantly, it also involves an ideological quasi-naturalization of 'globalization' as a legitimating narrative for neo-liberal developments in local and regional policy: a 'mythical' view that disguises 'globalization' as a strategic-discursive construct related to a profound re-organization of capitalism, and the restructuring of geographical scales – the 'local' and the 'regional' – as its spatial expression (Harvey 1995; Swyngedouw 2000; Massey 2005).

Governance and the Redefinition of Relations Between Politics and Spatiality

The constitution of new governance spaces redefines the nexus between politics and spatiality. The changing spatiality of governance practices, in fact, conveys a change in the way the public interest is defined. The rescaling of governance may be seen in this respect as an expression of a renewal of politics in which interest representation is being redefined – beyond sovereignty and territoriality rules – through new spatialized relationships among state and non-state actors.

Governance practices in cities and regions – particularly in European socio-economic contexts – have developed in the last few decades along a shift 'from welfare-distributive modes of governance to localized supply-side measures aimed at enhancing economic performance', 'from nationally-based, process-oriented governing arrangements to locally based, product-oriented ones', and 'from vertical integration, standardised rules, clear lines of authority, accountability and national equity to horizontal integration, flexibility, networking, problem solving and the realisation of economic potential through strategic competition and collaboration' (Harding 1997: 295). Territorial policies have been accordingly characterized by a broadening of issues – to include structural political-economic strategies, active labour and human capital policies, RTD policies, locational and environmental policies, territorial marketing – and by a parallel broadening of actors and organizations involved.

Parallel to a narrowing-down of governmental role to formal institutional competencies, the intermediate space between state and market rationales has expanded and increasingly become crowded with representatives of private interest associations, corporatist organizations and stakeholders. The governance settings provided for their representation and involvement are seen as alternatives to centralized public action and to its perceived deficits in effectiveness and problem-solving capacity. The result, however, is the emergence of highly fragmented and volatile policy arenas.

In this perspective, reference to a distinction between government and governance, to a dualism between statutory settings and actual practices of governance and regulation, gains a peculiar semantic bearing. If in fact 'local-regional government' is defined as a field of public action structured into statutory levels of competencies and roles coincident with a definite territorial articulation, according to a classic model of sovereignty, 'local governance' is rather defined as an activity of regulation and decision-making of which local government is only one of the players, of the actors possibly involved. The notion of the 'local' governance refers therefore to a fundamental discontinuity in the practices of governing territories (Cox 1993, 1997; Le Galès 2002; Harding 2005).

Rather than representing a given socio-spatial order, the meaning of the 'local' and the 'regional' is re-shaped according to a tension between de- and re-territorialization processes. By this, the meaning of territoriality itself is redefined. No longer primarily defined as the domain of exercise of state sovereignty through a hierarchical spatial articulation of its authority, territoriality re-emerges as a social construction and a processual outcome. In the politics of neo-localism and neo-regionalism, inscribed in a discourse of territorial competition and competitiveness, the operation of public actors and institutions is redefined as a reflective and interactive contribution to the effective integration of multiple forms of regulation within concrete action spaces (Bagnasco 1988). The promotion of new forms of territorial governance descends therefore from an understanding of the spatial embeddedness of modes of regulation. It implies 'an understanding of the linkage of different types of regulation in a territory in terms of political and social integration and at the same time in terms of capacity of action' (Le Galès 1998: 495).

Redefining local-regional politics as a question of governance, therefore, implies a properly political dimension, related to a radical restructuring of relations between public institutions and social actors.

The transition from a Fordist to a flexible regime of capital accumulation, from relatively enclosed and protected national economies to 'globalized' competition between firms, is accompanied by a progressive 'withdrawal of the state' from the role previously assumed in social welfare policies. This also involves a revision of the territorial division of labour between state and local governments in reproducing conditions for economic development. Cities and regions become increasingly dependent on decentralized forms of self-governance and self-promotion, and new forms of performative pressure frame the changing relationship between institutional and economic actors at the local level (Harvey 1989; Jessop 1990, 1995). In the framework of local-regional governance arrangements aimed at the promotion of territorial development, the active inclusion of non-institutional actors and of intermediate, informal and associative forms of action expresses the role played by the state in enacting a 'local state' defined around new enlarged and 'inclusive' political arenas. Aggregation of interests, commitments to development-oriented partnerships and, eventually, consolidation of development 'regimes' and 'coalitions' become crucial factors for local-regional politics (Stoker 1990; Stoker and Mossberger 1994). 'Meso-level' neo-corporatist settings take the place of former generalist welfare-oriented corporatist systems of representation and are redirected towards local forms of concerted action (Heinze and Schmid 1997; Schmitter and Grote 1997). The resulting policy initiatives develop peculiarly 'experimental' forms of localism and regionalism, featuring high levels of self-organization and low levels of institutionalization, which frequently situate them in an intermediate, transitional domain between classic governmental settings and emergent governance regimes. Similarly, these new forms of territorial governance appear defined by a shift in the conception of public action: from social control to social production, from compliance to collective action, from top-down direction to local concerted initiative. As forms of collective action, they are reliant on, and at the same time constitutive of, specific socio-political milieux and identities: 'artificial communities' (De Rita and Bonomi 1998) or 'invented spaces' (Liepitz 1994), as it were, constituted through their very enactment.

Thus, local-regional societies are set in a tension between 'exogenous' imperatives of economic attractiveness and competitiveness on one side, and 'endogenous' aims of social integration on the other. This bears potentials for innovative forms of cooperation and collective action, but also uncertainties and threats connected to an increasing dependence on a 'coercive consensus' with regard to the quasi-natural imperatives of economic competitiveness and performance. Local governance does not in fact only represent an (unequal) horizon of opportunities, but also an (unequal) distribution of benefits and risks. Under conditions of increasing territorial self-reliance, 'a progressively more concrete interdependence is constituted between local economic processes and welfare-state processes', which may result as such in 'a fragmented and potentially highly unbalanced supply of social services tied to the respective economic "performance" of the region and dependent on the abilities, political priorities and mobilization of local political actors' (Mayer 1996: 22–3).

These shifts in governance practices may thus bear significant potentials for the empowerment of local societies, but also significant challenges to democratic representation and accountability. Governance structures – as highlighted by network-theoretical interpretations (Rhodes 1996) – may develop tendencies to autonomization and resistance to external control and regulation. Moreover, the distribution of resources for influencing policy agendas, organizational settings and regulatory inputs is relatively independent of political representation and liable to structural unequality in opportunities, with potential for conflicts of interests and representation (Painter and Goodwin 1995). In this respect, the local dimension of governance most vividly highlights the need for a renewal of democratic theory and practice.

Governance, Space and Politics: Implications for Planning Theory

In discussing 'governance', I have pointed out the importance of distinguishing between its assumption as a policy concept – with its normative undertones – and as an analytic concept, with an emphasis on its critical-interpretive implications. It is now time to draw some conclusions on the latter. For this purpose, it is useful to get back to the question earlier introduced, whether 'governance' is a notion that simply 'extends' our understanding of political steering, or rather one that implies a paradigmatic change in understanding the state, politics and the nature of public policy. Critical governance research, in fact, points to a more radical interpretive dimension.

Key to this is understanding governance in the light of changing conceptions of the state. As Mayntz (2005) points out in reviewing its genealogy, political steering theory – as the expression of a central steering function by the state – remains a dominant paradigm in thinking about 'governance' as long as belief in the effectiveness and legitimacy of state action is not questioned. Political steering theory, as defined within this paradigm, however, is dependent on a contingent, continental-European notion of the state: in it, the state as the steering subject and its purposive action is at the forefront of attention, while the nature of this purpose and of its objects is conveyed by a welfarist idea of the 'public interest'. The nature of this purpose and of its objects comes into question as a late result of the emerging effectiveness and legitimacy crisis of the state. Governance discourse arises therefore from a fundamental crisis of this conception. This happens in connection with the increasing fragmentation and relativization of both the subject (the state as a site of regulation), and the object (domains and forms of regulation) of public steering.

This leads to the crux of the matter. If we are to understand what is specific in governance discourse and practice, we need to look for its foundation in a changing understanding of the state; and, if we are to understand its spatial implications, we need to look at change in the spatiality of state action.

Assuming steering as the function of a political actor, and assuming the 'public' as its object and recipient, implies assumptions about a distinction between the subject and the object of politics, and this distinction strictly relies on a peculiar conception of the legitimacy of state action. In the wake of the emergence of the idea of a 'cooperative state', and of its embodiment in governance discourse, however, such a distinction between subject and object of regulation begins to blur. Political steering is no more identifiable with state action as expressed by its political-administrative structures, but is rather the result of the contingent interaction between different forms of regulation. It is a pervasive but emergent mode of agency, a construct that stresses the co-constitutive relationship between structure and agency, between governance as regulatory structure and governance as regulatory process, and the 'cooperative' pursuit of the collective goals defined by the involvement of market and societal actors.

In this sense, reference to 'collective goals' in defining governance practices (Jessop 1995: 317) must be understood no more as the expression of a normative orientation of the state towards the achievement of a collective welfare function, assumed as the foundation for a politics of the 'public interest', but as an emergent construct defined by specific policy arenas and specific policy objects. Accordingly, governance is no more primarily defined by a focus on regulatory structures, but rather by a focus on regulatory effects taking contingent forms through a combination of different regulatory means in a variety of policy arenas.

This leads to another key issue: that of the 'problem-solving bias' common to political steering theory and most current governance theory. Their dominant assumption – despite their relative shift in perspective – is that of an orientation of political action to the solving of collective problems. While political steering theory conveys this bias through assumptions on the motivation of the political system

– the pursuit of a 'public interest' – governance theory conveys it 'through the functionalist misassumption that existing institutions have emerged in the interest of solving collective problems' (Mayntz 2005: 18). But this view, as we have seen, is radically challenged by the fact that the production and delivery of public goods is increasingly co-determined by or delegated to market exchange rationales, and by the fact that this is reflected in the institutional design of decentralized and fragmented partnership arrangements and delegation mechanisms.

In as far as it remains 'trapped' in its 'problem-solving bias' – that is, in the assumption of a centrality of agency towards the resolution of collective problems – the notion of 'governance' shares in the same, if extended, paradigmatic horizon as theories of political steering. If, however, governance research questions this assumption, and points to a more general dynamics of hegemony formation, then a paradigmatic break with this tradition is in view. An alternative understanding of the way in which public policy is defined and discursively constructed becomes possible.

What is at stake here is a question which, if addressed in its full implications, bears a crucial importance for planning theory: the question of how far governance practices may represent not only, or primarily, an emergent form of institutionalization of interest-based politics – and governance discourse a creeping legitimation of it – but also an expression of the decline of democratic politics. If loosened from the assumption of the centrality of regulation of collective interests, and if rather directed towards understanding the selective, power-dependent effects of its practices on the definition of the 'public', governance research opens the way to a critical interpretation of the dynamics of political power and hegemony. It emphasizes the post-political and post-democratic dimension of state action and the governmentality effects realized in and by state-promoted policy spaces that are increasingly 'externalized' from of the political system.

In this sense, it shows affinities with research on the post-political and post-democratic dimension of contemporary governing practices (Crouch 2004) as well as with research inspired by Foucault's late work (e.g. 1991, 1997) on the 'governmentality' effects of modern political practices and on their role in the definition of political power and hegemony (Dean 1999; Lemke 2002; Swyngedouw 2005; Huxley, this volume).

Foucault notoriously based his notion of 'governmentality' on a rejection of a traditional focus on a juridical model of power and on its institutionalized expression – the constitutionally or contractually sanctioned apparatus of state sovereignty. In contrast, his heuristics and methodology are a plea for turning the philosophical foundations of political analysis upside down (Foucault 1997). In his approach to the analysis of political power, the question addressed by Foucault is no longer how power is based on the constitution of sovereignty at the centre, at the core of political institutions, but how effects of power result from the regulation of social practices at the periphery of political institutions, in their diffuse, everyday-life effects on conduct. In this perspective, the primary domain of analysis is not juridical right, but human sciences, and the code of power is not juridical norm, but concrete practices of normalization, of regularization of social conduct. Sovereignty rights and regulatory apparatuses and practices both represent constitutive parts of mechanisms of power: but Foucault invites us to rethink their interaction and mutual influence as well as to understand their relative shifts in the process of constitution of a modern conception of political power.

As a paradigmatic expression of politics in late modernity, governance appears to fulfil, in both discourse and practice, what Foucault hinted at, in a broader genealogical perspective, as a shift from a logic of sovereignty to a logic of regulation in defining political power.

A logic of regulation defines the way by which politics is primarily inscribed in actual rules of conduct, frames and practices, rather than by the way it fits a system of rights and deeds. Within a logic of regulation, political power finds its expression through the institution of a 'body of practice', rather than by defining and applying a legal framework of sovereignty. Its foundation is hence a technology, rather than a juridical model, and its effectiveness and legitimacy are increasingly defined as inherent to the selective contingency of concrete practices and of their goal- or performance-orientation, rather than by reference to a universal system of rights.

The 'governmentality' of governance appears to be precisely defined by the constitution of a regime of practices that becomes increasingly quasi-autonomous from sovereignty rule and that – even more importantly – tendentially reverses the criteria for effectiveness and legitimacy that are typical of representative political institutions. Governance discourse and practices become a new technology of government that mirrors Foucault's notion of governmentality in that they are both 'internal' and 'external' to the state: they redefine the meaning of politics and the state from the inside out, but do this essentially by decentralizing and by ever more externalizing the locus of politics. Governance appears hence as the expression of a state governmentality based on practices that mark a progressive autonomization of public policy from a politically accountable pursuit of collective ends.

The spatial dimension of governance practices is a remarkable embodiment of this trend. It expresses a shift from a general juridical model of territorial relationships, based on hierarchical, 'nested' relationships between 'bounded spaces' and on the public policy arenas they define, towards a negotiated or contractual model based on non-hierarchical, 'interconnected' and ad hoc relationships among public, private and civic actors that contingently define their policy arenas.

In such governance arrangements, we experience a shift in the logic of the social contract. Recourse to contractualization is functionalized: it is based on a functional, 'working model' rather than on a constitutional or 'political' model of the social contract. Moreover, contractualization is 'localized'. Recourse to contractualization is context specific: it is not territorially bounded, but aimed at bounding actors and interests to a specific territorial policy initiative. Its territoriality is therefore not a framework condition, but the expression of a 'local' agreement defined – and valid – within a specific constellation of actors and interests. As a result, the conception of territory as a policy domain is also revised. It is the activation of resources in a spatialized, 'local' frame of cooperation practices which constitutes the territory, rather than a juridical system of spatial relationships based on sovereignty rule. In this process of relativization of a nested hierarchy of sovereignty, territory becomes redefined: from a juridical object – as, for instance, a unit of administration – to an active subject – as, for instance, a performative 'unit of competition'.

What is particularly important, in a spatial perspective, is that this change in conception, as it is conveyed by governance discourse and practices, pervades the way public policy is conceived throughout all scales, through its embodiment in a variety of new spatial configurations that are being constituted with the active support of the state. Governance entails a redefinition of policy objects and policy arenas as well as of their constitutive spatial features. These are increasingly independent from rules of territorial sovereignty and from related territorially-based representative democratic rules politics, and increasingly dependent on ad-hoc, selective and negotiated policy arrangements. But this entails a radical change in understanding of public policy. The relative self-referentiality by which governance arrangements define their own policy spaces and arenas, largely in autonomy from representative political institutions, redefines the meaning of democratic participation and accountability. In this, they bear significant contradictions but, above all, a potential redefinition of the political.

The planning enterprise, as it shares in governance discourse and practices, should be concerned with a critical reflection on its manifestations and consequences. This is anything but easy, as everyday planning practices are mutually implied in constituting this form of governmentality. In this perspective, three aspects emerge from governance research that may serve as critical entry points of inquiry for planning theory.

The first concerns the need for a peculiar 're-spatialization' of planning theory. If governance is defined by complex sets of practices which, to an increasing extent, define their own spatiality, and constitute themselves as new policy spaces, then understanding planning practice requires awareness of the emergent spatial configurations in which it takes place. As these spatial configurations increasingly overlap and even challenge formal-institutional rationales of space and territoriality, it becomes key to direct inquiry towards the role of governance practices in defining new modes of 'production of space' and their trajectories of institutionalization – both material and discursive.

The second concerns questioning governance practices and their spatial features as the expression of a collective endeavour, inquiring into the way they constitute and express collective identities and preferences. If governance practices become mainstream, in contemporary politics, as an approach to collective problem-solving, and if governance actors and arenas are increasingly defined by the contingent interests and forms of representation expressed in those practices, then the 'everyday' dimension of governance is likely to become a framework for new 'local' forms of hegemony. This is, to be sure, not something happening 'out of the state'. State agency, rather, is increasingly legitimized precisely by procedurally enabling and facilitating such collective practices, in contrast to directly performing collective tasks: by its ability to exert a 'meta-governance' function, rather than by the direct pursuit of a collective function. By this, however, collective problem-solving progressively moves away from a representative-democratic perspective on the definition of the 'public interest'. This changes not only traditional arenas and forms of political deliberation and agency, but the essence of political discourse.

The third concerns the role of the public and civil society. Beyond the rhetoric of the 'cooperative state' and of problem-solving oriented collaborative relationships between societal sub-sectors, a critical, state-theoretically grounded approach to governance should recognize that the way markets and civil society are involved in governance discourse and practices is anything but an alternative to government and the state, but rather an expression of how the state as a materialization of social relations is currently undergoing change. In a neo-Gramscian perspective, understanding governance as an expression of state change is key in order to understand how civil society and the public sphere are being redefined as a site for expression of social and political struggles.

Along a critical reflection on these issues, planning theory can re-establish the link with a tradition of critical theory as a form of theorizing projected towards alternative practices. This, however, is unlikely to be effective, in the current post-political conjuncture, if addressed in abstraction from the pervasive presence of governance discourse and practices. It is unlikely to be effective, in other words, if addressed either by adopting a neo-pragmatist ideal of collective problem-solving that does not question its embeddedness in governance discourse and practices and the way these frame the meaning of the 'public', or by advocating an ethics of rights and political citizenship that neglects a reality of governance practices in the name of a juridical model of the 'public'. Rather, if it has to play such a role in critical theorizing, planning theory should commit itself to reflective experimentations. It should address the issue of how spatial practices can actively contribute to (re)defining arenas for the expression of collective preferences and political interests – at all spatial scales and across spatial scales – in a domain of practices that appears increasingly defined in post-political, post-national and post-territorial terms. It should address the issue of how spatial practices can contribute to (re-)establishing an effective and legitimate linkage between different societal roles – producer/consumer, decision-maker/constituent, supplier/end-user, and the like – within specific policy contexts, beyond reliance on a juridical model of territorially-based representative democracy.

References

Anderson, B. (1991) *Invented Communities: Reflections on the Origin and Spread of Nationalism*. London: Verso.

Appadurai, A. (1996) *Modernity at Large: Cultural Dimensions of Globalization*. Minneapolis, MN: University of Minnesota Press.

Arrow, K.J. (1963) *Social Choice and Individual Values*. New York: Wiley & Sons.

Bagnasco, A. (1988) *La Costruzione Sociale del Mercato: Studi sullo Sviluppo della Piccola Impresa in Italia*. Bologna: Il Mulino.

Bardach, E. (1977) *The Implementation Game: What Happens When a Bill Becomes a Law*. Cambridge MA: MIT Press.

Barret, S. and Fudge, C. (eds) (1981) *Policy and Action: Essays on the Implementation of Public Policy*. London: Methuen.

Boudon, R. (1977) *Effets Pervers et Ordre Social*. Paris: Presses Universitaires de France.

Brenner, N. (1997) 'Global, fragmented, hierarchical: Henri Lefebvre's geographies of globalization' *Public Culture* 24: 135–67.

Crouch, C. (2004) *Post-Democracy*. Oxford: Blackwell.

Cox, K.D. (ed.) (1997) *Spaces of Globalization*. New York: Guilford Press.

Cox, K.R. (1993) 'The local and the global in the new urban politics: a critical view' *Environment and Planning D: Society and Space* 11: 433–8,

De Rita, G. and Bonomi, A. (1998) *Manifesi. per lo Sviluppo Locale: Dall'azione di Comunità ai Patti Territoriali*. Torino: Bollati Boringhieri.

Dean, M. (1999) *Governmentality: Power and Rule in Modern Society*. London: Sage.

Downs, A. (1957) *An Economic Theory of Democracy*. New York: Harper & Row.

Foucault, M. (1991) 'Governmentality', in Burchell, G., Gordon, C., and Miller, P. (eds) *The Foucault Effect: Studies in Governmentality*. Hemel Hempstead: Harvester Wheatsheaf, 87–104.

Foucault, M. (1997) *Il Faut Défendre la Société: Cours au Collège de France 1976*. Paris: Gallimard/Seuil.

Giddens, A. (1984) *The Constitution of Society*. Cambridge: Polity Press.

Goodwin, M. (2001) 'Regulation as process: regulation theory and comparative urban and regional research' *Journal of Housing and the Built Environment* 16(1): 71–87.

Harding, A. (1997) 'Urban regimes in a Europe of the cities?' *European Urban and Regional Studies*, 4(4): 291–314.

Harding, A. (2005) 'Governance and socio-economic change in cities', in Buck, N., Gordon, I., Harding, A., and Turok, I. (eds) *Changing Cities: Rethinking Urban Competitiveness, Cohesion and Governance*. Basingstoke: Palgrave, 62–77.

Harvey, D. (1985) 'The geopolitics of capitalism', in Gregory, D., and Urry, J. (eds) *Social Relations and Spatial Structures*. London: Macmillan, 128–63.

Harvey, D. (1989) 'From managerialism to entrepreneurialism: the transformation in urban governance in late capitalism' *Geografiska Annaler*, 71 B(1): 3–17.

Harvey, D. (1995) 'Globalisation in question' *Rethinking Marxism* 84: 1–17.

Heinze, R.G. and Schmid, J. (1997) 'Industrial change and meso-corporatism: a comparative view on three German states' *European Planning Studies* 5(5): 597–617.

Héritier, A. (ed.) (2002) *Common Goods: Reinventing European and International Governance*. Lanham, MD: Rowman and Littlefield.

Hollingsworth, J.R., and Boyer, R. (eds) (1997) *Contemporary Capitalism: The Embeddedness of Institutions*. Cambridge: Cambridge University Press.

Hooghe, L., and Marks, G. (2001) *Multi-level Governance and European Integration*. Lanham, MD: Rowman and Littlefield.

Hooghe, L. and Marks, G. (2003) 'Unraveling the central state, but how? Types of multi-level governance' *American Political Science Review* 97(2): 233–43.

Jessop, B. (1990) 'Regulation theories in retrospect and prospect' *Economy and Society* 19(2): 153–216.

Jessop, B. (1995) 'The regulation approach, governance and post-Fordism: alternative perspectives on economic and political change?' *Economy and Society* 24(3): 307–33.

Jessop, B. (2000) 'The crisis of the national spatio-temporal fix and the tendential ecological dominance of globalising capitalism' *International Journal of Urban and Regional Research* 24(2): 323–60.

Jessop, B. (2002) *The Future of the Capitalist State*. Cambridge: Polity Press.

Jones, M.R. (1997) 'Spatial selectivity of the state? The regulationist enigma and local struggles over economic governance' *Environment and Planning A* 29: 831–64.

Kohler-Koch, B., and Eising, R. (eds) (1999) *The Transformation of Governance in the European Union*. London: Routledge.

Kooiman, J. (ed.) (1993a) *Modern Governance*. London: Sage.

Kooiman, J. (1993b) 'Findings, speculations, and recommendations' in Kooiman, J. (ed.) (1993a), 249–62.

Le Galès, P. (1998) 'Regulations and governance in European cities' *International Journal of Urban and Regional Research* 22(3): 482–506.

Le Galès, P. (2001) 'Urban governance and policy networks: on the urban political boundedness of policy networks' *Public Administration* 79(1): 167–84.

Le Galès, P. (2002) *European Cities: Social Conflicts and Governance*. Oxford: Oxford University Press.

Lemke, T. (2002) 'Foucault, governmentality, and critique' *Rethinking Marxism* 14(3): 49–64.

Liepitz, A. (1994) 'The national and the regional: their autonomy vis-à-vis the capitalist world crisis' in Palan, R., and Gills, B. (eds) *Transcending the State-Global Divide*. Boulder, CO: Lynne Rienner, 24–43.

Marston, S.A. (2000) 'The social construction of scale' *Progress in Human Geography* 24(2): 219–42.

Massey, D. (2005) *For Space*. London: Sage.

Mayer, M. (1996) 'Postfordistiche Stadtpolitik: Neue Regulationsformen in der lokalen Politik und Planung' *Zeitschrift für Wirtschaftsgeographie* 40(1–2): 20–7.

Mayntz, R. (1987) 'Politische Steuerung und gesellschaftliche Steuerungsprobleme: Anmerkungen zu einem theoretischen Paradigma' *Jahrbuch zur Staats- und Verwaltungswissenschaft*, Vol. 1 Baden Baden: Nomos, 89–110.

Mayntz, R. (2004) 'Governance im modernen Staat' in Benz, A. (ed.) *Governance – Regieren in komplexen Regelsystemen*. Wiesbaden: VS Verlag für Sozialwissenschaften, 65–76.

Mayntz, R. (2005) 'Governance Theory als fortentwickelte Steuerungstheorie?', in Schuppert G.F. (ed.) *Governance-Forschung: Vergewisserung über Stand und Entwicklungslinien*. Baden-Baden: Nomos, 11–20.

Mayntz, R., and Scharpf, F.W. (1995) *Gesellschaftliche Selbstregelung und politische Steuerung*. Frankfurt a.M: Campus.

Mayntz, R., and Scharpf, F.W. (2005) 'Politische Steuerung – Heute?' *Zeitschrift für Soziologie*, 34(3): 236–43.

North D.C. (1981) *Structure and Change in Economic History*. New York: Norton.

North D.C. (1990) *Institutions, Institutional Change and Economic Performance*. New York: Cambridge University Press.

Olson, M. (1965) *The Logic of Collective Action: Public Goods and the Theory of Groups*. Cambridge, MA: Harvard University Press.

Osborne, D. and Gaebler, T. (1993) *Reinventing Government*. New York: Plume Press.

Paasi, A. (2001) 'Europe as a social process and discourse: considerations of place, boundaries and identity' *European Urban and Regional Studies* 8(1): 7–28.

Painter, J. and Goodwin, M. (1995) 'Local governance and concrete research: investigating the uneven development of regulation' *Economy and Society* 24(3): 334–56.

Peck, J. and Tickell, A. (1995) 'Social regulation after Fordism: regulation theory, neo-liberalism and the global-local nexus' *Economy and Society* 24(3): 357–86.

Pressman J.L. and Wildavsky, A. (1973) *Implementation*. Berkeley, CA: University of California Press.

Rhodes, R.A.W. (1996) 'The new governance: governing without government' *Political Studies* 64: 652–67.

Rosenau, J.N. and Czempiel, E.-O. (eds) (1992) *Governance without Government: Order and Change in World Politics*. Cambridge: Cambridge University Press.

Schmitter, P.C., and Grote, J.R. (1997) *The Corporatist Sisyphus: Past, Present and Future*. Florence: European University Institute, EUI Working Papers SPS 97/4.

Selznick, P. (1949) *TVA and the Grass Roots: A Study of Politics and Organization*. Berkeley, CA: University of California Press.

Smith, N. (1995) 'Remaking scale: competition and cooperation in prenational and postnational Europe', in Eskelinen, H., and Snickars, F. (eds) *Competitive European Peripheries*. Berlin: Springer, 59–74, now in Brenner, N. et al. (eds) (2003) *State/Space*. Oxford: Blackwell, 229–38 (references are to 2003 reprint).

Stoker, G. (1990) 'Regulation theory, local government, and the transition from Fordism', in King, D., and Pierre, J. (eds) (1990) *Challenges to Local Government*. London: Sage.

Stoker, G. (1998) 'Governance as theory: five propositions' *International Social Science Journal* 50(155): 17–28.

Stoker, G. and Mossberger, K. (1994) 'Urban regime theory in comparative perspective' *Environment and Planning C: Government and Policy* 12: 195–212.

Streeck W. and Schmitter P.C. (eds) (1985) *Private Interest Government: Beyond Market and State*. London: Sage.

Swyngedouw, E. (1997) 'Neither global nor local: globalization and the politics of scale', in Cox, K.D. (ed.) *Spaces of Globalization*. New York: Guilford Press, 137–66.

Swyngedouw, E. (2000) 'Authoritarian governance, power, and the politics of rescaling' *Environment and Planning D: Society and Space* 18: 63–76.

Swyngedouw, E. (2005) 'Governance innovation and the citizen: the Janus face of governance-beyond-the-state' *Urban Studies* 42(11) 1991–2006.

Williamson, O.E. (1975) *Markets and Hierarchies: Analysis and Antitrust Implications.* New York: Free Press.

Williamson, O.E. (1985) *The Economic Institutions of Capitalism: Firms Markets, Relational Contracting.* New York: Free Press.

Informality and the Politics of Planning

Ananya Roy

The twenty-first century will be an urban century. For the first time in human history more people will live in cities than in any other form of human settlement. Much of this urban growth and urbanization will take place in the cities of the global South. In these cities, significant proportions of urban citizens rely on informal work and informal settlements as means of survival, mobility, and accumulation. Yet, planning theory has been strikingly silent on such issues. It is as if the great urban revolution of modern history is a casual backdrop to the planning debates about communication and collaboration and even to the planning debates about knowledge and power. While much of the world is enmeshed in a complex urban reality, planning theorists continue to be barely interested in what Yiftachel (2006) calls 'the transformation of space'. It is my contention that planning theorists have thus rendered themselves irrelevant to one of the most important processes of the *fin-de-millénaire*: the struggle for the city. Since economic globalization is closely linked to urbanization and urbanism, planning theorists have thus also rendered themselves irrelevant to the study and analysis of global economic change and international development.

In this chapter, I seek to establish a theoretical agenda that revives the 'urban question'[1] in planning theory. I do so by focusing in particular on that which is often seen to lie well outside the safe boundaries of Euro-American planning theory: informal modes of organizing space, livelihood, and citizenship. Imagined as unplanned, chaotic and disorderly forms of urbanism, these modes are in fact deeply entangled with structures of planning and thus are central to any analysis of state power and community action in contemporary cities. While often perceived to be located solely in the cities of the global South, urban informality is in fact a pervasive phenomenon. More significantly, as detailed in this essay, informality is an important analytic tool in understanding the practice of planning and the production of space.

---

1   The concept of the 'urban question' comes of course from Castells (1977).

Recently, planning theorists have sought to take up the concept of informality. For example, an article in the flagship *Journal of the American Planning Association* by Judith Innes, Sarah Connick and David Booher (2007: 207) presents informality as a 'valuable strategy of planning'. For these authors, the term 'informality' signifies planning strategies that are 'neither prescribed nor proscribed (in) any rules ... The idea of informality also connotes casual and spontaneous interactions and personal affective ties among participants'. While attention by planners to practices of informality is welcome, this use of the concept reduces it to a mode of social behaviour, detaching it from the global and urban political economy that gives shape and form to systems of informality.

By contrast, in this chapter, I return to the several decades of rich theoretical work on informality. Instead of presenting a single, unified paradigm of informality, I seek to highlight a diversity of theoretical ideas, thus putting forward four different perspectives on the concept. I argue that such a debate, which is both analytical and political, opens up new and interesting questions for spatial planning. I also argue that these diverse ideas must be understood in their historical and regional contexts of knowledge production. Such genealogies are essential to confront and critique the disembedded and depoliticized use of the concept of informality that seems to be at risk of taking hold in planning theory. In the chapter, I organize these four prominent theoretical perspectives into two ensembles of argument and critique: the first concerned with the logic of global and urban capitalism; the second focused on questions of rule, sovereignty, citizenship, and politics. In each ensemble, informality plays a central role. In a final section, I explore the implications of the concept of informality for a type of planning theory that is able to confront and analyze the urban transformations of the twenty-first century in robust fashion.

Ensemble 1: Informal Capitalism

The brutal years of neo-liberal austerity were followed, in the mid-1990s, by a new formation of political economy. Billed as 'kinder and gentler', this approach sought to 'embed' the market in social relations and subjugate it to considerations of social justice.[2] There were varied manifestations of this formation. In the Anglo-American context, the Blair-Clinton paradigm of the 'Third Way' aimed to create a form of governance that reconciled laissez-faire and redistributive philosophies. Globally, the 'structural adjustment' of the 1980s was replaced by a renewed Keynesianism that made poverty alleviation and human development a priority. Indeed, the very economists who had once unflinchingly advocated 'shock therapy' for Third World economies were now calling for massive investments in physical and

---

2   The idea of 'embedding' the market in society comes from Polanyi (1944) and is often invoked to indicate a form of 'embedded liberalism' that stands in contrast to the free market ideology of neo-liberalism.

human infrastructure to help countries escape the 'poverty trap'. A visible symbol of this 'change of heart' is of course Jeffrey Sachs and his agenda of an 'end of poverty' (Sachs 2005). 'Millennial development', as I have come to call it (Roy 2010), thus exists in a complex relationship to the stark neo-liberalism that preceded it. It is hailed by Washington insiders such as former World Bank president, James Wolfensohn, and former World Bank economist turned critic, Joseph Stiglitz, as reform – a 'post Washington consensus' that rejects the neo-liberal (and faulty) tenets of unadulterated liberalization and privatization. On the other hand, 'millennial development' can be read as a reworking of neo-liberalism to manage the social costs of neo-liberalism, or even as a strengthened configuration of market ideologies and practices that opens up untapped frontiers of dispossession and accumulation. Informality is central to such debates, for, in the mid-1990s, as a new political economy was forming so was informality rediscovered.

The Rediscovery of Informality

The rediscovery of informality is a key component of 'millennial development'. This rediscovery is marked by three propositions: that informality embodies the entrepreneurial energies of the 'people's economy'; that the vitality of the informal economy is shaped by non-economic forces, particularly social capital; and that the value latent in informality can be activated and converted into fungible capital by integrating the informal into formal capitalism. Each proposition is worth discussing in greater detail and each has important implications for how the political economy and politics of planning can be understood and transformed.

In his influential vision for the 'end of poverty', Sachs (2005) outlines a mild global Keynesianism that promises to take developing countries up the ladder of modernization, a plan that bears strong echoes of Rostow's (1960) explicitly 'non-communist' teleology of economic growth. Such ideas are formally stated in the Millennium Development Goals, ratified by the member nations of the United Nations in 1999. Understood as a global social contract for human development, the MDGs act as a moral compass for those, such as Sachs, who push for more aid to, and public investment in, physical and human capital. It is against this vision that William Easterly (2006) presents a provocative counter-vision. Critiquing Sachs as a Planner, Easterly condemns these new modernizations as Big Western Plans, as neocolonial forms of utopian social engineering that are bound to fail and to possibly do more harm than good. Easterly contrasts Planners with Searchers, with the grassroots and self-help activities that are incremental, efficient, effective and accountable. His idea is pithy: that 'the poor help themselves' (Easterly 2006: 27) and that they do so through 'economic freedom', which is 'one of mankind's most underrated inventions' (72). Perhaps his most powerful argument against planning is this: that 'the rich have markets, the poor have bureaucrats' (Easterly 2006: 165). In other words, Easterly calls for the liberation of the poor from the bureaucratic chains of international aid and state planning. He argues that the poor are Searchers and that left to their own devices they can craft and run systems of great entrepreneurial energy.

Easterly's economic libertarianism draws inspiration from at least one key figure involved in the rediscovery of informality: Hernando de Soto. De Soto's arc of work, from *The Other Path* (1989) to *The Mystery of Capital* (2000), presents the informal sector as an 'invisible revolution' (the subtitle of *The Other Path*), a grassroots uprising against the bureaucracy of state planning. As Bromley (2004) notes, this 'other path' is also meant to be the alternative to the political radicalism of the Shining Path, the guerilla movement that waged a class war in Peru, de Soto's home, and the setting for *The Other Path*. In *The Mystery of Capital*, de Soto extends his arguments about the 'people's economy' by arguing that the poor are 'heroic entrepreneurs'. He insists that the poor already possess considerable assets and estimates that such assets amount to $9 trillion, far exceeding any transfers of aid and assistance that can be directed to them: 20 times the direct foreign investment in the Third World since the Berlin Wall fell and more than 46 times as much as the World Bank has lent in the last three decades. The cause of poverty is not the lack of assets but rather that the poor are relegated to the informal sector in their ownership and use of such assets. The cause of poverty, then, is the bureaucracy that makes it difficult for the poor to participate in the formal sector, a system that de Soto calls 'legal apartheid'. Thus, Bromley (2004) rightly notes that de Soto's work most closely hews to the ideas of Friedrich von Hayek and its depiction of the state as a bureaucratic obstacle to economic freedom.

The second proposition associated with the rediscovery of informality is less beholden to Hernando de Soto. While de Soto is interested in the forms of 'extra-legal regulation' that govern the informal sector, he does not provide a thorough analysis of such forms of regulation. But in the policy work of 'millennial development', the forms of governance are more clearly identified. They are seen to be primarily non-economic and to constitute 'social capital'. Across the political spectrum, from Francis Fukuyama to Joseph Stiglitz, social capital is seen to be a constellation of non-economic forces that make markets work, and work better. The World Bank defines social capital thus:

> *Social capital refers to the institutions, relationships, and norms that shape the quality and quantity of a society's social interactions. Increasing evidence shows that social cohesion is critical for societies to prosper economically and for development to be sustainable. Social capital is not just the sum of the institutions which underpin a society – it is the glue that holds them together.* (<http://web.worldbank.org/>)

While social capital is assumed to be found in all domains, it is seen to be particularly important in the workings of the informal economy or 'microenterprises'. It is thus that the popular policy intervention of 'millennial development' has been microcredit, which distributes tiny loans to the poor and deploys various forms of class and gendered norms, from community discipline to self discipline, to ensure loan repayment. But these norms have, in rather euphemistic fashion, been celebrated as the workings of 'social capital', an indication not only that the 'poor always pay back' but also that poor communities can be rich in types of social capital. In short, the informal economy is conceptualized as a solidarity economy.

Of course the idea of social capital is not new. In the work of Pierre Bourdieu (1977; 1986) for example, social capital, along with cultural and symbolic capital, helps create and maintain social distinctions. It is, in short, a key instrument of class differentiation and reproduction. However, the new political economy of the 1990s reframed 'social capital' through rational choice microeconomics. The information-theoretic economics that accompanied the 'post-Washington consensus' is primarily concerned with the social institutions and transactions that mitigate market failure. In this work, social capital plays a central role helping complete what Stiglitz (in Fine 2001a: 8) describes as 'incomplete information, incomplete markets, incomplete contracts'. World Bank reports (e.g. Narayan and Pritchett 1997) emphasize the role of social capital in increasing income. And the pervasive influence of Robert Putnam (2000) presents and reiterates the argument that social capital is a collection of social networks and norms of reciprocity and trustworthiness, and that these constitute the basis of civic engagement, associational life, and ultimately economic prosperity. Such framings make it possible to imagine social, political, and cultural worlds while simultaneously subjugating them to the overwhelming logic of the liberal economy. Fine (2001b: 136) thus notes that 'social capital is the dream concept of the new consensus'.

The significance of this second proposition about social capital is most evident when one returns to recent invocations of informality in planning theory, as in Innes, Connick, and Booher (2007). There is an uncanny ideological resonance between the formulation of informality as a type of 'organic' 'interaction order' and the 'thin' theories of social capital that animate the new political economy. Both genres of work suggest that norms of reciprocity and trust are solutions to various market and institutional failures, especially to collective action failures. The historical emergence of such cultures of solidarity remains unexplained, and the entanglement of cultures of solidarity with forms of power and hierarchies of distinction are rendered invisible. The designation of such types of exchange and transaction as 'informality' deepens these elisions of power, for in a manner similar to de Soto's work, this framework presents informal collaboration as the 'other path', the alternative to power-laden, bureaucratic planning.

The third proposition in the rediscovery of informality is the integration of the informal into formal systems of capitalism. This is a tricky proposition, potentially rife with contradictions, because how can one formalize informality while also maintaining its unique energies and capacities? One solution lies in the wildly popular text, *The Fortune at the Bottom of the Pyramid*, by C.K. Prahalad. In keeping with the subtitle of the text, 'eradicating poverty through profits', Prahalad (2004) argues that the poor surviving in informal and rural economies, often making less than $2 a day, must be seen as consumers. The more global capitalism seeks to tap such emerging markets through new consumer products and services, the more the poor will benefit from these economies of scale and choice. Prahalad dubs this virtuous, invisible hand, linkage between the formal and the informal, between multinational corporations and poor consumers, an ecosystem for wealth creation.

An equally popular method of integration comes from Hernando de Soto. Recall that de Soto estimates that the world's poor have accumulated assets worth $9 trillion. Why then are they poor? The answer, according to de Soto, lies in the fact that these assets are held in a defective form; they are 'dead capital'. Existing outside of formal and legal systems of regulation and exchange, these assets do not serve their owners as active and productive forms of capital, for example as collateral. He estimates that in Egypt alone 92 per cent of urban housing and 83 per cent of rural housing are held in the form of 'dead capital', yielding an untapped 'dead capital' base of $240 billion. De Soto thus calls for the legalization of these extra-legal assets.

The formalization of informality and the legalization of informal land titles may seem to be a rather radical approach, one that breaks with the Hayekian underpinnings of de Soto's ideology. Yet, as I have argued elsewhere (Roy 2005), de Soto is not calling for the redistribution of property. A closer look shows that his approach is not so much about property rights as it is about the right to participate in property markets. This became apparent in a debate that played out in the *Journal of the American Planning Association*. In a review of De Soto's *The Mystery of Capital*, Keyes (2003: 104), argued that his scheme was unfeasible because 'accumulation-hungry capitalists, by the logic of capital, do not wish to dilute their wealth, and the distribution of capital to the world's poor would do just that'. In a response, Schaefer (2003: 316), director of the Washington DC branch of De Soto's Institute of Liberty and Democracy, pointed out that Keyes had confused De Soto's efforts with traditional land reform programs:

> De Soto's proposal is not wealth transfer but wealth legalization. The poor of the world already hold trillions in assets now. De Soto is not distributing capital to anyone. By making them liquid, everyone's capital pool grows dramatically.

Schaefer's rather blunt statement about the difference between wealth transfer and wealth legalization is crucial. De Soto's ideas are seductive precisely because they only guarantee the latter but in doing so promise the former. But can such a promise be sustained in the context of brutally unequal national property regimes and dramatically skewed global hierarchies of wealth and asset ownership? What then does it mean to create a new 'asset class' that is the formalization of the informal and which is served by this new liquid capital?

Neo-liberal Populism

This talk of the entrepreneurial poor, of their social capital, and of the transformation of 'dead capital' into 'liquid capital', weaves a magical spell. The magic is that of capital. In this account, poverty is a disadvantage but the poor also belong to the 'people's economy', an informal domain marked by entrepreneurship, solidarity, associational norms, and extralegal asset ownership. Through simple interventions that 'include' the informal in the systems of formal capitalism, the assets of the poor can be made fungible and the disadvantage of poverty can be ended. Here is the compelling image of 'a billion bootstraps' (Smith and Thurman 2007) as numerous micro-economies convert their assets into fungible capital, and enter the great ecosystem of wealth creation.

However, this is a very particular view of capital and of contemporary capitalism. Against this optimistic read of the 'people's economy' is a more grim and sombre portrait of the world system, its economic logic, and the role of informality at the turn of the century. The most apocalyptic version of this account is presented by Mike Davis (2006) who imagines a 'planet of slums', a warehousing of the 'surplus humanity' released by deproletarianization and agricultural deregulation in hazardous and miserable forms of urban settlement. For Davis (2006: 14–15), informal urbanization is a stark manifestation of 'overurbanization' or 'urbanization without growth', which in turn is 'the legacy of a global political conjuncture – the worldwide debt crisis of the late 1970s and the subsequent IMF-led restructuring of Third World economies in the 1980s'. To this of course can be added the types of homegrown neo-liberalism that have led many economies to actively court and support extractive forms of global capital, what Shiva (2004) calls the 'suicide economy of corporate globalization'.[3] Davis's work is part of a substantial genre of research that traces the formation of a 'new urban marginality' – not only in the Third World but also in Europe and the Americas. While in the 1970s, researchers undermined the 'myth of marginality' (Perlman 1977), arguing that the informalized poor were integrated into the labour markets, social life, and political systems of the city, they are now making the case for the 'reality of marginality' (Perlman 2004). Wacquant's work (1996, 1999, 2007), for example, documents the emergence of an 'advanced marginality' that is linked to the 'territorial stigmatization' faced by residents of marginalized spaces: the ghetto, the banlieue, the favela. Similarly, Auyero (2000) charts the emergence of the 'hyper-shantytown'. Such research is united in its emphasis on the connections between such 'advanced marginality' and the hollowing out of economies and welfare states through neo-liberal capitalism. The 'hyper-shantytown' is thus produced by 'hyper-unemployment' (Auyero 1999), a systematic process of deproletarianization and labour informalization. While the theorists of 'advanced marginality' acknowledge the poverty-targeting efforts of the state (for example, in Brazil, the upgrading of favelas through the provision of services), they insist that such programs are minor palliatives in the face of a massive structural crisis. In particular, they argue that the communities of the urban poor are now overwhelmed by violence: the violence of state repression, the symbolic violence of stigma and discrimination, and the material violence of poverty and unemployment (Perlman 2004). My own work

---

3   Shiva's title refers to the suicides of Indian farmers, deaths that she attributes to the decimation of Indian agriculture by India's liberalization policies.

in India (Roy 2003, 2007) traces the ways in which the crisis of Indian agriculture, catalyzed by the auto-liberalization of the Indian economy, has created a state of territorialized vulnerability for the rural-urban poor, manifested in a 'footloose condition' between city and countryside.

Such structural understandings of informalization as a key feature of late capitalism and advanced marginality are an important counterpoint to the romanticized and sanitized account of informality that is part and parcel of 'millennial development'. However, it is important to see this latter account not simply as a 'thin' or 'failed' explanation but rather as a series of insights into the logic of the new political economy. Following Gore (2000: 176), I designate this logic as a 'neo-liberal populism', one that seeks to create new frontiers of capital accumulation through projects of inclusion, such as the inclusion of the people's economy. It is thus that Elyachar shows how, in Egypt, the management of the informal economy was an attempt to manage the social costs of liberalization and to thus manage 'the generation of structural adjustment', those 'freed' into the space dubbed the 'informal economy' (Elyachar 2005: 30). But more powerfully she shows how strategies of microenterprise development sought to transform the 'relational value' and 'ethical value' of the informal sector into 'economic value' (Elyachar 2005: 7–9). In similar fashion, Weber (2002) links microfinance and poverty reduction strategies to a 'global development architecture'. She conceptualizes these development interventions both as 'novel experimentations' in appeasing the political protests that have accompanied liberalization in many different nations and as forms of market restructuring that create local economies that have been ' adjusted' for new forms of accumulation (Weber 2002: 55). Rankin (2001) shows how such forms of governing take place through the instrument of the 'rational economic woman', a figure crucial to the functioning of successful micro-economies. In other words, neo-liberal populism is engendered by the activation and deployment of the class and gender hierarchies that lurk in the 'people's economy'. The bottom of the pyramid, is a vast and tempting market for global capital but it is also one that has to be made legible, transparent, and visible in order for its 'relational' and 'ethical' value to be transformed into 'economic' value, for 'dead capital' to circulate as 'liquid capital'. This is the significance of the rediscovery of informality for it transforms the margins of the global economy into an 'asset class' fit for the speculative appetite of late capitalism.

I must advance a word of caution here. It is not my intention to suggest a functionalist argument whereby the complex politics of millennial development are neatly and inevitably reduced to a self-perpetuating neo-liberal populism. Indeed, my current work (Roy 2010) is focused on the lively struggles over meanings and markets, over ideas and institutions, which mediate the relationship between millennial development and neo-liberal populism. As this relationship is marked by the functional logic of capital accumulation, so it is constantly disrupted by multiple political planes, ranging from global social movements to postcolonial nationalism. There is nothing guaranteed about neo-liberal populism but it is a formation that is dominant, even hegemonic, as an ideology and practice. It is naïve, even irresponsible, to celebrate the rediscovery of informality without taking into account this conjuncture. Especially significant here is the conceptualization of 'capital' that undergirds the rediscovery of informality. I have already made note of how 'thin' theories of 'social capital' elide forms of power, authority, and distinction. It is equally important to understand Hernando de Soto's calculus of 'dead capital'. For de Soto, capital is a representation; he therefore writes:

> In the West ... every parcel of land, every building, every piece of equipment, or store of inventories is represented in a property document that is the visible sign of a vast hidden process that connects all these assets to the rest of the economy ... Third World and former communist nations do not have this representational process. As a result, most of them are undercapitalized ... The enterprises of the poor are very much like corporations that cannot issue shares or bonds to obtain new investment and finance. Without representations, their assets are dead capital. ... The poor inhabitants of these nations – five-sixths of humanity – do have things, but they lack the process to represent their property and create capital ... This is the mystery of capital. (de Soto 2000: 6–7)

The transformation of 'dead capital' into 'liquid capital' is thus a process by which the assets of the poor come to be represented differently – under the visible sign of the legal title. Setting aside the mechanics and politics of such titling, it is worth noting what capital is not for de Soto. It is not a form of surplus value produced by the exploitation of labor. The 'defect' of the informal sector is thus a defective form of representation rather than the vulnerability that is associated with relations of production. Indeed, as Bromley (2004: 273) notes, de Soto is 'remarkably silent about the wage labor relationships that prevail in such sectors as domestic service and construction'. This idea of poverty as a lack of capital or a lack of fungible capital is a prevalent feature of millennial development. It is for this reason that, in my recent work, I characterize millennial development as 'the end of political economy'. In *An Archaeology of Knowledge*, Foucault (1969) charts the shift, in the eighteenth century, from a classical analysis of wealth to political economy, i.e. an analysis of wealth in relation to production and labour. In many ways, the millennial development and the attendant rediscovery of informality marks what can be seen as the end of political economy: a return to a classical analysis where wealth is understood as a system of circulation and exchange, the pure fiction of money constituted as a representation. In such a framework, political economy, as an analysis of the production of value, not as a sign, but as a product of labour, is no longer possible.

Ensemble 2: Rule, Sovereignty, and Citizenship

A second ensemble of argument and critique about informality is concerned with questions of rule, sovereignty, and citizenship. This ensemble commands much less public attention than the rediscovery of informality but also contains within it interesting bursts of optimism, albeit for reasons that are much more robust than those that celebrate the 'people's economy'. The optimism associated with this ensemble relates to how informality, as a set of claims to urban space, livelihood, and citizenship, generates a politics of the possible.

In the seminal text, *The City and the Grassroots*, Castells (1983) presents an ambitious theory of urban social movements. Studying both formal political organizations and the mobilizations of informal squatter communities, Castells acknowledges the central role of politics in the transformation of the capitalist city but also analyzes the limits of such politics. In particular, he designates the populist politics of squatter communities as a symptom of the 'dependent city', a 'city without citizens'. He argues that while squatters mobilize to secure access to land, services, jobs, and at times even tenure, they are simultaneously co-opted into systems of political patronage. Thus, they are clients rather than citizens, disciplined subjects of urban populism rather than active agents of structural change. Castells's work on the patronage politics of informality has influenced an entire genre of research and analysis. My own work in the city of Calcutta depicted a socialist regime skilled at populist politics (Roy 2003). In this system of territorialized uncertainty, and in sharp contradiction to de Soto's argument, the tenure claims of the poor could never be formalized and made secure for if they were, the populist calculus would be severed. For Calcutta's poor, informality is on the one hand a vital mode of access to services, shelter and livelihood (a manifestation of substantive citizenship), but on the other hand is a regime of calculated uncertainty and unrequited hope (the hoax of formal citizenship).

However, a growing body of work is much more optimistic about the politics of informality. Thus, Asef Bayat (2000) working in the context of Middle Eastern cities, outlines the repertoire of tactics through which urban 'informals' appropriate and claim space. According to him, this 'quiet encroachment of the ordinary' by subaltern groups creates a 'street politics' that shapes the city in fundamental ways. Bayat's analysis draws inspiration from Michel de Certeau's (1984) conceptualization of the 'practice of everyday life' as a set of tactics that can undo the oppressive grid of power and discipline. While planners and rulers seek to create and enforce the 'economy of the proper place' through strategies of rule, everyday and commonplace tactics refuse this discipline. In somewhat similar fashion, Abdoumaliq Simone (2006) presents the African city as 'pirate towns', where urban residents develop forms of everyday practice that allow them to operate resourcefully in underresourced cities. This is a context of crisis, where 'production possibilities' are severely limited; but this is also a context where 'existent materials of all kind are to be appropriated' (Simone 2006: 358). While Simone does not use the term 'informality', his analysis suggests that he is describing practices that can be designated as such:

> African cities are characterized by incessantly flexible, mobile, and provisional intersections of residents that operate without clearly delineated notions of how the city is to be inhabited and used. ... These conjunctions become an

> *infrastructure – a platform providing for and reproducing life in the city.*
> *(Simone 2004: 407–8)*

While Bayat is interested in the spontaneous and uncoordinated spatial practices of informality, other theorists seek to understand the forms of political society associated with informality. For example, in his work on South Asian cities, Partha Chatterjee (2004: 38) makes a distinction between 'civil' and 'political' societies. Civil society is bourgeois society and in the Indian context, an arena of institutions and practices inhabited by a relatively small section of people able to make claims as fully enfranchised citizens. By contrast, political society is the constellation of claims made by those who are only tenuously and ambiguously right-bearing citizens. Chatterjee (2004: 41) writes that civil society, 'restricted to a small section of culturally equipped citizens, represents in countries like India the high ground of modernity. ... But in actual practice, governmental agencies must descend from that high ground to the terrain of political society in order to renew their legitimacy as providers of well-being'. The ' paralegal' practices and negotiations of this political society are for Chatterjee the politics of much of the people in most of the world:

> *The paralegal then, despite its ambiguous and supplementary status in relation to the legal, is not some pathological condition of retarded modernity, but rather part of the very process of the historical constitution of modernity in most of the world. (Chatterjee 2004: 75)*

Chatterjee's work echoes that of Arjun Appadurai (2002) who finds in the political actions of Mumbai's slum-dwellers a form of 'deep democracy'. Appadurai, writing about the Alliance (which brings together SPARC, an NGO; the National Slum Dwellers' Federation, a grassroots organization; and Mahila Milan, an organization of poor women), is interested in how the poor negotiate access to land, urban infrastructure, and services. While Castells (1983) designated the 'dependent city' as a 'city without citizens', Appadurai (2002: 26) argues that the urban poor of Mumbai are 'citizens without a city': a 'vital part of the urban workforce' and yet with few of the amenities and protections of urban living. He is inspired by the Alliance because of its ability to politicize and mobilize the urban poor in ways that reject patronage politics as well as the dominance of experts. Appadurai draws attention to the technologies of auto-planning that are used by the Alliance. These forms of 'countergovernmentality', as Appadurai calls this, should be of special interest to planners for they indicate the appropriation of the planner's toolkit by poor and informal communities. It is worth quoting at length:

> *Not only has it placed self-surveying at the heart of its own archive, the Alliance is also keenly aware of the power that this kind of knowledge – and ability – gives it in its dealings with local and central state organizations (as well as with multilateral agencies and other regulatory bodies) ... But none of them knows exactly who the slum dwellers are, where they live, or how they*

are to be identified. This fact is of central relevance to the politics of knowledge in which the Alliance is perennially engaged. All state-sponsored slum policies have an abstract slum population as their target and no knowledge of its concrete, human components. Since these populations are socially, legally, and spatially marginal – invisible citizens, as it were – they are by definition uncounted and uncountable, except in the most general terms. By rendering them statistically visible to themselves, the Alliance comes into control of a central piece of any actual policy process – the knowledge of exactly which individuals live where, how they make their livelihood, how long they have lived there, and so forth. Given that some of the most crucial pieces of recent legislation affecting slum dwellers in Mumbai tie security of tenure to the date from which occupancy of a piece of land or a structure can be demonstrated, such information collection is vital to any official effort to relocate and rehabilitate slum populations. (Appadurai 2002: 35–6)

But as I continue to argue in my work on informality, it is important not to overdraw the distinction between civil and political societies, between what is legal and what is paralegal. Political society exists not in opposition to the state or civil society but rather is entangled with such regimes of rule. Appadurai and Chatterjee both use the Foucauldian concept of 'governmentality' to analyze the politics of informality. For Appadurai, the self-rule of slum-dwellers is 'governmentality from below'. For Chatterjee (2004: 37) political society is 'political' not as a revolutionary force but rather as 'populations connected to governmental agencies pursuing multiple policies of security and welfare'. This is appropriate, for political society often maintains the mentalities and rationalities of government and self-government. My own work goes even further, viewing the politics of informality as a 'civic governmentality', represented by an infrastructure of populist mediation, such as NGOs, and shaped by the rules and norms of the bourgeois city (Roy 2009).

A highly sophisticated account of the politics of informality is provided by Holston's recent work. Holston lauds the 'insurgent citizenship' of Brazil's urban poor, noting that since the 1970s members of this social class 'became new citizens not primarily through the struggles of labor but through those of the city' (2007: 4). Holston argues that such forms of insurgent citizenship have destabilized 'entrenched' forms of citizenship in Brazil and have included not only the production of urban space (as in the autoconstruction of the urban peripheries) but also the democratization of urban space (as in the institutionalization of the 'right to the city' through participatory forms of planning). However, Holston notes the limits and paradoxes of insurgent citizenship. The formalization of the 'right to the city' and of the 'social function of property' has been accompanied by dramatic increases in violence, including class violence (Holston 2007). Further, Holston (2007: 13) demonstrates that insurgent citizenship itself remains beholden to many of the rules and norms of the bourgeois city, such as property ownership. There is, for example, considerable hostility between those who purchase land in the informal subdivisions of the periphery and those who are perceived to be squatters (Holston 2007: 171). Thus while insurgent citizenship democratizes and even disrupts the Brazilian city, it also reinforces some of the key tenets of propertied notions of urban citizenship.

The Informalization of the State

One of the enduring features of most theoretical frameworks of informality is the assumption that poverty and informality are synonymous, i.e. that informality is the entrepreneurial strategy or tactical operations of the poor in marginalized spaces. While this may be true, informality can be equally associated with forms of wealth and power. In our edited volume, *Urban Informality*, Nezar AlSayyad and I (2004) argued that the informal is not a distinct and bounded sector of labour, housing, and governance, but rather is a 'mode' of the production of space. This in turn implies three things.

First, informality is not a sign of a pre-capitalist economy awaiting integration with formal capitalism, as de Soto and others would have us believe. Informality is a fully capitalized domain of property and is often a highly effective 'spatial fix' in the production of value and profits. My work in Calcutta (Roy 2004) shows that the differential value attached to what is 'formal' and what is 'informal' creates a patchwork of valorized and devalorized spaces that is in turn the frontier of primitive accumulation and gentrification. In this way informality produces an uneven geography of spatial value thereby facilitating the urban logic of creative destruction. Indeed, it may be argued that in Third World cities where a significant proportion of economy and space is informalized, the urban frontier is more often extended, developed and gentrified through informality rather than other means. In this sense, informality is a capitalist mode of production, par excellence. Here informality far exceeds the logic of patronage and urban populism often associated with it. It becomes much more than the relationship between the poor and political parties, much more than the struggle for shelter and livelihood. Informality can be all of these things, but it is also a form of creating exchange-value for property, of commodifying space, and of establishing a frontier of urban development. The actors of informality then are a much broader realm than is often acknowledged – from real-estate developers to state bureaucrats to property-owning classes.

Second, such a framework highlights how informality is internally differentiated. The splintering of urbanism does not take place at the fissure between formality and informality but rather, in fractal fashion, *within* the informalized production of space. A closer look at the metropolitan regions of much of the world indicates that informal urbanization is as much the purview of wealthy urbanites and suburbanites as it is that of squatters and slum-dwellers. With the consolidation of neo-liberalism, there has also been a 'privatization of informality'. While informality was once primarily located on public land and practised in public space, it is today a crucial mechanism in wholly privatized and marketized urban formations, as in the informal subdivisions that constitute the peri-urbanization of so many cities. These forms of informality are no more legal than squatter settlements and shantytowns. But they are expressions of class power and can thus command infrastructure, services, and legitimacy in a way that marks them as substantially different from the landscape of slums.

Third, the legitimacy of informal peri-urbanization and the illegitimacy of slums and squatter settlements raises the issue of the role of the state in informality. It is the state that often determines what is informal and what is not, thus allowing the sprawling, elite 'farm houses' on the edges of Delhi to function legally as appendages of the agrarian land laws while squatter settlements throughout the city are criminalized and violently demolished (Roy 2007a). If informality creates geographies of differentiated value, which in turn makes possible urban development, then the state plays a crucial role in assigning and fixing such value. The important work of Yiftachel and Yacobi (2004) indicates that such work is not simply that of the state but rather of the nation-state as it seeks to consolidate projects of nationalism and ethnocracy. My work on Calcutta (Roy 2003) goes a step further. It indicates that the state is not only an arbiter of value but is itself an informalized entity that actively utilizes informality as an instrument of both accumulation and authority. This informalization of the state has obvious and crucial consequences for how we conceptualize the mandate and role of planning and its relation to the public interest. Here are a few examples of the informalization of the state.

While it has been often assumed that the modern state governs its subjects through technologies of visibility, counting, mapping and enumerating, in *City Requiem, Calcutta*, I argue that regimes of rule also operate through an 'unmapping' of cities (Roy 2003). This is particularly evident on the peri-urban fringes of Calcutta where the lack of centralized and certain knowledge about land allows the state a territorialized flexibility necessary for its dual imperatives of developmentalism (conversion of land to urban use) and populism (political ties to sharecroppers and squatters). Such planning regimes function through ambiguity rather than through rigidity. However, such ambiguity is a sign of a strong, even authoritative state, rather than one that is weak or unsure of its power. An example of these types of state power is provided by Aihwa Ong (2006) in her analysis of neo-liberal forms of government. She shows that sovereign rule often uses zoning technologies to create zones of exception. Such invocations of exception produce a 'pattern of noncontiguous, differently administered spaces of graduated or variegated sovereignty' (Ong 2006: 7).

Yet another example comes from the work of Janet Roitman (2005). In an analysis similar to that of Simone she shows how forms of piracy, theft and violent expropriation have become everyday practices of accumulation and modes of subjectivity in the Chad Basin. These processes, according to Roitman, must be understood in the context of an economic crisis such that small arms trade, money counterfeiting, smuggling and road banditry all emerge as important, often sole, sources of livelihood in a region devastated by deindustrialization, the terms of global trade, structural adjustment, and military demobilization. Here informal, even violent, forms of appropriation become routine; theft becomes work. But while the state seems absent from such processes, it is the entity that sets the norm. Thus Roitman (2005: 428) quotes a young man who works the unregulated border trade:

> The state steals from the whites; the civil servants steal from the state; the
> merchants steal from the civil servants by selling them products at prices
> incompatible with their standard of living or making them pay exorbitant
> rents on housing and the bandits steal from the merchants and civil servants
> who together transformed the state into a criminal entity. But the whites
> always stole from Africa.

This inevitably political relationship between what is legal and illegal, what
is legitimate and illegitimate, what is authorized and unauthorized, forces us
to reconsider the very authority and legitimacy of the state itself. In this sense,
informality acts as a heuristic device calling into question the very basis of planning
knowledge and action: maps, surveys, property, zoning, and most important, the
law. In his analysis of the politics of citizenship in Sao Paulo, Holston (2007: 228)
thus notes that Brazilian cities are marked by an 'unstable relationship between
the legal and illegal'. While it may seem obvious and apparent that the urban
poor are engaged in an informal and illegal occupation of land, much of the city
itself is occupied through the 'misrule of law': 'Thus in both the wealthiest and the
poorest of Brazilian families we find legal landholdings that are at base legalized
usurpations' (Holston 2007: 207). What is the relationship between planning and
this sanctified 'misrule of law'? Who then is authorized to (mis)use the law in such
ways to declare property ownership, zones of exception, and enclaves of value? The
democratization of urban space in Brazil, Holston (2007: 204) argues, is a process
by which the urban poor have learned to use the law and legitimize their own land
claims; 'they perpetuate the misrule of law but for their own purposes'.

Conclusion: The Politics of Planning

Informality allows us to study cities that exceed and even defy current theoretical
models of urbanism: cities whose histories cannot be understood as the teleology
of liberal democracy and cities whose economies remain largely informal and
contingent. These cities, usually located in the global South, have been vilified as
cities that are anomalous and deviant, failures and problems in the world hierarchy
of cities. The study of informality allows us to study such cities as experiments and
projects of living, planning, and making. It reveals forms of knowledge, expertise,
imagination, and innovation that often remain invisible in planning theory. What
does it mean to study not only a city's formal regulations and master plans but also
the improvisational creativity of its shanty towns? What are the ways in which
squatter communities appropriate and mimic the instruments of planning, such
as the cadastral survey and its demarcations of property? What then is expert
knowledge? Or, since planning theory is often concerned with 'coping with
uncertainty' (Christensen 1985), what does it mean to study the forms of ambiguity,
contingency, and speculation associated with the informal organization of space?
What are the ways in which planners are also speculators, managing uncertainty

through zoning regulations, which are in effect urban forecasts? In short, the study of informality can greatly enrich planning theory, including those strands of theorization that are primarily focused on the communicative norms and everyday practices of planning. But this can only happen when planning theorists are willing to see informality as something more than a communicative process and to engage directly with the production of space and the politics of place.

The most obvious and necessary form of disruption to planning theory comes from the straightforward fact that the cities of the world, and thus their planning regimes, are inextricably entangled with the logic of late capitalism. Informality, as I have shown, is a key element of this logic. On the ground, planning encounters this logic in both everyday and extraordinary ways: in the hollowing-out of public employment and services; in splintered infrastructures and enclave urbanism; in the reliance of the marginalized on a parastatal apparatus of aid and development. Yet planning theory remains curiously distant from it. Thus Watson (2002: 39) notes the striking disjuncture between 'normative planning theories' and urban life in sub-Saharan Africa. She emphasizes that the most striking aspect of these economies in the last decade is their 'growing informalization'. Such forms of informalization are a far cry from the entrepreneurialism that Easterly, Prahalad, and de Soto assign to the informal sector. Instead, as Watson notes, the increase in informality is directly tied to survival strategies that are meant to cope with seismic shifts in global regimes of governance, trade, and production. Her cautionary note, 'it is not possible to think about planning in Africa outside of the issue of development more generally' (Watson 2002: 46) is one that needs to be taken up in much more substantial ways in planning theory. For the implications for planning are critical. Easterly (2005: 60) notes that one cannot plan a market. But under conditions of late capitalism, market economies are precisely what are being planned; everything else is shot to hell.[4] How then can planning regulate these market economies? Or is planning now relegated to the planning of the market, including the marketplace of urban space?

Equally important therefore is careful consideration of planning's role in the forms of development that accompany late capitalism. Recently in India, for example, there has been a vicious criminalization of rural-urban poverty with the state moving to demolish urban slums and evict squatters and sharecroppers from the urban periphery. In doing so, the state hopes to make space for transnational investment housed in 'special economic zones' and to remake Indian cities as global venues. Such evictions have been supported, and at times even instigated, by elite and middle-class civil society associations that organize around the themes of 'environmental improvements' and 'quality of life'. Analyzed incisively by Baviskar (2003), as 'bourgeois environmentalism', in Indian city after city, such environmental and consumer rights groups have led the battle against slums and squatter settlements. Through the filing of public interest litigation, they have managed to criminalize poverty and assert the values of 'leisure, safety, aesthetics,

---

4   The idea that markets are planned (and that planning is not) comes from Polanyi (1944).

and health' (Baviskar 2003: 90). Where, in all of this, are planners? Are they the keepers of the 'public interest' and thus of 'bourgeois environmentalism'? Are they simply technocratic handmaidens of the state's developmental agenda? Or are they insurgent planners able to present an alternative vision of the democraticization of urban space? The difficult answers to these simple questions indicate the ways in which regimes of planning far exceed the acts and practices of planners. Regimes of planning are assemblages of state power (including technologies of exception and the misrule of the law), global terms of trade and governance, spatial modes of accumulation, associations of citizenship (be they those of civil society or of political society), and much more. Communication, mediation, and collaboration may be part of the planner's toolkit but these techniques do not even begin to capture the forms of rule, sovereignty, and citizenship that constitute the politics of planning. The study of informality is thus a reminder of the ways in which regimes of planning exceed the figure of the planner.

For those planning theorists for whom Mike Davis's 'planet of slums' feels quite literally to speak to another world, another planet, it is worth reiterating that informality is not necessarily about conditions of extreme, Third World poverty. Informality is a mode of the production of space. It is often a process through which space is deregulated and restructured. Such forms of deregulation of space are amply evident in the fragmented and fractal spaces of the contemporary city, what AlSayyad and I (2006) have termed 'medieval modernity'. Naomi Klein's (2007a) recent analysis of the disaster capitalism complex makes evident how the deregulation of political economies is tied to the deregulation of space. She shows how, in the last decade, there has been the emergence of a parallel, privatized disaster infrastructure that caters exclusively to the wealthy and the 'chosen' (Klein 2007b). Thus as wildfires raged through suburban communities in Southern California, residents in the wealthiest ZIP codes in the country were able to rely on a special service, Firebreak, offered to customers of the insurance giant, American International Group (AIG). 'Members of the company's Private Client Group pay an average of $19,000 to have their homes sprayed with fire retardant. During the wildfires, the "mobile units" – racing around in red firetrucks – even extinguished fires for their clients' (Klein 2007b). Klein notes that the rise of such privatized disaster response services that provide VIP rescue missions and premium tiered services for the wealthy, create zones of exception that are akin to the forms of informality that I discussed earlier in this paper. But particularly important here is the relationship between state power and such technologies and spaces of exception:

> *The emergence of this parallel privatized infrastructure reaches far beyond policing. When the contractor infrastructure built up during the Bush years is looked at as a whole, what is seen is a fully articulated state-within-a-state that is as muscular and capable as the actual state is frail and feeble. This corporate shadow state has been built almost exclusively with public resources (90% of Blackwater's revenues come from state contracts), including the training of its staff (overwhelmingly former civil servants, politicians, and*

soldiers). Yet the vast infrastructure is all privately owned and controlled. The citizens who have funded it have absolutely no claim to this parallel economy of its resources. (Klein 2007a: 417)

This is a world, as Klein notes (2007a: 420), where the wealthy can opt out of the collective system, where the idea of the public interest loses all meaning, and where the city becomes a 'world of suburban Green Zones ... as for those outside the secured perimeter, they will have to make do with the remains of the national system'. This, in my opinion, is the urban catastrophe of the twenty-first century. No overcrowded, miserable slum can be as resource-greedy as these privatized and secured enclaves; no form of informal or illegal occupation of land by Third World squatters can be as defiant of public norms and laws as these parallel, mercenary economies. And what does this urban catastrophe mean for planning? Does it signal the end of planning? Or does it simply make visible the technologies of exception that planning has always utilized; that the state, at its core, is informalized, and is thus able to exercise both territorial flexibility and territorial authority? Or can planning be a more insurgent enterprise, one that mimics and appropriates such forms of sovereignty, rule and citizenship to democratize urban space?

References

AlSayyad, N. and Roy, A. (2006) 'Medieval modernity: on citizenship and urbanism in a global era' *Space and Polity* 10(1): 1–20.

Appadurai, A. (2002) 'Deep democracy: urban governmentality and the horizon of politics' *Public Culture* 14(1): 21–47.

Auyero, J. (1999) '"This is a lot like the Bronx, isn't it?": Lived experiences of marginality in an Argentine slum' *International Journal of Urban and Regional Research* 23: 45–69.

Auyero, J. (2000) 'The hyper-shantytown: Neoliberal violence(s) in the Argentine slum' *Ethnography* 1: 93–116.

Baviskar, A. (2003) 'Between violence and desire: space, power, and identity in the making of metropolitan Delhi' *International Social Science Journal* 55(175): 89–98.

Bayat, A. (2000) 'From "dangerous classes" to "quiet rebels": the politics of the urban subaltern in the global South' *International Sociology* 15(3): 533–57.

Bourdieu, P. (1977) *Outline of a Theory of Practice*. Cambridge: Cambridge University Press.

Bourdieu, P. (1986) 'Forms of Capital', in Richardson, J. (ed.) *Handbook of Theory and Research for the Sociology of Education*. Westport, CT: Greenwood Press.

Bromley, R. (2004) 'Power, property, and poverty: why de Soto's "mystery of capital" Cannot Be Solved', in Roy, A. and AlSayyad, N. (eds) *Urban Informality: Transnational Perspectives from the Middle East, Latin America, and South Asia*. Lanham, MD: Lexington Books, 271–88.

Castells, M. (1977) *The Urban Question*. Cambridge, MA: MIT Press.

Castells, M. (1983) *The City and the Grassroots*. Berkeley, CA: University of California Press.

Chatterjee, P. (2004) *The Politics of the Governed: Reflections on Popular Politics in Most of the World*. New York: Columbia University Press.

Christensen, K. (1985) 'Coping with uncertainty in planning' *Journal of the American Planning Association* 51: 63–73.

Davis, M. (2006) *Planet of Slums*. New York: Verso.

De Certeau, M. (1984) *The Practice of Everyday Life* (trans. Rendall, S.). Berkeley, CA: University of California Press.

de Soto, H. (1989) *The Other Path: The Invisible Revolution in the Third World*. London: I.B. Taurus.

de Soto, H. (2000) *The Mystery of Capital: Why Capitalism Triumphs in the West and Fails Everywhere Else*. New York: Basic Books.

Easterly, W. (2006) *The White Man's Burden: Why the West's Efforts to Aid the Rest Have Done So Much Ill and So Little Good*. New York: Penguin Press.

Elyachar, J. (2005) *Markets of Dispossession: NGOs, Economic Development, and the State in Cairo*. Durham, NC: Duke University Press.

Fine, B. (2001a) 'Neither the Washington nor the post-Washington consensus: an introduction', in Fine, B., Lapavitsas, C. and Pincus, J. (eds) *Development Policy in the Twenty-First Century: Beyond the Post-Washington Consensus*. New York: Routledge.

Fine, B. (2001b) ' The social capital of the World Bank' in Fine, B., Lapavitsas, C., and Pincus, J. (eds) *Development Policy in the Twenty-First Century: Beyond the Post-Washington Consensus*. New York: Routledge.

Foucault, M. (1969) *The Archaeology of Knowledge*. New York: Routledge (1972 edition).

Gore, C. (2000) 'The rise and fall of the Washington consensus as a paradigm for developing countries' *World Development* 28(5): 789–804.

Holston, J. (2007) *Insurgent Citizenship: Disjunctions of Democracy and Modernity in Brazil*. Princeton, NJ: Princeton University Press.

Innes, J., Connick, S. and Booher, D. (2007) 'Informality as planning strategy: collaborative water management in the CALFED Bay-Delta Program' *Journal of the American Planning Association* 73(2): 195–210.

Keyes, J.L. 2003. 'Review of *The Mystery of Capital*' *Journal of the American Planning Association* 69(1): 103–4.

Klein, N. (2007a) *The Shock Doctrine: The Rise of Disaster Capitalism*. New York: Metropolitan Books.

Klein, N. (2007b) 'Rapture rescue 911: disaster response for the chosen' *The Nation*, 19 November.

Narayan, D. and Pritchett, L. (1997) *Cents and Sociability: Household Income and Social Capital in Rural Tanzania*. Washington, DC: World Bank.

Ong, A. (2006) *Neoliberalism as Exception: Mutations in Citizenship and Sovereignty*. Durham, NC: Duke University Press.

Perlman, J. (1977) *The Myth of Marginality*. Berkeley, CA: University of California Press.

Perlman, J. (2004) 'Marginality: from myth to reality in the favelas of Rio de Janeiro', in Roy, A. and AlSayyad, N. (eds) *Urban Informality: Transnational Perspectives from the Middle East, Latin America, and South Asia*. Lanham, MD: Lexington Books.

Polanyi, K. (1944) *The Great Transformation: The Political and Economic Origins of Our Time* (2001 edition). Boston, MA: Beacon Press.

Prahalad, C.K. (2004) *The Fortune at the Bottom of the Pyramid: Eradicating Poverty through Profits*. Cambridge, MA: Wharton School Publishing.

Putnam, R. (2000) *Bowling Alone: The Collapse and Revival of American Community*. New York: Simon & Schuster.

Rankin, K. (2001) 'Governing development: neoliberalism, microcredit, and rational economic woman' *Economy and Society* 30(1): 18–37.

Roitman, J. (2005) 'The garrison-entrepôt: a mode of governing in the Chad Basin' in Ong, A. and Collier, S. (eds) *Global Assemblages: Technology, Politics, and Ethics as Anthropological Problems*. Cambridge, MA: Blackwell Publishing.

Rostow, W. (1960) *The Stages of Economic Growth: A Non-Communist Manifesto*. Cambridge: Cambridge University Press.

Roy, A. (2003) *City Requiem, Calcutta: Gender and the Politics of Poverty*. Minneapolis, MN: University of Minnesota Press.

Roy, A. (2004) 'The gentleman's city' in Roy, A. and AlSayyad, N. (eds) *Urban Informality: Transnational Perspectives from the Middle East, South Asia, and Latin America*. Lanham, MD: Lexington Books.

Roy, A. (2005) 'Urban informality: toward an epistemology of planning' *Journal of the American Planning Association* 71(2): 147–58.

Roy, A. (2007) *Calcutta Requiem: Gender and the Politics of Poverty*. New Delhi: Pearson Press (New edition of *City Requiem, Calcutta: Gender and the Politics of Poverty* (2003) Minneapolis, MN: University of Minnesota Press).

Roy, A. (2009) 'Civic governmentality: the politics of inclusion in Mumbai and Beirut'. *Antipode* 41(1): 159–179.

Roy, A. (2010) *Poverty Capital: Microfinance and the Making of Development*. New York: Routledge.

Roy, A. and AlSayyad, N. (eds) (2004) *Urban Informality: Transnational Perspectives from the Middle East, Latin America, and South Asia*. Lanham, MD: Lexington Books.

Sachs, J. (2005) *The End of Poverty: Economic Possibilities for Our Time*. New York: Penguin.

Schaefer, P. (2003) 'Review off target: letter to the editors' *Journal of the American Planning Association* 69(3): 316.

Shiva, V. (2004) 'The Suicide Economy of Corporate Globalisation'. Available online: http://www.countercurrents.org/glo-shiva050404.htm

Simone, A. (2004) 'People as Infrastructure: Intersecting Fragments in Johannesburg' *Public Culture* 16(3): 407–29.

Simone, A. (2006) 'Pirate towns: reworking social and symbolic infrastructures in Johannesburg and Douala' *Urban Studies* 43(2): 357–70.

Smith, P. and Thurman, E. (2007) *A Billion Bootstraps: Microcredit, Barefoot Banking, and the Business Solution for Ending Poverty*. New York: McGraw Hill.

Wacquant, L. (1996) 'The rise of advanced marginality: notes on its nature and implications' *Acta Sociologica* 39: 121–39.

Wacquant, L. (1999) 'Urban marginality in the coming millennium' *Urban Studies* 36: 1639–47.

Wacquant, L. (2007) 'Ghetto, banlieue, favela, etc.: tools for rethinking urban marginality, in *Urban Outcasts: A Comparative Sociology of Advanced Marginality*. Cambridge: Polity.

Watson, V. (2002) 'The usefulness of normative planning theories in the context of sub-Saharan Africa' *Planning Theory* 1(1): 27–52.

Weber, H. (2002) 'The imposition of a global development architecture: the example of microcredit' *Review of International Studies* 28(3): 537–55.

Yiftachel, O. (2006) 'Re-engaging planning theory? Towards "south-eastern" perspectives' *Planning Theory* 5(3): 211–22.

Yiftachel, O. and Yacobi, H. (2004) 'Control, resistance, and informality: urban ethnocracy in Beer-Sheva, Israel' in Roy, A. and AlSayyad, N. (eds) *Urban Informality: Transnational Perspectives from the Middle East, Latin America, and South Asia*. Lanham, MD: Lexington Books, 209–39.

Coexistence: Planning and the Challenge of Indigenous Rights

Richard Howitt and Gaim James Lunkapis

In Indigenous[1] domains, the oppressive legacies of colonial administration have had a profound and continuing effect on the interests of Indigenous peoples. Coexistence of Indigenous peoples, and their underlying claims and interests in the land, resources and places that constitute the modern postcolonial states that are governed by a variety of planning systems, is an important area in which social theory can contribute to improved planning practices. One of the key challenges for planning theory, then, is to acknowledge and address the coexistence of peoples with very different sorts of claims to, relationships with and understandings of place – and each other – and its implications for just, equitable and sustainable decision-making in planning systems.

The experience of sharing space is often (mis)represented as a frontier of civilization, settlement, order and governance, moving through uncivilized and anarchic Indigenous domains leaving the rule of law and the order of democracy in its wake. Urban, regional and land use planning have been key technologies in both colonial encounters and postcolonial experiences of coexistence. In many places the experience of coexisting pre-colonial, colonial and postcolonial social formations is disciplined by urban and regional planning systems, land use zoning regimes and the strict oversight of property markets, development approval regimes and legally

---

1   The term Indigenous has no simple, unambiguous definition. It is often used interchangeably with a range of other terms such as 'aboriginal', 'native', 'original', ' first nations' and 'tribal' or other similar concepts. In this chapter, the approach adopted is that exemplified by the International Working Group on Indigenous Peoples (IWGIA) whose mission statement notes that 'Indigenous peoples, belonging to the most marginalized and impoverished groups in the world have the right to be recognized and to have their basic human rights respected. In particular Indigenous peoples have the right to be able to survive as peoples and to maintain and develop their cultures based on their own aspirations, visions and identity, and generally' (<http://www.iwgia. org/sw17673.asp>). Following the practice recommended by Johnson et al., the terms Indigenous, Native and Aboriginal are generally capitalized in this chapter (Johnson et al. 2007).

enforceable rights. In many modernising societies, Indigenous peoples' customary laws and informal economies and cultures have persistent footprints in urban, peri-urban and rural environments that challenge both the colonial assumptions about the incompatibility of indigeneity and urban places and the professional practices of development, modernization and nation building.

Modernist state practices such as urban, land-use and environmental planning are commonly used as technologies to assert discipline and order to the development and governance process. They do, however, often erase, restrict and transform Indigenous peoples' spaces of coexistence and participation, constrain Indigenous peoples' customary and contemporary relationships with their territories, and limit the roles available to them in contemporary society. Indeed, urban and regional land use planning has not only enabled modernizing governments to transform Indigenous territories into managed landscapes subject to development controls and the practices of professional planning.[2] Planning practices have also disciplined and controlled the ancient jurisdictions of Indigenous governance to create new spaces for development within existing natural and cultural landscapes and managed the legal, social, political, discursive and territorial spaces of pluralist coexistence.

Although extremist spatial disciplines such as genocide, ethnic cleansing and mass relocation are increasingly discredited as planning tools,[3] even minimalist models of pluralist coexistence such as Australia's Native title regime, Canada's modern treaties, the United States' doctrine of limited First Nation sovereignty, and Malaysia's accommodations of *adat* (pre-colonial customary) law, come under enormous pressure to simply render up Indigenous interests as a set of quaint, antiquated echoes of history to be extinguished and (in more generous regimes)

---

2   In the Australian case, the legal notion that the colonizing state acquired radical underlying title to all territory on settlement (see also Howitt 2006 for discussion), meant that all land became state property for disposal to preferred others through lease, freeholding, sale and grant. Prior to the Native title cases in the mid-1990s, then, all 'Aboriginal Land' was held under title created by governments, not customary law. In Malaysia, formal acknowledgement of legal pluralism and *adat* law did not effectively insulate Indigenous peoples' property and civil rights. Transition to the post-colonial era saw the construction of state power for the newly-independent states over local society with a concomitant marginalization of 'Natives' from economic opportunities (e.g. Doolittle 1998). This was largely achieved through political and legal interpretation of land related laws and regulations. For example, the postcolonial state found it useful to use the *Town and Country Planning Ordinance, 1950*, to provide land use conditions to all land and waters throughout state territories which required formal registration of traditional interests and rights – but this registration was not prioritized or supported and many traditional domains were alienated as a result. Registration, while available as a means of securing formal recognition was, at best, uneven across Sabah, as discussed in detail below.

3   Sadly, such practices in many conflicts across the globe remind us that these methods continue to be seen as suitable tools for national development planning in some settings.

compensated. Mature postcolonial democracies have struggled to develop mainstream planning systems that can recognize, accommodate and support the coexistence of persistent Indigenous rights, cultures and aspirations alongside mainstream manifestations of dominant culture in spaces where planners are empowered to oversee the creation and management of space.

In this chapter, we pose as a major challenge to planning theory the task of establishing and supporting planning systems that acknowledge and engage with pluralist coexistence in ways that protect and support Indigenous peoples' rights and secure avenues for Indigenous peoples' participation in contemporary society. Failure to address this challenge will see planning continue to be marshalled and refined as a technology for state domination and oppression of minority and Indigenous rights in pluralist societies. The persistence of Indigenous peoples' customary rights to (along with their claims upon and contemporary uses of) lands, waters and natural resources in their customary domains is in deep tension with modern statist and developmentalist ideologies that rely on planning for their realization. Against these custom- and practice-based claims, modern states' planning systems all too easily construct Indigenous interests as anachronistic, parochial and antagonistic to modern nation building – and consequently excluded from the public interest represented by the state.

Using examples from Malaysia and Australia, this chapter investigates the power of planning discourse in dealing with Indigenous interests in pluralist democracies. It considers how claims about development, culture and custom are addressed in planning systems' implementation of technologies such as land use zoning, development approval and plan making. It suggests that conventional planning practices reflect and reinforce state power in ways that marginalize, exclude and caricature Indigenous peoples' claims for recognition and empowerment within their own cultural landscapes. We are particularly interested in the use of planning in urban and industrializing landscapes, where developmentalist ideologies often assume the absence of Indigenous interests because (by definition) these are spaces of planning and development – not the cultural landscapes of ancient and apparently fading cultures. As a result, Indigenous peoples in urban settings are often treated as if they are somehow out of place, not entitled to recognition, but perhaps needing to be acknowledged in terms of need because of backwardness or underdevelopment. Such paternalistic characterizations of Indigenous interests in the spaces of planning and development allow history and geography to be rewritten – often with planners as a front line in states' erasure of customary rights and interests. We are, therefore, interested in considering:

- how different understandings of place, culture and coexistence are embedded in the practices of planning;
- how the implications of land use policies and practices are understood within planning discourses; and
- how practices of planning, community mapping and social impact assessment might be reframed to facilitate a rethinking of the role of planners in pluralist and multicultural environments.

We recognize that cultural differences constitute the relationships to place that underpin the contemporary geographies of coexistence of Indigenous and state rights in urban and industrial development settings. Planners and state administrators, officials and politicians who deny, erase or trivialize cultural diversity and the historical and geographical circumstances that underpin coexistence are deeply implicated in discourses that entrench disempowerment and marginalization of Indigenous groups in these settings. The wider political challenge, then, is to contribute to planning theory and discourses that can utilize planning technologies to open new opportunities for practising coexistence by acknowledging and respecting Indigenous experience of space and place as foundational for just, sustainable and equitable urban and industrial development processes. Planning systems discipline the ways in which land use change occurs. How contemporary land use change is interpreted, however, and how the processes of interpretation unfold at different scales, opens space for theoretically reframing planning systems differently in relation to the challenges of coexistence and pluralism, in terms of local procedures, policy formulation and implementation and institutional capacity at different geographical scales. It is to this task that the chapter turns in developing a wider reading of the experiences reported from Australia and Malaysia, with a view to better understanding the politics through which Indigenous peoples' resistance to change creates new possibilities for how spaces might be governed and regulated.

Planning and Native Title in Australia

Australia is a federation of six former British colonies in which powers to manage land, resources and local and regional planning are lodged constitutionally at the provincial scale of the state governments. Some specific planning powers rest with the national government. For example, management of uranium mining and nuclear materials is governed by the Commonwealth *Atomic Energy Act 1953* and environmental planning is largely governed by the Commonwealth *Environment Protection and Biodiversity Conservation Act 1999*. A referendum in 1967 reserved to the Commonwealth Government powers to make laws in relation to Aboriginal and Torres Strait Islander peoples – the Indigenous peoples of the continent. While some legislation enacted using this power affects the professional practices of urban and regional planning in Australia – for example, the Commonwealth *Native Title Act 1993* – planning is largely in the hands of state and territory governments and the local government authorities established under state and territory legislation. This framing of planning legislation and practice at the local and provincial scale, and of Indigenous affairs at the national scale, reflects a complex politics in which erasure of Indigenous scales of governance and autonomy has been commonplace

(Howitt 2006). Sue Jackson (1996, 1997) suggests that professional planners in Australia and their professional bodies and employers have been hostile to a view of the public interest that recognizes urban Indigenous groups (and a continuing set of distinctive rights) as coexisting appropriately in modern urban places.

In this context, planning has been specifically used by governments hostile to the principles of Indigenous self-determination and cultural identity as a strategic tool to render Indigenous interests out of place in the domains of planning practice. Indeed, to thwart the legitimate claims of Aboriginal traditional owners in the Northern Territory, the Northern Territory Government gazetted the City of Darwin as the world's largest urban area because Aboriginal land claims could not be made over urban land under the *Aboriginal Land Rights (Northern Territory) Act 1976* (Jackson 1997). While the colonial and even racist intent of such actions has been clear, the construction of planning as what Deborah Rose has identified as 'deep colonising' practices (Rose 1999) makes it an insidious threat to Indigenous rights. Indeed, as Escobar has noted, of all the terms in the developmentalist lexicon, 'no other concept has been so insidious [nor] ... gone so unchallenged' as planning (Escobar 1992: 132). It has simply been accepted as an invisible and largely benign technology for managing the movement from governments' policy objectives to practical social outcomes in Indigenous affairs. Historic failure to achieve policy objectives (even if one accepts those objectives as appropriate – which in the Australian setting would be an unjustified leap of faith indeed!) is generally seen by governments and the general public not as a failure of planning, but as indicating the need for further planning activities. Inevitably, this perception calls forth more planning practices to discipline the spatial practices (and persistent presences) of Indigenous peoples.

Howitt and Suchet-Pearson observe that in Indigenous affairs 'planning exercises are entrenched in many government, non-government agency and community association procedures' (2006: 328). Yet planning is certainly not as neutral and innocent as it has been thought. Planning in its most common manifestations is fundamentally Eurocentric. It is:

> ... predicated ontologically on a linear, progressivist view of time and a bounded, static notion of space. A future is envisioned, one which is open to deliberate human intervention. Achieving that preferred future involves prioritizing becoming, moving towards, achieving and goal-setting. It requires planning. Change is disciplined to a static, singular view of what is worthwhile, valued and desirable. (Howitt and Suchet-Pearson, 2006: 329)

While there has been some critical discussion of planning in terms of its roles in disciplining space and citizens to conform to rationalist visions of the future (see, for example, Beauregard, 1989; Healey, 1997), and some discussion of planning theory in terms of marginality, identity and difference (see, for example, Sandercock, 1995; Jackson, 1997, 1998), critical discussion of planning has often been focused on how to include those such as Indigenous people that planning has conventionally excluded. This limited critique of planning needs to be extended considerably in the context of Indigenous Australia if we are to secure a more constructive role for planning in Indigenous futures.

The notion of coexistence has taken a particular form in Australia because of Native title legislation. The Australian High Court constructed a complex and slippery notion of coexistence in deciding the key Native title decisions in *Mabo* and *Wik*.[4] According to the Australian High Court, the legal notion of coexistence is not acknowledgement of the coexistence of Indigenous and non-Indigenous people and their lives, needs and cultures in particular places, but an abstract legal idea that allows legally recognizable interests in property to exist together. The slipperiness of the High Court's formulation was that it constructed the rights created by the persistent presence of Aboriginal people in the cultural landscapes of Australia to be configured legislatively as fragile and vulnerable to extinguishment by the rights created by the legal imaginary of *terra nullius*. The High Court's notion of coexistence was particularly slippery because at precisely the moment that it displaced *terra nullius* as a continuing principle of Australian law and property systems, it also constructed Native title rights as amenable to discipline by state planning legislation. Politically, this meant that conservative interests sought to ensure that Native title could be corralled into spaces that were generally remote from the spaces of urban and regional development. While the impact of Native title on developmentalist projects in the resources sector was generally recognized as inevitable, its intrusion into urban spaces and the planning-ordered domains of settlement was a source of great uncertainty and hostility in the dominant culture.

Native title, even in the highly circumscribed form arising from the Australian High Court's 1992 decision in *Mabo*, presented a challenge to the spatial discipline of Australian property and planning systems. In systems that had been developed on the assumption of *terra nullius* – the extraordinary proposition that Indigenous peoples across the continent had no property rights, no systems of recognizable law and governance, and were, effectively, no more entitled to recognition by the colonizing power than native animals – the *Mabo* decision suddenly proposed that Australian governments were obliged to recognize and acknowledge systems of rights and entitlement that pre-dated the creation of the colonial states. In many jurisdictions, the settled spatial discipline that created the tenure and property rights that underpinned urban, industrial, agricultural and economic systems was suddenly revealed as a fabrication that shared many characteristics of the emperor's new clothes in the Hans Christian Anderson story.

Political responses varied, but were often dedicated to constructing 'certainty' – usually for non-Indigenous interests whose previously unchallenged rights to

---

4   Australia's *Native Title Act 1993* arose from the High Court decision in Mabo (*Mabo and Others v Queensland (No 2) (1992) 175 CLR 1*). The decision in Wik (*Wik Peoples v State of Queensland; Thayorre Peoples v State of Queensland* [1996] HCA 40) included clarification of the idea of coexistence, where persistent Native title rights were found to survive the issue of certain land titles such as leases by state authorities and to coexist with those titles. The Wik decision produced significant (and controversial) amendment of the *Native Title Act* in 1997.

create and use spaces had become questionable, and restricting the impact of Native title to remote and marginal spaces away from settled Australia. In such places, for example in the Aboriginal Reserves of the Northern Territory, South Australia, Western Australia and Queensland, local government jurisdictions had never been created and large areas were left as 'unincorporated' into regular planning systems. The conservative Prime Minister John Howard appeared on television brandishing a map that seemed to threaten the 'loss' of large parts of Australia to Native title (see Markus 2001: 42; Holmes 2006), as if he wanted to produce a map that would restrict Native title to a few remote areas, limiting its disruption of planning and development in settled Australia and allowing business- (and planning-) as-usual in most places.

But Native title was not able to be spatially contained in this way. Western Australia's efforts to legislatively extinguish Native title and convert it from a property right to a set of usufructory rights was found to breach the Australian Constitution (Bartlett 1995). And, unlike the rights created by land rights legislation which generally precluded Indigenous claims to urban land (see Jackson 1996, 1997), the High Court found that Native title was able to persist in urban areas. Indeed, the first successful Native title claims under the *Native Title Act* included claims in urban areas of New South Wales and the Northern Territory.

The first successful Native title claim on the Australian mainland was the Dunghutti peoples' claim over Vacant Crown Land in the small coastal town of Crescent Head, New South Wales (Blackshield 1997). The land in question was subject to urban subdivision and development by the state government. The urban development needed to be brought into compliance with the provisions of the *Native Title Act* once they took effect in 1994. By negotiated agreement, the successful claimants received compensation for work that had been authorized by the government prior to the *Native Title Act 1993* coming into force, and payment for compulsory acquisition by the government of land subject to subdivision, and they authorized further development on the land in return for a percentage of sales revenue. Blackshield (1997) offers a detailed account of the legal complexities in this case, but for the planning system in New South Wales, the acknowledgement that Native title had not been extinguished in a long-settled area such as Crescent Head was a wake-up call that local and state government planning processes could no longer operate as if the legal principle of *terra nullius* continued to hold in the post-*Mabo* period.

Prior to the Native title processes, local government planning across Australia had generally dealt with Indigenous interests in terms of heritage and archaeology. In both cases, it was non-Indigenous experts who were empowered within planning systems rather than Indigenous people themselves. Expert reports were used by planners to decide whether or not a particular site could be developed. The cultural landscapes of Indigenous Australia were rendered invisible in this way, reduced to a series of discrete sites of more and (more usually) less significance. The consent to destroy Indigenous sites was central to the planning powers in most jurisdictions, and power to give that consent was vested in state agencies and government ministers, who acted on expert rather than community advice. In New South Wales, for example, Aboriginal sites were long designated as 'relics' and managed under the *National Parks and Wildlife Act*. In managing resource development consents in Western Australia, it was the Mining Warden's Court and the West Australian Museum that provided the institutional foundations for the planning system that affected Indigenous groups' capacity to protect their traditional domains.

In these settings, the reality of coexisting rights in space and time was overwhelmed by Eurocentric visions of development and governance which denied standing or significance to contemporary Indigenous governances. For such systems, the High Court's recognition of Native title challenged fundamental verities. In many ways, the Alice Springs Native title claim brought the challenge into the heart of urban Australia. Lhere Artepe Aboriginal Corporation was established as the body that holds Native title of lands within the Alice Springs town area for the Mparntwe, Antulye and Irlpme family groups, whose claim was accepted by the Federal Court in 1999.

In many places, the historical exclusion of Indigenous people from decision-making about their communities and futures has created deep legacies of mistrust in mainstream planning institutions. Jackson (1996), for example, documents the ways in which such histories have affected land-use planning negotiations around Broome, in Western Australia. In South Australia, some of those legacies have been addressed in developing new protocols and institutions for planning and decision-making (Agius et al. 2004; Agius et al. 2007). Throughout Australia, Indigenous Land Use Agreements (ILUAs) under the *Native Title Act* have demonstrated that planning and development can accommodate Indigenous interests, and the interests of governments and developers. Indeed, partnerships that are inclusive and open avenues for Indigenous participation and benefit in domains and activities from which they were previously excluded, provide windows on the fragile practices of coexistence that are emerging in post-*Mabo* planning systems in Australia. This move towards negotiated agreements as the basis for addressing the challenges and demands of coexistence rather than the top-down imposition of planning protocols that respond poorly to the local geographies and histories of coexistence is a promising 'frontier' for planning theory and practice in relation to Indigenous groups.

Planning and the Erasure of Native Rights in Sabah, Malaysia

Such negotiations, however, are less familiar in the planning systems of Sabah in Malaysia, where planning protocols are a relatively recent development. In Malaysia, planning is widely seen a key characteristic of good governance. Indeed, as in many colonies, spatial planning was central to the capacity of Sabah's colonial regime to govern, to create property rights that underpinned wealth, and controlled colonial subjects' behaviours and capacities to disrupt the colonial order of things. In postcolonial Malaysia, planning laws and regulations have been modified from the former colonial masters to suit local conditions but, most importantly, planning instruments have become powerful tools to aid the development model of the newly independent state. Planning laws and regulations are most often promoted in tandem with developmentalist ideologies as an instrument to deliver greater state control over vast territory and resources. This situation is common in newly independent nations. In Malaysia at independence, a conglomeration of relatively separate or different cultures with a multitude of ethnic groups occupied a portion of the contiguous territory (see, for example, Peluso 1993). Further, like most post-independence Asian countries, Malaysia has successfully established itself as an ethnically homogeneous nation-state with an ethnically-divided society (see Bunnell 2002: 109). In order to take charge in such a situation, a certain degree of control had to be exercised from the central and provincial governments – and the planning system is directly implicated in this in Malaysia. This has resulted in a 'second wave of colonialism' (see Kitingan 2006; Pepinsky 2007; Scott 1996) where the lines of arbitrary exclusion were not erased but merely shifted from the Western colonizing state to the local elite.

In Malaysia, where development programmes and planning controls are based on an *elite-mass* relationship,[5] the planning system has become a useful instrument to deliver nationally driven administrative and planning strategies throughout the national territory. This is in line with the 'controlled democracy' style of governance (see Hashim 2005) which is useful as an instrument for prohibiting the propagation of racial prejudice and discrimination (Sani 2008: 86). Based on this relationship, Malaysia has so far been considered as one of the most advanced nations compared with other nations that gained independence at about the same period within the Asian region. This has further assured the central leadership that such a relationship would fulfill Malaysia's development aspirations in the shortest possible period. In order to achieve its ambition, it was necessary for the central leadership to acquire appropriate power and control and to take charge of situations at all levels of governance.

Sabah is the second largest state in the Federation of Malaysia after Sarawak and is located at the top end of the island of Borneo. Together, Sabah and Sarawak are home to the largest non-Malay/non-Muslim Indigenous peoples of Malaysia (Luping 1994: 11). In the case of Sabah, the *elite-mass* relationship underpinned the *National Physical Plan* (Malaysia 2000), and was executed through the *Town and Country Planning Ordinance, Sabah, 1950*. This ordinance was carried forward from existing laws available in the pre-independence state into the post independence era. It went through a series of amendments to suit the nationally endorsed planning and development strategy. For example, in 2002, Part IA, Section 1 to

---

5   See, for example, Case (1996) and Hashim (2005). In such cases, where the elite represents the administrative machinery, using a top-down approach to planning is possible because the elite holds information and has the capacity to collect, to analyze, to interpret and to store data and information. On the other hand, the masses do not have the capacity to do so and as such it is far easier for the state to exercise top-down planning powers than it is for local populations to respond in systemic ways.

4 was added to this Ordinance in order to make way for the preparation of the *Sabah State Structure Plan* (see Table 3.1), a progression of the *National Physical Plan* at state level.[6] Unfortunately, proper understanding and sensitivity to local conditions has not been properly addressed and local practices of land use access, uses and livelihood strategy are now at risk. Consequently, there is an urgent need to develop better understanding of how the planning process intersects with local, national and global discourses of development, human rights, sustainability and justice in line with the dynamic relationship between races in Malaysia. We now provide a brief account of historical events that lead to the formation of the Malaysian federation in 1963.

Table 3.1   Level of spatial planning activity

Physical Plan	Corresponding Legislation	Jurisdictions	Map Scale
National Physical Plan	Town and Country Planning Act 1976, revised 2001	National (Federal)	1:50,000–1:500,000
Regional Plan	Town and Country Planning Act 1976, revised 2002	Regional (Federal)	1:25,000–1:100,000
State Structure Plan	Town and Country Planning Ordinance 1950, revised 2002	State (State and Federal)	1:25,000–1:50.000
District Land Use Plan	Town and Country Planning Ordinance 1950, revised 2002	State and Local Authority	1:10,000–1:25,000
Local Plan	Town and Country Planning Ordinance 1950, revised 2002	Local Authority	1:5,000–1:10,000

Source: Town and Country Planning Department, Malaysia.

Towards the end of the 1950s and the early part of the 1960s, the independent colonial states of Malaya (West Malaysia), Singapore, Sarawak and Sabah (then called North Borneo) decided to form a Federation called Malaysia based on equal partnership (Chin 1997; Ongkili 1992). Each of these four independent states under the British Colony specifically emphasized a special condition prior to joining the newly-agreed federation. Such a condition was intended as an instrument to

---

6   The Constitution of Malaysia divides the political jurisdiction into federal and state levels, and the administration division into federal, state and local levels. Although the judicial powers of the Federal and State are independent, there is a uniform system of administration between the Federal and State levels; with a unique additional structure for the various states of Malaysia, especially Sabah and Sarawak which have their own State Constitutions, but most often state administrative machinery is under Federal directives.

safeguard and to maintain each state's rights and identity within the newly-formed partnership. Malaya, for example, agreed to form the Federation based on certain conditions relating to equities of citizenship and social conditions. This condition is known as the 'social contract' which propagates the concepts of *Ketuanan Melayu* or Malay Supremacy (see Abbott and Franks 2007: 346–8).

Singapore, too, agreed to join on condition that there was equal partnership in terms of leadership, political control and equity. But, in 1965, it opted to leave the newly-formed Federation upon realizing that the original condition was not easily implemented. Some, however, argued that the real reason that Singapore joined the Federation initially was as a short cut to gain independence from Britain. The British were willing to grant independence to Singapore only on condition that the elites of the major races in Malaya were able to form a government in which they would work together amicably (see, for example, Milne 1966). For Sarawak also, its agreement to join the Federation was conditional on state control of immigration, land and state administration. British North Borneo (now Sabah) also agreed to join the Federation on condition that certain safeguards were maintained and left under the state control through the '20 Points Agreement' (Ongkili 1992: 531). Thus, at the time of the Malaysian federation, each of the colonies joining the Federation saw planning as a crucial element of the local states' strategic priority, and this was reflected in agreements addressing detailed conditions prior to the formation of Malaysia through a document called 'the Inter Governmental Committee's Reports', signed in London on July 9, 1963.[7]

At the time of writing this chapter, all points in the original agreement have gone through a series of alterations and changes to suit the nationally driven agenda, except point number 19, the name of the state. Spatial planning based on the *National Physical Plan* and *Sabah State Structure Plan* was one of many instruments used to convey nationally driven economic development that has found its way into the state. Vast land areas have been re-zoned to make way for the national development agenda. The Federal Land Development Authority (FELDA), a national agency specializing in estate development of mostly oil palm and rubber, and the Federal Land Consolidation and Rehabilitation Authority (FELCRA), a national agency specializing in rural development and small scheme development, offer examples. Through both land schemes, thousands of families from the west of Malaysia were resettled in Sabah. Thus, all settlers are not local, while local Indigenous people were evicted in the process (see for example, Colchester, et al. 2007 ; *Daily Express* 2007; Hai 2000). These schemes have created totally new space and environment while the rural landscape of Sabah has changed to endless scenes of oil palm plantation with scattered settlements along the major infrastructure routes weaving through these plantations. New settlements and downstream

---

7   Inter-Governmental Committee (ICG) Report 1963. This report contained a framework for Malaysia as a newly-formed Federation. Part of this report contained the 20 Points Agreement as conditions and safeguards of Sabah to be part of the Malaysia Federation, an agreement signed in London on July 9, 1963. This document is also available from Sabah Annual Report, 1962, Jesselton, pp. 24–6.

services were created and a whole new social landscape now dominates areas once under the domain of Indigenous people.

Indigenous peoples' have resolved to make persistent efforts to maintain control and to continue living in their ancestral land, and to air their struggle through several means, notably through local newspapers, through their local elected representatives and through local NGOs. Unfortunately, the nationally driven agenda seems to supersede local requirements while Indigenous pleas to be heard have fallen onto the deaf ears of the national leadership. The recent extension of the Malaya-based political party, the United Malay National Organization (UMNO), into the political arena of Sabah was seen as one further manifestation of the *elite-mass* model of governance (see Ahmad 1986; Chin 1994; 1997; 1999; Moten 1999; Ongkili 1992; Osman 1992). Box 3.1 provides examples of Indigenous persistence in place aired through local media in Sabah.

In view of the current struggle of Indigenous people in Sabah to maintain control over their domain, it is necessary to look at the operational systems of town and regional planning in Malaysia where formal planning systems may be able to accommodate and to provide room for the Indigenous people to register their interest. Table 3.1 indicates the five levels of spatial planning hierarchy that apply to all states in the federation of Malaysia. The *National Physical Plan* translates policy statements under the *Five Year Malaysia Plan*. This is followed by the *Regional Plan* which further refined the National Physical Plan. The *State Structure Plan* defines the broad framework for the spatial development of the State while the *District Land Use Plan* provides a spatial plan covering the whole district and the *Local Plan* contains a detailed plan of a specific area at local level. The basic legislation regulating land use in Sabah was established in the *Town and Country Planning Ordinance, Sabah 1950*, with the main planning objective of making provision for the orderly and progressive development of land, towns and other areas, whether urban or rural, to preserve and to improve the amenities thereof and other matters connected therewith (Sabah 1950). Thus, the Planning Ordinance provides the organizational and planning framework in Sabah. By 2003, with the help of an international funding agency and through local government initiatives, most districts in Sabah had completed their District and Local Plan at the map scale of 1:20,000 and 1:10,000 respectively.

The levels of physical planning described in Table 3.1 demarcate land for specific purposes and are usually referred by the planning term – 'Land Use Zones'. Land use zones are prepared using the cadastral boundaries covering the whole district. Through these zoning exercises, specific land use zones are clearly demarcated on maps. Land previously under the Indigenous peoples' domain has been fragmented into several uses, particularly the conservation zone, and agriculture, rural and other development zones, although Indigenous customary use is notably absent from zoning categories. Arising from these conditions, the scenario on the ground concerning local resource use, access and Indigenous customary rights claims, therefore, is a complex one. One possible explanation for this was that, under the practices of modern governance, all lands are enshrined as state property, with the exception of individually titled land.

Box 3.1   Recent media reports concerning Indigenous peoples' persistence in place

Example 1: State meet Federal over FELDA Scheme, *Daily Express*

7 January 2004

The State of Sabah was prepared to meet the Federal Government, specifically the Federal Land Development Authority (FELDA) to overcome weaknesses in land development programmes in Sabah. The issue identified was the transfer of 176,681 hectares in Tungku, and Umas-Umas from 1976 to 1985. Based on the original plan, the State has allowed FELDA to develop these lands so that Indigenous families would be assisted and allocated about 6 hectares each to plant oil palm and to settle within the estate area with modern services and facilities. Unfortunately, such a plan never materialized. Instead, the lands involved are now owned by FELDA while landless Indigenous peoples are squatting on lands they once owned.

Example 2: State agencies and not FELCRA should be developing Banggi, *Daily Express*

9 September 2007

The Federal government allocated substantial amount of budget for rural development projects in Sabah but insisted that such projects must be carried out in accordance with the nationally endorsed Development Plan and to be advanced through federal agencies notably through the Federal Land Development Authority (FELDA) and Federal Land Consolidation and Rehabilitation Authority (FELCRA). In 2007, Sabah identified a 4,000 hectares site in Banggi Island suitable for a rubber plantation development. This area is home of the Bongi Indigenous people. Consequently, the spokesperson for the Indigenous Bongi, Salmah Marail, claimed to have received reports that the Village Head would lose their post if they opposed this project. The position of Village Head is a State appointed person to head each of the respective villages who receives a substantial monthly allowance. Salmah further claimed that *'the 80 villagers have refused to move out from the land as they believe they have native customary rights over it'*. The group further insisted that they are not opposed to the development project provided their rights are properly dealt with and that the project should be carried out by state agencies instead of FELCRA as experiences through similar projects elsewhere in the state suggest that Federal involvement has done more harm to the Indigenous people. Instead of improving their daily livelihood, access and land ownership was taken away from them to make way for large scale plantation projects.

Example 3: Memo on land claims submitted – *Daily Express*
28 February 2008

A memorandum containing 32,352 land claims from Indigenous people across Sabah covering a total area of 339,984 acres from 18 districts was submitted to State Governor, Tun Ahmadshah Abdullah and Chief Minister Datuk Seri Musa Aman. Partners of Community Organisations (PACOS), a local NGO, led by coordinator Galus Ahtoi and 95 others representing several divisional Indigenous groups from 17 districts have gathered to discuss, exchange experiences and to formulate collective action plans to address the erosion of Native Customary Rights in Sabah. The group is considering taking this matter to court after exhausting all possible avenues to get the State to take a look at the demands from the Indigenous people. PACOS felt that State must do something by conducting a general land inquiry based on Native Customary Rights as stated in Section 13, 14, 15, 65, 66 and Part IV of the Sabah Land Ordinance 1930, Chapter 68, which commits the State to identifying and detaching all land of Native Customary Rights status throughout Sabah. '*These include all land of NCR status that has been given to outsiders inclusive of any State agencies that do not respect the NCR ownership*'. This group further demand that State should have acknowledged and declared that lands they inherited are owned by the Indigenous people based on their native customary rights. The group spokesperson claimed that after years of efforts to have Native Customary Rights land recognised, respected and protected, State did very little to this effect. He said '*The Government must act now and not just make more promises to us*'.

It is pertinent to mention here that privately owned property is subject to government interest, especially land owned by a large corporation with substantial state investment. Land use strategy implemented through the nationally endorsed National Physical Plan can indicate the future direction and land use strategy at the local level. Thus, the current planning hierarchy deserves full attention in the course of implementing the nationally endorsed *National Physical Plan* at the local level. It is also pertinent to mention that customary rights claims in the case of Sabah, Malaysia are fully recognized under the provision of the existing legislation as described in the following section.

Native Customary Rights within the Spatial Planning Spheres

Regulations concerning land use and ownership in Sabah are provided under the *Land Ordinance 1930* and the *Town and Country Planning Ordinance, 1950*, while local customary practices are both recognized under the *Adat* systems and *Land Ordinance 1930*. Even within the realm of modern land use legislation, there are quite often differences as regards land use strategy and sustainability concepts (Long et al. 2003). For example, land use conditions granted under the *Sabah Land*

Ordinance 1930 normally designate Indigenous Land based on Native Titles, Field Register, Country Lease and Provisional List. However, this does not correspond to the actual land use on the ground based on the *Town and Country Planning Ordinance 1950*, where the ordinance supersedes any title condition granted under the *Land Ordinance 1930* (Sabah 1950).

Contrary to land use under the Land Ordinance, land use provision under the *Town and Country Planning Ordinance* normally designates land uses as commercial, industry, residential, agriculture, sports and recreation, tourism, livestock farming, fisheries, parks and open spaces, infrastructure, utilities, and government reserve. Zoning and sub-zoning drew on more than 30 zoning provisions, but with no land use zone designated for Indigenous reserve and Indigenous land use (Lunkapis 2005). As a result, all land previously used by Indigenous people is fragmented into the land uses mentioned above and customary tenures are erased in the process. This scenario implies that the local implementation of the nationally endorsed *National Physical Plan* is in direct contradiction of *Section 15* of the *Sabah Land Ordinance 1930* where Indigenous people can own, use and access a vast land area based on criteria spelled out under this ordinance (see Section 15, Sabah 1930).

The traditional land ownership and the precolonial governance of Indigenous people in Sabah Malaysia were largely centred in the traditional systems which are collectively referred to as *adat*. The *adat* systems function as guidelines for peaceful and harmonious coexistence between members of a community and their environment. Drawing from several research findings (for example, Tongkul 2002; Woolley 1953) there were at least ten categories of traditional systems in the Indigenous Kadazandusun community in Sabah, including belief, social, cultural, education, health, politics and administration, judicial, economic, resource management and agriculture. Each of these systems deals with different aspects of livelihood and environment. Subsequently Tongkul (2002) noted that such a system was characterized by a very advanced traditional knowledge about sustainable land use and communal livelihood based on traditional practices.

The imposition of colonial governance marks the beginning of modern systems of access and use, where the governing body assumes control and rights to land and natural resources. Through the introduction of codification systems, rights to use and access were granted only through issuance of land title. Cleary (2002: 26) noted that such a system was driven by several factors. Firstly, land sales and the establishment of secure titles were necessary to attract foreign investment especially on tobacco and rubber plantations. Secondly, the agricultural practices of Indigenous people, in particular that of shifting cultivation, were seen as destructive to the environment and uneconomical. Thirdly, it was anticipated that through land codification practices, state revenues could be increased through quit-rent and exploitation of natural resources, notably forest timber and mineral extractions.

The postcolonial period saw the handing over of laws and regulations from the colonial state to the newly-established state elite. More importantly, however, was that the 'politics of sustainability' (see Majid Cooke 1999, 2002; Ngidang 2005) began to take centre stage of the state's development agenda. Based on this, lands, forests and natural resources were used as a vehicle to raise state wealth. Extraction of natural resources, notably timber and mineral resources for exports, immediately replaced by large scale oil palm plantation, was promoted and encouraged. Unfortunately, according to Ngidang (2005), all these activities took place within the Indigenous customary domain, which became an easy target for planning-based alienation and development because all these are fertile lands. Indigenous ownership claims over these lands required clear evidence of ownership. Ngidang (2005: 67) further argues that central to such economic linkages are the state power structures that act not only as a conduit but also as a powerful legitimizing authority, which provides official sanctions in the form of provisional lease protocol to enable both local and outside economic elites to gain access to huge tracks of lands and forest concession licences for extracting timber from the rainforest. Consequently Indigenous peoples are being evicted from their lands to make way for timber extraction and plantations.

In line with the state interest to regulate access, allocation and land uses, several supporting pieces of legislation were produced to suit state needs. For example, land alienation and occupation, land acquisition and the proper utilization of the rural areas are regulated by the State Department of Lands and Survey through the power vested to it by the *Land Ordinance, 1930; Land Acquisition Ordinance, 1950* and the *Country Land Utilization Ordinance, 1962*. The Land Acquisition Ordinance authorizes the acquisition of land for public purposes while the *Country Land Utilization Ordinance* provides for the proper uses of alienated rural lands. Land uses in urban and rural areas are governed through the *Town and Country Planning Ordinance, 1950*.

Discussion and Conclusions

This brief evaluation of the ordinances underpinning planning systems in both Australia and Malaysia reveals that they have had different impacts in different contexts – and the implications of particular planning systems and tools need to be considered in context rather than assumed. Despite the cultural pluralism of both nations, the complex political and legal circumstances created by persistent Indigenous rights, and the political and legal complexity created by uneven recognition, protection and acceptance of those rights within and between various jurisdictions and planning systems, has been taken as excusing professional planners from addressing the challenges of coexistence. In both nations, any early colonial recognition of traditional rights and customary laws was circumscribed by the expectation that Indigenous interests would be subsumed by the needs of the colonial administration, and later the post-colonial state (eg. Reynolds 1998, 2006; Doolittle 1998). For example, Sabah found it useful to use the *Town and Country Planning Ordinance, 1950* to provide relatively new land use conditions to all land and waters throughout state territories. Through this ordinance, each district was required to produce district and local land use zoning maps designating all land to be zoned and accorded specific land uses. Given the circumstances of their construction, however, such maps are unlikely to coincide with or acknowledge local and Indigenous land use traditions or customary access and use rights. While the opportunity might exist to formally register customary rights using specific legislation such as the Australian *Native Title Act 1992* or the *Sabah Land Ordinance 1930*, the technical requirements and practical circumstances involved in achieving such registration, and the effectiveness of registration in delivering practical improvements at the local scale, have reduced the value and accessibility of such tools as a means of making planning systems accountable to local and Indigenous needs and values. In both Australia and Malaysia, protests about the failures of such systems persist.[8]

In view of the endless tussle between state authority and existing rights and practices of local peoples, one avenue that might provide better recognition of Indigenous land use practices is community mapping. Community mapping, along with a variety of participatory mapping and GIS methods, aims to produce maps that reflect local communities' needs and aspirations (see for example Majid Cooke 2003; Herlihy and Knapp 2003; Bujang 2005; Momberg et al. 1996; Fox et al. 2005a; Chapin et al. 2005; Chapin and Threlkeld 2001; Fox et al. 2005b; Tobias 2000). In formal land use planning systems such as those under construction in Malaysia and common in Australian local government councils, integration of community-based mapping into the planning system might be intellectually possible, but it cannot succeed without a shift in resources to support the production of maps, and a shift in thinking to acknowledge what we have framed in this discussion as the challenges that coexistence presents to planning theory.

Looking at community mapping from a larger perspective, town and regional planning practices often involve the creation of spaces, where the boundaries proposed to define the newly-created spaces are problematic in terms of their implications for existing patterns of land use, tenure and governance. This contestation of the boundaries that planners intend to use to resolve disputes suggests that geopolitical processes need to be taken as seriously at local scales as the more commonly recognized scale of international relations, and that planning systems need to come to terms with local and Indigenous concepts of place, space and boundaries rather than assuming that the precision of geographical information systems makes them adequate or appropriate for the task of community mapping, land use planning and the just and equitable governance of communities of difference. Thus between communities, when it comes to planning exercises such

---

8   For example, in Sabah, an incident occurred on 28 February 2008 when a memorandum about land issues was submitted to the State Governor, Tun Ahmadshah Abdullah and Chief Minister, Datuk Seri Musa Aman urging the State to revise a provision concerning Native land customary rights based on the Section 13, 14, 15, 65, 66 and Part IV of the *Sabah Land Ordinance, 1930* (*Daily Express* 2008). In Australia, continuing criticism of the technical complexity of the *Native Title Act* and the system it has generated has led to persistent demands for change and reliance on negotiated rather than litigated outcomes as a means of securing beneficial outcomes – although that pathway is also fraught with pitfalls for Indigenous groups (e.g. Langton et al. 2004; O'Faircheallaigh and Corbett 2005; Agius et al. 2007).

as in community mapping projects, overlapping claims may occur and become problematic. Perhaps this confusion is better understood using the 'dynamics of boundaries', as in Howitt's (2001) discussion of frontiers, borders and edges using the coastal zone analogy. Coastal zones, for example, are not clearly identified by straight lines as perceived by many, but subject to changes due to weather conditions, human activities and the generation of new ecosystems resulting from the dynamics of the coastal zone itself. Thus, lines and edges from the perspective of local communities are different from what is understood in modern zoning and land use planning practices where exact boundaries are drawn and marked as lines in a cadastral map. Likewise, spatial planning at community level must involve local communities and combine effort using modern concepts of land use planning systems with techniques such as mapping exercises. This would bring a new dimension to planning theory and practice.

In instances such as those discussed in this chapter, Indigenous concepts of space must be fully understood prior to any commencement of development projects and proposals. Lack of local understanding in term of customs and Indigenous peoples' knowledge has often jeopardized well-intended development projects. Apart from that, it is equally important to determine who will control the creation of places and governance of spaces within a given community, and likewise who will control the production and use of the maps that are intended to record Indigenous communities' rights and claims. Fox (2002: 75), for example, believes that the most important aspect of mapping is who controls the maps. This is important for at least two reasons. First, whoever controls the maps can use them to tell their story and secondly, how the controller uses the map has implications for the surveillance and privacy of local informants. In the case of community mapping, Indigenous peoples' direct participation is necessary while state acceptance of community maps will provide for the integrity of maps at the community level.

State arguments about the use of legislation to regulate land use and development policies are often unilateral declarations of the need to promote and regulate development and land uses in line with state and national agendas for development. Historically, such declarations have not only excluded proper consideration of Indigenous interests, but have often been antagonistic to them. This is true, for example, in both Australia and Malaysia. This history implicates contemporary planning in the historical and continuing erasure and threats to Indigenous survival and burdens efforts to marshal planning theory to contribute constructively to just and sustainable coexistence in postcolonial settings. The use of planning laws and systems to circumscribe and even eliminate Indigenous rights in land, land use and development is commonly disguised as an appeal to order and development. Indigenous landowners are all-too-often pressured to accept planning as a suitable and reasonable means of having their lands, resources and interests integrated into the national development project of state building and economic development without full understanding of the implications, or full recognition of their persistent rights and interests. Through these processes, state planning systems are part of the modern technology that marginalizes and devalues Indigenous people as members of complex post-colonial societies.

In both Australia and Malaysia, the democratic rhetoric of consensus based decision-making and participation is advocated by the state and supported by planning professionals who discount the historical processes that create the structures of exclusion, marginalization and racism in modern pluralist societies. The tyranny of consensus creates enormous pressures for compliance from local planning officials in their relationships with local Indigenous groups. In our view, planning education and continuing professional development must recognize that such outcomes represent a failure of planning rather than a success! Reducing the complex challenges of coexistence, justice and sustainability in land use and development planning systems to imposed consensus formed as a top-down development or land use plan is a shortsighted failure of planning theory, as is state insistence on conformity and compliance at the cost of cultural diversity, traditional and customary rights and equitable participation in and access to benefits and opportunities of development processes. Such practices are a clear violation of local customary practices. They bypass, and in the process produce erasure of, customary law and governance structures. Further, such action quite often disrupts local social and economic relationships and alters existing local cultural and physical landscapes and their accessibility to, and meaning for, the Indigenous community. The emerging Australian practice of negotiated agreements offers one avenue for considering alternatives to such planning regimes and the social, cultural and environmental consequences – although it is also acknowledged that simply replacing one top-down state-based elite system with another customary elite without the protection of broad human rights in pluralist societies opens avenues for other forms of abuse and tyranny. So the challenge is one to be continually negotiated rather than simply 'settled'.

Characteristics of a community within the cultural and physical landscape are reflected through the dimensions in which particular communities are shaped and presented (see, for example, Becker et al. 2003). A community's natural environment, for example, includes local characteristics like fields, rivers and the attractiveness of the surrounding scenery and the quality of the region's natural environment. Similarly, general values about, and aspirations for, quality of life, along with culturally-based understandings of the value and meaning of place, community and development all contribute to local definitions and contestations of the character of a community. Of particular importance are those aspects of community life that are a result of residents' relationships with each other and the surrounding natural environment. In such instances, the intention of the nationally endorsed development plan might have been intended to improve the existing lifestyle of Indigenous people. But without the consent and consultation of a local community, a well-intended development proposal could often lead into a different understanding and may cause a negative impact on local livelihood. Local Indigenous livelihood, access and use to their ancestral lands and natural resources must be protected and maintained, to allow Indigenous people to participate in the mainstream development and modernity on their own terms and consistently with their own sense of place and history.

Several decades ago, Tuan (1974) advocated the idea of 'topophilia' as a way to conceptualize the bonds of connection and belonging that develop between people and places. Despite the significant efforts of planning theorists to advocate a break from the modernist paradigm of 'comprehensive plans, master plans, and physical development plans' (Healey 1999: 111), state regulation of Indigenous property rights still relies heavily on such spatial and land use planning tools as technologies of erasure and denial. Postcolonial planning systems face the challenge of acknowledging and addressing multiple and conflicting narratives of connection and belonging, each with power for those whose social histories, cultural biographies and imagined geographies are woven from them. In such circumstances, promotion of a singular statist vision of regulated development as if it were the only possible narrative of topophilia in a particular planning system's jurisdiction is to return to a practice of land use planning as a technology of dispossession, exclusion and erasure.

In modern democratic states, state insistence on such forms of social exclusion is not only unfashionable and unethical. It is also unnecessary and unjustifiable. Planning theory increasingly offers a discourse in which communicative action (e.g. Brand and Gaffikin 2007; Fischler 2000; Healey 2003; Hillier 2003; Hoch 2007; Huxley 2000; Huxley and Yiftachel 2000; Margerum 2002), transformational planning (e.g. Lane and Hibbard 2005; Purcell 2009) and so-called 'insurgent planning'(e.g. Miraftab 2009; Miraftab and Wills 2005; Roy 2009) provide models of practice for planning as a technology for nurturing more just, sustainable and inclusive engagement with diversity and empowerment in managing development processes. Planning as a discipline has established a range of tools, techniques and practices capable of integrating the varied narrative strands of peoples' and people's relationships of connection and belonging into more nuanced understandings of diversity, sustainability and coexistence. In many systems, we already see considerable movement towards such practices in state planning systems, where regional land use plans extend recognition, rights and opportunities to all citizens of the state whose authority underpins the planning system, rather than insisting on compliance with a top-down planning regime as a condition for recognition of citizenship (e.g. Flyvbjerg 2002).

The experience of coexistence, its history, geography and sociality, cannot be negated by the imposition of top-down, state-imposed development plans. Nor can it be converted into a story of peaceful and productive coexistence simply by restating contested and conflicting narratives of connection and belonging; possession and loss; victory and erasure. For planning systems engaged with Indigenous groups, such as discussed in this chapter in Australia and Malaysia, to transcend their colonial antecedents in their relationships with Indigenous groups, the urgent need is to transform contemporary practice in line with theoretical developments that are themselves integrative and transcendent rather than simply technical. It is not that techniques such as land registration, community mapping or participatory planning can, by themselves, produce better plans as a basis for more just, sustainable and inclusive communities and states. Rather, what is needed in these situations is planning theory that guides – even insists on – engagement with the narratives of connection and belonging in ways that grapple with messy coexistence from the ground up, rather than imagining that coexistence is something that can be planned and governed by state regulation and the imposition of planning technologies from above, as if diverse Indigenous groups and local communities had no interest in their own places. In meeting this challenge, planning discourses will need to reach out to new partners in cultural, social, environmental and philosophical studies for the language, concepts and tools required to move forward. Given that such tools are increasingly readily available, just how long does it take to transform planning practices in some jurisdictions in their relations with Indigenous rights?

References

Abbott, J.P. and Franks, O.S. (2007) 'Malaysia at fifty: conflicting definitions of citizenship' *Asian Affairs* 38(3): 337–56.

Agius, P., Davies, J., Howitt, R., Jarvis, S. and Williams, R. (2004) 'Comprehensive Native Title Negotiations in South Australia', in Langton, M., Teehan, M., Palmer, L. and Shain, K. *Honour Among Nations? Treaties and Agreements with Indigenous People*. Melbourne: Melbourne University Press, 203–19.

Agius, P., Jenkin, T., Jarvis, S., Howitt, R. and Williams, R. (2007) '(Re)asserting indigenous rights and jurisdictions within a politics of place: transformative nature of native title negotiations in South Australia' *Geographical Research* 45(2): 194–202.

Ahmad, Z.H. (1986) 'Malaysia in 1985: the beginnings of sagas' *Asian Survey* 26(2): 150–7.

Bartlett, R. (1995) 'The High Court: racism and the WA government' *Aboriginal Law Bulletin* 73(3): 8–9.

Beauregard, R.A. (1989) 'Space, time, and economic restructuring', in Beauregard, R.A. (ed.) *Economic Restructuring and Political Response*. Newbury Park, CA: Sage Publications, 209–40.

Becker, D.R., Harris, C.C., McLaughlin, W.J. and Nielsen, E.A. (2003) 'A participatory approach to social impact assessment: the interactive community forum' *Environmental Impact Assessment Review* 23(3): 367–82.

Blackshield, S. (1997) 'Crescent Head Native title agreement' *Aboriginal Law Bulletin* 88: 9.

Brand, R. and Gaffikin, F. (2007) 'Collaborative planning in an uncollaborative world' *Planning Theory* 6(3): 282–313.

Bujang, M. (2005) 'Community-based mapping: a tool to gain recognition and respect of native customary rights to land in Sarawak', in Fox, J., Suryanata, K. and Hershock, P. (eds) *Mapping Communities: Ethic, Values, Practice*. Honolulu: East-West Center: 87–96.

Bunnell, T. (2002) '(Re)positioning Malaysia: high-tech networks and the multicultural rescripting of national identity' *Political Geography* 21(1): 105–24.

Case, W.F. (1996) 'Can the "Halfway House" stand? Semidemocracy and elite theory in three Southeast Asian countries' *Comparative Politics* 28(4): 437–64.

Chapin, M., Lamb, Z. and Threlkeld, B. (2005) 'Mapping indigenous lands' *Annual Review of Anthropology* 34(1): 619–38.

Chapin, M. and Threlkeld, B. (2001) *Indigenous Landscape: A Study in Ethnocartography*. Arlington, VA: Centre for the Support of Native Lands.

Chin, J. (1994) 'The Sabah state election of 1994: end of Kadazan unity' *Asian Survey* 34(10): 904–15.

Chin, J. (1997) 'Politics of federal intervention in Malaysia, with reference to Sarawak, Sabah and Kelantan *The Journal of Commonwealth and Comparative Politics* 35(2): 96(25).

Chin, J. (1999) 'Going east: UMNO's entry into Sabah politics' *Asian Journal of Political Science* 7(1): 20–40.

Cleary, M. (2002) 'Codifying the land: colonial land regulation in early 20th-century British Borneo' *Landscape Research* 27(1): 25–37.

Colchester, M., Pang, W.A., Chuo, W.M. and Jalong, T. (2007) *Land is Life: Land Rights and Oil Palm Development in Sarawak*. Moreton-in-Marsh, UK: Forest Peoples Programme and Perkumpulan Sawit Watch, Bogor.

Daily Express (2004) 'State meet federal over FELDA scheme' *Daily Express*, 7 January 2004.

Daily Express (2007) 'State agencies and not Felcra should be developing Banggi, says Pasok' 6 September 2007: 2.

Daily Express (2008) 'Memo on land claims submitted' 28 February 2008.

Doolittle, A. (1998) 'Historical and contemporary views of legal pluralism in Sabah, Malaysia (North Borneo)' *The Common Property Resource Digest* 47: 1–5.

Doolittle, A. (2005) *Poverty and Politics in Sabah, Malaysia: Native Struggles Over Land Rights*. Seattle and London: University of Washington Press.

Doolittle, A. (2007) 'Native land tenure, conservation, and development in a pseudo-democracy: Sabah, Malaysia' *Journal of Peasant Studies* 34(3): 474–97.

Escobar, A. (1992) 'Planning', in Sachs, W. (ed.) *The Development Dictionary*. London, Zed Press: 132–45.

Fischler, R. (2000). 'Communicative planning theory: a Foucauldian assessment' *Journal of Planning Education and Research* 19(4): 358–68.

Flyvbjerg, B. (2002) 'Bringing power to planning research: one researcher's praxis story' *Journal of Planning Education and Research* 21(4): 353–66.

Fox, J. (2002) 'Siam mapped and mapping in Cambodia: boundaries, sovereignty, and Indigenous conceptions of space' *Society and Natural Resources* 15(1): 65–78.

Fox, J., Suryanata, K. and Hershock, P. (eds) (2005a) *Mapping Communities: Ethics, Values, Practice*. Honolulu, HI: East-West Center.

Fox, J., Suryanata, K., Hershock, P. and Pramono, A.H. (2005b) 'Mapping power: ironic effects of spatial information technology', in Fox, J., Suryanata, K. and Hershock, P. (eds) *Mapping Communities: Ethics, Values, Practice*. Honolulu, HI: East-West Centre, 1–10.

Hai, T.C. (2000) *Land Use and the Oil Palm Industry in Malaysia*. Kuala Lumpur: WWF Malaysia.

Hashim, R. (2005) *Pengurusan Pembangunan (Development Management)*. Kuala Lumpur: Dewan Bahasa dan Pustaka.

Healey, P. (1997) *Collaborative Planning: Shaping Places in Fragmented Societies*. London: Macmillan.

Healey, P. (1999). 'Institutionalist analysis, communicative planning, and shaping places' *Journal of Planning Education and Research* 19(2): 111–21.

Healey, P. (2003) 'Collaborative planning in perspective' *Planning Theory* 2(2): 101–23.

Herlihy, P.H. and Knapp, G. (2003) 'Maps of, by, and for the Peoples of Latin America' *Human Organization* 62(4): 303–14.

Hillier, J. (2003) ' "Agon"izing over consensus: why Habermasian ideals cannot be "Real" ' *Planning Theory* 2(1): 37–59.

Hoch, C.J. (2007) 'Pragmatic communicative action theory' *Journal of Planning Education and Research* 26(3): 272–83.

Holmes, J. (2006) 'The role and locale of international geographical conferences: a preliminary geographical interpretation. Opening address to the International Geographical Union Regional Conference, Brisbane, July 2006' *Geographical Research* 44(4): 435–7.

Howitt, R. (2001) 'Frontiers, borders, edges: liminal challenges to the hegemony of exclusion' *Australian Geographical Studies* 39(2): 233–45.

Howitt, R. (2006) 'Scales of coexistence: tackling the tension between legal and cultural landscapes in post-Mabo Australia' *Macquarie Law Journal* 6: 49–64.

Howitt, R. and Suchet-Pearson, S. (2006) 'Rethinking the building blocks: ontological pluralism and the idea of "management"' *Geografiska Annaler: Ser B, Human Geography* 88(3): 323–35.

Huxley, M. (2000) 'The limits to communicative planning' *Journal of Planning Education and Research* 19(4): 369–77.

Huxley, M. and Yiftachel, O. (2000) 'New paradigm or old myopia? Unsettling the communicative turn in planning theory' *Journal of Planning Education and Research* 19(4): 333–42.

Jackson, S. (1996) 'Town country: urban development and Aboriginal land and sea rights in Australia', in Howitt, R., Connell, J. and Hirsch, P., *Resources, Nations and Indigenous Peoples: Case Studies from Australasia, Melanesia and Southeast Asia*. Sydney: Oxford University Press, 90–103.

Jackson, S. (1997) 'A disturbing story: the fiction of rationality in land use planning in Aboriginal Australia' *Australian Planner* 34(4): 221–6.

Jackson, S. (1998) Geographies of Coexistence: native title, cultural difference and the decolonisation of planning in north Australia. Ph.D. thesis, School of Earth Sciences, Macquarie University.

Johnson, J.T., Cant, G., Howitt, R. and Peters, E. (2007) 'Creating anti-colonial geographies: embracing Indigenous peoples' knowledges and rights' *Geographical Research* 45(2): 117–20.

Kitingan, J.G. (2006) *Justice for Sabah*. Kota Kinabalu: Shelma Publication and News Agency.

Lane, M.B. and Hibbard, M. (2005) 'Doing it for themselves: transformative planning by Indigenous peoples' *Journal of Planning Education and Research* 25(2): 172–84.

Langton, M., Teehan, M., Palmer, L. and Shain, K. (eds) (2004) *Honour Among Nations? Treaties and Agreements with Indigenous People*. Melbourne: Melbourne University Press.

Long, B., Henriques, J., Andersen, H.S., Gausset, Q. and Egay, K. (2003) 'Land tenure in relation to Crocker Range National Park' *ASEAN Review of Biodiversity and Environmental Conservation* (January–March 2003): 1–11.

Long, B. (2006) *The Political Ecology of Tenure Struggles in Sabah*. Thesis submitted: Geography/International Development Studies Projects, Roskilde University Copenhagen.

Lunkapis G.J. (2005) 'Indigenous self-organized mental maps and conservation ideas: case study of Tuaran interior', in *Third International Conference Bornean Biodiversity and Ecosystem Conservation*, Kota Kinabalu, 55–67.

Luping, H.J. (1994) *Sabah's Dilemma: The Political History of Sabah 1960–1994*. Kuala Lumpur: Magnus Books.

Majid Cooke, F. (1999) *The Challenge of Sustainable Forest: Forest Resource Policy in Malaysia, 1970-1995*. Honolulu: Allen and Erwin.

Majid Cooke, F. (2002) 'Vulnerability, control and oil palm in Sarawak: globalization and a new era?' *Development and Change* 33(2): 189–211.

Majid Cooke, F. (2003) 'Maps and counter-maps: globalised imaginings and local realities of Sarawak's plantation agriculture' *Journal of Southeast Asian Studies* 34(2): 265–84.

Malaysia, Government of (2000) *National Physical Plan*. Kuala Lumpur: Government of Malaysia. Available online at: <http://www.google.com.au/url?sa=t&source=web&ct=res&cd=5&ved=0CBUQFjAE&url=http%3A%2F%2Fintranet.nahrim.gov.my%2Ffiles%2FNationalPhysicalPlan(NPP)2.doc&rct=j&q=national+physical+plan+2000+Malaysia&ei=uh0nS6bPMcuHkAWYofXyDA&usg=AFQjCNFKG9gAgIq2f7r4ueCvNUo0_8q1tg> [accessed December 2009].

Margerum, R.D. (2002) 'Collaborative planning: building consensus and building a distinct model for practice' *Journal of Planning Education and Research* 21(3): 237–53.

Markus, A. (2001) *Race: John Howard and the remaking of Australia*. Sydney: Allen & Unwin.

Milne, R.S. (1966) 'Singapore's exit from Malaysia: the consequences of ambiguity' *Asian Survey* 6(3): 175–84.

Miraftab, F. (2009) 'Insurgent planning: situating radical planning in the global South' *Planning Theory* 8(1): 32–50.

Miraftab, F. and Wills, S. (2005) 'Insurgency and spaces of active citizenship: the story of Western Cape anti-eviction campaign in South Africa' *Journal of Planning Education and Research* 25: 200–17.

Momberg, F., Dedy, K., Jessup, T. and Fox, J. (1996) 'Drawing on local knowledge: community mapping as a tool for people's participation in conservation management' *The Fourth Biennial Conference of the Borneo Research Council*, Bandar Sri Begawan, 10–15 June 1996.

Moten, A.R. (1999) 'The 1999 Sabah state elections in Malaysia: the coalition continues' *Asian Survey* 39(5): 792–807.

Ngidang, D. (2005) 'Deconstruction and reconstruction of Native customary land tenure in Sarawak' *Southeast Asian Studies* 43(1): 47–75.

O'Faircheallaigh, C. and Corbett, T. (2005) 'Indigenous participation in environmental management of mining projects: the role of negotiated agreements' *Environmental Politics* 14(5): 629–47.

Ongkili, J.F. (1992) 'Federalism and parochialism: relations between Kuala Lumpur and Sabah' *Journal of Contemporary Asia* 22(4): 529–45.

Osman, S. (1992) 'Sabah state elections: implications for Malaysian unity' *Asian Survey* 32(4): 380–91.

Peluso, N.L. (1993) 'Coercing conservation? The politics of state resource control' *Global Environmental Change* 3(2): 199–217.

Pepinsky, T. (2007) 'Autocracy, elections, and fiscal policy: evidence from Malaysia' *Studies in Comparative International Development (SCID)* 42(1) 136–63.

Purcell, M. (2009) 'Resisting neoliberalization: communicative planning or counter-hegemonic movements?' *Planning Theory* 8(2): 140–65.

Reynolds, H. (1998) *This Whispering In Our Hearts*. Sydney: Allen & Unwin.

Reynolds, H. (2006) 'Reviving Indigenous sovereignty' *Macquarie Law Journal* 6: 5–12.

Rose, D.B. (1999) 'Indigenous ecologies and an ethic of connection', in Low, N. (ed.) *Global Ethics and Environment*. London, Routledge: 175–87.

Roy, A. (2009) 'Strangely familiar: planning and the worlds of insurgence and informality' *Planning Theory* 8(1): 7–11.

Sabah (1930) *Sabah Land Ordinance 1930*. Kota Kinabalu: Government Printing.

Sabah (1950) *Town and Country Planning Ordinance 1950.*, Kota Kinabalu: Government Printing.

Sandercock, L. (1995) 'Voices from the borderlands: a meditation on a metaphor' *Journal of Planning Education and Research* 14(2): 77–88.

Sani, M.A.M. (2008) 'Freedom of speech and democracy in Malaysia' *Asian Journal of Political Science* 16(1): 85–104.

Scott, C. (1996) 'Indigenous self-determination and decolonization of the international imagination: a plea' *Human Rights Quarterly* 18(4): 814–20.

Tobias, T.N. (2000) *Chief Kerry's Moose: A Guidebook to Land Use and Occupancy Mapping, Research Design and Data Collection*. Vancouver: The Union of BC Indian Chiefs and Ecotrust Canada.

Tongkul, F. (2002) *Traditional Systems of Indigenous Peoples of Sabah, Malaysia*. Kota Kinabalu: PACOS Trust.

Tuan, Y.-F. (1974) *Topophilia: A Study of Environmental Perception, Attitudes, and Values*. Englewood Cliffs, NJ: Prentice-Hall.

White, N.J. (2004) 'The beginnings of crony capitalism: business, politics and economic development in Malaysia, c.1955–70' *Modern Asian Studies* 38(2): 389–417.

Woolley, C. (1953) 'Dusun Adat: some customs of the Dusun of Tambunan and Ranau' *Native Affairs Bulletin* 1953(5): 21.

Problematizing Planning: Critical and Effective Genealogies

Margo Huxley

Introduction

It may seem odd to bring history into debates about the relations between theory and practice in spatial planning, but if so, then this is an odd chapter. In it, I want to revisit suggestions (e.g. Boyer 1983; Fischler 1998b, 2000) that planning history as it has been conventionally told, contributes to an unquestioning acceptance of something called 'planning' that has identifiable points of origin and a more-or-less continuous identity over time. According to these narratives, if planning has not always been as 'good' or socially just as it might, could or should be – if it has a 'dark side' that needs to be acknowledged – these are unfortunate occurrences that can, and indeed must, be rectified. But such histories, of taken-for-granted yet disparate set of practices, tend to gloss over the contingent discursive and practical struggles through which 'planning' has come into being as a form of spatial government, an academic discipline and as a self-fashioning of both practitioners and 'participants' (that is, anyone who has to deal with or is affected by land use/spatial planning). Planning history (in the singular) as a seamless narrative, obscures opportunities for creative disruptions of the present, and plays a part in uncritical repetition, both of theoretical assumptions and of regulatory practices.

In this chapter, I argue for a different kind of approach to the emergence of 'planning' – a conceptual challenge from a genealogical perspective that poses potentially practically productive questions about current concepts, routine regulations and taken-for-granted practices.

However paradoxical it may seem and however difficult to put into effect, critical, sceptical forms of historical analyses that take nothing for granted and constantly question everyday assumptions about how things should be done, can open up practice to creative possibilities for change. These are what can be called (following Nietzsche) critical and effective histories, or genealogies (Foucault 1986a, 1988, 2003; see also Dean 1994).

In making a case for the practical and theoretical relevance of such genealogies in planning, I am not considering various forms of planning theories; nor am

I commenting on developments of, and debates about critical approaches in the discipline of history, although the exchanges about the distinction between 'social history' and 'a history of the social' are pertinent here (see Joyce 1997; and the debates reproduced in Jenkins 1997). In addition, I do not explicitly elaborate on planning as 'governmentality', although clearly this is a consideration in examining histories of the practices of 'town planning' (see, for instance, Huxley 2006, 2008a, b). Instead, in this chapter I want to focus on planning history and to suggest that, rather than being a narrative of a taken-for-granted trajectory of something called (urban/city/town and regional/ land use) 'planning', planning history itself contributes to the constitution of a subject and object, discipline and practice known as 'planning'. Concentrating mainly on UK/Anglophone examples, I briefly overview conventional planning history and discuss some of the critiques coming from 'within' planning, before setting out – all too briefly – the chief characteristics of a genealogical perspective. Finally, I indicate some ways in which productive genealogical sensibilities might be put to work to unsettle planning and its history, and to ask us to think again about our present.

Planning History

By and large until relatively recently, Anglophone (urban/city/town and country/ spatial) planning history and theory have generally been unreflexive about their search for reformist origins and justifications of the practice and profession of town planning, and tend to rest on a priori assumptions about the necessity for planning and the positive outcomes of planning activity. Where planning is seen to fail, it is because of the difference between Utopian visions or improving regulations of planning and grubby practices 'on the ground'; or because of the 'distortion' of the original ideals by subsequent advocates and misunderstood or mistimed applications (see, for instance, Hall 2002: 2–3) (For a comprehensive critique of this form of planning historiography, see Long 1981.)

That is, many stories of the history of planning take for granted that planning is, could, or should be, A Good Thing. Critiques of these narratives have been made from a number of positions: however, what most of these critiques have in common with 'standard' histories is a quest to save planning from its 'dark side' and to indicate ways in which planning's progressive promises might best be fulfilled. A genealogical perspective, in contrast, does not pose such questions nor seek such redemptive goals. In order to illustrate this difference, the next section examines examples of 'standard' planning history, before outlining critiques of these approaches, mainly coming from critical Marxian, feminist and multicultural perspectives; and looks at the potentials of perspectives derived from Foucauldian-inspired approaches.

Searching for Planning's Origins and Purposes

There are at least three approaches to planning history discernable in the 'mainstream' or 'progressivist' planning literature that is usually taught in (admittedly mainly Anglophone/UK based) planning schools. Although there has been much critical work (see below), these are still the kind of texts that are drawn on in teaching English planning history – where it is taught at all. They are what might be called: Utopian histories; regulatory histories; and histories of diffusion.

First, Utopian histories are those that seek the origins of planning in visionary attempts to imagine better societies. They look to the anarchist or communitarian antecedents to Ebenezer Howard's Garden City (e.g. Freestone 1989; Hall 2002; Hardy 1991; Ward 1992) and/or seek the origins of planning in the distant past of urban form, seeing in the ideals of (Western) architecture and the search for the good city, the seeds of the practice and discipline of town planning (e.g. Houghton-Evans 1975). They also tend to distinguish between such visionary ideals and mundane regulations for the management of the use and development of space.

Thus, for historians who see the origins of planning in the Garden City movement, the state regulation of suburban expansion represents a failure of nerve by the legislators (e.g. Hall 2002). They agree with Ebenezer Howard (1902/1965) that Garden Suburbs only served to prop up existing cities and perpetuate their evils, both physical – slums, smoke, disease, poverty – and social and economic dysfunction – greed, speculation, unproductive wealth accumulation – while doing nothing about rural poverty and depopulation. The foundation of Garden Cities, on the other hand, had the potential to solve both the problems of cities and prevent the depopulation of the countryside, by simultaneously providing healthy living for urban populations and employment for rural workers. Thus, the Garden City becomes the culmination of the visionary thought about the city that had gone before; the anticipation of the good city to come; and the touchstone against which to measure success or failure (e.g. Hall 2002; Hardy 1991; 2000; Osborne 1965).

Secondly, there are histories of urban planning that trace the accretion of nineteenth century urban reforms, and the advent and consolidation of state planning legislation and spatial regulation (e.g. Ashworth 1954; Booth 2003; Cherry 1974). These studies tend towards forms of progressivist teleology, seeing planning as a necessary response to the evils of unbridled development. Setbacks to progress and regulatory cul-de-sacs are noted, but in general, historical milestones in English planning, like the building of Garden Cities or the passing of the 1909 *Housing, Town Planning, Etc. Act*, are staging posts along the way to the 1947 *Town and Country Planning Act* (Ashworth 1954; Cherry 1996; Ward 1994), which sets the framework for what are sometimes seen as the halcyon days of post-war English planning.

Alternatively, the inevitable rise and spread of the planning profession and planning practice may be charted, as in Mel Scott's (1969) early exposition, *American City Planning Since 1890*.

Although 'Utopian' narratives tend to see histories of regulations as mere pragmatic watering down of planning's values, and regulatory histories tend to see the emphasis on the visions of great men as impractical idealism, both Utopian and regulatory stories of planning are generally told through the thoughts, writings and acts of individuals, gathered under the umbrella of forerunners and founders of 'planning' – Kropotkin, Howard, Geddes; or Horsfall, Nettlefold, Burns, Abercrombie, Burnham – who shape the aims and achievements of twentieth century English-speaking planning. However, the thoughts and acts of women working for urban reform (e.g. Octavia Hill, Jane Addams, Catherine Bauer) have, until recently, rarely been recorded in these histories, as Sandercock (1998b) points out.

A third type of planning history examines the diffusion of planning ideals and ideas – usually postulating origins in Europe, the UK or the US – and tracing the means by which planning concepts circulated between countries, and were instantiated in colonial settlements. More generally, diffusionist history shows how 'originary' ideas of city form, land use regulation and zoning were 'borrowed' or 'imposed' in different contexts and how, once again, they all too often fell short of their originators' aspirations (e.g. Cherry 1980; Home 1997; Sutcliffe 1981; Ward 2002). Hall (2002: 58–62), for example, is dismissive of American-style zoning (which was influenced by German examples): he sees zoning as a purely pragmatic protection of property values and a vehicle for racial segregation. He distinguishes it from (real) 'planning' driven by the ideals of the 'founding fathers', however incompletely achieved.

Similar 'diffusionist' (colonialist) stories are exemplified in Australian planning histories that see early advocates of planning in Australia as heavily influenced by English or American examples; they tend to give less prominence to the particular conditions that evoked local responses (e.g. Freestone 1989; Freestone 2000b; Freestone and Grubb 1998; Hamnett and Freestone 2000). Or as Powell argues, in his historical geography of Australia,

> the international diffusion of the great Garden City schema was almost invariably accompanied by a dilution of its imaginative ideals – that is, it was emasculated [sic]. In Australia, as elsewhere, it appeared as the 'Garden Suburb', nothing more. (Powell 1991: 33)

The best of these planning histories are rich with contextual material about the problems of cities, and abounding with details of the 'quirksy and creative and surprising' (Hall 2002: 4) lives of their main protagonists. But, with varying emphases, they also share other common features: a largely unproblematized belief in the virtue of planning and in the attempts to implement its originary ideas about the good life in the good city; a tendency to emphasize historical actors whose inspiration gives expression to formative ideas; an object called 'planning' that has a context in which its origin can be identified; an underlying teleological view of the necessity of planning for bringing about progressive improvement, however much such visionary or rational reforms are continually thwarted. And finally, such planning histories tend towards models of diffusion between 'centres' and from 'centres' to 'peripheries' – usually from 'Western' nations to colonial outposts – in which the peripheral instance has often been depicted as an inadequate copy of the central origin.

Where planning history is taught at all (and demands on planning curricula – in the UK at least – often mean that planning history is reduced to a few lectures at most), it is usually told in terms of these narratives, presenting an unbroken and unproblematic development that produces a singular object called 'planning' that can be traced from before Babylon to London and New York. To be sure, this object has sub-sets and specialisms, often with their own trajectories of development, but in historical terms, they are usually seen as sharing similar origins and aims.

However, of course, there are many approaches that provide critical perspectives on shortcomings, exclusions and blind alleys of past planning theories and practices, of which the next section provides examples.

Some Critical Histories

The notion that planning is an inherently benign practice, its good intentions frustrated by selfish politics or well-meaning misapplications, is critically examined in histories that measure the aspirations of planning against analyses of planning's place in wider social formations of inherent or persistent inequalities. Of these critical approaches to the premises of planning, Marxian perspectives, feminist and what might be called 'multicultural' and 'post-colonial' positions are examined here. Finally, there are historical approaches to the development of planning theories, regulations and practices that draw on Foucauldian perspectives (see Huxley 2008a)

Planning in the Interests of Capital

Broadly speaking, Marxian-inspired analyses of urban planning see it as serving the needs of capital, attempting to iron out the contradictions of capitalist production, consumption, reproduction and accumulation as inevitably spatially-mediated processes (e.g. Castells 1977; Harvey 1985; Scott 1980). Histories of planning from Marxian or political economy standpoints place planning in the context of historically developing economic relations of inequality, which planning's search for ideal environments can do little to alleviate. The succession of various planning theories and practices, and the 'great men' that espouse them are reflections of, and are inevitably constrained by, the cyclical processes of capital accumulation (Harvey 1985; Roweis 1981).

Nevertheless, within these constraints, and especially from positions that emphasize class struggle as enabling significant change, such histories have assessed planning's attempts to ameliorate the worst conditions of spatial inequalities and have described the aspirations of the public and political individuals who espoused it (e.g. Benevolo 1967; Fogelsong 1986; Harvey 1985, 1996: 405–407; Kirk 1980; Sandercock 1977). These attempts are usually seen to have, at best, only short-term or localized effects, mystifying the underlying relations of capitalist exploitation and in the long run, perpetuating them.

However, a class perspective can also suggest that the outcomes of planning projects and legislation are not necessarily such completely foregone conclusions, for either good or ill. For instance, Benevolo suggests that the schemes of the Utopian planners were technical proposals that were

> easily separated from social innovations and utilized by paternalistic reformers, precisely to conserve the social balance … [but equally] the various enterprises fostered by conservative forces … were able to develop in a sense completely contrary to their original conception, and … be transformed into weapons to overturn the systems they had been supposed to consolidate. (Benevolo 1967: 146–7)

The introduction of planning legislation in the twentieth century can similarly be seen as the result of the outcomes of working class demands that made themselves felt at a particular time in a particular configuration of forces (e.g. McDougall 1979 on the English 1909 *Housing, Town Planning, Etc. Act*; or Sandercock 1977 on the introduction of planning legislation in the Australian States).

Marxian inspired planning histories, thus, have been invaluable in drawing attention to the economic and social inequalities in which planning is enmeshed, and asking questions that challenge the more sanguine views of planning's aims and effects. But they also have a tendency to provide mono-causal, meta-theoretical explanations for its persistent failures and occasional successes, rooted, in the last instance, in the relations of capitalism (as noted by Sandercock 1998b: 19–20).

Similar social-theoretic explanations of planning's 'failures' can be found in some feminist histories that see planning as inevitably entangled in the reproduction of unequal gender relations.

Planning in the Interests of White, Able-bodied Patriarchy

Feminist approaches to planning history have set out to uncover, not only the inequalities and biases inherent in planning ideals and practices, but also the invisible histories of women's reforming and subversive actions in urban space (e.g. Allport 1986; Greed 1994; Hayden 1984). For radical feminists, planning has always reflected the structural imperatives of patriarchal domination and, in arguments paralleling Marxian analyses, the real solution to the gendered spatial inequalities perpetuated by planning lies in the complete revolution of social and economic relations.

Spatial divisions are exacerbated by design practices and planning regulations, especially those of US-style zoning (e.g. Ritzdorf 1994). Over time, the regulation of the built environment, it is argued, from house design to zoning, has produced spatial arrangements that impose mobility configurations and time-budget restrictions on women, making the work of household management – which is still very much women's responsibility – even more onerous (Huxley 1993; Roberts 1991; Weisman 1992). These spatial configurations reflect and reinforce historical structures of patriarchy that render women's work and life experiences invisible.

However, in contrast to histories told from the perspective of systemic patriarchy, other analyses suggest possibilities for the elimination of both spatial inequalities and professional and institutional gender bias. Gender sensitive practice, better education and further (action-based, participatory) research will have positive effects in bringing about improved spatial outcomes. Historical studies uncovering the work of women housing reformers and planners, like Octavia Hill, Jane Addams or Catherine Bauer, and other less-well-known women associated, for instance, with the Garden City Movement or the promotion of planning in Australia (Freestone 1995), produce alternative planning histories and hitherto invisible practices of planning and place-making (Sandercock 1998a; see also Allport 1986; Greed 1994; Hayden 1984).

Planning histories that uncover gendered inequalities in the built environment, modernist homogenizations of urban space, and heteronormative assumptions embedded in liberal democratic theories of equality, also bring to light the cross-cutting and mutually reinforcing ways in which multiple 'Others' are constituted, in part through planning's political and social assumptions about normality and difference (e.g. Fenster 1999). They examine planning's overt and tacit implications in racial segregation (e.g. Mabin and Smit 1997; Robinson 1996; Silver 1991; Thomas 1998; Yiftachel 1995), and trace histories of how planning exacerbates the disadvantages experienced through different bodily capacities (e.g. Gleeson 1998).

In his examination of colonial histories of planning, King (1980) rightly points out that much of the literature in the 1970s on the 'diffusion' of planning throughout British colonial and ex-colonial countries, and the biographies of the 'great men' who designed new towns, and new capital cities (Geddes, Abercrombie, Le Corbusier, and the exodus of British planners after the 1947 Act) were at best, imperialist, and at worst, racist. King points to the assumptions that colonial planning was done in the interests of the local population, and that it was a force for good in either fostering 'civilization of backward countries' or promoting progress in 'developing' nations. King's critique was almost unique at the time in pointing out the governmental projects of control and power involved in colonial city planning.

Subsequent critiques from postcolonial standpoints have also highlighted the ways in which colonial practices of planning and urban management were, in effect, experiments, the results of which 'returned' to become embodied (and contested) in the domestic planning and housing policies of the colonial powers (e.g. Jacobs 1996; Legg 2007; McGuiness 1999; Rabinow 1989).

Urban histories that do not necessarily start from the standpoint of planning also provide valuable insights into the underlying impulses to manage and reform unruly urban spaces and subjects. For instance, in Wilson's (1991) analysis of the gendered nature of discourses of the control of public space in the Victorian city, and of schemes for urban reform such as the Garden City, planning is seen as one effect of these multiple discourses, produced by, and producing, gendered practices that position women in particular ways. Similarly, there are historical studies of the fears of sexualities that differ from the white, male norm (e.g. Chauncey 1994 on gay New York).

So while not all of these studies are undertaken from the standpoint of planning, their various critiques point to conventional planning history's previous failures to acknowledge the cultural assumptions and exclusionary impulses (e.g. see Kruekeberg 1997) lying at the base of reformist aims. They intersect with 'multicultural' planning histories of difference and diversity, which, Sandercock (1998b: 30) suggests, can assist planning to become more culturally sensitive, equitable and democratic. 'If we want to work toward a policy of inclusion, then we had better have a good understanding of the exclusionary effects of planning's past practices and ideologies'.

Such critical planning histories thus have a valuable role to play in evaluating the effects of past practices and theories; and for instance, journals such as *Planning Perspectives* or the *Journal of Planning History*, and collections like Freestone (2000a) or Sandercock (1998a), provide many salutary instances – both positive and negative – of the effects of planning practices. However, studies from Foucauldian perspectives develop these insights from slightly different angles.

Foucauldian Planning Histories

In one of the first major studies of planning making use of Foucauldian ideas, Boyer (1983) examines the 'myth of American city planning' and the introduction of both zoning and regional planning. She describes planning as a 'quest for disciplinary control' (1983: 9) and draws heavily on Foucault's (1979) *Discipline and Punish*. But while she pays exemplary attention to the minutiae of regulation, nevertheless, her analysis appears to owe more to Marx than Foucault, since the control planning imposes is seen to necessarily arise from, and act in, the all-pervasive interests of capital.

In contrast, Sandercock's (1998a) ground-breaking critical historiography, *Making the Invisible Visible* – a 'collection of multicultural planning histories' – encapsulates many critical concerns in envisioning different planning pasts, uncovering unacknowledged influences and exposing the absences in standard accounts. Sandercock (1998b: 13–20) and several of the contributors to the volume, explicitly invoke Foucauldian insights into histories of power as important means for unsettling meta-narratives and instead directing attention to the ways in which 'power begins in little places and in terms of little things' (1998b: 20).

In particular, Wirka's (1998) chapter on 'city planning for girls' points out, in a discussion of attempts to regulate young women in public spaces in the early twentieth century American city, that these regulatory practices are performed by women as well as by men (in contrast with Wilson (1991), for instance). This detaching of essentialized characteristics of gender shows that, in taking up dominant discourses, women also act as 'disciplining professionals' – 'patrolling behaviours, policing norms, establishing new forms for the regulation of women in the city' (Wirka 1998: 159; see also Cruikshank 1999; for an alternative view of the power of 'lady visitors', see Robinson 2000).

Fischler (1998a; b) also employs Foucauldian perspectives to produce alternative planning histories, examining the 'little things' of the introduction of zoning and urban regulation in the US (see also Huxley 1994 on zoning in Australia). Like Sandercock (1998b: 30), he stresses the importance of knowledge of mundane histories of planning regulations for the improvement of current planning practices (Fischler 2000).

While productively drawing on elements of Foucauldian perspectives on history (see next section) and in particular, focusing on invisible narratives or often-overlooked aspects of regulation, many of these studies, nevertheless, share presumptions about the regulatory practices called 'planning', and they indicate prescriptive pathways to save planning from itself. Their starting point is the existence of planning, and the study of history is undertaken in order to suggest how it might be improved. To this extent then, even while acknowledging the 'noir' or 'dark side' of planning, these studies share the aim of justifying planning, with the additional purpose of using history in order to avoid both the mistakes of 'standard' planning history and the mistakes of the past (e.g. see also Birch 2006; Birch and Silver 2009; Fischler 2006; Freestone 2000b; Kruekeberg 1997; Thomas 2006).

This focus on the history of a taken-for-granted object called 'planning' tends to reinforce accepted assumptions about its existence and unproblematic nature, its aims and ideals, and the hopes and aspirations of its advocates.

But it is the 'decentring' of planning and setting aside searches for its origins, continuities and justifications that mark Foucauldian genealogical approaches. Seeing planning as an intersection of historically unsecured and continuously unstable sets of practices and regulations opens up possibilities for 'thinking otherwise' about spatial government. Suggesting this, however, requires some indication of what a genealogical approach entails.

Critical and Effective Genealogies

In his re-reading of Nietzsche's genealogy of the 'will to power', and in his linking of power to the materiality of discursive practices, Foucault (1986a, 1988, 2003) proposes genealogy as a 'critical' and 'effective' (Nietzsche's *wirkliche Historie*) form of historical analysis (see Dean 1994; Gordon 1980; Smart 2002). Critical and effective histories question all constants, essentialisms and teleological narratives of progress: they examine the specificity and the entanglement of 'events' in the struggles over discourses, vocabularies, knowledges and power; and acknowledge the role of chance and contingency in the effects of these struggles. They approach the study of the mundane, taken-for-granted and everyday – for instance, the body, nutrition, digestion, sex (or indeed, development control, zoning, planning permissions), as if they were unusual, strange and in need of exacting attention to expository detail.

Genealogy rejects the notion of an essential, self-identical origin of a social phenomenon or historical process that needs to be retrieved as the starting point of a teleological narrative. Neither should an origin be seen to respond to some predetermined need or necessity (Elden 2001; Foucault 1986a; Smart 2002), such as 'the march of progress', the functioning of capitalism, or the necessary creation of healthy environments. Rather, what are traced are 'descents' and 'emergences' – discontinuities, indeterminacies and multiplicities of events surrounding possible historical confluences, and contingent, provisional conditions that surround any identifiable continuities. Such an analysis avoids 'placing present needs at the origin ... [or positing] an obscure purpose that seeks its realisation at the moment it arises': neither does it see the present as 'the final term of a historical development' (Foucault 1986a: 83). The present is not end-point or culmination, but neither is it a radical departure – for instance, a new era of globalization, of migration, of social fragmentation – but '... a day like every other, or much more, a day which is never like another' (Foucault 1996b: 358), freighted with contingent possibilities, accidental openings and indeterminate opportunities.

From this perspective on 'who we are', genealogy acts as a 'diagnostic' of the present, examining how contemporary problems are formulated and showing that other problematizations and solutions have been, and therefore are, possible. What can be said, what truth is, are the outcomes of discursive and material exercises of power, and compose the conditions within which the contingent, accidental and indeterminate effects of actions, programmes, plans are played out. This emphasis on contingency and indeterminacy enables the possibility of seeing how things might have been different, and how fragile and unstable are the apparently commonplace structures of the present (Foucault 1986a: 89–90, 1988: 36–37).

Although it is not possible to give a full exegesis of this position here, it should be noted that one of the most difficult aspects of Foucault's Nietzschean genealogical examinations is the idea that history or society are not founded on the transcendental or free-willed subject of humanist philosophy as sources of historical change and social relations (e.g. Foucault 1994; see Patton 1998 on Foucault's 'thin' conception of the subject and the problem of human agency). Instead, in proposing a 'historical ontology of the subject', Foucault emphasizes that, like 'truth', the subject is not prior to history, but is historically constituted. 'The subject is a form, not a thing, and this form is not constant, even when attached to the same individual' (O'Farrell 2005: 113)

Thus, genealogy seeks to show the recurrence of taken-for-granted notions, seemingly without a history, like truth, the subject, '... love, conscience, instincts ... not in order to trace the gradual curve of their evolution, but to isolate the different scenes where they engaged in different roles' (Foucault 1986a: 76).

Rather than seeking a 'total' explanation that assumes the possibility of a complete knowledge or theory of 'man' or 'the social' based in philosophy or the human sciences, genealogy requires attention to the specific discourses and practices which constitute subjects as having particular attributes, at the confluences of which they come to (partially) recognize themselves. However, these conditions of existence of subjects/objects are neither finalized nor determinate, but 'go on changing in relation to one another, and thus go on modifying this field of experience itself' (Foucault 1994: 318). Genealogy indicates that 'truths' about, and 'problematizations' of, social relations are the products of conflicts and struggles over knowledge and power. Thus, conceptions such as 'society' 'the social', 'social relations', 'the economy', are discursively constituted, and are themselves open to genealogical analysis (see Dean 1999; Joyce 1997; Rose 1999). Tracing how the effects of these struggles in discourse and practice are materialized in repeated performance and congealed into taken-for-granted realities is the object of critical histories of the present (Foucault 1979: 31; Dean 1994: 50–5; Elden 2001: 112–14).

But this is not the same as denying the materiality of the subject, nor does it deny that actions have effects (see Patton 1998). 'What is done' by subjects is a field of practices constituted in and through historically specific ways of acting and thinking (a perspective Foucault set out most strictly in *The Order of Things* (1974) and subsequently modified to take account of power and transformation). For Foucault, practices are

> *more or less regulated, more or less conscious, more or less goal-orientated [ways of doing things], through which one can grasp the lineaments both of what was constituted as real for those who were attempting to conceptualise and govern it, and of the way in which those same people constituted themselves as subjects capable of knowing, analyzing, and ultimately modifying the real.*
> *(Foucault 1994: 318)*

Genealogies of 'planning' then, could uncover the different historical and local conditions of how, when and where certain discourses enabled the identification of a field of problems, and by what strategies and tactics certain subjects came to be constituted and to constitute themselves as 'planners' with expertise in this field.

This kind of 'radical agnosticism' (Dean 1996: 5), 'methodological scepticism' (Gordon 1980: 239) and suspension of prescriptive judgement (Kendall and Wickham 1999: 10–20) are what distinguish genealogy from other ways of approaching history. Genealogy 'tries to argue against an impoverished imagination that is caught in a certain perspective by confronting it with another one'; while acknowledging that all perspectives are 'immersed in power relations' (Biebricher 2005: 11). It can be productively applied to examining both the discourses and problematizations that brought 'the slum', 'housing', 'sanitation', 'the city' into view as objects of concern, and through modulations of which 'town planning' emerged as a solution (see Huxley 2006).

Genealogies of Spatial Reform

So for instance, genealogies of the complex interconnection of knowledge, space and urban regulation can be found in Paul Rabinow's (1989) *French Modern*. He shows how knowledges – statistics, medicine, biology, architecture and building, regional geography; and the 'technicians of general ideas' or 'specific intellectuals' whose writings addressing problems of government, are located somewhere between high culture and everyday life (1989: 9). Practices of architecture, colonial rule, working class reform, and sanitary infrastructure, are intertwined in nineteenth century French colonial experiments with 'urbanism'. This material discursive confluence of knowledges, practices and regulations attempts to create *milieux* that aim to induce and maintain specific and differentiated 'norms', embodied in the built 'forms of the social environment'. This study can be read as an examination of the 'thought', practices and materialities at work in nineteenth century projects of French spatial and urban reform, some of which disappear and some of which become modulated into a 'middling modernism' of the early twentieth century.

Or again, in histories of urban problematisations, Osborne and Rose (1999, 2004) conduct Foucauldian-Deleuzean examinations of the nineteenth century English industrialized city and practitioners of urban reform. However, while providing broad-brush insights into the 'mentalities' underpinning reforming impulses, their approach tends to lack detailed engagement with contemporaneous interplays of practices and regulations with theories or 'truths' about the relations between subjects, spaces and environments. As a result, it appears to produce somewhat abstract and epochal readings that obscure the contingent, unstable, partial, overlapping and conflicting nature of ways of visualizing and constituting the objects of regulation and reform.

In contrast, Long's (1981, 1982) sadly neglected two-part critique of planning historiography challenges the supposed continuity of nineteenth century practices of urban reform as teleological progress towards the coming of planning in the early twentieth century. Long (1981) draws on Foucauldian methods to scrutinize standard planning histories, and demonstrates that nineteenth century projects of urban reform problematize a 'social economy' that does not necessarily reflect the same discursive universe as current 'planning'. 'Social economy' and associated social and slum reforms, focused on the figure of the 'pauper' (see also Dean 1991); but the discourses of 'citizenship' and 'national efficiency' that appeared at the end of the nineteenth century constitute a different set of problems and aims, in which the emergence of 'town planning' is implicated (Long 1982: 67–8). In this way, 'planning' is not assumed to pre-exist its emergence from a network of competing and conflicting discourses in particular ways at particular times and in particular places.

Similarly, the complexity of the relations between the constitution of problems and the regulation of spaces and subjects is well illustrated in Gibson's (2001) study of how discourses of economic development and regional planning in the coal mining and electricity generating industries of the La Trobe Valley, Australia, in the 1920s, actively contributed to the production of 'regional subjectivities' – individuals and communities whose subjecthood was bound to the region and its economic activities. The certainties of 'the Economy', and the place of subjects and regions in it, were disrupted in the face of withdrawal of investment and government support in the 1980s. In official discourses promoting restructuring (of economy and subjects), 'The Economy' became the ultimate 'real', while 'the Region' – through which most residents constructed their identities – was configured as an artificial and investment-inhibiting fiction. Re-interpreting this discursive history and re-configuring 'discourses of decline' to focus on the productive nature of 'informal' activities already taking place in the region becomes a possible pathway for residents to shift to more positive subject positions.

From these kinds of historical, genealogical studies, practices of urban reform – physical and moral – can be seen to be based in assumed 'truths' about causal relations between environments and subjects. Genealogies of disparate and diverse programmes and practices of reform show that in different times and places, already existing practical and theoretical constitutions of problems were available for mobilization in the production of subjects who come to see themselves as 'planners'. From such a perspective, it is possible to trace diverse and obscure tracks and alleys, forgotten problematizations and debates, that serve to productively unsettle our assumptions about what we are as academics and practitioners, about what planning is or could be.

Some Possible Genealogies

In order to illustrate the potentials of genealogical approaches, I sketch two areas that might repay further exploration: planning history and land use regulation.

A Genealogy of Planning History

Rather than starting with 'planning', we can ask: how has it become possible to speak of something – or possibly different things – called (land use/urban/city/regional/spatial/environmental) planning? Taking a genealogical perspective on the constitution of planning, and detaching 'planning' from 'planning history', enables an examination of planning history as one form of the attempts to stake out a claim to disciplinary knowledge and professional expertise.

The emergence of town (and country) planning in the late nineteenth and early twentieth century 'North/West' has been portrayed as a logical consequence of concerns about the industrial city and the increasing role played by the state in managing economic and social life (e.g. Ashworth 1954; Cherry 1974; 1996). Certainly, the practices of sanitary, medical and moral reform; the growth of professional expertise; political demands and the extension of the franchise; and economic threats from international competition, all contributed to the conditions in which disparate sets of statements, concerns and practices coalesced under the name of 'town planning'.

However, as I have argued above (and elsewhere: see Huxley 2006), the multiple underlying assumptions about urban, spatial and environmental management from which 'town planning' emerges as a set of regulatory practices, are more complex and less continuous than this (see Long 1981). And, rather than accepting the narratives presented in much town planning history, we could examine how the writing of 'town planning' history itself provides support for claims to a body of knowledge and expertise about the effects of space and environment on the bodies and minds of individuals and populations, with the aims of creating the conditions for good lives in good cities.

The first recorded use of the phrase 'town planning' in English appears to have been in a paper to the Australasian Association for the Advancement of Science by John Sulman in 1890 (Sulman 1890, 1921: Appendix; Freestone 1983, 1996; see also King 1982). However, this date is not necessarily significant as an 'origin', 'discovery' or 'invention', but rather is indicative that such a practice and its objects had become 'thinkable' and 'sayable'. In the process of constituting 'town planning' out of haphazard arrays of practices and discourses coalescing around problematized objects (e.g. the city, slum housing) to which expertise could be applied (e.g. 'town planning'), knowledges were claimed and disciplinary boundaries were carved out of already existing discourses. The individuals who were concerned about urban conditions – philanthropists, scientists, statisticians, sanitarians, housing legislators, Utopian visionaries, etc. – were as Foucault (1996a: 26) says of the thinkers of the eighteenth century, 'caught up in the network of all those who speak "of the same thing", who are contemporary to them or follow them: this network that envelopes them outlines these ... figures without a social identity that one calls "mathematics", "history" or "biology"': that is, they did not speak as 'planners'.

But in less than 20 years, texts were being written about the history and practice of this discipline. Producing a history is one of the ways in which an object of intervention can be identified, and a field of knowledge claimed by experts of a discipline, who can then suggest solutions. Thus, almost all early twentieth century town planning texts identify an object – the city – and construct a history of conscious direction of its form; such identification is crucial to the delineation of the subject matter of the discipline and the profession. Much detailed attention is given to historical town layouts in texts ranging from advocacy of the virtues of town planning to how-to-do-it manuals. Books such as Triggs (1909) *Town Planning: Past, Present and Possible*; Unwin (1909) *Town Planning in Practice: An Introduction to the Art of Designing Cities and Suburbs*; Taylor (1914) *Town Planning for Australia*; Aldridge (1915) *The Case for Town Planning: A Practical Manual for the Use of Councillors, Officers and Others Engaged in the Preparation of Town Planning Schemes*; Sulman (1921) *An Introduction to the Study of Town Planning in Australia*; Adams (1935) *Outline of Town and City Planning: A Review of Past Efforts and Modern Aims* (intended for a North American audience); all begin with one or more chapters on the long and honourable history of consciously designed urban forms. These historical excurses covered millennia of urban development in order to show that town planning was not a 'modern fad' but 'one of the oldest arts evolved in the slow development of organized civic life in civilised countries' (Aldridge 1915: 9).

What this suggests is that 'history' itself needs interrogation. Planning history was already being written at the point when 'town planning' becomes a way of identifying a set of practices and an argument for legislation. History then, is but one aspect of the work that was (and is) necessary to produce 'town planning', and seeing it in this light opens up further questions to be pursued about the self-evidence of planning. Specific histories of the discursive presuppositions and tussles constituting 'planning' or 'urbanism' in different conditions and situations will further illustrate the indeterminate and often contradictory practices that are simultaneously gathered and scattered under this designation (see for instance, Novik 2007).

Along with the construction of a history, haphazard selections of regulatory practices emerge from contingent historical struggles over truth, knowledge and the power of the state and become entrenched in mundane routines of planning; but also inform the assumptions behind policy concepts and indeed, academic debates. Such routines and concepts can persist unquestioned until further problematizations – arising either from 'external' events (e.g. supposed housing shortages), or from the perceived 'internal' failures of the regulations themselves (e.g. planning 'obstructions' to development) – pose challenges to certain assumptions (or occasionally, to the whole system). Such questions and challenges can be turned to good effect, even at the mundane level of land use regulation.

Unsettling Land Use Regulation

A critical genealogy of (Anglophone) planning regulation might see in detailed zoning ordinances, use class orders or land use regulations reflections of disparate, historically contingent rationalities of environmental causality. These regulations are ramshackle collections in which spaces, environments, built forms, uses and users have become entangled in accretions of categories and boundaries that often no longer answer to any immediate or identifiable sets of interests or even technically rational goals (in the narrow sense). Some regulations call to mind Foucault's (1974: xv) description of Borges's (fictional) Chinese dictionary – 'the exotic charm of another system of thought … the stark impossibility of thinking *that*'.

Nevertheless, each set of regulations has a history of rationales that needs to be uncovered and examined in their own particularity (Fischler 1998a, b; Huxley 1994). But each particular regulatory regime also offers opportunities for questioning its self-evidence, through which practical tactics for change can grapple with specific regulations. As Sandercock (1998b: 19) suggests, 'definitions of order and disorder … are necessarily a preoccupation not only of planning historians and theorists but also of people in cities, taking to the streets to claim their rights to public space and public resources'.

An example is how, in Toronto, the use of zoning regulations to exclude homeless shelters from middle-class areas in Toronto was challenged (Valverde 2005, 2006). The restrictions were taken to the courts as infringements of citizen rights, but these appeals were lost. Valverde (2005, 2006) argues that a more productive strategy was to seek minor amendments to the regulations, which, because they dealt with the concept of 'amenity' rather than with 'rights', did not require legislative approval. The effect could be more practically positive in that small-scale adjustments to boundary regulations could enable more homeless shelters to be provided.

So, zoning rules and land use regulations should not be dismissed as either trivial and irrelevant; or as (irrational) infringements of rights that need to be fought for in other arenas (Valverde 2006: 19–20). Knowledge of the tangled history of such regulations, the discursive construction of concepts like 'amenity', and the mode of their operations can be presented in practical ways for use by groups engaged in specific struggles around inequalities in the management of the environment.

In this way, genealogy can contribute to productive questioning of 'planning' itself and how it came to be as it is; and can engender ways of thinking differently about planning practices that provide practical assistance in wearing away their obviousness in order to open up spaces for inventive transformations.

Conclusion

> … I am not looking for an alternative; you can't find the solution of a problem in the solution of another problem raised at another moment by other people … [W]hat I want to do is not the history of solutions, and that's the reason why I don't accept the word alternative. I would like to do the genealogy of problems … My point is not that everything is bad, but that everything is dangerous … If everything is dangerous, then we always have something to do. So my position leads not to apathy but to hyper- and pessimistic activism. (Foucault 1986b: 343)

In this chapter, I have tried to suggest how genealogical approaches to histories of the planning present have the potential to engage with the fields of 'what is done' (Foucault 1994: 318), examining how planning and its knowledges were made, and the ways in which planners 'constituted themselves as subjects capable of knowing, analysing, and ultimately modifying the real' (Foucault 1994: 318). Planning history can be approached in this light to examine its role in the constitution of the objects of planning, and claims to expertise in relation to them. Such reflexive examinations are required not only of those planning histories which take for granted the existence of planning and its potential for good, but also to more critical stances that question planning's self-image.

Critical and progressive approaches alike tend to place at the centre of reform, the figure of the insurgent, or communicative or multicultural planner who has knowledge of 'what must be done' to produce positive outcomes, and who can lead, or work with, repressed or disadvantaged groups to bring about radical change. However, from a Foucauldian perspective, the answers to general questions of inequality or repression in society at large cannot be prescribed in advance, nor can the liberating effects of radical action be guaranteed. Rather, the assessment of what can be transformed is specific to each instance where practices and institutions become problematized – challenged in practice and subjected to critical analysis in thought.

But genealogical thinking and the implications of problematizing planning pose considerable challenges, and do not come easily to a discipline and practices committed to normative justifications for progressive aims and future improvement – the good life in the good city. The de-centering of the subject (of the planner, of the 'participant', of the politician); the 'de-facing' of power (Hayward 1998); the avoidance of prescription; and the questioning of progressive aims and of planning itself, seem to lead inevitably to pessimistic and dystopian conclusions, leaving theoreticians and practitioners alike stranded and paralyzed, without purpose or room for action.

But this is far from the case, as work like the Community Economies Network (<www.communityeconomies.org>) shows: (partly Foucauldian-inspired) academic critique and transformative action can productively and inventively inform each other (see Gibson et al. Chapter 10 in this volume).

Such critical thinking about past, present and possible future practices should not be consigned to the prison of 'policy relevance'.

> The necessity of reform mustn't be allowed to become a form of blackmail serving to limit, reduce or halt the exercise of criticism. Under no circumstances should one pay attention to those who tell one: 'Don't criticize, since you're not capable of carrying out a reform.' That's ministerial cabinet talk. Critique doesn't have to be the premise of a deduction which concludes: this then is what needs to be done. It should be an instrument for those who fight, those who resist and refuse what is. Its use should be in processes of conflict and confrontation, essays in refusal. It doesn't have to lay down the law for the law. It isn't a stage in a programming. It is a challenge directed to what is. (Foucault 1991: 84)

The fact that such work will always be difficult to fit with the subject positions and routine practices of planners in government and consultancy does not mean that it is impossible. But it does require on-the-spot 'lateral thinking' and a willingness and courage to ask awkward questions, searching for different ways of proceeding (Foucault 1991: 84). The fact that the outcomes of such action are indeterminate and are not necessarily founded on optimistic expectations of 'success', does not mean that these risks are not worth taking.

References

Adams, T. (1935) *Outline of Town and City Planning: A Review of Past Efforts and Modern Aims.* London: J. & A. Churchill.

Aldridge, H. (1915) *The Case for Town Planning: A Practical Manual for the Use of Councillors, Officers and Others Engaged in the Preparation of Town Planning Schemes.* London: The National Housing and Town Planning Council.

Allport, C. (1986) 'Women and suburban housing: post-war planning in Sydney, 1943–61', in McLoughlin, J.B. and Huxley, M. (eds) *Urban Planning in Australia: critical readings*. Melbourne: Longman Cheshire, 233–48.

Ashworth, W. (1954) *The Genesis of Modern British Town Planning: A Study in Economic and Social History of the Nineteenth and Twentieth Centuries*. London: Routledge and Kegan Paul.

Benevolo, L. (1967) *The Origins of Modern Urban Planning* (trans. Landry, J.). Cambridge, MA: MIT Press.

Biebricher, T. (2005) 'Habermas, Foucault and Nietzsche: a double misunderstanding' *Foucault Studies* 3: 1–26.

Birch, E. (2006) 'Five questions and their (varied answers) about the use of planning history' *Journal of Planning History* 5(4): 323–8.

Birch, E. and Silver, C. (2009) 'One hundred years of city planning's enduring and evolving connections' *Journal of the American Planning Association* 75(2): 113–22.

Booth, P. (2003) *Planning by Consent: The Origins and Nature of British Development Control*. London: Routledge.

Boyer, M.C. (1983) *Dreaming the Rational City: The Myth of American City Planning*. Cambridge, MA: MIT Press.

Castells, M. (1977) *The Urban Question: A Marxist Approach*. London: Edward Arnold.

Chauncey, G. (1994) *Gay New York: Gender, Urban Culture, and the Making of the Gay Male World 1890–1940*. New York: Basic Books.

Cherry, G. (1974) *The Evolution of British Town Planning*. London: Leonard Hill.

Cherry, G. (ed.) (1980) *Shaping an Urban World*. (Volume 2 of *Planning and the Environment in the Modern World*). London: Mansell.

Cherry, G. (1996) *Town Planning in Britain since 1900: The Rise and Fall of the Planning Ideal*. Oxford: Blackwell.

Cruikshank, B. (1999) *The Will to Empower: Democratic Citizens and Other Subjects*. Ithaca and London: Cornell University Press.

Dean, M. (1991) *The Constitution of Poverty: Toward a Genealogy of Liberal Governance*. London: Routledge.

Dean, M. (1994) *Critical and Effective Histories: Foucault's Methods and Historical Sociology*. London: Routledge.

Dean, M. (1996) 'Putting the technological into government' *History of the Human Sciences* 9(3): 47–68.

Dean, M. (1999) *Governmentality: Power and Rule in Modern Society*. London: Sage.

Elden, S. (2001) *Mapping the Present: Heidegger, Foucault and the Project of a Spatial History*. London: Continuum.

Fenster, T. (ed.) (1999) *Gender, Planning and Human Rights*. London: Routledge.

Fischler, R. (1998a) 'The metropolitan dimension of early zoning: revisiting the 1916 New York City Zoning Ordinance' *Journal of the American Planning Association* 64(2): 170–88.

Fischler, R. (1998b) 'Toward a genealogy of planning: zoning and the Welfare State' *Planning Perspectives* 15: 389–410.

Fischler, R. (2000) 'Linking planning theory and history: the case of development control' *Journal of Planning Education and Research* 19: 233–41.

Fischler, R. (2006) 'Teaching history to planners' *Journal of Planning History* 5(4): 280–8.

Fogelsong, R. (1986) *Planning the American City: The Colonial Era to the 1920s*. Princeton, NJ: Princeton University Press.

Foucault, M. (1974) *The Order of Things: An Archaeology of the Human Sciences*. London: Routledge.

Foucault, M. (1979) *Discipline and Punish: The Birth of the Prison*. New York: Vintage Books.

Foucault, M. (1986a) 'Nietzsche, genealogy, history', in Rabinow, P. (ed.) *The Foucault Reader*. Harmondsworth: Peregrine Books, 76–100.

Foucault, M. (1986b) 'On the genealogy of ethics: an overview of work in progress', in Rabinow, P. (ed.) *The Foucault Reader*. Harmondsworth: Peregrine Books, 340–72.

Foucault, M. (1988) 'Critical theory/intellectual history', in Kritzman, L. (ed.) *Michel Foucault: Politics, Philosophy, Culture*. New York: Routledge, 17–46.

Foucault, M. (1991) 'Questions of method', in Burchell, G., Gordon, C. and Miller, P. (eds) *The Foucault Effect: Studies in Governmentality*. London: Harvester Wheatsheaf, 73–86.

Foucault, M. ('Maurice Florence') (1994) 'Foucault, Michel, 1926–', in Gutting, G. (ed.) *The Cambridge Companion to Foucault*. Cambridge: Cambridge University Press, 314–20.

Foucault, M. (1996a) 'The discourse of history', in Lotringer, S. (ed.) *Foucault Live*. New York: Semiotext(e), 19–32.

Foucault, M. (1996b) 'How much does it cost for reason to tell the truth?', in Lotringer, S. (ed.) *Foucault Live*. New York: Semiotext(e), 348–62.

Foucault, M. (2003) *Society must be Defended: Lectures at the Collège de France 1975–1976* (trans. Macey, J.). London: Allen Lane/Penguin.

Freestone, R. (1983) 'John Sulman and the laying out of towns' *Planning History Bulletin* 5: 18–24.

Freestone, R. (1989) *Model Communities: the Garden City Movement in Australia*. Melbourne: Nelson.

Freestone, R. (1995) 'Women in the Australian town planning movement 1900–1950' *Planning Perspectives* 10(3): 259–78.

Freestone, R. (1996) 'Sulman of Sydney: modern planning in theory and practice 1890–1930' *Town Planning Review* 67(1): 45–63.

Freestone, R. (ed.) (2000a) *Urban Planning in a Changing World: The Twentieth Century Experience*. London: E. & F.N. Spon.

Freestone, R. (2000b) 'Learning from planning's histories', in Freestone (ed.) (2000a), 1–19.

Freestone, R. and Grubb, M. (1998) 'The Melbourne Metropolitan Town Planning Commission 1922–1930' *Journal of Australian Studies* 57: 128–44.

Gibson, K. (2001) 'Regional subjection and becoming' *Environment and Planning D: Society and Space* 19: 639–67.

Gleeson, B. (1998) 'Justice and the disabling city', in Fincher, R. and Jacobs, J. (eds) *Cities of Difference*. New York: The Guilford Press, 89–119.

Gordon, C. (1980) 'Afterword', in Gordon (ed.) *Michel Foucault: Power/Knowledge. Selected interviews and other writings 1972-1977*. Brighton: The Harvester Press, 229–60.

Greed, C. (1994) *Women and Planning: Creating Gendered Realities*. London: Routledge.

Hall, P. (2002) *Cities of Tomorrow: An Intellectual History of Urban Planning and Design in the Twentieth Century*, third edition. Oxford: Blackwell.

Hamnett, S. and Freestone, R. (eds) (2000) *The Australian Metropolis: A Planning History*. Sydney: Allen & Unwin.

Hardy, D. (1991) *From Garden Cities to New Towns: campaigning for town and country planning, 1899–1946*. London: E. & F.N. Spon.

Hardy, D. (2000) 'Quasi Utopias: perfect cities in an imperfect world', in Freestone (ed.) (2000a), 61–79.

Harrison, M. (1991) 'Thomas Coglan Horsfall and the "example of Germany"' *Planning Perspectives* 6: 297–314.

Harvey, D. (1985) 'On planning the ideology of planning', in *The Urbanization of Capital: Studies in the History and Theory of Capitalist Urbanization*. Oxford: Basil Blackwell, 165–84.

Harvey, D. (1996) *Justice, Nature and the Geography of Difference*. Oxford: Blackwell.

Hayden, D. (1984) *Re-designing the American Dream: The Future of Housing, Work and Family Life*. New York: W.W. Norton.

Hayward, C. (1998) 'De-facing power', *Polity* 31(1): 1–22.

Home, R. (1997) *Of Planting and Planning: The Making of British Colonial Cities*. London: E. & F.N. Spon.

Horsfall, T. (1904) *The Improvement of the Dwellings and Surroundings of the People: The Example of Germany*. Manchester: Manchester University Press.

Houghton-Evans, W. (1975) *Planning Cities: Legacy and Portent*. London: Lawrence and Wishart.

Howard, E. (1902/1965) *Garden Cities of Tomorrow* (edited by F.J. Osborne). London: Faber & Faber.

Huxley, M. (1993) 'Feminisms/urbanisms: women and cities in Australia' *Trames: revue de l'amenagement* (University of Montreal) 8: 126–31.

Huxley, M. (1994) 'Planning as a framework of power: Utilitarian reform, Enlightenment logic and the control of urban space', in Ferber, S., Healy, C. and McAuliffe, C. (eds) *Beasts of Suburbia: Reinterpreting Cultures in Australian Suburbs*. Melbourne: Melbourne University Press, 148–85.

Huxley, M. (2006) 'Spatial rationalities: order, environment, evolution and government' *Social and Cultural Geography* 7(5): 773–87.

Huxley, M. (2008a) 'Planning, space and government', in Cox, K., Low, M. and Robinson, J. (eds) *The Sage Handbook of Political Geography*. Thousand Oaks, CA: Sage, 123–40.

Huxley, M. (2008b) 'Space and government: governmentality and geography', *Geography Compass* 2(5): 1635–58.

Jacobs, J.M. (1996) *Edge of Empire: Postcolonialism and the City*. London: Routledge.

Jenkins, K. (ed.) (1997) *The Postmodern History Reader*. London: Routledge.

Joyce, P. (1997) 'The end of social history?', in Jenkins (ed.) (1997), 342–65.

Kendall, G. and Wickham, G. (1999) *Using Foucault's Methods*. London: Sage.

King, A. (1980) 'Exporting planning: the colonial and neo-colonial experience', in Cherry, G. (ed.) (1980), 203–26.

King, A. (1982) 'Town planning: a note on the origins and use of the term' *Planning History Bulletin* 4(2): 15–17.

Kirk, G. (1980) *Urban Planning in Capitalist Society*. London: Croom Helm.

Kruekeberg, D. (1997) 'Planning history's mistakes' *Planning Perspectives* 12: 269–79.

Ladd, B. (1990) *Urban Planning and Civic Order in Germany, 1860-1914*. Cambridge, MA: Harvard University Press.

Legg, S. (2007) *Spaces of Colonialism: Delhi's Urban Governmentalities*. Oxford: Blackwell.

Long, M. (1981) 'Planning: "Birth" or "Break"? Problems in the historiography of British town planning', Working Paper 18, Liverpool: Department of Civic Design, University of Liverpool.

Long, M. (1982) 'Moral Regime and Model Institutions: precursors of town planning in early Victorian England', Working Paper 20, Liverpool: Department of Civic Design, University of Liverpool.

Mabin, A. and Smit, D. (1997) 'Reconstructing South Africa's cities? The making of urban planning 1900–2000' *Planning Perspectives* 12(2): 193–223.

McDougall, G. (1978) 'The state, capital and land: the history of town planning revisited' *International Journal of Urban and Regional Research* 3(3): 361–80.

McGuiness, M. (1999) 'Post-Colonial Spaces? Interrogating the spaces of planning and theory', Doctoral thesis, School of Geography and Environmental Sciences, University of Birmingham.

Novik, A. (2007) 'City planning and urban history', in Stiftel, B., Watson, V. and Acselrad, H. (eds) *Dialogues in Urban and Regional Planning, Vol. 2*. Abingdon: Routledge, 268–96.

O'Farrell, C. (2005) *Michel Foucault*. London: Sage.

Osborne, F.J. (1965) 'Preface', in Howard, E. (1902/1965), 9–28.

Osborne, T. and Rose, N. (1999) 'Governing cities: notes on the spatialisation of virtue' *Environment and Planning D: Society and Space* 17: 737–60.

Osborne, T. and Rose, N. (2004) 'Spatial phenomenotechnics: making space with Charles Booth and Patrick Geddes' *Environment and Planning D: Society and Space* 22: 209–28.

Patton, P. (1998) 'Foucault's subject of power', in Moss, J. (ed.) *The Later Foucault: Politics and Philosophy*. London: Sage, 64–79.

Phillips, W. (1996) 'The "German example" and the professionalization of American and British city planning at the turn of the century' *Planning Perspectives* 11: 167–83.

Powell, J. (1991) *An Historical Geography of Modern Australia: The Restive Fringe*. Melbourne: Cambridge University Press.

Rabinow, P. (1989) *French Modern: Norms and Forms of the Social Environment*. Chicago: The University of Chicago Press.

Ritzdorf, M. (1994) 'A feminist analysis of gender and residential zoning in the United States', in Altman, I. and Churchman, A. (eds) *Women and the Environment*. New York: Plenum Press, 255–79.

Roberts, M. (1991) *Living in a Man Made World*. London: Routledge.

Robinson, J. (1996) *The Power of Apartheid: State, Power and Space in South African Cities*. Oxford: Butterworth Heinemann.

Robinson, J. (2000) 'Power as friendship: spatiality, femininity and "noisy surveillance"', in Sharp, J., Routledge, P., Philo, C. and Paddison, R. (eds) *Entanglements of Power: Geographies of Domination/Resistance*. London: Routledge, 67–92.

Rose, N. (1999) *Powers of Freedom: Reframing Political Thought*. Cambridge: Cambridge University Press.

Roweis, S. (1981) 'Urban planning in early and late capitalist societies: outline of a theoretical perspective', in Dear, M. and Scott, A. (eds) *Urbanization and Urban Planning in Capitalist Society*. London: Methuen, 159–77.

Sandercock, L. (1977) *Cities for Sale: Property, Politics and Urban Planning in Australia*. Melbourne: University of Melbourne Press.

Sandercock, L. (ed.) (1998a) *Making the Invisible Visible: A Multicultural Planning History*. Berkeley, CA: University of California Press.

Sandercock, L. (1998b) 'Introduction: framing insurgent historiographies for planning', in Sandercock, L. (ed.) (1998a), 1–36.

Scott, A. (1980) *The Urban Land Nexus and the State*. London: Pion.

Scott, M. (1969) *American City Planning since 1890*. Berkeley: University of California Press.

Silver, C. (1991) 'The racial origins of zoning: southern cities from 1910-40' *Planning Perspectives* 6: 189–205.

Smart, B. (2002) *Michel Foucault* (revised edition). London: Routledge.

Sulman, J. (1921) *An Introduction to the Study of Town Planning in Australia*. Sydney: Government Printer, NSW.

Sutcliffe, A. (1981) *Towards the Planned City: Germany, Britain, the United States and France 1780-1914*. Oxford: Blackwell.

Taylor, G. (1914) *Town Planning for Australia*. Sydney: Building Ltd.

Thomas, J.M. (1998) 'Racial inequality and empowerment: necessary theoretical constructs for understanding U.S. planning history', in Sandercock (ed.) (1998a), 198–208.

Thomas, J.M. (2006) 'Teaching planning history as a path to social justice' *Journal of Planning History* 5(4): 314–22.

Triggs, I. (1909) *Town Planning Past, Present and Possible*. London: Methuen & Co.

Unwin, R. (1909) *Town Planning in Practice: An Introduction to the Art of Designing Cities and Suburbs*. London: T. Fisher Unwin.

Valverde, M. (2005) 'Taking "land use" seriously: toward an ontology of municipal law', *Law Text Culture* 9(1): 34–59.

Valverde, M. (2006) 'A parliament of uses? A post-humanist approach to zoning law and politics in urban North America'. Paper to symposium on 'Local Spaces, Law and Rights' Bristol University School of Law, School of Geographical Sciences and Institute for Advanced Studies, 23 June. Unpublished ms.

Ward, S. (ed.) (1992) *The Garden City: Past, Present and Future*. London: E. & F.N. Spon.

Ward, S. (1994) *Planning and Urban Change*. London: Paul Chapman Publishing.

Ward, S. (2002) *Planning the Twentieth-Century City: The Advanced Capitalist World*. Chichester: John Wiley & Sons.

Weisman, L. (1992) *Discrimination by Design*. Urbana, IL: University of Illinois Press.

Wilson, E. (1991) *The Sphinx in the City: Urban Life, the Control of Disorder, and Women*. London: Virago Press.

Wirka, S. (1998) '*City Planning for Girls*: exploring the ambiguous nature of women's planning history', in Sandercock, L. (ed.) (1998a) *Making the Invisible Visible: A Multicultural Planning History*. Berkeley, CA: University of California Press. 150–62.

Yiftachel, O. (1995) 'The dark side of modernism: planning as control of an ethnic minority', in Watson, S. and Gibson, K. (eds) *Postmodern Cities and Spaces*. Oxford: Blackwell, 216–42.

Is This How It Is, or Is This How It Is Here? Making Sense of Politics in Planning

Wytske Versteeg and Maarten Hajer

I've been very disillusioned. Of course people are going to be self-interested, but I was surprised at the degree to which that's true, and at how people work very long and very hard simply to protect their own interests ... This is the first planning job I've had, and I often find myself wondering, 'Is this how it is, or is this how it is here?' ... It's also been a learning experience. This is my first job, and even though sometimes I'm not real happy with the way things go, I'm still learning a lot about politics.

The quotation above comes from John Forester's interview with the young planner Kristin (Forester 1993). Her words echo her disappointment now her first job as a planner has turned out to be full of politics. The transcript of the interview was published in 1990, so Kristin is probably an experienced planner by now. Yet her early observations about her experience with politics in planning are still of relevance. The step from planning school towards the daily practice of planning turned out to be the first time that Kristin was really confronted with politics in action. Of course, she knew that people were 'going to be self-interested', but that abstract textbook wisdom is hardly comparable to an encounter with politics real-life. It is the experience of politics that creates understandings that truly stick. But what *is* politics actually? What do we mean when we talk about power and politics in planning?

When it comes to politics, theoretical definitions abound. Politics is 'the authoritative allocation of values for a society' (Easton 1953), or the game that determines 'who gets what, when, and how', to use Lasswell's equally classic definition (Lasswell 1936). And Dahl describes his 'intuitive idea of power' as: 'something like this: A has power over B to the extent that he can get B to do something that B would not otherwise do' (Dahl 1957: 202), a definition later complemented by Lukes to include the less tangible forms of power as well (Lukes 1974). But these theoretically useful descriptions remain more or less at the same level of abstraction as the knowledge that 'of course people are going to be self-interested'. They tell us about the mechanisms of a phenomenon called politics, but they don't explain how people 'sense' power, or how the experience of power produces its social effects. Can we observe it, can we find ways to handle it in its manifestations?

These are questions that have deeply affected the communicative turn in planning. Stated differently, it was one of the core ideas of those theorists whose work later came to be known under the general heading of 'the communicative turn' that:

> communicative practices, that is, how people 'make sense' (Forester 1989) and generate energy in social interaction, are critical to the quality of developing intersubjective understanding and the mobilisation of attention. (Healey 2008: 9)

and that:

> the quality of planning practice therefore depends not solely on competence in analytical, design, engineering and management technique, but on 'communicative performance' and the ability to work with (to co-labour) with others with different perspectives and competences. (Healey 2008: 9)

Therefore, we do not need to ask ourselves whether or not the planning process is political, but *how* politics and the political manifest themselves within the planning process. Or, as Forester put it:

> we cannot just keep talking about power, power, power ... today we surely need to be more specific about 'power'. We need to ask how specifically it is political, and how does the variation – different political pressures in different circumstances – matter practically? (Forester 1999: 176)

Starting from Dewey's persuasive argument that the public will only be able to find its substance when communication is improved (Dewey 1927), we will here try to rethink the concept of politics in planning by focusing on its physical and spatial enactment in the context of governance networks. We argue that, whereas the communicative turn has paid ample attention to the discursive dimension of planning, it has generally underestimated the importance of its dramaturgy (see Hajer 2009 for an integrated approach). Studying the way in which planning is discursively and dramaturgically *performed* provides a starting point to analyze what constitutes a legitimate and literally 'representative' decision within the context of the newly-formed institutional sites within which planning activity is undertaken.

The New Spaces of Planning

The differentiation of planning from politics, and the attempt to separate facts and values, which dominated twentieth century planning theory, have been problematized by a whole generation of scholars. A substantial chunk of the work in planning theory during the 1970s and 1980s was devoted to finding, criticizing and handling power in planning (Healey et al. 1982). And even before then, some of the most famous studies in planning theory were devoted to precisely this issue (see Meyerson and Banfield 1955, and Banfield 1961). But since then, planning practices have changed and so has the issue of how politics features in planning activities.

Characteristic for our day and age is that standing representative institutions and top-down government intervention are often unable to solve pressing societal problems, whereas open-ended ad hoc arrangements demonstrate remarkable problem-solving capacity (Hajer and Wagenaar 2003). Under conditions of interdependence and radical uncertainty, interest-based collaborative governance networks of actors might solve problems that traditional legislative institutions cannot deal with. Governance networks are relatively stable sets of interdependent, but operationally autonomous actors, focused on joint problem solving. The networks characteristically consist of a polycentric, often transnational and almost necessarily multicultural collaboration of actors. They employ a strange mixture of formality and informality, and typically transgress the limits of traditional administrative units and layers, being somewhere 'in between' (see also Gualini in Chapter 1).

The implications of this development for the issue of politics in planning are far reaching. Whereas in the 'old' paradigm the threat was the 'iron triangle' formed by interest groups that clustered around the elected political leaders, this at least assumed a clear centre of power. In the current situation those who were on top of the classical-modernist democratic order – the elected representatives – are often portrayed as occupying a more marginal place. An indication of this is the sigh that can be heard when the actors cooperating in a governance network have worked out a solution that all regard as fair and intelligent: 'now, what do we do with the elected representative?' Governance networks typically thrive in the shadow; they remain invisible for the majority of citizens.

Simultaneously, there has emerged what might be called an industry of citizen forums, public hearings, public workshops and other forms of citizen participation. Interest groups, once the key threat to good political practice, have returned as 'stakeholders' and are, suddenly, seen as the solution to the problems of politics. The planning field has become pre-occupied with public participation: 'is there enough, is it the right sort, has sufficient account been taken of it?' (Rydin 1999: 84) Citizen input seems to be regarded as an almost universal good, so much so that some elected politicians feel unable or unjustified to decide without a 'sufficient' number of public workshops or hearings. As Campbell and Marshall observed:

161

A political adviser to a local politician commented that, ' We can only make a decision if we've had enough workshops'. This she regretted, stating that she hoped 'Berkeley would grow up' and consequently 'feel less guilty about exercising its authority and making decisions based on information and analysis and not political pressure'. (Campbell and Marshall 2000: 337)

Both in theory and in practice, the idea of citizen input tends to be regarded as motherhood and apple pie, as an almost universal good. But the focus on public participation can become problematic when normative and functionalist reasoning get conflated, when the move towards a more participative planning is justified *both* in terms of its effectiveness for the planning system, *and* as part of a grand normative endeavour towards a more communicative democracy. Inclusion of citizens in planning processes can be defended on the basis of normative reasons. The argument then is that institutions of strategic planning are not truly democratic, since they sustain inequality in political decision-making (for example, by the naturalization of routines, the canonization of texts and the exclusion of certain actors) and fail to provide sufficient *public* deliberation. Participation is then meant to find the 'right' solutions. A second line of argument would be functionalist in nature. New participants are approached as sources of previously institutionally suppressed knowledge, and public deliberation would help to provide solutions and take the 'better' decisions for pressing societal problems that existing institutions cannot deal with. This argument is well-expressed in a paper of Booher and Innes, on the topic of collaborative planning in the network society:

effective forms of strategic planning today are characterized by two features in particular: they are collaborative and they are self-organizing and adaptive to many unique conditions and problems. They are not hierarchical or bureaucratic, not dependent on authoritarian leadership, and not primarily grounded in the advice of technical experts. ... The knowledge they rely on is socially constructed and shared among experts and non-experts. The approach involves vision, but it is collectively created rather than the product of a single visionary. These strategies depend on power, but it is the power of networked relationships, shared information, identity and meaning. They produce coordinated action, not because of rules, top-down control or even formal requirements for coordination, but because players develop shared understandings, use similar heuristics and are governed by common norms. (Booher and Innes 2000: 176)

We here recognize the hope for progress, for 'a project of becoming' that is unquestionably characteristic for the communicative turn. Booher and Innes (2000: 189) presume that not only traditional planning procedures but also the very nature of representative democracy will change. Legislative institutions will become as ceremonial as the current monarchies, as the real decisions are made elsewhere. In contrast to this strong vision, most theorists presume that governance networks will not cause the state to wither away, but instead will continue to exist alongside the representative institutions and to complement these. According to this perspective, networks and participatory practices are particularly strong in solving a triple deficit hindering the effectiveness of classical-modernist practice – an implementation deficit, a learning deficit and a legitimacy deficit (Hajer 2009, chapter one). The *implementation deficit* describes the familiar situation in which a policy that has been politically agreed upon does not get implemented either because of practical realities that do not fit the policy plan, or because of resistance among key actors or citizens. The *learning deficit* refers to the difficulties in mobilizing and incorporating practical, often tacit, 'field' knowledge all through the various 'phases' of policy making (although the vocabulary of distinct phases is itself deeply problematic as collaborative planning suggests a continuous interaction). Collaborative governance networks and participatory practices imply a different organization of planning and policy making that allows for more regular interaction with those acting in the field, and are thus regarded as possible solutions for these two deficits. Finally, the *legitimacy deficit* refers to the complications that arise now the most pressing policy problems no longer respect the territorial scales along which constituencies are traditionally organized. As collaborative governance networks are organized along functional lines, ideally involving all those that are potentially affected by the decisions to be taken, it might help to solve this deficit. The same applies to participatory processes that draw on ideas of either direct or deliberative democracy.

Yet whereas collaborative processes might have the potential to solve or ameliorate these deficits, they should not be regarded as a panacea. The broader risk of a capture of the political process by interest groups should be a continued concern which goes to the heart of the theory of governance (see the response by Lowi 1999 to Sabel et al. 2000). The above quoted study by Campbell and Marshall (2000) provides us with a telling example of how participative practices often remain far removed from the effective ideal as imagined by Booher and Innes (2000). In this study, politicians showed themselves frustrated by the public hearings, and reacted by trying to find a course of action that would upset as few people as possible – that is, among those who were physically present. Their observation that 'the discussion has considerably muddied the waters' (Campbell and Marshall 2000: 337) might be attributed either to the 'bad quality' of that particular discussion, leading to a failure to generate any intelligent communication, or on the contrary to the fact that it had brought in relevant information that might slow down the policy process. In the latter case, it would certainly not be the first time in planning history for actors to be delegitimized because their concerns did not fit the terms like 'order', 'efficiency', 'environmental protection' and 'social learning' that planning histories are written around (Yiftachel 2002). The awareness of this bias in planning has been an important stimulus for encouraging the input of local, collectively created knowledge in planning processes.

Starting from that awareness, the longing expressed by the political adviser quoted above to 'feel less guilty about … making decisions based on information and analysis and not political pressure' (Campbell and Marshall 2000: 337) could be easily placed within the well known classical-modernist repertoire in which science could still speak 'truth to power' (Wildavsky 1979). Yet such a categorization would perhaps too easily neglect a legitimate wish to replace the haphazard participatory practices (as experienced by this political adviser) by an intelligent planning process. Critics warn that supplying local communities with proper information will not necessarily lead to wise participatory decision making (Rydin 1999). Others argue that the problem of legitimacy has been replaced by a problem of extension, that is, an indefinite extension of technical decision-making rights, dissolving any boundary between public and experts (Collins and Evans 2002). The plea for caution is timely and apposite; governance networks, participative politics and consensus building networks have altered the political landscape and the character of planning by providing institutional sites and solutions that the state cannot provide on its own.

Now that networks are a crucial part of planning practice, there is ample reason to take them as point of departure to formulate a new agenda. How is power exercised within these environments? How can it be kept in check? How can we evaluate the quality of public decisions, both in terms of their legitimacy and intelligence? To further this agenda we start by considering the way in which 'real' network governance matches the normative criteria and ideals as outlined in the theoretical literature on deliberative governance.

The Not so Ideal Speech Situation: Deliberation between Practice and Theory

To the extent that the literature is concerned with the normative aspects of network governance, it has become customary to assess the quality of these forms by applying continental European ideas on discourse ethics or American rules of deliberative democracy (see Habermas 1984, and Gutmann and Thompson 1996). The starting point for Habermas's concept of communicative reason is a question: how can people with different concepts of the good life reasonably shape their co-existence in a pluralist society? According to Habermas, a norm can only be valid if all those who might be affected by it reach (or would reach) agreement that the norm is valid. Validity claims are based on sincerity (the absence of deceit), rightness (or appropriateness within a given dialogical context) and truth (or representational adequacy). Thus, every form of authority has to be legitimated by a process of intersubjective judgment, governed by the force of better argument and a system of discursive ethics. The Habermasian model is idealist, in so far as it regards language and the exchange of ideas expressed in language as a source of social critique and reform, and knowledge as essentially emancipatory. In contrast to a more Foucauldian perspective, the ideal speech situation envisages power as subject to reason; the possibility of power free rationality – the force of the better argument – is the condition of Habermas's political thought (see, for example, Blotevogel 2000). The Habermasian 'ideal speech situation' can be used as a point of reference for evaluating actual practices of political deliberation, while still acknowledging that existing power relations do not, and probably could never, meet the criteria of these idealized circumstances. Communicative ethics is then used as a probing tool that helps to differentiate among forms of public debate.

Whether or not the Habermasian-inspired ideals can be realized in the real world remains the subject of debate. Some authors have pointed to the potential of deliberation to produce more tolerant, autonomous, sophisticated citizens, but other studies have shown that these positive findings are by no means self-evident (see Ryfe 2005 for an overview). Indeed, the ideals of a deliberative approach to planning are often inherently contradictory. For instance, Dryzek argues 'that outcomes are legitimate to the extent they receive reflective assent through participation in authentic deliberation by all those subject to the decision in question' (Dryzek 2001: 651). This leads Parkinson (2006: 4) to conclude that, as authentic deliberation can only be conducted with a very small number of participants and it is practically impossible to let 'all those subject to the decision' participate in governing, 'deliberative democratic practices cannot deliver legitimate outcomes as the theory defines them'. The work of Carolyn Lukensmeyer's *America Speaks*, staging deliberation among more than 1,000 participants at a time, suggests otherwise. Evaluations of her events are mixed but theorists like Fung, Poletta and Hajer have come up with favorable assessments (Polletta 2008; Hajer 2009). Hence the true empirical question is what it is that makes one practice of engagement successful while others are so obviously not delivering high quality ideas and broad legitimation.

Probably the most well known problem is the fact that white, educated middle class groups tend to be overrepresented in deliberative exercises. Political participation is easier for those who belong to groups that emphasize civic identity, and are well aware of the modes of conduct, accepted ways of argumentation, and particular logics of appropriateness in a political discussion. This kind of biased participation would hardly promote equality, legitimacy or the development of an encompassing deliberative mind. It is unlikely that political conflicts or questions of diversity are raised within homogeneous groups and if they are, they will be raised according to the frame characteristic of the particular group that dominates the deliberative setting.

Another dilemma is that between representation (or legitimacy) and learning. For obvious reasons, not all of those concerned can actively participate in the deliberations. The view of communities will have to be represented by individuals, even if it is not always clear what these communities are. When the deliberation is successful, the representative will learn from the views of other actors and initiate a change of perspective – she will learn, but with the risk that she ceases to represent her own community.

Political psychologists have pointed out that people are far less rational than most deliberative theories tend to assume. They are neither willing nor able to gather all relevant information, but form judgments and take decisions on the basis of routine scripts and snap shot information, media images, framing, symbols, existing affiliations, personal likings, etc. Reasoning, psychologists and cognitive scientists argue, tends to be unconscious rather than deliberative, even in small group settings (Lakoff 1996). If the explicit goal of deliberation is to disrupt routinized cognitive scripts and everyday reasoning habits, individuals have to be highly motivated to take this risk and the stress that inevitably comes with it. Three conditions are crucial to attain this motivation: accountability, diversity and high stakes. To be prepared to deliberate (which is not the same as to deliberate successfully!), one has to feel accountable to others, encounter others that are different from oneself and last but not least, feel *threatened* by others or by one's environment (Ryfe 2005: 56–57).

If we take the above into account, it is perhaps less surprising that a deliberative encounter leaves participants with feelings of frustration and disempowerment concerning their ability to influence the course of affairs on a particular topic. Indeed, they may grow doubtful whether there is a correct decision to be found at all ('the discussion has muddied the waters') or they may find themselves involved in taking a decision that is in conflict with their own opinion and is later regretted (Ryfe 2005: 54). Deliberative theorists sometimes promote participation as a goal in itself, but they tend to forget that intensive political participation occurs in most cases because people feel threatened, for example, by the decision to build a facility near to a beloved neighbourhood or park. It is hard to see how participants, starting from such an acute threat, should be able to see their situations in terms of flexible preferences instead of static interests, all the more so because they are often not allowed to discuss that very threat in the participative process. After all, such a self-interested stance conflicts with deliberative ideals of a civic identity and a common good. In most participatory processes, the accepted way of arguing is to reason in terms of the best possible outcome for the community as such, but this is a precondition that worried parents (to name just one example) do not (want to) meet, at least not initially. Moreover, participation processes typically allow for the discussion of the details of decisions, but not for debating the need of the decision itself. This is understandable in the light of political logic but can be deeply frustrating for participants. Arnstein (1969) has warned us about the different forms that 'participation' might take in practice and Amy's classic research into this matter (Amy 1983) showed, quite early on, that, whatever happens in participatory processes, 'the road gets built'. Frustrations that cannot be discussed can then create a sphere of antagonism between citizens and government representatives or between the various groups of stakeholders, leading to stultifying and bigoted debates (Campbell and Marshall 2000: 335).

All these findings suggest that we should be cautious both with the model of the ideal speech situation as a metaphor that easily steers our thinking, and with defending participation on the basis of a mixture of normative and functionalist arguments. Collaborative processes can provide a space for dialogue, but this depends heavily on the conditions under which they are conducted. The ideal of players collectively creating a joint vision, sharing information, appreciating identities and meaning, governed by common norms, conflicts with the preconditions of deliberation in the first place. Success is perhaps not the exception, but nor is it the rule. And, even when a legitimate consensus is reached in the collaborative process, decisions are often set aside by the standing institutions. Participating actors then might have to face a decision with which they do not agree, but against which they can hardly protest because they were involved in the preceding process. The unclear roles that collaborative processes can create might foster deception and distrust instead of active trust. Collaborative processes can disguise, rather than resolve, conflicts of interest (Abram 2000: 352–3).

In short: we value the communicative standards outlined by deliberative theory as a measuring rod to assess the legitimacy of the practices of the newly-emerging governance networks. But the cleavage between theoretical deliberative criteria on the one hand and empirical practice on the other hand (but see Thompson 2008), suggests that the concept of legitimacy might need further refinement in order to be of practical guidance. There might be an alternative way of thinking about sincerity, appropriateness and representational adequacy, and it is to this that we now turn.

Representing the Public

What exactly do we mean when we say a decision is 'legitimate'? Fung (2006: 70) calls a public policy or action legitimate when 'citizens have good reasons to support or to obey it'. Legitimacy would be endangered when a rift or disconnection emerges between public opinion and elected officials, a situation more likely to occur now the circles in which policy makers operate become more distant from those of ordinary citizens. In other words, a decision becomes illegitimate when those who take it do not sufficiently *represent* the general citizenry – if one can still speak of a 'general' citizenry in a society as fragmented as ours. The term representation is used most often in the context of an individual defending (or pretending to defend) the political interests of a larger group, and as such is strongly associated with the practices of the classical-modernist system. But it has an underlying, less cognitivist, meaning, namely the portrayal of something abstract or absent (Latour 2005). In this sense, parliament both literally and physically *re-presents* the demos, even if this is done in an imperfect way, and criticized by citizens (often rightly). How would we be able to understand 'democracy' when we could not engage in experiential practices such as the ritual of voting or the passing of a Bill? What would we make of parliamentary democracy if we could see or enter, that is directly experience, our parliamentary buildings, the site where important decisions are made (Mumford 1952; Goodsell 1988)?

However, although these classical-modernist symbols are still prominent in the media portrayal of politics, they hardly 'represent' the current practice of politics, policy and planning as outlined above. The governance networks as described above tend to be inchoate, lacking clear contours as they transgress the limits of traditional administrative units and layers, being somewhere 'in between'. As a consequence of these conditions – that form the very basis of their effectiveness in solving the implementation and the learning deficit, they literally show no face and often remain invisible to anyone not deeply involved. Thus, instead of simply solving the legitimacy deficit, the dominance of collaborative governance networks might merely lead to a different legitimacy problem.

For one, the invisibility of the new sites makes it hard to monitor and control the decisions that are made 'for the public good', but this invisibility also causes an even more fundamental complication. The classical-modern order presupposes an already existing, more or less coherent public whose representatives can deliberate and vote about planning decisions, which are subsequently implemented by administrators. In practice, a public is often only formed *after* decision making has taken place or, in other words, only when abstract politics has become concrete in a way that touches the very life of the 'citizens on standby' (Hajer 2003). This was one of the reasons behind the implementation deficit of classical-modernist politics. When planning tends to take place more and more in the context of multiple 'invisible' networks so that politics remains inchoate, this can inhibit the very *formation* of a public – with obvious consequences for the democratic quality of decision making.

Traditionally, planning activity has not been oriented to the sum of interests of the various groups of residents, but to an organic, unitary interest intrinsic to the city as a whole (Beauregard 2004: 148). Planners were trained to see themselves as the defenders of 'the public interest'. But as the advocacy planning of Davidoff *cum suis* has shown decades ago, 'the' public interest is hard to define, and the communicative turn has paid ample attention to that difficulty in subsequent years. But in the 1990s, attention to structural power and biased information systems made way for a more optimistic view of discursive communities, facilitated by planners, shaping their own future. It is perhaps significant that in 1989, Forester published a book with the cautious title *Planning in the Face of Power*, which was generally seen as a first landmark of the communicative turn, whereas a decade later he published *The Deliberative Practitioner* – a far more optimistic, but also a much more agency-focused and less political title.

Following this optimistic view, a certain current within the communicative turn tends to portray the planner as someone standing more or less outside the political process, helping the weaker groups to voice their concerns, guiding the deliberation towards a consensus and moving the planning process in some universal best direction. This representation runs the risk, argues Jean Hillier, that 'the identity and "facts" of the planner are essentialized as intrinsically rational, good and truth-bearing' (Hillier 2003). In line with an idealized view of deliberation and participation, he/she might be described as a process manager (as in collaborative planning), a storyteller (Mandelbaum) or a planner-author (e.g. Throgmorton). What these terms have in common is that they lack any obvious political connotation. Of course, authors like Throgmorton have emphasized time and again that the transformation of stories into narratives and the subsequent representation or telling of these narratives is necessarily selective and therefore inherently political. Nevertheless, the dominant impression remains that the planner herself has no real political power and continuously has to avoid being made either the handmaid or the dupe of the 'real' political actors in the process (Booher and Innes 2000: 6). For instance, although Throgmorton (2003) emphasizes the importance of representative power, he also states that 'planners could help imagine and create sustainable places by making space for diverse locally grounded common urban narratives (or community stories)'.

The problem in that endeavour is the suggestion that the construction of places is a matter of imagination. When Throgmorton stipulates that 'we choose to tell certain stories because they matter to us, and we tell them in certain ways because those ways of telling *feel* right' (2003: 145, emphasis in text), he emphasizes the agency of the planner and the actors involved – as if telling 'the' right story in the right way would ensure a 'right' planning process. In essence, the planner remains a blank figure – a neutral, benevolent storyteller engaged in the 'project of becoming'.

However, such an overtly optimistic perspective is dangerous as it overestimates the agency and discursive equality of the various actors within the planning process. For instance, local actors will often find it hard to defend their interests in the planning process because their worries frequently meet with an accusation of NIMBYism. Abram (2000) cites a case in which planners were so influenced by their ideal of providing homes for the homeless that they could only regard the concerns of residents of wealthy villages with a deep suspicion of elitism and exclusivity. This led them to ignore the real existing risk of social disorder and environmental degradation when the villages would be expanded into towns. Examples like these are a reminder of the fact that, even when the planner genuinely believes in serving 'the' public interest, there is a range of ideas and ideals that have to be balanced against each other. The judgment about which ideals should prevail cannot be solved by simply 'making space' for conflicting narratives, as these are often mutually exclusive. Thus any judgment is inherently political, as is the role of the planner as a persuasive storyteller. Any framework of criteria for both a legitimate and an intelligent planning process would therefore have to involve an assessment of what stories are judged to be persuasive and why, and why certain narratives have proved to be sustainable throughout the process whereas others seem to have simply disappeared. The question then becomes whether our current analytical tools are sufficient to be able to study those questions.

The Problem of Method

Following from the above, categories like politics, the public or power all become subject to *empirical* definition, that is to say categories for which we need to investigate the particular way in which they feature in the planning process. But how can we investigate politics in a scientifically sound way? Traditionally, the communicative turn has focused on language to answer that question. Discourse analysis and communicative research in general are employed to help discover the exercise of these more subtle types of power, for instance by exposing the non-naturalness of planning routines, discourses and the conditionality of expert authority. Moreover, many communicative theorists have confined themselves to the analysis of micro-practice, the '*fine grain of interaction*' (Healey 2003: 106). Highly detailed, ethnographic case studies might be called typical for the communicative turn. In-depth case studies do indeed provide a rich source of information and are necessary for discursive analysis, because only a high level of detail can generate knowledge about the particular way in which language is drawn upon in situated contexts, meaning is allocated and policy visions are translated in concrete practices. The studies of John Forester in particular clearly illustrate the value of such an approach.

But the disadvantage of narrowing the analytical scope to do justice to detail is that thick description can easily become a goal in itself. Context, first problematized because it was used as an exogenous explanation, at some point disappears. For instance, Hoch (1996: 43, as quoted in Fischler 2000) went as far to say that planning theorists would 'be better off becoming storytellers of practice', to reconstruct the personal and institutional narratives of struggle produced by practitioners. But by focusing solely on the micro-practice of the planner, the analysts run the risk of reification as they will not be able to study the more subtly pervasive forms of power. For instance, the analyst that uncritically accepts the transformative perspective of 'the planner as storyteller' runs the risk of uncritically accepting the goals of a planner or a planning procedure as they are officially stated. Yet spatial planning has been used more than once as a double-edged sword, simultaneously facilitating a 'rational' intervention and oppressing a minority or subordinate group. Even bottom-up planning procedures draw on the resources and regulations of state-related institutions. Thus, any analyst aiming to study politics in planning processes should keep an eye on the manifestation of these wider context dynamics within the particular planning process. After all, we cannot know whether this is how it is, or how it is *here* if we only study how it is here. The communicative turn would lose one of her most important trump cards – the questioning of normality – and any 'project of becoming' would be lost.

The above is not a new observation. It has also been recognized by some of the leading authors of the communicative turn. They developed analytical frameworks in order to be able to study the variation of different political pressures in different circumstances. Forester followed Lukes (1974), Habermas (1984) and Foucault (1980), and discerned three types of 'power': 1) the ability to make decisions; 2) the ability to filter issues; and 3) the ability to shape others' perceptions of issues, needs and even themselves (Forester 1999: 185). The first type of power – the power of decision making – is relatively well-known and easy to observe. The second and third types are more complicated to study, but have grown in importance with the emergence of governance networks. These are the powers that determine which issues are put on the agenda and receive political attention, and which do not; the powers of inclusion and exclusion, of the active shaping of publics and identities and even of defining normality. Surely this power will manifest itself in the micro-interaction between the actors of a collaborative network and is thus observable, but it is ultimately connected to influence structures on a meso- and macrolevel. Recognizing this, Healey and Coaffee (2003) developed an analytical framework in which they discern three levels of power relations present in any interaction. At the microlevel, there is the power of specific episodes; the power of interpersonal relationships, of actors, arenas or institutional sites and ambiances or communicative repertoires. At a more mesolevel, one finds the power relations of governance processes and the bias that is mobilized in institutionalized practices; stakeholder selection procedures, networks and coalitions, discourses (including the way in which issues are framed) and practices (defined as routines and repertoires for action) are situated here. Finally, there is the level of governance cultures; the range of accepted modes of governance, embedded cultural values and the (in)formal cultures of policing discourses and practices.

Collaborative governance networks have to keep relating to these institutional environments in order to be politically successful, or even sustainable. Thus, any attempt at persuasion has to connect to the accepted communicative repertoires, but also to practices and embedded cultural values. Research into planning processes should embrace at least these three levels. When the planner has to be a persuasive storyteller in order to be politically successful, the question is not only what his persuasion consists of within the specific episode and the interpersonal relations of the planning process, the concrete power of decision making. We should also ask how his or her persuasion fits (or does not fit) in the power relations of governance processes and institutional practices, and finally in the governance cultures and embedded cultural values, as it is in these higher levels that the ability to filter issues and shape perceptions manifests itself.

Of course, the above strategy runs a risk of circular reasoning, when it would be suggested that a story line is persuasive because it fits the power relations of governance, etc. This risk is aggravated by the tendency to focus on case studies, analyzing only a tiny fragment of the policy process. The trick to avoid this risk (or the scientific rigour, if you like), is that the researcher investigates the ways in which the various levels of power relations get mobilized, even if this is only through an anticipation of the limits set by certain contextual 'variables', something which one might find out through in-depth interviewing and longitudinal cases that would enable us to study long-term developments.

A final methodological problem in analyzing how power is mobilized and assessing the legitimacy of collaborative governance networks seems to be the way in which our theoretical standards are overtly rationalist and language based. For instance, Tait and Campbell (2000) observed that there are important difficulties in connecting the ideas of both Habermas and Foucault to everyday planning practice. Both theories fail to connect language to its local, ambiguous, material practices, that is, to the detailing of how the discursive moment is given specific form. Ryfe suggests that:

> [I]f we grant that deliberation looks like storytelling, then we have to rethink the theoretical link between reason and autonomy ... The cognitive literature suggests that we will find deliberation to be episodic, difficult, and tentative. Within any particular interaction, deliberation may ebb and flow as participants alternately resist and accept the challenge of deliberation. And we will find that deliberation sustains itself through these conversational

> *eddies by means of the co-construction of identities and values that keep*
> *people motivated and engaged. (Ryfe 2005: 59–60)*

When we conceptualize the participative process as the building of a shared identity, we see how ideas about sincerity, appropriateness and representational adequacy are gradually and intersubjectively construed and negotiated. These norms and the relationships between the various actors do not develop solely by means of cognitivist language, but in an embodied spatial-temporal interaction. Although the literature manifests a strong awareness that people do things with words (Austin 1962), we sometimes forget that settings do things with people too.

We argue that there is a need to enhance insight into the link between the discursive and the non-discursive, material practices that together constitute the cultural context of collaborative governance networks. When we want to understand how collaborative governance networks can come to a legitimate and intelligent decision, we need to analyze the way in which such a network develops itself as a temporary community, including its narratives, myths and logics of appropriateness (or accepted modes of behaviour, see below). Here a performative approach might help to bridge the gap between discursive and material practices, and between the micro, and the meso and macrolevel (Hajer 2005b). Planning should then not only be analyzed as a discursive exchange, but also in dramaturgical terms.

The Project of Becoming: The Manifestation of Politics in Planning Processes

The dramaturgical take on processes of planning or policy making is of course not new. Its origins might be found in Aristotles' account of rhetorics. More recent examples of this tradition include Burke (1969), Edelman (1964), Goffman (1959), Merelman (1969), Alexander et al. (2006) and Hajer (2009). The planning field is a profession where language is non-verbal at least as often as it is verbal. As Forester argues:

> *planners need to solve analytic problems ... in spatial and political contexts*
> *in which the way in which they articulate their results will matter. Analytic*
> *techniques matter, but so do strategies of representation (visual and textual,*
> *graphical and electronic), and capacities of argumentation, mediation, and*
> *public deliberation – and all these can be done better or worse. [italics in*
> *original] (Forester 1999: 176)*

Images increasingly receive a coordinating role and can serve as glue – or, on the contrary, as the origin or the first clear manifestation of conflict in the vulnerable interaction of a collaborative network. Neuman describes how Spanish planners used a gradually evolving, conceptual image to craft and implement a planning strategy – 'drawing the sketch was the first thing that interviewees did when explaining the project' (Neuman 1996: 305). Images, Neuman argues, are relevant to planning because we see issues in a new light by changing our mental, internal image. The importance of images as nodal points only grows as metropolitan planning and governance become more fragmented.

According to a dramaturgical perspective, practices of participation 'construct' their participants not only by the type of arguments that can be raised, but also by the physical, technical or theatrical conditions (compare for example, Jasanoff 1990). When we argue that the planning process is *performed,* we refer to the way in which the contextualized interaction itself produces social realities including understandings of the problem at hand, knowledge and new power-relations. This becomes all the more important if we examine planning activities taking place in networks and discourses that are relatively unstable as compared to the continuity of the classical-modernist system. Whereas established institutions can generally draw on a culture that has been in place for years (and carefully designed, see (Heurtin 2005), this does not apply to ad hoc governance networks, citizen forums and mini publics. As analysts, we have to appreciate how those newly-formed networks, often consisting of actors from different cultural backgrounds, gradually develop a shared convention. However, there exists a strong tendency to distinguish in a normative way between form and function, between ritual and substance. For instance, Campbell and Marshall observe that:

> It is ... striking in listening to participatory encounters how little of the discussion is devoted to substance and how much to the maintenance of meetings. The example of WOCAG is intriguing in this connection as it consisted entirely of members of the community and therefore in theory should not be constrained in its practices by the norms of bureaucratic agencies. Despite such circumstances the membership showed a positive desire to adopt the trappings of public-sector organizations and establish order through similar procedural devices. The ground rules set out in these procedures were crucial in establishing who could speak and when, who could sit where, when a motion could be made and by whom and whose comments were recorded and in what form. The ritualistic qualities of the discussions about such matters and their regular re-enforcement during the course of a meeting are inherent to the shadow boxing which goes on within any group of personalities. (Campbell and Marshall 2000: 337)

What is here described as 'trappings' or 'shadow boxing' might be a crucial element of the process – an element with the ability to reflect, reproduce, but also the potential to change the power relationships of both the group and the wider context in which it has to operate. Before even being able to speak about the problem at hand, which in itself might be different for the different actors involved, group members have to develop a consensus about what are and what are not accepted modes of behaviour (see Hajer and Versteeg 2005). March and Olsen (1989) define this as a *logic of appropriateness*. Actors have to find out their role during the process.

They will have to establish an identity within the group and sort out the obligations and entitlements that come with it. 'Common sense' will have to be collectively created: one or several group rationalities might emerge during the planning process and subsequently acquire a binding function. These rationalities serve to lend legitimacy to the process in the eyes of the actors involved, help to develop a shared identity and – in the ideal case – a language that all actors can relate to. They can, however, just as well exclude certain groups, thus threatening the legitimacy of the process.

Material dimensions are of crucial importance for the development of any logic of appropriateness, as the room in which a particular meeting takes place will provide actors with cues about what is expected from them. As Perrin put it:

> ... the setting in which a citizen finds herself helps structure whether, and how, she talks about important issues ... Talk is not political, democratic or imaginative in the abstract ... And, crucially, the parameters and group style of a setting can make talk less political, less democratic, and less imaginative. Settings are sites that promote and inhibit the development and expression of the democratic imagination. [italics in original] (Perrin 2006: 52)

If we want to assess the legitimacy of a particular planning process, we therefore should investigate the *setting*, the physical situation(s) in which the interactions take place. The active manipulation of the setting is called *staging*, including the use of existing symbols and the invention of new ones, as well as the distinction between active players and the (presumably) passive audience. For instance, the degree of formality (or, in Goffman's terms, 'tightness') of a particular governance network can be conveyed by markers such as the location of meetings, the spatial arrangement of the physical environment, the demeanour of the principal participants, their physical proximity to the audience within the setting and the degree to which the sequence of acts and the range of activities permitted during a meeting are codified in advance (Futrell 1999: 503). Efforts to create a setting by determining the characters in the process and to provide cues for appropriate behavior, are here referred to as *scripting*. Planners will not always be able to script a planning process, and they will seldom be able to script a process without being confronted with counter scripts. Often, the evolving logic of appropriateness within the collaborative network will cause them to improvise, drawing maps and sketches on the spot – but always in the awareness of an audience.

But 'audience' might be the inappropriate term, having an implication of passivity. Perhaps we should better ask ourselves under what circumstances a passive audience is transformed into an active public, if we want to address the question of legitimacy in planning processes. In trying to answer this question, Dewey (1927) emphasized the importance of face-to-face dialogue. Shared signs, symbols and language of immediate interaction would instantiate, revitalize and complete the broken, frozen written words. It is hard to envisage his idea of a great community of shared communication. After all, it seems as impossible to identify one public within a planning process as it is to defend a single 'public interest'.

Even when we regard the planning process as one single drama, consisting of a series of (often not logically ordered) performances and the planner as one of the protagonists, we have to consider the different languages he or she speaks in various situations. Different publics ask for different approaches. The meaning of things is dependent upon the perspective of the viewer. What can be inviting for one potential public, can be repulsive for another. Different publics will sometimes read settings and storylines in radically different ways, as their experience and previously existing knowledge influences their categorizing of events. It therefore requires a thorough contextual knowledge to be able to interpret how an event will be 'read' by a particular public (see Hajer and Versteeg 2008). In a sense, content here follows form; the fluency with which the planner speaks the language of the public will be a crucial factor in the decision of the latter whether or not to trust the planning process. The planner in turn will often have to connect these different audiences with their conflicting interests, to get the various actors behind a single plan. In order to attain a legitimate decision, this plan has to be both understandable for and acceptable to all those involved.

It is not only that the performance of the planning process is itself framed by rules, such as about what is and what is not appropriate behaviour for a planner vis-à-vis his/her audience or for an audience vis-à-vis 'the experts', but also that it generates a new reality, with its owns norms and values about how to behave. Within the context of the planning process, actors negotiate and renegotiate identities, while proposing and trying out actions and stories that might express or contest existing normative orders. In order to be able to tell a persuasive story, the planners have to be aware of the different ways in which the various publics feel themselves connected to the places involved. They have to deal with the emotions and conflicts that might come about as a consequence of the questions raised by the confrontation between various narratives and with the transformations that can or will occur in the identities of the public during the planning process. It is crucial to appreciate that a (proposed) planning decision might *in itself* create new publics and can change relationships between actors in a radical way (Hajer 2003).

Artefacts play a crucial role in this collective process of sense-making. These are props that can be used, more or less successfully, to address a particular audience. Graphics, maps and images often function as focal points for collaborative meetings, and some artefacts come with particular assumptions about what behaviour is appropriate. For instance, the maps that are used in a particular planning process can be easy to understand for the general public, thereby *drawing* in the audience and creating a 'dramaturgical loyalty' (Goffman 1959; Benford and Hunt 1992) to the process (see Hajer 2005b, 2009), or in the terms we used before; transforming a passive audience into a participating public. Or they can be very technical, abstract and hard to read, emphasizing the expert authority of the planners responsible and enlarging the gap between them and the public. Or maps that actors have commonly drawn in a design session can painfully visualize the gaps between the different visions of the various actors that had until then happily cooperated (Poorter and Versteeg 2006). Interestingly, the website of a community consultation initiative like Planning for Real® describes the consultation process largely in terms of its artefacts: (blank) option cards, three-dimensional model making and visual hands-on techniques. On a far less technical level than these participatory GIS projects, policy makers are aware of the dramaturgical dimension as well. For instance, planners from the Dutch Ministry of Transport, Public Ways and Water Management told us how they had pondered about the apt place for a first meeting with farmers. Should the farmers be invited to a posh meeting hall in the city to show them they were taken seriously, or should the planners travel to the small village involved and organize the meeting in a community house in order to diminish the gap?

Both planners and policy makers are often surprisingly well aware of their audiences – of the fact that they are performing and that they are being watched and judged for their performance, including the *mise-en-scène*. This is also where the correction to more traditional communicative accounts lies. These tend to describe the participants as alternatively speakers and listeners, engaged in a cooperative effort to achieve mutual understanding. However, it is far more likely that some specialization will occur, with the majority taking a supporting role, while only a few occupy centre stage. Communication then becomes oriented to persuading the audience, not necessarily physically present in the room, instead of achieving mutual understanding with one's interlocutors (Parkinson 2007: 5). Any communicative repertoire has to connect to a broader discourse – both influenced by and influencing networks and political coalitions – that is again related to the accepted modes of governance. In other words: the stories that are told in the planning process are not freely floating around. Even in local planning processes, the media can play a crucial role in favoring the 'story suitability' (Gans 1979) of some stakeholders rather than others. Neither the planner nor the other actors are free to simply tell a story that 'feels right'; scripting, setting and staging are factors that can influence the durability of a particular claim or storyline within the policy process. A setting is not chosen freely, but in line with the political goals to be attained and with the existing informal policy culture. Put alternatively, if a setting is chosen freely it might run the risk of being irrelevant in the context of a given power network. Persuasive as a story may be, ultimately it also has to be told to and implemented by institutions that follow their own stories, procedures and rules. A strong awareness both of the broader political-economic context and the way in which this broader context is instantiated, played out and changed in a micro-context of setting and staging, is crucial for any planner to be successful.

Does this imply research into planning and politics should be conducted with two feet on the ground? Yes it does, but let's not forget the lessons learned since the days of the neo-Marxist and structuralist hegemony. The emergence of the communicative paradigm in the 1990s was also a re-appreciation of the contingency of planning processes. Not all is set in stone. The study of the rebuilding of Ground Zero in New York is a case in point (Hajer 2005a, 2009). Although the legal rights to rebuild were clear, and although the economic power of the developer and the owner of the land was unrivalled, the process nevertheless took many different turns as the planning process was not only about those interests. It had a profound symbolic dimension as well. While this might be simple to accept in the case of

Ground Zero (with 'survivors' and families of 'victims' as stakeholders that could not be discounted), the principles are the same everywhere. Even if there is a layer of basic interests and legal rights, there is always also a layer at which those interests and rights can be questioned, changed or transformed. The physical conditions – the staging and scripting – of a collaborative process can heavily influence its quality and openness. The staging and scripting of a planning process influences which roles the actors receive, who are the active participants, who is to be the audience, who is to be persuaded. These are crucial themes for empirical planning studies, leading us to investigate the particular conditions under which the questioning and potential transformation of interests and rights may or may not occur, and to explain why. The answers to questions like these will ultimately determine both the quality and the legitimacy of any collaborative process.

The Articulation of Conflict

Unfortunately, adding a dramaturgical dimension is not solving all our problems and again, the risk of reification is looming. A dramaturgical approach could reduce the 'project of becoming' to a smoothly scripted process (see Maginn 2007). The planning process could acquire temporal performative legitimacy by means of collectively experienced transition rituals, or well-orchestrated moments of staged consensus, but ultimately fail in the follow-up with potentially disastrous results for the authority and legitimacy of the procedure. This happened, for instance, in the way in which architect Daniel Libeskind enchanted the public with his very personal presentation of his plans for the rebuilding of the WTC or the way in which Carolyn Lukesmeyer and *America Speaks* performed the public participation in the setting of the Jarvis Center in one single day with more than 5,000 people present. Scripting, setting and staging are crucial elements for attaining legitimacy in today's unstable policy environments, but a persuasive planning procedure is not necessarily democratic or honest for all actors involved. One only needs to think of the persuasive, theatrical powers of authoritarian regimes. Nor does it have to lead to 'the best' qualitative result in terms of content. The actor who knows best to engage his audience does not have to have the best plans. Moreover, a presentation or image that works well in a specific episode – Libeskind's 'Life Victorious' is probably the best example – does not always connect to the relevant governance processes and cultures, as became painfully clear in New York (see Hajer 2005a).

For the analyst, this implies a need to zoom out, asking whether a particular performance brings about a transformation not only in terms of specific episodes, but also on the level of governance processes and even governance cultures. The important question is not in the first place whether consensus is reached, but whether the performances of the planning process create a meandering conversation that allows a variety of people to join the policy deliberation in a meaningful way and that allows for new points of view, new insights, new knowledges, to be taken into account. Moreover, we should ask ourselves which publics, perspectives and narratives are supported and carried forward throughout the process, and which seem to simply 'disappear' during the consensus building dialogues, and why this is the case. We might have to look for what is not as much as for what is.

The possibility of conflict helps to allow for a variety of expressions and, in the words of Chantal Mouffe (1999), to transform 'antagonisms' into 'agonisms', that is, to make conflicts among enemies who turn against the system into conflicts among adversaries who share a commitment to the system (compare for instance Hillier 2003). This is a crucial quality of democracy. A setting would acquire democratic quality if it allows for, or indeed triggers or provokes, an interplay of opinions that allows for interactive preference formation. A basic criterion for legitimacy would be whether or not the process allows for the articulation of conflict – not only on the level of specific episodes, but also on the level of governance processes and cultures. Relevant questions could be whether all potential audiences are addressed, including those publics that are themselves created through the very planning decision; in what ways the different audiences are addressed; what – if any – possibilities there are for role changes from audience to actor and vice versa; to what extent can the scripting and staging be influenced by the various actors concerned; to what extent can the different persuasive stories exist next to each other; in what ways they can relate and interact with each other; which publics are sustained and which are not; etc. In sum, we have to ask ourselves in what concrete forms the politics of persuasion manifests itself within the planning process. The perception of issues – the most subtle form of power – is shaped not only by the force of the better argument, but also and crucially by the staging, setting and scripting that influence what can be said and what can be said with influence. In that sense, the planning process could literally be analyzed as a 'project of becoming'.

Conclusion

Communicative planning theory has added valuable insights to our understanding of how power can be exercised by language, rituals, procedures, and of how political interests are formed in the first place. This is all the more important now collaborative networks seem to have fundamentally altered the planning landscape, whereas we still lack the criteria to judge their democratic legitimacy. Although the communicative turn has concerned itself with the ways in which the planner has to persuade actors within the context of collaborative networks, it has often overemphasized the role of the planner as a benevolent, helping actor. For future empirical analysis, it seems crucial not only to acknowledge the importance of discursive power and politics for the planning process, but to further develop a sophisticated account of the specific ways in which power manifests itself within the material dimensions and the (re)presentation of the planning process. A performative approach could be of help in the attempt to bridge the gap between micro- and macro context, and between discursive and non-discursive practices.

The move from communicative planning to performing deliberative planning is not at all a trivial project. We are currently experiencing a host of initiatives which employ dramaturgical techniques, not to allow people in, or to try and come to the best possible solution or to maximize the legitimacy of a solution, but to simply stylize politics as if this is the case. These days publics are not so much heard as created. Recent research by Reynolds and Szerszynski (Reynolds et al. 2007) showed how the UK government uses particular techniques to differentiate the 'true' public and the 'real' citizen from the partisan publics and stakeholders. Yet what they illuminate is that in this process of differentiation the government basically excluded everybody with a considered opinion from the 'general public'. This example is a reminder that public opinion does not exist but is performed, whether through opinion polls, media portrayal or participatory practices. It is our task to illuminate the influence of the process on the opinion and on the outcome. And it remains our task to think about the most appropriate ways of conducting planning processes, in the awareness that they are always performed.

References

Abram, S.A. (2000) 'Planning the public: some comments on empirical problems for planning theory' *Journal of Planning Education and Research* 19: 351–57.

Alexander, J., Giesen, B. and Mast, J. (2006) *Social Performance: Symbolic Action, Cultural Pragmatics and Ritual.* Cambridge: Cambridge University Press.

Amy, D. (1983) 'The politics of environmental mediation' *Ecology Law Quarterly* 11: 1–19.

Arnstein, S. (1969) 'A ladder of citizen participation' *Journal of the American Planning Association* 35: 216–24.

Austin, J. (1962) *How to do Things with Words.* Cambridge, MA: Harvard University Press.

Banfield, E. (1961). *Political Influence: A New Theory of Urban Politics.* New York: Free Press.

Beauregard, R. (2004) 'Mistakes were made: rebuilding the World Trade Center, phase 1' *International Planning Studies* 9: 139–53.

Benford, R.D. and Hunt, S.A. (1992) 'Dramaturgy and social movements: the social construction and communication of power' *Sociological Inquiry* 62.

Blotevogel, H. (2000) 'Rationality and discourse in (post)modern spatial planning', in Salet, W. and Faludi, A. (eds) *The Revival of Strategic Spatial Planning.* Amsterdam: KNAW.

Booher, D. and Innes, J. (2000) *Network Power in Collaborative Planning.* University of California at Berkeley Institute of Urban and Regional Development.

Burke, K. (1969) *A Grammar of Motives.* Berkeley, CA: University of California Press.

Campbell, H. and Marshall, R. (2000) 'Public involvement and planning: looking beyond the one to the many' *International Planning Studies* 5: 321–44.

Collins, H. and Evans, R. (2002) 'The third wave of science studies' *Social Studies of Science* 32: 235–96.

Dahl, R.A. (1957) 'The concept of power' *Behavioural Science* 2: 201–15.

Dewey, J. (1927) *The Public and its Problems.* New York: Henry Holt and Company.

Dryzek, J. (2001) 'Legitimacy and economy in deliberative democracy' *Political Theory* 29: 651–69.

Easton, D. (1953) *The Political System.* New York: Alfred A. Knopf.

Edelman, M. (1964) *The Symbolic Uses of Politics.* Urbana, IL: University of Illinois Press.

Fischler, R. (2000) 'Communicative planning theory: a Foucauldian assessment' *Journal of Planning Education and Research* 19: 358–68.

Forester, J. (1989) *Planning in the Face of Power.* Berkeley, CA: University of California Press.

Forester, J. (1993) 'Learning from practice stories' in Fischer, F. and Forester, J. (eds) *The Argumentative Turn in Policy Analysis and Planning.* Durham, NC: Duke University Press.

Forester, J. (1999) 'Reflections on the future understanding of planning practice' *International Planning Studies* 4: 175–93.

Foucault, M. (1980) *Power/Knowledge: Selected Interviews and Other Writings 1972–1977.* New York: Pantheon.

Fung, A. (2006) 'Varieties of participation in complex governance' *Public Administration Review* 66: 66–75.

Futrell, R. (1999) 'Performance governance: impression management, teamwork, and conflict containment in city commission proceedings' *Journal of Contemporary Ethnography* 27: 494–529.

Gans, H. (1979) 'Deciding what's news: story suitability' *Society* 16: 65–77.

Goffman, E. (1959) *The Presentation of Self in Everyday Life.* New York: DoubleDay.

Goodsell, C.T. (1988) *The Social Meaning of Civic Space: Studying Political Authority through Architecture.* Lawrence, KS: University Press of Kansas.

Gutmann, A. and Thompson, D. (1996) *Democracy and Disagreement.* Cambridge, MA: Harvard, Belknap Press.

Habermas, J. (1984) *The Theory of Communicative Action.* Boston, MA: Beacon Press.

Hajer, M. (2003) 'A frame in the fields: policymaking and the reinvention of politics', in Hajer, M. and Wagenaar, H. (eds) *Deliberative Policy Analysis; Understanding Governance in the Network Society.* Cambridge: Cambridge University Press, 88–110.

Hajer, M. (2005a) 'Rebuilding Ground Zero. The politics of performance' *Planning Theory and Practice* 6: 445–64.

Hajer, M. (2005b) 'Setting the stage: a dramaturgy of policy deliberation' *Administration and Society* 36: 624–47.

Hajer, M. (2009) *Authoritative Governance: Policy-making in the Age of Mediatization.* Oxford: Oxford University Press.

Hajer, M. and Versteeg, W. (2005) 'Performing governance through networks' *European Political Science* 4: 340–7.

Hajer, M. and Versteeg, W. (2008) 'The limits to deliberative governance' *Annual Meeting of the American Political Science Association Conference.* Boston.

Hajer, M. and Wagenaar, H. (2003) *Deliberative Policy Analysis: Understanding Governance in the Network Society.* Cambridge: Cambridge University Press.

Healey, P. (2008) 'The idea of "communicative" planning: practices, concepts and rhetorics; talk to MIT series on the "History of Planning Ideas", Boston. 2nd draft 10 April 2008. To be published in forthcoming volume, *History of Planning Ideas.* Editors: Sanyal, B., Vale, L. and Rosan, C.

Healey, P. and Coaffee, J. (2003) ' "My voice, my place": tracking transformations in urban governance' *Urban Studies* 40: 1979–99.

Healey, P., McDougall, G. and Thomas, M. (1982) *Planning Theory: Prospects for the 1980s.* Oxford: Pergamon.

Heurtin, J.-P. (2005) 'The circle of discussion and the semicircle of criticism' in Latour, B. and Weibel, P. (eds) *Making Things Public; Atmospheres of Democracy.* Karlsruhe: ZKM/MIT Press, 754–69.

Hillier, J. (2003) ' "Agon"izing over consensus; why Habermasian ideals cannot be "Real"' *Planning Theory* 2: 37–59.

Hoch, C. (1996) 'A pragmatic inquiry about planning and power', in Mandelbaum, S.J., Mazza, L., and Burchell, R.W. (eds) *Explorations in Planning Theory.* New Brunswick, NJ: Center for Urban Policy Research, Rutgers University, 30–44.

Jasanoff, S. (1990) *Risk Management and Political Culture.* New York: Russell Sage Foundation.

Lakoff, G. (1996) *Moral Politics: How Liberals and Conservatives Think.* Chicago, IL: University of Chicago Press.

Lasswell, H. (1936) *Who Gets What, When, and How?* New York: McGraw-Hill.

Latour, B. (2005) *Making Things Public: Atmospheres of Democracy.* Karslruhe: ZKM/ MIT Press.

Lowi, T. (1999) 'Frontyard propaganda' *Boston Review,* 24.

Lukes, S. (1974) *Power: A Radical View.* New York: Macmillan.

Maginn, P. (2007) 'Deliberative democracy or discursively biased? Perth's dialogue with the city initiative' *Space and Polity* 11: 331–52.

March, J.G. and Olsen, J.P. (1989) *Rediscovering Institutions: The Organizational Basis of Politics.* New York: Free Press.

Merelman, R. (1969) 'The dramaturgy of politics' *The Sociological Quarterly* 10: 216–41.

Meyerson, M. and Banfield, E. (1955) *Politics, Planning, and the Public Interest: The Case of Public Housing in Chicago.* Glencoe: The Free Press.

Mouffe, C. (1999) 'Deliberative democracy or agonistic pluralism? *Social Research* 66: 745–58.

Mumford, L. (1952) *Art and Technics.* New York: Columbia University Press.

Neuman, M. (1996) 'Images as institution builders: metropolitan planning in Madrid' *European Planning Studies* 4: 293–312.

Parkinson, J. (2006) *Deliberating in the Real World.* Oxford: Oxford University Press.

Parkinson, J. (2007) 'Does democracy require physical public space?' *Democracy: Theory and Practice Conference.* Manchester Centre for Political Theory.

Perrin, J. (2006) *Citizen Speak: The Democratic Imagination in American Life*. Chicago: University of Chicago Press.

Polletta, F. (2008) 'Just talk: public deliberation After 9/11' *Journal of Public Deliberation*, 4.

Poorter, M. and Versteeg, W. (2006) *ICES-KIS: Grenzen aan publieke participatie bij waterbeheer*. Noordwaard, Amsterdam.

Reynolds, L., Szerszynski, B., Kousis, M. and Volakakis, Y. (2007) GM Food – The Role of Participation in a Techno-Scientific Controversy, final report of WP6, Work Package 6, of the EC project Participatory Governance and Institutional Innovation (PAGANINI). (available at http://www.univie.ac.at/LSG/paganini/output.htm).

Rydin, Y. (1999) 'Public participation in planning'. in Cullingworth, B. (ed.) *British Planning: 50 Years of Urban and Regional Planning*. London: The Athlone Press, 184–97.

Ryfe, D. (2005) 'Does deliberative democracy work?' *Annual Review of Political Science* 8: 49–71.

Sabel, C., Fung, A., Karkkainen, B., Cohen, J. and Rogers, J. (2000) *Beyond Backyard Environmentalism*. Boston: Beacon Press.

Tait, M. and Campbell, H. (2000) 'The politics of communication between planning officers and politicians: the exercise of power through discourse' *Environment and Planning A* 32: 489–506.

Thompson, D. (2008) 'Deliberative democratic theory and empirical poltical science' *Annual Review of Political Science* 11: 497–520.

Throgmorton, J.A. (2003) 'Planning as persuasive storytelling in a global-scale web of relationships' *Planning Theory* 2: 125–51.

Wildavsky, A. (1979) *Speaking Truth to Power: The Art and Craft of Policy Analysis*. Boston: Little Brown.

Yiftachel, O. (2002) 'The dark side of modernism: planning as a control of an ethnic minority', in Bridge, G. and Watson, S. (eds) *The Blackwell City Reader*. Boston: Blackwell.

Role Conflict: Planners Torn Between Dialogical Ideals and Neo-liberal Realities[1]

Tore Sager

Introduction: Roles and Values

The purpose of this chapter is to show that the current role of planners, in a number of societies where neo-liberal ideas play an important part in shaping economic-political life, contains tensions which affect negatively the everyday working conditions of many planners. Although planners in a variety of administrations and public agencies will presumably recognize the conflicting demands analyzed in this chapter, the planners most likely to feel the cross pressure are employed in the regional or county offices of national or state agencies (for example, in Norway, the Public Roads Administration or the Water Resources Administration). They work on local plans and projects developed through processes that include citizen participation, and their administration has in many cases been reorganized in accordance with neo-liberal management ideals.

The tensions under scrutiny here spring from differences between Communicative Planning Theory (CPT) and New Public Management (NPM) regarding the kind of behaviour expected from public planners. NPM is a set of ideas applying neo-liberalism to public sector management. CPT has been important in forming planners' ideals and professional values and attitudes over the last couple of decades, most often linking up to Habermasian discourse ethics, dialogue, and ideas of deliberative democracy (see the previous chapter). On the other hand, NPM had crucial economic-political influence on the public sector over the same period in most of the Western world, transforming the planning bureaucracies of many countries in line with principles of competitiveness, market-orientation and economic accountability. In some of these countries, for example the UK and Norway, government is pursuing both a social democratic agenda of consultation

---

1   This chapter is developed from my article, 'Planners' role: torn between dialogical ideals and neo-liberal realities', *European Planning Studies* 17(1): 65–84.

and a competitive market agenda. The social forces surrounding many planners seem simultaneously to produce dialogical ideals pulling them in one direction and efficiency-obsessed leadership pushing in a different direction.[2]

In periods throughout the twentieth century, the role of the public planner was intensely debated. The socialism versus liberalism debate before and just after the Second World War was also a debate for and against public planning, albeit mostly at the macro level. The planner was seen by some as the guarantor of welfare and by others as a guide on the road to dictatorship (Hayek 1944; Wootton 1945).[3] By the end of the 1970s, the public choice school in economics had demonstrated the strong tendency in planning-related disciplines to regard individuals as self-centred utility maximizers when acting in the market, and as altruistic pursuers of the public interest when acting in governmental hierarchies (Lane 2000a: 205–10). This methodological inconsistency engendered an interventionist bias. Observed market imperfections tended to be taken as sufficient reason for publicly planned solutions, even if government imperfections might in practice be more severe. The public choice critique eroded the planner's role as finding bureaucratic substitutes for market solutions, and strengthened the planner's role as designer of efficient and democratically acceptable market institutions. Public choice theory also provided an important basis for neo-liberalism and thus the reform movement NPM, to be outlined in an ensuing section of this chapter.

The planning literature is replete with references to tasks that planners are supposed to carry out (Hoch 1994). There are also attempts at identifying more comprehensive roles for planners (Beckman 1964; Howe 1980). Every familiar mode of planning implies a particular role for the planner, such as the following examples making up Hudson's (1979) famous SITAR:

Synoptic (rationalistic) planning: Technical-economic expert
Incrementalism (disjointed):   Coordinator of input brought forth by various interests
Transactive planning: Manager of interpersonal relations (doing societal guidance)
Advocacy planning: Advocate
Radical planning: Change agent

The role of the communicative planner has notable procedural aspects in that she or he facilitates discussion and attempts to involve even marginalized interests (Campbell and Marshall 1999: 473). Those emphasizing participation and dialogue tend to see the role of planners more as that of a facilitator and mediator and less as

---

2   Nalbandian (2005) has observed a similar tension in the role of local government professionals. They 'find themselves in the middle of two dynamic forces: administrative modernization and citizen engagement. Attention to one without recognition of the other renders governance ineffective' (311). Related tensions caused by the neo-liberal agenda in Britain are analyzed by Campbell and Marshall (2000).

3   Even though Friedrich Hayek was a paragon liberal rather than a neo-liberal, Pennington's (2003) comparison of Hayek's market-oriented philosophy and contemporary communicative planning supplements the value differences identified in this chapter.

that of a technical-economic expert. Neo-liberals, on the other hand, see the planner role primarily as providing expertise in substantive and legal-procedural matters rather than promoting participation, consensus building, and empowerment of weak groups. Even planned solutions should be in harmony with the market, according to neo-liberalism, thus leaving less room for politics.

Tensions in the planner role are created by external pressure on the planner to act contrary to her values, and by recurring tasks that imply hard choices, that is, the need to trade off different values. Values define what is right and what is wrong. They are central concepts or beliefs regarding final states or desirable behaviour that transcend specific situations, guide decisions and their ex post evaluation, and therefore human conduct, becoming an integral part of an individual's way of being and acting (Argandoña 2003: 16; Schwartz and Bilsky 1987: 551).[4] Values are resistant to change, and this continuity separates them from preferences and opinions. 'Values run deeper than interests ... (W)hen we give up something we value, we often feel we give up part of ourselves, and that's very difficult, very threatening, and hardly compensated by some gain somewhere else' (Forester 1999: 463). Attitudes ('valences') are less abstract than values and linked to a specific context. They 'refer to the subjective attractiveness or aversiveness of specific objects and events within the immediate situation' (Feather 1995: 1135).

The following few examples are selected from Rokeach's (1973) list of 'life values'. Their description is modified to make it more suggestive of how an individual might act on them in his or her capacity as a planner:

> *Freedom, independence, free choice, asserting that adult persons are themselves the right judges of what public goods will serve them best.*

> *Helpfulness, showing social solidarity, implying that society should help individuals out of poverty, and that increasing the capabilities of people should be a primary policy concern.*

> *Responsibility, taking care of the social and natural environment required to uphold the quality of life for everyone.*

> *Social recognition, showing respect, protecting integrity, identity, and things held sacred from being traded off for economic gain.*

Overly economistic ideology threatens the values above, in that all relevant consequences of plans are measured in monetary terms, decisions rest on utilitarian considerations, and efficiency-oriented management is given priority

---

4   Van Wart (1998) offers a comprehensive discussion of values in public administration, presenting the major schools of thought. Scott (2002) applies content analysis to identify five organizational moral values: honest communication, respect for property, respect for life, respect for religion, and justice.

over democracy. These are features that can be recognized in the normative claims of neo-liberalism (and thus NPM) as briefly outlined below.

Neo-liberals espouse economic liberalism as a means of promoting economic development and securing political liberty. Political liberty is seen as the freedom of the individual from outside compulsion; for example, from intervention by the state or other government hierarchies. In order to promote economic development, it is important that political liberty also provides opportunities to act: the individual has a moral claim to freedom of action. Neo-liberalism promotes individualism, stressing human independence and individual self-reliance, primarily achieved by acting in markets. Competitive markets are hailed both as the crucial way to disperse power and to provide an institutional framework for transactions that are economically beneficial to all parties. As a consequence, following Brown (2003), neo-liberalism seeks to disseminate the logic of the market to all institutions and all social action dimensions of human life, making the market the organizing and regulative principle of the state and society. It is a corollary that a generalized calculation of cost and benefit is to become the measure of state practices. According to Brown:

> (E)qually important is the production of all human and institutional action as rational entrepreneurial action, conducted according to a calculus of utility, benefit, or satisfaction against a micro-economic grid of scarcity, supply and demand, and moral value-neutrality. Neo-liberalism does not simply assume that all aspects of social, cultural and political life can be reduced to such a calculus, rather it develops institutional practices and rewards for enacting this vision ... Importantly then, neo-liberalism involves a normative rather than ontological claim about the pervasiveness of economic rationality and advocates the institution building, policies, and discourse development appropriate to such a claim. (Brown 2003: 4)

The train of reasoning throughout the present chapter goes as follows. The prominent values of CPT are outlined and linked to the role of the communicative planner. Then NPM is presented, with special attention given to market orientation and the aim for economic efficiency. Some values are deduced from this and contrasted with CPT values. A separate section explores patches of common ground between CPT and NPM, especially the common concern for service quality and responsiveness to users. This common interest makes it more difficult to read, from empirical studies of planner values and attitudes surveyed in the subsequent section, whether their practices reflect support for communicative planning or managerialism. The discussion section preceding the conclusion argues that this difficulty can be overcome. It is therefore hypothesized that the attitudes of the typical Nordic planner are much closer to CPT than to NPM. Hence, many planners are assumed to experience a tension in their perceived role between dialogical ideals and the neo-liberal realities conveyed by NPM. Finally, theoretical developments are mentioned that might change public administration so as to ease this role conflict.

Communicative planning and New Public Management (NPM) are both modes of governance. The communicative approach makes sense for planning tasks that require citizen deliberation. Other tasks, such as the routine of issuing permits for uncontroversial changes of built structures, might lend themselves to market adaptations involving people in their capacity as consumers. Agencies working according to NPM principles might provide such a service in a satisfactory way. Communicative planning and NPM both take an adaptive and pragmatic approach towards the management of complex coordination problems. The two modes of governance are, however, very different with respect to purpose, ideological foundation, area of application, and potential for transforming organizations in line with the needs of the capitalist economic system. A systematic comparison of communicative planning and NPM is pointless in the present context. Instead, the next two sections demonstrate that these modes of governance encourage conflicting types of behaviour on the part of the planner.

Values and Communicative Planning

This section defines communicative planning and briefly outlines the planner role and values associated with it. In later sections, role and values will be juxtaposed with the ideas of New Public Management and with the attitudes of practising planners.

Communicative planning demands more than communication with stakeholders and an involvement process merely informing the public. This planning style is commended as a respectful, interpersonal discursive practice adapted to the needs of liberal and pluralist societies where one social group cannot legitimately force its preferred solutions to collective problems on the other groups. The aim is to promote the deliberative aspect of democracy and create and protect the conditions for deep and genuine civic discourse (see the previous chapter and Verma (this volume).

Communicative planning is an open and participatory enterprise involving a broad range of affected groups in socially oriented and fairness-seeking developments of land, infrastructure, or public services guided by a consensus building process designed to approach the principles of discourse ethics. The process of communicative planning is open in the sense of being inclusive and transparent. The public can gain knowledge of what is going on. Development efforts are socially oriented when they aim to further the interests of large segments of society rather than the interests of a few stakeholders only. Development is fairness-seeking when it aims to improve the living conditions of deprived groups, and when its substantive results observe the rights of all groups. The principles of discourse ethics state that the communicative process should be open, undistorted, truth-seeking, and empathic – in line with (A)-(D) below (compare Allmendinger 2002: 188 and Innes and Booher 1999: 419):

(A) Openness as formulated by Habermas (1990: 89):
1. Every subject with the competence to speak and act is allowed to take part in a discourse.
2a. Everyone is allowed to question any assertion whatever;
2b. Everyone is allowed to introduce any assertion whatever into the discourse;
2c. All speakers are allowed to express their attitudes, desires, and needs.
3. Speakers may not be prevented, by internal or external coercion, from exercising their rights as laid down in (1) and (2).
(B) The communication between participants should be comprehensible, factually true, sincere, and legitimate within the normative context of public planning.
(C) Nothing should coerce a participant except the force of the better argument.
(D) Participants should be committed to reaching mutual understanding in dialogue free from strategic action.

The idea is that, with communication approaching the principles of discourse ethics, participation would more likely be empowering, and decision-making would be deliberative and democratic. The ideal of deliberative democracy is to reach a decision through debate rather than voting, although practice calls for both modes of making decisions, most often with careful exploratory debate preceding voting (Bohman and Rehg 1997).

The role of the communicative planner is to make stakeholders and affected groups collaborate with each other in a creative process generating opportunities that offer each participating group more than it would have been able to achieve for itself in alternative processes. The planner facilitates the process, mediates conflict, and exposes domination by recognizing and avoiding distortions. Forester suggests

> a distinctively counterhegemonic or democratizing role for planning and administrative actors: the exposure of issues that political-economic structures otherwise would bury from public view, the opening and raising of questions that otherwise would be kept out of public discussion, the nurturance of hope rather than the perpetuation of a modern cynicism under conditions of great complexity and interdependence. (Forester 1993: 6)

Technical-economic expertise features less prominently in communicative planning than in some other modes of planning, but this does not imply the levelling down of planners' role to that of any other stakeholder, as is sometimes asserted (Allmendinger 2001: 134). Nevertheless, as for every other participant in dialogue, planners must act openly and honestly, be prepared to see their values subjected to scrutiny and criticized by stakeholders, and to yield in the face of arguments that others find more convincing. Throgmorton (2000) describes the planner's role as that of being a 'skilled-voice-in-the-flow'of persuasive argumentation. The planner must take on tasks related both to process and substance. It is in the planner's role to advance plans that are fair and to the advantage of deprived groups, as well as to design a process based on open exchange of sincere and honest arguments.

It is evident from the above definition of communicative planning and the associated planner role that values peculiar to this mode of planning are closely related to dialogue, communicative rationality, and fairness in the social possibilities to express oneself. The following values implicit in CPT provide a basis for comparison with stated planner attitudes later in the chapter:

- Empathy: open-minded, a good listener, aiming to understand others' point of view.
- Equality: equal opportunities for communicative action across race, sex, and religion.
- Fairness: serving people according to criteria of need and communicative difficulties rather than power, money, and social status.
- Honesty: sincere and truthful, abstaining from deception and manipulation.
- Responsiveness: to other parties in the planning process and to the general public, willingness to engage in dialogue.
- Self-government: defending every citizen's right to influence collective decisions in matters that concern them.

Responsiveness is a basic value in communicative planning. There can be no dialogue unless the parties involved are willing to listen to each other and respond to each other's utterances and arguments. '(P)racticing responsiveness by developing the ability to listen skillfully reduces the tension between administrative effectiveness and democratic accountability' (Stivers 1994: 364). It is considered rude in many cultures to ignore what other interlocutors say in ordinary conversation. Unresponsiveness is a way to exclude a person and breaks with the openness (feature A) required by discourse ethics above.

Critical pragmatists (Forester 1993) aim to counteract unfavourable effects of biased power relations in the planning process, as they interfere with the above values. They want to increase the transaction costs of those trying to have things their way by putting forward power-based arguments (Sager 2006). The planner arranges the process so as to support those who use honest and fair arguments instead of manipulation, threats, misinformation and other power strategies.

Communicative planning seeks an enlargement of egalitarian values, principally through the extension of cultural respect and moral consideration for a wider range of human and natural communities. According to Gleeson and Low (2000: 146), '(i)t is precisely this "meta-concern" of progressive planning that is directly imperilled by the neo-liberal project'. The rest of the chapter provides a background for assessing this statement. NPM is outlined in the next section to facilitate consideration of its compatibility with the values of communicative planning.

New Public Management – the Efficiency Features

This section describes briefly the economizing core features of NPM. The efficiency-oriented view of NPM is supplemented in the next section, dealing with the aim for consumer satisfaction and related characteristics of NPM that seem to be more in line with communicative planning. This mode of planning is not intrinsically against efficiency, as that would mean being in favour of wasting resources. The aim for efficiency is seen as reasonable to the extent that it is compatible with a democratic and fair process. Communicative planners should consider the risk that, without discipline in all activity areas of the budget, resources meant for participation and dialogue might instead be used for covering deficits in budget chapters that the economizing 'new public managers' hold to be more important.

The neo-liberal shift in the organization of government is a broad trend including aspects such as entrepreneurialism (Harvey 1989), depoliticization (Flinders and Buller 2006), and outsourcing of governmental tasks and activities to separate agencies (Christensen and Lægreid 2006). Entrepreneurialism reflects the widening responsibility of urban politicians from provision of services, facilities and benefits to local development and employment growth. The notion of a public-private partnership is the centrepiece of this development. Depoliticization is the process of placing at one remove the political character of decision-making (see Harmes 2006: 732–34 for the separation of economics and politics in neo-liberalism). This is a precondition for the disaggregation of integrated administrative structures into single purpose semi-independent agencies. Large public agencies are split up to create units that are fit for market competition. In the railway industry, for example, construction and maintenance of infrastructure have been separated from operation of the trains. The purpose is to arrange for competition on the railway network in conditions where the owner of the tracks lacks the motive for giving one operator preferential treatment.

New Public Management (NPM) is a reform movement challenging the traditional political-administrative systems of Western democracies (Hood 2002; Lane 2000b). It is part of the broader current of neo-liberal thinking which has strongly affected right-of-centre politics and even made an impact far into the social democratic parties of many countries (for instance, in the UK, New Zealand and Scandinavia). NPM's stress on delegation, devolution and decentralization, as well as the subsequent need for coordination, has profoundly changed the central agencies and departments where many planners are working (Hart 1998). The aim of the brief account given here is to make clear that the core ideas of NPM differ from the values which in the previous section were found to guide communicative planning. See Gualini (this volume) for a more general discussion of the implications for planning theory of recent developments in governance.

Traditional government systems 'are based on a complex and often ambiguous set of norms and values related to political-administrative control, codes of professional behaviour, due process and government by rules, democratic responsibility, public service ethics, and participation of affected groups' (Christensen and Lægreid 2001a: 93). NPM offers an economic model of governance claiming that market and business rationality can be made to operate as effectively in the public interest as it does in securing private interests. Similarities between the public and private sectors are accentuated, and NPM encourages organizational forms that increase the autonomy and freedom of choice of managers in order to enhance agency efficiency. This aim is also pursued by performance contracts and other financial incentives for public servants. It is further emphasized that administrative bodies at all levels should be competitive, should have a management orientation and customer-focused quality improvement systems, and should pay attention to results (benchmarking). The public sector should give lower priority to rules, processes, and various internal considerations, such as expert jurisdictions and job security.

Under NPM, less weight is put on political signals, professional interests, rights, equality and the preferences of affected third parties (Christensen and Lægreid 2001b: 67). This means that traditional bureaucratic virtues are placed more in the background, such as formally equal treatment and always acting in conformity with specified rules grounded on technical knowledge. Devolution and management by contract rather than control via hierarchy are among the core elements in a reform where cost effectiveness takes centre stage. Financial targets, budget discipline, and monitoring of service provision and performance are standard features. Other means to achieve the efficiency goal are internal accounts, tendering, privatization, outsourcing, and separation of political and administrative functions.

NPM brings to the fore an inherent rhetoric aiming to give administrative efficiency and economic freedoms more impetus than a rigid command structure aiming at political control. More weight is put on economic indicators of the effectiveness of the political management system, and less weight is put on indicators measuring the democratic aspects of politics. The idea is that the market should discipline politics, which is contrary to the traditional view that politics should discipline the market (ibid: 69). The prevailing attitude among planners has probably been to embrace neither politics nor markets, but rather to opt for professionally good solutions. In order to implement these solutions, however, planners tend to argue for the transfer of tasks from markets to public hierarchies, even if this implies the acceptance of political steering. NPM, on the other hand, seeks to limit the scope and forms of public intervention.

In contrast to communicative planning theory, NPM has given much attention to problems of accountability, meaning answerability for performance and being subject to sanctions for failure to meet defined criteria (Thomas 1998: 352). With the increased discretion granted to managers under NPM, relatively more emphasis is put on managerial accountability than political responsibility. Extending freedom to managers without strengthening their accountability would undermine the power of politicians. By managerial accountability is meant the obligation to provide an account of one's actions to those in superior positions of authority (Christensen and Lægreid 2002: 277). Accountability under NPM is mainly based on output measurement, competition, transparency and contractual relations.

It is a problem, however, that political-administrative processes often do not generate the kind of precise, clear-cut objectives and criteria that are necessary for managerial accountability to be a relatively neutral and value-free exercise. The most common techniques for checking given accounts involve monitoring, audits, and investigation of possible wrong-doings.

Managerial accountability is mainly performance-based as opposed to compliance-based. The last type requires rule-based processes, so that whether an agency works in conformity with process regulations can be checked. 'Performance-based processes are more concerned with establishing measures of desirable outcomes and using these tools to measure performance than they are with monitoring compliance with rules' (Jos and Tompkins 2004: 259). Indeed, impatience with restrictions, rules and procedures is a dominant theme in NPM. Measuring the performance of processes poses particular difficulties, as discussed by Agger and Löfgren (2008) and Carmona and Sieh (2008). This is more of a problem for CPT than for NPM, as the latter has a more pronounced emphasis on specifying the quality of services rendered.

Critics maintain that NPM is 'threatening to eliminate democracy as a guiding principle in public-sector management' (Box et al. 2001: 608). This is controversial, however, and the aim towards devolution, decentralization and delegation might be interpreted as signalling democratic concern (Harmes 2006). A case can also be made that NPM supports efforts to strengthen consumers' interests by widespread consultation (as dealt with in the next section). Furthermore, NPM supports consumers' voice and choice, that is 'consumer sovereignty' and 'freedom of choice', but the individualism behind these values might also lead to selfishness (Maesschalck 2004: 476). Selfishness stands in contrast to the empathy and mutual understanding encouraged in CPT.

The present section does not give a full picture of NPM, as will shortly be shown. It is nevertheless clear from the above that planners working in line with the NPM ideology would have to give priority to economic arguments and make the striving for efficiency a prominent part of their professional role. The NPM values of not wasting resources and exercising budget discipline are quite different from the values of communicative planning identified in the previous section. Moreover, dialogical processes are time consuming, and the solutions emerging from dialogue might challenge expertise and management preferences. Both elements can cause conflict between the values of NPM and communicative planning.[5] The next section will nevertheless examine whether there are similar features of NPM and communicative planning which point to shared values.

---

5 Value differences between NPM and communicative or collaborative processes for planning and decision-making do not prevent governments from embracing both modes of governance. For example, New Labour under Prime Minister Blair was widely held to institutionalize neo-liberal ideas (Bevir 2003; Fyfe 2005), yet it simultaneously initiated a range of participatory policies (Barnes et al. 2004; Newman et al. 2004).

Only Irreconcilable Differences, or Patches of Common Ground?

The techno-bureaucratic style of planning and governance, so strongly advocated in the mid twentieth century is confronted both by CPT and NPM. Both styles challenge the traditional roles of politicians and professionals, but in different ways. This section draws attention to some other correspondences between communicative planning and NPM. It turns out, however, that even apparent similarities might conceal significant divergences. The basic contrasts are first recapitulated. The interest of both CPT and NPM in involvement and user satisfaction is then discussed. Finally, it is considered whether – intended or unintended – both modes of governance benefit strong developers by putting more emphasis on local negotiations.

Summing up the Contrapositions

In the face of competing values and role ambiguities, according to Hendler (1991: 156), planners tend to choose one of the following conflicting responses when forming their own professional role:

- Retreating to a more value-neutral role of technical advisor to politicians.
- Pursuing a value-laden, normatively directed course of action. This is often, but not necessarily, aimed at enhancing social equity and conserving the natural environment.

The first is the traditional expert role, which is readily combined with NPM. The second role allows for taking sides more openly, without perforce throwing overboard the notion of widely shared interests. This position is chosen by many communicative planners and can be recognized, for example, in John Forester's sympathy for equity planning (Krumholz and Forester 1990).

Most planners are reluctant to give up their expert status, and some might be tempted to bring the first role above into dialogical planning processes. According to Tewdwr-Jones (2002: 73), however, they are caught in a trap: 'to be a professional requires possessing a specialised area of knowledge for which they are rewarded and this fact rests heavily on their mind. But the communicative turn argues for a more pluralistic and equal relationship between 'the planner' and the planned ...' In a conscious or subconscious attempt to retain prestige and rewards, planners might hesitate to question their supposed professional status even if they share the values that underpin communicative planning (ibid: 73).

In communicative planning, the planner 'should continually foster participatory processes to expand democratic rights, and access to those rights, to support citizens' voices, and to redirect resources to the most needy' (ibid: 66). Communicative planning fosters deliberative democracy. NPM, on the other hand, conceives the welfare state as a market-based delivery system, and its aim is to satisfy customers and free managers from political shackles and unions' idiosyncrasies. The main feature of NPM is its one-dimensional emphasis on economic norms and values. Tensions between these positions have been noted and discussed also in the planning of health services (Parkinson 2004; Rowe and Shepherd 2002).

Some further tensions between NPM and communicative planning can be read from Imrie's (1999) critique of the regime shift from bureau-professionalism to managerialism. This shift paved the way for business or corporate values and technical-economic procedures and discourses. For planning, the efficiency goal of NPM entails speeding up the turnaround of planning applications, faster completion of local plan preparation, facilitation of development objectives, and the streamlining of procedures. Important procedures in the present context are those arranging for public consultation. The risk is that the pressures on local planning authorities to streamline procedures and reduce delays in plan preparation and development control could diminish the time devoted to public involvement in planning processes (Imrie 1999: 117; Campbell and Marshall 2000: 307). If so, there is the risk of extra costs further down the line, if objectors resort to direct action or the courts.

The splitting up of strong public agencies and the privatization of their entrepreneurial and commercial divisions have made it difficult in many cases to build large-scale infrastructure as a purely public undertaking. Planners are increasingly being encouraged towards management practices premised on the development of associative and collaborative networks to enable the attainment of planning objectives (Imrie 1999: 111). Public-private partnerships are therefore more often becoming a necessary solution, and both parties might have a financial stake. As argued by Campbell and Marshall (2000: 303), there are considerable risks in these circumstances that profit maximization will subvert planning considerations. Commitment might shift from widely shared interests to more narrowly defined intra-organizational goals.

The Mutual Focus on Users' Needs

The individualism of neo-liberalism and the collective nature of discourse ethics (Habermas 1990) lead to quite different sets of values in NPM and CPT. Nevertheless, should there be some patches of common ground, it might ease the tension felt by planners if they could be identified and provide a basis for (at least some) action that would be seen as meaningful both from the managerial and the dialogical perspective. In fact, NPM and CPT appear to have a central theme in common. Both theories stress the importance of involvement and client satisfaction, and they have a common interest in being responsive to the users or consumers of public plans. However, communicative planners have much broader commitments. There is a crucial difference between serving the consumers, for instance the users of a planned new trunk road, and taking into account all the groups and interests affected by the road. Christensen and Lægreid place the critique in a wider democratic setting:

(W)hile the term 'customer' is meant to empower the public, it may actually turn out to be a more limited role than that of citizen. The rights of a customer are really quite minimal compared to those of a citizen and the relationships to public employees/service providers are short-term and temporal in nature. Reform efforts that focus on the aggregation of individual customer preferences ignore and weaken the fundamental democratic trusteeship required of both public bureaucrats and citizens. (Christensen and Lægreid 2002: 283)

Citizens are bearers of rights and duties within the context of a wider community. Customers are different in that they do not share common purposes but rather seek to optimize their own individual benefits (Denhardt and Denhardt 2003a: 60).

Imrie (1999: 116) makes the additional point that consumer influence depends on expressing a preference in a market place through willingness to pay. Willingness is highly correlated with ability to pay. Thus, while planners may be attentive to social difference and unequal opportunities, the consumerist conception of the public seems inattentive to issues of inequality of access to the public realm. Therefore, 'public participation in planning, along consumerist lines, has the capacity to reinforce social exclusions by doing little more than maintaining the power of the professionals to design, develop and implement the range of planning services' (ibid: 116).

Purely technical or managerial decisions might easily fall foul of complex political reality. A demand for extensive public consultation therefore came hand in hand with NPM in several countries (OECD 2001; Commission of the European Communities 2001).[6] The main idea is that public plans and services should become more in line with citizen preferences, not that those consulted should also be the decision-makers. The coupling of participation with decision-making is more in demand when people are seen as citizens in a democracy (as in CPT), than when they are regarded as clients or consumers (as in NPM). From the NPM perspective, public involvement is closely linked to the aim of driving up public sector performance (Barnes et al. 2004). To improve accountability, there is increased emphasis on formal control and concomitant transparency, 'because the theory behind the consumer orientation holds strongly that people need access to detailed information in order to make informed decisions about preferred goods and services' (Aberbach and Christensen 2005: 240). The consumer orientation of NPM fits the neo-liberal idea of the citizen, as defined by individual preferences and rights. However, it de-emphasizes collective traditions, as embedded for example in discourse ethics and CPT, which underline common goods and collective

---

6   OECD (2001: 23) defines three levels of involvement. The lowest level is information given in a one-way relationship. The medium level is consultation, which implies a two-way relationship. Governments define the issues for consultation, set the questions and manage the process, while citizens are invited to contribute their views and opinions. The highest level is active participation in a relation based on partnership with government. Citizens actively engage in defining the process and content of policy-making.

action through political parties, social movements, neighbourhood groups and participation in community activities (ibid: 241).

Preventing the potential abuse of power is the ultimate goal of the numerous accountability arrangements of NPM and other democratic modes of governance. Keeping illegitimate use of power from influencing public plans is also a central concern of critical communicative planning (Forester 1993; Sager 2006), and one might thus expect that accountability has been thoroughly discussed in CPT. This is not the case, despite the usefulness of dialogue in improving accountability (Roberts 2002), even if Agger and Löfgren (2008), Blair (2000) and Tait and Campbell (2000) touch on the theme.

The customer service ideal of the NPM, and the aim to empower affected lay people in communicative planning, both lead to a profound reorientation of accountability relationships compared to the compliance orientation of traditional bureaucracy. The accountability needs of the manager and the planner become more complex. There is still a chain of command, so managers and planners have to justify their actions up the hierarchy. In addition, however, responsiveness to customers, clients, and the general public becomes the central aspect of accountability (Thomas 1998: 355–6). Responsiveness is essential in what Romzek (2000) calls political accountability relationships. They afford NPM-managers and communicative planners the discretion of being responsive to the concerns of key stakeholders, such as elected officials, clientele groups, and the public at large (ibid: 27). In NPM, the responsiveness is often linked to the use of customer satisfaction surveys and other output performance measures. In communicative planning, on the other hand, responsiveness tends to be regarded as a value in itself, independent of the service improvements it might bring about. There is scepticism in CPT towards citizens being seen as consumers. Public life should not be 'reduced to a series of isolated transactions from which individuals come away feeling more or less satisfied that they have received value for money' (Thomas 1998: 378).

It can be concluded that even in the main area of common interest to NPM and communicative planning – involvement and user satisfaction – there are profound differences between these modes of governance. Two additional differences which are likely to create tensions when the two modes are combined, warrant emphasis:

- Communicative planning opens up the process and welcomes all sincere arguments from involved parties. NPM narrows the public debate, in the sense that cost-effectiveness is given a hegemonic position among the arguments.[7]

---

7   This contention is valid even though the cost-benefit analysis, often used for assessing projects under NPM, is gradually becoming more comprehensive. The range of environmental effects included is expanding, and cultural heritage (Navrud and Ready 2002) and health effects (Sælensminde 2004) are making their entry. This is still part of the effort to estimate the social benefit-cost ratio, however. The focus is on economics as before.

- NPM seems to induce a depoliticization of decision-making in the public sector, placing at one remove the political character of decision-making, while communicative planning engenders a politicization of public planning by bringing a wide range of interests to the table.

In response to the first point above, one might question the idea of opening up the planning process to extensive and effective lay involvement if it is already given that cost-effectiveness arguments are to be decisive. Aware of the NPM ideology and neo-liberal leanings of her or his agency and its political principals, is the planner really in the position to act sincerely when propagating dialogue and participation? Or does manipulation sneak into her professional role despite the dislike of manipulation expressed by the typical planner (see the empirical material in the next section)? An affirmative answer to the last question would suggest that tensions easily arise between the role expectations faced by communicative planners.

The second point invites the objection that communicative planning cannot stimulate political processes, as it is striving for rational solutions and not compromises achieved by political means. Mouffe (1999) surmises that advocates of deliberative democracy conceive political questions as being of a moral nature and therefore susceptible of being decided rationally. 'This means that they identify the democratic public sphere with the discursive redemption of normative validity claims' (ibid: 746).[8] While the point mentions a concrete and practical characteristic of communicative planning, Mouffe's criticism relates to the theoretical model in which dialogue is communicatively rational. There is admittedly a dilemma here: communicative planners have to choose between a political participation process on the one hand, and a communicatively rational process that will by itself guarantee the legitimacy of consensus solutions on the other hand.

Actually, even if a political process is chosen, that is, a collaborative and stakeholder-based process that might be quite exclusive and far from the Habermasian dialogical ideal, critics hold that depoliticization can take place. Swyngedouw et al. (2002) studied large-scale urban development projects in Europe, which are 'emblematic examples of neoliberal forms of urban governance' (ibid: 543). They found that the collaborative partnerships and networks often set up to organize the projects tend to 'compete with and often supplant local and regional authorities as protagonists and managers of urban renewal … a process that can be described as the "privatization of urban governance" ' (ibid: 573). It can be questioned, though, how much of the depoliticization is due to the general neo-liberal transfer of competencies, decision-making power, and funding from the public to the private sector, and how much follows from the collaborative mode of project planning.

---

8   See also Kapoor's (2002) clear exposition of Mouffe's argument. Dahlberg (2005) defends
     Habermas's public sphere conception against critique from the 'difference democrats',
     Mouffe among them.

Flexible Planning Decisions Heeding Local Knowledge and Preferences

Recent managerial restructuring of government has aimed at depoliticizing decisions by making them a matter of operational management. The dispersal of state functions to a range of extra-governmental organizations makes this evident (Flinders and Buller 2006). Social and political issues are reformulated so as to fit market solutions, or they are translated into problems to be managed. Imrie (1999) makes use of this to build a case against communicative planning, contending that it 'is a powerful conception in legitimising a managerialist approach to the problems confronting the planner' (ibid: 119). Organizing networks, forging partnerships, and developing processes are seen as managerial tasks, but Imrie also views them as core tasks of communicative planning. Although Imrie has a point, he ignores the contrasting reasons for the process-orientation. The proponents of NPM want to make issues less political and opt for a streamlined managerial process. Communicative planning theorists focus on the process because they acknowledge that the issues are political, and that the groups and interests affected should therefore have a say. Moreover, the process should be participatory and fair not only because this is valuable in itself, but because the process will usually affect the final plan. Taking an interest in process does not therefore imply indifference to substance.

We now turn to a critique of communicative planning put forward by Bengs (2005a, b). He observes that, in many Western countries, the deregulation of real estate markets and the decentralization of land use decision-making coincide, although this connection is rarely made by either the proponents of NPM or by communicative planning theorists. Bengs contends that CPT is a means to argue for social institutions consistent with neo-liberal society, that is to say, institutions that match and advance development and the free flow of investments. The common interest of CPT and NPM is, allegedly, manifest in their endorsement of '(a) new planning regime with a minimum of predefined restrictions and guidelines and ample possibilities for striking deals on the local level …' (Bengs 2005b: 6).

As mentioned, NPM is interested in having satisfied users. This follows from market logic rather than democratic logic, although satisfaction with public service would presumably help politicians get uncomplaining voters. Displeased customers impair the accountability of the manager and reduce the agency's or company's opportunities for supplying the same type of projects or plans in the future. Flexible local planning decisions are attractive to NPM – which has a managerial and entrepreneurial focus – as they give managers (developers) more leeway to negotiate locally instead of risking to be stopped by general regulations. Big land developers, often with several prospective projects in the municipality, might have a strong hand in negotiations with local stakeholders.

Sure enough, CPT recommends that solutions be searched for in dialogue with local interests. The democratic values that are involved are a core concern of communicative planning theorists. Local knowledge should be respected in decisions on local matters. Decisions should be made by political bodies as close as possible to where the development takes place. This is assumed to give more power to people directly affected by the plans.

Critics contend that communicative planners acting on the democratic values above unwittingly risk transferring power to developers. The strength of developers can be balanced by the power of national authorities. Therefore, at the national level, laws, regulations and political guidelines can be enacted, which serve widely shared interests. At lower administrative levels, communities often compete for the employment opportunities, activities and tax revenues following from development projects. Developers are hence often in the position to play local politicians off against each other. This can bias local power relations to the developers' advantage and hence bias initiatives in collaborative problem-solving, although this effect may be modified by other local actors.

This critique of CPT is not equally strong in all institutional contexts. The position of developers is stronger when industry is footloose and thus can locate anywhere, and when the market for land is free enough to supply a choice of plots fit for development in several adjacent administrative districts. Developers are also stronger when they operate in a monopolistic market allowing them to accumulate profit, and making it more difficult for local administrations to start negotiations with competitors. Finally, developers will have an advantage in local negotiations if they are backed by an entrepreneurial urban regime (Harvey 1989), and if widely shared environmental interests are insufficiently protected by law.

This section has compared selected aspects of NPM and communicative planning. Even if reasons differ, some forms of participative practices are supported by both modes of governance. However, the patches of common ground should not be allowed to overshadow the value differences pointed out in previous sections. The consequences of these differences will depend on the typical values and attitudes of practising planners. The next section examines whether the average planner is closer to the NPM values or the values of CPT.

Typical Planner Values and Attitudes

What then do we know of the values and attitudes of the 'average planner'? This section briefly reviews results from the empirical literature on European planners' values and attitudes to assess how far the problem analyzed in this chapter is a real one. That is, the aim is to show that many planners actually express values that make it reasonable to assume that they experience tension between conflicting sets of values and experiences. The empirical results are considered only in so far as they record such tensions. The national differences in institutions and social conditions that might affect the results are not discussed.

The values and attitudes of planners have been studied empirically in several countries. The research design developed by Howe and Kaufman (1979; 1981) has been replicated to study the attitudes of planners in Israel (Kaufman 1985), the Netherlands, Spain and the US (Kaufman and Escuin 2000), Sweden (Khakee and

Dahlgren 1990), and Norway (Olsen 2000). Most of the results referred to here are from these studies, and the similar questionnaires facilitate comparisons.[9] The samples of planners studied in European countries are small and probably not statistically representative. The smallest is the Spanish sample of 19 planners questioned in 1995, and the biggest consists of 77 Norwegian planners questioned in 1998.[10] The Swedish and Dutch studies were carried out in 1988 and 1995, respectively. The typical attitudes of Nordic planners which emerge from these studies correspond to the ideals and values embedded in communicative planning, while private and market-oriented development is regarded with considerable scepticism.

Negative attitudes to the neo-liberal NPM were indicated by planners' scepticism towards private developers, as revealed in the empirical studies above. From the questionnaires of those studies, the following five characterizations were selected:

- Developers have a bad image, not unjustified.
- Developers have a complaint against many communities for imposing unnecessary and cost-increasing requirements on their development, the complaints are not legitimate.
- There should be tighter controls on private development to protect the public interest.
- Private developers have little or no concern for the good of the community as a whole.
- Developers are only concerned to make money for themselves.

---

9   The values of planners can also be elicited indirectly, for example by asking what are considered important competencies by planning professionals (Seltzer and Ozawa 2002; Guzzetta and Bollens 2003). Communicative skills seem to be valued more than technical and quantitative knowledge, although professional communication should build on a base of broad analytic skills. A more reliable and representative source of knowledge about the values of planners is the professional codes of organizations like the American Institute of Certified Planners in the US and the Royal Town Planning Institute (RTPI) in the UK. Their web addresses are, respectively: <www.planning.org/ethics/conduct.html>, and <www.rtpi.org.uk/about-the-rtpi/codecond.pdf>. The codes are discussed by Hendler (1991; 2005) and Lucy (1996). The codes take a stand against discrimination on the grounds of race, sex, religion and sexual orientation, and they promote equality of opportunity. Even the educational guidelines of the professional organizations reveal values. Poxon (2001) comments on the guidelines of the RTPI, which promote an appreciation of and a respect for the role of government and public participation in a democratic society, among other things.

10   Abram (2004) studies ethical problems of planning officials in a Norwegian municipality. She shows that in public administrations and agencies, the typical values of planners might easily place them in conflict between loyalty to budgetary limitations and loyalty to political decisions. Professionalism may be difficult to pair with loyalty to politicians' criteria for service distribution (ibid: 29).

Planners were asked how far they agreed with these statements. Norwegian planners turned out to be the most sceptical to private developers. This negative attitude is taken to indicate scepticism towards the neo-liberal (and NPM) ideas of transferring more urban land use decisions to private markets. Planners from Spain, Sweden and the Netherlands reveal less distrustful attitudes towards private developers. In addition, Olsen (2000) shows that European planners typically hold positive attitudes towards dealing with local public transport, low-income groups and minorities, and the natural environment. These are themes that are not usually thought to be well catered for in market-led processes favoured by neo-liberalism.

Such attitudes give some support to the conception of planners and neo-liberals as natural adversaries, as Gleeson and Low report from Australia:

> *What is new ... about the contemporary attack on planning is its conceptual and political reach: neo-liberals desire both to contract the domain of planning (deregulation) and then to privatise segments of the residual sphere of regulation (out-sourcing). In both instances, the raison d'etre of planning as a tool for correcting and avoiding market failure is brushed aside in favour of a new minimalist form of spatial regulation whose chief purpose is to facilitate development. (Gleeson and Low 2000: 135)*

Indications of planners' attitudes towards openness and citizen involvement were also deduced from the empirical studies above, by utilizing planners' responses to the following four questionnaire themes:

- In a democratic system opposition to a policy held by one's own agency should be just as normal and appropriate as support for it.
- Planners should be open participants in the planning process, staking their values in competition with others, and openly striving to achieve their ends.
- No one can better define the needs of a community than its residents.
- Planners should involve citizens in every phase of the planning process.

The responses to the first two statements indicate that planners from all four European countries are in favour of open planning processes. However, the last two statements, dealing directly with citizen involvement, reveal significant differences. The typical Norwegian planner is clearly in favour of involving the public, and more so than was found in Sweden. The Dutch and Spanish planners were more cautious and ambivalent about the role of citizens in the planning process.[11]

In CPT, much emphasis has been put on counteracting manipulation and other distortions of information. Critical questioning has been a main strategy for fighting

---

11   Two focus groups studied by Campbell and Marshall (2001) in 1996 confirm that the view on citizen involvement varies among planners. The more senior British planners, in particular, emphasized the importance of consultation in order to 'give people a say'. What came through on a fairly general basis, however, was the importance of not romanticizing public participation (ibid: 102).

power-based argumentation (Forester 1993; Sager 1994). Howe and Kaufman (1979) drew up 15 planning scenarios that were designed to elicit planners' opinions on what constitutes ethical and unethical professional behaviour. Their study was replicated in Sweden, where 40 planners were questioned in 1988 (Khakee and Dahlgren 1990). Six of the scenarios were also used in the Norwegian study from 1998 (Olsen 2000). The Swedish results show that wilful distortion of information is considered very unethical planner behaviour. Examples of such behaviour include deliberate omission of facts that erode arguments in favour of the planner's preferred solution, and falsely claiming to have support from groups or agencies that have not backed the planner's solution. The Norwegian planners are also strongly opposed to communicative distortions, and more so than what is typical among the 616 US planners questioned by Howe and Kaufman. The strong dislike of distorted information is here taken as an indication of sympathy with the values of communicative planning.

Among the countries contributing empirical data, Norwegian planners display the attitudes most closely aligned to CPT and most disassociated from the neo-liberalism of NPM. They are both the most positive to public participation and the most sceptical to private developers. Swedish planners are also favourable to citizen involvement and express some doubt about private development. On this basis I put forward the hypothesis that the attitudes of the typical Nordic planner are much closer to communicative planning theory than to NPM (the pro-CPT hypothesis).[12]

Planners from the US are also typically of the opinion that citizens should be involved in every phase of the planning process, and that this involvement should go beyond merely allowing citizens to be heard (Kaufman and Escuin 2000: 41). However, the average US planner is considerably more positive towards private development than Norwegian planners, making it more uncertain where the American planners stand in relation to neo-liberalism and NPM. Empirical results for European planners outside the Nordic countries disclose only lukewarm attitudes towards citizen involvement. There is no strong evidence to suggest that the attitudes of Israeli or non-Nordic European planners are much closer to CPT than to NPM. The differences between countries may be due to a number of factors, for example, the attitudes in the wider society towards the state and towards private land ownership, but explanatory variables for these differences are not studied further here.

The dialogical ethos and the neo-liberal managerial ethos pull the role of the planner in different directions. New Public Management is likely to be the strongest influence, as it is aligned with predominant trends in contemporary

---

12   Lapintie and Puustinen (2002) report from a survey of the values of 233 Finnish planners that their attitudes towards the idea of communicative planning and participation were quite positive. Seventy-eight per cent of the respondents agreed that participation practices increase the meaningfulness of their work. On the other hand, 36 per cent agreed that participation practices are wearisome and consume too much planning resources.

market-oriented politics. However, communicative planning seems to better match the typical values and attitudes of Nordic planners. The result is a value conflict which is likely to be felt by many in the planning community, presumably also by many reformist planners outside the Nordic countries. This statement and possible steps to take if it is correct, are discussed in the next section.

Discussion

This section discusses the reasonableness of the hypothesis that the attitudes of the typical Nordic planner are much closer to CPT than to NPM. Then follows a brief account of how NPM has affected government structures and how it is likely to change the working conditions of planners in executive agencies. This is a backcloth for considering whether the New Public Service – a recently presented alternative set of ideas for public management – offers a possibility of bringing the values of public administration into harmony with those of communicative planning.

Is the Pro-CPT Hypothesis Reasonable?

The European studies of planners' values and attitudes are scattered over a ten year period from 1988 to 1998, and hence none of them are quite up to date. The attitudes both towards communicative planning and NPM might have changed as planners acquired more experience with the practices following from these sets of ideas.

However, the most serious challenge to the pro-CPT hypothesis is that CPT and NPM might have sufficiently much in common through their mutual interest in user involvement and 'customer' orientation, that planner attitudes in favour of participation could also be interpreted as support of NPM. The question is whether the statements in the questionnaire designed by Howe and Kaufman (1979; 1981) allow the distinction between support for citizen participation with a democratic purpose and support for customer consultation with the more narrow purpose of service quality check. If such a distinction is impossible, most of the empirical research on planner values and attitudes cannot be used to make a case for the pro-CPT hypothesis.

Returning to the bullet points concerning openness and consultation, it is possible to infer that the planner responses reflect participation from the perspective of improving democracy. The request for general openness in planning processes, which is explicit in the first two statements on the list, points far beyond the need for consultation to improve the quality of publicly supplied service. The last two statements are directly related to citizen participation. One statement focuses on 'the needs of a community' rather than the quality of service experienced by individual customers or clients. The last statement is about involving citizens 'in every phase of the planning process'. This is usually seen as necessary when the aim is democratic decision-making, but it is quite needless when the purpose is to advise on how to improve service quality.

The conclusion is that the statements on openness and consultation deal with wide participation with the aim of democratic decision-making rather than narrow consultation aiming for product development. Hence, attitudes manifested through strong agreement with the statements indicate sympathy with the kind of citizen involvement required by communicative planning. Such openness and democratically grounded participation would be incompatible with administrative processes in which it is predetermined what arguments are going to count as important. Therefore, open processes do not go well with NPM where market-orientation and economic efficiency are predetermined core considerations.

NPM and Trends in the Structure of Government: Consequences for Planners

The main conclusion of Norway's second official study of social power relations is that all elements of popular self-government are being weakened (Østerud et al. 2003: 295; Selle and Østerud 2006). Some of the reasons are peculiar to Norway, but in the present context it is of more concern that some noted changes in the structure of government are due to the dissemination of NPM:

- The distinction between politics and administration has become clearer and more formal. More discretion has been granted to executive directors of public agencies and public enterprises without any formal political responsibility. The state apparatus has been hollowed out and become more fragmented, and politically accountable bodies have lost or delegated power (Østerud et al. 2003: 290).
- The National Assembly has tighter control over a more restricted domain following from the implementation of NPM in public administration.
- Through market-orientation, privatization, and forms of public enterprise exempt from political dictate, areas of economic life previously controlled by politicians are transferred to the neo-liberal governance mechanisms of competitive markets (ibid: 292).
- Democratic self-government at the local level has been sapped of much content by a combination of state directives, laws granting citizens the right to certain types of service, and limited budgets (compared to assigned tasks). The public persona of Norwegians is undergoing a change from citizen to service recipient and customer (ibid: 293).
- In the sum of the current processes of change – including the transfer of authority to administration, independent organizations, judicial system, and markets – a retreat of politics is embedded. The chain of parliamentary steering is growing weak in all links (ibid: 294–5).

Due to the international impetus of NPM ideas, the above points seem to be valid far beyond the Norwegian borders. A reasonable supposition might be that planners in executive agencies will become less dependent on political principals as NPM procedures become firmly established. If neo-liberal influence remains strong, they will probably be able to plan with less direct intervention from politicians in the future. They might, however, be working under stricter intra-organizational regimes due to NPM. Much will depend on how the wider governance landscape in particular contexts is being transformed (see Gualini's chapter in this volume).

With regard to democracy, planners can inform and vitalize public debate on the physical development of places, facilitate public involvement, expose and criticize repressive use of power, and check that market forces are played out within the framework of laws and political guidelines. Judging from the official Norwegian study of social power, it seems more important than ever to develop an interface between the prevalent styles of public planning and public administration that strengthens democracy. Such compatibility of communicative planning and administration can be achieved by substituting the New Public Service (explained below) for NPM as the prominent ideology of public sector organization.

New Public Service

Denhardt and Denhardt (2003a, b) outline a system of ideas for administering the public sector which offers an alternative to NPM. This ideology is coined New Public Service, and it puts collective decisions based on dialogue at the centre stage to the displacement of individual decisions based on rational choice. Perry (2007) juxtaposes New Public Service with related ideas about a public sector ethos. The contrast to NPM is underlined by the maxim that '(g)overnment shouldn't be run like a business; it should be run like a democracy' (Denhardt and Denhardt 2003a: 3). The roots of New Public Service are ideas of citizenship, community, organizational humanism and civil society (ibid: chapter 2). The Denhardts propose replacing the ethos of NPM – based on market and customers – with a public service ethos that re-establishes the centrality of citizens, democracy and the public interest. This mode of governance 'seeks shared values and common interests through widespread dialogue and citizen engagement' (ibid: 170):

> *From this perspective, the role of public administrator is to bring people 'to the table' and to serve citizens in a manner that recognizes the multiple and complex layers of responsibility, ethics, and accountability in a democratic system. The responsible administrator should work to engage citizens not only in planning, but also implementing programs to achieve public objectives. This is done not only because it makes government work better, but because it is consistent with our values. The job of the public administrator is not primarily control or the manipulation of incentives; it is service. (Denhardt and Denhardt 2003a: 170)*

Denhardt and Denhardt (2003b: 9) delineate the principles of New Public Service, summarized below. The primary role of the public servant is helping citizens articulate and meet their shared interests and commit to shared responsibility. This can be most effectively achieved through collective efforts and collaborative processes. The preferred tool is dialogue for eliciting shared values and building relationships of trust and mutual respect. Public servants must be attentive to more than the market; they must also attend to statutory and constitutional law, community values, political norms, professional standards and citizen interests.[13]

Perry (2007: 7) aims to contrast NPM and New Public Service, and starts by condensing the many aspects of NPM into the following four points:

- Catalytic government, steering rather than rowing.
- Customer-driven government, meeting the needs of the customer, not the bureaucracy.
- Community-owned government, empowering rather than serving.
- Enterprising government, earning rather than spending.

New Public Service, on the other hand, is built on seven mutually reinforcing ideas (ibid: 8):

- Serve citizens, not customers.
- Seek the public interest.
- Value citizenship over entrepreneurship.
- Think strategically, act democratically.
- Recognize that accountability is not simple.
- Serve rather than steer.
- Value people, not just productivity.

These points are not meant to sideline values such as efficiency and productivity. However, in a democratic society, democratic values should be paramount in the way we think about public administration.

The gist of the principles is that widely shared interests are better advanced by public servants and citizens committed to dialogue than by entrepreneurial managers acting on market incentives. The accentuation of involvement and dialogue, and the attention given to democratic accountability at the expense of

---

13   Some traits of New Public Service are similar to characteristics of the post-bureaucratic organization, as outlined by Alvesson and Thompson (2005), Heckscher and Donnellon (1994), and Iedema (2003). The latter explains that the post-bureaucratic organization dissimulates authority 'by reducing hierarchy, devolving decision-making power, setting up collaborative decision-making forums, emphasizing flexibility, and dissolving inside-outside boundaries and rigidities' (Iedema 2003: 193). Post-bureaucratic work is not principally about following pre-determined rules, but about enacting some kind of rule-making. The role of trust is also discussed in the literature on post-bureaucracy, for example by Grey and Garsten (2001).

efficiency and cost-effectiveness, would bring public administration in line with communicative planning practice. New Public Service is much closer to the values of CPT than the ideals of NPM. The similarity of the ideas is acknowledged by Hefetz and Warner (2005, 2007), stating that the reform has been coined 'new public service' in public administration and 'communicative planning' in the planning field. Behind both is the idea of deliberative democracy, where 'the cooperative search of deliberating citizens for solutions to political problems takes the place of the preference aggregation of private citizens or the collective self-determination of an ethically integrated nation' (Habermas 2006: 413).

Conclusion on Tension in the Role of Planners

Several studies of the values and attitudes of planners confirm their inclination to be in favour of public involvement and open processes and opposed to manipulation and lenient control of developers. The evidence is sufficient to put forward the hypothesis that the attitudes of the typical Nordic planner, in particular, are much closer to communicative planning theory than to New Public Management. Discourse ethics and theories of deliberative democracy have provided inspiration and supportive ideas to planners since the early 1980s. It is nevertheless questionable whether these ideas can stand up to the pressure from main trends in politics, economy, and administration – such as the market orientation and rational choice perspective of New Public Management. This set of neo-liberal ideas has a marked influence on the planning of many types of public infrastructure and service provision both at the national and the local level. The planner role is currently under contradictory pressures from conflicting values and expectations held by educators and part of the professional community influenced by communicative planning theory on the one hand, and politicians and administrators promoting New Public Management on the other. However, patches of common ground have also been identified and analyzed, especially the concern for user influence, service quality and client satisfaction.

Imrie (1999: 111) notes the dilemma of the present situation, in which 'pressures for community involvement in planning policy processes, and the democratisation of policy practices, are heightening in a context whereby planners are increasingly having to justify their actions by recourse to measures of efficiency and value for money'. In the present confrontation between the one-dimensional economic approach of the NPM and the open and multi-dimensional dialogue recommended by CPT, it seems important that planning retains a critical function (Forester 1993; Sager 2006).

Planners can take on many different roles, but in the light of the present discussion of CPT and NPM, and putting nuances aside, there are the following two extremes on the range of possibilities:

- Role 1: The planner as intermediary between the multiplicity of society and the economism of neo-liberal public administration. The planner interprets reality in managerial NPM terms. The planner makes a note of the retreat of politics and becomes part of the reductionist movement, working in the service of efficiency and cost-effectiveness only.
- Role 2: The planner conveys the variety of views in the polity to the public administration at national and local levels. The planner regards it as a task to prevent the many-faceted public discourse from collapsing into one dimension as issues are filtered through the preparatory stages of planning and policy-making on their way to political decision-makers. The planner brings the outcome of deliberative democracy into planning documents and recommendations.

The present challenge is to simultaneously ease planners' tension and stimulate democracy by forging workable compromises from the stylized planner roles above. New Public Service has a value content bridging the present gap between the ideals of prominent theories of public administration and of planning. Hence, by struggling to give the dialogical and democratic ideals of New Public Service a solid foothold in public administration and breaking the hegemony of NPM, planners would also relax the contradictory claims that CPT and NPM make on their role in society. This would ease the role tension that might currently be felt by communicative and collaborative planners in particular, as CPT and New Public Service are related in that both aim to strengthen the deliberative qualities of democracy.

References

Aberbach, J.D. and Christensen, T. (2005) 'Citizens and consumers: an NPM dilemma' *Public Management Review* 7(2): 225–45.

Abram, S. (2004) 'Personality and professionalism in a Norwegian district council' *Planning Theory* 3(1): 21–40.

Agger, A. and Löfgren, K. (2008) 'Democratic assessment of collaborative planning processes' *Planning Theory* 7(2): 145–64.

Allmendinger, P. (2001) *Planning in Postmodern Times*. London: Routledge.

Allmendinger, P. (2002) *Planning Theory*. Basingstoke: Palgrave.

Alvesson, M. and Thompson, P. (2005) 'Post-bureaucracy?', in Ackroyd, S., Batt, R., Thompson, P. and Tolbert, P. (eds) *The Oxford Handbook of Work and Organization*. Oxford: Oxford University Press, 485–507.

Argandoña, A. (2003) 'Fostering values in organizations' *Journal of Business Ethics* 45(1): 15–28.

Barnes, M., Newman, J., and Sullivan, H. (2004) 'Power, participation, and political renewal: theoretical perspectives on public participation under New Labour in Britain' *Social Politics* 11(2): 267–79.

Beckman, N. (1964) 'The planner as a bureaucrat' *Journal of the American Institute of Planners* 30(4): 323–7.

Bengs, C. (2005a) 'Time for a critique of planning theory' *European Journal of Spatial Development*, <http://www.nordregio.se/EJSD/editorials.html> (Editorial no. 3, June).

Bengs, C. (2005b) 'Planning theory for the naïve?' *European Journal of Spatial Development*, <http://www.nordregio.se/EJSD/debate050718.pdf> (Debate and Miscellaneous, July).

Bevir, M. (2003) 'Narrating the British state: an interpretive critique of New Labour's institutionalism' *Review of International Political Economy* 10(3): 455–80.

Blair, H. (2000) 'Participation and accountability at the periphery: democratic local governance in six countries' *World Development* 28(1): 21–39.

Bohman, J. and Rehg, W. (eds) (1997) *Deliberative Democracy.* Cambridge, MA: MIT Press.

Box, R.C., Marshall, G.S., Reed, B.J. and Reed, C.M. (2001) 'New Public Management and substantive democracy' *Public Administration Review* 61(5): 608–19.

Brown, W. (2003) 'Neo-liberalism and the end of liberal democracy' *Theory and Event* 7(1) <http://muse.jhu.edu/journals/theory_and_event/v007/7.1brown.html>

Campbell, H. and Marshall, R. (1999) 'Ethical frameworks and planning theory' *International Journal of Urban and Regional Research* 23(3): 464–78.

Campbell, H. and Marshall, R. (2000) 'Moral obligations, planning, and the public interest: a commentary on current British practice' *Environment and Planning B: Planning and Design* 27(2): 297–312.

Campbell, H. and Marshall, R. (2001) 'Values and professional identities in planning practice', in Allmendinger, P. and Tewdwr-Jones, M. (eds) *Planning Futures. New Directions for Planning Theory.* London: Routledge, 93–109.

Carmona, M. and Sieh, L. (2008) 'Performance measurement in planning – toward a holistic view' *Environment and Planning C: Government and Policy* 26(2): 428–54.

Christensen, T. and Lægreid, P. (2001a) 'New Public Management – undermining political control?', in Christensen, T. and Lægreid, P. (eds): *New Public Management: The Transformation of Ideas and Practice.* Aldershot: Ashgate, 93–119.

Christensen, T. and Lægreid, P. (2001b) 'New Public Management i norsk statsforvaltning' (New Public Management in the Norwegian public administration), in Tranøy, B.S. and Østerud, Ø. (eds) *Den fragmenterte staten. Reformer, makt og styring* [The Fragmented State. Reforms, Power and Steering]. Oslo: Gyldendal, 67–95.

Christensen, T. and Lægreid, P. (2002) 'New Public Management: puzzles of democracy and the influence of citizens' *Journal of Political Philosophy* 10(3): 267–95.

Christensen, T. and Lægreid, P. (2006) 'Agencification and regulatory reforms' in Christensen, T. and Lægreid, P. (eds) *Autonomy and Regulation: Coping with Agencies in the Modern State.* Cheltenham: Edward Elgar, 8–49.

Commission of the European Communities (2001) *European Governance: A White Paper.* Brussels: European Commission.

Dahlberg, L. (2005) 'The Habermasian public sphere: taking difference seriously?', *Theory and Society* 34(2): 111–36.

Denhardt, J.V. and. Denhardt, R.B (2003a) *The New Public Service: Serving, not Steering*. Armonk, NY: ME Sharpe.

Denhardt, R.B. and Denhardt, J.V. (2003b) 'The New Public Service: an approach to reform' *International Review of Public Administration* 8(1): 3–10.

Feather, N.T. (1995) 'Values, valences, and choice: the influence of values on the perceived attractiveness and choice of alternatives' *Journal of Personality and Social Psychology* 68(6): 1135–51.

Flinders, M. and Buller, J. (2006) 'Depoliticization, democracy and arena shifting', in Christensen, T. and Lægreid, P. (eds) *Autonomy and Regulation: Coping with Agencies in the Modern State*. Cheltenham: Edward Elgar, 53–80.

Forester, J. (1993) *Critical Theory, Public Policy, and Planning Practice: Toward a Critical Pragmatism*. Albany, NY: State University of New York Press.

Forester, J. (1999) 'Dealing with deep value differences', in Susskind, L., McKearnan, S. and Thomas-Larmer, J. (eds) *The Consensus Building Handbook*. Thousand Oaks, CA: Sage, 463–93.

Fyfe, N.R. (2005) 'Making space for "neo-communitarianism"? The third sector, state and civil society in the UK' *Antipode* 37(3): 536–57.

Gleeson, B. and Low, N. (2000) 'Revaluing planning: rolling back neo-liberalism in Australia' *Progress in Planning* 53(2): 83–164.

Grey, C. and Garsten, C. (2001) 'Trust, control and post-bureaucracy' *Organization Studies* 22(2): 229–50.

Guzzetta, J.D. and Bollens, S.A. (2003) 'Urban planners' skills and competencies' *Journal of Planning Education and Research* 23(1): 96–106.

Habermas, J. (1990) *Moral Consciousness and Communicative Action*. Cambridge, MA: MIT Press.

Habermas, J. (2006) 'Political communication in media society: does democracy still enjoy an epistemic dimension? The impact of normative theory on empirical research' *Communication Theory* 16(4): 411–26.

Harmes, A. (2006) 'Neoliberalism and multilevel governance' *Review of International Political Economy* 13(5): 725–49.

Hart, J. (1998) 'Central agencies and departments: empowerment and coordination', in Peters, B.G. and Savoie, D.J. (eds) *Taking Stock. Assessing Public Sector Reforms*. Canadian Centre for Management Development, Montreal: McGill-Queen's University Press, 285–309.

Harvey, D. (1989) 'From managerialism to entrepreneurialism: the transformation in urban governance in late capitalism' *Geografiska Annaler. Series B, Human Geography* 71(1): 3–17.

Hayek, F.A. (1944) *The Road to Serfdom*. London: Routledge and Kegan Paul.

Heckscher, C. and Donnellon, A. (eds) (1994) *The Post-bureaucratic Organization*. Thousand Oaks, CA: Sage.

Hefetz, A. and Warner, M. (2005) 'No room for simple solutions: combining markets with planning in US city services'. Paper presented at the *46th Annual Conference of the American Collegiate Schools of Planning*, Kansas City, MO, 27–30 October 2005.

Hefetz, A. and Warner, M. (2007) 'Beyond the market versus planning dichotomy: understanding privatisation and its reverse in US cities' *Local Government Studies* 33(4): 555–72.

Hendler, S. (1991) 'Do professional codes legitimate planners' values?' in Thomas, H. and Healey, P. (eds) *Dilemmas of Planning Practice.* Aldershot: Avebury: 156–67.

Hendler, S. (2005) 'Towards a feminist code of planning ethics' *Planning Theory and Practice* 6(1): 53–69.

Hoch, C. (1994) *What Planners Do.* Chicago, IL: APA Planners Press.

Hood, C. (2002) 'New Public Management', in Smelser, N.J. and Bates, P.B. (eds) *International Encyclopaedia of the Social and Behavioral Sciences. Volume 8.* Oxford: Elsevier, 12553–6.

Howe, E. (1980) 'Role choices for planners' *Journal of the American Planning Association* 46(4): 398–410.

Howe, E. and Kaufman, J. (1979) 'The ethics of contemporary American planners' *Journal of the American Planning Association* 45(3): 243–55.

Howe, E. and Kaufman, J. (1981) 'The values of contemporary American planners' *Journal of the American Planning Association* 47(3): 266–78.

Hudson, B.M. (1979) 'Comparison of current planning theories: counterparts and contradictions' *Journal of the American Planning Association* 45(4): 387–98.

Iedema, R. (2003) *Discourses of Post-bureaucratic Organisation.* Amsterdam: John Benjamins.

Imrie, R. (1999) 'The implications of the "New Managerialism" for planning in the millennium', in Allmendinger, P. and Chapman, M. (eds) *Planning Beyond 2000.* New York: John Wiley, 107–20.

Innes, J.E. and Booher, D. (1999) 'Consensus building and complex adaptive systems: a framework for evaluating collaborative planning' *Journal of the American Planning Association* 65(4): 412–23.

Jos, P.H. and Tompkins, M.E. (2004) 'The accountability paradox in an age of reinvention. The perennial problem of preserving character and judgment' *Administration and Society* 36(3): 255–81.

Kapoor, I. (2002) 'Deliberative democracy or agonistic pluralism? The relevance of the Habermas-Mouffe debate for Third World politics' *Alternatives: Global, Local, Political* 27(4): 459–87.

Kaufman, J. (1985) 'American and Israeli planners – a cross-cultural comparison' *Journal of the American Planning Association* 51(3): 352–64.

Kaufman, J.L. and Escuin, M. (2000) 'Thinking alike: similarities in attitudes of Dutch, Spanish, and American planners' *Journal of the American Planning Association* 66(1): 34–45.

Khakee, A. and Dahlgren, L. (1990) 'Ethics and values of Swedish planners: a replication and comparison with an American study' *Scandinavian Housing and Planning Research* 7(2): 65–81.

Krumholz, N. and Forester, J. (1990) *Making Equity Planning Work.* Philadelphia, PA: Temple University Press.

Lane, J.-E. (2000a) *The Public Sector* (3rd edition). London: Sage.

Lane, J.-E. (2000b) *New Public Management.* London: Routledge.

Lapintie, K. and Puustinen, S. (2002) 'Towards a reflexive planner: the planning profession and the communicative challenge', Unpublished manuscript available from the authors, Helsinki University of Technology.

Lucy, W.H. (1996) 'APA's ethical principles include simplistic planning theories', in Campbell, S. and Fainstein, S. (eds) *Readings in Planning Theory.* Cambridge, MA: Blackwell, 479–84.

Maesschalck, J. (2004) 'The impact of New Public Management reforms on public servants' ethics: towards a theory' *Public Administration* 82(2): 465–89.

Mouffe, C. (1999) 'Deliberative democracy or agonistic pluralism?' *Social Research* 66(3): 745–58.

Nalbandian, J. (2005) 'Professionals and the conflicting forces of administrative modernization and civic engagement' *American Review of Public Administration* 35(4): 311–26.

Navrud, S. and Ready, R.C. (eds) (2002) *Valuing Cultural Heritage.* Cheltenham: Edward Elgar.

Newman, J., Barnes, M., Sullivan, H. and Knops, A. (2004) 'Public participation and collaborative governance' *Journal of Social Policy* 33(2): 203–23.

OECD (2001) *Citizens as Partners: Information, Consultation and Public Participation in Policy Making.* Paris: Organization for Economic Co-operation and Development.

Olsen, K.H. (2000) *Ethics, Attitudes and Values of Norwegian Planners.* Working Papers from Stavanger University College 81/2000. Stavanger: Stavanger University College.

Østerud, Ø., Engelstad, F.and Selle, P. (2003) *Makten og demokratiet* (Power and Democracy). Oslo: Gyldendal.

Parkinson, J. (2004) 'Why deliberate? The encounter between deliberation and new public managers' *Public Administration* 82(2): 377–95.

Pennington, M. (2003) 'Hayekian political economy and the limits of deliberative democracy' *Political Studies* 51(4): 722–39.

Perry, J.L. (2007) 'Democracy and the New Public Service', *American Review of Public Administration* 37(1) 3–16.

Poxon, J. (2001) 'Shaping the planning profession of the future: the role of planning education' *Environment and Planning B: Planning and Design* 28(4): 563–80.

Roberts, N.C. (2002) 'Keeping public officials accountable through dialogue: resolving the accountability paradox' *Public Administration Review* 62(6): 658–69.

Rokeach, M. (1973) *The Nature of Human Values.* New York: Free Press.

Romzek, B.S. (2000) 'Dynamics of public sector accountability in an era of reform' *International Review of Administrative Sciences* 66(1): 21–44.

Rowe, R. and Shepherd, M. (2002) 'Public participation in the new NHS: no closer to citizen control?' *Social Policy and Administration* 36(3): 275–90.

Sælensminde, K. (2004) 'Cost-benefit analyses of walking and cycling track networks taking into account insecurity, health effects and external costs of motorized traffic' *Transportation Research A* 38(8): 593–606.

Sager, T. (1994) *Communicative Planning Theory*. Aldershot: Ashgate.

Sager, T. (2006) 'The logic of critical communicative planning: transaction cost alteration' *Planning Theory* 5(3): 223–54.

Schwartz, S.H. and Bilsky, W. (1987) 'Toward a universal psychological structure of human values' *Journal of Personality and Social Psychology* 53(3): 550–62.

Scott, E.D. (2002) 'Organizational moral values' *Business Ethics Quarterly* 12(1): 33–55.

Selle, P. and Østerud, Ø. (2006) 'The eroding of representative democracy in Norway' *Journal of European Public Policy* 13(4): 551–68.

Seltzer, E. and Ozawa, C.P. (2002) 'Clear signals: moving on to planning's promise' *Journal of Planning Education and Research* 22(1): 77–86.

Stivers, C. (1994) 'The listening bureaucrat: responsiveness in public administration' *Public Administration Review* 54(4): 364–9.

Swyngedouw, E., Moulart, F., and Rodriguez, A. (2002) 'Neoliberal urbanization in Europe: large-scale urban development projects and the new urban policy' *Antipode* 34(3): 542–77.

Tait, M. and Campbell, H. (2000) 'The politics of communication between planning officers and politicians: the exercise of power through discourse' *Environment and Planning A* 32(3): 489–506.

Tewdwr-Jones, M. (2002) 'Personal dynamics, distinctive frames and communicative planning', in Allmendinger, P. and Tewdwr-Jones, M. (eds) *Planning Futures. New Directions for Planning Theory*. London: Routledge, 65–92.

Thomas, P.G. (1998) 'The changing nature of accountability', in Peters, B.G. and Savoie, D.J. (eds) *Taking Stock: Assessing Public Sector Reforms*. Montreal: Canadian Centre for Management Development and McGill-Queen's University Press, 348–93.

Throgmorton, J.A. (2000) 'On the virtues of skillful meandering' *Journal of the American Planning Association* 66(4): 367–75.

van Wart, M. (1998) *Changing Public Sector Values*. New York: Garland.

Wootton, B. (1945) *Freedom under Planning*. Westport, CT: Greenwood Press.

Enhancing Creativity and Action Orientation in Planning

Louis Albrechts

Introduction: The Revival of Strategic Spatial Planning

The problems and challenges that places are confronted with cannot be tackled and managed adequately with the intellectual apparatus, concepts and mind-set of traditional spatial planning. This chapter argues that planning must involve a strategically-focused, creative effort to imagine structurally different answers, and to bring this creative imagination to bear on political decisions and the implementation of these decisions into transformative practices. Hence the chapter constructs the outline of a 'new' strategic spatial planning approach open to transformative practices. Transformative practices focus on the structural problems of our society, elaborate images of a preferred outcome and propose how to implement them. Envisioning as a learning process is used to broaden the spectrum of possible futures. In a final section, the chapter reflects on the role planners may play in substantiating transformative practices.

The word strategy originated within the military context as the 'science and art of employing the political, the economic, psychological and military forces of a nation or group of nations to afford the maximum support to adopted policies in peace or war' (Webster 1970: 867).

In the US, government leaders became increasingly interested in strategic planning as a result of the wrenching changes – the oil crisis, demographic shifts, changing values, a volatile economy (Eadie 1983; Bryson and Roering 1988). In north-western Europe, early traces of strategic spatial planning were closely linked to the idea of the modern nation state (Mastop 1998). The differences in origin and traditions between the US and Europe reflect the historical 'statist' traditions of many post-war European states, which are linked to a battery of welfare state policies (Batley and Stoker 1991; Esping-Anderson 1990, cited by Healey 1997b).

In a number of Western European countries, strategic spatial planning evolved in the 1960s and 1970s towards a system of comprehensive planning, understood as the integration of nearly everything (Perloff 1980), at different administrative levels. In the 1980s, when the neo-liberal paradigm replaced the Keynesian-Fordist one and when public intervention retrenched in all domains (Martinelli 2005), Europe witnessed a retreat from strategic spatial planning fuelled not only by the neo-liberal disdain for planning, but also by postmodernist scepticism, both of which tend to view progress as something which, if it happens, cannot be planned (Healey 1997b). Instead the focus of urban and regional planning practices shifted to projects (Secchi 1986; Motte 1994; Rodriguez and Martinez 2003), especially for the revival of rundown parts of cities and regions, and to land use regulations.

The growing complexity, an increasing concern about the rapid and apparently random development of cities and regions, the problems of fragmentation, the increase in interest (at all scales, from local to global) in environmental issues (global warming …), the need for governments to adopt a more entrepreneurial style of planning in order to enhance competitiveness, a longstanding quest for better coordination, both horizontal and vertical, a re-emphasis on the need for long-term thinking and the aim to return to a more realistic and effective planning approach, all served to expand the agenda (Harvey 1989; Breheny 1991; Healey 1997b; Newman and Thornley 1996; Freestone and Hamnett 2000; Landry 2000; Cars et al. 2002; Le Galès 2002; Swyngedouw et al. 2002; Gibelli 2003; Friedmann 2004). There is ample evidence, however, that the problems and challenges that places are confronted with cannot be tackled and managed adequately either with the neo-liberal perspective or with the intellectual technical-legal apparatus and mind-set of traditional land-use planning. In response, more strategic approaches, frameworks and perspectives for cities, city-regions, and regions became fashionable again by the late 1980s and the 1990s (Healey et al. 1997; Pascual and Esteve 1997; Albrechts 1999; Salet and Faludi 2000; Hamnett 2000; Lennon 2000; Albrechts et al. 2001; Albrechts et al. 2003; Pugliese and Spaziante 2003; Martinelli 2005 ; Albrechts 2001, 2004, 2006). But, just as in planning generally speaking, there are different traditions of strategic spatial planning. I argue that only a kind of strategic planning open to transformative practices is suited to cope with the continuing and unabated pace of change driven by the structural developments and challenges in our Western society. Consequently, the chaper constructs the outline of a new strategic planning. Imagining transformative practices and how to implement them needs creativity in all phases of the planning process. Since transformative practices are so all pervasive, envisioning these practices is looked upon as a learning process. Moreover, a focus on transformative processes brings us to reflect on the role planners have the potential to play in instantiating these practices. For my discussion, I draw on a selective reading of the literature and my own practical experience.

Towards an Outline for a 'New' Strategic Spatial Planning

Transformative practices focus on the structural problems in society (see Friedmann 1987: 389 for transformative theory, and Sandercock 2003: 157–79 for transformative practices). They construct images/visions of preferred outcomes and how to implement them (see Friedmann, 1987). Transformative practices mean structurally different solutions/responses and not just variations on the same theme. This takes decision-makers, planners and citizens out of their comfort zones and compels them to confront the key-beliefs, to challenge conventional wisdom, and to look at the prospects of 'breaking-out-of-the-box'.

The way I conceive the outline of a 'new' strategic planning contains three components: a what, a how and a why.

What?

'New' strategic spatial planning is a transformative and integrative, (preferably) public sector-led socio-spatial process through which visions, coherent actions and means for implementation are produced that shape and frame what a place is and what it might become (Albrechts 2001, 2004, 2006). The term 'spatial' brings into focus the 'where of things', whether static or dynamic – the creation and management of special 'places' and sites; the interrelations between different activities and networks in an area; and significant intersections and nodes in an area which are physically co-located (Healey 2004; 46). Cities and regions possess a distinctive spatiality as agglomerations of heterogeneity locked into a multitude of relational networks of varying geographical reach (Amin 2004: 43). Strategic spatial planning processes with an appreciation of 'relational complexity' demand a capacity to 'hear', 'see', 'feel' and 'read' the multiple dynamics of a place in a way that can identify just those key issues that require collective attention through a focus on place qualities (see Healey 2005, 2006). Strategic spatial planning is not just a contingent response to wider forces, but is also an active force in enabling change. This strategic planning cannot be theorized as though its approaches and practices were neutral with respect to class, gender, age, race and ethnicity (Sandercock 1998; Albrechts 2002).

The focus on the spatial relations of territories allows for a more effective way of integrating different agendas (economic, environmental, cultural, social and policy) as these agendas affect places. It also carries a potential for a 'multiscaling' of issue agendas down from the national or state level and up from the municipal and neighbourhood level. The search for new scales of policy articulation and new policy concepts is also linked to attempts to widen the range of actors involved in policy processes, with new alliances, actor partnerships and consultative processes (Albrechts et al. 2003). Moreover, a territorial focus seems to provide a promising basis for encouraging levels of government to work together (multi-level governance) and in partnership with actors in diverse positions in the economy and civil society.

How?

The 'new' strategic spatial planning focuses on a limited number of strategic key issues. It takes a critical view of the environment in terms of determining strengths and weaknesses in the context of opportunities and threats. Strategic spatial planning focuses on place-specific qualities and assets (social, environmental, economic, cultural, intellectual, as well as qualities of the urban tissue – physical and social) in a global context. It studies the external trends, forces and resources available. Strategic spatial planning as a practice identifies and gathers together major actors (public and private). It allows for a broad and diverse involvement of actors (public, economic, civil society) during the planning process. It works across the levels of government and governance (multi-level governance). It creates solid, workable long-term visions and perspectives through generating a geography of the unknown (Albrechts 2004) and strategies at different levels, taking into account the power structures (political, economic, gender, cultural), uncertainties and competing values. Strategic spatial planning designs plan-making structures and develops contents, images and decision frameworks for influencing and managing spatial change. It is about building new ideas and processes that can carry them forward, thus generating ways of understanding, ways of building agreements, and ways of organizing and mobilizing for the purpose of exerting influence in different arenas. Finally, strategic spatial planning, both in the short and the long term, focuses on framing decisions, actions, projects, results and implementation, and incorporates monitoring, feedback, adjustment and revision.

Why?

The why question deals with values and meanings, with 'what ought to be' (Ozbekhan 1967) and what 'could be'. Without the normative, we risk adopting a pernicious relativism where anything goes (see Ogilvy 2002). In a conscious, purposive, contextual, creative and continuous process, the new strategic planning aims to develop openness to new ideas, and to understand and accept the need and opportunity for change. Transformative practices oppose a blind operation of market forces and involve constructing 'desired' answers to the structural problems of our society. To will particular future states into being is an act of choice involving valuation, judgment and the making of decisions that relate to human-determined ends and to the selection of the most appropriate means for coping with such ends. 'Futures' must symbolize some good, some qualities and some virtues that the present lacks (diversity, sustainability, equity, spatial quality, inclusiveness, accountability). Speaking of quality, virtues and values is a way of describing the sort of place we want to live in, or think we should live in.

Making New Strategic Planning Operational Through a Four-track Approach

The 'new' strategic (spatial) planning approach becomes operational in a four-track approach. The four tracks (Albrechts et al. 1999; see also Van den Broeck 1987, 2001) can be seen as working tracks: one for the vision, one for the short-term and long-term actions, a third for the involvement of the key actors and, finally, a fourth track for a more permanent process (mainly at the local level) involving the broader public in major decisions. The proposed tracks should not be viewed in a purely linear way. Indeed, strategic planning does not flow smoothly from one phase to the next. It is a dynamic and creative process. The context forms the setting of the planning process but also takes form and undergoes changes in the process (see Dyrberg 1997).

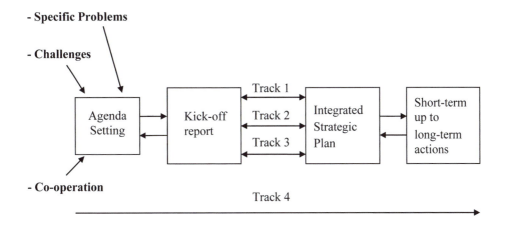

Figure 7.1   A possible macro-structure for the overall strategic
              planning process

In the **first track** the emphasis is on long-term visions. Visions are constructed in relation to the social values to which a particular polity is historically committed (see Ozbekhan 1969). The creation of visions is a conscious and purposive action to represent values and meanings for the future. Hence the need to shift from analysis, which seeks to discover a place that might exist, towards design (in its broadest sense), which creates a place that would not otherwise exist. This is similar to Habermas's *knowing* (understanding the challenges and the options available) and *steering* (the capacity to take action to deal with the challenges) (Habermas 1996). Power is at the heart of these values and meanings. To avoid pure utopian thinking, the views of social critics such as Harvey (1973), Friedmann (1987), and Krumholz (1982) need to be integrated into the process for creating visions.

In **track 2** the focus is on creating trust by solving problems through actions which may even have a very short-term timespan. It concerns acting in such a way as to make the future develop towards the visions constructed in track 1 and to tackle problems in the light of these visions. Strategic spatial planning is about action, about implementation. Things must get done! By providing a qualitative, adequate and timely response to problems, challenges faced by a polity – trust, understanding and confidence, are built up in the process, between the actors and in planning practice (Albrechts and Van den Broeck 2004). A combination of a long-term perspective (visions) with short-term actions makes visions tangible and makes it possible to react almost immediately to certain urgent problems with a clear perspective as to where to go and what the likely impacts of decisions are. This means that spatial planners, politicians, people at large who are involved in spatial planning activity, need visions that embody the long-term strategy. They need concrete short-term actions in response to the everyday problems, while longer-term actions are needed for the realization of possible futures.

As spatial planning has almost no potential for concretizing strategies, so **track 3** involves relevant actors needed for their substantive contribution, their procedural competences and the role they might play in acceptance, in getting basic support and in providing legitimacy. Both the technical skills and the power to allocate sufficient means to implement proposed actions are usually spread over a number of diverse sectors, actors and departments. Integration in its three dimensions – substantive, organizational and instrumental (legal, budget) – is at stake here.

The **fourth track** is about an inclusive and more permanent empowerment process (Forester 1989; Friedmann 1992) involving citizens in major decisions. In this process, citizens learn about one another and about different points of view, and they come to reflect on their own points of view. In this way a store of mutual understanding can be built up, a sort of 'social and intellectual capital' (see Innes 1996; but see also the more critical view of Mayer 2003). Arenas, in which the relevant actors meet, are used not as locations devoid of power, but rather as vehicles that acknowledge and account for the working of power and for the passionate commitment of planners and other actors who care deeply about the issues at stake (Flyvbjerg 2002).

The proposed four-track approach cannot change the power relations, but I am confident that empowerment, as developed in track 4, supports wider, collective efforts to change such relations (see also Forester 1989; Sager 1994; Innes et al. 1994; Healey 1997a).

The 'end' product of the process presented above may consist of an analysis of the main processes shaping our environment, which amounts to dynamic, integrated and indicative long-term visions (frames), plans for short-term and long-term actions, budgets, and strategies for implementation. It constitutes a consensus or (partial) (dis)agreement between the key actors. For the implementation, credible commitments to action engagement (commitment package), and a clear and explicit link to the budget are needed where citizens, the private sector, different levels of governance and planners enter moral, administrative and financial agreements to realize these actions (collective spatial agreement) (for an example see Albrechts and Van den Broeck 2004).

Strategic spatial planning activity needs a fine-grained analysis of what actually takes place in formal decision-making and implementation, in the transition from plan to formal adoption of (parts of) the plan and in its actual implementation, as opposed to what they normatively would like to see happen (see Friedmann 1998). Research by Flyvbjerg (1998) makes it clear that critical analysis of cases is needed to discover the 'whys and wherefores' of how elected representatives or privileged actors change the plan and why and how executive officers depart from the formally approved plan. Change is the sum of a great number of acts (individual, group, institutional) of re-perception and behaviour change at every level. Not everyone (individual planners, groups, institutions, citizens) wants to give up power associated with the status quo.

Strategic spatial planning is not a single concept, procedure or tool. In fact, it is a set of concepts, procedures and tools that must be tailored carefully to whatever situation is at hand if desirable outcomes are to be achieved. Strategic spatial planning is as much about process, institutional design and mobilization as it is about the development of substantive theories, analyses and policy solutions. Content relates to the strategic issues selected in the process. The capacity of a strategic spatial planning system – formal, informal and as a set of more theoretical concepts to deliver and implement the chosen strategies – is dependent not only on the system itself, but also on the broader conditions underlying it. These conditions, including political, cultural, economic and professional contexts and attitudes, affect not only the ability of the system to provide conditions for implementing chosen strategies but the development and processes of choosing between strategies as well (see also Law 2004).

Strategic planning is selective and oriented to issues that really matter. As it is impossible to do everything that needs to be done, 'strategic' implies that some decisions and actions are considered more important than others and that much of the strategy-making and implementation process lies in making the tough decisions about what is most important for the purpose of producing fair, structural responses to problems, challenges, aspirations and diversity (Albrechts 2004: 751–2).

(How) Can Creativity Enhance Transformative Practices?

Transformative practices focus on new concepts and new ways of thinking that change the way resources are used, (re)distributed and allocated, and the way the regulatory powers are exercised. They mobilize all necessary resources, they develop the power to 'travel' and 'translate' into an array of practice arenas, and they transform these arenas, rather than merely being absorbed within them. Those concepts and ways of thinking that accumulate sufficient power to become routinized may then 'sediment' down into the cultural ground, which sustains ongoing processes and feeds into new strategic spatial processes (Hajer 1995; Albrechts and Liévois 2004; Healey 2005: 14–8; Healey 2006: 532). Transformative change rarely occurs in instant revolutions. Changes evolve in many small ways, building a ground of understanding and experiences which, over time, eventually come together in what history may then describe as 'a transformative moment' (Healey 2005: 158; Healey 2006: 541).

Integrating Back-Casting and Forecasting

Those involved in transformative practices simply refuse to accept that the current way of doing things is necessarily the best way; they break free from concepts, structures and ideas that only persist because of the process of continuity. It is precisely the discontinuity that forces us outside the usual boundaries of 'reasonableness' (see De Bono 1992). Discontinuity builds on a contrary assumption based on a psychological notion of time (a normative approach: see Berger 1964; De Jouvenel 1964; Ozbekhan 1969; Jantsch 1970). Normativity indicates the relations with specific values, desires, wishes or needs for the future. In the psychological notion of time an action point of view is taken. This is opposite to an exploratory approach based on an abstract notion of time (an observer's point of view). So the normative approach creates (see Ozbekhan 1969), invents (see Gabor 1969) or constructs (see Massé 1965) more desirable futures (Ozbekhan 1969), the good society (Friedmann 1982) and betterment. This intellectual tradition yields the idea that futures can be willed into being (Ozbekhan 1969; Jantsch 1970; Berger 1964; Dubos 1969) and is developed further in the French intellectual tradition of 'les futuribles' (De Jouvenel 1964). The latter deploys a conception of 'futures' that transcends mere feasibility and that results from judgments and choices formed, in the first place, with reference to the idea of 'desirability', to the idea of 'betterment' and to the practice of the good society (Friedmann 1982). To will a particular future state into being is an act of choice involving valuation, judgment and the making of decisions that relate to human-determined ends and to the selection of the most appropriate means for coping with such ends. Transformative practices become the activity whereby (within certain boundaries) that which can be *willed* is 'imposed' on that which *is*, and it is 'imposed'[1] for the purpose of changing what *is* into what is *willed*. Such an activity differs from the established or traditional way of thinking, in which there is no choice and we are not even aware of other possibilities. The normative approach invents, or creates, practices – in relation to the context, the social and cultural values to which a particular place/society is historically committed – as something new rather than as a solution arrived at as a result of existing trends. It is only by working backwards ('reverse thinking', 'back casting') that we are able to open up and use other directions.

A society is not bound by its past to live out a future that is predetermined and therefore predictable. A willed future is a clear reaction against the future as a mere extension of the here and now. On the other hand, the spectrum of possible futures cannot be so open that anything is possible, as if we could achieve anything we wanted to achieve (Ozbekhan 1969; Berger 1964; Ogilvy 2002). Conditions and constraints on 'what is' and 'what is not' possible are placed by the past and the present. These conditions and constraints have to be questioned and challenged in the process, given the specific context of place and time. So, in order to imagine

---

1   Although 'imposed' may refer to a top down jargon, I use the term very deliberately. As soon as directions based on an emancipatory practice are agreed upon, they must be imposed for action.

the conditions and constraints for the future differently, we need to deal with history and to overcome history. Therefore, we also need an exploratory approach. The interrelation between the normative and the exploratory approach (so-called 'prospective thinking', see Ozbekhan 1969) defines the boundaries of a fairly large space between openness and fixity.

Transformative practices result from judgments and choices formed with reference to the ideas of desirability and betterment. For spatial planning, the concepts of both sustainable development and spatial quality provide lenses through which we can give substance to desirability, the good society and betterment. These are potentially rich concepts that may help to drive the policy integration of economic, environmental and socio-cultural objectives in their spatial manifestation. In addition, our concepts of sustainable development and spatial quality cannot be imagined without acknowledging a politics of difference. As there is growing evidence that 'more of the same'– be it more market, more technology or just keeping to vested concepts, discourses and practices – is not suited to provide the answers needed, a clear statement must be made against any notion of a purely quantitative approach to growth (see Hamilton 2004) and in favour of the need for a 'just' use of resources and for social cohabitation. In the instance of planning activity, we must link spatial quality and sustainability to all phases in the process, to every single step, to all strategies, to all actions. We must make the culture of attention to spatial quality and sustainability an integral part of the big picture. These values must be stressed at the highest levels and innermost circles of governance. Spatial planners, politicians and society at large have to accept that spatial quality and sustainability are not 'happy accidents' and that, subsequently, we have to create/manage them in an intentional and systematic fashion.

If we look at spatial plans today, most, if not all of them embrace some unspecified notions of sustainability and spatial quality, though almost none of them questions growth as such.

The creative challenge of imagining and creating instances of a new practice should balance freedom and discipline, unite stakeholders behind the creative effort and evince empathy for the difficulties of the creative process.

From Visions to Envisioning as Learning Processes for Transformative Practices

Spatial planners, politicians, people at large, feel uncomfortable when challenged to think beyond the short term and to reflect on multiple futures, and consequently they take an unconsciously deterministic view of events. How can they be convinced that they can have meaningful choices and will not have to be a complete prisoner of circumstances? How can different groups in a place be made aware that they are interdependent, that they share the same physical space and may therefore face similar problems, and that there are some problems that they cannot solve on their own? How can they be made aware that they may loose if they do not cooperate?

How can they be persuaded to consider alternatives that may broaden the scope of possible answers? Yet when the sustainability, quality and equity of places are at stake, then this is exactly what may be needed: to imagine visions of alternatives in order to grasp the opportunities available in changing how things go on. As visions are not just 'out there', waiting to be discovered, those doing planning work have to construct them. Such visions help us to think about how places/institutions will operate under a variety of future possibilities and they enable decision-makers and civil society to detect and explore all or as many alternative futures as possible in order to clarify present actions and subsequent consequences. For Schwartz (1991: 192), this is 'rehearsing the future'. This is not a linear, but rather a dialectic (back casting and forecasting) process. Visions themselves may not be seen as static descriptions of futures. They need to reflect an understanding of development and portray its dynamic nature, changing challenges and contexts. We cannot confront complex dynamic realities with a language designed for simple static problems (Senge 1990). Hence the need for ways of thinking and for tools that help planners to cope with change in a dynamic environment (see also Winch 1998). The ability to practically shape and develop an idea is just as important as the ability to imagine the idea in the first place. Imagination and analysis are equal partners in creativity (Plsek 1997: 30).

Envisioning is the process by which individuals – or preferably groups – develop visions of future states for themselves, their organization, their city or their region that are sufficiently clear and powerful to arouse and sustain the actions necessary for (parts of) these visions to become a reality (see Goodstein et al. 1993). The active participation in an envisioning process may generate trust as participants in the process are likely to find that – and to understand why – some visions present a future that certain of them would like to inhabit, while other possible futures are considered highly undesirable. The process helps the participants to think more broadly about the future and its driving forces, and to realize that their own actions may move a place towards a particular kind of future. Moreover, envisioning can become a learning process if it looks in an open way to the future, if it integrates the knowledge of what might happen with an understanding of the driving forces and a sense of what a vision means to a place and its citizens.

A broad involvement of actors in the envisioning process plays a crucial role in the sense that it helps to cope with the danger of manipulation and one-sidedness (for instance an elitist concept of spatial quality) (see Godet 2001). Envisioning as a collective process is based on a trust in creativity from below, the wisdom of crowds (Surowiecki 2005). This needs a constant awareness of problems of aggregation, inclusiveness and power. Envisioning focuses on the collective intelligence of the group as being greater than the intelligence of the individual.

Some of the driving forces are fixed in the sense that they are completely outside our control and will play out in any narrative about the future. Hence, visions must be placed within a specific context (economic, social, cultural, political and power), place, time and scale regarding specific issues that are of interest and within a particular combination of actors. The context provides the setting for the process but also takes form and undergoes changes in the process. To avoid naïve utopian thinking and to avoid visions that are just exercises in 'banalization', 'woolly thought' or pseudo-legitimation for a number of measures and projects connected only on paper (see Borja and Castells 1997), visions must be rooted in an understanding of the basic processes that shape places. This must be done recognizing conditions of power, inequality and diversity. Whose vision is created remains a basic question to be asked.

Envisioning does not claim to eliminate uncertainty with predictions. Instead, it seeks to work with uncertainty as well as possibility, and to enable people to make decisions in view of desired futures. According to Godet (2001: 8), envisioning is above all a state of mind (imagination and anticipation) that leads to behavior (hope and will). With *envisioning*, we focus on 'what ought to be'. In the final analysis, we must come back to what 'is' if we want to present ideas and concepts that are solid, workable and of testable value. To get to these ideas, we need both the solidity of the analysis and the creativity of the design of alternative futures. To avoid naïve thinking, all of this must be rooted in an understanding of the basic processes that shape places.

In strategic planning, envisioning enables openness to new ideas, and helps to understand and accept the need and opportunity for change. Envisioning of discontinuous futures involves change, so all the usual forms of resistance to change (and definitely to structural change) are likely to be present.

Since envisioning is so central to the strategic planning process and so all pervasive, it cannot be confined to a single actor or institution in the process. We consider envisioning to be a collective process that concerns futures for which citizens are themselves responsible. Their vision, then, is more than a wish list. It involves commitment to the realization of the vision through practice (Friedmann 1987). Visions provide citizens with views of the future that can be shared – a clear sense of direction, a mobilization of energy, and a sense of being engaged in something important (see Goodstein et al. 1993). A vision is 'communicatively rational' to the degree that it is reached consensually through deliberations involving all relevant stakeholders, where all are equally empowered and fully informed, and which reaches towards the conditions of the ideal speech situation model as articulated by Habermas (see Innes 1996). Spatial planners, politicians and people at large have to be aware that these Habermasian ideals are only guaranteed in a limited number of situations. The images provided in a vision involve a dynamic interaction between the relevant actors in the process rather than a unidirectional flow. The reiterative process occurs at the moment of creating the vision, as well as throughout the process of its implementation. The values and images of what a society wants to achieve must be discussed in the envisioning process. Values and images are not generated in isolation but are socially constructed and given meaning and validated by the traditions of belief and practice. They are reviewed, reconstructed and invented through collective experience (see Ozbekhan 1969; Foucault 1980: 11; Hillier 1999; Elchardus et al. 2000: 24). We must be aware of the impact on the social and psychological milieu of the consumer society, which teaches citizens how to think about themselves and their goals. Citizens' tastes, priorities and value systems are, to a large degree, manipulated by the very markets that are supposed to serve them (Hamilton 2004: 66). Within (and constrained by) this established framework of the market society, places and communities face the challenge of constructing (or rejecting) and implementing the discourses of cultural diversity, sustainability and place quality and, hence, of creatively transforming their own functioning and practice.

Envisioning reveals how things can be different, how things could be truly better, how people can be innovative, how we can unlock the natural creativity of the citizens to improve our cities and regions, how we can legitimize these natural tendencies that are typically inhibited or suppressed by the daily demands of our governance systems. The construction of different futures, which lies at the very heart of the transformative practices, requires creativity and original synthesis (Ozbekhan 1969: 87).

The process helps the participants to think more broadly about the future and its driving forces and to realize that their own actions may move a place towards a particular kind of future. The process allows participants to step away from entrenched positions and identify positive futures that they can work at creating. It allows for a high degree of ownership of the final product and illustrates that citizens do have a responsibility for the(ir) future. So the real test is not whether anyone has fully achieved the 'conceived' future, but rather whether anyone has changed his or her behaviour because he or she saw the future differently (Schwartz 1991).

Re-emphasizing the Role Planners Have to Play in Substantive Issues

I have linked envisioning to transformative practices. Transformative practices involve constructing 'desired' and 'possible' responses – images/visions and strategies for action – to the structural problems of our society. For me it is unthinkable that planners would refrain from playing a role in constructing visions/images and act as mere neutral observers.

Planners are necessarily involved with and instrumental in substantiating/formulating and implementing images/visions (see also Forester 1989). In this way they take a stand on substantive issues. For spatial planners, more specifically, spatial quality and sustainable development are key substantive issues. They form the core of their discipline. Spatial planners capitalize on the 'locus' using the characteristics of space and place – the natural as well as the built environment, the socio-spatial structure, the flows and the spatial and social tissue. Space and place serve as a medium and as an integration frame for human activities. In this sense space gets its own relative autonomy. This is somehow at odds with some tendencies in collaborative and communicative approaches/practices that seem to push planners more and more into a role as facilitator.

Planners must use the power and the imagination available to them to contribute to spatial quality and to sustainable development. The power comes from their specific body of knowledge (typo-morphological research, research on visual form and visual perception, research by design ...), their skills, their ability to grasp and to work with the characteristics of a place and its potentials. In practice, however, there is a danger that the concern for the substantive is snowed under with the process (involvement of citizens, processes of democratization). No doubt all these issues are extremely important. The point I want to make is that what processes are significant will depend on the specific exercise. A community planner or social planner will focus on citizen participation for the sake of empowering these citizens, to make the process more democratic, to fight exclusion. Although, as a strategic spatial planner, I deeply share these values, my purpose is different. I do not get involved in participation and empowerment processes 'per se' but because and in so far as these processes contribute to spatial quality and to sustainable development, to the implementation of spatial strategies. The role of a spatial planner is to systematically cultivate awareness about spatial quality and sustainable development. Indeed, a lack of awareness leads to the worst kind of myopia: that of a place lumbering into the future. Planners need to lure citizens and politicians outside the comfort and familiarity of their traditional mind-sets, concepts and modes of operation. They need to mutually explore a set of distinctive, plausible, qualitative and sustainable (in the broadest sense) futures that could unfold. This demands imagination and a thorough understanding and analysis of the driving forces of change and of what might be. This brings us back to a transformative agenda.

Imagination is like a muscle: it strengthens through use. And nothing uses it better than looking beyond the domain of what we know (Kao 1997). Imagination generates a type of strategic spatial planning that embraces creativity and critical analysis and encourages a contemporary utopian tradition (in the broadest sense). In a utopia, there is the dimension of the 'radically new', the transformative, the dimension of bringing something new into being and the dimension of values related to spatial quality and sustainability. Creativity challenges 'mental models' – of planners, governors and citizens – about the quality of places and their sustainability. It lifts the 'blinkers' that limit the creativity for designing and formulating structurally new concepts and discourses (see Schwartz 1991). Planners must be able to grasp the momentum and they must try to come up with many different responses, some of which are unconventional and possibly unique (see Michalko 2001: 2). Hence planners need a mind-set that is willing to force their thinking into the unknown, to trigger insights and unleash ideas, to explore new concepts and new ideas and to look for alternatives. Alternatives mean structurally different futures. Conceptions of alternatives are so desperately needed in the face of the challenge to find sustainable pathways and not just variations on the same theme. Planners must help to create empathy for the difficulty of change. As indicated before, change is dynamic and ongoing. This involves understanding the process, the motivation for and the consequences of change.

Creativity in the long-term perspective is important and possible as long as it is combined with creativity in the short-term actions. Planners must make the images around spatial quality and sustainability highly specific, descriptive and detailed.

If these images are not accessible, if they cannot be understood, no one will be able to act on them.

Epilogue

The challenges society is faced with are huge. There is growing evidence that 'more of the same', be it more market, more technology or just keeping to vested concepts, discourses and practices, is not suited to provide the answers needed.

To develop a strategic spatial planning open to transformative practices, a climate and environments conducive to new ideas and in which creative people (planners, politicians, civil servants and citizens) can flourish must be created. Planners, civil servants and governments need to think beyond customary job descriptions and traditional government structures, to address problems in new ways, and to accept that the past is no blueprint for how to go forward. Governments and planners need to trust the creativity of residents. They must acknowledge that there are multiple publics and that planning and governance in a new multicultural era requires a new kind of multicultural literacy and a new kind of democratic politics, which is more participative, more deliberative and more agonistic.

My focus on transformative practices does not imply that day-to-day problems are not important. They are! But there is evidence that, for whatever reasons, spatial planners are left out (or put themselves aside) when major decisions are at stake. The argument I want to make in this chapter is that spatial planners have to take part in a very proactive way to bring structural issues onto the political agenda and to give substance to the transformative practices that are needed.

Acknowledgment

I thank Jean Hillier and Patsy Healey for their constructive comments on an earlier version of this chapter.

References

Albrechts, L. (1999) 'Planners as catalysts and initiators of change. The new Structure Plan for Flanders' *European Planning Studies* 7(5): 587–603.

Albrechts, L. (2001) 'In pursuit of new approaches to strategic spatial planning' *International Planning Studies* 6(3): 293–310.

Albrechts, L. (2002) 'The planning community reflects on enchancing public involvement: views from academics and reflective practitioners' *Planning Theory and Practice* 3(3): 331–47.

Albrechts, L. (2004) 'Strategic (spatial) planning reexamined' *Environment and Planning B* 31: 743–58.

Albrechts, L. (2005) 'Creativity as a drive for change' *Planning Theory* 4(2): 247–69.

Albrechts, L. (2006) 'Shifts in strategic spatial planning? Some evidence from Europe and Australia' *Environment and Planning A* 38(6): 1149–70.

Albrechts, L., and Liévois, G. (2004) 'The Flemish diamond: urban network in the making' *European Planning Studies* 12 (3): 351–70.

Albrechts, L., and Van den Broeck, J. (2004) 'From discourse to facts. The case of the ROM project in Ghent, Belgium' *Town Planning Review* 75(2): 127–50.

Albrechts, L., Alden, J., and Da Rosa Pires, A. (2001) (eds) *The Changing Institutional Landscape of Planning*. Aldershot: Ashgate.

Albrechts, L., Healey, P., and Kunzmann, K. (2003) 'Strategic spatial planning and regional governance in Europe' *Journal of the American Planning Association* 69: 113–29.

Albrechts, L., Leroy, P., van den Broeck, J., van Tatenhove, J., and Verachtert, K. (1999) 'Opstellen van een methodiek voor geintegreerd gebiedsgericht beleid' [A methodology for integrated area development] Leuven: KU Leuven, KU Nijmegen, copy available from author.

Amin, A. (2004) 'Regions unbound: towards a new politics of place' *Geografisker Annaler* 86B: 33–44.

Batley, R., and Stoker, G. (eds) (1991) *Local Government in Europe*. London: Macmillan.

Berger, G. (1964) *Phénoménologie du Temps et Prospective*. Paris: P.U.F.

Borja J., and Castells, M. (1997) *Local and Global: Management of Cities in the Information Age*. London: Earthscan.

Breheny, M. (1991) 'The renaissance of strategic spatial planning?' *Environment and Planning B: Planning and Design* 18: 233–49.

Bryson, J.M. and Roering W.D. (1988) 'Initiation of strategic spatial planning by governments' *Public Administration Review* 48: 995–1004.

Cars, G., Healey, P., and Madanipour, A. (eds) (2002) *Urban Governance, Institutional Capacity and Social Milieux*. Aldershot: Ashgate.

De Bono, E. (1992) *Serious Creativity. Using the Power of Lateral Thinking to Create New Ideas*. New York: Harper Business.

De Jouvenel, B. (1964) *L'art de la Conjecture*. Monaco: Du Rocher.

Dubos, R. (1969) 'Future-oriented science', in Jantsch, E. (ed.) *Perspectives of Planning*. Paris: OECD, 157-75.

Dyrberg, T.B. (1997) *The Circular Structure of Power*. London: Verso.

Eadie, D.C. (1983) 'Putting a powerful tool to practical use: the application of strategic spatial planning in the public sector' *Public Administration Review* 43: 447–52.

Elchardus, M., Hooghe, M., and Smits, W. (2000) 'De vormen van middenveld participatie', in Elchardus, M., Huyse, L., and Hooghe, M. (eds) *Het Maatschappelijk Middenveld in Vlaanderen*. Brussels: VUB Press, 15–46.

Esping-Anderson, G. (1990) *The Three Worlds of Welfare Capitalism*. Cambridge: Polity Press.

Flyvbjerg, B. (1998) *Rationality and Power: Democracy in Practice*. Chicago, IL: University of Chicago Press.

Flyvbjerg, B. (2002) 'Bringing power to planning research: one researcher's praxis story' *Journal of Planning Education and Research* 21(4): 357–66.

Forester, J. (1989) *Planning in the Face of Power*. Berkeley, CA: University of California Press.

Foucault, M. (1980) *The History of Sexuality*. New York: Vintage.

Freestone, R., and Hamnett, S. (2000) 'Introduction', in Hamnett, S., and Freestone, R (eds) *The Australian Metropolis*. St Leonards: Allen & Unwin, 1–10.

Friedmann J. (1982) *The Good Society*. Cambridge, MA: MIT Press.

Friedmann, J. (1987) *Planning in the Public Domain: From Knowledge to Action*. Princeton, NJ: Princeton University Press.

Friedmann, J. (1992) *Empowerment: The Politics of Alternative Development*. Oxford: Blackwell.

Friedmann, J. (2004) 'Strategic spatial planning and the longer range' *Planning Theory and Practice* 5(1): 49–62.

Friedmann, J., and Douglas, M. (1998) 'Editor's introduction', in Douglas, M. and Friedmann, J. (eds) *Cities for Citizens*. Chichester: John Wiley & Sons, 1–6.

Gabor, D. (1969) 'Open-ended planning', in Jantsch, E. (ed.) *Perspectives of Planning*. Paris: OECD, 329-47.

Gibelli, M.C. (2003) 'Flessibilita e regole nella pianificazione strategica: buone pratiche alla prova in ambito internazionale' in Pugliese, T., and Spaziante, A. (eds) *Pianificazione Strategica*. Milano: Franco Angeli, 53–78.

Goodstein, L., Nolan, T., and Pfeiffer, J. (1993) *Applied Strategic Planning*. New York: McGraw-Hill.

Godet, M. (2001) *Creating Futures*. London: Economica.

Habermas, J. (1996) 'Normative content of modernity', in Outhwaite, W. (ed.) *The Habermas Reader*. Cambridge: Polity, 341–65.

Hajer, M. (1995) *The Politics of Environmental Discourse*. Oxford: Oxford University Press.

Hamilton, C. (2004) *Growth Fetish*. London. Pluto Press.

Hamnett, S. (2000) 'The late 1990s: competitive versus sustainable cities', in Hamnett, S., and Freestone, R. (eds) 2000 *The Australian Metropolis*. St Leonards: Allen & Unwin, 168–88.

Hamnett, S., and Freestone, R. (eds) 2000 *The Australian Metropolis*. St Leonards: Allen & Unwin.

Harvey, D. (1973/1989) *Social Justice and the City*. London: Edward Arnold.

Harvey, D. (1989) 'From managerialism to entrepreneurialism: formation of urban governance in late capitalism' *Geografisker Annaler* 71B: 2–17.

Healey, P. (1997a) *Collaborative Planning, Shaping Places in Fragmented Societies*. London: Macmillan.

Healey, P. (1997b) 'The revival of strategic spatial planning in Europe', in Healey, P., Khakee, A, Motte, A., and Needham, B., *Making Strategic Spatial Plans*. London: UCL Press, 3–19.

Healey, P. (2004) 'The treatment of space and place in the new strategic spatial planning in Europe' *International Journal of Urban and Regional Research* 28: 45–67.

Healey, P. (2005) 'Network complexity and the imaginative power of strategic spatial planning' in Albrechts, L., and Mandelbaum, S. (eds) *The Network Society: A New Context for Planning?* New York: Routledge, 146–60.

Healey, P. (2006) 'Relational complexity and the imaginative power of strategic spatial planning' *European Planning Studies* 14(4): 525–46.

Hillier, J. (1999) 'What values? Whose values?' *Ethics, Place and Environment* 2(2): 179–99.

Innes, J. (1996) 'Planning through consensus-building: a new view of the comprehensive planning ideal' *Journal of the American Institute of Planners* 62 (4): 460–72.

Innes, J., Gruber, J., Thompson R. and Neuman M. (1994) *Coordinating Growth Management through Consensus Building: Incentives and the Generation of Social, Intellectual and Political Capital*. Berkeley, CA: University of California at Berkeley, Institute of Urban and Regional Development.

Jantsch, E. (1970) 'From forecasting and planning to policy sciences' *Policy Sciences* 1(1): 79–88.

Kao, J. (1997) *Jamming: The Art and Discipline of Business Creativity*. New York: HarperCollins.

Kaufman, J.L. and Jacobs, H.M. (1987) 'A public planning perspective on strategic spatial planning' *Journal of the American Planning Association* 53 (1): 21–31.

Krumholz, N. (1982) 'A retrospective view of equity planning, Cleveland, 1969-1979' *Journal of American Planners Association* 48(4): 163–74.

Landry, C. (2000) *The Creative City: A Toolkit for Urban Innovators*. Earthscan: London.

Law, J. (2004) *After Method*. Routledge: London.

Le Galès, P. (2002) *European Cities: Social Conflicts and Governance*. Oxford: Oxford University Press.

Lennon, M. (2000) 'The revival of metropolitan planning', in Hamnett, S., and Freestone, R. (eds) *The Australian Metropolis*. St Leonards: Allen & Unwin, 149–67.

Martinelli, F. (2005) 'Introduzione' in Martinelli, F. (ed.) *La Pianificazione Strategica in Italia e in Europa: Metodologie ed Esiti a Confronto*. Milano: Franco Angeli, Milano, 11–31

Martufi, F. (2005) 'Pesaro futuro con vista', in Martinelli, F. (ed.) *La Pianificazione Strategica in Italia e in Europa: Metodologie ed Esiti a Confronto*. Milano: Franco Angeli.

Massé, P. (1965) *Le Plan ou l'anti-hasard*. Paris: Collection Idées, Gallimard.

Mastop, H. (1998) 'National planning. New institutions for integration'. Paper for the XII AESOP Congress, Aveiro.

Mayer, M. (2003) 'The onward sweep of social capital: causes and consequences for understanding cities, communities and urban movements' *International Journal of Urban and Regional Research* 27(1): 110–32.

Michalko, M. (2001) *Cracking Creativity*. Berkeley, CA: Ten Speed Press.

Motte, A. (1994) 'Innovation in development plan-making in France 1967–1993' in Healey, P. (ed.) *Working Paper 42*. Department of Town and Country Planning, University Newcastle upon Tyne: 90–103.

Newman P., and Thornley, A. (1996) *Urban Planning in Europe*. London: Routledge.

Ogilvy, J. (2002) *Creating Better Futures*. Oxford: Oxford University Press.

Ozbekhan, H. (1967) *The Triumph of Technology: 'Can' Implies 'Ought'*. Professional paper. System Development Corporation Santa Monica, California, SP 2830.

Ozbekhan, H. (1969) 'Towards a general theory of planning', in Jantsch, E. (ed.) *Perspectives of Planning*. Paris: OECD, 45–155.

Pascual, I., and Esteve, J. (1997) *La Estrategia de las Ciudades. Planes Estratégicos como Instrumento: Métodos, Téchnicias y Buenas Practices*. Barcelona: Diputacion de Barcelona.

Perloff, H. (1980) *Planning and the Post-Industrial City*. Washington, DC: Planners Press.

Plsek, P. (1997) *Creativity, Innovation and Quality*. Wisconsin, WI: ASQ Quality Press.

Pugliese, T., and Spaziante, A. (eds) (2003) *Pianificazione Strategica per le Città: Riflessioni dale Pratiche*. Milano: Franco Angeli.

Rodriguez A., and Martinez, E. (2003) 'Restructuring cities: miracles and mirages in urban revitalization in Bilbao, in Moulaert, F., Rodriguez, A., and Swyngedouw, E. (eds) *The Globalized City. Economic Restructuring and Social Polarization in European Cities*. Oxford: Oxford University Press, 181–207.

Sager, T. (1994) *Communicative Planning Theory*. Aldershot: Avebury.

Salet, W., and Faludi, A. (eds) (2000) *The Revival of Strategic Spatial Planning*. Amsterdam: Royal Netherlands Academy of Arts and Sciences, 1–10.

Sandercock, L. (2003) *Cosmopolis II. Mongrel Cities in the 21st Century*. London: Continuum.

Schwartz, P. (1991) *The Art of the Long View*. New York: Doubleday Currency.

Secchi B. (1986)'Una nuova forma di piano' *Urbanistica* 82: 6–13.

Senge, P. (1990) *The Fifth Dimension*. New York: Century/Doubleday.

Surowiecki, J. (2005) *The Wisdom of Crowds*. New York: Anchor Books.

Swyngedouw, E., Moulaert, F., and Rodriguez, A. (2002) 'Neoliberal urbanization in Europe: large-scale urban development projects and the new urban policy' *Antipode* 34(6): 542–77.

Van den Broeck, J. (1987) 'Structuurplanning in praktijk: werken op drie sporen' *Ruimtelijke Planning* II.A.2.C: 53–119.

Van den Broeck, J. (2001) *Informal Arenas and Policy Agreements Changing Institutional Capacity*. Paper to the First World Planning School Congress, Shanghai.

Webster, N. (1970) *Webster's Seventh New Collegiate Dictionary*. Springfield: Merriam.

Winch, G. (1998) 'Dynamic visioning for dynamic environments' *The Journal of the Operational Research Society* 50(4): 354–361.

PART TWO
CONCEPTUAL CHALLENGES
FOR SPATIAL PLANNING
THEORY

Introduction to Part Two

Jean Hillier

There is a lot of theoretical re-thinking that is needed (Harvey 2009: np)

The so-called economic 'crisis' which has unfolded as a global event since 2008 has generated, for many people, a rupture in the nature of socio-economic life. Changes in the organizational structure of capitalism – of attempts by state and supra-state architectures to regulate capital and of networks of governance attempts to manage impacts as diverse as increases in poverty and welfare need or decaying commercial areas on declining rate incomes – epitomize instability and uncertainty. If we also include the environmental crises of floods, droughts and global warming, the *raison d'être* of spatial planning faces substantial conceptual challenges.

Economic markets, nature and cities are complex, non-linear systems of networks whose future behaviour is essentially unpredictable. The days of spatial planning researchers and practitioners being able to fall back for help on, for instance, classical location theory or notions of the city as a closed system, are long gone. As the chapters in this volume demonstrate unequivocally, there is a need to develop and reference theories which will help practitioners to understand and to cope with the messiness of uncertainty.

There has been, and will always be, strong debate between those who regard the primary purpose of planning theory as explanatory, improving understanding of issues, from which appropriate responses will flow (eg. McConnell 1981; Cooke 1983), and those who regard theory as primarily normative or prescriptive: what ought to happen (e.g. Breheny 1983).[1] Peter Hall (2002: 371) explains 'the agony of the dilemma' as: either theory is about unpacking and understanding historical logics of particular issues and circumstances or it is about prescription for action. As Dempster (2006) points out, however, descriptive/explanatory and prescriptive elements of planning are sometimes conflated, with consequent loss of recognition of the role of values. 'The ease with which what *is* is taken to imply what *should be* points to a reason for ensuring clarity' (2006: np, emphasis in original).

Whilst some authors distinguish between the theoretical, the analytical and the normative, I believe that boundaries are fuzzy, as analysis demands a theoretical foundation and may often lead to a preferred (perhaps implied) normative.

---

1   See Alexander (1992); Hendler (1995) and Dempster (2006) for more detailed discussion.

Moreover, the theoretical foundation selected tends to be linked to a much broader social philosophy (see Reade 1982; Sandercock 1998). Spatial planning theory, therefore, needs to pay ethical attention to the interrelations between economic, socio-cultural, environmental, political and administrative dynamic forces.

The recent essay by Hubert Law-Yone (2007) and the responses by Bish Sanyal (2007) and Huw Thomas (2007), in the journal *Planning Theory*, discuss the issue of what planning theory is and does. Law-Yone (2007: 315-16) accuses the 'field' of planning theory of having become 'formless and sporadic, with no signs of convergence towards a unified body of knowledge'; 'a patchwork of individual interpretations' (2007: 321). I disagree, however, with Law-Yone's view that there should be one meta-theory. I thus welcome a diversity of theoretical views. I agree with Huw Thomas (2007) that planning theories are inevitably grounded in different ways of conceptualizing and understanding and that this is no bad thing. My question is, therefore, not what should be *the* planning theory, but rather, what kinds of theoretical approaches might be relevant to spatial planning.

Volume 3 of the *Critical Essays* collection (Hillier and Healey 2008c), to which this volume is Companion, includes papers 'representative' of several contemporary movements in planning theory. Papers include theories relating to communicative and collaborative planning, institutional approaches, relational concepts, complexity, psychoanalysis, non-representation, insurgence and informality, many of which are not mutually exclusive. Current 'planning theory' thus embraces a multiplicity of different ways of thinking as theorists struggle to make sense of worlds characterized by uncertainty, insurgence and complexity.

Many of the chapter authors in this Part would probably describe their work as poststructuralist. One of the current 'frontiers' of planning theory is that of relating poststructuralist theories to planning. Poststructuralism has become rather an umbrella term for a range of theories which are often grounded in the work of French scholars, including Jacques Derrida, Michel Foucault, Gilles Deleuze, Félix Guattari and Jacques Lacan. Poststructuralist theories typically do not reject structures (such as capital, class, linguistics etc.), but argue that structures are not primordially determinate: 'the relationship between structure and agency is undecidable' (Hillier and Healey 2008c: 410). As are both structures and agents themselves: agents are part of indeterminate structures which are unable to fully determine the subject. A dualist ontology is thereby displaced by a relational one.

As Mauz (2005: 161) describes, 'certitudes waiver in the face of the general production of incertitude ... [M]astered know-how gives way to improvisation' (cited in Buller, 2008: 1588). I would argue for an ontology of indeterminacy and an epistemology of a lack of accurate knowledge. I suggest, moreover, like Bruce Braun (2008: 671), that ontology and epistemology cannot be held entirely distinct, 'since we know the world through specific, embodied practices; in turn, these practices encounter neither a passive nor undifferentiated world'.

As editors, we have specifically invited contributions to this Part from a multidisciplinarity of authors. Many of the important conceptual challenges for planning theory over the years have originated in disciplinary areas such as biology (see the paper by Patrick Geddes, in Hillier and Healey 2008a), management science, psychology and politics (e.g. Herbert Simon), economics (e.g. Kenneth Arrow), philosophy (e.g. C.W. Churchman's pragmatist influence and Stan Stein), sociology (e.g. Karl Mannheim (in Hillier and Healey, 2008a), Pierre Bourdieu and Anthony Giddens), civil engineering (e.g. Lewis Keeble), geography (e.g. David Harvey, Nigel Thrift and Doreen Massey), cybernetics and operations research (e.g. Stafford Beer and others' influence on Brian McLoughlin, in Hillier and Healey 2008a). We should not find such influences surprising, as planning as a discipline is but 'a diminutive newcomer surrounded by larger, more established disciplines' as Campbell and Fainstein (2003: 4) point out.

The discipline of geography, in particular, has had a strong impact especially on postmodern planning theories (Cooke 2008; Phelps 2008). However, Phelps and Tewdwr-Jones (2008) suggest that whilst planning theorists have integrated geographical concepts into their thinking (see, for instance, McLoughlin 1994), as 'an enlarged theoretical "front-end"' (Phelps and Tewdwr-Jones 2008: 576), interdisciplinary work across the two disciplines has been noticeably lacking. Geographers, in particular, have tended to ignore ideas which originate from planning sources.

As geographer, Doreen Massey, wrote, '[t]here are always connections yet to be made, juxtapositions yet to flower into interaction' (1999: 284). Whilst Massey was referring to space, I think that the statement also applies to planning theory. The disciplinary origins and current locations of the authors in this Part range from geography, philosophy, film, computer science, architecture and sociology to bio-engineering. I hope that their chapters may form a porous intertwining of ideas. I regard one of the aims of this Introduction as drawing out some of the connections between them, with specific reference to spatial planning theory.

Although the emphasis in these chapters is on planning theory, theory is related to practice as we editors constantly recognize (see also Patsy Healey's Introduction to Part 1). All the authors in this Part relate their theoretical approaches to the reality of planning practice and/or its built and natural environments. They offer a range of responses to the editorial question which we posed in the Introduction to Volume 3 of the *Critical Essays* (Hillier and Healey 2008c: xii): can we develop theories and practices of provisionality, which 'rely less on closure and more on discovery, which reveal potentialities and opportunities and which open up difficult ambiguities'?

In the remainder of this Introduction, I present brief outlines of some of the key terms used by several of the authors; in particular, concepts of assemblages, materialities and expressivities. Locating the papers in the current problematic of global economic recession, I indicate how the authors offer us theoretical tools to understand conditions of possibility of what happened (Manuel DeLanda, Joris Van Wezemael); to consider alternatives to the hegemony of mainstream capitalism (J.K. Gibson-Graham and Jenny Cameron) and to the implications of reconsidering nature (Erik Swyngedouw). Planning practice is concerned with imagining futures and with hoping for better, rather than worse, futures to eventuate.[2] As such, the

---

2   I refer readers back to the discussion of underlying values and planning interventions in the Overall Introduction to this volume.

chapter by John Pløger on the vitalism of urbanity offers some new and challenging conceptualizations.

Assemblages, Materialities, Expressivities

Very few, if any, countries of the world have been unaffected by the global economic recession caused, as the International Trade Union Confederation claims, by 'unfettered casino capitalism' (ITUC, cited in Wachman 2009: 29). As Lovering (2009) indicates, in the UK at least, the collapse of finance markets has precipitated a dramatic decline in investment and consumption by individuals, the public, private and voluntary sectors alike. Cranes stand idle on skylines as urban regeneration projects have halted. Local planning authority staff in many areas of the UK have been offered voluntary redundancy packages and contracts have not been renewed as the numbers of development applications have decreased substantially. I argue that before we can begin to imagine futures, we need to understand how we/our cities/regions/nations, got into such situations. What were the main drivers; the conditions of possibility? In considering this question, I first present the concept of assemblages, to which several authors refer.

Assemblages

As David Harvey (2009) argues, to understand the current (2009) economic situation, there is a need to go beyond simply looking at labour processes or toxic debt. It is more informative to consider the complex connectivities or relationships – assemblages – around the state, production and labour processes; around finance and the wider range of speculative and derivative markets which have been created.

An assemblage is a multiplicity. A poststructuralist theory of assemblages, their creation, temporary stabilization and disjunction, was developed by the French philosopher, Gilles Deleuze (1991, 1994; Deleuze and Guattari 1987). Since then, it has gained widespread use and acceptance in the social sciences (see, for example, DeLanda 2002, 2006, this Part; Thrift 2004; Olds and Thrift 2005; Venn 2006; Hillier 2007; Harman 2008a; Van Wezemael 2008, this Part; Farias and Bender 2009). An assemblage is an entity constructed from heterogeneous parts. It can refer to atoms, biological organisms, species, ecosystems, social human and non-human entities, from a subjective state of cognition and experience to 'objective relations, a material structure-like formation, a describable product of emergent social conditions; a configuration of relationships among diverse sites and things' (Marcus and Saka 2006: 102, cited in Hillier 2007: 61). What is particularly important about an assemblage is the relations (especially the power or force relations) between the heterogeneous parts or elements. Relational interaction and connectivity are vital, especially if the assemblage is to develop agency. Nevertheless, as Thrift (2005: 469) points out, assemblages do not exist in isolation, but in relation to a 'whole series of worlds which are more or less attuned to each other and which have more or less resonance in and with each other'. Even Darwinian evolution has now convincingly been demonstrated to be a tangled network of assemblages rather than a hierarchical tree (Doolittle 2000a, 2000b; Woese 1998, 2004).

Van Wezemael (2008) illustrates how assemblages may be analyzed along two axes: according to the *processes* by which relations between elements territorialize or stabilize and deterritorialize or destabilize an assemblage, and also according to the *roles* which assemblages can play. Components can be either material and/or expressive/discursive. I explain these in turn.

Materialities

Social scientists are increasingly recognizing that many materials possess agentic capacity. They act as agents, occasionally with powerful consequences – which Jane Bennett (2004) terms 'thing-power'. Material components of an assemblage include elements such as bodies, time, energy, buildings, technology, laws, each of which can be enforced/stabilized or challenged/destabilized (Hillier 2009). The material parts of a social assemblage, such as a design competition assessment panel, as Joris Van Wezemael demonstrates (this Part), consist of the energy and labour involved in viewing and assessing the proposals, establishing and maintaining relations between panel members and negotiating a competition winner.

Expressivities

Expressive components of an assemblage include texts, such as area action plans, reports, petitions and nonlinguistic visibilities such as gestures, charisma, architectural style, the skyline of a city and so on (see DeLanda 2006).

With regard to both materialities and expressivities, it is important to consider not only their properties, but also their capacities – what can something or someone *do*; its potential to affect or be affected by other entities with which it interacts. For instance, we recognize the capacity of a person's smile to give someone else a 'warm' feeling; the capacity of an installation of iron bodies on a beach to induce emotions of joy, anger or sadness (Hillier 2008a, 2008b).

Conceptualizing Challenges and Opportunities

Applying such concepts, Manuel DeLanda (this Part) traces the development of cities, regions and states. His non-reductionist, pluralist assemblage approach indicates how social entities 'emerge from the interactions among entities operating at a smaller scale' (2006: 118) and form an assemblage which 'does not harmonize its different components but interlocks them while respecting their heterogeneity' (2006: 119). DeLanda argues that 'a reified generality like "society as a whole" can be replaced by a multiscaled social reality, as long as the part-to-whole relation is correctly conceptualised to accommodate all their complexity' (2006: 34).[3]

DeLanda views multi-scalar spatial relations as crucial in the stabilization or territorialization of locales.[4] He asks what components play material roles in locale assemblages, and emphasizes the relevance of physicalities such as the local square, churches, pubs, shops and streets in addition to infrastructures of pipes, cables and wires. With regard to expressive roles, he particularly identifies architectural style, vistas and skylines.

Manuel DeLanda's conceptual challenge for planning theory lies in his 'new model' of philosophy, which commentators such as Graham Harman (2008b: 367) regard as holding 'a surprising possible future' for the field. DeLanda's realist ontology (real things exist apart from us humans and from each other) argues that assemblages – and particularly the relations between elements – potentially catalyze effects and generate the new through emergence.[5]

In his chapter, Joris Van Wezemael applies assemblage theory as a conceptual methodology which facilitates our comprehension of the pluralism constitutive of planning design competitions, which, in a period of economic recession, are often seen as a relatively 'cheap' means of obtaining high quality development proposals. Van Wezemael illustrates how human and non-human actants are folded together in an assemblage of relational materialities and expressivities: of models, images, texts, speech utterances and so on. He shows how the dynamics of the competition are not determined as the component parts can play many roles and generate different tendencies of becoming. Van Wezemael concludes by making some suggestions for improving the release of a competition's 'innovative energy'.

Returning to my theme of economic recession, I argue that actants should regard it as an opportunity for change and to release innovative energy: to address long-term problems and to do something different, rather than reconstructing capitalism in its previous image. Whilst some commentators, such as Amartya Sen (2009), argue a need for capitalism to be reconstructed via a more accurate reading of Adam Smith, others, such as David Harvey (2009), call for the 'people' to take command of productive absorption of the capitalist surplus. Harvey advocates 'popular revolt' against the old regime in a reconfiguration of the economy. He calls for strategic thinking about 'the social economy in some alliance with labour

---

3   There appears resonance between DeLanda's conceptualization of pluralism and that of John Dewey, the North American pragmatist philosopher introduced in Volume 2 of the *Critical Essays* (Hillier and Healey 2008b), whose work, *The Public and its Problems* (1927), has influenced planning theorists.

4   See also the chapter by Enrico Gualini, this volume, for a similar argument from a different philosophical grounding.

5   For definition and explanation of the concept of emergence, see the Introduction to Part 3, this volume.

and ... municipal-based movements' (2009: np).[6] In addition, John Lovering (2009: 4) suggests that 'central strategic place' should be given to the goals of 'maximising local economic welfare' and 'strengthening community resources and non-market opportunities' (2009: 5).[7]

Reading Harvey and Lovering together leads me to the paper by J.K. Gibson-Graham and Jenny Cameron and the conceptual challenge of alternative, non-exploitative economic relations in destabilizing the dominance of capitalocentric economic thinking. The authors develop their feminist-inspired critique of capitalocentric perspectives (for detail, see Gibson-Graham 1996), which has been intrinsically practice-linked through their participatory action research with communities in particular sites in Australia and the US. Such work has enabled community members, NGOs and local governments to both imagine and enact alternative economic development trajectories which are not reliant on capitalist 'growth' (see also, Cameron and Gibson 2005; Gibson-Graham and Roelvink 2008). Theirs is a prime example that economic change does not have to involve whole-scale, structural transformation, but that small, local, changes can be valuable, especially to the socially excluded (Gibson-Graham 1996: 160).

Gibson-Graham and Cameron argue the importance of distinguishing analytically between different types of economic practices and for legitimizing such diversity (community enterprises, household production, for example) with regard to both the conditions of existence and the effects of such practices. They also argue for promoting existing forms of non-capitalist production, appropriation and distribution, including within households, co-operatives, family partnerships and so on. The current recession offers an almost unique opportunity for agencies of governance to make a choice: either to reconstruct capitalism '(as we knew it)' or to support non-capitalist alternative conceptions of economic relations so that they eventually transform the economic landscape into something less oppressive, more just and more socially beneficial.

Gibson-Graham and Cameron's chapter may be contextualized within a broader field of social innovation literature which 'valorizes the knowledge and cultural assets of communities and which foregrounds the creative reconfiguration of social relations' (MacCallum et al. 2008: 2). The work of Frank Moulaert (2008; Moulaert et al. 2007; Moulaert and Sekia 2003; Moulaert and Nussbaumer 2005) is particularly relevant, as is his Integrated Area Development (IAD) approach which has specific territorial and spatial planning implications (Moulaert et al. 2000; Moulaert and Nussbaumer 2004). Focused on the improvement of life quality for disempowered inhabitants of 'deprived' urban neighbourhoods, particularly through action research programs, IAD links the satisfaction of human needs to innovation in the social relationships of governance, social economy, welfare, education and so on (Moulaert 2009).

---

6   But Harvey is less clear about how a 'people' might come together with the force to eventuate such changes to the capitalist system.

7   See Ananya Roy's chapter in this volume for a possible response to Lovering on this point.

Much of Erik Swyngedouw's work also falls within the rubric of social innovation (e.g. Swyngedouw 2008). In his chapter in this Part, Swyngedouw conceptualizes the challenge of problematizing Nature beyond its traditional reductionism to an imaginary 'object' or 'the environment'. (See also Braun 2005, 2006; Castree 2005, 2010; Gandy 2006.) I find such problematization stimulating. In the current global recession, there have been several calls for a Green New Deal (GND) which would grasp the opportunity to do something about the financial crisis in a 'green' manner that would also decelerate the rate of global warming and oil-dependence (<www.greennewdealgroup.org>). Recognizing the connectivities between global economies, energy and nature, the GND calls for a restoration of economic stability and environmental sustainability: to 'lay the foundations for the emergence of a set of resilient low-carbon high well-being economies, rich in jobs and based on independent sources of energy supply' (The Green New Deal Group 2009: 19).

In 2009 the summit of G20 nations effectively ignored such advice in its recommendations for reconstituting capitalism in much its former state. This potentially does little for the plight of many of the world's environments which face possible ecological collapse. For instance, global warming is melting the Arctic ice-cap at an unprecedented rate, endangering animals such as polar bears and arctic foxes. However, while EU reports continue to comment favourably on ice-melt in terms of 'the increased accessibility of the enormous hydrocarbon resources in the Arctic region' (HREC 2008: 8, cited in Traynor 2008: np) and the exposure of vast oil, gas and mineral riches (chiefly diamonds, nickel, copper, zinc, lead sulphide, lead and zinc), it remains unsurprising that states, such as the US, refuse to support or enact legislation to protect polar bears as an endangered species (Goldenberg 2009). Economic considerations outweigh even photogenic species in this instance. Nature has become an empty signifier, depoliticized except as the object of an unseemly political scramble to colonize its meaning and control economic returns. Alternative socio-natural arrangements appear foreclosed in the Arctic, where Nature is passively represented as an economic resource.

Erik Swyngedouw's political ecology approach challenges the 'fantastic' concepts of sustainability and sustainable planning, such as the above, which 'sustain a post-political arrangement sutured by fear and driven by a concern to manage things so that we can hold on to what we have' (see also Swyngedouw 2007; Dean 2009 and Tambakaki 2009, for further discussion of the post-political). Swyngedouw argues that 'feel-good' depoliticized sustainability policies are grounded in several assumptions which require challenge. The assumptions include: social and ecological problems are external side-effects of, rather than integral to, the workings of liberal politics and capitalist economics; Nature and the environment are universalized imaginaries; environmental problems can be managed through a dialogical politics which depoliticizes Nature and its demands.

The challenges for spatial and so-called 'natural resource' planning thus require new, politicized, understandings of Nature: as meshworks of various assemblages; in encounters with humans and other non-humans and, in particular, with the violences of law and of urbanity. As Halsey (2009: 241) claims, 'it is the city that brings about a relation with the earth that is peristaltic and predatory rather than fluid and mutually agreeable'.

Is fluid urbanity possible? In his chapter, John Pløger clarifies our understanding of 'urbanity', demonstrating how, all-too-often, spatial planners have interpreted the term to mean 'socio-spatial experiences in cities' relating to the 'city as a form'. He suggests that spatial planners should, instead, regard urbanity as a mental disposition of living in the city: of experiences and values, of significations, attitudes and norms, rather than as a relatively 'passive use of space' represented by life-form typologies and demographic mappings.

Pløger's urbanity is grounded in rethinking the concept of vitalism. He argues that because of the vitality of human and non-human life and the 'lived contingency' of cities, urbanity is inevitably fluid, or 'in-becoming'. Pløger suggests that spatial planners should consider actants' lived schemes of significations and lived identifications (including their own, I would add), if they are to begin to understand the topology of cities.

The conceptual challenge of vitalism reminds us that strategic spatial planning must always be an act of experimentation. We can never guarantee outcomes over short, medium and, especially, over long terms. Vitalism also teaches us, as Bruce Braun (2008: 676) comments, that 'dreams of mastery' which presume that we can plan 'without any surprises, are the height of hubris, and harbour the possibility of catastrophe'. The dramatic failure of such 'dreams of mastery' were exemplified, some 30 years ago, by Peter Hall's catalogue of Great Planning Disasters (1980), but we continue to master-plan and construct monumental megaprojects.[8]

A key value of vitalism may, therefore, lie in its epistemological ethical imperative, forcing us to think about the limits of our knowledge (Braun 2008; Greco 2005). 'Vitalism functions in part as an ongoing form of resistance to reductionism and to the temptation of premature satisfaction, closure, denial or ignorance' (Fraser et al. 2005: 2, cited in Braun 2008: 676).

Admitting uncertainty and 'not knowing' should not be anathema to the strategic task of planners to imagine futures. What the authors in this Part (and in Part 3) argue is to imagine futures on the basis of greater pragmatic[9] understanding of the relational links between actants[10] and drivers of change. Spatial planning practice, by its very nature, entails attempting to imagine one, or several, future(s) which are different to the actualities that actors know (see Albrechts, this volume). John Friedmann (2002) identifies two moments of futures thinking:

---

8   In 2010, several of Hall's examples would not now be regarded as such 'disasters' (for instance, the Sydney Opera House, San Francisco's BART), whilst many others could be nominated for inclusion (such as development of Dubai's Palm Islands and World archipelago, only four metres above sea-level, residential development in flood-prone areas in the UK and high-rise outer suburban public housing estates throughout the Western world).

9   That is, in terms of practical consequences.

10   See footnote 6, Overall Introduction.

critique and constructive vision. We tend to criticize aspects of present situations and conditions – injustice, inequality, exclusion, environmental degradation and so on. Out of such critiques may develop constructive visions of the future. Such visions carry a range of values, meanings and purposes (Friedmann 2002). They also carry hope.

David Pinder explains in his chapter that for several hundred years, theorists and planners have imagined ideas of the 'good city' and the 'utopian city' as solutions to perceived urban ills or dis-eases. From the cities proposed by Plato (1992 [c.380BC]) and Thomas More (1965 [1516]) onwards, scholars, planners and politicians have dreamed of and fantasized 'good' or 'better' futures. From Boullée to Saint-Simon and Comte, through Ebenezer Howard, Patrick Geddes, Frank Lloyd Wright, Le Corbusier and the British New Towns movement, to the theoretical work of David Harvey and Leonie Sandercock and the physical dreamings of Robert Moses in New York and the New Urbanists such as Andres Duany, Elizabeth Plater-Zyberg and Peter Katz, authors' imaginaries have been (explicit or implicit) visions of a better world.

Resonating with Margo Huxley's chapter in Part 1, Pinder seeks more nuanced understandings of how utopias have been and are conceived. He searches for the often obscured impulses which lay behind or buried within utopian plans and regulatory projects, to ask what and whose interests and/or anxieties they assert; who were or would be included and who excluded from such ordered states.

As Pinder explains, however, there is still a role for conceptualizing how socio-spatial relations might be transformed for the better; a 'provocative dreaming', shifting the terms of debate about urban form and function away from identification with formal plans or schemes. In this vein, the work of Ernst Bloch (1986, 2000) offers a broader, 'utopic' impression of utopia as 'spatial play' (Marin 1984). The utopic is not a normative prescription, blueprint, or master plan, but rather a speculative force. It is a desire for a different way of living which can incorporate different voices and ways of being, which is a trajectory rather than a point and which becomes an immanent transcendence rather than a transcendent vision.

Hope is central to Blochian thought. Hope enables the present to be prospected outside itself into the future. This is Bloch's 'not-yet', which embodies an immanent future as already-always present. It involves unpacking what constitutes a 'good city' and opening up visions of alternatives, rather than closing down on 'a' vision of 'a' better city or society; one which often benefits the few, rather than the many. It is about what moves us to hope for, and to cultivate, alternative possibilities; and it is about establishing the conditions for the development of such alternatives. (See also Gibson-Graham and Cameron, Swyngedouw, this volume; Fournier 2002; Gunder and Hillier 2007). Such *visions, foresights or prospectives* (see Albrechts, this volume) represent a means of re-introducing hope to spatial planning theory and practice: hope that too-often becomes lost under routines of ticking boxes, following government policy guidance and so on.

Conclusions

Conceptual challenges for planning theory link to philosophical questions of ontology and epistemology. As argued in the Overall Introduction to the set of *Critical Essays* (Hillier and Healey 2008a: xxiii), '[t]he planning idea is oriented towards shaping futures in which better conditions for human life and planetary survival can be achieved'. The authors in this Part illustrate the complexity of the relations through which futures actualize or eventualize and the uncertainty and unpredictability attached to any planning intervention with future-shaping intent. There are many potential futures. Which of the potential futures become possible and actual depends on a politics of futures – of theoretical and practical knowledges and their mobilizations; of power-games.

What might be the ambition of future planning theory? O'Neill (2009) argues that theories should be enacted rather than applied. Enacted, theories can provide a basis for practical judgement in spatial planning. Through constructing, supporting or challenging and deconstructing the institutional, cultural, economic and political structures and agencies of planning practice, theories can offer strong foundations on which to base practice decisions in the face of messy actualities.

With regard to conceptual challenges for planning theory, Geoff Bennington, in 1983, suggested several defining elements of theory, including its reflexivity and its paradoxical nature. What I find most appealing, though, is the suggestion that 'theory thrives by uncovering and working against the doxa, the set of unfounded assumptions that common opinion holds dear' (cited in Scholar 2006: 41). Whether this is in postcolonial theorization of spatial planning, theories of informality and insurgence, of security-related issues, or of how planning practitioners 'learn', long may planning theorists be paradoxical!

References

Alexander, E.R. (1992) *Approaches to Planning: Introducing Current Planning Theories, Concepts and Issues* (2nd edn). Amsterdam: Gordon and Breach.

Allmendinger, P. and Tewdwr-Jones, M. (eds) (2002) *Planning Futures: New Directions for Planning Theory*. London: Routledge.

Bennett, J. (2004) 'The force of things: steps toward an ecology of matter' *Political Theory* 32(3): 347–72.

Bennington, G. (1983) 'Theory: they or we?' *Paragraph* 1(4): 1–8.

Bloch, E. (1986) [1955-1959] *The Principle of Hope*, 3 Volumes. Oxford: Blackwell.

Bloch, E. (2000) [1923] *The Spirit of Utopia*. Stanford, CA: Stanford University Press.

Braun, B. (2005) 'Writing a more-than-human urban geography' *Progress in Human Geography* 29(5): 635–50.

Braun, B. (2006) 'Environmental issues: global natures in the space of assemblage' *Progress in Human Geography* 30(5): 644–54.

245

Braun, B. (2008) 'Environmental issues: inventive life' *Progress in Human Geography* 32(5): 667–79.

Breheny, M. (1983) 'A practical view of planning theory' *Environment and Planning B, Planning and Design* 10(1): 101–15.

Buller, H. (2008) 'Safe from the wolf: biosecurity, biodiversity, and competing philosophies of nature' *Environment and Planning A* 40: 1583–97.

Cameron, J. and Gibson, K. (2005) 'Alternative pathways to community and economic development: the LaTrobe Valley Community Partnering Project' *Geographical Research* 43(3): 274–85.

Campbell, S. and Fainstein, S. (2003) 'Introduction: the structure and debates of planning theory', in Campbell, S. and Fainstein, S. (eds), *Readings in Planning Theory* (2nd edition). Malden, MA: Blackwell, 1–16.

Castree, N. (2005) *Nature*. London: Routledge.

Castree, N. (2010) *Making Sense of Nature*. London: Routledge.

Cooke, P. (1983) *Theories of Planning and Spatial Development*. London: Hutchinson.

Cooke, P. (2008) 'Locality debates', in Kitchin, R. and Thrift, N. (eds) *The International Encyclopaedia of Human Geography*. Oxford: Elsevier. <http://www.dime-eu.org/files/active/0/Cooke%2006%20Locality%20Debates%5B1%5D.pdf> [accessed 26/04/2009].

Dean, J. (2009) 'Politics without politics' *parallax* 15(3): 20–36.

DeLanda, M. (2002) *Intensive Science and Virtual Philosophy*. New York: Continuum.

DeLanda, M. (2006) *A New Philosophy of Society: Assemblage Theory and Social Complexity*. New York: Continuum.

Deleuze, G. (1991) [1953] *Empiricism and Subjectivity: An Essay on Hume's Theory of Human Nature* (trans. Boundas, C.). New York: Columbia University Press.

Deleuze, G. (1994) [1968] *Difference and Repetition* (trans. Patton, P.). London: Athlone.

Deleuze, G. and Guattari, F. (1987) [1980] *A Thousand Plateaus: Capitalism and Schizophrenia* (trans. Massumi, B.). London: Athlone Press.

Dempster, B. (2006) *Categories of Planning Theory*. <http://www.sympoiesis.net/plancat> [accessed 28/04/2009].

Dewey, J. (1927) *The Public and its Problems*. Athens, OH: Ohio University Press.

Doel, M. (1996) 'A hundred thousand lines of flight: a machinic introduction to the nomad thought and scrumpled geography of Gilles Deleuze and Félix Guattari' *Environment and Planning D, Society and Space* 14: 421–39.

Doolittle, W.F. (2000a) 'The nature of the universal ancestor and the evolution of the proteome' *Current Opinion in Structural Biology* 10(3): 355–8.

Doolittle, W.F. (2000b) 'Uprooting the tree of life' *Scientific American* February: 90–5.

Farias, I. and Bender, T. (2009) *Urban Assemblages: How Actor-network Theory Changes Urban Studies*. London: Routledge.

Fournier, V. (2002) 'Utopianism and the cultivation of possibilities: grassroots movements of hope', in Parker, M (ed.) *Utopia and Organisation*. Oxford: Blackwell, 189–216.

Fraser, M., Kember, S. and Lury, C. (2005) 'Inventive life: approaches to the new vitalism' *Theory, Culture and Society* 22(1): 1–14.

Friedmann, J. (2002) *The Prospect of Cities*. Minneapolis, MN: University of Minnesota Press.

Gandy, M. (2006) 'Urban nature and the ecological imaginary', in Heynen, N. and Swyngedouw, E. (eds) *In the Nature of Cities*. New York: Routledge, 63–74.

Gibson-Graham, J.K. (1996) *The End of Capitalism (as we knew it)*. Cambridge, MA: Blackwell.

Gibson-Graham, J.K. and Roelvink, G. (2008) 'Social innovation for community economies', in MacCallum, D., Moulaert, F., Hillier, J. and Vicari Haddock, S. (eds) *Social Innovation and Territorial Development*. Aldershot: Ashgate, 25–37.

Goldenberg, S. (2009) 'US denies polar bears protection from climate change' *The Guardian*, Friday 8 May, <http://www.guardian.co.uk/environment/2009/may/08/polar-bears> [accessed 08/05/2009].

Greco, M. (2005) 'On the vitality of vitalism' *Theory, Culture and Society* 22(1): 15–27.

Gunder, M. and Hillier, J. (2007) 'Planning as urban therapeutic' *Environment and Planning A* 39(2): 467–86.

Hall, P. (1980) *Great Planning Disasters*. London: Weidenfeld.

Hall, P. (2002) *Cities of Tomorrow* (3rd edition). Oxford: Wiley-Blackwell.

Halsey, M. (2009) 'Deleuze and deliverance: body, wildness, ethics', in Herzogenrath, B. (ed.) *Deleuze and Guattari and Ecology*. Basingstoke: Palgrave Macmillan: 233–50.

Harman, G. (2008a) *The Assemblage Theory of Society*. <http://nsrnicek.googlepages.com/HarmanGraham.TheAssemblageTheoryofSoc.pdf> [accessed 05/05/2009].

Harman, G. (2008b) 'Deleuze's ontology: assemblage and realism' *Continental Philosophy Review* 41: 367–83.

Harvey, D. (2009) 'The crisis and the consolidation of class power. Is this really the end of neoliberalism?' (transcribed by Ferguson, K.) *Counterpunch* <http://www.counterpunch.org/harvey03132009> [accessed 23/03/2009].

Hendler, S. (1995) 'Ethical theory and planning theory', in Hendler, S. (ed.) *Planning Ethics: A Reader in Planning Theory, Practice and Education*. New Brunswick, NJ: Rutgers University, Centre for Urban Policy Research, 3–10.

High Representative and the European Commission (HREC) (2008) *Climate Change And International Security*. Paper from the High Representative and the European Commission to the European Council, 14 March 2008, S113/08. <http://www.consilium.europa.eu/ueDocs/cms_Data/docs/pressData/en/reports/99387.pdf> [accessed 05/05/2009].

Hillier, J. (2007) *Stretching Beyond the Horizon: A Multiplanar Theory of Spatial Planning and Governance*. Aldershot: Ashgate.

Hillier, J. (2008a) 'Do we know what a body can do? Emergent subjectivities in Another Place' *Rhizomes* 17(winter): <http://www.rhizomes.net/issue17/hillier/index.html>

Hillier, J. (2008b) *Do we know what a body can do? Emergent subjectivities in Another Place*. Paper presented at The First International Deleuze Studies Conference: 'One or Several Deleuzes?', Cardiff University, Wales, 11–13 August. Copy available from author.

Hillier, J. (2009) *Encountering Gilles Deleuze in Another Place*. Paper presented at Roskilde University, Denmark, 30 April. Copy available from author.

Hillier, J. and Healey, P. (eds) (2008a) *Critical Essays in Planning Theory, Volume 1, Foundations of the Planning Enterprise*. Aldershot: Ashgate, ix–xxvii.

Hillier, J. and Healey, P. (eds) (2008b) *Critical Essays in Planning Theory, Volume 2, Political Economy, Diversity and Pragmatism*. Aldershot: Ashgate.

Hillier, J. and Healey, P. (eds) (2008c) *Critical Essays in Planning Theory, Volume 3, Contemporary Movements in Planning Theory*. Aldershot: Ashgate.

Law-Yone, H. (2007) 'Another planning theory? Rewriting the meta-narrative' *Planning Theory* 6(3): 315–26.

Lovering, J. (2009) 'The recession and the end of planning as we have known it', *International Planning Studies* 14(1): 1–6.

MacCallum, D., Moulaert, F., Hillier, J. and Vicari Haddock, S. (2008) 'Introduction', in MacCallum, D., Moulaert, F., Hillier, J. and Vicari Haddock, S. (eds) *Social Innovation and Territorial Development*. Aldershot: Ashgate, 1–8.

Marcus, G. and Saka, E. (2006) 'Assemblage' *Theory, Culture, Society* 23(2-3): 101–6.

Marin, L. (1984) *Utopics: Spatial Play*. London: Macmillan.

Massey, D. (1999). 'Spaces of politics', in Massey, D., Allen, J. and Sarre, P. (eds) *Human Geography Today*. Cambridge: Polity Press, 279–94.

Mauz, I. (2005) *Gens, Cornes et Crocs*. Paris: Cemagref.

McConnell, S. (1981) *Theories for Planning*. London: Heinemann.

McLoughlin, J.B. (1994) 'Centre or periphery? Town planning and spatial political economy' *Environment and Planning A* 26: 1111–22.

More, T. (1965) [1516] *Utopia*. Harmondsworth: Penguin.

Moulaert, F. (2008) 'Social innovation: institutionally embedded, territorially (re)produced', in MacCallum, D., Moulaert, F., Hillier, J. and Vicari Haddock, S. (eds) *Social Innovation and Territorial Development*. Aldershot: Ashgate, 11–23.

Moulaert, F. (2009) 'Theories of social innovation from past to present', in Moulaert, F., Vicari, S., Cassinari, D. and d'Ovidio, M. (eds) *WP4 Social Innovation, Final Report*. Katarsis, EU Contract No. 029044 (CIT5), <http://katarsis.ncl.ac.uk/wp4/documents/D4final.pdf> [accessed 01/08/2009].

Moulaert, F. and Nussbaumer, J. (2004) 'Integrated Area Development and social innovation in European cities: a cultural focus' *City* 8(2): 249–57.

Moulaert, F. and Nussbaumer, J. (2005) 'Defining the social economy and its governance at the neighbourhood level: a methodological reflection' *Urban Studies* 42(11): 2071–88.

Moulaert, F. and Sekia, F. (2003) 'Territorial innovation models: a critical survey' *Regional Studies* 37(3): 289–302.

Moulaert, F., Delvainquière, J-C. and Demazière, C. (2000) *Globalization and Integrated Area Development in European Cities*. Oxford: Oxford University Press.

Moulaert, F., Martinelli, F., Gonzalez, S. and Swyngedouw, E. (2007) 'Introduction: social innovation and governance in European cities – urban development between path dependency and radical innovation' *European Urban and Regional Studies* 14(3): 195–209.

O'Neill, O. (2009) 'Applied ethics: naturalism, normativity and public policy' *Journal of Applied Philosophy*, 26(3): 219–30.

Olds, K. and Thrift, N. (2005) 'Cultures on the brink: reengineering the soul of capitalism – on a grand scale', in Ong, A. and Collier, S. (eds) *Global Assemblages*. Oxford: Blackwell, 270–90.

Phelps, N. (2008) 'Doreen Massey: Spatial Divisions of Labour, 1984', in Hubbard, P., Kitchin, R. and Valentine, G. (eds) *Key Texts in Human Geography*. Sage: London: 81–91.

Phelps, N. and Tewdwr-Jones, M. (2008) 'If geography is anything, maybe it's planning's alter-ego? Reflections on policy relevance in two disciplines concerned with place and space', *Transactions of the Institute of British Geographers* NS 33: 566–84.

Plato (1992) [*c.*387-380 BC] *The Republic*. Indianapolis, IN: Hackett.

Reade, E. (1982) 'The theory of town and country planning', in Healey, P., McDougall, G. and Thomas, M.J. (eds), *Planning Theory: Prospects for the 1980s*. Oxford: Pergamon Press, 43–58.

Sandercock, L. (1998) *Towards Cosmopolis*. New York: Wiley.

Sanyal, B. (2002) 'Globalization, ethical compromise and planning theory' *Planning Theory* 1(2): 116–23.

Sanyal, B. (2007) 'Déjà-vu' *Planning Theory* 6(3): 327–31.

Scholar, R. (2006) 'Two cheers for free-thinking' *Paragraph* 29(1): 40–53. <http://muse.jhu.edu/demo/paragraph/v029/29.1scholar.pdf> [accessed 30/04/2008].

Sen, A. (2009) 'Capitalism beyond the crisis' *The New York Review of Books* 56(5), 26 March, <http://www.nybooks.com/articles/22490> [accessed 23/03/2009].

Swyngedouw, E. (2007) 'Impossible "sustainability" and the postpolitical condition', in Krueger, R. and Gibbs, D. (eds) *The Sustainable Development Paradox*. New York: Guilford Press, 13–40.

Swyngedouw, E. (2008) 'Civil society, governmentality and the contradictions of Governance-beyond-the-State: the Janus-face of social innovation', in MacCallum, D., Moulaert, F., Hillier, J. and Vicari Haddock, S. (eds) *Social Innovation and Territorial Development*. Aldershot: Ashgate, 63–78.

Tambakaki, P. (2009) 'When does politics happen?' *parallax* 15(3): 102–13.

The Green New Deal Group (2009) *The Green New Deal*. <http://www.greennewdealgroup.org/?page_id=19> [accessed 05/05/2009].

Thomas, H. (2007) 'From radicalism to reformism' *Planning Theory* 6(3): 332–5.

Thrift, N. (2004) 'Summoning life', in Cloke, P., Crang, M. and Goodwin, M. (eds) *Envisioning Human Geography*. London: Arnold, 81–103.

Thrift, N. (2005) 'From born to made: technology, biology and space' *Transactions of the Institute of British Geographers* NS 30: 463–76.

Traynor, I. (2008) 'Europe takes first step towards "Arctic policy" to protect energy security', *The Guardian* <http://www.guardian.co.uk> [accessed 20/11/2008].

Van Wezemael, J. (2008) 'The contribution of assemblage theory and minor politics for democratic network governance' *Planning Theory* 7(2): 165–85.

Venn, C. (2006) 'A note on assemblage theory' *Theory, Culture and Society* 23(1-2): 107–8.

Wachman, R. (2009) 'Unions press G20 leaders to end "casino capitalism"', *The Guardian*, 1 April: 29.

Woese, C. (1998) 'The universal ancestor' *Proceedings of the National Academy of Sciences* 95(12): 6854–9.

Woese, C. (2004) 'A new biology for a new century' *Microbiology and Molecular Biology Reviews* 68: 173–86.

Cities and Nations

Manuel DeLanda

Interpersonal networks and institutional organizations may be studied without reference to their location in space because communication technologies allow their defining linkages and formal positions to be created and maintained at a distance, but as we move to larger scales spatial relations become crucial. Social entities like cities, for example, composed of entire populations of persons, networks, and organizations, can hardly be conceptualized without a physical infrastructure of buildings, streets and various conduits for the circulation of matter and energy, defined in part by their spatial relations to one another. In fact, sociologists discovered the social relations generated by territoriality in the 1920s when the famous Chicago school began its studies of urban contexts, viewed both as spatial localities as well as sites structured in time by habitual or customary practices (Park 1984). More recently sociologists like Anthony Giddens, influenced in part by the work of urban geographers, have returned to this theme, re-conceptualizing social territories through the notion of a 'regionalized locale'.

As Giddens writes:

> Locales refer to the use of space to provide the settings of interaction, the settings of interaction in turn being essential to specifying contextuality ... Locales may range from a room in a house, a street corner, the shop floor of a factory, towns and cities, to the territorially demarcated areas occupied by nation states. But locales are typically internally regionalized, and the regions within them are of critical importance in constituting contexts of interaction ... One of the reasons for using the term 'locale' rather than place is that the properties of settings are employed in a chronic way by agents in the constitution of encounters across space and time. [Locales can be] 'stopping places' in which the physical mobility of agents' trajectories is arrested or curtailed for the duration of encounters or social occasions ... 'Regionalization" should be understood not merely as localization in space but as referring to the zoning of time-space in relation to routinized social practices. Thus a private house is a locale which is a 'station' for a large cluster of interactions in the course of a typical day. Houses in contemporary societies are regionalized into floors, halls and rooms. But the various zones of

the house are zoned differently in time as well as space. The rooms downstairs are characteristically used mostly in daylight hours, while bedrooms are where individuals 'retire to' at night. (Giddens 1986: 118–19)[1]

Giddens' description of regionalized locales, as physical territories structured in time by social rhythms, lends itself nicely to an assemblage approach, providing his definition is augmented with the expressive elements with which locales and regions distinguish themselves from each other. The stress on rhythmic or periodic routines, however, would seem to present a problem. I have argued in previous chapters that, except in the most uneventful situations, routine behaviour must be complemented with deliberate decision-making in the explanation of social action. But when studying the effect of human behaviour on the form of urban components the emphasis on routine activity is justified because, as the historian Fernand Braudel reminds us, urban forms tend to change extremely slowly. A house, as he says, 'wherever it may be, is an enduring thing, and it bears witness to the slow pace of civilizations, of cultures bent on preserving, maintaining, repeating' (Braudel 1992: 267). Given this slowness it seems correct to emphasize those human activities that are so regular they have a chance to impinge on urban form in the long run, such as the journeys to work or journeys to shop that give cities their daily rhythms. On the other hand, in those cases where we witness historical accelerations of this slow pace we will have to add choice to routines since acceleration in the change of urban form typically implies breaks with tradition and hence, deliberate design.

Let's now give an assemblage analysis of these regionalized locales, starting with individual buildings. The material role in buildings is played, first of all, by those components that allow them to be successful *load-bearing structures*. For buildings that are a few stories high, the walls themselves perform this task, in conjunction with columns and independent beams, but large governmental, religious and corporate buildings must make use of more sophisticated techniques as they become taller. As skyscraper designers know well, radical changes in form may be needed once a critical height has been reached, such as the use of an interconnected iron or steel frame which, beginning in the 1850s, liberated walls from their load-bearing duties, transforming them into mere curtains. Other components playing

---

1   Giddens' treatment of regionalized locales is similar to Deleuze and Guattari's concept of a territory, a concept they develop in relation to animal territories but that is not confined to this example. To see the parallel, we must add to Giddens' definition in terms of rhythmic or periodic routines the expressive marking of boundaries. A territory is, in this sense, 'an act of rhythm that has become expressive' (Deleuze and Guattari 1987: 315). Actually, there are three elements in the definition of a territorial assemblage. One needs 'a block of space-time constituted by the periodic repetition of [a] component' (ibid: 313) made into a territory by marking its boundaries, drawing 'a circle around that uncertain and fragile center, to organize a limited space' (ibid: 311). And, in addition to rhythm and boundary, there must be the possibility of opening up the circle, of venturing away from home through a gap in the border. This, of course, corresponds to the processes of deterritorialization which can open up an assemblage to future possibilities or even change its identity.

a material role are those determining the *connectivity* of the regions of a building. If locales are stations where the daily paths of individual persons converge, the regions that subdivide them must be connected to each other to allow for the circulation of human bodies and a variety of other material entities (Vance 1990: 24–5). In a simple dwelling, this connectivity is effected via doors, hallways and staircases shaping the flow of people, and by windows for the circulation of air and light. In taller buildings, on the other hand, internal transportation technology may be needed. Thus, the same decade that saw the introduction of the internal metallic frame also witnessed the transformation of old mechanical lifting devices into the earliest elevators, and a corresponding transformation in the vertical connectivity of buildings.

Changes in connectivity, in turn, impinge in a variety of ways on the social activities performed in a given locale. Fernand Braudel, for example, argues that the connectivity of some residential buildings in the eighteenth century changed dramatically at the same time that the function of the rooms became more specialized, with the bedroom in particular becoming a fully detached region. As he writes, the new connectivity contrasted sharply with that which characterized previous buildings: 'In a Parisian town house of the seventeenth century, on the first floor, which was the noble storey, reserved for the owners of the house, all the rooms – antechambers, salons, galleries and bedrooms – opened off each other and were sometimes hard to tell apart. Everyone, including servants on domestic errands, had to go through all of them to reach the stairs' (Braudel 1992: 308). A hundred years later, some rooms had become public while others remained strictly private, partly as a result of the fact that the routine circulation through a house was now constrained by a different distribution of doors and hallways. Privacy, in a sense, was created by the new regionalization of these locales. In non-residential buildings the changes in connectivity brought about by elevators altered the form of the circulation of employees, from a horizontal to a vertical form, whenever firms were not able to secure nearby buildings to accommodate a larger number of workers. As the urban geographer James Vance writes:

> For the financial district [the] mechanical lift was of critical importance, because much of the movement tended to be internal to a rather clearly defined group of employees in a single organization or in a modest number of commonly related organizations. In that situation the walking zone limits could be reached within a few adjacent buildings, as in the structures built to house a legal community, a medical one, or even a very large single insurance company ... It seems to me not at all a matter of chance that the earliest skyscrapers to be built, those in New York and Chicago, were constructed predominantly for insurance companies and were among the earliest buildings to be equipped with elevators. Large metropolitan newspapers were other early entrants into the construction of skyscrapers, again finding a great advantage in piling large numbers of workers on top of each other and thus, by elevator, being able to secure rapid personal communication. (Vance 1990: 416)

The introduction of internal transportation also had expressive effects. Thus, the apartment buildings that were constructed prior to the elevator, in Paris for example, displayed a clear vertical stratification in which the social status of the inhabitants decreased with height. After the elevator was introduced, this stratification of regions was reversed, with apartments higher up expressing increased status (Vance 1990: 378). Other expressive components vary with the activities housed by the building. In the case of residential buildings, the distinctive furniture of their internal regions and the decorative treatment of walls, floors and ceilings, have often played a role in the marking of social class territories. Ostentatious displays in the aristocratic homes of Renaissance Italy, as Braudel reminds us, were in fact a way of using luxury as a means of domination. But as he goes on to argue, this luxury was purely expressive since until many centuries later it was not associated with any kind of material confort (Braudel 1992: 310). In the case of public buildings, a particularly important example are cathedrals, churches, mosques, and synagogues, locales used for worshipping services, processions and religious ceremonies. These buildings must demarcate a sacred territory from a profane one through the expressive use of geometry and proportion. In medieval Europe, for example, the overall cruciform shape, arcaded cloisters, and rhythmic patterns in stained windows, were all sacred territorial markers. No doubt, these spatial expressions often coexisted with religious representations. The fan vaults of some English gothic churches, for instance, with their series of ribs radiating upwards, express an expansive, ascending motion well suited to mark a sacred territory. This physical expression, of course, must work in conjunction with linguistic ones (the belief that, for example, heaven is above the earth) but it is not reducible to them.

What are the processes that stabilize or destabilize the identity of these assemblages? In the Chinese, Indian and Islamic civilizations, as well as among the European poor, the weight of tradition seems to have been almost overwhelmingly stabilizing when it comes to building techniques and materials, as well as the evolution of furniture and other elements of interior decoration. This evolution, when it took place, occurred at a glacial pace. The birth of *fashion*, on the other hand, had deterritorializing effects, although these were at first confined to the European rich. Fashion greatly accelerated the pace at which the interior and exterior decoration of buildings evolved, although it was not until the 1700s that the rate of change approximated the speed to which we have become accustomed today (Braudel 1992: 317). The motor behind fashion was not just the desire to mark social class territories through the way bodies and homes were dressed but the added fact that, in Europe, aristocracies saw their distinguishing expressive markers constantly under threat by the increased social mobility of rich merchants and artisans. This resulted in a spiralling 'arms race' that drove change. As Braudel writes: 'I have always thought that fashion resulted to a large extent from the desire of the privileged to distinguish themselves, whatever the cost, from the masses that followed; to set up a barrier ... Pressure from followers and imitators obviously made the pace quicken. And if this was the case, it was because prosperity granted privileges to a certain number of *nouveaux riches* and pushed them to the fore' (Braudel 1992: 324).

Another process deterritorializing the identity of buildings is drastic changes in the routines which give them a temporal rhythm. In the case of organizations possessing an authority structure, changes in either practices of legitimization or enforcement may affect the identity of locales. As new enforcement routines replaced old ones in the seventeenth and eighteenth centuries, for example, they generated a distinct regionalization and connectivity in the buildings of factories, prisons, hospitals and schools. As Michel Foucault writes, these buildings have 'an architecture that is no longer built simply to be seen (as with ostentatious palaces), or to observe the external space (cf. the geometry of fortresses), but to permit an internal, articulated and detailed control – to render visible those who are inside it ... The old simple schema of confinement and enclosure – thick walls, a heavy gate that prevents entering or leaving – began to be replaced by the calculation of openings, of filled and empty spaces, passages and transparencies' (Foucault 1979: 172). We can extend these remarks to other types of locales, such as office buildings. The bodies of bureaucrats, for example, must also be analytically distributed in space, pinned down to their offices, and separated from any activity not directly related to their jobs. 'The physical separation of offices', Giddens writes, 'insulates each from the other and gives a measure of autonomy to those within them, and also serves as a powerful marker of hierarchy' (Giddens 1986: 152).

The changes brought about by fashion, or by the disciplinary use of space, already point to the fact that buildings exist in collectivities of similar assemblages, since in both cases we are concerned with how new forms propagate over time through an entire population. These populations of buildings, in turn, form larger assemblages such as residential neighbourhoods, commercial, industrial or government districts, or even moral zones, such as red light districts. What components play a material or expressive role in these larger assemblages? On the material side we must list all the physical locales defining stations for the periodic intersection of the life paths of neighbours (the local square, churches, pubs, shops) as well as the streets providing the necessary connectivity among them. A whole underground infrastructure, starting with water and sewage pipes and conduits for the gas that powered early street lighting, was added in the nineteenth century, and the twentieth contributed with electricity cables and telephone wires.

On the expressive side it was the exterior of buildings, that is, the decoration (or lack thereof) of their façades, that defined the personality of a neighbourhood. In residential neighbourhoods where streets were narrow and their layout formed a complex maze, the frontage of houses remained rather plain. Hence, expressive exteriors appear first in public buildings. These were typically located on a central square in which the surrounding space opened up vistas, that is, opportunities for unusual visual experiences, an effect enhanced by a straight street leading to the church, administrative building, or monument. Aristocratic residential buildings joined public ones by the fifteenth century as the European rich began to deliberately pick observable sites for the location of private houses. Only when enough space was left open around these buildings could expressive ostentation, and the interclass competition that fuelled it, begin to touch the external surfaces (Vance 1990: 175). Besides opening up vistas, the central square of a town played another expressive role: as a centre determining the location of residential neighbourhoods, with proximity to it expressing greater social prestige. This concentric arrangement was characteristic of many European medieval towns but it was more prevalent south of the Alps. In the north, where merchants or craftsmen dominated their settlements, a marketplace occupied the centre of the city, and accessibility to it determined the desirability of a location. This functional rather than social separation led to a more egalitarian form of expressivity, particularly in those planned towns named 'bastides' which were used in the late Middle Ages as a means to colonize economically backward areas within Europe (Vance 1990: 120 and 184–5).[2]

Next we must list the processes that sharpen the boundaries and increase the internal homogeneity of a given neighborhood. The processes of *congregation and segregation* are among those that perform this territorializing function. As James Vance writes:

> *The activities that grow up in cities show a strong tendency to come together in limited areas of specialization drawn into a congregation by the internalizing linkages among them. Whether it be the use of shared sources of materials, the selling to a common body of customers, the practice of a given religion, or the speaking of a particular language, the institutional practice shapes the process of congregation, which is internally induced and highly responsive to matters of scale. A few persons doing a particular thing normally congregate, but not in an obvious congregation. When numbers are increased to the point that they present an areally extensive pattern, then a geographical congregation is to be seen ... In contrast to a congregation is a similarly extensive grouping of ostensibly similar individuals induced by external forces. Instead of being drawn together, they are forced together by segregation. (Vance 1990: 36–7)*

Commercial and industrial neighbourhoods have often been subject to the processes of congregation and segregation: similar crafts and trades have traditionally tended to congregate, while certain noxious activities like slaughtering have often been the target of institutional segregation. But residential neighbourhoods too acquire relatively well-defined borders, and a uniform internal composition, through these processes. The case of institutionalized segregation is perhaps the clearest example, since in this case both the boundaries and composition of a neighbourhood are codified by law and enforced by government organizations. But congregation may also result in a relatively homogenous composition (by race, ethnic group, class, language) even when one assumes a desire by residents to live in a relatively integrated neighbourhood. If people who do not actively discriminate also prefer not to be in the minority, whether relative to their immediate neighbours or relative to their overall proportion in the neighbourhood, there will be critical thresholds

---

2   'The central morphological truth learned in the bastides was that inter accessible and proportionate layout of the town is one of the more concrete expressions of functional equality, and a strong bulwark in its defense' (Vance 1990: 200).

in the composition of a neighbourhood beyond which a chain reaction takes place causing a flight away from the locale by one of the groups.[3]

Important examples of processes of deterritorialization are increased *geographical mobility* and the effect of *land rents* on the allocation of uses for a particular neighbourhood or district. As the sociologists who pioneered urban studies pointed out long ago, segregation sharpens the boundaries of residential areas whereas transportation tends to blur them (Park 1984: 9). A good example of the destabilizing effects of the increased mobility afforded by mechanical transportation are the changes that working class neighbourhoods underwent towards the end of the nineteenth century. These neighbourhoods had sharply defined borders when the journey to work was on foot, but as the electric trolley became available the need to live near the factory was removed and new working class suburbs with more porous boundaries emerged. As Vance summarizes the situation:

> *The fundamental assemblage of buildings and uses in the English industrial city was the working class district composed of row housing ranged around one or several factories and served by quite local shops and pubs. The locating factor was the factory, because the hours of labor were long and the virtually universal way of going to work was on foot. The result was the creation of a city, or even a metropolis, of small, very definite neighborhoods, which contained the life of most people save for weekly or less frequent visits to the market square, the market hall, or the street market for the buying of items of clothing, house furnishings, or perishable food. This parochial existence was enforced by conditions of work and housing and the economic unavailability of access to mechanical transportation. Only later in the nineteenth century, when the bicycle, the trolley, and finally the cheap excursion to the seaside by train began to come into the life of the working class, did any appreciable breaking out of this narrow geographical frame of life occur. (Vance 1990: 316)*

Increased geographical mobility, in turn, interacted with the way in which land assignment and land use were determined to produce more drastic changes in the identity of neighbourhoods. Central authorities have always had a say in these allocative decisions, and they still do, their zoning regulations having a territorializing effect. Land rents, on the other hand, when they became sufficiently fluid to give rise to economic speculation, were a powerful deterritorializing force, divorcing the reasons for land ownership from any consideration of the activities taking place in it, and promoting the relatively rapid displacement of one land use by another. Early urban sociologists referred to this phenomenon as *land succession*, after

---

3   As the economist Thomas Schelling has shown, the dynamics behind these processes are those of people responding to an environment which consists of people responding to each other: given a group of people's preferences to live in proximity to similar groups, each decision made to move into or out of a neighbourhood will change the neighbourhood itself influencing the future decisions of current residents and of people wanting residence there. (See Schelling 1978: Chapter 4.)

the ecological process in which a given assemblage of plants gives way to another assemblage as an ecosystem grows towards its climax mix of vegetation. Instead of plants these sociologists were concerned with land uses and modelled this succession as a concentric expansion away from a city's centre. The core was taken over by a central business district, encircled by a zone in transition, with light manufacture and deteriorating residential neighbourhoods. Next came a ring of working class neighbourhoods, followed by middle and upper class neighbourhoods, and finally the suburbs or the commuters' zone (Burgess 1984: 50).

Those early studies, however, focused on a single city (Chicago) and did not give a full explanation of the mechanisms involved in succession. The concentric ring model seems to be valid for many cities in the US, where incomes do tend to rise with distance from a city's centre, but not for many parts of continental Europe where the reverse is the case (Hohenberg and Lees 1985: 299). This may explained by the older age of European cities and the fact that, as I mentioned before, proximity to the centre was very prestigious earlier in their history. At the core, the displacement of residential by commercial uses in the nineteenth century was a kind of territorial invasion which produced the central shopping district. While a wholesalers' location was determined by proximity to the port or the railroad station, the location of retail shops became increasingly determined by the intensity of pedestrian traffic and the convergence of transportation lines (Vance 1990: 409). Having conquered its territory near the centre, retail itself differentiated into speciality shops (with more locational freedom) and commodity-combining shops, such as the centrally located department store, the first example of which emerged in Paris in the 1850s (Vance1990: 412–13. In addition, retailing had to compete with activities involving the exchange of information – as it occurs among brokers, bankers, couriers and other traffickers of knowledge – and its shops with the office space sought out by these service providers. Eventually, taller buildings decreased the intensity of the competition by giving the territory a vertical differentiation, with shops occupying the first floor and offices those higher up.

Explaining the process of land succession already involves going beyond individual neighbourhoods to a consideration of populations or collectivities of neighbourhoods interacting with one another. Moreover, since these interactions depend on the relative location of members of these populations with respect to a central locale, land succession implies the existence of larger assemblages of which neighbourhoods and districts are component parts: towns and cities. The identity of these larger assemblages, in turn, may be affected by the succession processes taking place within them. As I argued above, the centre of a city, particularly when there is a single one, is a privileged locale which plays a large role in defining its identity. A central square may owe its location to the building which served as a nucleus for the urban settlement, a church or a castle, for example, and to this extent may serve as an expression of the historical origins of the town. Likewise, when the centre is occupied by a marketplace, the commercial character of the town is expressed by that very fact. Thus, when a city loses its *mono centricity* its historical identity may be affected. This multiplication of centres occurred in many countries after 1945, as suburbanization and the increased use of automobiles made the city's core a less promising place for retail activities, and as shopping centres in outlying locations became increasingly common.

But even before the proliferation of suburbs and industrial hinterlands the identity of urban settlements depended on their relationship with their surroundings. Until relatively recently this meant the countryside and its rural villages. A town may emerge within a pre-existing rural area, a process referred to as *synoecism*, or on the contrary, it may be planted in an area lacking previous rural inhabitants with urban life projected outwards on surrounding areas, a process called *dioecism* (Vance 1990: 74–7). But whether it is through a rural implosion or an urban explosion that the difference between town and countryside is established, it is this difference that constitutes them both, a difference in their mix of routine activities and in their density of population. The distinction of routine activities is based on the oldest form of division of labour, that between agricultural activities, on one hand, and those of commerce, industry and formal government, on the other. Until the last two centuries, this separation of activities was not abruptly discontinuous: towns kept vegetable gardens and raised farm animals within their walls, while rural villages engaged in small-scale industry (Braudel 1992: 484–9). The distinction in terms of demographic density also varied in sharpness but it was always there, however blurry. Some big villages may have been larger than some small towns, but the latter always packed more people in the same amount of space.

The relations between town and countryside may be characterized in terms of the resources with which they supply one another. A medieval town of 3,000 inhabitants, for example, needed the land of about ten villages (or 8.5 kilometres) to generate enough food for its inhabitants (Braudel 1992: 486). But those villages, in turn, needed services from the town, from the commercial services provided by its marketplace to the legal, medical, financial and educational services supplied by its organizations, as well as the military protection afforded by its walls and armies. Yet, despite the mutuality of resource dependencies, cities have always tended to dominate the countryside because of the cumulative, *self-stimulating dynamics* that characterize them. There are many models of these dynamics, some stressing the mutual stimulation between the accumulation of workers in a place and the availability of economic investment, private or public, in that place; others focusing on the mutual stimulation between different economic activities that supply each other with materials and services and provide demand for each other's products. In all models, however, 'spatial concentration itself creates the favorable economic environment that supports further or continued concentration' (Fujita et al. 1999: 486).[4] These self-stimulating dynamics can make towns grow much faster than their countryside, increasing their influence and breaking the symmetry of the resource dependencies.

In fact, an assemblage analysis of urban centres must take into account not only town and countryside, but also the geographical region they both occupy. This region is an important source of components playing a material role in the assemblage. The geographical site and situation of a given urban settlement provides it with a

---

4   See also Allen 1997: 27.

range of objective opportunities and risks, the exploitation and avoidance of which depends on interactions between social entities (persons, networks, organizations) and physical and chemical ones (rivers, oceans, top soil, mineral deposits). In addition to ecological components there are those making up the infrastructure of a city, that is, its physical form and its connectivity. While the physical form of some towns may result from a mere aggregation of its neighbourhoods, some aspects of its connectivity (those related to citywide mechanical transportation) tend to have properties of their own, and are capable of affecting the form of the neighbourhoods themselves. The best example is perhaps that of locomotives. Their large mass made them hard to stop as well as to accelerate again and this demanded the construction of elevated or underground tracks whenever they had to intermesh with pedestrian traffic. The same physical constraints determined an interval of two or three miles between train stops, directly influencing the spatial distribution of the suburbs which grew around railroad stations, giving this distribution its characteristic bead-like shape (Vance 1990: 373).

The components playing an expressive role in an urban assemblage may also be a mere aggregation of those of its neighbourhoods, or go beyond these. Let's take for example the silhouette which the mass of a town's residential houses and buildings, as well as the especially decorated tops of its churches and public buildings, cut against the sky. In some cases, this *skyline* is a mere aggregate effect but the rhythmic repetition of architectural motifs – belfries and steeples, minarets, domes and spires, even smokestacks, water towers and furnace cones – and the way these motifs play in counterpoint with the surrounding features of the landscape, may result in a whole that is more than a simple sum.[5] Either way, skylines, however humble, greeted for centuries the eyes of incoming people at the different approaches to a city, constituting a kind of visual signature of its territorial identity. This was particularly true before the blurring of city boundaries by suburbs and industrial hinterlands, but cities endowed with large skyscrapers continue to possess this physical expressivity even in these new conditions. In some cases, however, as the architectural historian Spiro Kostoff reminds us, the process through which old and new skylines become territorial signatures involve a variety of visual representations, such as those found in coins, paintings and prints aimed at tourists (Kostoff 1991: 284–5).

The processes that stabilize a city's identity concern both the sharpness of its physical borders as well as the routine human practices taking place within those borders, in particular, the form taken by *residential practices*. In ancient Greek towns, for example, a substantial part of the population returned to their rural homes in summer months or in times of economic trouble. This custom, in turn, affected the process of congregation that formed neighbourhoods within towns: residents tended to congregate by their rural place of origin and maintained their geographical

---

5   Deleuze and Guattari view rhythmically repeated motifs and the counterpoints they create with the external milieu as the two ways in which expressive components self-organize in territorial assemblages, including animal assemblages, transforming what was mere signature into a style. See Deleuze and Guattari (1987): 317.

loyalties (Vance 1990: 56). In addition, military threats made the inhabitants of a Greek town disperse rather than hide behind its walls. This combination of factors resulted in towns that, in a sense, blended with their countrysides and therefore did not have a sharply defined identity. The opposite case is exemplified by medieval European towns, where fortified walls provided not only protection to the rural population during a siege, but also a sense of security against undefined outsiders, a sense which, even in the absence of obvert conflict, helped to make citizens into clearly defined insiders. In addition, the stone walls marked the point beyond which the exclusivity of citizenship and its privileges ended, unlike the Greek case in which citizenship could be held by those who practised a duality of residence. Overall, medieval towns had a much sharper identity as locales. These cities, as Braudel writes, 'were the West's first focus of patriotism – and the patriotism they inspired was long to be more coherent and much more conscious than the territorial kind, which emerged only slowly in the first states' (Braudel 1992: 512).

The native town in ancient Greece and the walled medieval town represent two extreme forms which city boundaries may take. An interesting intermediate case was created by the rise of the suburb in the nineteenth century, and its proliferation in the twentieth. Whereas at first suburbs and industrial hinterlands simply blurred the outer boundaries of cities which otherwise retained their centre, and hence their old identity, after the Second World War not only the area which suburbs occupied but the variety of their land uses (retail, wholesale, manufacturing, and office space) multiplied, recreating the complex combinations that used to characterize the old central business district. As I noted before, this process created brand new centres in the suburban band. In some cases, the urban realms around these centres were so self-sufficient that the daily paths of their residents could be contained within their limits (Vance 1990: 502–4). Thus, by creating a true multi-centered urban space, suburban growth – and the changes in connectivity brought about by the automobile and the freeway – acted as a powerful deterritorializing force.

As usual, an assemblage analysis of singular, individual entities must be complemented by a study of the populations formed by those entities. An important property of populations of towns and cities is the birth rate of new urban settlements, as well as the rate at which old settlements disappear. These determine the overall *rate of urbanization* of a particular geographical region. In the case of Europe, urbanization intensified in the eleventh and twelfth centuries, accelerated again in the sixteenth, and picked up speed once more in the centuries following the Industrial Revolution. Between 1350 and 1450, and between 1650 and 1750, both the human population and the overall rate of urbanization declined.[6] The first wave of city building took place against the background of feudalism, creating densely occupied areas in which a certain autonomy from feudal relations could be achieved – the city's land still belonged to a bishop or a prince but the city as a whole paid the rent – as well as areas with lower urban density in which cities could not shed their shackles.

---

6   See Hohenberg and Lees (1985), pp. 20–3 (for the period between the years 1000 and 1300), pp. 106–7 (1500–1800) and pp. 217–20 (1800–1900).

Higher density affected not only the relations of cities with feudal organizations, making them more contractual and less directly tributary, but also the intensity of the economic interactions between cities. In the period between the years 1000 and 1300, cities in the low-density feudal areas (Spain, France, England) did not develop systematic relations among themselves, remaining within relatively closed politico-economical domains in which trade relationships were mostly local. In the high-density areas (Northern Italy, Flanders, the Netherlands, some parts of Germany), on the other hand, the regularity of trade was greater, its volume higher, and it covered much larger areas. This led to the generation of more systematic and enduring relations among urban centres, creating the conditions for the emergence of larger assemblages: hierarchies and networks of cities. Much as the differentiation between a city and its surrounding countryside involved breaking the symmetry of its resource dependencies through self-stimulating accumulations, other cumulative processes – related to differential degrees of autonomy from feudal organizations, the relative speed of different forms of transportation, differences in volume and intensity of trade – destroyed the possibility of a uniformly sized population of towns with symmetric resource dependencies.

In formal models of urban dynamics, assemblages of cities of different sizes emerge from a sequence of symmetry-breaking events, as each town confronts centripetal processes, like the capture of population, investment and other resources, as well as centrifugal ones, like congestion, pollution, traffic. At the tipping point, when one set of forces begins to dominate the other, a town may grow explosively or shrink to a small size in the shadow of a larger one (Fujita et al. 1999: 34). In computer simulations the actual pattern that emerges *is not unique* – as if there existed a single optimal pattern to which the urban dynamics always tended – but is, on the contrary, highly sensitive to the actual historical sequence of events. For this reason, the emergent pattern of urban centres is like a memory of this symmetry-breaking sequence 'fossilized in the spatial structure of the system' (Allen 1997: 53).

A recurrent emergent pattern in these formal models is one familiar to geographers: a hierarchy of *central places*. In its original formulation, central place theory was an attempt to describe the hierarchical relations among regularly spaced urban centres, with larger ones displaying a greater degree of service differentiation than smaller ones. In the hierarchies that emerged in medieval Europe, for example, the smallest towns offered a small marketplace as a service to their rural surroundings; medium-sized towns added to this marketing function religious services, as well as some simple administrative ones, like county jails, which they offered to their countrysides as well as to lower-ranked towns. Larger towns, in turn, multiplied the variety of marketing, administrative and religious services and added new ones, like the educational services provided by universities (Hohenberg and Lees 1985: 51–4). In short, in a central place hierarchy each rank offers all the services of the immediately lower rank and a few more, and these added services create resource dependencies across ranks. To these it must be added the economic dependencies which trade may create, since larger towns typically offered a larger variety of products than smaller ones, as well as political dependencies derived from the fact that the largest towns at the top of the hierarchy were usually regional or provincial capitals. In addition to landlocked central place hierarchies, trade among the European population of towns in the Middle Ages generated extensive *networks of maritime ports* in which cities were not geographically fixed centres but changing relays, junctions or outposts. As the urban historians Hohenberg and Lees write:

> *Instead of a hierarchical nesting of similar centers, distinguished mainly by the number and rarity of services offered, [a maritime network] presents an ordering of functionally complementary cities and urban settlements. The key systemic property of a city is nodality rather than centrality, whereas hierarchical differences derive only partly from size and more from the nature of the dominant urban function. Control and innovation confer the most power and status, followed by transmission of goods and messages, and finally by execution of routine production tasks. Since network cities easily exercise control at a distance, the influence of a town has little to do with propinquity and even less with formal control over territory. (Hohenberg and Lees 1985: 240)*

Each node in these networks specialized on a subset of economic activities not shared with the rest, with the dominant nodes typically monopolizing those that yielded the most profits. Since rates of profit vary historically, as sources of supply change or as fashion switches demand from one luxury product to another, the mix of activities in each node of the network also changed, and this, in turn, affected the dominance relations between nodes. For this reason, the position of dominant node, or 'core', as it is sometimes referred to, changed over time, although it was always occupied by a powerful maritime port. The sequence of cities occupying the core was roughly this: Venice was dominant in the fourteenth century, followed by Antwerp in the fifteenth, Genoa in the sixteenth, Amsterdam in the seventeenth, London in the next two centuries, and New York in the twentieth (Braudel 1992: 27–31). Besides economic specialization, Hohenberg and Lees mention control at a distance as a characteristic of city networks, a relative independence from spatial proximity made possible by the much higher speed of transportation by sea relative to that over land. Faster transportation implied that nodes in the network were in a sense closer to each other than to the landlocked cities in their own backyard: news, goods, money, people, even contagious diseases, all travelled more rapidly from node to node than they did from one central place to another.

As assemblages, central place hierarchies and maritime networks have different components playing material and expressive roles. Materially, they vary in both geographical situation and connectivity. On one hand, the geographical siting of central places always gave them command over land resources, farm land in particular. By contrast, the cities in maritime networks, particularly the dominant nodes, were relatively poor in these terms: Venice was so ecologically deprived it was condemned to trade from the start, and Amsterdam had to be constantly reclaiming land from the waters. In terms of connectivity, roads linked central places following the ranks of the hierarchy: there were seldom direct land routes connecting the smaller towns to the regional capital. Also, the relative slowness of terrestrial transportation forced towns to cluster together since the services offered by larger centres could only be enjoyed if the smaller ones were located at relatively short distances, the distance its inhabitants would be willing to walk to get the needed service. Maritime ports were not subject to these constraints. Not only were long distances less of a problem given the faster speed of their ships but they could all be directly connected to one another regardless of rank. The key to this connectivity was the sea. During the first wave of urbanization, for instance, 'the two inland seas, the Mediterranean-Adriatic and the Channel-North Sea-Baltic, served to unite trading centers rather than to separate them' (Braudel 1992: 66). After that, first the Atlantic Ocean, and later on the Pacific, became the connecting waters of a network that by the seventeenth century had acquired global proportions.

While the expressive components of these assemblages may be a mere aggregate of those of the towns that are their component parts, the aggregate may have a pattern of its own. In the case of central places, if we imagine travelling from the smallest and simplest towns up the ranks until we reach the regional capital, this experience would reveal a pattern of increased complexity in the expressive elements giving towns their personality: taller and more decorated churches and central plazas, more lavish religious and secular ceremonies, a greater variety of street and workshop activities, as well as more diversified and colorful marketplaces. In the case of maritime networks, it was not the increased differentiation of one and the same regional culture that expressed a dominant position but the gathering of expressions from all over the world. The core cities, in particular, always had the highest cost of living and the highest rate of inflation, so every commodity from around the world, however exotic, tended to flow towards their high prices. 'These world-cities put all their delights on display', writes Braudel, becoming universal warehouses, inventories of the possible, veritable Noah's Arks (Braudel 1992: 30–1).

Territorialization in these assemblages is performed by the processes that give an entire region a certain homogeneity. The largest central places, often playing the role of political capitals, attracted talented people from the lower-ranked towns, people who brought with them linguistic and non-linguistic elements of their own local culture. Over time, these capitals gathered, elaborated and synthesized these elements into a more or less homogenous product which was then re-exported back to the smaller centers (Hohenberg and Lees 1985: 6). The *higher prestige* of the more differentiated culture at the top acted as a magnet for the short-distance migratory patterns of cultural producers, and gave the synthesized cultural product the means to propagate throughout the region. Long distance trade, on the other hand, had deterritorializing effects. The nodes of a maritime network often played the role of *gateways to the outside*, opening up to foreign civilizations, so they housed a more colourful and varied population. Having a larger proportion of foreign merchants than central places, maritime ports offered their inhabitants the opportunity to be in more regular contact with outsiders and their alien manners, dress and ideas. The existence of dominant nodes implies that the more cosmopolitan culture of urban networks was not egalitarian, but its heterogeneity was preserved since it was 'superimposed on a traditional periphery with no attempt at integration or gradual synthesis' (Hohenberg and Lees 1985: 281).

Moving from the scale of city assemblages to that of territorial states may be done in an abstract way, simply noting that the landlocked regions organized by central place hierarchies and the coastal regions structured by maritime networks are today component parts of nation-states. But this would leave out the historical process behind the absorption of cities into larger entities, as well as the resistance offered by urban centres to such an integration. In Europe, the outcome of this process varied depending on the segment of the population of cities that was involved. In the densely urbanized regions, cities managed to slow down the crystallization of territorial states until the nineteenth century, while in the areas of low density they were quickly absorbed. In particular, unlike the central place hierarchies just examined, those that emerged in the areas where feudalism remained dominant tended to adopt distorted forms with excessively large cities at the top. These disproportionately populous and powerful centers formed the nucleus around which empires, kingdoms and nation-states grew by a slow accretion of territory and, in time, they became the national capitals of these larger assemblages.

Although the incorporation of cities in the sixteenth and seventeenth centuries was performed through a variety of means, direct military interventions were often involved. In some cases the rulers of kingdoms or empires made claims to the territory on which cities were located, claims legitimated by inheritance or marriage but often enforced through the use of organized violence. But warfare also influenced the outcome of the contest between cities and territorial states indirectly through the enormous expense that armies and fortified frontiers implied. Only large, centralized governments, commanding the entire resources of a land and its inhabitants, could afford to stay in the arms races that developed between new weapons (such as mobile artillery) and defensive fortifications. As the historian Paul Kennedy writes:

> Military factors – or better, geostrategical factors – helped to shape the territorial boundaries of these new nation-states, while the frequent wars induced national consciousness, in a negative fashion at least, in that Englishman learned to hate Spaniards, Swedes to hate Danes, Dutch rebels to hate their former Habsburg overlords. Above all, it was war – and especially the new techniques which favored the growth of infantry armies and expensive fortifications and fleets – which impelled belligerent states to spend more money than ever before, and to seek a corresponding amount in revenues ... In the last few years of Elizabeth's England, or in Phillip II's Spain, as much as three-quarters of all government expenditures was devoted to war or to debt repayments for previous wars. Military and naval endeavors may not always have been the raison d'etre of the new nation-states, but it certainly was their most expensive and pressing activity. (Kennedy 1987: 70–1)

The historical period that sealed the fate of autonomous cities can be framed by two critical dates, 1494 and 1648, a period that witnessed warfare increasing enormously in both intensity and geographical scope. The first date marks the year when Italian city-states were first invaded and brought to their knees by armies from beyond the Alps, the French armies under Charles VIII whose goal was to enforce territorial claims on the kingdom of Naples. The second date celebrates the signing of the peace treaty of Westphalia, ending the Thirty Years' War between the largest territorial entity at the time, the catholic Habsburg Empire, and an alliance between France, Sweden and a host of protestant states. When the peace treaty was finally signed by the exhausted participants, a unified, geopolitically stabilizing Germany had been created at the centre of Europe, and the frontiers that defined the identity of territorial states, as well as the balance of power between them, were consolidated. Although the crucial legal concept of 'sovereignty' had been formalized prior to the war (by Jean Bodin in 1576) it was during the peace conference that it was first used in practice to define the identity of territorial states as legal entities (Barker 2000: 5–8).[7] Thus, international law may be said to have been the offspring of that war.

As I argued in the previous chapter, it is important not to confuse territorial states as *geopolitical entities* with the organizational hierarchies that govern them. Geopolitical factors are properties of the former but not of the latter. As Paul Kennedy argues, given the fact that after 1648 warfare typically involved many national actors, geography affected the fate of a nation not merely through 'such elements as a country's climate, raw materials, fertility of agriculture, and access to trade routes – important though they all were to its overall prosperity – but rather [via] the critical issue of strategical *location* during these multilateral wars. Was a particular nation able to concentrate its energies upon one front, or did it have to fight on several? Did it share common borders with weak states, or powerful ones? Was it chiefly a land power, a sea power, or a hybrid – and what advantages and disadvantages did that bring? Could it easily pull out of a great war in Central Europe if it wished to? Could it secure additional resources from overseas?' (Kennedy 1986: 86, emphasis in original).

But if territorial states cannot be reduced to their civilian and military organizations, the latter do form the main actors whose routine activities give these largest of regionalized locales their temporal structure. A good example of the new organizational activities that were required after 1648 were the fiscal and monetary policies, as well as the overall system of public finance, needed to conduct large-scale warfare. On the economic side there were activities guided by a heterogeneous body of pragmatic beliefs referred to as 'mercantilism'. The central belief of this doctrine was that the wealth of a nation was based on the amount of precious metals (gold and silver) that accumulated within its borders. This monetary policy, it is clear today, is based on mistaken beliefs about the causal relations between economic factors. On the other hand, since one means of preventing the outward flow of precious metals was to discourage imports, and this, in turn, involved the promotion of local manufacture and of internal economic growth, mercantilism had collective unintended consequences that did benefit territorial states in the

---

7   On the five year negotiation period see Parker (1987): 170–8.

long run (Braudel 1979a: 544–5). For this reason, however, it is hard to consider the people making mercantilist policy decisions the relevant social actors in this case. Another reason to consider the activities of organizations the main source of temporal structure for territorial states is that many of the capacities necessary to conduct a sound fiscal policy were the product of *slow organizational learning*, a feat first achieved in England between the years of 1688 and 1756. As Braudel writes:

> *This financial revolution which culminated in a transformation of public credit was only made possible by a previous thoroughgoing remodeling of the kingdom's finances along clearly defined lines. Generally speaking, in 1640 and still in 1660, English financial structures were very similar to those of France. On neither side of the Channel did centralized public finance, under the exclusive control of the state, exist. Too much had been abandoned to the private initiative of tax-collectors, who were at the same time official money lenders, to financiers who had their own affairs in mind, and to officeholders who did not depend on the state since they had purchased their posts, not to mention the constant appeals that were made to the City of London, just as the king of France was always calling on the goodwill of Paris. The English reform, which consisted in getting rid of parasitic intermediaries, was accomplished steadily and with discretion, though without any discernible plan of action.* (Braudel 1979a: 525, my emphasis)

An assemblage analysis of organizational hierarchies was already sketched in the previous chapter so what remains to be analyzed is the territorial states themselves. Among the components playing a material role we must list all the resources contained within a country's frontiers, not only its natural resources (agricultural land and mineral deposits of coal, oil, precious metals) but also its demographic ones, that is, its human populations viewed as reservoirs of army and navy recruits as well as of potential taxpayers. As with all locales, the material aspect also involves questions of connectivity between regions, a question that in this case involves the geographical regions previously organized by cities. Territorial states did not create these regions, nor the provinces that several such regions formed, but they did affect their interconnection through the building of new roads and canals. This is how, for example, Britain stitched together several provincial markets to create the first national market in the eighteenth century, a process in which its national capital played a key centralizing role. And, as Braudel argues, without the national market 'the modern state would be a pure fiction' (Braudel 1992: 527).

Other countries (France, Germany, the US) accomplished this feat in the following century through the use of locomotives and telegraphs. The advent of steam endowed land transportation with the speed it had lacked for so long, changing the balance of power between landlocked and coastal regions and their cities, and giving national capitals a dominant position. With the rise of railroads, as Hohenberg and Lees write, although 'many traditional nodes and gateways continued to flourish, the pull of territorial capitals on trade, finance, and enterprise could grow unchecked. With their concentration of power and wealth, these cities commanded the design of rail networks and later of the motorways, and so secured the links on which future nodality depended. Where once the trade routes and waterways had determined urban locations and roles in the urban network, rail transportation now accommodated the expansion needs of the great cities for both local traffic and distant connections' (Hohenberg and Lees 1985: 242).

On the expressive side, the most important example was the use of national capitals as a means to display central control. This was achieved through the so-called 'Grand Manner' of Baroque urban design pioneered in Europe by the absolutist governments of the seventeenth and eighteenth centuries. Italian cities created the basic elements of the Grand Manner, but it was in France after 1650 that these elements became codified into a style: residential blocks with uniform façades acting as frames for sweeping vistas which culminated with an obelisk, triumphal arch or statue, acting as a visual marker; long and wide tree-lined avenues; a use of the existing or modified topography for dramatic effect; and the coordination of all these elements into grand geometric configurations (Kostoff 1991: 211–15). Although the use of symbols and visual representations was also part of this global approach to urban design, it can be argued that the overall theatricality of the Grand Manner, and its carefully planned manipulation of a city's visual experience, physically expressed the concentration of power. To quote Spiro Kostoff:

> *If the Grand Manner is routinely associated with centralized power, we can readily see why. The very expansiveness it calls for, and the abstraction of its patterns, presuppose an untangled decision-making process and the wherewithal to accomplish what has been laid out. When such clear cut authority cannot be had the Grand Manner remains on paper ... It was not an accident that Washington was the only American city to celebrate the Grand Manner unequivocally ... This was the only city in the United States that had a centralized administration, however deputized, being under direct authority of Congress. Elsewhere one could only resort to persuasion, and try to advance whatever fragments of the overall plan one could through the tangles of the democratic process ... The presumption of absolute power explains the appeal of the Grand Manner for the totalitarian regimes of the Thirties – for the likes of Mussolini, Hitler and Stalin. (Kostoff 1991: 217)*

The stability of the identity of territorial states depends in part on the degree of uniformity (ethnic, religious, linguistic, monetary, legal) that its organizations and cities manage to create within its borders. A good example of homogenization at this scale is the creation of standard languages. In the areas which had been Latinized during the Roman Empire, for example, each central place hierarchy had its own dominant dialect, the product of the divergent evolution that spoken or vulgar Latin underwent after the imperial fall. Before the rise of national capitals the entire range of romance dialects that resulted from this divergent differentiation coexisted, even as some cities accumulated more prestige for their own versions. But as territorial states began to consolidate their grip the balance of power changed. In some cases, special organizations (official language academies) were created to codify the dialects of the dominant capitals and to publish official dictionaries, grammars and books of correct pronunciation. This codification, however, did not manage to propagate the new artificial languages throughout the entire territory. That process had to wait until the nineteenth century for the creation of a nationwide system of compulsory elementary education in the standard. Even then, many regions and their cities resisted this imposition and managed to preserve their own linguistic identity, a resistance that was a source of centripetal forces. Although in some countries, such as Switzerland, political stability coexists with multilingualism, in others (Canada, Belgium) even bilingualism has proved to be a destabilizing force.[8]

In addition to internal uniformity, territorialization at this scale has a more direct spatial meaning: the stability of the defining frontiers of a country. This stability has two aspects, the control of the different flows moving across the border, and the endurance of the frontiers themselves. The latter refers to the fact that the annexation (or secession) of a large piece of land changes the geographical identity of a territorial state. Although these events need not involve warfare aimed at territorial expansion (or civil war aimed at secession) they often do, and this shows the importance of deploying armies near the border or constructing special fortifications for the consolidation of frontiers. A few decades after the Treaty of Westphalia was signed, for example, France redirected enormous resources to the creation of coherent, defensible boundaries, through the systematic construction of fortress towns, perimeter walls, and citadels – separate star-shaped strongholds sited next to a town's perimeter. In the hands of Sebastien Le Prestre de Vauban, the brilliant military engineer, France's defining borders became nearly impregnable, maintaining their defensive value until the French Revolution. Vauban built double rows of fortresses in the northern and southeastern frontiers, so systematically related to each other that one 'would be within earshot of French fortress guns all the way from the Swiss border to the Channel' (Duffy 1985: 87).

Migration and trade across national borders tend complicate the effort to create a single national identity, and to this extent they may be considered deterritorializing. The ability to reduce the permeability of frontiers depends to a large degree on the conditions under which a territorial entity comes into being. Those kingdoms and empires that crystalized in the feudal areas of Europe had an easier task creating internal homogeneity than those in the densely urbanized areas that had to cope with the split sovereignty derived from the coexistence of many autonomous city-states (Taylor 1985: 113–15). Similarly, territorial states born from the collapse of a previous empire or from the break-up of former colonial possessions can find themselves with unstable frontiers cutting across areas heterogeneous in language, ethnicity or religion, a situation which militates against a stable identity and complicates border control. A more systematic challenge to border control and territorial stability has existed since at least the seventeenth century. As the identity of the modern international system was crystallizing during the Thirty Years War,

---

8   I attempted to synthesize all available materials on the political history of languages and dialects in DeLanda (1997): Chapter 3.

the city of Amsterdam had become the dominant centre of a transnational trade and credit network that was almost as global as anything that exists today. If the rise of kingdoms, empires and nation-states exerted territorializing pressures on cities by reducing their autonomy, maritime networks not only resisted these pressures but were able then, and still are today, of deterritorializing the constitutive boundaries of territorial states. The pressure on these boundaries has intensified in recent decades as the ease with which financial resources can flow across state boundaries, the degree of differentiation of the international division of labour, and the mobility of legal and illegal workers, have all increased.

That networks of cities, and the transnational organizations based on those cities, can operate over, and give coherence to, large geographical areas cutting across state boundaries, has been recognized since the pioneering work of Fernand Braudel, who refers to these areas as 'world-economies'.[9] It is too early, however, to tell whether these world-economies are as real as the other regionalized locales that have been analyzed in this chapter. Some of the processes that are supposed to endow these economic locales with coherence, such as the synchronized movement of prices across large geographical areas following long temporal rhythms (the so-called 'Kondratieff waves') remain controversial. But what is clear even at this stage of our understanding is that approaches based on reductionist social ontologies do not do justice to the historical data. This is particularly true of macro-reductionist approaches, such as the so-called 'world-systems analysis' pioneered by Immanuel Wallerstein, in which Braudel's original idea is combined with theories of uneven exchange developed by Latin American theorists (Wallerstein 2004: 11–17). In Wallerstein's view, for example, only one valid unit of social analysis has existed since the end of the Thirty Years war, the entire 'world system'. Explanations at the level of nation-states are viewed as illegitimate since the position of countries in the world-system determines their very nature (Wallerstein 2004: 16).[10] An assemblage approach, on the other hand, is more compatible with Braudel's original idea. Although he does not use the concept of 'assemblage', he views social wholes as 'sets of sets', giving each differently scaled entity its own relative autonomy without fusing it with the others into a seamless whole (Braudel 1979a: 458).

It has been the purpose of this chapter to argue the merits of such a non-reductionist approach, an approach in which every social entity is shown to emerge from the interactions among entities operating at a smaller scale. The fact that the emergent wholes react back on their components to constrain them and enable them does not result in a seamless totality. Each level of scale retains a relative autonomy and can therefore be a legitimate unit of analysis. Preserving the ontological independence of each scale not only blocks attempts at micro-reductionism (as in Neoclassical economics) and macro-reductionism (as in world-systems analysis)

---

9   Braudel introduced the term 'world-economy' to discuss the Mediterranean as a coherent economic area in Braudel (1995): 419. He attributes the original concept to two German scholars in Braudel (1979b): 634, footnote 4.

10 Wallerstein's macro-reductionism derives directly from his use of Hegelian totalities to conceptualize large-scale social entities. See Wallerstein (1993): 4.

but also allows the integration of the valuable insights that different social scientists have developed while working at a specific spatio-temporal scale, from the extremely short duration of the small entities studied by Erving Goffman to the extremely long duration of the large entities studied by Fernand Braudel. Assemblage theory supplies the framework where the voices of these two authors, and of the many others whose work has influenced this chapter, can come together to form a chorus that does not harmonize its different components but interlocks them while respecting their heterogeneity.

References

Allen, P.M. (1997) *Cities and Regions as Self-Organizing Systems*. Amsterdam: Gordon and Breach Science Publishers.

Barker, J.C. (2000) *International Law and International Relations*. London: Continuum.

Braudel, F. (1979a) *The Wheels of Commerce*. New York: Harper & Row.

Braudel, F. (1979b) *The Perspective of the World*. New York, Harper & Row.

Braudel, F. (1992) *The Structures of Everyday Life*. Berkeley, CA: University of California Press.

Braudel, F. (1995) *The Mediterranean and the Mediterranean World in the Age of Philip II. Volume One*. Berkeley, CA: University of California Press.

Burgess, E.W. (1984) 'The growth of the city', in Park, R.E. and Burgess, E.W. (eds) *The City*. Chicago, IL: University of Chicago Press.

DeLanda, M. (1997) *A Thousand Years of Nonlinear History*. New York: Zone Books.

Deleuze, G. and Guattari, F. (1987) *A Thousand Plateaus*. Minneapolis, MN: University of Minnesota Press.

Duffy, C. (1987) *The Fortress in the Age of Vauban and Frederick the Great*. London: Routledge and Kegan Paul.

Foucault, M. (1972) *Discipline and Punish: The Birth of the Prison*. New York: Vintage Books.

Fujita, M., Krugman, P. and Venables, A.J. (1999) *The Spatial Economy: Cities, Regions, and International Trade*. Cambridge, MA: The MIT Press.

Giddens, A. (1986) *The Constitution of Society*. Berkeley, CA: University of California Press.

Hohenberg, P.M. and Lees, L.H. (1985) *The Making of Urban Europe 1000–1950*. Boston, MA: Harvard University Press.

Kennedy, P. (1987) *The Rise and Fall of the Great Powers: Economic Change and Military Conflict from 1500 to 2000*. New York: Random House.

Kostoff, S. (1991) *The City Shaped: Urban Patterns and Meanings Throughout History*. London: Bulfinch Press.

Park, R.E. (1984) 'The city: suggestions for investigation of human behavior in the urban environment', in Park, R.E. and Burgess, E.W. (eds) *The City*. Chicago, IL: University of Chicago Press, 4–6.

Parker, G. (1987) *The Thirty Years' War*. London: Routledge and Kegan Paul.

Schelling, T.C. (1978) *Micromotives and Macrobehavior*. New York: W.W. Norton and Co.

Taylor, P.J. (1985) *Political Geography*. New York: Longman.

Vance, J.E. Jr (1990) *The Continuing City: Urban Morphology in Western Civilization*. Baltimore, MD: The Johns Hopkins University Press.

Wallerstein, I. (1993) *The Capitalist World-Economy*. Cambridge: Cambridge University Press.

Wallerstein, I. (2004) *World-Systems Analysis: An Introduction*. Durham, NC: Duke University Press.

Modulation of Singularities
– A Complexity Approach to
Planning Competitions

Joris E. Van Wezemael

Introduction

What lies at the heart of the complexity turn for planning is that complexity is no longer placed on the plane of interpretation – of meanings, of linguistic structures – but on the plane of a relational materiality and a realistic constructivism. In this chapter I discuss the consequences of this shift in worldview for the conception of decision-making in planning. I illustrate my argument by referring to planning competitions as a specific practice in Switzerland. Planning competitions (architectural, urban design and urban planning competitions) are a widely used instrument in Switzerland and form an important part of the planning culture (Van Wezemael 2009). In this chapter I will also elaborate on a conceptual perspective that helps us with the question of how planning competitions as a particular practice could be designed so that innovative energy may be released.

Planning competitions are broadly considered as a method to encourage innovation and quality in the design of urban projects and buildings. Furthermore, they are said to produce solutions that dispose of a 'self-evident legitimacy' on the basis of their assessment by an 'independent and competent jury' (Stiftung Forschung Planungswettbewerbe 2007). The quality of a competition thus depends on the alleged 'independence'[1] of both the result (winning project) and the competition

---

1 The claim for independence and objectivity triggers suspicion against the background of findings on agonism and antagonism in adjacent fields of urban decision-making (is there a Habermasian dictate of the 'best solution'?) as well as with regard to the political fabric of competitions (see below). As we can learn from Latour (1987) different knowings from various practices (or perspectives) are not expected to produce one coherent set of knowledge. This means that we cannot expect an objectively 'best' solution to be produced by adding up professional (as well as lay) knowings in a competition.

process. Such normative notions tend to veil the real processes that constitute and stabilize planning competitions as heterogeneous assemblages and their capacities. Neither are they fit to analyze planning competitions as regulatory devices; as 'sorting machines' of urban futures, and thus as generative procedures.

In planning competitions many relational settings are connected and densified. On the basis of these relations a constellation emerges that regulates and empowers specific solutions. The relations of forces in competition settings relate inwards and outwards as they fold together relations from economic, political, and architectural fields. The resulting relational complexity of an architectural competition makes it an institution that enables a society's ideals and objectives to be transcribed into its built environment.

How can we adequately conceptualize planning competitions as regulatory devices? How might we address the relations that eventualize the power to govern specific solutions? I conceptualize planning competitions by drawing on what has come to be known as the 'complexity turn' (Urry 2000). The radicalism of contemporary approaches to social complexity, such as assemblage theory (DeLanda 2006a, 2006b) or actor-network theory (Latour 1987; 2005), lies in the recognition of complexity *as a property of reality* and not as a property of humans interpreting reality. I work towards a perspective that recognizes the complexity of planning competitions.

I view the process of opening up, producing ideas, determining a solution and actualizing this multitude into another fixed set of materials as the realm of the competition. At the outset of a competitions process, a given, actual site is opened up towards a virtual space of potential. Then its potential becomings are individuated into representations (projects submitted by the participants) which are contested on the basis of economic relations, statics and material properties, power relations among the networks which are folded together through the jury, design paradigms, political struggles and so on. The competition process moves step by step towards a new possible actualization of a place, separating out most potential solutions and manifesting only one urban future.[2] Therefore planning competitions refer to what is actualized, to what remains virtual, and to the way a planning or building problem is being posed and 'solved' by means of the competition as a socio-technical process. I propose to view design competitions as sites where 'singularities' (see below) that shape planning and design solutions are modulated and eventually actualized.

This perspective calls for a foundation of planning decision-making in complexity thinking. Competitions can be viewed as urban laboratories from which we might also gain a better understanding of how our cities are shaped, and about the relationship of design and the political.[3] Manuel DeLanda's Deleuzian-inspired

---

2   Be there 7, 17 or 77 contributions to a design competition – they illustrate that we could solve an urban situation *differently* (Kohoutek 2005).

3   Here we can also relate to the chapter by Versteeg and Hajer in this volume. They conceptualize 'performance' as the way in which the contextualized interaction itself produces social realities. They use the concepts of 'setting', 'staging' and 'scripting'. They argue that planning should be analyzed with regard to investigating the setting,

approach to social complexity will be used as a foundation for the conception of planning competitions on the basis of complexity thinking. The theory of social assemblages and the processes that create and stabilize their historical identity delivers a conceptual basis for the connection of heterogeneous elements in planning competitions and for decision-making as the modulation of singularities.

In what follows I introduce *exterior relations, singularities* and *assemblages as individuals* as key concepts for thinking social complexity. I then elaborate a relational materialism which allows planning to acknowledge complexity as based on relational materialism and realistic construction. On this basis I reconceptualize planning competitions as a modulation of singularities. This grounds a reflection on doing decision-making analysis in social complexity. In conclusion I emphasize some practical gains of the mooted conceptual approach.

Key Concepts for Social Complexity

The Nature of Relations

The predominant conceptualization of the relations between parts and wholes in social sciences can be addressed as 'relations of interiority'. In assemblage theory relations are conceptualized as 'exterior' ones. While relations of interiority imply that 'the component parts are constituted by the very relations they have to other parts in the whole' and the whole in turn 'possesses an inextricable unity in which there is a strict reciprocal determination between parts' (DeLanda 2006a: 9), the exteriority of relations implies 'a certain autonomy for the terms they relate, ... it implies that a relation may change without the terms changing' (DeLanda 2006a: 11). Hence, a part detached from a whole represented by relations of interiority 'ceases to be what it is, since being this particular part is one of its constitutive properties' (DeLanda 2006a: 9). In contradiction, a component part of a whole characterized by relations of exteriority 'may be detached from it and plugged into a different assemblage in which its interactions are different' (DeLanda 2006a: 10). It 'is always possible to detach an entity from one particular set of relations, and insert it instead in a different set of relations, with different other entities' (Shaviro 2007: n.p.).

In planning competitions many relational settings are connected and densified. On the basis of these relations a constellation emerges that regulates and empowers specific solutions. Kohoutek (2005) refers to such relational settings as he explains that beauty, truth, justice and profit are not naturally compatible, and that we are in

---

including the physical situation in which the interaction takes place to thereby acknowledge the hybrid character of the planning process. Staging refers to the active manipulation of the setting. Scripting refers to the effort to create a setting by determining the characters in the process and providing cues for appropriate behaviour.

need of couplings in order to establish communication. Exterior relations allow for conceptualization of couplings with regard to planning competitions. For instance, a member of a jury in one competition (A) can, at the same time, be a member of an association of planners (B) and a collaborator in a planning or architectural firm (C). All the different relations that make her B or C will affect her capacity to form sets of relations of diverse, heterogeneous elements spontaneously in A, without determining her role. Changes in one set of relations, however, may affect the capacities of a component part in other sets of relations. Change thus becomes immanent to assemblages as it is driven by differences, which are not in the order of things, but generated in the relations that produce it. Changes in those fields that are folded into a competition (because component parts of the competition as an assemblage belong to other assemblages at the same time) can manifest themselves in the competitions. For example, if the architectural firm (relation 'C') wins a competition that is heavily criticized in the architects' community, the capacity for the jury member (relation 'A') to form certain coalitions will be affected.

Relations of exteriority imply that the properties of a whole are not the result of an aggregation of the components' own properties, but the actual exercise of the components' capacities to interact with each other. Component parts include 'things' such as plans, maps, models, or images. Agency is thus not the *starting point* for the formation of a coalition (or a centre of involvement, or an assemblage), *but its product*. Every relation has a localized motive, a singular moment in the onset of turbulence, or the birth of a vortex of involvement. Exterior relations, therefore, may change without their terms changing (Deleuze and Parnet 2002). Involvement in one assemblage, however, can be limited by involvement in other assemblages. For instance, being involved in a community group can limit one's involvement in other juries, or the submission of a project to one competition may be so time consuming that other opportunities cannot be taken; the formation of a set of relations in a jury that gives rise to one project as a winner limits the formation of other coalitions in favour of another project, and so on. As soon as assemblages emerge on the basis of their components' connections they start providing resources for their components as well as constraining them. This then introduces a top-down aspect into the theory.

Singularities

Assemblages are not only actual formations but also virtual ones. In addition to the roles and processes yet described, an assemblage is characterized by what Deleuze refers to as a diagram, 'a set of universal singularities … , that would structure the space of possibilities associated with the assemblage' (DeLanda 2006a: 30). To elaborate, 'analysis in assemblage theory is not conceptual but causal, concerned with the discovery of the actual mechanisms operating at a given spatial scale' whereas 'the topological structure defining the diagram of an assemblage is not actual but virtual and mechanism-independent, capable of being realized in a variety of actual mechanisms, so it demands a different form of analysis' (DeLanda 2006a: 31). As a statistical product of lower-scale connections an assemblage displays emergent properties. However, its properties are not 'given'. When not exercised they are merely possible. Real assemblages consist of a field of actualities (exercised properties), a field of virtuality (potential properties), and a generative field: the intensive, individuating level. All are equally real, but the virtual has no form. The virtual is necessarily structured since different assemblages exhibit different sets of capacities. Singularities are virtual, but they are individuated in assemblages, and so they are vital to the operation of those assemblages (Deleuze and Guattari 1987: 100). We can address the virtual by means of a 'diagram' in terms of unactualized tendencies ('singularities') and unactualized capacities to affect and be affected ('affects') (DeLanda 2002: 62).

Singularities can be thought of as a set of attractors, which allow for a variety of actualizations to one problem. Since actualizations are (temporary) solutions which are derived from processes of individuation, real (not actual) problems are defined by singularities. Problems therefore maintain a certain autonomy from their particular solutions.

The capacity to affect refers to the potential to form assemblages of diverse, heterogeneous elements spontaneously. The virtual-intensive-actual distinction enables us to account for unpredictability in systems while maintaining a consistent materialism. Since attractors are forms of self-organization, systems can become organized, even if currently random or laminar. However, *singularities do not exist independently of the specific assemblage in which they are expressed* and thus incarnated. On the basis of different connections of component parts, *singularities are modulated*. In a planning competition assemblage, the changing relations of jurors (as components of many other assemblages) with submitted projects, other jurors and so on also *modify the space of possibilities as constituted by singularities*. Thus, the changing relations in the process of 'finding a winner' literally modulate the singularities which govern the actualization of decision-making and thus the selection of winning projects. More generally this means that everything that exists in the actual can be considered as an 'answer' to some problem. The concept of singularities allows addressing the distribution of the relevant as a 'structure' of the virtual.

In this strategy we can distinguish between universal singularities (e.g. all juries display some degree of heterogeneity and intensity and open up a space of potential) and individual singularities (each jury displays a singular, distinct degree of heterogeneity and creates intensity in a specific way). Consequently the space of potential for finding a specific competition winner is organized around an individual set of singularities.

Assemblages as Singular Individuals

The identity of any assemblage at any level of scale[4] is always the product of a historical process.[5] There are, as in the vortices of involvement, many levels of emergence in assemblage theory. The identity of an assemblage, large or small, is always precarious, since processes of deterritorialization or decoding can destabilize it, as explained below. Therefore, the ontological status of an assemblage of any size 'is always that of unique, singular individuals' (DeLanda 2006a: 28). Every single design competition as an assemblage is a unique entity with its own history and trajectories. The population of design competitions (as in Switzerland) also has its own history and trajectories on another spatio-temporal scale and is also viewed as an assemblage. Although we should think of universal singularities in the sense of a 'problem' to which all planning competitions give an (individual) answer, there is no role model or 'type' of 'the competition' because every individual competition is 'locally' actualized around individual sets of singularities.

Heterogeneity and a Relational Materialism

I view planning competitions as densifications of relational networks that create a specific interface or platform between the generation of urban texture and architectural, political and economic sets of relations. Today, Anglo-Saxon urban studies view urban areas as locked into a multitude of relational networks of varying geographical reach (Amin 2004). In such a relational perspective urban areas are viewed as second-order phenomena: they emerge from the superimposition and intertwining of multiple layered networks (Schmid 2007). Planners are familiar with a key characteristic of such networks: they cannot be reduced simply to (networks of) human subjects and organizations. For instance, building materials deteriorate; even cyber-businesses require physical locations and resources; data-speedways need glass fibre cables and server farms need a considerable amount of electric energy; the mass of a train and its engine power determine minimum stopping point intervals which affects the urban structure; and flying to a planning conference may affect the world's future climate. Indeed, networks are heterogeneous, intrinsically hybrid with regard to their constitution from relations of non-human and human component parts. They are only ever meta-stable and cannot be determined by a finite set of relations.

---

4   'Scale' is not used in a strictly geographical sense. It rather follows a topological sequence of emergence.

5   In DeLanda (2006b) an individual person, a population of individual persons, friendship networks, interpersonal networks, organizations, inter-organizational networks (clusters, etc.), cities and territorial states are all conceptualized as assemblages on different 'scales', which do not differ in ontogenetic status: they are all historically produced, singular individuals.

But how does their hybrid nature affect the way they can be analyzed? How does this relate to the point of view of the analyst or practitioner? What does this mean for the conception of planning competitions? Planners are used to analysing such networks from the point of view of their human components – an anthropocentric worldview – and to organizing development strategies around the intents of human subjects or groups. I would like to argue that this is related to a very important, and originally positive, development with respect to the planner's worldview. Communicative rationality (Habermas 1981) has – as a side effect – reinforced a perspective where almost everything is related to hermeneutic, linguistic or sociological constructions. In the sense of Giddens' (1984) 'double hermeneutics', I argue that this shift in wider social sciences had a great impact on planning theory and practice (Forester 1999; Healey 1996).

The so-called linguistic turn helped to acknowledge the active involvement of the observer of society and the open, complex nature of social life as the focus of analysis. Wider social sciences have reconciled themselves with the idea of observers as active participants in the research of social reality, giving them a central and pivotal role. This social scientific perspective, however, provides a second order representation by reading all instances of human/non-human relations as somehow culturally determined (Hinchcliffe 2003) and this, as a consequence, enables a (social) constructivist approach to planning issues. Reality is now exposed to the interpretation of the 'active human participant'. However, the 'realities' of the objects of study were inevitably substituted by the analyst's interpretations of the objects or were equated with deeper linguistic structures. This effectively vapourized the relational materiality of social structures into conceptual, idealistic constructions.

Although in the context of post-modernism and post-structuralism, the fluidity, uncertainty and complexity of the social world has been brought to the fore (Arbor and Hirt 2003; Doel 1992; Doel and Matless 1992), recognition of the open and complex nature of social life tends to take place in the symbolic/linguistic dimension. Almost unperceived by many, for most social scientists a sort of linguistic idealism[6] has become a predominant paradigm that has accepted the fortification of the symbolic/linguistic dimension and an anthropomorphic view of the world.

However, I would like to point out that the corresponding anthropocentrism creates fundamental difficulties when dealing, as planners do, with socio-technical and environmental issues. As a consequence of the modernist essentialist perception of matter as inert, passive and docile, the constructional nature of reality (be it 'natural' or 'social') is entirely attributed to human intervention. Or, as DeLanda (1998) argues, we have made the world open and complex at the expense of giving up its objectivity. In other words, the world becomes open only through human intervention. This, in turn, overestimates the capacity of human action as it is cut

---

6   As a consequence of the 'linguistic turn' the term 'construction' is not used in the sense in which Foucault, for example, talks of the construction of soldier bodies through drill and discipline, but to the way our minds 'construct' the world of appearances via linguistic categories. (DeLanda et al. 2006)

off from the relations of forces that govern hybrid and non-human systems. With regard to what it means to plan and govern in complexity, the following questions arise:

- Is a mostly unconsidered, and subsequently 'naturalized', anthropocentrism an unfortunate point to begin theoretization of strategic planning and urban governance?[7]
- If many open systems are involved in the creation of our cities (see above), then why should we conceptualize urban development solely from a human perspective?
- How could a less anthropocentric perspective contribute to our understanding of the dynamics of urban development?

I would like to draw on two examples in order to illustrate my argument:

- Recall that it was a groundbreaking decision in the days of Copernicus to move the virtual point of the observer from the earth to the sun in order to give the empirical data more coherence. Could a shift in our perspective on the becoming of urban areas similarly generate an improved picture of what we planners are dealing with? Could, indeed, a view that moves the narrator of the (hi)story of urban development away from a solely social (constructivist) and anthropocentric perspective clear the field for alternative problems and solutions, for alternative (hi)stories? Could this provide an alternative basis for the potentials of 'steering' (planning, governance)? And how could such a view change our understanding of, for instance, design competitions?
- In his book *War in the Age of Intelligent Machines* (2003), DeLanda attempts to re-tell the history of warfare neither from the point of view of great commanders, nor from the perspective of human victims, but by asking how would the evolution of warfare be seen, analyzed, and accordingly also told by, 'artificial' intelligence? An (however unlikely) anthropomorphic robot historian would trace the various technological lineages that gave rise to their species. Although these lineages would surely involve humans, however, the history of armies would depict humans as component parts of a war machine. Commanders would be catalysts that work on specific critical points in the self-assembly of war machines.

Should planners, investors or community groups be conceptualized as catalysts in the self-assembly of cities? Would planning competitions depict sites where critical points in the self-assembly of cities are manifested? Clearly I argue here that the processes that literally – not phenomenologically – create an urban area (processes of morphogenesis), exceed the constructions of linguistic categories. They need a conception of morphogenetic processes and emergent characteristics on the basis

---

7   It may even be one reason for the bemoaned 'failure' of planning polity and policy on many scales and in many places.

of a relational materialism. Complexity thinking is helpful here because it enables the acknowledgement of 'the unmanageability of the contemporary world whilst also holding open the possibility that novel forms of organisation or structuring might emerge spontaneously out of a sea of dense and disorderly interaction (Cilliers 2005: 166). In planning competitions specific relations of human agents, architectural models, fragments of discourses etc. eventually pick up speed and display the emergent property of capacity to empower specific solutions (Van Wezemael 2009). They can also be depicted as transductions (Mackenzie 2002) as they transcribe societal/cultural variables into the built environment. I next turn to the issue of how we can understand planning competitions.

Decision-making as Modulation of Singularities: The Complexity of Planning Competitions

On the basis of the argument so far, the notion that planning competitions are temporal couplings between diverse fields can be further specified. Each of those fields inherits dynamics that may be understood as relations of forces that are structured by specific critical points which I refer to as singularities. Experimentation and creativity in planning competitions – as in all forms of spatial planning – can be understood as a tracing of critical points that are generated by relations of forces, both human and non-human. Accordingly, the submitted projects in planning competitions are viewed as lines that are mapping out spaces of potential – as a 'phase space' (DeLanda 2002). Every proposed project simultaneously positions itself in many fields, and each of them implies specific forces (or attractors, DeLanda 2002). The space of potential should be viewed as a relational space that disposes of slopes, gravitational fields and so on.

Submitted projects in planning competitions can be viewed as exploring multiple trajectories that are governed by economic tipping points, physical singularities, liminal spaces that are generated by meshworks of overlapping regulations and institutions, financial conditions, material properties, energy flows, building regulations, the discursive field of architecture, fragments of past discourses on 'the good' home, city or museum, etc. They serve to stratify the plane on which a project unfolds. It is the relation of the positionality of the planning suggestions in all the above dimensions – which of course interfere with each other – which gives rise to emergent properties of each of the projects.

The sum of the proposed solutions generates a relational space of possible solutions to the problem as outlined in the planning competition's programme brief. With regard to decision-making this means that each project involves an initial 'judgement': the planners who submit projects try to anticipate the relations of trade-offs between the interfering fields, which they believe the jury might honour. However, a planning competition implies three different judgements: the judgements which submitting planners make with regard to what they believe the jury might honour; the judgement of the jury which eventually picks a winner and which unfolds in a relational space as opened up by the projects; and the judgement of the public with regard to the outcome of the competition, which is also, of course, a judgement on both of the prior ones.[8] However, the programme brief should not be confused with what will actually be required in the competition (Kreiner 2008), or put differently: with those criteria that eventually select the winning project. The second 'judgement' – the jury eventually picks a winner – will *experimentally unfold* in the interaction with the space as generated by the submitted projects. The decisive *criteria thus co-evolve* with the projects that are proposed. The unfolding trajectories of 'what the jury wants' should therefore be viewed as a tracing of the singularities of that relational space which is mapped out by the competition entries. Those singularities emerge only piecemeal. The jury process is thus an experimental modulation of those singularities and depicts an open process of becoming. This process cannot be reduced to discourse since the folding together of heterogeneous relations exceeds linguistic representation. Empirical research[9] shows that the 'direct expression' (or the 'suggestive character', as jury members state) of models, drafts, renderings, etc. immediately shapes members of the jury's perceptions of a project's positives (formations) and negatives (limitations).

A planning competition is a procedure that aims at fathoming a wide range of solutions to one problem. This means that the diversity among the proposed solutions should be great. The composition of the jury should allow for *a real exploring of the space of potential solutions*. Competitions should allow for the connection of the many, which means that early identitarian attractors in the spaces of potential should be avoided (Van Wezemael 2008a). In studies of 'learning environments' it is suggested that the concept of *enduring heterogeneity* keeps processes away from being locked into one single basin of attraction.[10] The soundness of a competition procedure, therefore, significantly relies on the *heterogeneity of the perspectives* of the jury members and also on the diverse knowings (Ibert 2007; Van Wezemael 2008b)

---

8   The idea of viewing the judgement process in planning competitions as threefold stems from Jean-Pierre Chupin (personal communication).

9   Jan Silberberger and Sofia Paisiou from the Geography Unit at the University of Fribourg are working on Swiss design competitions with a social complexity approach. The projects combine ANT inspired qualitative in-depth analysis with model-based approaches to complexity.

10   We can learn from organization science and studies on knowledge-creation that there are conditions which are more likely to trigger the emergence of new forms (organizational solutions, designs, technical innovations, etc.) than others (Chia 1997; Gibbons et al. 1994; Grabher and Maintz 2006; Kamoche and Cunha 2004; Nonaka and Konno 1998; Schön 1995; Senge 1990; Tsoukas and Chia 2002). Van Wezemael (2008a) suggests that 'we can learn from the analysis of project ecologies (Grabher 2004), geographies of knowledge-creation (Ibert 2007), or from science and technology studies (Latour 1987), [that] learning processes are fuelled by the connection of heterogeneous elements (practices which belong to different places or to different projects or organizations) and – given a learning environment – from the encounter with novel and unexpected processes or "anomalies".'

and truths of different professional and non-professional groups which enter the collective decision-making process. This latter is usually mirrored in the composition of the jury, which often includes representatives of the municipal council, of the landowner, community associations, real estate investors, funds managers, or representatives of diverse societal associations. As Gilbert and Jormakka (2005) explain, it is common practice that a jury be composed of a group of individuals who represent a certain spectrum of professional views, interests and inclinations that populate the vocation. It is generally thought that heterogeneity of position will at least in part balance an extreme reaction to a project by any one particular jury member.

Thus, since jury members as externally related components (see above) are always part of several organizations, institutions or groups, these components of the competition's environment are folded into the competition and become part of the process of transcribing societal ideals and objectives into its built environment. In that way planning competitions create a flow of information that enables them to adapt to flux or changes in the wider environment.[11] However, since all agents involved primarily see only their own respective perspective, there is no overview position. Since diverse fields are folded together – its component parts (e.g. jury members) are organized and related to many spatio-temporal 'scales'– a specific planning competition is at the same time local *and* cuts across multiple scales. The unpredictable outcome of a planning competition should be understood in the sense of an emergent effect, generated from the interactions of the component parts. The competition as a whole displays unpredictable global behaviour. Sometimes competitions do not produce a solution at all, and sometimes the solution is very predictable. Competitions operate somewhere between order and chaos and thus point towards a conception of non-equilibrium. This critical stand highlights the importance of the third mode of judgement (see above). This is the judgement in the reception of the planning competitions by the public. We can now clearly see a universal singularity of a 'failed' planning competition when the anticipated judgement of the participants, the emerging judgement by the jury, and the judgement of the outcome by the public, diverge.

In order to develop an understanding of decision-making in competitions we must ask how forces of relations cluster around a project – or put differently: how do they emerge spontaneously and form temporary structures with a capacity to act? Furthermore, what kind of relations are involved in the conception of the folding together of heterogeneous fields into the competition?

---

11   Versteeg and Hajer (in this book) point out that stories told in a planning process are not freely floating around. Rather, there is a strong awareness both of the broader political-economic context and the way in which this broader context is instantiated, played out and changed in a micro-context of 'setting' and 'staging'. A competition is also a micro-cosmos and both the entries and the jury's trajectories can be referred as a 'staging' of the setting that embeds the competition process.

Coalitions Pick up Speed

Why and how do some of the relations form coalitions and develop more dynamics and more internal cohesion than others? How do forms of organization or structuring emerge out of a sea of dense and disorderly interaction (Cilliers 2005: 166)? Research in planning decision-making suggests that collective processes tend to gather around identitarian attractors, which are reinforced in the case of external conflict (Hillier and Van Wezemael 2008a, 2008b). This sharpens the boundaries between 'us' and 'them' (Van Wezemael 2008a). The distribution of what will be relevant in finding a winning project actively evolves in this process of stabilizing and freeing-up relations – it is not at all given at the start of the process (Kreiner 2008). As patterns of interaction stabilize, an entity develops a sense of itself in relation to a field of action. Summers-Effler (2007) illustrates this by reference to a loose growing network of friendly neighbours which became a 'neighbourhood' with a clear sense of itself as a political actor when local politicians proposed changes in neighbourhood policing. The transition from emergence to organization happens almost instantly when historical referencing decouples action from the immediate environment.[12] In a jury, referring to 'similar' problems or solutions from past and often famous planning competitions creates a sense of belonging for members, which stabilizes their connection to some solutions while turning others into veto-projects. However, this decoupling through naming or referencing is less an emancipation, but rather a suppression of minor connections. Through such defensive strategies entities may gain persistence. However, they also limit the path for action (Summers-Effler 2007).

Empirical Analysis of Assemblages

In order to analyze assemblages, assemblage theory draws on two analytical 'axes'. The *first analytic axis* defines the variable roles that an assemblage's components may play, from a purely material role at one extreme of the axis, to a purely expressive role at the other extreme. 'These roles are variable and may occur in mixtures, that is, a given component may play a mixture of material and expressive roles by exercising different sets of capacities' (DeLanda 2006a: 12). However, expressivity – in assemblage theory – is not reduced to language and symbols; there are also bodily and behavioural forms of expression, as well as the direct expression of colour or design and so on.

---

12   Here we may refer to the basic idea in Badiou's naming of events: in order to really become an event Badiou argues that not only a (potential) event must occur, but also that someone must recognize and name the event as an event whose implications concern the nature of the entire situation. This initial naming is called intervention. It is the first moment in a process of fundamental change, which Badiou terms fidelity or a generic truth procedure (Badiou 2006: 20–1). This procedure can be related to the role of language as a catalyst in assemblage theory.

The material parts of a design competition consist of the energy and labour involved in setting up and maintaining a jury, patching together provisional coalitions, hiding internal struggles from public view. The representation hardware – plans, texts, design models, computer animations – plays a material role, too. Kohoutek (2005) also points out that in competitions, various levels of communication and modes of representation – expressive roles – are intertwining: images, text, models, spoken discourse in pre-negotiation or jury meetings.

DeLanda argues that *specialized expressive media* (such as language) can be seen as an additional dimension or a differentiation of the expressive roles in social assemblages. Specialized expressive media consolidate and rigidify the identity of the assemblage (e.g. by shared stories, metaphors, professional design discourses and architectural 'schools of thought') or allow the assemblage certain latitude for more flexible operation while benefiting from linguistic (and other) resources in processes of coding and decoding. (DeLanda 2006b: 18–19).

The *second analytic axis* in assemblage theory concerns 'variable processes in which these components become involved: processes either stabilizing or destabilizing the identity of an assemblage (DeLanda 2006a: 12). The former are referred to as processes of (re-)territorialization, the latter as processes of deterritorialization. De- and re-territorialization may be understood as a *movement which produces change*. It indicates the creative potential of an assemblage to become; to connect differently and to grow in a disorganized way. The emergence of semi-stable patterns, of coalitions between projects and people can be viewed as movements that introduce change into other coalitions. To de-territorialize means to free up the fixed connections which contain an assemblage, all the while exposing it to new organizations (re-territorialization). Processes of (re-)territorialization increase an assemblage's degree of internal homogeneity or the degree of sharpness of its boundaries. For example the first stage of a two-stage architectural competition, that is the process of the jury picking suitable candidates to develop planning solutions to the posed problem, (re-)territorializes the competition. The selection occurs according to a mixture of criteria – mainly the candidate's experience in dealing with the task in demand plus their references, but also whether the jury generally likes the candidate's 'style of architecture'.

By contrast, processes of deterritorialization either destabilize an assemblage's boundaries or increase its internal heterogeneity. As an example of deterritorialization, think of replacing one member of a jury which consists of a close-knit personal network (where all the members know and like each other) with a complete stranger (e.g. someone who has a fundamentally different professional background, or an ill-tempered user-to-be).

In fact, 'one and the same assemblage can have components working to stabilize its identity as well as components forcing it to change or even transforming it into a different assemblage' and 'one and the same component may participate in both processes by exercising different sets of capacities' (DeLanda 2006a: 12). Thus, an argument in favour of one particular project may stabilize a set of relations – a coalition that pushes for this project – and at the same time free up relations that would push for another project.

Think of an architectural drawing that may, on the one hand, create and unify a coalition of jury members which then pushes the respective project due to the 'surprising and unpredictable' architectural solution that it dangles; yet the same drawing might at the same time destabilize that coalition due to fear of 'incalculable' building costs that it provokes.

Conclusion

In this chapter I have worked towards a theoretically-informed conception to analyze decision-making in planning. I have used planning competitions as an illustration for my argument and thus as a playground to think about conceptual challenges for planning in complexity. Assemblage theory, as a theoretical basis, allows for an understanding that it is not enough to 'trace' the processes of planning competitions from actual events. Rather, we should embrace the space of potential, and thus 'counter-actualize' the becoming of the competition-setting and decision-making in the process. The relations of forces that generate the dynamics of the jury are also fuelled by the folding together of heterogeneous fields in the sense of exterior relations in an assemblage. However, these dynamics and their de-/re-territorialization are not determined. Rather, the component parts can play many roles and thus generate rather different tendencies of becoming. Since the component parts include both human and material elements, their relation generates a realistic construction on the basis of a relational materialism. The focus in the analysis of assemblages on the roles that components play moves the research perspective beyond a merely anthropocentric view.

In order to understand when and how planning competitions may release creative energy we should think of how the competition brief opens up a space of potential that is subsequentially explored by the submitted planning projects. The assessment of the competing projects by the jury, then, is an interaction with the assemblage of the projects and thus with its space of potential. This space is not a merely discursive one, as projects should be viewed as an exploration of multiple alternative trajectories that are governed by economic and physical singularities; by liminal spaces that are generated by overlapping regulations and institutions. This again highlights the recognition of complexity as a property of reality rather than a mere property of humans interpreting reality. Thus, decision-making by the jury is a *modulation of the singularities* of the space of potential as generated by the presented solutions, which, again, evolve in an experimental interaction with the programme brief.

The conceptual perspective, as outlined in this chapter, also helps us with the question of how planning competitions might be improved in their design as a particular practice so that innovative energy is released. One practical gain from the conceptual perspective tells us that bringing the jurors together for their first meeting around the project proposals tends to lead to lock-in situations. This is likely to happen because the materiality of planning projects (plans, models, etc.)

and their direct expressivity act as a crystallization point for coalitions and set up boundaries between 'us and them': a territorialization without a prior exploration of the spaces of potential as generated by the competing projects, their material representation and the jury setting proper. Projects and their 'analogical' character (this is like thinking Bilbao! Barcelona!) tend to work as identitarian attractors and thus fuel pre-mature statements. Similarly, research shows that 'technologies' such as individual rating projects by jurors prior to debate kills a potentially creative process of stretching beyond the horizon (Hillier 2007) and thus limits the becoming of a specific place, a specific urban future.[13]

References

Amin, A. (2002) 'Spatialities of Globalisation' *Environment and Planning A* 34: 385–99.

Arbor, A., and Hirt, S. (2003) *Measuring Postmodernism: Placing Urban Planning in the Context of a Broader Cultural Values Tradition*. Paper presented at the 2003 Distinguished Faculty and Student Symposium: Crossing Disiplinary Boundaries in the Urban and Regional Context.

Badiou, A. (2006) *Infinite Thought*. London/New York: Continuum.

Chia, R. (1997) 'Thirty years on: from organisational structures to the organisation of thought' *Organization Science* 18(4): 685–707.

Cilliers, P. (2005) 'Complexity, deconstruction and relativism' *Theory, Culture and Society* 22(5): 255–67.

DeLanda, M. (1998) *Deleuze and the Open-ended Becoming of the World*. Available at: <http://www.cddc.vt.edu/host/delanda/pages/becoming.htm> [Accessed 9.12.2009].

DeLanda, M. (2002) *Intensive Science and Virtual Philosophy*. London: Continuum.

DeLanda, M. (2003) *War in the Age of Intelligent Machines*. New York: Zone Books.

DeLanda, M. (2006a) *A New Philosophy of Society: Assemblage Theory and Social Complexity*. London and New York: Continuum.

DeLanda, M. (2006b) 'Deleuzian social ontology and assemblage theory', in Fugslang, M. and Meier Sorensen, B. (eds) *Deleuze Connections*. Edinburgh: Edinburgh University Press, 250–66.

DeLanda, M., Protevi, J., and Thanem, T. (2006) 'Deleuzian interrogations: a conversation with Manuel DeLanda, John Protevi and Torkild Thanem. *Journal of Critical Postmodern Organisation Science*. Retrieved 15.01.2007 from <http://www.tamarajournal.com>

Deleuze, G., and Guattari, F. (1987) *A Thousand Plateaus: Capitalism and Schitzophrenia*. Minneapolis, MN: University of Minnesota Press.

Deleuze, G., and Parnet, C. (2002) *Dialogues II*. New York: Columbia University Press.

---

13   See footnote 9.

Doel, M.A. (1992) 'In stalling deconstruction: striking out the postmodern' *Environment and Planning D: Society and Space* 10(2): 163–79.

Doel, M.A., and Matless, D. (1992) 'Geography and postmodernism' *Environment and Planning D: Society and Space* 10(1): 1–4.

Forester, J. (1999) *The Deliberative Practitioner*. Cambridge, MA: MIT Press.

Gibbons, M., Limoges, C., Nowotny, H., Schwartzman, S., Scott, P., and Trow, M. (1994) *The New Production Knowledge: The Dynamics of Science and Research in Contemporary Societies*. London: Sage.

Giddens, A. (1984) *The Constitution of Society: Outline of the Theory of Structuration*. Cambridge, MA: Polity Press.

Gilbert, M., and Jormakka, K. (2005) 'The willing suspension of disbelief' *Wettbewerb! Competition! Ö. G. f. Architektur*. Wien: ÖGFA.

Grabher, G. (2004) 'Temporary architectures of learning: knowledge governance in project ecologies' *Organization Studies* 25(9): 1491–514.

Grabher, G., and Maintz, J. (2006) 'Learning in personal networks: collaborative knowledge production in virtual forums', in *Working Papers of the Center on Organizational Innovation*. New York: Columbia University.

Habermas, J. (1981) *The Theory of Communicative Action*. London: Beacon Press.

Healey, P. (1996) 'The communicative turn in planning theory and its implications for spatial strategy formations' *EBP* 23(2): 217–34.

Hillier, J. (2007) *Stretching Beyond the Horizon: A Multiplanar Theory of Spatial Planning and Governance*. Aldershot: Ashgate.

Hillier, J., and Van Wezemael, J.E. (2008a) ' "Empty, swept and garnished": the Public Finance Initiative case of Throckley Middle School' *Space and Polity* 12(2): 157–81.

Hillier, J., and Van Wezemael, J.E. (2008b) 'Tracing the disorderly real: performing civic engagement in a complex world', in Yang, K. and Bergrud, E. (eds) *Civic Engagement in a Network Society*. Charlotte, NC: Information Age Publishing.

Hinchcliffe, S. (2003) 'Inhabiting: landscapes and natures', in Anderson, K., Domosh, M., Pile, S., and Thrift, N. (eds) *The Handbook of Cultural Geography*. London: Sage, 207–25).

Ibert, O. (2007) 'Towards a geography of knowledge-creation: the ambivalences between "Knowledge as an Object" and "Knowing in Practice"' *Regional Studies* 41(1): 103–14.

Kamoche, K., and Cunha, M.P.E. (2004) 'Improvisation, knowledge and the challenge of appropriation' *CIMOC Working Paper Series*, 1/2004.

Kohoutek, R. (2005) Der unmögliche Wettbewerb. *Wettbewerb! Competition! Ö. G. f. Architektur*. Wien: ÖGFA, 124–9.

Kreiner, K. (2008) 'Architectural competitions. Empirical observations and strategic implications for architectural firms', paper presented at the Nordic Symposium, Stockholm: 16–18 October 2008. Conference Proceeding (CD ROM, KTH Stockholm).

Latour, B. (1987) *Science In Action: How to Follow Scientists and Engineers Through Society*. Cambridge, MA: Harvard University Press.

Latour, B. (2005) *Reassembling the Social*. New York: Oxford University Press.

Mackenzie, A. (2002) *Transductions: Bodies and Machines at Speed*. London: Continuum.

Nonaka, I., and Konno, N. (1998). 'The concept of "Ba": building a foundation for knowledge creation' *California Management Review* 40(3): 40–54.

Schmid, C. (2007) 'Die Wiederentdeckung des Städtischen in der Schweiz', in Lampugnani, V.M., Keller, T.K., and Buser, B. (eds) *Städtische Dichte*. Zürich: Verlag NZZ.

Schön, D.A. (1995) *The Reflective Practitioner: How Professionals Think in Action*. Aldershot: Arena.

Senge, P. (1990) *The Fifth Discipline*. New York: Doubleday Books.

Shaviro, S. (2007) *De Landa: A New Philosophy of Society*. Available at: http://www.shaviro.com/Blog/?p=541 [accessed 26.4. 2007]

Stiftung Forschung Planungswettbewerbe (2007) *Forschung Planungswettbewerbe*. Zürich (self-published).

Summers-Effler, E. (2007) 'Vortexes of involvement: social systems as turbulent flow' *Philosophy of the Social Sciences* 37(4): 433–48.

Tsoukas, H., and Chia, R. (2002) 'On organizational becoming: rethinking organizational change' *Organization Science* 13(5): 567–82.

Urry, J. (2000) *Sociology beyond Societies: Mobilities for the Twenty-first Century*. London: Routledge.

Van Wezemael, J.E. (2008a) 'The contribution of assemblage theory and minor politics for democratic network governance' *Planning Theory* 7(2): 165–85.

Van Wezemael, J.E. (2008b) 'Knowledge creation in urban development praxis', in Baum, S., and Yigitganlar, T. (eds) *Knowledge-based Urban Development*. Hershey, PA: Idea, 1–20.

Van Wezemael, J.E. (2009) *Mattering the Res Publica – Design Competitions as Foucauldian Dispositif*. Paper presented at the Annual Conference of the Association of American Geographers, Las Vegas, 22–28 March.

Community Enterprises: Imagining and Enacting Alternatives to Capitalism

J.K. Gibson-Graham and Jenny Cameron

Introduction

If the rise of the World Social Forum is any indication, there is a groundswell of support for alternatives to capitalism. But within this movement that links North and South, 'developed' and less 'developed' nations worldwide, the debate as to what constitutes an economic alternative is fraught with judgments about the purity or contamination of what is on offer. Wholehearted experimentation with the premise that 'other economies are possible' is held back by the critical voices (many in our own heads) arguing that this or that element of an alternative project is no different from capitalism or is insufficient to withstand the colonizing forces of the 'capitalist' market. J.K. Gibson-Graham's recently published book *A Postcapitalist Politics* (2006) argues that the danger of taking too much notice of these objections is that desires for alternatives become destabilized and the intentional practice of building alternatives gets undermined. It seems that a prerequisite for enacting economic alternatives to capitalism is an affective stance that will enable us, as authors, researchers and activists, to be a condition of possibility (rather than impossibility) for the emergence of other worlds and other economies. In this short chapter we discuss how we have cultivated a stance that enables possibility, while building economic alternatives alongside or perhaps outside of something called 'capitalism'.

For some years we have been engaged in participatory action research with community members, NGOs and local governments to imagine and enact alternative economic development pathways that are not reliant on the promises of capitalist growth. Action research involves participating in creating new realities rather than simply describing or analyzing existing situations; working 'with' people and not 'on' them (Cameron 2007; Cameron and Gibson 2005a). Our action research has been aimed at building 'community economies' and it is part of a larger intellectual project of deconstructing capitalism, deflating the representation of a systemic economic power that dominates and constrains social life (Gibson-Graham 1996/2006). The community economies project attempts to 'take back' the economy as a space of decision and ethical practice (see <www.communityeconomies.org>).

As a result of our collaborative action research interventions in regional Victoria, suburban Brisbane, the Pioneer Valley of Massachusetts, USA, and the rural and semi-rural communities of Jagna and Linamon in the Central Visayan and Southern regions of the Philippines, a number of community-based manufacturing, agricultural and service-oriented enterprises have been formed. Some are providing income support for participants and small surpluses that are allocated to community ends, while some are a focus for volunteer labour and are reliant on gifts as well as market transactions; some are still going six to ten years after their initiation, others have folded; some community members have stayed involved, others have moved through these projects into higher education, community work of a different nature or new enterprise development.

When we talk about this research to academic and activist audiences we often get a somewhat negative, or at least quizzical, reaction. The best-mannered version of this response takes the form of a figurative yawn, followed by what are seen as the cold hard facts: co-operatives, communes and community enterprises were all tried 20 years ago when there was a lot more interest in economic alternatives but now they are a thing of the past. The more stroppy version points to the inevitable limitations placed on any kind of economic experiment by 1) market forces that cannot be out-competed, 2) the state that's ready to jump in and co-opt community enterprise to its neo-liberal agenda of shifting responsibility on to the household and community, 3) the global capitalist system whose hegemonic power will not be thwarted by any small, local intervention, let alone experiments that cannot immediately be seen to have growth or 'scale-up' potential, and 4) the inherent self-interest of community members who, once abandoned by the social scientists who have 'engineered' community enterprise development, revert to self-serving activities that advance the march of consumerism and individualist identity.

Over the past decade we have thought our way through answers to these objections. The 2006 re-issue of J.K. Gibson-Graham's *The End of Capitalism (As We Knew It): A Feminist Critique of Political Economy* (1996/2006) gave us the opportunity, in the new introduction, to address our critics. It seems that for many people, and perhaps most of all for those who are interested in resisting or replacing it, capitalism has no outside. If there is nothing untouched by capitalism, there is no place to stand from which to combat it or construct something that is 'non-capitalist'. Without a ground upon which to build an alternative it is no wonder that allegiances and support for experimentation shift and shake.

In *The End of Capitalism*, to escape the double bind of wanting change but being unable to conceive of it as a possibility, we downsized our understanding of capitalism, refusing to conflate it with commodity production and market activity, limiting it to the class relations in which non-producers appropriate surplus labour in value form from free wage labourers and distribute it to a variety of social destinations, including themselves. From this perspective capitalism becomes recognizable as a set of practices scattered over a landscape in formal and informal enterprise settings, practices that interact with non-capitalist firms as well as other sites and processes, activities and organizations in a diverse economy. De-linked from the structural necessity of facilitating capital accumulation or legitimation, state activities can then be seen as variously supporting and regulating diverse economic practices that range from capitalist, cooperative and self-employed enterprises, to household and neighbourhood non-market exchanges, to slavery (in the prison system, for example) and voluntarism. By recognizing the contingency of capitalism we expand the number of empirical questions we can ask and multiply the points of possible economic intervention.

In *A Postcapitalist Politics* we suggest that this theoretical approach requires a distinctive affective stance that abandons the deep-seated negativity often associated with critical, radical and left-oriented thinkers and activists. This means challenging those habits of feeling and thinking that push us towards advancing strong theories of what *is*, but blind us to what this type of theorizing *does*. It means questioning the emotional and affective investments that attach us to the political victories of yesteryear, prompting us to belittle the political opportunities at hand. These affective investments shore up the reactive stance of the victim and invoke a moralistic attitude toward engagement with the powerful (Gibson-Graham 2006: 5–6). We advocate, instead, a practice of theorizing that can help us to see openings, that provides/performs a space of freedom and possibility; a practice of thinking undertaken with a reparative motive that fosters connection and coexistence and offers care of the new; a practice that produces positive affect and energizes our interest in experimentation. It is from this stance that we read the success of the Mondragón Co-operative Corporation (MCC), the longstanding experiment in rebuilding a regional economy in Spain's Basque north west centred on 'people not profits' (Gibson-Graham 2006: Chapter 5). From a social base in the late 1940s that was divided by ideological differences, with a physical infrastructure destroyed by civil war, the Mondragón community, under the guiding philosophy of Catholic priest Father Arizmendiarrieta, has built perhaps the most successful and well-recognized complex of worker-owned industrial, retail, service and support co-operatives in the world (Mathews 1999). The MCC offers the example of an alternative development pathway in which the social objectives of regional employment, social welfare and Basque cultural survival have been uppermost while business objectives have been subordinated, but by no means ignored. The ways in which the owner-worker co-operators of the MCC have negotiated the dilemmas of maintaining their commitment to co-operativism and Basque solidarity in the face of significant economic pressures offer lessons in enacting an ethical economic politics. Such a politics views threats as something to struggle against, not as structural limits that set the bounds of what is possible.

In the last few years greater attention has been drawn in Australia to the range of enterprises whose 'core business' is not to maximize private benefit but to produce community well-being directly, particularly for marginalized groups. Many of these businesses focus not only on servicing community needs but on actively building new kinds of community. To offer just a few examples, a community-building social enterprise may involve a disadvantaged neighbourhood in food security projects such as community gardening and food banking; it may attempt to sustain a marginalized ethnic group through livelihood provision or affordable housing; it may undertake recycling projects that provide environmental education and experiences of collective stewardship to at-risk youth, and so on. In terms of creating and working towards alternative economies, for us the important questions are: How might we think about these community enterprises in a way that strengthens their ability to offer a non-capitalist model of enterprise? What kind of stance might we need to cultivate towards these experiments so that they succeed not just as viable businesses but as 'laboratories for alternative futures' (Rose 1999: 279) where new kinds of economic subjects can be nurtured?

First we might need to relax our knee-jerk suspicion of state support. At present there is growing interest by Australian governments in putting substantial resources into developing community enterprises with the hope that they will expand opportunities for economic and social participation. For example, since 2000 the Victorian government has allocated $9.2 million to their community enterprise strategy (Department for Victorian Communities 2006) and, in partnership with the Brotherhood of St Laurence (BSL), is supporting 42 localities across the state to develop community enterprises (Brotherhood of St Laurence 2006). These initiatives appear to be influenced by policy developments in the United Kingdom (UK) where the growth of social enterprises has been a key plank of the Blair administration's 'Third Way'. The UK government has provided this growing sector with increased financial and bureaucratic support (Cabinet Office 2006). It has registered a new legal form of Community Interest Company (CIC) (Todres et al. 2006: 62) and formally defined social enterprises (or community enterprises in our terms) quite explicitly as:

> [A] business with primarily social objectives whose surpluses are principally reinvested for that purpose in the business or in the community rather than being driven by the need to maximize profits for shareholders and owners. (UK Department of Trade and Industry 2002: 7)

For some, this kind of government interest signals co-optation of the highest order and is proof that these enterprises are just part of the neo-liberal roll back of the welfare state. For us, it is intriguing to see an authoritative definition of business activity that legitimizes the notion that surplus is indeed produced in the context of business operations and that its social distribution is something that can build community capacity. Such a clear focus on surplus distribution has the potential to challenge the dominant view that capitalist business activity produces benefit for all by focusing attention on how surpluses generated in private enterprise flow exclusively to shareholders and owners who are only minimally taxed.

Increased interest in the social sector of the economy, including community enterprises as well as charitable, voluntary and all non-profit organizations, has generated economic statistics that can play an important role in destabilizing the 'capitalist' identity of our national economy. The 'capitalist' designation is based on the accounting of those formal market exchanges, waged and salaried employment and private 'capitalist' business activity that comprise the most visible parts of the economy. Yet in 1999/2000 the social sector in Australia employed 6.8 per cent of the labour force and generated an income of $33.5 billion, a contribution equal to that of agriculture (ABS 2002). When the value of volunteer labour is imputed, the economic contribution is greater than that of key sectors such as government administration and defence, or mining (ABS 2002). This is a sizeable economic sector in which surplus production and appropriation is taking place *outside* of formal market, capitalist wage labour and private ownership relations. When we add to this picture the findings of economist Duncan Ironmonger (1996), who has estimated that the value of goods and services produced in households by unpaid workers in Australia is almost equivalent to the value of the goods and services produced by paid workers for the market, we start to see a national economy made up of many sectors in which capitalist class relations are absent. Ironmonger proposes that the value of unpaid household work be called Gross Household Product (GHP), and he argues that the System of National Accounts should be revised so that the total measure of economic performance, Gross Economic Product, be 'comprised of Gross Household Product and Gross Market Product' (1996: 38–9).

Gaining greater public recognition for the economic contribution made by the household and social sectors is part of a discursive strategy of destabilizing the dominance of *capitalocentric* economic thinking (Cameron and Gibson-Graham 2003). A *capitalocentric* perspective denies difference by seeing all economic activity as either the same as, the opposite of, a complement to, or contained within capitalism (Gibson-Graham 1996/2006: 6; 35). But the strategy of showcasing economic diversity (whether the growing number of community enterprises or the extent of household production) is not sufficient in itself to help build alternatives to capitalism. There is more work to be done.

At present, models of business behaviour and management are based on those of conventional private enterprise, which are not wholly applicable to community enterprises (Bull and Crompton 2006; Jones and Keogh 2006). Indeed, there is a concern that over-reliance on mainstream business models to guide the community enterprise sector will potentially undermine its diversity and ability to achieve the social objectives that are its 'core business' (Reid and Griffith 2006). Yet increased government interest in social enterprises has heightened the need to assess their 'success' and sustainability (Amin et al. 2002) and has promoted, if not required, the application of measurement technologies. The problem is, as Bull and Crompton note in the UK context (2006: 57), that while there are many ways of measuring the *business* success of social enterprises, there are few ways of assessing the success of their *social* agenda. Given the availability of business models of accountability and the time pressures of running a community-focused enterprise it is tempting to apply these more developed techniques with only slight modification (Pearce 2003). The success of a community enterprise is often simply equated with its ability to function independent of grant and government support (Reid and Griffith 2006), or is gauged by its volume of business or numbers of employees. Importantly, there are very few vehicles by which enterprise members themselves can be involved in developing appropriate 'measures' of enterprise viability (Todres et al. 2006).

Our experience with community enterprise development highlights the unpredictable nature of community building outcomes. As we have found, the closure of a community enterprise after a number of years may not necessarily be deemed by all stakeholders as a 'failure' (Cameron and Gibson 2005b). For example, members may go on to develop other enterprises and contribute to community building in other ways. As with mainstream business, community enterprise failure is common, yet with each breakdown the knowledge of that experiment has the potential to contribute to the next. By too readily deeming experiments as failed, useful knowledge is likely to be discarded. The community enterprise and social enterprise literatures and our own research experiences demonstrate the pressing need for more information about how to define and assess success and failure in the sector. It is here that we need to step in to assist community enterprises to develop ways of evaluating their experimental pathways that do not set up unrealistic expectations but that help to strengthen their performance of economic alterity.

In an action research project currently being planned we aim to involve members of the community enterprise sector in generating more useful definitions and techniques of assessing performance, based on their own organizational histories and the ethical decision-making that has shaped their enterprise. The research will enrol community enterprise members in self-study of both well-established and newly-established enterprises. Our research is in its early stages but from what we have discovered it appears that some of the campaigners who led the way, building economic alternatives in the 1970s, are among the organizers of the new networks that have sprung up to support and forward the social enterprise agenda today. Such networks include Social Enterprise Partnerships, the Employee and Community Buyouts Network, Community Co-operative Connections, the New Mutualism Group and the Social Enterprise Hub.

What does this say for the resilience of a movement for economic alternatives that puts people before profits? We have a choice: to see the ephemeral nature of public organizing around the possibility of 'other economies' as evidence of the superior power of a global, neo-liberal capitalist machine; or to see it as a reminder that the desire for a more just economy is never completely suppressed. Just as the feminist social transformation we have experienced over the last century began with small scattered experiments that gradually linked up to produce a discursive and material shift of tectonic proportions, so might our repeated attempts at building non-capitalist economic relations eventually transform the economic landscape. Inspiring examples of success and failure are all around us. They require theorizing in an open-hearted, affirming and practical way that is not lured by the temptations of judgement, nostalgia or conspiratorial thinking but also does not deny the problems and ethical dilemmas posed by alternatives. Releasing ourselves from an affective stance that has (de-)energized the left for too long is, we argue, a vital ingredient of strengthening and expanding alternative economic possibilities. Against the 'profit at all costs is good for you motif' of capitalism, community enterprises stand as contemporary experiments in producing well-being directly and surpluses that are publicly accessible. The support we offer them will contribute to continued disruption of the *capitalocentric* thinking that denies them centre stage in building alternative futures.

References

Australian Bureau of Statistics (2002) *Australian National Accounts: Non-Profit Institutions Satellite Account*, 5256.0, 1999–2000, Canberra: ABS.

Amin, A., Cameron, A. and Hudson, R. (2002) *Placing the Social Economy*. London: Routledge.

Brotherhood of St Laurence (2006) *Community Enterprise Development Initiative*. Melbourne: Brotherhood of St Laurence. URL <http://www.bsl.org.au/main. asp?PageId=3561> (consulted 5 March 2007).

Bull, M., and Crompton, H. (2006) 'Business practices in social enterprises' *Social Enterprise Journal* 2(1): 42–60.

Cabinet Office (UK)(2006) *Social Enterprise Action Plan: Scaling New Heights*. London: Cabinet Office.<http://www.cabinetoffice.gov.uk/media/cabinetoffice/third_ sector/assets/se_action_plan_2006.pdf>. [Accessed 10 December 2009).

Cameron, J. (2007) 'Linking participatory research to action: institutional challenges', in Kindon, S., Pain, R., and Kesby, M. (eds) *Participatory Action Research Approaches and Methods: Connecting People, Participation and Place*. London: Routledge.

Cameron, J., and Gibson, K. (2005a) 'Participatory action research in a poststructuralist vein' *Geoforum* 36: 315–31.

Cameron, J., and Gibson, K. (2005b) 'Alternative pathways to community and economic development: the Latrobe Valley Community Partnering Project' *Geographical Research* 43(3): 274–85.

Cameron, J., and Gibson-Graham, J.K. (2003) 'Feminising the economy: metaphors, strategies, politics' *Gender, Place and Culture* 10(2): 145–57.

Department for Victorian Communities (2006) *Enterprising Communities: The Victorian Government's Community Enterprise Strategy*. Melbourne: Victorian Government. <http://www.dvc.vic.gov.au/Web14/dvc/rwpgslib.nsf/ GraphicFiles/Enterprising_communtiies_brochure_homepage.pdf/$file/Enterp rising+communities+brochure+homepage.pdf> (Consulted 8 March 2007).

Gibson-Graham, J.K. (2006) *A Postcapitalist Politics*. Minneapolis, MN: University of Minnesota Press.

Gibson-Graham, J.K. (1996/2006) *The End of Capitalism as we Knew It: A Feminist Critique of Political Economy*. Minneapolis, MN: University of Minnesota Press.

Ironmonger, D. (1996) 'Counting ouputs, capital inputs and caring labor: estimating gross household product' *Feminist Economics* 2 (3): 37–64.

Jones, D., and Keogh, W. (2006) 'Social enterprise: a case of terminological ambiguity and complexity' *Social Enterprise Journal* 2(1): 11–26.

Mathews, R. (1999) *Jobs of Our Own: Building a Stake-holder Society*. Sydney: Pluto Press Australia.

Pearce, J. (2003) *Social Enterprises in Anytown*. London: Calouste Gulbenkian Foundation.

Reid, K., and Griffith, J. (2006) 'Social enterprise mythology: critiquing some assumptions' *Social Enterprise Journal* 2(1): 1–10.

Rose, N. (1999) *Powers of Freedom: Reframing Political Thought*. Cambridge: Cambridge University Press.

Todres, M., Cornelius, N., Janjuha-Jivral, S., and Woods, A. (2006) 'Developing emerging social enterprise through capacity building' *Social Enterprise Journal* 2(1): 61–72.

United Kingdom Department of Trade and Industry (2002) *Social Enterprise: A Strategy for Success*. Social Enterprise Unit: DTI.

Trouble with Nature: 'Ecology as the New Opium for the Masses'[1]

Erik Swyngedouw

Let's start by stating that after 'the rights of man', the rise of the 'the rights of Nature' is a contemporary form of the opium for the people. It is an only slightly camouflaged religion: the millenarian terror, concern for everything save the properly political destiny of peoples, new instruments for control of everyday life, the obsession with hygiene, the fear of death and catastrophes … It is a gigantic operation in the depoliticization of subjects. (Badiou 2008: 139)

Every time we seek to mix scientific facts with aesthetic, political, economic, and moral values, we find ourselves in a quandary … If we mix facts and values, we go from bad to worse, for we are depriving ourselves of both autonomous knowledge and independent morality. (Latour 2004: 4)

Nature Does Not Exist!

Several decades ago, Raymond Williams argued that 'Nature is perhaps the most complex word in the language', wrought with all manner of histories, geographies, meanings, fantasies, dreams, and wish images (Williams 1988: 221). Yet, he also concurred that Nature is socially and politically one of the most powerful and performative metaphors of language (Williams 1980). In the wake of the current environmental 'crisis', it has gained considerable purchase in political debate, economic argument, and public intervention. If there is a conceptual challenge in need of exploration for planning theory, Nature must undoubtedly rank very highly. And this is all the more urgent as the socio-ecological conditions – the 'states of nature' as it were – in many places on earth as well as globally are under serious stress.

Nature is indeed very difficult to pin down. Is it the physical world around and inside us, like trees, rivers, mountain ranges, HIV viruses, microbes, elephants,

---

1   The subtitle of this chapter is taken from Žižek (2008a). See also Badiou (2008).

oil, cocoa, diamonds, clouds, neutrons, the heart, shit, etc. ...? Does it encompass things like roses in a botanical garden, freshly-squeezed orange juice, Adventure Island in Disneyland (one of the most bio-diverse eco-topes on earth), a Richard Rogers skyscraper, sewage flows, genetically-modified tomatoes, and a hamburger? Should we expand it to include greed, avarice, love, compassion, hunger, death? Or should we think about it in terms of dynamics, relations and relational processes like climate change, hurricane movements, speciation and species extinction, soil erosion, water shortages, food chains, plate tectonics, nuclear energy production, black holes, supernovas, and the like?

In his recent book, provocatively titled *Ecology without Nature*, Timothy Morton calls Nature 'a transcendental term in a material mask [that] stands at the end of a potentially infinite series of other terms that collapse into it' (Morton 2007: 14). He distinguishes between at least three places or meanings of nature in our symbolic universe. First, as a floating signifier, the 'content' of Nature is expressed through a range of diverse terms that all collapse in the Name of Nature: olive tree, parrot fish, SARS virus, love, reproduction, the Alps, mineral water, markets, desire, profits, CO_2, money, competition ... Such metonymic lists, although offering a certain unstable meaning, are inherently slippery, and show a stubborn refusal to fixate meaning durably or provide consistency. Nature as metaphor remains empty; its meaning can only be gleaned from metonymic references to other, more ordinary signifiers.

Second, Nature has 'the force of law, a norm against which deviation is measured' (Morton 2007: 14). This is the sort of invocation of Nature that is mobilized, for example, to normalize heterosexuality and to think queerness as deviant and unnatural or that sees competition between humans as natural and altruism as a produce of 'culture' (or vice versa). Normative power inscribed in Nature is invoked as an organizing principle that is transcendental and universal, allegedly residing outside the remit allocated to humans and non-humans alike but that exercises an inescapable performative effect and leaves a non-alienable imprint. This is a view that sees Nature as something given, as a solid foundational (or ontological) basis from which we act and that can be invoked to provide an anchor for ethical or normative judgments of ecological, social, cultural, political or economic procedures and practices. Consider, for example, how many recent sustainable planning efforts legitimize their activities by invoking some transcendental view of a Nature that is out of synch and requires re-balancing.

And, third, Nature contains a plurality of fantasies and desires, like, for example, the dream of a sustainable nature, the desire for love-making on a warm beach under the setting sun, the fear for the revenge of Nature if we keep pumping CO_2 into the atmosphere. Nature is invoked here as the stand-in for other, often repressed or invisible, longings and passions – the Lacanian *object petit a* around which we shape our drives and that covers up for the lack of ground on which to base our subjectivity (Žižek 1999). This is a procedure by which we invest in Nature, displaced on to the plain of an 'Other', our libidinal desires and fears, a displacement of the abyss that separates the disavowed Real 'hard' kernel of being from the symbolic world in which we dwell. It is the sort of fantasy displayed in calls for the restoration of a true (original but presumably presently lost) humane harmony by restoring the world's ecological balance. Here, Nature is invoked as the 'external' terrain that offers the promise, if attended to properly, for finding or producing a truly happy and harmonious life (see Stavrakakis 1997a).

In sum, the very uses of Nature imply simultaneously an attempt to fixate its unstable meaning while being presented as a fetishized 'Other' that reflects or, at least, functions as a symptom through which our displaced deepest fears and longings are expressed. As such, the concept of Nature becomes ideology par excellence and functions ideologically – and by that I mean that it forecloses thought, disavows the inherent slipperiness of the concept, and ignores its multiplicities, inconsistencies, and incoherencies (Morton 2007: 24). Every attempt to suture, to fill in exhaustively and to colonize the meaning of Nature is part of hegemonizing drives that are inherently political, but are not recognized as such (Laclau and Mouffe 2001; Stavrakakis 2000). Suturing Nature's meaning is of course systematically undertaken in almost all public debates, policy documents and planning discourses that invoke Nature or the environment. The disavowal of the empty core of Nature by colonizing its meaning, by filling out the void, staining it with inserted meanings that are subsequently generalized and homogenized, is the gesture par excellence of de-politicization, of placing Nature outside the political, that is, outside the field of public dispute, contestation and disagreement.

It is in this sense that Morton proposes 'to think ecology without nature', to abandon the concept of Nature altogether. This is not a stupid or silly gesture to disavow 'the Real' of all the things, feelings and processes associated with Nature that I listed above. On the contrary, it is exactly the recognition of the inherent slipperiness and multiplicities of meaning suggested by such metonymic lists of really existing things, emotions and processes that urges us to consider that perhaps the very concept of Nature itself should be abandoned. Slavoj Žižek makes a similar point when he states that 'Nature does not exist!' (Žižek 1992; 2002). His Lacanian perspective insists on the difference 'between [a] series of ordinary signifiers and the central element which has to remain empty in order to serve as the underlying organizing principle of the series' (Žižek 2000: 52). Nature constitutes exactly such a central (empty) element whose meaning only becomes clear by relating it to other more directly recognizable signifiers. While every signifier is to a certain extent floating (that is, undecided with respect to its associated referent), it is much easier to imagine, say, what 'CAT' stands for (despite the great number of different sorts of cats, let alone the infinite emotive and other meanings individuals associate with these creatures) than what Nature stands for. For Žižek, any attempt to suture the meaning of empty signifiers is a decidedly political gesture. Yet, for him, the disavowal or the refusal to recognize the political character of such gestures, the attempts to universalize the situated and positioned meanings inscribed metonymically in Nature lead to perverse forms of depoliticization, to rendering Nature politically mute and socially neutral (Swyngedouw 2007a).

Bruno Latour, albeit from a completely different perspective, equally proposes to ditch the concept of Nature. For Latour, there is neither such thing as Nature in itself and for itself, nor something like Society (or Culture) (Latour 1993). For him, the collection of things (human and non-human) that fill in the world consists of continuously multiplying nature-culture hybrids. With Michel Serres and others, Latour argues that these socio-natural 'messy' things are made up of proliferating sets of networked socio-natural assemblages that are defined as quasi-objects; they stand between the poles of nature on the one hand and culture on the other. They are simultaneously both and neither, yet they are socio-ecologically significant and politically performative (Latour 2005). They form the socio-natures that define, choreograph and sustain everyday lives and things (Swyngedouw 1996). Think of, for example, greenhouse gases, Dolly the cloned sheep, a dam, a bottle of milk, water networks, or electromagnetic waves. They are simultaneously social/cultural and natural/physical, and their coherence, i.e. their relative spatial and temporal sustainability, is predicated upon assembled networks of human and non-human relations (Swyngedouw 2006). This perspective, too, rejects retaining the concept of Nature and suggests in its stead to consider the infinite heterogeneity of the procedures of assembling – dissembling – reassembling the rhizomatic networks through which things, bodies, natures and cultures become enrolled and through which relatively stable quasi-objects come into purview (Castree 2003; Braun 2006). The world is radically heterogeneous, and the more-than-human (human and non-human assemblages like a cow, a personal computer, the parliament, irrigation systems, a transport network) 'collectives' that constitute the almost infinite collection of things we call 'world', 'earth', or 'cosmos' congeal relationally constituted assemblages that 'are of a highly variable duration and spatial extent – sometimes very durable, sometimes of seemingly well-bounded extent' (Henderson 2009: 284). This Latouran gesture also attempts to re-politicize Nature, to let quasi-objects enter the public assembly of political negotiations and considerations. For Latour too, there is nothing left to retain from the concept of Nature (Latour 2004).

Despite the rejection of the concept of Nature advanced by these theorizations, it is indisputably the case that many of the world's environments are in serious ecological trouble and planners, policy-makers and activists desperately search or call for urgent and immediate action in the face of the clear and present danger posed by environmental degradation and possible ecological collapse. For those attuned to the mess many of the world's environments are in, linguistic acrobatics as those introduced above might sound esoteric at best and nonsensical and counter-productive at worst, coming from the usual suspects of critical social theorists and sexy, but politically vacuous and pragmatically impotent, cultural musings. Interestingly, however, some 'hard' scientists seem to echo these critical social theory perspectives, albeit with a slightly different terminology and from an altogether different vantage point. The exemplary work of Levins and Lewontin (Levins and Lewontin 1985) (Lewontin and Levins 2007), Harvard University biologists and ecologists, comes to strikingly similar conclusions, yet does so from a Marxist dialectical materialist perspective. They too agree that Nature has been filled in by scientists with a particular set of universalizing meanings that ultimately depoliticize Nature, and evoke a series of distinctly ideological principles that facilitated particular mobilizations of such 'scientifically' constructed Nature.

While eighteenth and nineteenth century scientific views of nature were enthralled by notions of change, revolution, and transformation, twentieth century biology, Levins and Lewontin argue, settled Nature down, and reduced it to a homeostatic constellation. As they put it:

> We are at the End of Natural History. The world has settled down, after a rocky start, to a steady state. Constancy, harmony, simple laws of life that predict universal features of living organisms, and self-reproduction and absolute dominance of a single species of molecule, DNA, are the hegemonic themes of modern biology. (Lewontin and Levins 2007: 13–14)

Of course, modern biology does not reject the radical environmental transformations affecting our living environments. However, unforeseen changes are seen either as the effect of 'externalities', i.e. humans' irresponsible intervention in the steady state/evolution of a mechanical nature, or as catastrophic turbulence resulting from initial relations that spiral out in infinitely complex and greatly varying configurations such as those theorized by Chaos or Complexity Theory. While the former insists on nature's innate stabilizing force disrupted by external (human) agency, the latter reduces the complex vagaries of environmental change to the unpredictable outcome of forces immanent in simple original conditions. Both perspectives deny that the biological world is inherently relationally constituted through contingent, historically produced, infinitely variable forms in which each part, human or non-human, organic or non-organic, is intrinsically bound up with the wider relations that make up the whole.[2] Levins and Lewontin abhor a simplistic, reductionist, teleological and, ultimately, homogenizing view of Nature. They too insist that a singular Nature does not exist, that there is no trans-historical and/or trans-geographical transcendental natural state of things, of conditions or of relations, but rather that there are a range of different historical natures, relations and environments that are subject to continuous, occasionally dramatic or catastrophic, and rarely, if ever, fully predictable changes and transformations. Their dynamics are shaped by the time-space specific relational configurations in which each part is inserted. Neither these parts nor the totality of which they are part can be reduced to a foundational given (whether 'mechanical' or 'chaotic'). They eschew such expressions as 'it is in the nature of things' to explain one or another ecological or human behaviour or condition. They hold to a relational and historically contingent view of biological differentiation and evolution. The world is in a process of continuous becoming through the contingent and heterogeneous recompositions of the almost infinite (socio-)ecological relations through which new natures come into being. They see the relations of parts to the whole and

---

2   Of course, the geophilosophical thought of Deleuze and Guattari articulates in important ways with complexity theory and has spawned an exciting, albeit occasionally bewildering, literature that takes relationality, indeterminacy and the radical heterogeneities of natures seriously (see, among others, Conley (1996); Deleuze and Guattari (1994); Herzogenrath (2008); Hillier (2009)).

the mutual interaction of parts in the whole as the process through which both individuals and their environments are changed (see also Harvey 1996). In other words, both individuals and their environments are co-produced and co-evolve in historically contingent, highly diversified, locally specific and often not fully accountable manners. For Levins and Lewontin, therefore, no universalizing or foundational claim can be made about what Nature is, what it should be or where it should go. For them too, Nature does not exist either.

This is also the view shared by the late evolutionary biologist Stephen Jay Gould who saw evolution not as a gradual process, but one that is truncated, punctuated, occasionally catastrophic and revolutionary but, above all, utterly contingent (Gould 1980). There is no safety in Nature – Nature is unpredictable, erratic, moving spasmodically and blind. There is no final guarantee in Nature on which to base our politics or the social, on which to mirror our dreams, hopes or aspirations. To put it bluntly, bringing down (or not as the case may be) CO_2 emission does affect the global climate and shapes socio-ecological patterns in distinct manners (that are of course worthy of both scientific exploration and ethical concern), but such a process, even if successful, would not produce in itself the 'good' society in a 'good' environment.

The critical cultural perspectives and anti-foundational evolutionary views explored above lead to a series of arguments and claims about Nature and how to think, conceptualize and/or politicize it. This is the conceptual conundrum I wish to disentangle further in this contribution. Dissecting the conceptual challenges posed by the mobilization of Nature in a wide range of social sciences, political discourses and policy/managerial practices is absolutely vital in a world in which socio-ecological dynamics like resource depletion, climate change or environmental degradation pose challenges that, if unheeded, might possibly lead to the premature end of civilization as we know it, to the end of us before our sell-by date has expired.

The main points of argument I wish to unfold in this chapter are as follows:

1. Nature and its more recent derivatives, like 'environment' or 'sustainability', are 'empty' signifiers.
2. There is no such thing as a singular Nature around which an environmental policy or an environmentally sensitive planning can be constructed and performed. Rather, there are a multitude of natures and a multitude of existing, possible or practical socio-natural relations.
3. The obsession with a singular Nature that requires 'sustaining' or, at least, 'managing', is sustained by a particular 'quilting' of Nature that forecloses asking political questions about immediately and really possible alternative socio-natural arrangements.
4. I conclude with a call for a politicization of the environment, one that is predicated upon the recognition of the indeterminacy of nature, the constitutive split of the people, the unconditional democratic demand of political equality, and the real possibility for the inauguration of different possible public socio-ecological futures that express the democratic presumptions of freedom and equality.

The Empty Core of Nature – Multiple Natures

As suggested above, it is difficult, if not impossible, to define exactly what Nature is. Every attempt to nail down or to fix its meaning seems futile at best and politically problematic at worst; Nature's content is like an eel, slipping away the very moment you think you have finally grasped it. Nature is an 'empty' or 'floating' signifier. 'Empty' signifiers gain a certain, yet unstable, contingent and contestable, temporary coherence or content (but, in the process, they are simultaneously emptied out of a determinate meaning – they are rendered 'floating') through the mobilization of a metonymic list, a chain of equivalences or equivalent signifieds that 'quilt' their meaning (Žižek 1989; Stavrakakis 1997b). The longer the list of signifiers (like fish, rain, orgasm, earthquake, evolution, skin pigment, greed, …) that have to be strung together to give a concept like Nature some sort of meaning/content, the more contested, indeterminate and inchoate the concept becomes. Nature becomes a tapestry, a *montage*, of meaning, held together with quilting points (like the upholstery of a Chesterfield sofa). For example, in today's environmental parlance, 'biodiversity', 'eco-cities', 'pollutants', 'CO_2' can be thought of as quilting (or *points de capiton*) points through which certain meanings of Nature are knitted together. Moreover, these quilting points are also more than mere anchoring points; they refer to a beyond of meaning, a certain enjoyment that becomes structured in fantasy (in this case, an environmentally sound and socially harmonious order).[3]

This emptying out of a fixed meaning of Nature has been a systematic feature of late modernity, particularly as signifying chains of what Nature 'really' is multiplied in parallel to the proliferation of socio-political, cultural or other differentiations. We shall briefly explore this multiplication of narratives of Nature. Consider, for example, how in pre-modern times Nature was signified through a divine order, God's creation, whereby Nature was relegated to the domain of the divine: Nature and God were interchangeable, offering a meaning of Nature that gained content through its relationship with a world order understood as Divine, given and beyond the mortal. With the advent of enlightenment and early modernity, Nature became quilted through referents such as science, rationality, truth and clockwork mechanics. A new Truth of Nature became gradually established, one of a singular Nature that behaved mechanically, and through the mobilization of the correct application of the technologies of rationality (i.e. the proper scientific method), its law-like operation could be deciphered and subsequently manipulated to serve human ends. Nature possessed an internal logic, teleology, a mode of arranging itself that was self-contained and self-organizing, one that did not require a referent like God or Man; a set of things that defied an articulation with both the divine and the human. It was a view of Nature that rapidly asserted itself as the 'true' view against all lingering 'superstitious' remainders, whether pagan or Christian. It was

---

3   This particular semiologic perspective draws on Slavok Žižek's reading of Jacques Lacan's psychoanalytic interpretations of the Imaginary, the Real and the Symbolic (see Žižek 1989; Lacan 1993; Lacan 1997).

also a view that increasingly considered Nature as distinct and separate from the constructed social and cultural world of human interactions (Smith 2008b).

Yet, this 'scientific' notion of Nature began to explode rapidly from the nineteenth century onwards. While the Nature/Science/Rationality imbroglio remained firmly in place and consolidated itself, primarily through the increasingly successful development of the natural sciences and its mesmerizing applications in all domains of life, a plethora of other signifying chains began to quilt Nature's meaning. Take, for example, the Romanticism of nineteenth century notions of Nature. At a time during which the frontiers of Nature (in the sense of the external de-humanized nature that enlightenment thinking had framed) receded through the spiralling mobilization of an expanding array of non-human things in capitalist production and consumption on the one hand, and colonial-imperial exploration and incorporation of 'new' lands and natures in a rescaled eco-political orbit on the other, Nature (including the 'non-civilized' peoples it contained, like Native Americans or enslaved/colonized Africans) became associated with untamed wilderness, (lost) originality, moral superiority (against the moral decay of the 'civilized' world), utopian idyllic Arcadia, and sublime awesome beauty. Or consider the signifying chain that emerged with the first signs of ecological crisis in late nineteenth century cities, something that was particularly prevalent in rapidly urbanizing societies where the deteriorating sanitary conditions, the bacteriological infestations, the metabolic rift produced by the separation of town and countryside, etc. ... opened up a tremendous new real and symbolic space for Nature. From then onwards, Nature would also be partly symbolized as dangerous and threatening, as fearful – yet man-made – in its urban manifestations (Kaika 2005; Gandy 2006).

In sum, modernization produced a cacophony of metonymic lists associated with Nature, none of which exhausted the vagaries, idiosyncrasies and heterogeneous acting of the different and changing forms of nature that composed the world. Moreover, these forms proliferated as the number of socio-natural things, these hybrids of human and of nature – what Bruno Latour calls quasi-objects (Latour 1993) or what Donna Haraway calls Cyborgs (Haraway 1991) – multiplied with the intensifying assembling of human and non-human processes (like in, for example, nuclear energy, the making of trans-uranium elements, genetic manipulation, techno-natural constructs like water systems, energy lines, mega-cities, and the like). In recent years, and in particular as a result of the growing global awareness of 'the environmental crisis', the inadequacy of our symbolic representations of Nature have become more acute again as the Real of Nature, in the form of a wide variety of ecological threats (global warming, new diseases, biodiversity loss, resource depletion, pollution) invaded and unsettled our received understandings of Nature, forcing yet again a transformation of the signifying chains that attempt to provide 'content' for Nature, while at the same time exposing the impossibility of capturing fully the Real of natures (Žižek 2008b). Ecologists (deep or otherwise), environmental modernists, post-materialists, a diversity of environmental movements, new insights generated by a still successful and sprawling natural science (but one somewhat more sensitive to ethical issues after the backlash unleashed by the perverse 'successes' of the 'nuclear' age), even the captains of industry and a new generation of political elites, began to extend, transform or re-invent the arsenal of meanings assigned to Nature.

The point of the above argument is that the natures we see and work with are necessarily radically imagined, scripted and symbolically charged as Nature. These inscriptions are always inadequate, they leave a gap, a remainder and maintain a certain distance from the natures that are there, which are complex, chaotic, often unpredictable, radically contingent, historically and geographically variable, risky, patterned in endlessly complex ways, ordered along 'strange' attractors (see, for example, Prigogine and Stengers 1985). In other words, there is no Nature out there that needs or requires salvation in name of either Nature itself or a generic Humanity. There is nothing foundational in Nature that needs, demands or requires sustaining. The debate and controversies over Nature and what to do with it, in contrast, signal rather our political inability to engage in directly political and social argument and strategies about rearranging the socio-ecological co-ordinates of everyday life, the production of new socio-natural configurations, and the arrangements of socio-metabolic organization (something usually called capitalism) that we inhabit. In the next section, we shall exemplify and deepen further this conceptual and theoretical analysis by looking at the notion of sustainability and sustainable planning/development, symptomatic concepts that have become the hegemonically and consensually agreed metaphors to signal the ecological quandary we are in. Indeed, one of the key signifiers that has emerged as the pivotal 'empty' signifier to capture the growing concern for a Nature that seemed to veer off-balance, is of course 'sustainability'.

The Fantasy of Sustainability and Sustainable Planning

There is now a widespread consensus that the earth and many of its component parts are in an ecological bind that may short-circuit human and non-human life in the not too distant future if urgent and immediate action to retrofit nature to a more benign equilibrium is postponed for much longer. Irrespective of the particular views of Nature held by different individuals and social groups, consensus has emerged over the seriousness of the environmental condition and the precariousness of our socio-ecological balance. BP has re-branded itself as 'Beyond Petroleum' to certify its environmental credentials; Shell plays to a more eco-sensitive tune; eco-warriors of various political or ideological stripes and colours engage in direct action in the name of saving the planet; New Age post-materialists join the chorus that laments the irreversible decline of ecological amenities; eminent scientists enter the public domain to warn of possible ecological catastrophe; politicians try to outmanoeuvre each other in brandishing the ecological banner; and a wide range of policy initiatives and practices, performed under the motif of 'sustainability', are discussed, conceived, and implemented at all geographical scales. Al Gore's *An Inconvenient Truth* landed him with the Nobel Peace prize, surely one of the most telling illustrations of how ecological matters are elevated to the terrain of a global humanitarian cause. While there is certainly no agreement on what exactly Nature is and how to relate to it, there is a virtually unchallenged consensus over the need to be more 'environmentally' sustainable if disaster is to be avoided.

In this consensual setting, environmental problems are generally staged as universally threatening the survival of humankind, announcing the premature termination of civilization as we know it and sustained by what Mike Davis aptly called 'ecologies of fear' (Davis 1998). The discursive matrix through which the contemporary meaning of the environmental condition is woven is one quilted systematically by the continuous invocation of fear and danger, the spectre of ecological annihilation or at least seriously distressed socio-ecological conditions for many people in the near future. 'Fear' is indeed the crucial node through which much of the current environmental narrative is woven, and that continues to feed the concern with 'sustainability'.

This cultivation of 'ecologies of fear', in turn, is sustained by a particular set of phantasmagorical imaginations (Katz 1995). The apocalyptic imaginary of a world without water or at least with endemic water shortages, ravaged by hurricanes whose intensity is amplified by climate change; pictures of scorched land as global warming shifts the geo-pluvial regime and the spatial variability of droughts and floods; icebergs that disintegrate around the poles as ice melts into the sea; alarming reductions in bio-diversity as species disappear or are threatened by extinction; post-apocalyptic images of derelict wastelands reminiscent of the silent ecologies of the region around Chernobyl; the threat of peak-oil that without proper management and technologically innovative foresight would return civilization to a stone age cave-like existence; the devastation wreaked by wildfires, tsunamis, spreading diseases like SARS, Avian Flu, Ebola, or HIV – all these imaginaries of a Nature out of synch, destabilized, threatening and out of control are paralleled by equally disturbing images of a society that continues piling up waste, pumping CO_2 into the atmosphere, deforesting the earth's lungs, etc. ... This is a process that Neil Smith appropriately refers to as 'nature-washing', whereby the socio-ecological origins of the problems are recognised while this socially changed nature becomes a new super determinant of our social fate' (Smith 2008a: 245). In sum, our ecological predicament is sutured by millennialism fears sustained by an apocalyptic rhetoric and representational tactics, and by a series of performative gestures signalling an overwhelming, mind-boggling danger, one that threatens to undermine the very co-ordinates of our everyday lives and routines and may shake up the foundations of all we took and take for granted.[4]

---

4   Of course, apocalyptic imaginaries have been around for a long time as an integral part first of Christianity and later emerging as the underbelly of fast-forwarding technological modernization and its associated doomsday thinkers. However, as Martin Jay argues, while traditional apocalyptic versions still held out the hope for redemption, for a 'second coming', for the promise of a 'new dawn', environmental apocalyptic imaginaries are 'leaving behind any hope of rebirth or renewal ... in favour of an unquenchable fascination with being on the verge of an end that never comes' (Jay

This scripting of Nature permits and sustains a post-political arrangement sutured by fear and driven by a concern to manage things so that we can hold on to what we have (Swyngedouw 2007a). This constellation leads Alain Badiou to insist that ecology has become the new opium for the masses, replacing religion as the axis around which our fear for social disintegration becomes articulated (but also from where redemption, if the warnings are heeded, can be retrieved). Such ecologies of fear ultimately conceal, yet nurture, a conservative or, at least, reactionary message. While clouded in rhetoric of the need for radical change in order to stave off imminent catastrophe, a range of technical, social, managerial, physical and other measures have to be taken to make sure that things remain the same, that nothing really changes, that life (or at least our lives) can go on as before. Is this not the underlying message of, for example, *An Inconvenient Truth* or of the report of the United Nation's Intergovernmental Panel on Climate Change (IPCC) on the human consequences of global climate change? Both these narratives, in their very different representational ways (popular/populist on the one hand, 'scientific' on the other), urge radical changes in the techno-organizational management of the socio-natural environment in order to ensure that the world as we know it stays fundamentally the same (Žižek 2008a). This sentiment is also shared by Fredric Jameson when he claims that 'it is easier to imagine the end of the world than it is to imagine the end of capitalism' (Jameson 2003: 76).

In the call for a rebalanced environmental condition, many actors with very different and often antagonistic cultural, economic, political or social positions, interests and inspiration can find common cause in the name of a socially disembodied humanity. *An Inconvenient Truth* becomes, strangely enough, a very convenient one for those who believe civilization as we know it (I prefer to call this capitalism) needs to be preserved, rescued from potential calamity and revolutionary change. It calls for the rapid development of a whole battery of innovative environmental technologies, eco-friendly management principles and sustainable organizational forms (something capitalist dynamics and relations excel in producing providing they conform to the profit principle (see Buck 2007)), so that the existing socio-ecological order really does not have to change radically. Consider, for example, how the real and uncontested accumulation of CO_2 in the atmosphere, the threat of peak-oil, the expanding demands for energy and other resources, are today among the greatest concerns facing large companies. Of course, BP, Shell, IBM or others are rightly worried that the model of unbridled capital accumulation upon which their success in the twentieth century rested so crucially may be faced by ecological constraints if not limits. Manchester University

1994: 33). As Klaus Scherpe insists, this is not simply apocalypse now, but apocalypse forever. It is a vision that does not suggest, prefigure or expect the necessity of an event that will alter history (Scherpe 1987). Derrida sums this up most succinctly: 'here, precisely, is announced – as promise or as threat – an apocalypse without apocalypse, an apocalypse without vision, without truth, without revelation ... without message and without destination, without sender and without decidable addressee ... an apocalypse beyond good and evil' (Derrida 1982: 94).

has recently founded a 'Sustainable Consumption Institute', funded by TESCO to the tune of £20 million. This testifies to the quest of leading companies to ensure the right techno-administrative arrangements can be invented and devised to permit consumers to buy ourselves out of the ecological pickle we're in. Provided the correct techno-administrative apparatuses can be negotiated (like Agenda 21, the Kyoto protocol, recycling schemes, eco-friendly hard and soft technologies, or biodiversity preservation management), the socio-ecological order as we know it can be salvaged, rescued from ecological Armageddon. Consider, for example, how the climate change argument often revolves around discussing technological fixes and searching for more energy effective and fossil fuel replacing technologies that, combined with market-conform policy arrangements (like the Kyoto Protocol or the various schemes for carbon off-setting), stand to guarantee that the current capitalist socio-ecological can be sustained for some time longer.

The container signifier that encapsulates these post-political attempts to deal with Nature is, of course, 'sustainability' (Gibbs and Krueger 2007). Even more so than the slippery and floating meanings of Nature, 'sustainability' is the empty signifier par excellence. It refers to nothing and everything at the same time. Its prophylactic qualities can only be suggested by adding specifying metaphors. Hence, the proliferation of terms such as sustainable cities, sustainable planning, sustainable development, sustainable forestry, sustainable transport, sustainable regions, sustainable communities, sustainable yield, sustainable loss, sustainable harvest, sustainable resource (fill in whichever you fancy) use, sustainable housing, sustainable growth, sustainable policy, etc... The gesture to 'sustainability' already guarantees that the matter of Nature and the environment is taken seriously, that our fears are taken account off by those in charge, that 'homeland security' is in good hands.

The fantasy of imagining a benign and 'sustainable' Nature avoids asking the politically sensitive, but vital, question as to what kind of socio-environmental arrangements and assemblages we wish to produce, how this can be achieved, and what sort of environments we wish to inhabit, while at the same time acknowledging the radical contingency and undecidability of Nature. This is the clearest expression of the structure of fantasy in the Lacanian sense. While it is impossible to specify what exactly sustainability is all about (except in the most general or generic of terms), this void of meaning is captured by a multiplying series of fantasies, of stories and imaginations that try to bridge the constitutive gap between the indeterminacies of natures on the one hand (and the associated fear of the continuous return of the Real of nature in the guise of ecological disasters like droughts, hurricanes, floods, etc...) and the always frustrated desire for some sort of harmonious and equitable socio-ecological living on the other, one that disavows the absence of a foundation for the social in a Nature that, after all, does not exist. 'Sustainability', or more precisely the quilting points around which its meaning is woven, is the environmental planner and activist's *objet petit a*, the thing around which desire revolves, yet simultaneously stands in for the disavowed Real, the repressed core, the denial of the state of the situation (i.e. the recognition that the world is really in a mess and really needs drastic and dramatic, that is revolutionary (a metaphor that of course can never be mobilized, that is banned, censured) action).[5] It is in this phantasmagoric space that the proper political dimension (on which more below) disappears to be replaced by a consensually established frame that calls for techno-managerial action in the name of humanity, social integration, the earth and its human and non-human inhabitants, all peoples in all places.

The sequence of the de-politicization of Nature placed under the banner of 'the environmental crisis', and reassembled post-politically under the sign of 'sustainability', corrals a series of interconnected processes that fuse together in the production of a rather unstable collective through which some sort of meaning to sustainability becomes articulated. First, it is based on the expertise of an assumedly neutral natural scientific knowledge aristocracy. Yet, these experts partake directly in policy domains and become, as expert managers, integral to policy making forums and institutions. Here is a fundamentally duplicitous science and scientists at work, whereby 'matters of fact' are seamlessly and without much political dispute translated into 'matters of concern'. This is a short-circuiting procedure, whereby 'fact' and 'value' are mixed, sometimes interchanged, and invariably translated without proper public political intermediation (Latour 2004). These normative values (like the idealized climate we ought to return to) become then universalized in the sustainability discourse. This discourse invokes THE people (as well as non-humans) as a whole. Although socio-spatial differences and inequalities are acknowledged, the environmental threat is global, and affects everyone and everything (Swyngedouw 2007a). 'Sustainability' does not identify a privileged subject of change (like the proletariat for Marx, women for feminists, or the 'creative class' for competitive capitalism), but instead invokes a common condition or predicament, the need for common humanity-wide action, mutual collaboration and co-operation. There are no internal social tensions or internal generative conflicts; it is a populist gesture that disavows the agonistic heterogeneity of 'the people'. Instead the 'enemy' is externalized and objectified. Its fundamental fantasy is that of *an intruder*, or more usually a group of intruders, who have *corrupted* the system. The empty signifier of sustainability needs a specific material quilting point around which a metonymic list can be assembled and a more or less stable narrative woven. These quilting points invariably refer to more or less specific fetishized objects, like CO_2 for 'climate change', gene pools for 'biodiversity', H_2O for 'droughts' or 'floods' (although each of these things are themselves multiple in their meaning and practice). The 'enemy' is externalized, vague, and ambiguous, socially empty, homogenized, vacuous, and, ultimately, fetishized. Consider, for example, how the Kyoto negotiations elevated CO_2 and its problems to quintessentially an issue of market failure that can be rectified by instituting a market where hitherto there was none (Liverman 2009; Bumpus and Liverman 2008). Problems, therefore, are not the result of the 'system' as such or a fatal flow inscribed in the system, but transposed on to the Thing itself, which is staged as some pathological excess. That is, of course, why the solution can be

5   For further details, see Lacan (1977).

found in dealing with the 'pathological' phenomenon, the resolution for which resides in the system itself.

Demands for sustainability are addressed to the elites, demands that fully operate within contours of the possible; it is a politics of the possible operative within the framework of the given situation. 'Sustainability' is hereby reduced to a practice of 'good environmental governance'. The architecture of such inherently populist governing takes the form of stakeholder participatory governance that operates beyond-the-state and permits a form of self-management, self-organization, and controlled self-disciplining (Dean 1999; Lemke 1999; Swyngedouw 2005, 2009b), under the aegis of a non-disputed liberal-capitalist order. It certainly does not include a visioning and associated naming of a proper name to its field of action; no proper names are assigned to such post-political politics (Badiou 2005). Only vague concepts like sustainable communities, sustainable forests, the sustainable city, the green city or the eco-city replace the proper names of politics.

In sum, post-political sustainability policies rest on the following foundations. First, the social and ecological problems caused by modernity/capitalism are external side-effects; they are not an inherent and integral part of the relations of liberal politics and capitalist economies. Second, a strictly populist politics emerges here; one that elevates the interest of an imaginary 'the People', Nature, or 'the environment' to the level of the universal rather than opening spaces that permit to universalize the claims of particular socio-natures, environments or social groups or classes. Third, these side-effects are constituted as global, universal, and threatening: they are a total threat. Fourth, the 'enemy' or the target of concern is thereby of course continuously externalized and disembodied. The 'enemy' is always vague, ambiguous, unnamed and uncounted, and ultimately empty. Fifth, the target of concern can be managed through a consensual dialogical politics whereby demands become depoliticized and politics naturalized within a given socio-ecological order for which there is ostensibly no real alternative (Swyngedouw 2009a).

CODA: The Nature of Planning

For Slavoj Žižek, Chantal Mouffe (Mouffe 2005), and others (see (Swyngedouw 2007b; 2009a), consensually established concerns, like 'sustainability', structured around ecologies of fear that nurture a reactionary stance and urge techno-managerial forms of intervention, are an expression of the current post-political and post-democratic condition, one that is arranged around distinct bio-political gestures. Post-politics refers to a politics in which ideological or dissensual contestation and struggles are replaced by techno-managerial planning, expert management and administration, 'whereby the regulation of the security and welfare of human lives is the primary goal' (Žižek 1999). Such post-political arrangement signals a depoliticized (in the sense of the disappearance of the democratic agonistic struggle over the content and direction of socio-ecological life) public space whereby expertise, interest intermediation, and administration through governance define the zero-level of politics (see Marquand 2004; Swyngedouw 2009d). This depoliticized consensual arrangement is organized through post-democratic institutions of governance, like the Kyoto protocol, the European Union or assorted other public-private governing arrangements, that increasingly replace the political institutions of government (see Crouch 2004).

The conceptual challenges explored above are, I would argue, of vital importance for grappling with this post-political condition, for exploding the infernal process of de-politicization marked by the dominance of empty signifiers like Nature or Sustainability, and for thinking planning again. The claim made above to abandon Nature in no way suggests ignoring, let alone forgetting, the Real of natures or, more precisely, the diverse, multiple, whimsical, contingent and often unpredictable socio-ecological relations of which we are part. The claim we make is about the urgent need to question legitimizing all manner of socio-environmental politics, policies and interventions in the name of a thoroughly imagined and symbolized Nature or Sustainability, a procedure that necessarily forecloses a properly political frame through which such imaginaries become constituted and hegemonized, and disavows the constitutive split of the people by erasing the spaces of agonistic encounter. The above reconceptualization urges us to accept the extraordinary variability of natures, insists on the need to make 'a wager' on natures, forces us to choose politically between this rather than that nature, invites us to plunge into the relatively unknown, expect the unexpected, accept that not all there is can be known, and, most importantly, fully endorse the violent moment that is inscribed in any concrete or real socio-environmental intervention.

Indeed, the ultimate aim of planning is intervention, to change the given socio-environmental ordering in a certain manner. Like any intervention, this is a violent act; it erases at least partly what is there in order to erect something new and different. Consider, for example, the extraordinary effect the eradication of the HIV virus would have on sustaining livelihoods (or should we preserve/protect the virus in the name of biodiversity?). In ways comparable to how private decisions, like buying a car, are violent intrusions in the socio-ecological order, or to business decisions to recycle computers in the socio-ecological wastelands of Mumbai's shantytowns, planning interventions are also irredeemably violent engagements that re-choreograph socio-natural relations and assemblages. The recognition that planning acts are singular interventions, that any form of spatialization/ environmentalization closes down, at least temporarily, the horizon of time, is of central importance. Such violent encounter, of course, always constitutes a political act, one that can be legitimized only in political terms, and not – as is customarily done – through an externalized legitimation that resides in a fantasy of Nature or Sustainability. Any political act is one that re-orders socio-ecological co-ordinates and patterns, reconfigures uneven socio-ecological relations, often with unforeseen or unforeseeable consequences.

Such interventions signal a totalitarian moment, the temporary suspension of the democratic, understood as the presumed equality of all. The dialectic between the democratic as a political given and the totalitarian moment of planning intervention as the suspension of the democratic needs to be radically endorsed.

While a pluralist democratic politics, founded on a presumption of equality, insists on difference, disagreement, radical openness and exploring multiple possible futures, concrete spatial-ecological intervention is necessarily about closure, definitive choice, a singular intervention and, thus, certain exclusion and silencing. The democratic planning process dwells, therefore, in two spheres simultaneously. Jacques Rancière (Rancière 1998) and others (see, for example, Marchart 2007, for a review) define these spheres respectively as 'the political' and 'the police' (the policy order). The (democratic) political is the space for the enunciation and affirmation of difference, for the cultivation of dissensus and disagreement, for asserting the presumption of equality of each and everyone (see Swyngedouw 2009c). In contrast, the practice of planning interventions, when becoming concretely geographical or ecological, is of necessity a violent act of foreclosure of the democratic political (at least temporarily), of taking one option rather than another, of producing one sort of environment, of assembling certain socio-natural relations, of foregrounding some natures rather than others, of hegemonizing a particular metonymic chain rather than another. And the legitimation of such options cannot be based on corralling Nature or Sustainability into legitimizing service.

In conclusion, while Nature and Sustainability do not exist outside the metonymic chains that offer some sort of meaning, there are of course all manner of environments and assemblages of socio-natural relations. Environments are specific historical results of socio-physical processes (Heynen et al. 2005). All socio-spatial processes are indeed invariably also predicated upon the circulation, the metabolism and the enrolling of social, cultural, physical, chemical or biological processes, but their outcome is contingent, often unpredictable, immensely varied, risky. These metabolisms produce a series of both enabling and disabling socio-environmental conditions (Swyngedouw 2006). Indeed, these produced milieus often embody contradictory tendencies. Processes of socio-metabolic change are, therefore, never socially or ecologically neutral. For example, the unequal ecologies associated with uneven property relations, the commodification of all manner of natures, the impoverished socio-ecological life under the overarching sign of the commodity and of money in a neo-liberal order, and of the perverse exclusions choreographed by the dynamics of uneven eco-geographical development at all scales suggest how the production of socio-ecological arrangements is always a deeply conflicting, and hence irrevocably political, process. All manner of social power geometries shape the particular social and political configurations as well as the environments in which we live. Therefore, the production of socio-environmental arrangements implies fundamentally political questions, and has to be addressed in political terms. The question is to tease out who gains from and who pays for, who benefits from and who suffers (and in what ways) from particular processes of metabolic circulatory change. These flows produce inclusive and exclusive ecologies both locally and in terms of the wider uneven socio-ecological dynamics that sustain these flows. Democratizing environments, then, become an issue of enhancing the democratic content of socio-environmental construction by means of identifying the strategies through which a more equitable distribution of social power and a more inclusive mode of producing natures (of producing metabolic circulatory processes) can be achieved. This requires reclaiming proper democracy and proper democratic public spaces (as spaces for the enunciation of agonistic dispute) as a foundation for and condition of possibility for more egalitarian socio-ecological arrangements and the naming of positively embodied ega-libertarian socio-ecological futures that are immediately realizable. In other words, egalitarian ecologies are about demanding the impossible and realizing the improbable.

References

Badiou, A. (2005). *Politics: A Non-Expressive Dialectics*. Paper read at 'Is The Politics of Truth still Thinkable?', a conference organized by Slavoj Žižek and Costas Douzinas, 25–6 November, at Birkbeck Institute for the Humanities, Birkbeck College, London.

Badiou, A. (2008) 'Live Badiou – Interview with Alain Badiou, Paris, December 2007', in Feltham, O. (ed.) *Alain Badiou – Live Theory*. London: Continuum, 136–9.

Braun, B. (2006) 'Environmental issues: global natures in the space of assemblage' *Progress in Human Geography* 30 (5): 644–54.

Buck, D. (2007) 'The ecological question: can capitalism survive?' in Panitch, I and Leys, C. (eds) *Socialist Register 2007 – Coming to Terms with Nature*. New York: Monthly Review Press, 60–71.

Bumpus, A., and Liverman, D. (2008) 'Accumulation by decarbonization and the governance of carbon offsets' *Economic Geography* 84 (2): 127–55.

Castree, N. (2003) 'Environmental issues: relational ontologies and hybrid politics' *Progress in Human Geography* 27 (2): 203–211.

Conley, V. (1996) *Ecopolitics: The Environment in Poststructural Thought*. London: Routledge.

Crouch, C. (2004) *Post-Democracy*. Cambridge: Polity Press.

Davis, M. (1998) *Ecology of Fear: Los Angeles and the Imagination of Disaster*. New York: Metropolitan Books.

Dean, M. (1999) *Governmentality – Power and Rule in Modern Society*. London: Sage.

Deleuze, G., and Guattari, F. (1994) *What is Philosophy?* New York: Columbia University Press.

Derrida, J. (1982) 'Of an apocalyptic tone recently adopted in philosophy' *Semeia* 23: 63–97.

Gandy, M. (2006) 'Urban nature and the ecological imaginary', in Heynen, N.K., Kaikam, M., and Swyngedouw, E. (eds) *In the Nature of Cities: Urban Political Ecology and the Politics of Urban Metabolism*. New York: Routledge, 63–74.

Gibbs, D., and Krueger, R. (eds) (2007) *The Sustainable Development Paradox*. New York: The Guilford Press.

Gould, S.J. (1980) *The Panda's Thumb*. New York: W.W. Norton.

Haraway, D. (1991) *Simians, Cyborgs and Women: The Reinvention of Nature*. London: Free Association Books.

Harvey, D. (1996) *Justice, Nature, and the Geography of Difference*. Oxford: Blackwell.

Henderson, G. (2009) 'Marxist political economy and the environment', in Castree, N., Demeritt, D., Liverman, D., and Rhoads, B. (eds) *A Companion to Environmental Geography*. Oxford: Wiley-Blackwell, 266–93.

Herzogenrath, B. (ed.) (2008) *An [Un]likely Alliance: Thinking Environment(s) with Deleuze/Guattari*. Newcastle upon Tyne: Cambridge Scholars Publishing.

Heynen, N., Kaika, M., and Swyngedouw, E. (eds) (2005) *In the Nature of Cities – The Politics of Urban Metabolism*. London: Routledge.

Hillier, J. (2009) 'On justice between absence and presence: the "ghost ships" of Graythorp', *International Journal of Urban and Regional Research* 33(3).

Jameson, F. (2003) 'Future City', *New Left Review* (21): 65–79.

Jay, M. (1994) 'The Apocalyptic Imagination and the Inability to Mourn', in Robinson, G., and Rundell, J. (eds) *Rethinking Imagination – Culture and Creativity*. New York: Routledge, 30–47.

Kaika, M. (2005) *City of Flows*. London: Routledge.

Katz, C. (1995) 'Under the falling sky: apocalyptic environmentalism and the production of nature', in Callari, A., Cullenberg, S. and Biewener, B. (eds) *Marxism in the Postmodern Age*. New York: The Guilford Press, 276–82.

Lacan, J. (1977) *The Seminar. Book XI. The Four Fundamental Concepts of Psychoanalysis*. London: Hogarth Press.

Lacan, J. (1993) *The Seminar of Jacques Lacan Book III. The Psychoses 1955–1956*. New York: W.W. Norton.

Lacan, J. (1997) *Ecrits*. London: Tavistock/Routledge.

Laclau, E., and Mouffe, C. (2001) *Hegemony and Socialist Strategy*. London: Verso.

Latour, B. (1993) *We Have Never Been Modern*. Cambridge, MA: Harvard University Press.

Latour, B. (2004) *Politics of Nature: How to Bring the Sciences into Democracy* Cambridge, MA: Harvard University Press.

Latour, B. (2005) *Reassembling the Social: An Introduction to Actor-Network-Theory*. Oxford: Oxford University Press.

Lemke, T. (1999) '"The Birth of Bio-Politics" – Michel Foucault's Lectures at the Collège de France on Neo-Liberal Governmentality' *Economy and Society* 30 (2): 190–207.

Levins, R., and Lewontin, R. (1985) *The Dialectical Biologist*. Cambridge, MA: Harvard University Press.

Lewontin, R., and Levins, R. (2007) *Biology under the Influence – Dialectical Essays on Ecology, Agriculture, and Health*. New York: Monthly Review Press.

Liverman, D. (2009) 'Conventions of climate change: constructions of danger and the dispossession of the atmosphere' *Journal of Historical Geography* [forthcoming].

Marchart, O. (2007) *Post-Foundational Political Thought – Political Difference in Nancy, Lefort, Badiou and Laclau*. Edinburgh: Edinburgh University Press.

Marquand, D. (2004) *Decline of the Public: The Hollowing Out of Citizenship*. Cambridge: Polity Press.

Morton, T. (2007) *Ecology without Nature*. Cambridge, MA: Harvard University Press.

Mouffe, C. (2005) *On The Political, Thinking in Action*. London: Routledge.

Prigogine, I., and Stengers, I. (1985) *Order out of Chaos: Man's New Dialogue with Nature*. London: HarperCollins.

Rancière, J. (1998) *Disagreement*. Minneapolis, MN: University of Minnesota Press.

Scherpe, K.R. (1987) 'Dramatization and de-dramatization of "The End": the apocalyptic consciousness of modernity and post-modernity' *Cultural Critique* 5 (Winter 1986–7): 95–129.

Smith, N. (2008a) 'Afterword to the third edition' in Smith, N. (ed.) *Uneven Development*..London: The University of Georgia Press, 239–266.

Smith, N. (2008b) *Uneven Development – Nature, Capital and the Production of Space (third edition, with a new afterword)*. London: University of Georgia Press.

Stavrakakis, Y. (1997a) 'Green fantasy and the real of nature: elements of a Lacanian critique of green ideological discourse' *Journal for the Psychoanalysis of Culture and Society* 2(1): 123–32.

Stavrakakis, Y. (1997b) 'Green ideology: a discursive reading' *Journal of Political Ideologies* 2(3): 259–79.

Stavrakakis, Y. (2000) 'On the emergence of green ideology: the dislocation factor in green politics', in Howarth, D., Norval, A.J., and Stavrakakis, Y. (eds) *Discourse Theory and Political Analysis – Identities, Hegemonies and Social Change*. Manchester: Manchester University Press, 100–18.

Swyngedouw, E. (1996) 'The city as a hybrid – on nature, society and cyborg urbanisation' *Capitalism, Nature, Socialism* 7(1) (25): 65–80.

Swyngedouw, E. (2005) 'Governance, innovation and the citizen: the Janus face of governance-beyond-the-state' *Urban Studies* 42(11): 1–16.

Swyngedouw, E. (2006) 'Circulations and metabolisms: (hybrid) natures and (cyborg) cities' *Science as Culture* 15(2): 105–21.

Swyngedouw, E. (2007a) 'Impossible/undesirable sustainability and the post-political condition', in Krueger, J.R. and Gibbs, D. (eds) *The Sustainable Development Paradox*. New York: Guilford.

Swyngedouw, E. (2007b) 'The post-political city', in BAVO (ed.) *Urban Politics Now: Re-imagining Democracy in the Neo-liberal City*. Rotterdam: Netherlands Architecture Institute NAI Publishers.

Swyngedouw, E. (2009a.) 'The antinomies of the post-political city: in search of a democratic politics of environmental production' *International Journal of Urban and Regional Research* 33(3).

Swyngedouw, E. (2009b) 'Civil society, governmentality and the contradictions of governance-beyond-the-state', in, MacCallum, D., Moulaert, F., Hillier, J.and Vicari-Haddock, S. (eds) *Social Innovation and Territorial Development* Aldershot: Ashgate.

Swyngedouw, E. (2009c) 'Where is the political?' Paper available from the author.

Swyngedouw, E. (2009d) 'The zero-ground of politics: musings on the post-political city' *New Geographies* (2).

Williams, R. (1980) *Problems of Materialism and Culture*. London: Verso.

Williams, R. (1988) *Keywords*. London: Fontana.

Žižek, S. (1989) *The Sublime Object of Ideology*. London: Verso.

Žižek, S. (1992/ 2002) *Looking Awry: An Introduction to Jacques Lacan Through Popular Culture, October Books Series*. Cambridge, MA: MIT Press.

Žižek, S. (1999) *The Ticklish Subject – The Absent Centre of Political Ontology*. London: Verso.

Žižek, S. (2000) *The Fragile Absolute*. London: Verso.

Žižek, S. (2008) *Censorship Today: Violence, or Ecology as a New Opium for the Masses* [accessed 5 August 2008]. Available from <http://fordiletante.wordpress.com/2008/05/07/censorship-today-violence-or-ecology-as-a-new-opium-for-the-masses/>

Žižek, S. (2008b) *In Defense of Lost Causes*. London: Verso.

Urbanity, (Neo)vitalism and Becoming

John Pløger

Introduction

Dictionaries define urbanity as the result of urban experiences which shape manners and ways of thinking and acting. Urbanity is a rarely used concept in urban theory and studies, and, if used, it mainly refers to public space as the centre of urban life. Urban sociology prefers the words 'urbanism as a way of life', and from an architect's point of view `urban life´ concerns how space and place should be ordered. The functional and aesthetic order of space is key to shaping the 'good' city life. These ideas can be found in classical urban sociology from Park and Wirth to Patrick Geddes, Jane Jacobs and Charles Booth (Osborne and Rose 2004). Early urban planning was concerned with how to give a moral order to cities through space (Joyce 2003). Others define urbanity as the product of the socio-spatial ontology (Amin and Thrift 2002) including acknowledging the 'throwntogetherness' of people in space, or to put it another way, 'cities are precisely arenas of chance encounters' (Massey 2005: 179). Others again emphasize aesthetic experiences and the pleasure of gazing stimulated by encounters with strangers and informal interaction in cities (Bauman 1993; Sennett 1991).

The major theorists concerned with urbanity remain Georg Simmel and Walter Benjamin. For them, the stranger, the gaze, signs, symbols, the 'reading' of space, and 'shock' experiences are all important. Furthermore, they argue that urban experiences (both as 'erfahrung' and 'erlebnis'[1]) are transformed into manners (social forms), codes, attitudes as well as desires, hopes, imaginaries and a restless identity-seeking (Sennett 1991; Simmel 1997). Metaphors and allegories are vital

---

1   'Erfahrung refers to experience as the accumulation of knowledge. It means experience in the sense of being widely travelled, of having witnessed many things, of having gained wisdom. Erlebnis is concerned with the domain of inner life, with the chaotic contents of psychic life. The shocks of the metropolitan environment are inassimilable by the consciousness of the individual, and are parried or deflected into the realm of the unconscious where they remain embedded' (Gilloch 1996: 143).

to urbanites as ways of understanding and reflecting on city life and ways of lives, which we can cautiously say point to the need to look at city life's 'mental space'. Another thread in urban studies since the 1990s has placed a greater emphasis on city life as desire, the imagined and the sensate, where body, affection, *jouissance*, sexualized spaces and 'thing-materiality' are 'actors' (Binnie 2006; Liggett 2003; Pile 2004; Thrift 2008). In line with this discussion, we have also seen a greater interest in the psychological and phenomenological aspects of city life (Liggett 2003; Pile 1996; Stevens 2007). Following philosophers such as Gilles Deleuze (Hillier 2007) and Michel Foucault (Pløger 2008), the trajectory in this chapter will be to reflect on forces of an urbanity-in-becoming made by numerous socio-spatial *dispositifs* of urban life.

Whether utilizing Simmel, Deleuze or Foucault as a starting point, a discussion of vitalism and vitalist forces is crucial if we are to understand the nature of becoming and the emergence of urbanity. If one follows this trajectory, it need not reduce urbanity to the non-representational. Rather we must take as our starting point that 'we live in a multiverse, not a universe, in which intersection, transfer, emergence and paradox are central to life' (Thrift 2004: 83, referring to the pragmatist William James). In other words, if we take seriously that 'life itself is a process of production of the new' (p. 85), we have to recognize that everyday life is virtual and vitalistic, and we have to consider this everyday life vitalism in its urban setting; in particular its temporary and – most often – instantaneous articulation as eventalisations affecting and affected by motive forces, sensibility, emotions and body-mind. We have to approach urbanity not only as socio-spatial ontology or from an architectural informed theory of spatiality, but as vitalism and a virtuality of city living (Rajchman 1998).

From here we consider a possible neo-vitalism that, for some, is shaped by new forms of communication (Lash 2006). Social becomings always rest provisionally as social forms. Urbanity is such provisionality as constituted immanently by form, content and becoming (Simmel 1997; Hansen 1991; Hillier 2007). Seeing urbanity as vitalism and becoming, however, opens up a whole range of possible perspectives such as ontology, the imaginary and representation, urbanity as lived and experienced, spatiality, non-representational forces and, not forgetting, the phenomenology of situations and the power of discourses. We have, in other words, to reflect on an urbanity-in-becoming shaped by everyday life experiences and practices and influenced in particular by its socio-spatial settings, imaginaries and other social representations. Following recent writings, a discussion of urbanity must consider vitalism as generative forces. Here we may consider two approaches: space and meaning, and their forming of transversal as well as rhythmic urban lives (Huxley 2006; Pløger 2008) and the sensate (Lash 2006). Everyday life spatialities are seen as agents, acting as constitutive of urbanity.[2] Looking at vitalism as generative also includes reflection on urban life becoming meaning and meaningful through

---

2   The particular density, social heterogeneity and intensity of urban space and the social
     forms, ways of life and attitudes it shapes make city life different to countryside ways
     of life (Simmel 1971: 324–9).

the imaginary, lived value-schemes, coding and re-coding, social constructions and deconstruction, words and discourses.

This chapter has a trajectory starting from the question of why urbanity should be considered as vague. The first section, *Urbanity is vague, ephemeral and fluid*, starts by acknowledging that urbanity is not only a concept, but life lived within new emergences, the imaginary, coding and values. In some countries, early modern urbanism and urban studies thought of city life as shaped by vitalist forces. The section, *Life as vitalism in cities*, shows how the idea of a 'vital impulse' (Bergson), which influenced not only French urbanism but a vitalist thread, can also be found in the writings of the theorist of urban life, Georg Simmel. The section, *Lived threads of vitalism*, then turns to contemporary ideas on urban vitalism; followed by the section, *Neo-vitalism, presence and emergence*, which discusses what contemporary urban vitalist forces might be (giving the examples of mobile phones and presence-events). The different sections all point to the need for urban theory, planning theory and practice to be more aware of city life as urbanity-in-becoming, rather than something we can understand through fixed typologies, fixed spatial schemes, or housing politics and social policies in themselves. Urbanity as a way of living and thinking, experiencing city spaces and lives is, so to say, on-the-move, contingent and ephemeral, pointing to the need to always try to see new threads emerging, and the forces of vitalism merging in new ways. The section, *Working with urbanity-in-becoming*, tries to inspire readers to acknowledge the fundamental differences between planning for urbanism and urbanity, and to see how these concepts themselves need to be considered as spatial and social before seeing them as relational. If planning for urbanity-in-becoming should work as a tool for urban planning, cities continually must work with lived schemes of signification, lived identifications, the meaningful life, vitalist forces of individuality and emerging social forces much more than with space.

Urbanity – Vague, Ephemeral and Fluid

Huxley (2006) and Osborne and Rose (1999), following Foucault, recognize that urban planning becomes the main tool of 'the neutralisation and control, at a social scale, of the logic of event, of the creation and production of the new' (Lazzarato 2006: 177). As socio-spatiality – the production of social forms – urban design and architecture give distance, proximity, nearness, seriality, and encounters as constitutive forms to presence in space. What counts in planning and urban politics is the taming of life through space. As Foucault states, the city form shapes conduct by ensuring 'a certain allocation of people in space, a *canalization* of their circulation, as well as coding of their reciprocal relations' (Foucault 1986: 253). Foucault (2008) called the wish to neutralize and control space the birth of a new bio-politics, constituted by a new dynamic between medicine, planning, and politics. This was part of an ensemble of *dispositif* forces of observations and calculation informing the government on how to tame space and shape a predictable and healthy workforce.

Self-regulation, manners and surveillance were crucial instruments of this bio-politics (Dillon 2007).

According to Foucault 'the new biopolitical *dispositifs* are born once we begin to ask ourselves, [w]hat is the correct manner of managing individuals, goods and wealth within the family ... and of making the family fortunes prosper – how are we to introduce this meticulous attention of the father towards his family into the management of the state?' (Lazzarato 2000: 2). What is important is that the bio-politic becomes part of the political economy of forces that 'encompasses power *dispositifs* that amplify the whole range of relations between the forces that extend throughout the social body ... rather than ... the relationship between capital and labour exclusively' (Lazzarato 2000: 3). What are confined are, according to Deleuze, multiplicity, the outside, 'the virtual, the power to metamorphosis, becoming' (Lazzarato 2006: 175). Bio-politics is a modality of power, where space plays a crucial role in 'a normation rather than normalization' of life (Foucault 2004: 57); a phrase Foucault uses to stress the primary of the norm to disciplines, and which again can be used to underline the normative aspect of the spatial *dispositifs* (Pløger 2008).

Numerous writers, intellectuals and academics try to understand their time, history, society and everyday life from theorizing and conceptualizing the city and its forces. As in so much art (expressionism, surrealism etc.), novelists such as Raban or Baudelaire, Calvino and Auster (to name a few), implicitly or explicitly write stories about subjects that appropriate urban life in a vitalistic way; expressively, gazing, involving, reflecting within cities' diversity and manifold encounters. We need to focus on the effect of urban presences – expressivity and reading/coding – trying to understand how city life is shaped by connectivities, assemblages, emergences, transformativity, transcendence, fluidity, (ephemeral) flows and (re)codings and how these modalities are made meaningful and what meaning they have.

Urbanity, in this manner, is life experienced in constellations and configurations of repetitive time-space geographies, in which significance also refers to manners and conventions, but there is too an active engagement with urban life and its challenges, choices and possibilities. Space surroundings and everyday life are lived through representations from which meanings derive and are made and from which choices occur. What is important is, as Liggett (2003: 90) makes clear, that 'encounters in the city between memory and experience are profoundly noninstrumental. They are examples of life as an engaged art'. Lefebvre (1991) is well-known for pointing to this relation between the lived, the perceived and conceived, although he sees space as 'passively experienced' through collective embodied 'associated images and symbols' and 'non-verbal symbols and signs' (Lefebvre 1991: 39). Lefebvre does not bring together 'the image, the imagined, and the imaginary' (to use Mendieta 2001b: 207) and thus does not focus on subjects as always active and instantaneous meaning-makers.

We are, as Sartre makes us aware, 'trained' in city living by experiencing and making meaningful/non-meaningful 'the life of persons, moving, sitting, talking, reflecting, objectifying, deceiving and trusting others, always under the look of others' (Mendieta 2001b: 209). It is fairly easy to see vitalism as a matter of sensing the city, but following Sartre and Mendieta, we also have to stress that humans approach the city for themselves, where its 'other' and 'the other' are 'necessary preconditions of my own consciousness' (2001b: 210). Representations, so seen, play a crucial role because people make the world understandable and adaptable through meaning, words, coding, re-coding and significative signs and representations. The city is made 'something' by, Foucault would say, discursive practices and its system of visibilities (Pløger 2008). Life is more than words and concepts – existence in itself – but we have to remember that 'forming concepts is a way of living and not a way of killing life; it is a way to live in a relative mobility and not a way to immobilize it …' (Foucault 1998: 475).

Urbanity is seen subjectively as vague; often like a feeling of being 'well situated' or 'this is me' feeling ('stimmtheit'), grounded on, for instance, an emphatic sensing of, and engagement with, urban living. Values ascribed to urbanity such as atmosphere, excitement, intensity, unpredictability, diversity, cosmopolism, proximity-to-everything or joyfulness are expressions of vagueness. The vagueness also refers to a 'mentality', a way of thinking and acting shaped by living lives grounded in imaginaries made by the vitalist, perceived and cognitive relation to one's city life experiences. Life changes and so do imaginaries and schemes of significations, as well as one's discourses and ways of experiencing. Lived urbanity will always, as we know from Sartre and Foucault (Seitz 2004), be situated as praxis and ways of thinking within intersubjective discourses, norms and codes, as moods or feelings. What is important, in order to understand urbanity, is the notion of indefinite and infinite becoming-selves, if we 'suggest that existentialism is a performance piece that is still becoming and will never be something definite or self-identical, that is never come and never went … ' (Seitz 2004: 103. As Sartre says, 'perhaps before anything else we are historical' (Seitz 2004: 99), meaning that we are situated in both past and present. The meaning of living in cities to each and every one changes through one's life-course and its life-phases.

Lately this urbanity, to feel one-self living as an urbanite, is touched on in planning and urban politics using surveys on value-schemes to implicate what it is. This is done from the perspective of the spatialization of everyday life, where what matters is how one's place of living and working works functionally, conveniently and rationally according to class and life-style (e.g. gentrification, creative class, career and the like). When urbanity is used as a concept in planning, it is similar to the idea of spatialized urbanism. Life is not there but we can find traces in urban planning where city life was thought of as vitalistic.

Life as Vitalism

One of the founding figures of French urbanism, Marcel Poëte, used Henri Bergson's philosophy of vitalism to inform his ideas on urban planning (Terranova 2008). Bergson's idea of 'the vital impulse' (l'élan vital) or 'spontaneous consciousness', his ideas of life as flux and becoming, made Poëte see 'the city as an always-changing object, the transformation of which is driven by the pure pulsing of life' so that 'urban changes occur in sudden jumps (*sauts brusques*)' (Terranova 2008: 924). Poëte talked about an 'urban organism' that was 'comparable to a sentient being' (p. 926), where 'reality' is 'mobile and changing; a fixation is nothing but an instant movement' (p. 929). The city is a place where 'life is always in flux, always becoming', and, therefore, urban life is characterized by a vital indetermination and the 'unforeseeable forms it (life) creates in the course of its evolution' (p. 925). For Bergson images, 'an existence halfway between the 'thing' and the representation' (Bergson, in Terranova 2008: 934), are a condition of/for life, and to Poëte urbanism must plan with and from these images in-between 'matter-in-motion and life-in-flux' (p. 935); that is, becomings.

To Bergson and Poëte, vitalist forces, such as desire, intention, the will-to-will, and values, precondition life as lived. Vitalism is an aspect of an urbanity-in-becoming. Vitalist forces have the potential to produce events, difference, distinction, contingency, as well as change. As such, vitalism should be of interest to planning and urban politics, because vitalist forces can move emotions, desires, intuition, and are therefore constitutive to the phenomenology of fluxes and everyday life flows, connectivities and chance. Vitalist forces not only influence and shape events and situations, but influence meaning and readings of space and give values to space, architecture, political issues and plans.

Simmel's vitalistic *lebenphilosophie* builds on Nietzsche as well as Schopenhauer (Simmel 1986) seeing society and life moved and changed by 'events' ('*geschehen*') (Pyyhtinen 2007: 112).[3] Events, to Simmel, happen on 'the axis between potentiality and actuality' along 'concrete socio-cultural phenomena, relations and formations' (p. 114). An event is thus part of life, a becoming of the social. Simmel sees society as 'a continuous process and eventing' (p. 115) that strives to find a form, but the unity of becoming and being in form is relative, unstable, provoked by events itself. There is a duality or dialectic between form and event which could be characterized as '*wechselwirkung*'[4] mediated by agents. The event occurring – the 'eventalization' of contexts – 'deprives individuals being the 'source' of social processes' (p. 117), and therefore opens up to a causality of another order; namely that between form and life, structures and subjects, space, materialities and acting subjects. Simmel (1997) discusses Schopenhauer and Nietzsche on life, and he tries to see how the idea of life as will (Schopenhauer) and life as 'will to will' (Nietzsche) could be seen as 'the struggle of life to be itself' (p. 81); in the stream of life itself. He criticizes philosophy for seeing life which either simply 'ascends as spirit' or 'descends as matter' (p. 85), because life

---

3   Several of Simmel's most used concepts such as '*Leben* (" life"), *Erlebnis* ("inner lived experience"), Form, *Geschichte* ("history"), *Worden* ("becoming") and *Schicksal* ("fate")' (Pyyhtinen 2007: 113) belong to his vital thought. '*Geschehen*' refers to 'happen' or 'occur', but Pyyhtinen prefers 'event' and 'eventalization'.

4   '*Wechselwirkung*' is more than interaction or acts, so pace Pyyhtinen (2007), I have otherwise translated it as 'interchange' and 'interchangeability' (Pløger 2006) to indicate the significance of mood, meaning, and sensuous factors.

'refuses to be governed by anything subordinated to itself, but it also refuses to be governed at all, even by any ideal realm with a claim to a superior authority' (p. 86). Life is a realm or reality, but never reducible to this, because of the will as energies, intuitions, affects, senses, emotions etc. occasionally 'becoming mind'. 'What we *are* is spontaneous life, with its equally spontaneous, un-analysable sense of being, vitality and purposiveness, but what we *have* is only a particular form at any time, which proves from the moment of its creation to be part of a quite different order of things' (p. 89). Form and life are 'conditions of each other' and therefore 'simultaneous cause and effect' (p. 118) in one and the same moment. Events are of life and are thus a result of a relation between the vital and the social, becoming something in-between form and life. For instance, relatively stable forms and becoming form make them traceable. Simmel's vital event gives 'primacy to process over substance' and underlines the social as 'movement, process, fluid, associations' (p. 124) creating a never-ending tension between life and forms. But still at points-in-time-and-space life 'settles' as cognition, values and forms with space as its point of articulation and emergence.

Life, for the philosophy of vitalism, is this will in all of us that has both 'causal and temporal link in our consciousness' (Simmel 1986: 23). Simmel continues, that life as 'this will is what we all are, beyond all distinctions' (p. 24), and it is therefore only an 'abstract name and unifying dimension for all of the singular energies and valuable states' (p. 137) in and of human lives. This life does not 'react' to some biological stimulus but to differences, and to differences in intensity from previous difference (p. 152), thus stimulated by senses, desires, passions, 'stimmung' or atmosphere; in fact all that makes a difference. Life is therefore not ' the vehicle of form' (p. 159), a life-form, or identity although we are all part of collective schemes of signification. Life is never pure form, only becoming and eventalisations, as Simmel would say.

Life is therefore not a realm in itself, but of itself; that is, the product of a continual 'coming into being' through vitalist processes. This life, however, according to Gilles Deleuze, comes into existence within a 'determinate social situation', so 'life flows along the axis of being and becoming' because 'life is incorporeal transformation; it is event' meaning life's possibility is not an 'an individual affair' but occurs through 'the various mechanisms of coding, overcoding and axiomatizing' (May 1991: 29, 26, 29). Life is also in society, in discourses, in disciplines. As Lash (2006: 324) says, 'vitalism presumes an emergent form'. Signs and events are thus two emergent vitalist forms influencing not only life but everyday living. The will is just as much related to 'soul' or 'spirit' (*geist*) as it is to body. A vitalist perspective stresses that life in itself is 'movement, becoming, contingent' (Fraser et al. 2005: 3) and so seen 'every time a rupture is identified, a new series of relations are established' (p. 4). The 'situative event [is] dependent on and generative of meaning and memory' (p. 7).

To Deleuze, life is both corporeal, linked to events, and incorporeal, linked to life's duration, but what makes life 'vital' 'is its capacity for disorganisation' (May 1991: 25) on the thresholds of what Paul Rabinow (inspired by Canguilhem) defines as 'life

325

[as] action, mobility and pathos' (cited in Rose 1998: 163). Even though everyday life is most often a desire for constancy, predictability, routines, habits, then life is always 'lines of flight that break with both the axioms and the codes of a given society in order to create new forms of life that are subversive to the repression of society' (May 1991: 32). Vitalism is then to be seen as a kind of resistance to life as determined form and the 'intuitive recognition' that life itself has power to change 'circumstances'. Life is, one might say, transversal to 'the givens' of society and everyday life, because it is a 'ceaseless movement of becoming, that finds a provisional form or arrangement of forces in "the human"' (Brown 2006: 331–2).

Lived Threads of Vitalism

Vitalism 'has had its time' (Kanamori 2005: 22), it is argued from biology, and in fact vitalism has 'always been under suspicion of corruption, by association with dubious influencies' (Maffesoli 2005: 203). Vitalism is read as being associated with life as will and 'our urge to live and our will to will are ultimately the same' (Arendt 1978: 164). Foucault (2003: 326) claims that 'life is "the root" to all existence'. Taking inspiration from Nietzsche and especially from Canguilhem, Foucault talks about life as form (*bios*) and as 'being alive' (*zoe*) (Rabinow 1998: 198). Norms play a role, because 'life is an activity that follows a norm' (197). In life, according to Canguilhem, form controls experience. However, life is also existential 'being alive' because of life's 'pathos'.

Vitalist forces work through affect, sense, sensation and perception. They also need coding (temporary fixity). Life is, therefore, both a potential and a power, which we may call virtual, alluding to Simmel's phenomenological *Lebenswelt* (life-world) (Lash 2006: 325–6). Life will always 'rest' in temporary social forms, and this resting is predicated on, and further moved by, articulated or actualized difference. Difference means differential content or there is no difference, which is exactly the point for Simmel, Nietzsche, Deleuze or Foucault. To them life is subjected to being relational and is, in particular, effected or affected by its relations to the social world of difference.

Vitalistic forces are 'life-as-becoming', 'a force *in* life (non-representational) and *of* life (reflexivity), folded and unfolding along the lines of life' (Pløger 2006: 386). For Deleuze, vitalism is linked to 'the profound unity between signs, events, life and vitalism' (1995: 142), that is, to 'the non-organic' (p. 142); a 'practical vitality', which makes 'thought to come into contact with power of life' (Marks 1998: 31). The body-mind relation of the sensate and recognition shapes 'readings of space', produces motives, values and signification as well as morals. These modalities of life are vital forces of life producing wills belonging to what Henri Bergson (1980) calls human 'vitalism'. Life is, so to say, always on-the-move, moved by vitalist energies and exigencies.

The flow of life will always become form as, for example, Simmel's social forms, Lefebvre's rhythms, Bourdieu's habitus, or De Certeau's habits and the habitual (the given, commonsense, tacit knowledge). This 'life, as it becomes mind' creates both culture and form, but still 'the forces of life erode every cultural form which they have produced' (Simmel 1997: 76). As Schrift (2000: 153) says, we always meet a life-enhancement that is indicative of 'a will to life' and a will to 'self-overcoming' represented in acts, styles, talking or kissing. Humans are also in these acts always producing a transition. Vitalism thus is not *'eigentlichkeit'* (a priori, 'before life') or ontological 'origin', but a force in and of life, of being a living human, a life-force of Heidegger's *Dasein*; of being-there in experience, sensing, differentiating, interpreting, or as a product of a situative atmosphere or 'moodness' (*stimmheit/ stimmung*). Nietzsche would remark that 'there is no will given: there is given points of will, that constantly formate or lose their power' (Houman 1996: 88). The power of the will of vitalism is always directed towards something and an effect of something. Vitalism is not teleological, theological or biological, but *'worden'* (coming into existence by will); it is a directedness towards the world as a perceiving and recognizing being. Vitalist life is only conceived in its manifestations, which is to see beyond being seen ontologically to see living as pathos, for instance. Life's 'way of living' is both desire, body and language, and all forms of life's existence will produce socially prescribed forms to space and place, but only in temporary, situated and circumstantial ways.

The fact that humans are attached to the world bodily, by sensing, by memory, by experiencing and imagination, has not moved urban studies to consider vitalism and the role of its forces in the production of social spaces and forms of urbanity. Amin and Thrift (2002: 8–9) hint in this direction and want us to recognize 'the varied and plural nature of urban life' and to acknowledge 'the multiple temporalities and spatialities of different urban livelihoods' as constitutive of the 'everydayness' of city life. They point to the reality of 'transitivity' and ' porosity' (p. 10) as part of the city as 'lived complexity' (p. 11). This may be why Amin (2007: 103) sees 'a vitalist phenomenological lens' developing in urban studies to help to 'read' the 'world of practices and the ebb and flow of matter of continual flux' in life and cities. People make both relatively stable and provisional schemes of signification from their experiences and images of space and place. Impression and expression thus, together with life (history) and experiences, produce micro or macro change in our schemes of signification, affectual reactions, and discourse about the city. They are thereby part of a continuous vitalist production of a liveable urbanity for subjectivities. Vitalism is not only an 'inner' force, but stimulated by relational spaces and socio-spatial folding of presences. It is the vitalism of presences – expressivity and reading/coding – that we need to focus on as we try to understand living in cities as shaped by connectivities, assemblages, emergences, transformability, transcendence, fluidity, (ephemeral) flows and (re)codings. Life's lived contingency is wonderfully described by Foucault as follows: 'Life has led to a living being that is never completely in the right place, that is destined to "err" and to be "wrong"' (Foucault 1998: 476). Life disturbs the given we believe in; for instance the stability, sameness, reliability, truth and so on.[5]

---

5   Foucault's reading of Kant's *'Aufklärung'* ('What is Enlightenment?') is significant on

Neo-vitalism, Presence and Emergence – the City

Deleuze has stated that 'a life contains only virtuals. It is made of virtualities, events, singularities. What we call virtual is not something that lacks reality, but something that enters into a process of actualisation by following the plane that gives its own reality' (Deleuze 1997: 5). One of these virtual realities – and to some the dominant vitalist force of our time – is the media (Lash 2006). The media is not to be understood as something in itself, but as 'life'; not as an extension of life, but as 'bio-media' coupling body and media in a 'genetic coding' (Lash 2006: 328). Life is not simply flows, but has vitalist roots in 'a media or information heuristic', where 'life itself is swept up in the global flows of finance, information and media' (p. 328). As such, consideration of neo-vitalism then should include reflections on the effects of the absent-present forces offered by world-wide information connections. Diagnosing contemporary neo-vitalism in such a way is to look for virtual forms influencing life. The media's new virtual forms might shape new social forms and contents not known before, such as cyber-sex or affectual virtual communication (internet flirting).

Virtualism – what is 'known only indirectly by its effects' including 'things' as 'code, habitus or class' (Shields 2006: 284) – is often a contingent potential to urban life as inventions, imaginations and passions that arise out of being situated in spaces of strangers, encounters, events-as-desire-production, and the unpredictability of urban life folding presences (to be grasped instantaneously). The neo-vitalist forces of urban life are linked to immediate emergences and presences themselves, partly deriving from the urban 'ontology of encounters' (Amin and Thrift 2002), on one side, and the connectivity of 'signs, events, life, and vitalism' (Deleuze) on the other. Vitalist forces thus find provisional resting or stability. The present vitalism is enforced by consumerism, event-seeking, pleasure-seeking, difference, distinction and subject positioning, or 'the sheer expressiveness and passion of [city] life' (Pile 2005: 2). Expressivity can include both the banal phenomena of everyday life, such as customs, habits, anxiety and style, as well as desire, dreams, eroticism and sublimity. The expressivity of city life has always been an inspiration to artists and painters and novelists (Pinder 2002), but the expressiveness of the city is, in fact, the banal reality of urbanism, because city spaces 'constantly [throw] people into contact with new experiences, new situations and new people' (Pile 2005: 17). Expressivity is situationism, intentions, (un)consciousness, urban imaginaries and 'phantasmagoria' in one (Donald 1999, Pile 2005).

Vitalism calls attention to these modes of life and to some of its characteristics; for instance that 'every time a rupture is identified, a new series of relations are established' (Fraser et al. 2005: 4) and that the 'situative event [is] dependent on and generative of meaning and memory' (p. 7). Hence, we should not miss Deleuze's point (as Hume taught him) that 'lives are something like "bundles" of virtualities'.

---

this, and clearly in his stating that to be modern, the task is 'to heroize the present' and to 'invent ourselves' indefinitely ('a permanent creation of ourselves in our autonomy') (Foucault 1986: 40 and 44).

It is from here that we might think of the building of cities as making 'dispositions'. Stating this, Rajchman saw Deleuze as a philosopher of 'the city and its modes of arranging or disposing persons and things – its *agencement* (assemblages[6])' (1998: 2). Not only this, but Deleuze also holds that the 'city of senses' includes 'voids and interstices' making chance a reality in its complexity (p. 6). In this way, the city vitalism, I would say, emerges in-between the virtual and the possible actualization of the virtual forces. This is 'the virtual [that] lies in those forces and potentials whose origins and outcomes cannot be specified independently of the open and necessarily incomplete series of their actualizations' (Rajchman 1998: 116). Virtuality is to be thrown into the unforeseen city or everyday world and thereby produces becomings and emergencies.

Following affect trajectories, the major contemporary form of neo-vitalism is *presence*, shaped by the desire for event experiences, intensity, and the search for involved 'affectedness' (Ziehe 1982). In this presence-vitalism the becoming of emergences become important modalities to affect the intensity, atmosphere and 'the shock' experience in Benjamin's sense, giving a particular vitalistic quality to place, space and time. The eventalization of space and its aesthetic-atmospheric quality is a crucial virtual quality of the contemporary city of consumption and event. This, however, reminds us of classical aspects of urban vitalism, because Simmel and others already identified these vitalist forces (for instance, the urban heterogeneity, the singularity of any event, and the effects of life itself). Significant neo-vitalist forces are to be found in new aspects of the event-quality, not from the spectacular event, but from the presence-quality of events.

The presence experience seems precarious to contemporary urban neo-vitalism – to be there, to be present, nearness, in an urban space that 'promises' events and desirous experiences. When Lash and Fraser, Kemper and Lury claim that virtual (internet, IT-communication etc.) mass communication is the neo-vitalist force of our time, it is I would say, possible because of their presence-possibilities. These are materialities that mediate an instantaneous immediacy, here-and-now force into everyday life by allowing the user to navigate through the city immediately and to make instantaneous shifts or moves if necessary.[7] Presence is to urbanity a mode of living as a seeking for the presence in events and its presumed (existing) eventalizations. Preferably spectacular and organized around art, performance, avant-garde, spontaneous gatherings, informal meetings, or mega-events, this presence and its modalities are crucial conditions to meaningful lived urbanity. The never-ending 'production of presences' (Gumbrecht 2004)[8] through presence-

---

6   '*Agencement*' is a 'process of agency – active bringing-into-existence of its own agency' (Hillier 2007b: 9) and '*agencement*' 'thus possesses an atmosphere of potential' (p. 11) and a potential for self-transformation.

7   Mobile phones make people able to connect at most points of time and place. Young people coordinate their everyday arrangements instantly via mobile calls rather than by pre-made arrangements.

8   Presence could be related to Walter Benjamin's concept of 'now-time' and Deleuze and Guattari's 'aeonic time' (Hutta 2009: 260), but these times only indirectly emphasize

materialities such as the mobile phone, internet, fashion, goods, art etc., as well as the desire for presence-feelings through events, experiencing and being particularities, and this desire for what emerges, is what makes *active presence* the dominant neo-vitalism of our time.

Events are, therefore, particular presence 'agencements'[9] shaping virtual social becomings as something in-between form and life. As such, there is a duality between form and event which could be characterized as *'wechselwirkung'* mediated by individuals 'throwntogetherness' (Massey 2005) in the virtual-real. There is, as said, a vitalist thread in Georg Simmel's urban writings, where he follows Nietzsche in advocating a human 'will-to-differentiate' (Simmel 1997: 174-186). Simmel sees this will as stimulated by cities' intensified spaces where individualities are shaped by the need to differentiate and positioning oneself in the face of always meeting strangers, being situated in places of social heterogeneity, and within a competitive money economy. These forces of city life produce particular social forms and manners. Looking at urbanity from here, we have to treat city life as 'immediate life' (Maffesoli 2005), 'presences' (Metcalfe and Game 2004), 'life' (Lash 2006) and intensity (Amin and Thrift 2002) as the real/lived constituencies, which also implies the significance of moods and feelings to understand the lived and willed urban life. The city as social space is a restless space of difference, sights, sighs, sounds, symbols and acts, where the use and meaning of spaces are affected by users' minds, motive forces, sensibilities and emotions.

We might say the city becomes a virtual vitalism; that is a place of potentials influencing the sensate living, experiencing, and 'reading' of unfolding lives. Urbanity, then, is also what comprises and signifies the relation between representation, body, interpretation, image, feelings, words, imaginaries and perceptions from being situated within changing virtual-real forces in time and space. Therefore, to discuss an urban neo-vitalism is to discuss contemporary becomings of the city body-mind shaped by affects, situations, durability as well as schemes of signification, and meaning. The forces of urban vitalism are, in particular, (a) events and eventalizations, (b) difference, otherness, social heterogeneity, (c) 'tension', intensity, challenges and (d) imagination, enchantment and dis-enchantment.

---

the aesthetic-affectual aspects of 'to-be-present' as Gumbrecht points out. However, Benjamin's *flâneur* and the street as the place for 'the gaze' certainly could be read as aesthetic presence, but 'the phantasmogoria' of the *flâneur* is to make 'typologies', 'to read labour, the origin and character of the face' (1990: 357), and search more for an expression and impression than a presence-feeling. Benjamin pays attention to the moment, *'jetz-zeit'*, not as being-there-in-presence, but always in history and lived experience. Presence-events – say football match (Gumbrecht 2004) or Pirate Parties (Pløger 2009) – are of another aesthetic kind. Deleuze and Guattari talk about 'the moment of the "now"' (Hutta 2009: 260) and recognize an event-as-becoming as a moment of possibilities.

9   To Deleuze 'agencement' has 'a very precise correspondence to the notion of the *event, becoming* and *sense'* (Philips 2006: 109).

Working With Urbanity-in-becoming

We may have a 'urbanity popular' in urban politics and planning in debates about gentrification, tourism, the pleasure of the event city, and the 'creative class'. Urbanity and city life are here shaped by the imperative performance of space through spectacular architecture, heritage, malls and shopping areas, anaesthetization of space, encounters with strangers, the atmosphere of crowds, or just gazing at people passing by. Benjamin could be read in this vein. To Benjamin, the *flâneur* epitomizes the modern form of urbanity: the stroller, the *derivé*, the daydreamer, the loafer in the street and in the passage or arcade (Benjamin 1991), and the figure may even be a symbol of 'urbanity popular' of today's consumer-society. Benjamin underlines the significance of the street imaginaries and citizens being part of 'the family of eyes' in the street (seeing and being seen, shifting subject-object positions) as a vital element in how people imagine themselves as urbanites. Everywhere citizens are haunted by this ambiguity of positions between the spectator and the seen in the urban street.

The late modern spatialization of urban life contrasts with that of ancient Greece where urbanity belonged to discursive practice and, in particular, to rhetoric. In Greece it was a matter of 'clever urbane expression' (*asteia*), humour or irony (*asteimos*) or 'the whole tone of speech' (*urbanitas*) (De Jonge 2004). The philosopher Cicero (80 BC) called for proper manners from urban citizens in order to stand against the plebeians' hedonistic, excessive, parasitic, and indecent living in cities. To Cicero urbanity is manners, such as ' literary manners, civility, presence of mind, and [to be] knowledgeable' citizens (Zerlang 1995: 269). Manners were necessary because of particular circumstances of living in the city (the proximity of the plebeians), and needed as a social-psychological reaction to the expressive city space.

The city, seen phenomenologically, is the social subject situated and unfolding within and against a particular spatio-temporal background of both non-human prosthetics and a social space of strangers, presences, events, flows as well as the lived life-world of desires, hopes and schemes of signification. If urbanism is the body or corporeal city of the habitable, urbanity is a product of socio-spatial foldings rather than something in itself. We must understand how the urban, as Mendieta (2001b: 204) says, 'is made accessible by a way of thinking'. We may therefore find 'traces of practices, representations, and experiences of space inescapably a product of the philosophical imaginary'. As Raban (1974: 4) says, 'we mould them [cities] in our image: they, in their turn, shape us by the resistance they offer when we try to impose our own personal form on them'.

Modern urban studies mostly approach urban life from the issue of space and, more precisely, space as determinate generative of social effect, whether we are talking about the Chicago School's study on poverty and segregation, Jane Jacobs' dense city, Michel de Certeau's 'walking stories' and 'spatial tactics', Manuel Castells' social movements, gender and embodiment, studies on gentrification politics or use of visual spaces in urban competition (Tonkiss 2005; Liggett 2003). When recent commentators on urbanism emphasize the city as a place of transition, fluidity, flows, mobility and the like (Amin and Thrift 2002; Hubbard 2006; Lefebvre 1991, 2006; Soja 1996; Stevens 2007), it is still mainly based on a spatial approach rather than on time (e.g. lived experiences, socialization). Although some would be hesitant to sign up to Soja's statement that 'I am an avowed spatialist, a determined advocate for the critical power of the spatial or geographical imagination', many agree with Soja about seeing 'space as both product and producer of social life' (2003: 271). Others emphasize that urbanism as a spatial approach 'overstates the city as a space of open flow, human interaction and proximate reflexivity', and lacks concern for 'the instituted, transhuman and distanciated nature of urban life' (Amin and Thrift 2002: 7). Amin and Thrift (pp. 10–11) prefer to talk about an urban porosity, lived complexity and transitivity grounded on a basic ontology of urban life; 'the ontology of encounter and togetherness based on the principles of connection, extension and continuous novelty' (p. 26). This is an urban life, where life is shaped by the effects of spatialized social interconnectivity thought of as encounters. The spatialized approach is apparent when the authors say that in cities humans as subjects are 'aggregates of numerous subject positions which are parts of numerous networks' (p. 29).

Amin and Thrift tend to be in line with Henri Lefebvre who sees urbanity as the 'simultaneity of many discrete social interactions brought together in a "centrality"'(Shields 1999: 145), where urbanity is implied from the spatialization of everyday life. We might call that perspective 'a dialectic of urbanism' (Lewandowsky 2005: 294); a thinking where space is determinant in forming and informing social action, well known from the history of urban planning (Huxley 2006; Joyce 2003; Osborne and Rose 1999). In urbanism and urban design, urban life becomes a product of a dialectic between spatial structures or materialities, embodied perceptions and practices shaped by society's collective culture and value schemes which designate common dispositions on how to use city spaces 'properly'. Even though some of the authors are aware of questions of subjectivity, of the city as a discourse to be read or, to paraphrase Lefebvre (1991), of the mental urbanity 'of, in and for' the city, subjectivity is not an objection to urbanism's understanding of urbanity.

Only a few urban theorists and planners will now claim to see space as a solely physical entity; it is always a socio-spatiality. Urban space design, architecture and settlement places are constitutive of a socio-spatial relationship where space forms the social field of action. Space signifies and symbolizes functionality, use and use-value, life-style or class, community or diversity. Space is the context of the banal urbanism of everyday life routines and its time-geographies as well as the desirous, presence-atmospheric, event spaces. Urban space is thought 'intentional' and users most often use it accordingly to its designed intention; for instance obeying its spatial design and urban prosthetics of traffic-lights, doors, metro-lines and the like. There are 'intricate inter-dependencies between humans and non-humans' (Amin 2007: 112) perhaps most obviously traced as lines of behaviour and repetitive time-space geographies. Urbanism is here the forming of conduct through the spatialization of everyday life necessities. This banal urbanism – the everyday life of seriality, routines and social commitments – is rarely mentioned in city branding and profiling, although it is still the main planning perspective of urbanism. But of equal importance to urban planning's understanding of city life in this respect should be ways of thinking and acting developed generatively by regarding the city as the place for the unfolding of life from 'concepts as embodied practices, and practices as interpretative or meaning-granting schemata, which in turn are seen as being part of a form of life, or socio-historical environment. There is no concept without a practice and no practice without a world'. Transformation of urban life, therefore, requires 'new conceptual matrixes ... to make sense of the emergent forms of life' (Mendieta 2001a: 5).

As such, urbanity is shaped by the entanglements of micro-social experiences, minglings, symbolisms, agonisms, strangenesses, normativities, surprises and so on. Urbanity is partly constituted within the complex, hybrid, multiverse socio-spatiality that we call the city. It is 'realized' or 'learned' both from cities' socio-materiality (form, architecture, design, prosthetics, art in space etc.) and social interaction (most often between strangers), embodied sensately and mentally by readings and reflecting from discourses, codes as well as circumstances. Somewhere, inbetween these entanglements, schemes of signification, values and beliefs develop, are challenged, and change during the life-course. It is here – somewhere – we find meaningful city life.

Cities, then, have (at least) three entry-points through which to plan for the lived or meaningful city life:

- Urbanism (1) referring to urban design through physical and spatial planning. This involves *dispositifs* coming from architectural theory and physical and spatial planning theory about form and functionality.
- Urbanism (2) referring to cities as part of societies' development and modernization structures and processes. Here one focuses on economy, politics, social and cultural modernization processes transformed to cities.
- Urbanity (1) referring to socio-spatial experiences in cities related to acts, use of space and place related to the city as a form. This urbanity is concerned with the habitual and, more or less, passive use of space often leading to typologies of life-forms, the life world[10] socio-economic typologies or mappings, or life-style types (creative class, gentrifiers, DINKs, SINKs etc.).

These ways of thinking about city life do not ensure that urban planning includes *subjectivization* and *subjectification*[11] stemming from mental dispositions, attitudes, subjectivities and the cognitive recognition of the city formed by nearness and

---

10   The life world includes '(1) *life conditions*, that make the background for (2) a number of *tendencies to draw up life's unfolding*, and those are contributing to the development of (3) certain socio-cultural *forms of life*'. Life forms – which are the product of life worlds as grounding modes of living, thinking and experiencing (Bech 1999) – are not necessarily given (although informed by collective life-forms), but emergent from eventalizations made by, let's say, experiencing cultural representations as directing life into forms and manners (Bech 1999: 13).

11   'Subjectivisation means "self-actualisation, or taking a subject position". Subjectification means "the subjective identification of others, or accordance of a subject-position"' (Hook 2007: 31, cited in Hillier, 2009: np).

presences as well as schemes of signification. *Imaginary cities* as dreams, desires, wants and needs from city life and one's self living there will also be absent. If planning for urban life as urbanity is not to be as a political timely rhetoric, it is to be clear that planning needs to work with how the 'why' and 'hows' of life endlessly change people's schemes of signification and use of city spaces. All forms of life and existence will contain both socially prescribed forms of lived and unexpected experiences and acts that mobilize vitalist forces. Life is about differences affecting senses. Vitalist forces make 'life as drive, life as lines of flight, life as some kind of energetics, and these things takes forms more or less' (Lash 2004: 102). I propose to add these points to the efforts to trace lived urbanity and its vitalist *dispositifs*. This means a call for continuing work with:

- *Urbanity (2)* referring firstly to life itself as social becomings, including vitalist forces and secondly, to the mental and word-ing effects of and affected by living in cities. That is the shaping of ways of thinking and acting that are only partly the product of the city as a space of particular experiences, values, schemes of significations, attitudes and norms. Urbanity is grounded in a vitalist mode of being and simultaneously with a cognitive and reflexive attitude towards presence experiences, everyday life symbols and representations.

Space is, of course, an important element of discussions on life as becoming, because life 'actualizes' itself in space as behaviour, bodies, gestures, conversations, connectivities, rhythms or seriality, and other forms of expressive acts. Amin, as mentioned above, finds a contemporary tendency to read differentiations and changes through a vitalist or phenomenological lens, however, claiming that the potentials of the actual matter-world are the becoming of 'entities/associations/togetherness' (Amin and Thrift 2002: 27) or one could say, the spatialization of sociabilities.

If urban spatial planners want to approach the vitalist urbanity-in-becoming from planning, they must relate to area-planning and urban design (Urbanism 1), clarification of structural forces (Urbanism 2), the use of, and experience from, everyday spaces (Urbanity 1) as well as the change of meaning and life itself. As part of strategic planning for creative cities some planners have started to focus on life-forms and values ascribed to city life (Copenhagen Municipality 2005). This way city politics and planning may approach the meaningful city life (Urbanity 2) in order to be able to work with the ongoing change of forces of city development and social lives as productive to cities short and long-termed (strategic) planning. Considering urbanity means seeing cities' social spaces as becomings, because they are constituted by multiple and vitalist forces made from the interconnectivity of habits and presences as well as a changing value-plural and cultural-plural city. Planners working with urbanity-in-becoming have then to include (1) lived schemes *of significations* and their subjective meaning, (2) lived *identifications*, not identity or identities in planning. This subjective life-world is from where citizens identify their particular city inbetween and imagined from experiencing its spaces and places and always in particular circumstances. Cities need to pay greater attention to (3) what is *meaningful* to lives lived in cities, and hence (4) *individualities* must be the point of departure and not predefined collectivities of whatever kind.

By Way of a Conclusion ...

In this chapter I offer a theoretical-philosophical ground from which to approach urban life as urbanity-in-becoming with vitalist forces such as social heterogeneity, schemes of signification, beliefs and readings. The vitalism of urban life is shaped by 'energies', which could be termed 'the property of generalised affectivity' (Thrift 2004: 85), and urban lives are affected and formed by non-cognitive and cognitive forces from where sensations and sensing are transformed to 'meaning' through 'reading'. Urbanity, seen in this way, starts with contextualized life containing life-constituencies such as desire, duration, will, existence and expectation shaped by living in cities' socio-spatial world of flows, structures, eventualities, acts, connectivities, assemblages, relations, and lived schemes of signification, leading to ever new emergences and becomings as well as new forms of habits and habitual living. Urbanity is constituted by the past as well as by everyday presences, absence-presences, experiences, life philosophy and what is meaningful. Talking about urbanity-in-becoming underlines a focus on chance, change and wills that again imply situations, differences, interpretations, interactions and indeterminacies (even, perhaps, indeterminabilities and indescribabilities) as constitutive of acting and of the ongoing constitution of meaning of one's urban living. Urbanity is immanently a matter of becoming, where becoming emerges out of (bodily) experiences, (phenomenological) recognition and (hermeneutical) practice.

Vitalism is a force in life-as-becoming, for instance, as a will-to-will (Nietzsche), a will to differentiate (Simmel) and 'subjectivation' (late Foucault) stimulated by situations, interactions, experiences as well as discourses. Humans are also always in acts and life producing transitions or 'self-overcomings'. Urban theory and urban planning studies have for a long time ignored urban life as vitalism, perhaps because Simmel's *Lebensphilosophie* and his understanding of the urban have been ignored.

Current perspectives on the urban as complex, plural, contingent, and how these forces shape an urbanity-in-becoming, call for an awareness of the 'minor' forces of change. Urban planners who want to plan for urbanity, therefore, should care more about doing detailed analysis of micro-social forces. We, as academics, need to stimulate planners' and institutions' curiosity for knowing 'what is going on' through ongoing interaction and small-talk with citizens. Here we need 'the wandering planner' who 'botanizes' (Benjamin 1990) the street meeting local needs, desires and wishes at eye-level. This kind of work requires a sensitive dialogue with subjects of 'otherness' and their feelings of being different or an-other, which might require planning institutions to work with 'not-understandable' ways of living and doing. Planning needs the capacity to understand and 'read' the subtle moves emerging on horizons and their schemes of signification about living in cities.

335

This would be a real bottom-up planning from where planners may be able pro-actively to anticipate changes in urban life before they are manifest. The challenge to urban planning working with urbanity-in-becoming is to work with life lived and imagined by looking at its vague becomings and representations in order to see its vague changes and moves. I have argued that vitalist and virtual presence forces are significant to understand the effect and affect of cities' complexities, multiplicities and becomings.

To sum up, urbanity-in-becoming does not have a substance, but is generated from discourses, manners and other *dispositifs*. The city is spatialized rhythms and time-space mechanisms, but city life is also a fluid, fragmentary and changing reality that informs everyday life schemes of signification. City life, of course, also contains imperative discourses, but is always influenced by life-in-becoming due to, among other things, the vitalism of life such as desire and wills. Urbanity, so seen, is made and changes inbetween the uncertain, the aleatory and forms of normalization: changing and resting, settled and disrupted.

Forces of ordering struggle with the disrupting need for urbanites to differentiate themselves in a symbolic, aesthetic and social competitive space. The serial life and the givens so dear to homogeneous societies, however, never fully count for the fact of the city as occurrence, circumstance, constellation and other unpredictable forces of change. People are inscribed in different value discourses and life-worlds (e.g. diaspora life worlds) and social tensions in spaces of chance events and circumstances. However, most people also try to make their lives at least temporarily 'safe' by making them habitual and making 'the everydayness of the everyday life' (Lefebvre 1987). People will the expressive city life as well as the private, invisible city life. Everyone relates to both the discursive and non-discursive city; its signs and representations, codes and practices. Cities not only 'abound with all manner of acts of mutuality, friendship, pleasure and sociality' (Thrift, in Amin 2006: 10–11), but also strangers, intensities, wills and uncertainties, as 'all that is solid melts into air' (Berman 1987). The 'throwntogetherness' of the known, the expected, and the new in space mean that meaning and the meaningful are always disturbed, disrupted, affected, and eventually transgressed. No-one and nothing in life is 'always there for ever', neither instantaneous on-the-move. Life is change.

Urbanity has no topos, only topological porous contours.

Acknowledgement

I want to thank Patsy Healey, Newcastle University, Margo Huxley, Sheffield University and Anne Jensen, Danish Environmental Research Institute, for invaluable comments on the first draft of the paper. In particular I want to thank Jean Hillier, Newcastle University, who has helped me to sharpen my focus and arguments by reading several drafts of the paper and giving sharp and precise comments all the way.

References

Amin, A. (2006) 'The good city' *Urban Studies* 43(5-6): 1009–23.

Amin, A. (2007) 'Re-thinking the urban social' *City: Analysis of Urban Trends, Culture, Theory, Policy, Action* 11(1): 100–14.

Amin, A., and Thrift, N. (2002) *Cities: Re-imagining the Urban*. Cambridge: Polity.

Arendt, H. (1978) *The Life of the Mind*. New York: Harcourt.

Barthes, R. (1969/1957) *Mytologier* [Mythologies]. København: Bibliotek Rhodos.

Barthes, R. (1994) *I tegnets tid* [The Time of the Sign]. Oslo: Pax forlag.

Bauman, Z. (1993) *Postmodern Ethics*. Oxford: Blackwell.

Bech, H. (1999) *Fritidsverden* [Leisure World]. København: Forlaget Sociologi.

Benjamin, W. (1969) *Bild och dialektik* [Picture and Dialectics]. Göteborg: Bo Caverfors Förlag.

Benjamin, W. (1990) *Paris 1800-talets hovudstad. Passagearbetet* [Paris the Capital of the 18th Century. Passagen-work/Das Passagenwerk]. Stockholm/Stehag: Symposion Förlag.

Bergson, H. (1981/1917) *Det umiddelbare i bevidstheden* [Essai sur les Données Immédiates de la Conscience)]. København: Vintens Forlag.

Berman, M. (1987) *Allt som er fast förflyktigas* [All that is Solid Melts into Air]. Göteborg: Arkiv Förlag.

Binnie, J. et al. (eds) (2006) *Cosmopolitan Urbanism*. London: Routledge.

Bleicher, J. (2006) 'Leben' *Theory, Culture and Society* 23(2–3): 343–5.

Brenner, N. (1994) 'Foucault's new functionalism' *Theory and Society* 23: 679–709.

Bridge, G. (2005) *Reason of the City of Difference: Pragmatism, Communicative Action and Contemporary Urbanism*. London: Routledge.

Brown, S.D. (2006) 'The determination of life' *Theory, Culture and Society* 23(2–3): 331–2.

Copenhagen Municipality (2005) *Kommuneplan 2005–2009* [Municipal Plan 2005–09], København, Københavns Kommune.

De Jonge, C. (2004) Demosthenes: asteios or agroikos? Dionysius of Halicarnassus and Other Ancient Literary critics on (the Lack of) Demosthenes' 'Urbanity'. Penn-Leiden Colloquia on Ancient Values III, Leiden University, 3–5 June.

Deleuze, G. (1995) *Negotiations*. New York: Columbia University Press.

Deleuze, G. (1997) 'Immanence: a life …' *Theory Culture and Society* 14(2): 3–7.

Dillon, M. (2007) 'Governing through contingency: the security of biopolitical governance' *Political Geography* 26: 41–7.

Donald, J. (1999) *Imagining the Modern City*. London: Athlone Press.

Foucault, M. (1977) *Overvågning og straf* [Surviller et Punir]. København, Rhodos Bibliotek.

Foucault, M. (1986) *The Foucault Reader* (ed. Rabinow, P.). New York: Peregrine.

Foucault, M. (1998) *Aesthetics, Method and Epistemology*, Vol. 2 (ed. Faubion, J.D.). New York: The New Press.

Foucault, M. (2004) *Security, Territory, Population. Lectures at the Collège de France 1977–1978*. New York: Palgrave Macmillan.

Foucault, M. (2008) *The Birth of Biopolitics. Lectures at the Collège de France 1978–1979*. New York: Palgrave Macmillan.

Fraser, M., Kemper, S. and Lury, C. (2005) 'Inventive life: Approaches to the new vitalism' *Theory Culture and Society*, 22(1): 1–14.

Gilloch, G. (1996) *Myth and Metropolis: Walter Benjamin and the City*. Cambridge: Polity.

Greco, M. (2005) 'On the vitality of vitalism' *Theory Culture and Society* 22(1): 15–27.

Groth, J. and Corijn, E. (2005) 'Reclaiming urbanity: indeterminate spaces, informal actors and urban agenda setting' *Urban Studies* 42(3): 503–26.

Gumbrecht, H.U. (2004) *Production of Presence: What Meaning Cannot Convey*, Stanford: Stanford University Press.

Gunder, M. and Hillier, J. (2007) 'Planning as urban therapeutic' *Environment and Planning A* 39: 467–86.

Hansen, N.G. (1991) *Sansernes Sociologi. Om Simmel og det moderne* [The Sociology of Senses. On Simmel and the Modern]. København: Tiderne Skifter.

Hillier, J. (2007a) *Stretching Beyond The Horizon*. Aldershot: Ashgate.

Hillier, J. (2007b) Inplenary Practice: Towards a Deleuzian-inspired Methodology for Creative Experimentation in Strategic Spatial Planning. Draft 15.11.2007 (copy), 1–34.

Hillier, J. (2009) 'Planning with a political "P"?' paper presented to *Space, Contestation and the Political: A Workshop on Planning, Development and Resistance*, Zurich, 12–13 February (17 pages).

Hook, D. (2007) *Foucault, Psychology and the Analytics of Power*. Basingstoke: Palgrave Macmillan.

Houman, I. (1972) *Nietzsche – Værdiernes krise* [Nietzsche – The Crisis of Values]. København: C.A. Reitzels Forlag.

Hubbard, P. (2006) *City*. London: Routledge.

Hutta, J.S. (2009) 'Geographies of *Geborgenheit*: beyond feelings of safety and the fear of crime' *Environment and Planning D: Society and Space* 27: 251–73.

Huxley, M. (2006) 'Spatial rationalities: order, environment, evolution and government' *Social and Cultural Geography* 7(5): 771–87.

Huxley, M. (2007) 'Geographies of governmentality', in Crampton, J.W. and Elden, S. (eds) *Space, Knowledge and Power: Foucault and Geography*. Aldershot: Ashgate, 185–204.

Joyce, P. (2003) *The Rule of Freedom: Liberalism and the Modern City*. London: Verso.

Kanamori, O. (2005) 'The problem of vitalism revisited: from Barthez to Bernard' *Angelaki* 10(2): 13–26.

KK (2005) *Byudviklingsstrategi* [Urban development strategy], The Municipal Plan 2005, Copenhagen.

Lash, S. (2004) 'Information is alive' in Gane, N. (ed.) *The Future of Social Theory*. London: Continuum, 91–102.

Lash, S. (2005) 'Lebenssoziologie: Georg Simmel in the information age' *Theory, Culture and Society* 22(3): 1–23.

Lash, S. (2006) 'Life (Vitalism)' *Theory Culture and Society* ('Problematizing Global Knowledge: Special Issue, eds Featherstone, M, Couze, V. Bishop, R., and Philips, J.) 23(2–3): 323–9.

Lazzarato, M. (2000) 'From Biopower to Biopolitics' *Pli: The Warwick Journal of Philosophy* (also *Multitudes* 1(2000): 45–57). Available at: <www.generation-online.org/c/fcbiopolitics.htm>. [accessed 25.06 2007]

Lazzarato, M. (2006) 'The concepts of life and the living in the societies of control', in Fuglsang, M., and Sørensen, B.M. (eds) *Deleuze and the Social*. Edinburgh: Edinburgh University Press, 171–90.

Lefebvre, H. (1987) 'The everyday and the everydayness' *Yale French Studies* 73: 7–12.

Lefebvre, H. (1991) *The Production of Space*. Oxford: Blackwell.

Lefebvre, H. (2006) *Writing on Cities* (eds Kofman, E., and Lebas, E.) Blackwell: Oxford.

Lewandowsky, J. (2005) 'Street culture: the dialectic of urbanism in Walter Benjamin's *Passagen-werk*' *Philosophy and Social Criticism* 31(3): 293–308.

Liggett, H. (2003) *Urban Encounters*. Minneapolis, MN: University of Minnesota Press.

Maffesoli, M. (2004) 'Everyday tragedy and creation' *Cultural Studies* 18(2/3): 201–10.

Marks, J. (1998) *Gilles Deleuze: Vitalism and Multiplicity*. London: Pluto Press.

Massey, D. (2005) *For Space*. London: Sage.

May, T. (1991) 'The politics of life in the thought of Gilles Deleuze' *Substance* #66 20(3): 24–35.

Mendieta, E. (2001a) 'Invisible cities: a phenomenology of globalization from below' *City: Analysis of Urban Trends, Culture, Theory, Policy, Action* 5(1): 7–26.

Mendieta, E. (2001b) 'The city and the philosopher: on the urbanism of phenomenology' *Philosophy and Geography* 4(2): 203–18.

Metcalf, A. and Game, A. (2004) 'Everyday presences' *Cultural Studies* 18(2/3): 350–62.

Osborne, T. and Rose, N. (1999) 'Governing cities: notes on the spatialisation of virtue' *Environment and Planning D: Society and Space* 17: 737–60.

Osborne, T. and Rose, N. (2004) 'Spatial phenomenotechnics: making space with Charles Booth and Patrick Geddes' *Environment and Planning D: Society and Space* 22: 209–28.

Parr, A. (2006) 'One nation under surveillance: turning striated space inside out' *Angelaki: Journal of Theoretical Humanities* II(1): 99–107.

Philips, J. (2006) 'Agencement/Assemblage' *Theory, Culture and Society* ('Problematizing Global Knowledge: Special Issue, eds Featherstone, M., Venn, C., Bishop, R., and Philips, J.) 23(2–3): 108–110.

Pile, S. (1996) *The Body and the City*. London: Routledge.

Pile, S. (2005) *Real Cities*. London: Sage.

Planning Theory and Practice (2003) 2 and 3 ('Interface').

Pinder, D. (2002) 'In defence of utopian urbanism: imagining cities after the "end of utopia"' *Geografiska Annaler* 84B(3–4): 229–41.

Pløger, J. (2006) 'In search of urban vitalis' *Space and Culture* 9(4): 382–99.

Pløger, J. (2008) 'Foucault's *dispositif* and the city' *Planning Theory* 7(1): 51–70.

Pløger, J. (2009) 'Presence experiences – the eventalisation of urban space' Paper forthcoming (2010) in *Environment and Planning D*.

Pyyhtinen, O. (2007) 'Event dynamics: the eventalization of society in the sociology of Georg Simmel' *Distinktion: Scandinavian Journal of Social Theory* 15: 111–32.

Raban, J. (1974) *Soft City*. London: The Harvill Press.

Rabinow, P. (1998) 'French enlightenment: truth and life' *Economy and Society* 27(2–3): 193–201.

Rabinow, P. and Caduff, C. (2006) 'Life – After Canguilhem' *Theory, Culture and Society* 23(2-3): 329–31.

Rajchman, J. (1998) *Constructions*. Cambridge, MA: MIT Press.

Rose, N. (1998) 'Life, reason and history: reading Georges Canguilhem today' *Economy and Society* 27(2&3): 154–70.

Schorske, C. (1963) 'The idea of the city in European thought: Voltaire to Spengler' in Handlin, O. and Burchard, J. (eds) *The Historian and the City*. Cambridge, MA: MIT Press, 95–113.

Schrift, A.D. (2000) 'Nietzsche, Foucault, Deleuze and the subject of radical democracy' *Angelaki: Journal of Theoretical Humanities* 5:2: 151–62.

Seitz, B. (2004) 'Sartre, Foucault, and the subject of philosophy's situation' *Sartre Studies International* 10(2): 92–105.

Sennett, R. (1991) *The Conscience of the Eye: The Design and Social Life of Cities*. London: Faber & Faber.

Shields, R. (1999) *Lefebvre, Love and Struggle*. London: Routledge.

Shields, R. (2006) 'Virtualities' *Theory, Culture and Society* ('Problematizing Global Knowledge: Special Issue, eds Featherstone, M., Venn, C., Bishop, R., and Philips, J.) 23(2–3): 284–86.

Simmel, G. (1971) *On Individuality and Social Forms* (ed. Levine, D.N.). Chicago, IL: The University of Chicago Press.

Simmel, G. (1981) *Hur er samhället möjligt? Och andre essä* [How is Society Possible? And Other Essays]. Göteborg: Bokomotiv.

Simmel, G. (1986) *Schopenhauer and Nietzsche*. Urbana and Chicago, IL: University of Illinois Press.

Simmel, G. (1997) *Simmel on Culture* (eds Frisby, D. and Featherstone, M.). London: Sage.

Soja, E. (1996) *Thirdspace*. Oxford: Blackwell.

Soja, E. (2003) 'Writing the city spatially' *City: Analysis of Urban Trends, Culture, Theory, Policy, Action* 7(3): 269–80.

Stevens, Q. (2007) *The Ludic City: Exploring the Potential of Public Spaces*. London: Routledge.

Terranova, C. (2008) 'Marcel Poëte's Bergsonian urbanism: vitalism, time, and the city' *Journal of Urban History* 34(6): 919–43.

Tester, K. (ed.) (1994) *The Flâneur*. London: Routledge.

Thrift, N. (2004) 'Summoning life', in Cloke, P., Crang, P., and Goodwin, M. (eds) *Envisioning Human Geography*. London: Arnold, 81–103.

Thrift, N. (2008) *Non-Representational Theory: Space/politics/affect*. London: Routledge.

Tonkiss, F. (2005) *Space, the City and Social Theory*. Cambridge: Polity.

Vigar, G., Healey, P. and Graham, S. (2005) 'In search of the city in spatial strategies: past legacies, future imaginings' *Urban Studies* 42: 1391–410.

Wirth, L. (1995/1938) 'Urbanism as a way of life', in Kasinitz, P. (ed.) *Metropolis: Center and Symbol of Our Times*. Basingstoke: Macmillan, 58–82.

Zerlang, M. (1995) 'Det urbane menneske' [The Urban Human], in Frandsen, J. (ed.) *Lys of blade. Sider af oplysningens litteratur*. Odense: Odense Universitetsforlag, 265–77.

Ziehe, T. (1982) *Ny ungdom og usædvanlige læreprocesser* [Plädoyer für Ungewöhnliches Lernen. Ideen zur Jugendsituation]. København: Politisk Revy.

Necessary Dreaming: Uses of Utopia in Urban Planning

David Pinder

Utopian thinking, the capacity to imagine a future that is radically different from what we know to be the prevailing order of things, is a way of breaking through the barriers of convention into a sphere of the imagination where many things beyond our everyday experience become possible ... We need a constructive imagination to help us create the fictive worlds of our dreams, of dreams worth struggling for. (John Friedmann 2002: 103)

Utopias relativise the present ... Utopias pave the way for a critical attitude and a critical activity... The presence of a utopia, the ability to think of alternative solutions to the festering problems of the present, may be seen therefore as a necessary condition of social change. (Zygmunt Bauman 1976: 13)

Utopian dreams in any case never entirely fade away. They are omnipresent in the hidden signifiers of our desires. (David Harvey 2000: 195)

Introduction

In an essay on new directions in planning theory published at the turn of the millennium, Susan Fainstein identified a return to many preoccupations of the nineteenth century reformers concerned with improving urban conditions and producing a more democratic and just society. Referring to several otherwise quite different approaches to planning theory, namely to what she termed the communicative model, the new urbanism, and the just city, she detected a new optimism and suggested that theorists concerned with outlining and advancing conceptions of the just city in particular have 'resurrected the spirit of utopia that inspired Ebenezer Howard and his fellow radicals' (Fainstein 2000: 473). Her arguments will be returned to later but I want to ask first, and more generally, what does it mean to invoke 'the spirit of utopia' in the current context? How and why might it be resurrected today? What is the significance of utopia so long after the grand utopian projects of those 'founding fathers' of modern urban planning from the late nineteenth and early twentieth centuries such as Howard? Why does the concept continue to matter in this field, and how should it be understood and used? Fainstein's reference might, after all, seem surprising given the disrepute and comparative invisibility into which utopia fell over the last few decades, and the ways in which utopian ideas and projects have been widely dismissed, both within the realms of planning and far beyond them.

Utopia is today often associated with impractical or escapist fantasizing. At best it is construed as a harmless exercise in drawing up an ideal world in another space or time, based on ruminations about alternative economic and political systems, living arrangements, daily routines, landscapes and the like. It may offer intellectual stimulation but apparently little purchase on contemporary daily life. The frequency with which 'utopian' is used in derogatory fashion and is connected with such terms as 'fanciful', 'fictional', 'impractical', 'chimerical', 'unrealistic', 'unreasonable' and the like implies as much (Bauman 2007: 102). The term has also become widely associated with the individualized pursuit of material satisfaction and with escape from, or innoculation against, less than ideal present conditions. Telling in this regard is its common appropriation by commercial enterprises and companies in search of catchy titles or appealing advertising script, among them providers of holidays, interior design, financial services, security, cosmetics, jewellery, clothes, computer games, bodily fitness and tanning and much else, who offer 'individual services to individuals seeking individual satisfactions and individual escapes from individually suffered discomforts' (Bauman 2007: 103).

More negatively, the presentation of utopias is frequently viewed as authoritarian and dangerous, as anything but innocuous in its effort to mould the world in all its messy complexities and imperfections into fixed plans. Pernicious rather than benevolent is how Karl Popper and many critics before and since have characterized 'utopian engineers' who, supposedly intoxicated by their dreams of a beautiful new world, aim to reconstruct society as a whole according to an absolute and unchanging ideal. Refusing to compromise with existing conditions, and brooking no dissent in their commitment to a chosen path, they depend upon centralized rule by a few – in all likelihood, a dictatorship – in order to realize their ambitions. Popper contends that, with utopia, the threats of tyrannical rule and totalitarianism are never far away. Indeed, all too often the best intentions of making heaven on earth only succeed in making hell (Popper 1945; see also Rouvillois 2000). Such criticisms of utopia gained strength in the closing decades of the twentieth century and particularly after 1989, when some critics asserted that 'the flying carpets of utopia [were] pulled out from under the feet of those who made themselves at home there', and welcomed the collapse of socialist bureaucratic states in Europe as, so they claimed, marking an end to 'the most disastrous moments of utopian thought: projective megalomania, the claim for totality, finality and novelty' (Enzensberger 1990: 3; cited in Faulenbach 1995: 139; for alternative perspectives, see Buck-Morss 2000; Jacoby 1999; Ray 2009).

For the moment I will put aside how the ensuing talk of the 'end of utopias' and the 'end of history' can itself be regarded as utopian, representative specifically of the 'utopia of global capitalist liberal democracy' that came to rule during the following decade (Žižek 2004: 122). The point to be made here, however, is that utopias might seem today to be of little use to urban planners, in particular those of more pragmatic (practical) persuasions who are concerned with addressing cities and built environments in the here and now. Does not an interest in utopias lead to irrelevance on the one hand, or to megalomania and terror on the other? Is not the term itself too compromised to remain critically useful? In this chapter, however, I want to argue that, on the contrary, utopia – a term coined originally by Thomas More in 1516 as a pun on the Greek words for 'good place' and 'no place' – remains vital for urban planning theory and practice. Two broad sets of reasons will be advanced. The first concerns the ways in which utopia provides a critical lens through which to interrogate planning, one that focuses attention on the visions, desires and interests that lie within conscious efforts to improve urban conditions. Of concern here are not only utopian plans, projects and schemes that project visions of 'good cities' and of the 'good life', and that have long played an important, if unevenly acknowledged role, in planning traditions, both mainstream and alternative. Also significant are the more diffuse utopian impulses that lie within diverse urban plans, projects and approaches, often buried or obscured. One reason for taking utopia seriously, then, is to uncover and to analyze critically these visions and impulses, to open up conceptions of cities involved to scrutiny, and to question the interests and views they assert and support. Conceptions of utopia tell us much about the hopes, anxieties and senses of possibility at play in particular periods and places.

The second set of reasons for addressing utopia lies in its significance for considering potential urban futures and for motivating critical perspectives on cities and social change today. How can cities be imagined differently? How can their social and spatial relations be transformed for the better? These questions are at the heart of utopian approaches, which are concerned with not only what is but also what *could be*. In this regard it will be argued that utopias are not simply of historical interest but also matter – indeed, are necessary – for current pressing discussions about how more humanizing urban spaces and ways of living might be struggled for and produced. In making this claim, I acknowledge the dark side of utopias in urban planning, in particular the long trail of disappointments, failures, and disasters that have been associated with utopian experiments in city building especially through the twentieth century. That trail has been subject to considerable historical scrutiny, one that, as Leonie Sandercock points out, is itself 'perhaps enough to discourage any further attempts at utopian thinking about the city' (2003: 2). Part of my argument is indeed about the need to analyze further the authoritarianism and other dangers associated with many urban utopias. Yet, as Sandercock also stresses, 'the utopian impulse is, and will hopefully remain, an irrepressible part of the human spirit', and my intention is similarly to defend utopianism against its detractors through exploring some of the progressive uses that utopias have played – and could play – within this field.

The chapter as a whole refuses commonplace and colloquial definitions of utopia of the kinds mobilized by Popper and many other critics. They typically understand utopia to be a perfect state to be realized through a fixed blueprint plan, and all too readily conflate it with what should be understood to be a quite different concept, namely totalitarianism. Instead I draw upon recent work in the interdisciplinary field of utopian studies that, inspired in turn by critical lineages of utopian thought, has reconceptualized utopia in more open ways, and that foregrounds in particular issues of imagination and desire. Utopias are here understood as expressions of desire for fundamentally better worlds and ways of living, an approach that opens up perspectives on their potential functions, including those of enabling critique and progressive social and spatial change (Levitas 1990; Sargisson 1996). While asserting the significance of utopia for efforts to imagine and construct cities otherwise, however, I also want to underline its ambiguities, tensions and transgressive qualities against any easy assimilation. A return to utopia today within planning risks becoming simply restorative of existing positions and compensatory at a time of gross inequalities and suffering. On this basis, so I will argue, utopia must be disruptive, a form of provocative dreaming that undermines and reaches beyond taken-for-granted assumptions on which planning and its conceptions of cities and urbanism depend.

Utopias and Histories of Urban Planning

The ties between utopias and cities are long-standing and deep. As Ash Amin notes, numerous utopian thinkers imagine 'the logos of utopia to be an ideal city, a visible emblem of order and harmony'. He continues, 'the city of concentric circles of function and purpose, the city of modernist planning, the city of contemplation or passion ordered through particular architectural rules, can all be seen as blueprints for urban organization in different parts of the world, intended to deliver the good life, however defined' (Amin 2006: 1010). The history Amin invokes is frequently traced from Plato via Thomas More to include Italian Renaissance designs such as Filarete's Sforzinda and Tommaso Campanella's City of the Sun. From there it incorporates conceptions of eighteenth-century Enlightenment thinkers such as Etienne-Louis Boullée and Claude-Nicholas Ledoux; proposals for communes and communities associated with utopian socialists such as Robert Owen, Saint-Simon and Charles Fourier; urban visions of the industrial age by the likes of Ebenezer Howard, Patrick Geddes, Frank Lloyd Wright and Le Corbusier; on to the contemporary new urbanism and eco-topias. While many ideal cities can be seen as the products of wishful architectural thinking, of fanciful dreaming or of speculative design, supported by and intended to gratify powerful patrons, others stem from efforts to engage critically with current urban conditions and to change them. Through imagining, outlining and advocating the construction of cities that are fundamentally different and better, their advocates seek also to create a better society. In these 'utopias in three dimensions', as Robert Fishman (1984) terms them, the emphasis is on building or rebuilding cities in order to bring about spatial *and* social change: urban design is held to be the key to total transformation that will usher in an ordered and harmonious existence. Geometry, symmetry, clean lines and immutable forms typically underpin their efforts to plan and regularize space in the name of a new harmonious socio-spatial order governed by reason, in which the physical environment itself is meant to embody the values of a new civilization based on the common good (see Eaton 2002; Fishman 1982; Harvey 2000; Miles 2008; Pinder 2005; Rosenau 1983).

The urge to confront existing urban conditions and to transform them for the better was particularly prominent in utopian designs for cities that poured forth in the late nineteenth and early twentieth centuries in Europe. In their efforts to address problems of the day associated with ill health, poverty, poor housing and sanitation and the like, their aim was neither piecemeal reform, nor was it tinkering with the urban system. Rather, it was building new healthy cities for a new modern era. The terrible conditions of the nineteenth century city became a spur to action, leading urban visionaries to strive for a clean canvas, either by escaping and building on fresh land, or by sweeping away the dark, decaying spaces of existing cities and replacing them with sparkling alternatives. For all their differences, what made such projects utopian was their effort through urban construction to bring about fundamental spatial and social change, to 'save' society from conflict and upheaval by providing more appropriate settings for urban living, and to open up paths to what was conceived as nothing less than a new civilization. Such urban utopias may have never been built as such according to their original conceptions, but many directly inspired grand urban construction projects, from the garden cities of Letchworth and Welwyn, which were established through Howard's movement in the UK, to the new modernist cities of Brasília and Chandigarh, which have typically been seen as the fullest realizations of the theories and tenets proposed by Le Corbusier and CIAM (Congrès Internationaux d'Architecture Moderne). Of further reaching significance, however, were the more diffuse and partial ways in which these utopian projects informed discourses and practices of urban planning and city building. This was as they entered into dialogue with, and were in turn shaped by, other ideas, norms and conventions; that is, as they developed '*constellations* of design ideas and sociological precepts' that allowed their imagery to be malleable, providing a broad vision around which different interests could gather, and that insulated them from criticism through claims that 'their proposals derived from the application of rational and moral principles to the needs of society' (Gold 2008: 74, 75).

Given their ambitions to bring about total change, it is not surprising that utopian visionaries have typically been viewed warily within professional planning and in their own time many were 'outsiders' (Fishman 1982; Hardy 2000). They have nevertheless since received prominent acknowledgement in many histories of modern urban planning for their roles in the foundation and development of the field, both in terms of how their ideas and ideals shaped subsequent debates and practices, and in relation to how they were drawn upon in different times and places to inform the actual building of cities, especially after the Second World War. 'The profession of city planning was born of a vision of the good city', notes Fainstein (2009: 19). 'Its roots lie in the nineteenth-century radicalism of Ebenezer Howard and his associates, in Baron Haussmann's conception of creative destruction, and in the more conventional ideas of the urban progressives in the United States and their technocratic European counterparts'. While noting their significant differences, she points to their common beginnings 'in a revulsion at the chaotic and unhealthful character of the industrial city' and to their common purpose 'to achieve efficiency, order, and beauty through the imposition of reason' (see also Meyerson 1961; Hall 2002; Hermansen 2010). Far from the utopianism of ideal cities hindering their capacity to sway others, Fishman asserts that 'it was precisely their total design; their deep connection between aesthetic and utopian change; and their remoteness from any immediate practical application that led to their essential influence' (1984: 97).

Interest in urban utopias has tended to centre on certain canonical movements and especially individual figures, usually white middle-class men, who are the focus of specific studies or are given leading parts in more general surveys. This is particularly the case with studies centred on the rise, institutionalization and achievements of the profession of planning, that is with what Sandercock terms 'mainstream planning history' or 'the official story' whereby 'the rise of planning is presented as a heroic, progressive narrative, part of the Western or Enlightenment project of modernization, part of the rise of liberal democracy with its belief in progress through science and technology and faith that "the rational planning of ideal social orders" can achieve equality, liberty, and justice' (Sandercock 1998: 3, citing Harvey 1989: 11–13). How utopian visionaries and their plans have been portrayed varies, with different heroes emerging from different narratives. But beyond these individuals, notes Sandercock (1998: 4), planning itself becomes 'the real hero' within mainstream histories, with the role of planners and planning been viewed as unproblematic and progressive (see also Huxley, this volume). Studying critically such urban utopias is therefore an important task for rendering the histories and geographies of influential ideas as well as planning ideals problematic, and for showing how they were not neutral or inevitable but embodied particular interests and desires.

In relation to calls for an ideal urban order that claim to speak for the general good it is always necessary to ask: whose order? Whose interests would be served, and what forms of regulation and control would be required? These questions have come to the fore through critical studies in planning that have drawn upon Marxist, feminist, poststructuralist, psychoanalytic and postcolonial theories so as to expose myths of value-neutrality and to consider the forms of power-knowledge through which planning processes operate to produce differential effects along lines of class, gender, ethnicity, sexuality, and disability (for example, Boyer 1983; Dear and Scott 1981; Foglesong 1986). Considering the modes of regulation, control, marginalization, erasure and oppression of spaces and bodies that lie behind utopian dreams of order is part of what some critics have referred to as a 'noir history' of modernist planning and an exploration of its 'dark side' (Sandercock 1998; 2003; Yiftachel 1998). To do so is not necessarily to deny the emancipatory intent of the urban utopias, nor the value of their efforts to transform cities fundamentally by improving living conditions, infrastructures, amenities and the like for working class populations. Rather, it is to bring out the politics of the visions and especially of the regulatory ambitions that are often masked by claims to be working for the universal good, not least through their common use of organic and medical metaphors, with attendant discourses of hygiene, health and disorder. It is to enquire into, for example, how their 'pure' spaces are based on certain kinds of class relationships, how they project and serve to certain kinds of male-female relationships, certain kinds of sexual relations and so on.

Addressing critically the utopianism of urban projects in particular focuses attention on the desires as well as the anxieties and fears apparent in their dreams of order, and can thus be a means of unsettling their self-presentation as disembodied rationalist and technical enterprises designed to cure cities of their ills (see Pinder 2005, Chapters 2–4). The work of feminist critics has been especially important in this regard for exploring how utopian plans may be read as responses to the threats of upheaval and disruption associated with the presence of women and the female body (Wilson 1991; Hooper 2002). So too have studies by postcolonial critics on the ways in which modernist urban utopias were constructed through orientalist fantasies of colonial 'others' (Çelik 1992), and work on sexuality that has revealed the psychosexual dynamics within certain notions of urban order and disorder with modern planning and architecture and cities (Colomina 1992; Wigley 2001). Others have challenged the utopian fantasies that underpin prescriptive ideals of the 'good' and 'healthy' city in strategic planning practice with its future oriented language of *ought* and *must* (Gunder and Hillier 2005).

Urban Utopias in a Cold Climate

Advocating the need to view urban utopias sceptically and to subject their forms to critique might seem almost unnecessary in the present era given the resistance and even hostility that they have faced in recent decades, as the term itself has come under considerable fire and there has been much talk of it coming to an 'end'. The predominant mood enveloping references to utopias within urban planning during the closing decades of the twentieth century would seem to be one of tragic decline. This was especially the case with respect to utopian schemes associated with 'high modernism' and its technocratic and rationalistic approach to planning ideal social orders (Harvey 1989: 35), and it is associated with the apparent gulf between what the projects set out to achieve, and what was accomplished in their name. For some critics the 'tragedy' relates to the ways in which the projects were taken up in different circumstances, transplanted in time and space by others leading to results that were often hard to recognize and at times catastrophic. For other critics, it lies in the repressive and authoritarian nature of the static and idealized visions themselves, and to the ways in which their will to order had an inherently dystopic side, notwithstanding their desires to improve urban conditions. Meanwhile, others have taken a more materialist approach, stressing how, in their efforts to be realized, such projects had to work with social, political and economic processes quite different from those originally imagined in their efforts to be realized, in particular those associated with authoritarian state power and capital accumulation (for varying accounts see, for example, Hall 2002; Harvey 2000; Scott 1998). However it is presented, the abandonment of utopian schemes as a viable means to improve cities since the early 1970s, following a previous decade that witnessed remarkable experimentation in this regard by planners, architects and others, certainly seems resounding. As one commentator puts it, 'there seems to be consensus that the age of utopian ideals of the good city is over and that the contemporary city is a piecemeal and dystopian product of struggles over space among various social groups and interests staking claims to the city' (Ruppert 2006: 4). As a consequence, so Fainstein states, planning has been characterized by 'greater modesty', with most planners and academic commentators believing that 'visionaries should not impose their views upon the public' – as if relinquishing matters to the 'free market' does not do this? – and with scepticism reigning 'over the possibility of identifying a model of the good city' (2009: 19).

Such 'consensus', however, underlines rather than obviates the need for critical enquiries into the roles played by utopianism. In place of general dismissals, more nuanced understandings of the concept of utopia and different ways of thinking about urban utopias in the past and present are required. Often being invoked is the understanding of utopia as a blueprint plan that depicts a perfect future and establishes this as the goal of change. This was the basis of Popper's attack on the 'utopian engineer' cited earlier, made in the aftermath of the Second World War, when he claimed that 'the Utopian method must lead to a dangerous dogmatic attachment to a blueprint for which countless sacrifices have been made' (Popper 1945: 144). It was on those grounds that he asserted utopianism's proximity to totalitarianism, and that he thus advocated abandoning 'dreaming about distant ideals and fighting over our Utopian blueprints for a new world and a new man' (Popper 1969: 380). In light of Popper's recognition that the 'heavenly vision' has, since Plato, often been imagined in terms of the city, it is telling that many other conservative and liberal critics have similarly attacked utopians not only as engineers but also as planners and architects who supposedly propagate blueprint plans that have repressive results. 'The supreme architect, who begins as a visionary, becomes a fanatic, and ends as a despot,' claimed Walter Lippman some years earlier. 'For no one can be the supreme architect of society without employing a supreme despot to execute the design' (1937: 364).

Yet the roles of neither utopia, nor utopian planners and architects, need to be understood in this way. Even if aspects of the liberal pluralist critique of the authoritarianism of utopia are conceded, they refer to a particular form of the utopian blueprint plan and to attempts at its realization as a perfect end state, rather than to utopia per se (Sargisson 2007). This is stressed by Harvey in his significant interventions into utopian thinking and spaces of hope, in which he criticizes 'utopias of spatial form', by which he means utopias based on fixed and formal designs concerned with promoting ideal cities as a means for securing a harmonious and stable social order. '[H]istory and change cannot be erased by superimposing a spatial form that locks down all desire for novelty and difference,' he argues. 'All such utopias of spatial form end up being repressive of human desire. And to the degree that they have been implemented, the results have been far more authoritarian and repressive than emancipatory' (Harvey 2009: 46; see also Harvey 2000). How much their 'failures' were due to the flawed qualities of the projects, and how much they were down to the necessity to compromise with social processes that were ultimately inimical to their ambitions in order to get support for their construction, is in fact a moot point for Harvey, yet he is highly critical of their emphasis on spatial form when that is interpreted as an attempt to freeze historical and geographical processes in some harmonious ideal end state. He indeed acknowledges that the dismal record of urban utopias might seem enough to justify abandoning the whole enterprise, and many have taken that route. But crucially, by focusing his criticisms on a certain kind of utopia, Harvey keeps open the opportunity to consider other ways of conceptualizing urban utopias, other uses to which they might be put.

Even the tradition of utopias of spatial form can be mobilized for more open purposes, so Harvey notes, enabling what can be termed after Louis Marin (1984) a kind of 'spatial play'. This term refers to how their different spatial forms can serve more experimental ends, no longer tied to some realized end state but instead inviting speculation about different ways of producing cities and different ways of living. Herein lies some of their continuing appeal, for they may be viewed as 'suggestions as to how we might re-shape urban spaces to our hearts' desires or, more cogently, to realize a certain social aim, such as greater gender equality, ecological sustainability, cultural diversity, or whatever' (Harvey 2009: 46). Taking utopia seriously within urban planning and using it as a lens through which to explore the field, as I am advocating here, provides a means of considering such potential functions of utopian proposals, beyond examining their roles as regulatory spatial plans and schemes as discussed above. For example, how can they open up spaces for criticism and imagination, even as they close down others? How can they challenge taken-for-granted assumptions about urban and social orders, so as to stimulate consideration of how they could be otherwise? What can critical readings of their forms tell us about fears, anxieties and the difficulties as well as possibilities of imagining change at the time? Contextualizing urban utopias in their times and places, and considering how they were part of struggles for urban and social change, bound up with different ideological and political positions, is valuable for bringing out dimensions beyond those most often acknowledged. This is especially significant at a time when urban utopias are so readily and apparently easily dismissed, in relation to which it is necessary to stress a further point: that criticism of urban utopias, including frequently vilified forms, should be conducted in the name of the utopian hope of building better futures that underpinned them rather than through renunciation of that hope and of the desire for urban change (cf. Buck-Morss 2000: xiv).

351

Rewriting Utopian Planning Histories

So far my focus has been on the critical analysis of urban utopias whose roles within histories of modern urban planning may be disputed but are nevertheless widely acknowledged. Another important side of critical discussion of utopia, however, involves questioning the partial nature of the 'canon' around which mainstream planning histories have been constructed, so as to explore other uses of utopia in this field. This involves developing critiques of the systematic exclusions through which certain kinds of utopian traditions have been constituted, and opening up consideration of other utopias in the past and present. It also requires a process of theoretically informed historical recovery that depends upon reading the past against the grain of triumphalist or linear histories, through which the story of planning is told in terms of its growing institutional presence and its 'great men'. 'Any project for future alternatives to the paralysis of the present needs to remain mindful of the narratives of the past,' notes Richard Kearney (1994: 394). 'The ethical imagination demands such an "anticipatory memory" – in order to reread history as a seed-bed of prefigured possibilities now erased from our contemporary consciousness. By contrast the remembrance of things past may become a "motive power in the struggle for changing the world" [Horkheimer and Adorno]: a reminder that the horizons of history are still open, that other modes of social and aesthetic experience are possible'.

As the epigraph for her study of feminist designs of homes, neighbourhoods and cities in the United States, Dolores Hayden (1982) takes a declaration from Susan B. Anthony, from 1871: 'Away with your man-visions! Women propose to reject them all, and begin to dream dreams for themselves'. Concerned with how the built environment may be constructed in ways more responsive to the needs of women, and with how cities may be made more egalitarian and socially just, she considers the interest in collective living arrangements and cooperative housekeeping among a range of urban visionaries. Among them are the literary utopian Edward Bellamy, whose proposals for domestic reform at the turn of the twentieth century gained much support among feminists, as well as from Ebenezer Howard. The latter, in turn, influenced designers with his plans and eventual construction of 'cooperative quadrangles' at Letchworth and Welwyn as integral components of his garden city vision. He intended them to be a means for reorganizing domestic work on a communal basis, and, after the first cooperative housekeeping project opened in the form of Homesgarth, composed of 32 kitchenless apartments in Letchworth, he and his wife Elizabeth became residents in 1913 (Hayden 1982: 147–48, 230–37). But beyond exploring typically overlooked gendered dimensions of prominent urban utopias, Hayden recovers the visions and plans of what she calls 'a lost feminist tradition', one that was comprised of three generations of 'material feminists' including Charlotte Perkins Gilman, Melusina Fay Peirce and Mary Livermore, who opposed the economic exploitation of women's domestic labour by men, and who sought the complete transformation of the material spaces of everyday life in the belief that 'women must create feminist homes with socialized housework and childcare before they could become truly equal members of society' (1982: 3).

As Hayden shows, recovering such ideas and experiments in putting them into practice provides vital resources for asking fundamental questions that remain pressing today, namely 'what would a non-sexist city be like?' (see also Hayden 1981).

Hayden is one of many feminist scholars who have opened up appreciation of traditionally marginalized utopian visions and demonstrated their historical significance for urbanism and urban planning (see also Anderson 1992; Bingman et al. 2002; Hayden 1995). Such work has thrown into relief the narrowness of many influential mainstream histories that, in focusing on the planning profession and its constitution and achievements, focus only on 'founding fathers' with the claim that there were 'almost no founding mothers' (Hall 2002: 7). As Sandercock notes, such exclusions are not innocent for they stem from ontological and epistemological positions 'concerning the subject and object of planning, concerning the writing of history, concerning the relationship of planning to power and the power of systems of thought' (1998: 13). Against 'the official story' with its heroic image of planning as the voice of reason, she asserts the need for 'insurgent planning histories', a term that she borrows from anthropologist James Holston (Sandercock 1998; 2003; Holston 1998). These insurgent planning histories challenge mainstream definitions of what constitutes planning, and seek to shatter their state-centred, class-based, masculinist and Eurocentric histories of the field through attending to the many stories of marginalized and oppressed groups. In place of the idea of a single history, there are thus plural histories, involving plural readings, depending on the theoretical lens deployed. For Sandercock, writing histories differently – making the invisible visible, in the title of her edited book, and forging connections between oppositional practices in the past with those in the present – is itself a crucial task for opening up spaces of possibility. As she puts it: 'Perhaps, to imagine the future differently, we need to start with history, with a reconsideration of the stories we tell ourselves about the role of planning in the modern and postmodern city'. She adds: 'In telling new stories about our past, our intention is to reshape our future' (Sandercock 1998: 29).

In relation to urban utopias, this emphasizes the need to reconsider their multiple and contested histories. Beyond the visions that have gained prominence in standard histories of twentieth century planning, also requiring attention are alternative currents of utopianism through which different groups have dreamed dreams for themselves, including those that have operated at a distance from, and in opposition to, the state and processes of capital accumulation. Among such currents of utopianism are those from within European modernism and the avant-gardes that form a critical counter-current to the modernist utopias that posited ideal spatial forms for new cities in the early twentieth century, as they imagined and sought to construct cities otherwise. They include groups such as the constructivists, the surrealists and, after the Second World War, the letterists and the situationists, the latter being vehemently opposed to planning as constituted under capitalist conditions while recognizing, as did their sometime associate Henri Lefebvre, with whom they developed some of their critical perspectives on cities, that transforming urban space is an essential part of the process of revolutionizing everyday life (Pinder 2005). They also include utopian Russian avant-gardes following the revolution of 1917, with their experimental architectural and planning projects for cities, public spaces, homes, monuments and much else that were intended to undermine the habits and practices of the bourgeois era, to eradicate the remnants of the capitalist city, and to cultivate new forms of collective living (Cooke 1995).

These cases attest to the ways in which modernist urban utopias were themselves plural and sharply contested, and harboured radically different visions of possible urban worlds. Alongside such histories should be considered the forms of utopianism evident in feminist designs for more egalitarian cities and living conditions discussed above, as well as those in the visions and insurgent practices of community organizations and grassroots activists and different ethnic and social groups. Attention might also turn to the multitude of efforts to establish alternative settlements around the world in both past and present. These range from various eco-topias, self-organizing cooperative housing initiatives and other 'practical utopias', that do not pretend to be ideal states but that nevertheless involve striving to live and build according to different ideals in the conviction that another world is possible, to intentional communities, that can be likened to 'concrete utopias', being 'physical, observable spaces in which people try to create a context in which their everyday lives are closer to their utopia' (Sargisson and Sargent 2004: xiv; see also Miles 2008). Of further significance are the utopian energies evident in more temporary, even fleeting spatial interventions that, in their own ways, also seek to forge other ways of being in cities, other possibilities beyond those defined under capitalist urbanization (for example Curran 2009).

Considering the diversity of urban utopias from the past is not simply a case of adding neglected ideas and practices to mainstream histories of urban planning, although that in itself can be significant, whether they are from within modernist movements, from theoretical and artistic projects, from political and grassroots mobilizations, or from everyday practices. More fundamentally, it is about shifting the terms of debate about the forms and functions of utopian urbanism. Certainly the significance of such urban utopias mentioned above cannot be gauged in the terms of mainstream planning debates in which they go largely unrecognized, forgotten or marginalized or to which they were opposed. Nor does it necessarily or solely lie in the extent to which they have found realization in practice, although in some cases their ability to shape environments and to improve people's lives, either temporarily or longer term, has obviously been crucial. In any case, their visions were typically not addressed to those in office, to the state administrators and functionaries of planning practice, with the aim of developing new methodologies or policy prescriptions. Instead, they sought to mobilize, to agitate and to criticize in the name of their alternatives. In an argument that will be revisited in the conclusion to this chapter, it might therefore be asserted that much of their significance therefore lies in the demands they put into play, in the challenges they pose to thinking about cities and urban life, in the desires and dreams that they articulate, some of which live on to be taken up by others, and consequently in the senses of possibility they open up. They also, in different ways, attest to the importance of addressing the transformation of space as part of the transformation of everyday life, posing critical questions not only about utopia's role within planning but also planning's potential roles within utopian projects.

Utopia as a 'Dirty Secret' of Planning

Using utopia as a lens through which to explore aspects of planning, as I have been suggesting, opens perspectives on a range of ways in which ideals and desires for fundamentally better ways of being have informed – and contested – this field. Most often this is thought about in terms of utopian projects, plans and schemes. Yet crucial to my argument is the need to reconceptualize utopia away from any necessary identification with a formal plan or scheme, especially of the blueprint variety. On this basis, a further significant critical task lies in considering utopian impulses that run through urban planning projects more generally, and specifically conceptions of the 'good city' and 'good life' that underpin them, whether or not the proponents described themselves as utopian. The architect Rem Koolhaas (2003: 393) has described utopia as 'the dirty secret of all architecture, even the most debased', arguing that 'deep down all architecture, no matter how naïve and implausible, claims to make the world a better place'. Marx's famous point about imagination being what distinguishes the worst of architects from the best of bees similarly invites attention to be paid to a utopian moment in attempts to imagine, order and construct urban spaces that is also essential to planning (see Harvey 2000: 200–2). Investigating such utopian impulses that lie within planning practices and projects can be described, after Ruth Levitas (2007), as an 'archaeological' practice, in that it requires excavating elements that may be implicit and buried, and piecing the fragments together so as to uncover the implicit utopia that lies buried within a project or programme. Drawing out and making visible conceptions and assumptions of projects is valuable for examining the particular positions, interests and ideologies involved, and for addressing how they might be contested.

This approach is significant not only for historical analysis but also for addressing contemporary situations, as a means of examining critically visions of what constitutes good cities and good urban life that currently circulate and shape planning debates and actions, even as they deny their own utopian status. It involves asking questions about how visions of the good city get defined in the current political-economic climate, for example in terms of competitive globalization? What functions do they play? What are their effects in defining parameters of what is possible and acceptable (Gunder and Hillier 2005)? In need of wider consideration in this regard is the way in which neo-liberalism has functioned as a powerful utopian rhetoric over the last three decades, promising a process through which prosperity and freedom will supposedly be delivered to populations as a whole. As has already been remarked, in the wake of the collapse of the utopian projects that were associated with the state socialist regimes in central and Eastern Europe, and with associated announcements of the 'end of history', the recent past has often been depicted as post-utopian. Yet, as Harvey and others have highlighted, there is critical value in addressing neo-liberalism *as* a utopia so as to draw out the specific values and class interests involved. This is something that has come into clearer focus with the economic crisis that has rendered attempts to present neo-liberalism as the only path and that there is no alternative, as the saying went, increasingly untenable. Considering neo-liberalism's utopian dimensions also provides perspectives on its failures, indeed its impossibility as it operates in 'no place', detached from the spatialization that is required when it comes to ground and that inevitably disrupts the purity of its assumptions and operations in practice (Harvey 2000, 2005; Baeten 2002).

This leads into the last point as to why utopia remains of more than historical interest for planners today, and that is the potential value of utopian perspectives for thinking critically about cities and urban life. There is an urgent need to discuss what kinds of urban futures can and should be created, and how urban spaces should be managed and produced. This is especially after a long period when the prospects for cities and their development have been so dominated by neo-liberal agendas and by assertions that the latter were the best guarantors of urban prosperity and wellbeing. A question that consequently arises, one that is especially important in the wake of the recent global economic crises is whether different paths can be forged. Is the only paradise on offer one construed by developers and global capital? Or can others be envisaged that give prominence to social justice and to the creation of cities in relation to the needs and desires of a multitudinous people? These questions underline the need to mobilize powers of the imagination as well as those of social movements, and to consider what roles planners and architects, as key shapers of urban imaginaries and environments, might have in this regard.

Utopian perspectives can continue to play a number of potential functions here. By way of conclusion in the final section, I want to remark briefly on some of the issues at stake by returning to the comments about the resurrection of 'the spirit of utopia' within planning theory from Fainstein that I cited at the beginning of this chapter. As she remarks, positive interest in utopianism within urban studies and planning is now less rare than it was, especially compared to the earlier critical turns against modernist utopias during the 1970s and 1980s and the development of 'postmodernist' challenges to foundationalist thinking. Detecting a broad move within post-positivist planning theory from 'a purely critical outlook' to 'one that once again offers a promise of a better life', Fainstein finds renewed optimism in a number of strands of progressive thought that, in different ways, seek to develop normative commitments and standpoints from which to make critical judgments on present cities and planning practices, and to outline the basis for better alternatives (2000: 472). As with the earlier utopian traditions that she evokes, associated with figures such as Ebenezer Howard, these strands are energized rather than enervated by the need to respond to the social and spatial injustices, inequalities, exploitation, violence and other negative characteristics of contemporary capitalist cities. The directions and forms they take are quite different from one another and frequently opposed, however, and considering some of these differences can help to clarify certain potential uses of utopia in urban planning.

Utopianism and Planning: Critical Prospects

Fainsteins's own focus in recent years has been on theories of 'just city' planning that combine a political economic perspective, which takes a normative stance concerning material well-being and the distribution of social benefits, with philosophical debates about justice. Her aim is to establish grounds from which can be derived a concept of the just city, in the belief that justice and its relationship with democracy and diversity are cornerstones of a 'good city' along with other sets of values around desirable physical form, environmental concerns, questions of authenticity and the like. She argues that outlining a concept of the just city is important for making explicit values that are often taken for granted or left unexamined in critiques of planning practice, and it is therefore a necessary step in what she presents as the object of planning theory, which is to formulate answers to the following two questions: '(1) Under what conditions can conscious human activity produce a better city for all citizens? (2) How do we explain and evaluate the typical outcomes of planning as it has existed so far?' (Fainstein 2005: 121). Her intention is to develop an urban vision that can establish and frame goals for urban development, and she asserts the significance specifically of calling for and conversing about a just city, noting how it can challenge popular discourse about cities and tendencies to exclude social justice from the aims of urban policy. Yet she is wary of utopian ideals as such, arguing that although they 'provide goals toward which to aspire and inspiration by which to mobilize a constituency, they do not offer a strategy for transition within given historical circumstances' (2009: 28). She insists that it is necessary to work within the parameters of the global capitalist political economy and its social and spatial processes, and to seek opportunities for better qualities of life in that context (see also Fainstein 1999: 2000).

Among writers that she cites approvingly in outlining the task of theorizing the just city are those who take a more explicit utopian stance. They include John Friedmann (2002) who, in his defence of utopian thinking cited at the head of this chapter, emphasizes its importance for 'breaking through the barriers of convention'. For him it involves two intertwined moments: critique and constructive vision. In identifying elements of the 'good city' as contributions to the latter, his aim is to establish not a singular blueprint but rather a guiding normative vision whose pillars rest on four material foundations: housing, affordable healthcare, remunerated work and adequate social provision. He also presents as the fundamental protagonist 'an autonomous, self-organizing civil society, actively making claims, resisting, and struggling on behalf of the good city within a framework of democratic institutions' (2002: 118). Despite his embrace of the term utopian, however, he shares Fainstein's concern to work within the context of global capitalism in a spirit of compromise and negotiation, and he refers to his project as 'a utopia of the possible' (2002: xxii).

A key aim is to provide 'a set of criteria against which actual cities can be assessed *by their own citizens*' (2002: xxv).

Those last lines are echoed by Amin in his own recent discussion of 'the good city', which he presents in terms of a 'pragmatism of the possible' or a 'practical urban utopianism' (2006: 1010, 1013). Again, this is proposed not as a blueprint plan but rather as a practical and unsettled achievement based on 'the challenge to fashion a progressive politics of well-being and emancipation out of multiplicity and difference and from the particularities of the urban experience' (1012). Similarly to Friedmann, he outlines key principles that he refers to as four registers of urban solidarity – repair, relatedness, rights and re-enchantment – through which he gives importance to such matters as service provision and privation, social justice and duties of care, openness and inclusion, active public engagement and dissent, association and sociality, and experimenting with everyday public spaces for transformative purposes. He suggests that together these registers 'act as a kind of democratic audit, through inculcating a particular kind of social ethos' (1021). Notable in the approaches adopted by these thinkers are the careful ways in which they position themselves within utopian traditions while distancing themselves from frequently associated tendencies to prescriptiveness, fixed plans, finality, moral absolutism and claims to the 'impossible'. This is also the path taken by Sandercock who, as indicated earlier, is critical of the 'noir' side of earlier utopian planning projects but who continues to advocate the envisioning of alternatives and what she terms '*dreaming cosmopolis*'. Her aim is to outline a planning imagination and practice suitable for confronting today's multicultural cities that is at the same time 'utopian and critical, creative and audacious' (2003: 2). In a manner that resonates with Amin's 'good city', utopia is here conceived as an open process rather than a static vision, something that is striven towards and emergent rather than settled and defined, but whose construction can be guided through outlining principles 'of social justice, of multicultural and urban citizenship, of coalitions building bridges of cooperation across difference' (2003: 212).

There are, however, other ways of conceiving of utopianism that similarly avoid the prescription of fixed spatial plans but that at the same time insist on the fundamental need to challenge dominant notions of 'practical possibility' so as to open up other paths. As has been noted, Fainstein is insistent that, when addressing normative questions, 'any meaningful effort in this direction must work within the context of economic, social, and political forces' (1999: 261), by which she means the context currently established within the capitalist present. To that end, as an actual model of a good city based on principles of social justice, she has frequently posited the case of Amsterdam. Her point is not that this is a utopia but that, relative to other cities, it embodies certain progressive values and elements of the just city from which lessons might be learned (see especially Fainstein 1999). That model and her deployment of it as a potential guide have recently been widely scrutinized and challenged (for example, Novy and Mayer 2009; Uitermark 2009), and Fainstein (2009: 32–3) has herself qualified her depiction of it. Beyond their arguments about the particularities of her chosen case and about the associated dangers of idealized models of the European City more generally, however, Johannes Novy and Margit Mayer raise concerns about her acceptance of the current regime of rights and freedoms and her assumption that 'urban social justice and a capitalist order can go hand in hand'. They argue that her approach to the just city in its current formulation 'unnecessarily constrains the struggle for urban social justice, sweeping alternative visions and alternative possibilities aside' (2009: 116). Among such visions and alternatives are those arising through recent progressive governance experiments in Latin America, and projects that retain the conviction that 'truly transformative change' is not illusionary or utopian, in the colloquial sense of impractical and fantastical, but something 'worth fighting for' (2009: 117; see also Potter and Novy 2009; and more generally the debates in Marcuse et al. 2009).

This returns us to questions about the potential uses of utopia for urban planning. Should its role be primarily inspirational, functioning as a model of a desired city so as to focus debate and to clarify whether 'we can build the cities we want', Fainstein (1999)? Should it concede to dominant understandings of what is feasible under current conditions, so as to avoid standard dismissals of impractical dreaming and to persuade audiences of the efficacy of its vision? Should it look to ground its perspective in current examples of success and failure in city building, in cases such as Amsterdam? Would it in fact be better, as Fainstein implies, to avoid the term utopia altogether? Or alternatively, and this is the position that I want to assert in concluding, is not what makes a project utopian the desire for fundamental social and spatial change, and the questioning of what gets designated as 'possible' and 'impossible' under current conditions? In which case, we could ask, what might be the significance for debates in urban planning of considering unashamedly utopian projects that focus not only on what the current social and economic order defines as possible, but also on struggles to reconfigure that order and its associated conceptions of justice and rights? That is, projects that refuse the proposal that there is no alternative to living under conditions of capitalist accumulation and associated processes of urbanization, and that seek to expand what is possible by charting paths towards cities and ways of urban life that, in the designation of the current order, are impossible. As Slavoj Žižek puts it: 'The "utopian" gesture is the gesture which changes the co-ordinates of the possible' (2004: 123).

Relevant in this regard is the recent explosion of interest within activist and academic circles around Lefebvre's term 'right to the city', where that right is understood not in individualized terms but as encompassing the right to make cities differently, to produce their spaces in keeping with collective needs and desires and, at the same time, to change everyday life (Lefebvre 1996 [1968]). Also significant are Harvey's efforts to address critically how concepts of justice and of rights relate to social processes, and to consider how utopian visions might help inform and guide a transformative process based on social movement struggles to remake social and spatial processes along emancipatory lines. Harvey insists that such utopias must be rooted in current conditions rather than abstract dreams, even as they search for alternative trajectories. His goal is to devise 'a utopianism of spatio-temporal process, a dialectical utopianism that combines the idea of radical changes in both space and time to fashion an entirely different imagination of what city life could be about' (2009: 47; see also Harvey 2000). There are many difficult questions requiring negotiation, as Harvey notes, and as an analogy for the tensions involved he significantly deploys the figure of the architect as someone who works with the circumstances and materials of the present but who also, through the play of imagination, conjures up and constructs other spaces.

Of further significance in this regard are the ranges of utopian experimentation from past and present noted earlier, in which efforts to transform space have been bound up with those to transform society, and vice versa. Included here are earlier radical modernist and avant-garde projects, too often dismissed through undifferentiated references to a singular modernist past, but from whose experimentations with ways of intervening in and revolutionizing spaces there is still much to learn. From such varied strivings 'to fashion an entirely different imagination of what city life could be about', it becomes clear that one of the significant roles of utopias lies not in restoring spaces of order and harmony, as much of the utopian tradition threading through influential thinkers such as Howard has suggested. Rather it entails rupturing dominant assumptions about the organization of cities and societies, and displacing the conceptual frameworks through which they are approached. It involves making space for considering other possibilities and desires, and for opening up different ways of thinking about urban futures. And in the process it puts radical demands in play, radical demands based on the potentialities of the here and now but whose realization would necessitate fundamental changes to cities and the social relations through which they are produced. In this way, utopias seek to chart paths for urban spaces and life beyond the closures of the present. They demand a dreaming beyond current configurations into what is not-yet-set.

References

Amin, A. (2006) 'The good city' *Urban Studies* 43: 1009–23.

Anderson, H. (1992) *Utopian Feminism: Women's Movements in Fin-de-Siècle Vienna.* New Haven and London: Yale University Press.

Baeten, G. (2002) 'Western utopianism/dystopianism and the political mediocrity of critical urban research *Geografiska Annaler B* 84(3–4): 143–52.

Bauman, Z. (1976) *Socialism: The Active Utopia.* London: Allen and Unwin.

Bauman, Z. (2007) *Liquid Times: Living in an Age of Uncertainty.* Cambridge: Polity.

Bingman, A., Sanders, L., and Zorach, R. (eds) (2002) *Embodied Utopias: Gender, Social Change and the Modern Metropolis.* London and New York: Routledge.

Boyer, M.C. (1983) *Dreaming the Rational City: The Myth of American City Planning.* Cambridge, MA: MIT Press.

Buck-Morss, S. (2000) *Dreamworld and Catastrophe : The Passing of Mass Utopia in East and West.* Cambridge, MA: MIT Press.

Çelik, Z. (1992) 'Le Corbusier, orientalism, colonialism' *Assemblage* 17: 59–76.

Colomina, B. (ed.) (1992) *Sexuality and Space*. New York: Princeton Architectural Press.

Cooke, C. (1995) *Russian Avant-Garde: Theories of Art, Architecture and the City*. London: Academy Editions.

Curran, G. (2009) '(Con)temporary utopian spaces', in Hayden, P. and el-Ojeili, C. (eds) *Globalization and Utopia: Critical Essays*. Basingstoke: Palgrave Macmillan, 190–206.

Dear, M. and Scott, A. (eds) (1981) *Urbanization and Urban Planning in Capitalist Society*. London: Methuen.

Eaton, R. (2002) *Ideal Cities: Utopianism and the (Un)Built Environment*. London: Thames and Hudson.

Enzensberger, H.M. (1990) 'Gangarten: Ein Nachtrag zur Utopie' *Kursbuch* 100 (June): 2–10.

Fainstein, S. (1999) 'Can we make the cities we want?', in Beauregard, R. and Body-Gendrot, S. (eds) *The Urban Moment*. Thousand Oaks, CA: Sage, 249–72.

Fainstein, S. (2000) 'New directions in planning theory' *Journal of Urban Affairs* 35(4): 451–78.

Fainstein, S. (2005) 'Planning theory and the city' *Journal of Planning Education and Research* 25: 121–30.

Fainstein, S. (2009) 'Planning and the just city', in Marcuse, P., Connolly, J., Novy, J., Olivio, I., Potter, C., and Steil, J. (eds) *Searching for the Just City: Debates in Urban Theory and Practice*. London and New York: Routledge, 19–39.

Faulenbach, B. (1995) 'Utopia at the end of the twentieth century: the current discussion in Germany', in Fiedler, J. (ed.) *Social Utopias of the Twenties: Bauhaus, Kibbutz and the Dream of the New Man*. Wuppertal: Müller and Busmann Press, 138–43.

Fishman, R. (1982) *Urban Utopias of the Twentieth Century: Ebenezer Howard, Frank Lloyd Wright, and Le Corbusier*. Cambridge, MA: MIT Press.

Fishman, R. (1984) 'Utopia in three dimensions: the ideal city and the origins of modern design', in Alexander, P. and Gill, P. (eds) *Utopias*. London: Duckworth, 95–108.

Friedmann, J. (2002) *The Prospect of Cities*. Minneapolis, MN: University of Minnesota Press.

Foglesong, R. (1986) *Planning the Capitalist City*. Minneapolis, MN: University of Minnesota Press.

Gold, J. (2008) 'Modernity and utopia', in Hall, T., Hubbard, P. and Rennie Short, J. (eds) *The Sage Companion to the City*. London: Sage, 67–86.

Gunder, M. and Hillier, J. (2005) 'Planning as urban therapeutic' *Environment and Planning A* 39(2): 467–86.

Hall, P. (2002) *Cities of Tomorrow: An Intellectual History of Urban Planning and Design in the Twentieth Century* (3rd edition). Oxford: Blackwell.

Hardy, D. (2000) 'Quasi utopias: perfect cities in an imperfect world', in Freestone, R. (ed.) *Urban Planning in a Changing World: The Twentieth Century Experience*. London: Routledge, 61–77.

Harvey, D. (1989) *The Condition of Postmodernity: An Enquiry into the Origins of Cultural Change*. Oxford: Blackwell.

Harvey, D. (2000) *Spaces of Hope*. Edinburgh: Edinburgh University Press.

Harvey, D. (2005) *A Brief History of Neoliberalism*. Oxford: Oxford University Press.

Harvey, D. with Potter, C. (2009) 'The right to the Just City', in Marcuse, P., Connolly, J., Novy, J., Olivio, I., Potter, C., and Steil, J. (eds) *Searching for the Just City: Debates in Urban Theory and Practice*. London and New York: Routledge, 40–51.

Hayden, D. (1981) 'What would a non-sexist city be like? Speculations on housing, urban design, and human work', in Simpson, C., Dixler, E., Nelson, M., and Yatrakis, K. (eds) *Women and the American City*. Chicago, IL: University of Chicago Press.

Hayden, D. (1982) *The Grand Domestic Revolution: A History of Feminist Designs for American Homes, Neighborhoods, and Cities*. Cambridge, MA: MIT Press.

Hayden, D. (1995) *The Power of Place: Urban Landscapes as Public History*. Cambridge, MA: MIT Press.

Hermansen, C. (ed.) (2010) *Manifestoes and Transformations in the Early Modernist City*. Aldershot: Ashgate.

Holston, J. (1998) 'Spaces of insurgent citizenship', in Sandercock, L. (ed.) *Making the Invisible Visible: A Multicultural Planning History*, Berkeley, CA: University of California Press, 37–56.

Hooper, B. (2002) 'Urban space, modernity, and masculinist desire: the utopian longings of Le Corbusier', in Bingman, A., Sanders, L., and Zorach, R. (eds) *Embodied Utopias: Gender, Social Change and the Modern Metropolis*. London and New York: Routledge, 55–78.

Jacoby, R. (1999) *The End of Utopia: Politics and Culture in an Age of Apathy*. New York: Basic Books.

Kearney, R. (1994) *The Wake of Imagination: Toward a Postmodern Culture*. London and New York: Routledge.

Koolhaas, R. (2003) 'Utopia station', in Koolhaas, R. and McGetrick, B. (eds) *Content*. Cologne: Taschen, 393.

Lefebvre, H. (1996 [1968]) 'Right to the city', in Lefebvre, H. *Writings on Cities* (trans. and ed. Kofman, E. and Lebas, E.). Oxford: Blackwell, 61–181.

Levitas, R. (1990) *The Concept of Utopia*. Hemel Hempstead: Philip Allan.

Levitas, R. (2007) 'The imaginary reconstitution of society: utopia as method', in Moylan, T. and Baccolini, R. (eds) *Utopia Method Vision: The Use Value of Social Dreaming*. Oxford: Peter Lang, 47–68.

Lippman, W. (1937) *The Good Society*. London: Allen and Unwin.

Marcuse, P., Connolly, J., Novy, J., Olivio, I., Potter, C., and Steil, J. (eds) *Searching for the Just City: Debates in Urban Theory and Practice*. London and New York: Routledge.

Marin, L. (1984) *Utopics: The Semiological Play of Textual Spaces* (trans. Vollrath, R.). Atlantic Highlands, NJ: Humanities Press International Inc.

Meyerson, M. (1961) 'Utopian traditions and the planning of cities' *Daedalus* 90: 180–93.

Miles, M. (2008) *Urban Utopias: The Built and Social Architectures of Alternative Settlements*. London and New York: Routledge.

Novy, J. and Mayer, M. (2009) 'As "just" as it gets? The European City in the "Just City" discourse', in Marcuse, P., Connolly, J., Novy, J., Olivio, I., Potter, C., and Steil, J. (eds) *Searching for the Just City: Debates in Urban Theory and Practice*. London and New York: Routledge, 103–19.

Pinder, D. (2005) *Visions of the City: Utopianism, Power and Politics in Twentieth Century Urbanism*. Edinburgh: Edinburgh University Press.

Popper, K. (1945) *The Open Society and its Enemies, Volume 1: The Spell of Plato*. London: Routledge and Sons.

Popper, K. (1969 [1947]) 'Utopia and violence', in Popper, K. *Conjectures and Refutations*, third edition. London: Routledge, 357–63.

Potter, C. and Novy, J. (2009) 'Conclusion – Just City on the horizon: summing up, moving forward', in Marcuse, P., Connolly, J., Novy, J., Olivio, I., Potter, C., and Steil, J. (eds) *Searching for the Just City: Debates in Urban Theory and Practice*. London and New York: Routledge, 229–39.

Ray, L. (2009) 'After 1989: globalization, normalization, and utopia', in Hayden, P. and el-Ojeili, C. (eds) *Globalization and Utopia: Critical Essays*. Basingstoke: Palgrave Macmillan, 101–16.

Rosenau, H. (1983) *The Ideal City: Its Architectural Evolution in Europe*, third edition. London: Methuen.

Rouvillois, F. (2000) 'Utopia and totalitarianism' (trans. Benabid, N.), in Schaer, R., Claeys, G., and Tower Sargent, L. (eds) *Utopia: The Search for the Ideal Society in the Western World*. Oxford: Oxford University Press, 316–32.

Ruppert, E. (2006) *The Moral Economy of Cities: Shaping Good Citizens*. Toronto, University of Toronto Press.

Sandercock, L. (1998) 'Introduction: framing insurgent historiographies for planning', in Sandercock, L. (ed.) *Making the Invisible Visible: A Multicultural Planning History*. Berkeley, CA: University of California Press, 1–33.

Sandercock, L. (2003) *Cosmopolis II: Mongrel Cities in the 21st Century*. London: Wiley.

Sargisson, L. (1996) *Contemporary Feminist Utopianism*. London and New York: Routledge.

Sargisson, L. (2007) 'The curious relationship between politics and utopia', in Moylan, T. and Baccolini, R. (eds) *Utopia Method Vision: The Use Value of Social Dreaming*. Oxford: Peter Lang, 25–46.

Sargisson, L. and Sargent, L.T. (2004) *Living in Utopia: New Zealand's Intentional Communities*. Aldershot: Ashgate.

Scott, J. (1998) *Seeing Like a State: How Certain Schemes to Improve the Human Condition Have Failed*. New Haven, CT: Yale University Press.

Uitermark, J. (2009) 'An in memoriam for the just city of Amsterdam' *CITY* 13(2): 347–61.

Wigley, M. (2001) *White Walls, Designer Dresses: The Fashioning of Modern Architecture*. Cambridge, MA: MIT Press.

Wilson, E. (1991) *The Sphinx in the City: Urban Life, the Control of Disorder, and Women*. London: Virago Press.

Yiftachel, O. (1998) 'Planning and social control: exploring the dark side' *Journal of Planning Literature* 12(4): 395–406.

Žižek, S. (2004) *Iraq: The Borrowed Kettle*. London and New York: Verso.

PART THREE
CONCEPTUAL CHALLENGES
FOR SPATIAL PLANNING IN
COMPLEXITY

Introduction to Part Three

Jean Hillier

[A]n experiment in knowledge: the creation of unforeseen compounds out of ephemeral elements that become obvious only after the event (Potts 2001: 422)

Introduction

The largely mechanistic epistemologies employed by strategic spatial planners have in the past regarded phenomena as 'objects which must be taken apart, abstracted and packaged into propositional statements in an instrumental manner' (Tsoukas 2005: 220). Such an 'if x, then y' approach to strategic planning, which binds the future to the present, is redundant at the beginning of the twenty-first century and I, like many other authors, argue for a turn to what is increasingly being referred to as post-normal thinking and practice.[1] This might well entail 'a reinvention of the ways in which we live' (Guattari 2000: 34) and plan: ways in which politics, economics, society and space are imagined, not as something 'out there' – contexts for planning practices – but as processes through which relations are constructed, entangled and disentangled. (See also the Introduction to Part One of this volume.)

The chapters in Part 3 of this volume all develop notions of relational complexity, including fragmented and folded conceptualisations of actants, including space, and demands for spatial planning theory and practice to be creative and experimental.

Niraj Verma argues that 'good governance' in the early twenty-first century should espouse 'a deliberate precariousness and a willingness to entertain competing perspectives'.

Luca Bertolini squares up to 'the challenge of irreducible uncertainty' – the chaotic and wicked nature of contemporary planning problems – by turning to an evolutionary theoretical viewpoint.

Nikos Karadimitriou also recognizes that spatial planning is concerned with complex socio-spatial systems. He argues that whilst total control of such systems is neither possible nor desirable, there is scope for planning practitioners to influence their trajectory and evolution.

---

1   See, for example, O'Connor (1999) and Frame and Brown (2008).

My chapter agrees that spatial planning practice in complexity must inevitably be speculative and experimental. I advocate a practice of strategic navigation as a means of 'negotiating unknown terrain and unprecedented complexity', whilst retaining integrity and relevance.

In the remainder of this Introduction, I provide a contextual background to facilitate understanding of the four chapters. My context is inevitably selective and, as such, reflects my position as a Caucasian, middle-aged woman steeped in poststructuralist theories. I apologize to those voices which I unwillingly, but inevitably, marginalize. Errors and omissions are my own.

There are several recurring themes in the chapters, including change, the unknowability of the future, relationality, networks, systems, complexity, pragmatism and the relationship between theory and practice. I concentrate below on understandings of pragmatism and complexity, as these concepts are evident in almost all of the chapters in this Part. There are clear links to the volumes of *Critical Essays* (Hillier and Healey 2008a; 2008b; 2008c) to which this collection is the Companion. I endeavour to draw out those links as appropriate.

Pragmatism

> *Deliberation is irrational in the degree in which an end is so fixed, a passion or interest so absorbing, that the foresight of consequences is warped to include only what furthers execution of its predetermined bias. Deliberation is rational in the degree in which forethought flexibly remakes old aims and habits, institutes perception and love of new ends and acts. (Dewey 1988: 138, cited in Tsoukas, 2005: 263)*

As Healey (2008; 2009) illustrates, the work of several early US-based pragmatist scholars has been highly influential on spatial planning theory, both directly – as in the work of John Dewey and William James – and indirectly, as in the case of Charles Peirce who influenced not only Jürgen Habermas' (1987; 1995) thinking on speech acts and communicative action, but also Gilles Deleuze's (1986) articulation of a non-linguistic theory of the sign.

As the above quotation from Dewey suggests, pragmatism is concerned with experimentation, flexibility and the new. Pragmatists emphasize the importance of practical wisdom and practical judgement in questioning assumptions and working through the consequences of possible actions; a 'what might happen if' approach also seen in my own ideas of strategic navigation (this volume).

The famous 1940s–1950s Chicago School of planning and policy science was grounded in part in pragmatism, as was the systems thinking of C. West Churchman (1968) which focused on the complex relations between parts and wholes in open, dynamic systems (Healey 2009). Churchman's influence on planning theorization is evident in the work of John Forester (1989, 1993, *Critical Essays*, Volume 2, Part

3), Hilda Blanco (1994) and Niraj Verma (1998; *Critical Essays* Volume 2, Part 3; and this volume) in particular.[2]

In his chapter for this volume, Niraj Verma references the work of pragmatist William James for his exploration of 'good governance' in network societies accustomed to broadband internet use. Can 'virtual' city halls and planning departments, now in operation from Albania to India, not only deliver more efficient services, but also revive 'the lost conviviality of spatial connectedness' via on-line network communities? Verma asks whether e-governance can be 'good governance', resting as it does on a pragmatic combination of reason and sentiment, rationality and passion, 'rigour and relevance'. As such, does e-governance possess the potential to restate the best traditions of planning or does it offer a fundamental challenge to planning theory and practice?

Pragmatist perspectives of process-philosophy have also influenced complexity-theorization in its refutation of the prediction of innovation. For Dewey (1988), potentiality cannot be teleologically determined as the achievement of a given end, but is rather interactively generated, as reflected in Deleuze's emphasis on force relations as the conditions of possibility for the production of something new in an unpredictable, experiential world (see Semetsky 2006; Hillier 2007). Deleuze's emphasis on connection or combination as critical in construction of the plane of immanence (see Hillier, this volume) resonates with Dewey's 'drawing of a ground-plan of human experience' (1980: 22). For Dewey, thinking 'in terms of relations of qualities' (1980: 46) comprises, in its multitude of relational combinations, Deleuze's multiplicities (Semetsky 2003). Moreover, Dewey recognized that 'a response to another's act involves contemporaneous response to a thing as entering into other's behaviour, and this upon both sides' (1958: 178, cited in Semetsky 2008: 87); a process similar to that of autopoiesis, found in many theories of complexity (see Karadimitriou, this volume; Hillier, this volume).

It is to the theorization of complexity that I now turn.

Complexity

> *No one has yet succeeded in giving a definition of 'complexity' which is meaningful. (Waddington 1977: 30)*

In this section, I first attempt to define some characteristics of complexity theories, before presenting a contextual overview of their development with specific reference to spatial planning. I pay particular attention to the gap which opened up in the latter half of the twentieth century between mathematical and non-mathematical ideas of complexity and to recent attempts to bridge this divide. I present some of the key terms found in complexity writings, employed in this

---

2   See Healey (2009) for more detail about pragmatist influences on spatial planning theorists. Also see chapters by Schön, Forester, Verma and Hoch in *Critical Essays*, Volume 2, Part 3 (Hillier and Healey 2008b).

volume by authors including Karadimitriou, Hillier, DeLanda and Van Wezemael. I then introduce evolutionary theories and complex adaptive systems as subsets of complexity thinking, indicating their particular relevance to strategic spatial planning. Issues of foresighting and anticipation raise strong ethical questions, which I outline briefly before concluding that there can be no universally applicable theory or practice of spatial planning. (See also the Overall Introduction and Introduction to Part 1 of this volume.) This is not, however, a reason for stasis. I argue a need for theorists and practitioners to respond to the many and diverse conceptual challenges of the twenty-first century with pragmatic spatio-temporally appropriate ways of thinking and acting in complexity. The issue, of course, is to judge what is appropriate.

There are several theories which inform the ideas of complexity. Their reduction to one 'complexity theory' would do violence to the many different ideas around. I should begin, however, by distinguishing between the words complex, complicated and complexity. 'Complex' and 'complicated' are often used interchangeably to indicate something which includes several elements plaited or folded together and which thus becomes difficult to comprehend, not easily disentangled or analyzed (Alhadeff-Jones 2008) and far from simple. 'Complexity', on the other hand, focuses on 'the dynamical properties and structural transformation of non-linear, "far-from equilibrium" systems' (Martin and Sunley 2007: 575).

Applied to assemblages (which might include planning authorities, cities, pressure groups and so on), Cilliers (2005a: 9–11) identifies some key characteristics of complexity:

- Relationships are vital – 'things happen during interaction' (Cilliers 2005a: 9).
- Organisations are open systems without clearly defined boundaries. Organizations interact with their contextual environments and cannot be understood independently from them.
- An organization's history of interactions co-determines its nature.
- Unpredictable and novel characteristics may emerge.
- Small causes can have large effects and vice versa: a principle of non-linearity. 'We should be prepared for the unexpected' (Cilliers 2005a: 10).
- Organizations can self-organize.
- Complex organizations are stultified by too much central control.
- Complex organizations work well with shallow structures.

Let me give an example. March 1994. Six months of hot weather and no rain in Western Australia culminated in a series of pyrotechnical lightning strikes which struck several telegraph poles and resulted in the whole of the South-West region (c.750,000 km^2, c.1.5 million people) losing electric power for up to two weeks. Traffic lights, computer-controlled entrances to office-complexes, bank ATMs, barcode-readers etc. all failed. Chaos ensued. Yet after a few hours, the traffic began to flow freely, slower than normally, with drivers approaching intersections carefully and giving way fairly. Order on the roads prevailed. Nobody had decreed this. There were no traffic police to be seen. It just happened.

Definitions of complexity include:

- the study of complex adaptive ('vital') matter that shows ordering but which remains 'on the edge of chaos' (Urry 2005: 1);
- 'the interdisciplinary understanding of reality as composed of open systems with emergent properties and transformational potential' (Byrne 2005: 97);
- 'an accretion of ideas, a rhetorical hybrid … representing a shift towards understanding the properties of the interaction of systems as more than the sum of their parts. This is, then, the idea of a science of holistic emergent order; a science of qualities as much as of quantities, a science of "the potential for emergent order in complex and unpredictable phenomena" (Goodwin 1997: 112), a more open science which asserts "the primacy of processes over events, of relationships over entities and of development over structure" (Ingold, 1990: 2009)' (Thrift 1999: 33);
- 'it is usually recognised that complexity includes a variety of branches, among them chaos theory, cellular automata, fractal theory, neural networks etc'. (Suteanu 2005: 115)

Moreover, Cilliers (2005: 258) suggests that

> *since different descriptions of a complex system decompose the system in different ways, the knowledge gained by any description is always relative to the perspective from which the description was made. This does not imply that any description is as good as any other. It is merely the result of the fact that only a limited number of characteristics of the system can be taken into account by any specific description. Although there is no a priori procedure for deciding which description is correct, some descriptions will deliver more interesting results than others.*

My history of complexity theories begins at the end of the nineteenth/beginning of the twentieth centuries, when chance circumstances provided a window of opportunity for thinking relationally and rebutting Cartesian science. Henri Poincaré, a mathematician and physicist, famous for his use of non-Euclidean geometry (1892–1909) and for describing the Hallmark of Chaos as sensitive dependence on initial conditions in which 'prediction becomes impossible' (1914); Albert Einstein's 1905 theory of relativity and Henri Bergson's ideas about *durée* (temporality and relational time) (1896, 1911, 1921), were all published. Also influential (as mentioned above) were the American pragmatists Charles Peirce, John Dewey and William James and the anarchist Piotr Kropotkin (who lived in France), whilst it is known that Einstein corresponded with Sigmund Freud (Novotny 2005) and that Picasso read Bergson's work and attended seminars by Einstein, Bergson and Poincaré, which had a bearing on the development of Cubism.

In 1941, through US Army research on anti-aircraft guns (Alhadeff-Jones 2008), the concept of cybernetics emerged, introducing the notions of information feedback and organizational self-directed change. The Second World War further stimulated the development of operations research in Britain to address naval and air force tactics and strategies in multidimensional, uncertain circumstances. Post-war, as mainframe computing systems became more widespread, scholars such as Ilya Prigogine (1955), studying chemical reactions and thermodynamics, biologist Ludwig von Bertalanffy (1951) and the US Rand Corporation's systems modelling for policy decision-making, identified the importance of connections and networks of flow in open systems. Cybernetics and operations research, investigating adaptive networks of relations, together with developments in neural networks, artificial intelligence and cognitive sciences, were increasingly applied to organizational decision making in the 1940s and 1950s by scholars such as Herbert Simon (1947, 1958, 1962), known in planning fields for his 'satisficing' ideas.

Two Trajectories: System Dynamics

Since the 1970s, complexity thinking has tended to follow two different paths, which are generally regarded as epistemologically antagonistic to each other. The first, based on 'system dynamics', has been described as logico-scientific, hard, computational and mathematical (Bruner 1986; Richardson and Cilliers 2001; Cilliers 2005b). In relation to spatial planning, Churchman's (1968) systems approach was influential (as above).

Mandelbrot's later work on fractals[3] (1975) indicated that 'if different points of view produce different results, this is not a problem to solve, but an opportunity to use' (Suteanu 2005: 116). He went on to develop mathematical methods of extracting the relations which connect the different views and in so doing demonstrated the importance of regarding a problem from multiple perspectives, with multiple possibilities of developing geometrical order. Meanwhile, Prigogine (1968; 1980) was concentrating on open and chance-governed non-linear systems evolution (Kwa 2002). His seminal volume, written with Isabelle Stengers (1984), has paved the way for subsequent thinking on complex systems including issues of far-from-equilibrium conditions, autopoiesis, irreversibility, path dependency and energized interaction (Kwa 2002; Smith and Jenks 2005).

Chaos theory (Gleick 1987) provided a theoretical lens through which to describe behaviour of systems which depend so sensitively on precise conditions that they are effectively unpredictable, but which can have highly significant impacts. The work of the Santa Fe Institute in the USA has developed 'emergence' as a prominent element of research, fostered by scholars such as Waldrop (1993) and Lewin (1993). This aspect of complexity theories has continued to develop, spurred by the

---

3   Infinitely complex shapes, such as snowflakes.

Report of the Gulbenkian Commission (Wallerstein 1996) on which Prigogine sat, the journal *Emergence* (now *E:CO*) founded in 1999 by Jeffrey Goldstein, and the Complexity Research Programme at the LSE (<http://is.lse.ac.uk/complexity>).

With regard to strategic spatial planning, Brian McLoughlin's (1969) systems approach was based in cybernetics and operations research. McLoughlin's attempt to construct a holistic, and also dynamic, model of evolving urban systems envisaged planning practitioners as 'steering' the system towards equilibrium, with urban development plans as critical ordering devices (see *Critical Essays*, Volume 1, Part 3, Hillier and Healey 2008a). However, the idea of cities and regions reaching states of 'equilibrium', together with practices of unchallenged rational scientific management, were always going to be utopian. In response, Friend and Hickling (1987, *Critical Essays*, Volume 1, Part 3, Hillier and Healey 2008a) presented management as operations research helping stakeholder partnerships to develop capacities to think and act creatively when faced with uncertainties (*Critical Essays*, Volume 1, Part 3, Hillier and Healey, 2008a).

In the UK, since the late 1960s, Mike Batty (e.g. 1969, 1994, 2005) has been working on modelling urban systems. Batty was probably one of the first exponents of complexity theories in Britain, paving the way for scholars such as Cletus Moobela (2005) and Angelique Chettiparamb (2006, *Critical Essays*, Volume 3, Part 3, Hillier and Healey 2008c). The Centre for Advanced Spatial Analysis (CASA) at University College, London (<www.casa.ucl.ac.uk>), directed by Mike Batty, develops and applies complexity theorization and emerging computer technologies to issues of city systems, urban growth and the built environment. As part of NEXSUS (the Network for Complexity and Sustainability), CASA is designing the new Complexity and Cities website. In addition, the journal *Environment and Planning B, Planning and Design*, edited by Batty, has become an important arena for publication of research on the application of computers to planning and design.[4]

Table III.1 gives an overview of some of the many complex systems approaches and their applications.

As Nikos Karadimitriou argues in his chapter in this Part, the challenge for planning theorists lies not so much in debating the relevance of complex systems approaches, but of working with them to suggest new practices and tools to increase the effectiveness of spatial planning. Grounded in cybernetics, synergetics and self-organized (autopoietic) criticality, Karadimitriou proposes some potential principles for the evolution of spatial planning as a 'structured adaptive response'.

---

4   See, for example, the paper by Frenkel and Ashkenazi (2008), which applies fractal geometry to measuring urban sprawl; that by Helbing et al. (2001) on self-organizing pedestrian movement; and Koenig and Bauriedel's (2009) application of cellular automata to the generation of settlement structures.

Table III.1   Comparison of complex systems approaches and applications

Structural complexity models

Approach	Common Applications	Particular focus	Constraints and advantages
Cellular automata	Simple land use change, urban developments, fire spread,	Spatial interactions, diffusion processes, pattern formation	Grid/discrete based. Mostly used for spatial phenomena.
Network analysis	Social networks, electricity transmission networks, transport and industrial networks	Interactions between nodes	Can be used to analyze structural features of interactions. Useful for mapping social relationships (SNA). Often relatively data hungry. Often mathematically demanding.
Systems dynamics	Water supply, carbon cycles, urban metabolism, resilience assessment	Dynamic systems with multiple interacting components involving feedback	Limited capacity for handling uncertainty. Can model feedback in systems. Good for exploring effects of non-linearity. Can show importance of initial and boundary conditions as well as finding stable and unstable regions, and attractors.
Evolutionary algorithms	Numerical optimization, learning, artificial life, robotics	Learning processes, evolutionary processes, optimization	Allows configurations to emerge without a designer. Can mimic real evolutionary processes. Allows for optimization over huge, undefined, complex and variable fitness landscapes.

Social complexity approaches

Approach	Common Applications	Particular focus	Constraints and advantages
Game theory (incl. evolutionary)	Economics, behavioural modelling, political science, biology	Decision making, behaviour and cooperation	Requires mathematical formulation. Usually assumes rational actors. Deals with issues of repeated interactions. Deals with issues of perfect and imperfect information. Provides formulation of social dilemmas.

| Heuristic decision making models | Resource use, psychology, computer science | Human decision making | Does not rely on assumptions of perfect information or rational actors. Can embed cultural and institutional aspects. Can feed into evolutionary algorithms. Allows for modelling adaptive behaviour. |
| Experimental economics | Economics, markets, auctions | Collecting information about decision making and preferences | Difficult to generalize findings. Requires considerable skill to set up experiments. Can uncover surprising and important insights. |

Hybrid approaches

Approach	Common Applications	Particular focus	Constraints and advantages
Agent based models	Markets, epidemics, social interactions, autonomous segregation of populations, traffic congestion modelling	Dynamic interactions between large systems of diverse agents. Integration framework for complexity models	Narratives can be used as input. Can have powerful visualization features. Good for scenario analysis. Can be linked to role-playing games. Very useful when the diversity of agents, and agent outcomes, is important.
Companion modelling	Natural resource problems	Social dilemmas. Rapid assessments. Mixing qualitative and quantitative information. Post normal dialectic.	Supports social learning and collective action. Relies on assumptions made by participants. Acknowledges multiple possible realities (post-normal). Allows for eliciting knowledge about complex human interactions. Relies on social validation.
Bayesian belief networks (graphical models)	Bioinformatics, decision support systems	Decision making under uncertainty and imperfect information	Interactions under uncertainty encapsulating beliefs. Excellent for risk assessments. Can incorporate stakeholder perceptions and evaluations. Doesn't really solve the problem of establishing causal relations. Computationally infeasible for large graphs.

Source: Adapted from <http://www.complexsystems.net.au/wiki/Comparison_of_Complex_Systems_Approaches_and_Applications> [accessed 05/02/2009]

Two Trajectories: Narrative Approaches

The second path which complexity theorists have taken – described as narrative (Bruner 1986), soft (Richardson and Cilliers 2001), baroque or critical (Cilliers 2005a) – can be traced from Henri Bergson (or even from Leibnitz and Spinoza). We can trace psychoanalytical trajectories through Sigmund Freud, Melanie Klein and Jacques Lacan and into French social theory (notably Gilles Deleuze, Félix Guattari, Michel Foucault, Michel Callon, Bruno Latour, Jacques Derrida, Michel Serres and others), whilst Morin's work (1977 onwards) on the anthropology of knowledge indicated relations between concepts across the disciplinary boundaries of philosophy, physics, biology and human sciences.[5] In Germany, the work of the Frankfurt School and early Jürgen Habermas also displayed significant influences, both from these sources (Habermas 1971, 1979) and from systems theory (Habermas 1976; Habermas and Luhmann 1971).

This group of scholars acknowledged the subjectivity of knowledge and the constructivist nature of meaning. They argue that there is no objective way to determine any 'correct' meaning. This insight resonated with ideas in cybernetics of actants as cybernetic systems, able to adapt to changes in their environments. Gregory Bateson (1972) wrote of 'not arriving at a place but following a path of continual questioning assumptions and values' (McWhinney 2005: 34). The path is non-linear; a spiral of connection and contradiction. Bateson applied his thinking to the ecological crisis (1972: 496–501) and to urban planning, stressing the importance of practitioners practising flexibility as 'uncommitted potentiality for change' (Bateson 1972: 505). Bateson had a profound influence on the work of Deleuze and Guattari (especially their *A Thousand Plateaus*, 1987), as did biologists and neurophysiologists Humberto Maturana and Francisco Varela (1980; 1987) who originated the concept of autopoiesis in addition to developing constructivist epistemology (see Guattari 1995, in particular).

With regard to strategic spatial planning, Karen Christensen's (1985, 1999) matrix of means, ends and uncertainty (*Critical Essays*, Volume 3, Part 3, Hillier and Healey 2008c) has become fundamental to development of many complexity analyses of spatial planning practice (see the chapter by Luca Bertolini in this Part). As David Byrne (2003) suggested, there is a 'necessary encounter' between planning and qualitative complexity theories; one which has been facilitated by authors including Juval Portugali (2000, 2008) and Gert de Roo (2007b). Alfasi and Portugali (2007) have developed a substantive-qualitative planning model which has, at its core, an appreciation of the relations between elements.

My chapter (this Part) also has relationality as a central theme. My work has come to complexity thinking through the French social philosophy of Michel Foucault, Gilles Deleuze and Félix Guattari. As Protevi (1999: 4) remarks, 'Deleuze was a "sensitive" who picked up currents in the air, and thought through, with Guattari, what a chaos/complexity approach to what a complex econo-psycho-politics might look like'.

---

5   Morin's term 'chaosmos' was developed by Félix Guattari (1995).

I fold together pragmatics and poststructuralism in a multiplanar theory of strategic navigation. I emphasize the importance of power or force relations between elements in a network or assemblage as influencing how things happen. Through understanding such conditions of possibility, how they were mobilized in the past and how they have influenced the shape of the present, we might be more able to understand what pressures and affects are working within and constituting our cities. Future-oriented planning practitioners could then map and experiment with potential force relations and conditions of possibility for emergent events or imaginary alternative worlds: a 'what might happen if?' approach.

Two Trajectories: Bridging Epistemological Gaps

Differences between the two epistemological paths of complexity theorization are increasingly being bridged (see Karadimitriou, Hillier, this volume). For instance, philosopher Manuel DeLanda (1997, 2002, this volume) and social scientist Isabelle Stengers (1997, 2000, 2004) are both concerned with investigating relations between scientific and social-philosophical thought. For them, complexity science provides 'a source of insight into the nature of virtual multiplicities' (Mackenzie 2005: 52).

Stengers (1997, 2000) adds a political dimension to complexity thinking. She distinguishes between the invention of complex objects and their mobilization and the 'problem posed in the future it creates' (Stengers 2000: 67) by becoming other than anticipated. She teaches us that:

- generalizable solutions pertain only to unproblematic (usually highly reductionist) aspects of situations (Mackenzie 2005);
- experimental practice is a way of posing relevant questions (Mackenzie 2005);
- we should expect the unexpected.

As Plummer and Sheppard (2006, 2007), Martin and Sunley (2007) and Bergmann et al. (2009) demonstrate, dialogues are taking place and resonances emerging as scholars recognize that each approach is 'no more than an emergent permanence', whose nature and properties are 'shaped through their relations with other ontologies and epistemologies' (Sheppard 2008: 2610). As such, Eric Sheppard argues that there is much potential benefit for researchers exploring these relationalities: an 'and … and … and' (Deleuze and Parnet 2002: 9) approach rather than an 'either/or' across the multiplicity of complexity-referential theories.

Sheppard (2008) presents an excellent comparative summary of DeLanda's thinking on assemblages, Ilya Prigogine on complexity and David Harvey's relational aesthetics, which I reproduce below (Table III.2).

As Hillier and Van Wezemael (2008) explain, there is value in different epistemological worldviews. A 'romantic' view 'from above' allows an explanatory overview of a situation which can lend itself to mathematical modelling using

Table III.2   Parallels between relational dialectics, assemblages, and complexity

Attributes	A. Relational dialectics (after Harvey 1996)	B. Assemblages (after DeLanda 2006)	C. Complexity (after Prigonine 1996)
Relational ontology	Entities have no stable, essential, characteristics, but are constituted through the 'internal' relations through which they are connected.	An assemblage is a whole, whose properties emerge through interactions amongst components.	Objects are relationally constituted.
Heterogeneity	All entries are heterogeneous, possessing internal contradictions.	Its componenets are heterogeneous, at all scales.	Object and systems are heterogeneous (at all scales).
Relational causality	Subject/object, cause/effect, are interchangeable; parts and wholes are mutually constitutive.	Assemblages at one scale emerge from relations between smaller scale components; components can be unplugged from assemblages, because their existence is not entirely determined by their relations, yet they are also internally related.	Local/global and short term/long term are mutually constitutive.
Socionature	Society and 'nature' are inseparable, dialectically related.	Assemblages are socionatural, with agency operating in all domains; components play roles that vary from material to expressive in nature.	Systems are socionatural, with agency operating in all domains.

Change	Change is a characteristic of all 'systems'; it is statis and 'permanence' that require explanation; transformative behavior is an emergent feature of the heterogeneities and contradictions within and between entities.	Immanent processes of emergence are driven by repetition and difference.	The system spends large amounts of time in motion, far from equilibrium; change is path dependent and potentially transformative.
Space-time	Space-time is contingent and relational, and contained within socionatural processes.	Components shape assemblages through mechanisms of territorialization (reinforcing homogeneity/identity) and deterritorialization (undermining homogeneity/identity)	Time is unidirectional and spatiotemporality is an emergent relational feature.
Open-endedness	Dialectical enquiry works with concepts and abstractions that are always subject to revision, and necessarily incorporates ethical and political choices given the always present possibility of the emergence of other possible worlds	The relations of an assemblage are not logically necessary but contingently obligatory, and must be revealed empirically.	The future is uncertain: minor events can have large and lasting effects.

Source: Sheppard 2008: 2607 [Table 1]

indicators which define a finite set of dimensions. In contrast, through 'baroque' 'looking down' or among, one may discover the many fragmented, heterogeneous worlds which comprise a multiplicity. Leibniz's (1998) 'ponds within the ponds' unfold a complex and hardly coherent pluriverse (Law and Urry 2004) which entangles distant and often unexpected issues and places. We thus need consideration of *both* vertical and horizontal connections between people and places, as rhizome-like processes through which collective relations are constructed and perform. We need to think entanglement rather than embedding[6] (Rabeharisoa and Callon 2002) and also to think non-human as well as human actants, as do both Manuel DeLanda and Erik Swyngedouw (this volume).

I now turn to a brief explanation of some of the key terms encountered in complexity theories, before moving on to discuss the subsets of evolutionary theory and complex adaptive systems in more detail.

A Brief Conceptual Vocabulary

I begin this section with a note on the use of metaphors, as they are frequently found in philosophical and, especially, poststructuralist texts.

Metaphor

It was traditionally thought in the natural and social sciences that metaphors performed as literary decoration, but they have now become accepted as central organizing principles of entire bodies of thought (Rigney 2001: 4), shaping social analysis. Theorists in philosophy, sociology, anthropology and political science compare societies to biological systems (from Auguste Comte, Emile Durkheim, Friedrich Nietzsche and the Chicago School onwards), machines (from Max Weber), wars (from Niccolò Machiavelli, Thomas Hobbes, Karl Marx), games (from Ludwig Wittgenstein) and theatre (from William Shakespeare, Erving Goffman). Poststructuralist thinkers, in particular, adopt metaphors, including Michel Foucault and war (see, Foucault 2003; 2007; Dillon and Neal 2008), Gilles Deleuze and machines (Deleuze and Guattari 1987), Hélène Cixous and theatre. In this volume see Versteeg and Hajer (theatre), Van Wezemael (machines), Hillier (machines) and Karadimitriou (machines)

Poststructural metaphors create 'multiple ways of bringing concepts together' (Koro-Ljungberg 2004: 340) through associated commonplaces rather than stable

---

6   Entanglement – two or more elements are non-hierarchically connected by participation or association in that none can be completely understood without reference to the other/s. Embedding – an element is contained within another, such as a subgroup within a group. Embedded journalists, for instance, worked within and were controlled by the forces of one side in the Gulf Wars.

sameness. They change an epistemology of objectivism and positivist views of producing truth to open up and create new meanings and multiple directions of possible understanding (Koro-Ljungberg 2004: 340).[7] As Davidson (1984: 263) suggests, attempts to give literal expression to metaphorical content are 'simply misguided'.

Matthew Gandy (2005: 40) writes that, 'the contemporary city needs a conceptual vocabulary that can give expression to the unknown, the unknowable and what is yet to come'. In this spirit I offer four keywords which recur in the chapters in this Part.

Emergence and Immanence

Whilst the concept of emergence had been widely used in the natural sciences since the seventeenth century, it became a key concept in complexity thinking to indicate the appearance of behaviour that could not be anticipated simply from knowledge of the elements of a system. 'Emergence' was used by the microbiologist René Dubois (1959) to describe 'rupture' in biological evolution; in particular, sudden upheavals of ecological systems that could not be predicted in linear terms or by looking at the system as a unitary whole. Emergence is concerned with the many local, micro interactions which generate macro or large-scale entropic transformation. (For more depth see Waldrop 1993; Holland 1995; 1998.)

Immanence is similar to emergence. It refers to creativity; the quality of an action which proceeds from the spontaneity essential to the living subject or agent. Immanence, in which new properties emerge, can occur autopoietically without need of external intervention or 'top-down' imposition (Clark 2005: 168; DeLanda 2002: 28). Immanence is both unpredictable, with no necessary proportionality between cause and effect (Urry 2003: 24), and irreversible, 'full of unexpected and irreversible time-space movements, often away from points of equilibrium' (Law and Urry 2003: 9). The multiple cocktail effects of air and water pollution exemplify immanence whereby individual elements, connected in new relationships, may interact and develop different collective properties not implicit within their singular components. What is particularly interesting here are the relations between elements which emerge and which become highly forceful in shaping what eventuates.

Chaos

Chaos is a particular nonlinear dynamic in which small differences in initial states eventually compound to create very different end states, as in the famous example of a butterfly flapping its wings in Brazil causing a tornado in Texas. Chaos is not disorder or anarchy, contrary to its more popular linguistic use. Rather, chaos is related to chance, randomness and incomprehensibility (for more depth see

---

7   Also see Nietzsche (nd)[1873]; Derrida (1982) and Morgan (1997) on this point.

Prigogine and Stengers 1984; Gleick 1987; Lorenz 1996.) It was a fear of chaos which grounded much of modernist planning thought in demands for certainty (see *CEPT*, Volume 1).

Autopoiesis

Introduced by Maturana and Varela (1972), autopoiesis means 'self-creation'. An autopoietic organization (such as a biological cell) is an autonomous and self-organizing, self-maintaining unity which contains component-producing processes. Through their interaction, the components recursively generate the same processes which produced them. In other words, the outputs of the system become its inputs. Maturana and Varela's autopoietic systems are structurally dependent and operationally closed.

The concept of autopoiesis has transferred from biology to disciplines including sociology and organizational management. The main author associated with autopoiesis of social systems is Niklas Luhmann (1995), who distinguished social autopoiesis from Maturana and Varela's biological autopoiesis by identifying communication as the basic element of social systems and by defining social systems, not in terms groups (of people), but as systems of meaning (King 1993). Social autopoiesis thus involves social systems, as networks of communication, producing their own meanings.

There are strong arguments advocating the autopoiesis of disciplines (such as law), of societies (Luhmann 1992; 1995), of administrative systems and of cities, as urban systems (Chettiparamb 2007). Others, however, argue that autopoiesis is too linear, too structural and too oversimplified to explain the reality of complex systems (e.g. Habermas 1987; Zolo 1992). Whilst I, personally, have doubts whether cities can be autopoietic, preferring to regard cities as complex open systems or complex assemblages (as I outline below), I agree with King (1993: 230) that thinking about autopoiesis can force researchers to concentrate simultaneously on 'the internal operation of different systems, the interfaces between these systems, and the different social worlds of meaning that each constructs'.

Evolutionary Theories

Evolutionary approaches to the complexity paradigm address the question, 'what is the origin of order, organisation and the apparent intelligence that we see around us?' (Heylighen 2000) Whilst some authors (such as Witt 1999, 2003; Marshall, 2008) have turned to Charles Darwin's theory of evolution for understanding cities, many consider Darwinism too restricted by its biological origins to be of significance to urban studies and spatial planning (e.g. Heylighen 2000; Lawson 2003). Biologist, Patrick Geddes, did, however, apply an organicist approach to economics and later to regional planning (see *Critical Essays*, Volume 1, Hillier and Healey 2008a;

Mehmood 2010) which was highly influential in the early twentieth century in Britain and in the US, via the Chicago School.

Meanwhile, Thorsten Veblen (1919), a friend of Geddes, was applying evolutionary thinking to economics. Evolutionary economics only became popular, however, after the 1960s developments in cybernetics which facilitated the generation of statistical models for understanding the chaotic, yet predictable, nature of emergence (see, for example, Gould and Eldredge 1977; Martin and Sunley 2007). As Potts (2000: 186) explains, evolutionary economics has become 'an eclectic rubric centred round the paradigm of the complexity of open systems processes' (cited in Martin and Sunley 2007: 582). In other words, evolutionary economics is concerned with the emergence and evolution of multiple networked connections.

Luca Bertolini's chapter in this Part addresses complex evolutionary possibilities of land use and transport policy and planning. Reformulating Karen Christensen's (1985) matrix with its four 'prototype' problems or conditions, depending on whether goals and techniques are known or unknown, Bertolini concentrates on Christensen's 'chaotic' situation where both goals and techniques are unknown. He advocates mapping partial models of goals and means onto each other, such that 'robust' combinations may be identified. Bertolini illustrates these ideas through a case of transportation planning in the Netherlands, demonstrating how relatively robust combinations of goals and means may emerge through evolutionary processes of renaming, reframing and removing, fuelled by reflection. There are links here to interpretive policy analysis and the work of Maarten Hajer (see the chapter by Versteeg and Hajer in Part 1 of this volume).

Bertolini's suggestion for an evolutionary approach to planning resonates somewhat with my own advocacy of Deleuzean-inspired tracing and mapping of the force relations of conditions of possibility. The grounds for such resonance lie in Deleuze's (1994; Deleuze and Guattari 1987) reading of evolutionary theory which locates change in 'a shifting, fluid set of milieus that effectively compose the individual organism' (Marks 2006: 94). As Marks explains, Deleuze appropriates the molecular aspect of evolutionary theory, but rejects its genetic determinism, proposing instead pure difference (differenciation). Deleuze's thinking thus foregrounds the idea of rupture and differenciation rather than that of homeostasis (organizational or identity conservation within the generation of variety) as in more autopoietic forms of evolution (see Ansell Pearson 1999; Hansen, 2000; DeLanda, 2002).

Complex Adaptive Systems

Evolutionary theories may suggest that agents act through some form of trial-and-error 'natural' selection of actions. This may mean that they tend to ignore other agents. Axelrod (1984) proposed, for instance, that agents commence co-operation with their neighbours only later. For example, taking productive land from group B may be the initial solution for group A's problem of population growth, but that action will be resisted by B, possibly with loss of life to both groups. Later, groups

A and B may co-operate, *adapting* their behaviour, with A perhaps deciding to live at higher densities and B providing A with extra food. Adaptation tends to involve dimensions of cognitive learning in that information is synthesized, leading to development of new understandings and preferences.

The expression, complex adaptive system (CAS), emerged in the 1980s with the work of the independent, interdisciplinary Santa Fe Institute in the US, attempting to understand the commonalities connecting artificial, natural and human systems (<www.santafe.edu>). Duit and Galaz (2008) and Jones (2003) identify several key traits of a CAS:

- a CAS consists of agents (such as humans, ants, starlings etc.) assumed to follow certain behaviours, including swarming;.
- there is no central control directing agent behaviour, which is self-organizing (autopoietic), acting on locally available information.;
- such co-evolutionary, adaptive processes generate temporary, unstable equilibria which, in turn, give rise to
- emergent behavioural patterns with limited predictability;
- a CAS does not respond to change in a continuous or linear manner. Instead, a CAS continues in much-the-same-way until it reaches a 'tipping point' when resilience ceases and large-scale changes (crises) occur (e.g. Antle et al. 2006; Coaffee and Murakami Wood 2009);
- a CAS comprises interconnected elements across multiple time-spaces whose interactions are often poorly understood, resulting in 'surprises' (e.g. Ellis 1998) on the crisis of Hong Kong's Mass Transit Railway in 1996);
- there are no neutral observers of a CAS. Anyone observing affects the system;
- there is no 'objective reality' which can describe a CAS;
- definitions of a CAS are inevitably arbitrary, since interconnectivity and adaptive transformation is pervasive.

As Martin and Sunley (2007: 578, n9) point out, there is a vital difference between a complex system and a complex *adaptive* system: a complex system can be simply chaotic and not necessarily self-organizing, whereas a CAS is, by definitional necessity, autopoietic.

There is currently much debate over whether governance systems and urban systems may be regarded as CASs and what identifiable characteristics might render them effective as CASs. With regard to governance systems, Duit and Galaz (2008), for instance, claim that adaptability depends on resolving the fundamental tensions between institutional stability and flexibility; something which is not likely to be easily achieved in practice. In addition, Filchakova et al. (2007: 228) conclude, from a review of studies applying thermodynamics and CAS concepts to urban systems, that most efforts 'to date have been based on somewhat questionable theoretical foundations' and that the indicators employed in several studies are 'neither succinct nor diagnostically useful' (2007: 227).

Nevertheless, since Nicolis and Prigogine's (1977) original suggestion that cities might be considered as CASs, several authors have applied complexity thinking to researching the spatial dynamics of urban land use (including Batty 1969, 1994, 2005; Allen 1984, 2003; Portugali 2000, 2008; Benenson and Torrens 2004; Pulselli et al. 2006) as Nikos Karadimitriou and Jean Hillier both explain in chapters in this Part.

In the UK, Will Medd and Simon Marvin (2005) have analyzed the regional water management system in North-West England as a CAS. They conclude both that 'localised activities of sustainable water management will require adaptability to specific sets of interests and socio-technical configurations' and also that 'localised activity forms part of a large-scale emergent dynamic' (2005: 503). The authors argue that such understanding should facilitate the introduction of changing technologies and patterns of practice in water management.

David Booher and Judith Innes (2006) have applied selected aspects of CAS interactions to analysis of the CALFED process in the San Francisco Bay-Delta area of the US. CAS features studied comprised agents, interactions, non-linearity, openness, unpredictability and emergence, adaptation and autopoiesis (self-reorganization). The authors concluded that CALFED's success was due largely to its functioning

Table III.3   Comparing traditional governance and collaborative CAS governance

Governance Dimension	Traditional Governance	Collaborative CAS Governance
Structure	Top down hierarchy	Interdependent network clusters
Source of direction	Central control	Distributed control
Boundary condition	Closed	Open
Goals	Clear with defined problems	Various and changing
Organizational context	Single authority	Divided authority
Role of manager	Organization controller	Mediator, process manager
Managerial tasks	Planning and guiding organization processes	Guiding interactions, providing opportunity
Managerial activities	Planning, designing, leading	Selecting agents and resources, influencing conditions
Leadership style	Directive	Generative
Nature of planning	Linear	Nonlinear
Criterion of success	Attainment of goals of formal policy	Realization of collective action
System behaviour	Determined by components	Determined by interactions
Democratic legitimacy	Representative democracy	Deliberative democracy

Source: Booher and Innes 2006: 19.

as a CAS. Booher and Innes (2006: 19) have produced a useful comparison between traditional and collaborative CAS governance approaches, which I present above (Table III.3) in order to assist readers' understanding of CASs and their potential applicability to strategic spatial planning and governance systems.

As hinted above, however, I personally have grave doubts about the possibility of cities or planning systems to be autopoietic. I, therefore, doubt whether cities or spatial planning systems of governance can be regarded as CAS, if autopoiesis is an essential characteristic. I regard the relationalities in play in cities and planning systems in several parts of the world as too regulated to offer much scope for self-organisation.[8] In England, at least, the role of strong central legislation and 'guidance' (such as Planning Policy Statements) induces what could be regarded as 'stability', 'inertia' or 'dependence' in local planning authorities and severely restricts practitioners' capacity and willingness to experiment and innovate with locally-appropriate practices. I prefer, therefore, to regard cities and spatial planning systems as complex assemblages.

Securing Complex Systems

One other disciplinary area in which complexity thinking is routinely applied is that of security. We were unfortunately unable to secure a chapter for this volume on security-related conceptual challenges for planning, so I offer an extremely short introduction to how notions such as networks, emergence and pre-emption have travelled into security discourse. From the molecular biological origins outlined earlier, where bacteria were regarded as CAS, spreading via networks, has come the notion of 'bacteria' as terrorists or guerrilla warriors (Cooper 2006). Duffield (2002: 156) points out that terrorist groups, such as al-Qaida, and international drug syndicates, have been operating in a complex adaptive manner for many years. With regard to bacterial epidemics, crime syndicates and terrorist threats, complexity analysis cultivates an alertness to the unpredictable; a response to the emergent before it has actualized – a 'speculative pre-emption' (Cooper 2006: 120) of the emergency of emergence (Dillon and Lobo-Guerrero 2009). Regarding CAS as networks of actors and information, the US Army Marine Corps Field Manual on Counterinsurgency (2006) describes the use of Social Network Analysis (SNA) as 'a powerful threat evaluation tool' (2006: B–1), for 'understanding the organizational dynamics of an insurgency and how best to attack or exploit it' (2006: B–10).

My chapter (this Part) gives further detail on SNA as applied to counterinsurgency and suggests a certain resonance with the technique of 'mapping' in strategic spatial planning. However, as I explain, Deleuzean-inspired cartography possesses several key differences from SNA which entails the (generally quantitative) study of system structure. Structure is derived from patterns of relationships between actors and as such, tends to reduce actors to points or nodes (see also the Introduction to Part 1). SNA describes individuals based on their network position in relation to that of all

---

8   See also Mingers' (2002) comments on autopoiesis and social processes.

other known individuals in the network. For instance, the strength of a relationship or tie between two nodes may be suggested by how often an actor communicates with another. Graphical analysis of overlapping ties allows identification of 'core members' of networks. The number of ties and network 'scores' indicates the degree of power and allegiance possessed by nodes or members (Holman 2008; Latour 1997). Based on calculations of centrality, network density and so on, decisions can be taken with regard to which actors should perhaps be 'removed' or 'infiltrated' to achieve the maximum impact on the effectiveness of that network. Many mathematical approaches to SNA have tended to treat data as either deterministic, or as indicating a strong probabilistic realization of an underlying tendency (Hanneman and Riddle 2005); a tendency which Latour (1997) criticizes as being inscribed by the mathematician.

My Deleuzean-inspired mapping is more interested in agency than structure and the conditions of possibility of agency which reside in the force relations between agents: the lines rather than the nodes. In Deleuzean-inspired analysis, actants and relations are conceived as variable flows, rather than as 'fixed' points, nodes or lines.

Ethical Implications

Interfering in complex systems to 'remove' actors or 'tweak' force relations raises a number of important ethical questions, of which the most important may well be: who has the power to 'play God' and decide who or what is a 'good' actor or network and who or what is a 'bad' one? Can one intervene (or plan) too little, or too much? Decision makers are forced to take up some sort of ethical position in situations in which 'black' and 'white' are never distinct, but rather overcast by messy shades of grey (see the paper by Campbell and Marshall in *Critical Essays*, Volume 3, Part 3, Hillier and Healey 2008c).

Given that 'good' and 'bad', 'friend' and 'enemy' are social constructs, products of 'temporary selection' (Deleuze and Guattari 1987: 10) by powerful actants – notwithstanding Campbell and Marshall's (2000, 2002) work on the 'bad breath' of utilitarianism and the public interest – I advocate consideration of Judy Brown's concept of dialogic accounting (Brown and Fraser 2006; Bebbington et al. 2007; Brown 2007; Frame and Brown 2008). Such accounting is not concerned with the discovery of an 'infallible truth', but rather with discussing actants' values and priorities in 'democratic' processes of decision making (Brown and Frame 2007). Who gets to discuss these values and priorities in what type of 'democratic' setting, however, poses yet another ethical issue.

Which leads me back to pragmatism. Pragmatism's emphasis on specific, context-based ethical decision-making offers spatial planning theorists and practitioners a useful frame for consideration of connections between ethical judgement and action.[9]

---

9   See, for instance, the work of Charles Hoch (2006, 2007a, 2007b) and Gerald Emison (1997, 2004a, 2004b), the latter being influenced, like several planning theorists, by the

Conclusions

Haridimos Tsoukas begins his book, *Complex Knowledge* (2005), with the parable of Professor Bleent, an entomologist, searching for the extremely rare, desert-dwelling Floon Beetle. Only one Floon Beetle ever lives at a time. It emerges from the sand to lay one egg every 1300 years. Estimating an appropriate passage of time, Professor Bleent travels to the desert where he finally spots a Floon Beetle in the sand. Hardly believing his incredible luck, the Professor kneels to inspect the Beetle through his magnifying glass. However, the rays of the scorching desert sun, concentrated through the magnifying glass, burn the Beetle to a cinder and it disappears in a sizzle before his eyes. The Professor's scientific expedition comes to a sad end, as does the Floon Beetle as a species. The method of Professor Bleent's investigation has destroyed the very object of his research.

My reasons for retelling this parable are twofold. Firstly, that it offers a valuable critique of some indicator-driven planning practices and their almost-obsessive use of quantitative indicators and structural rules and guidelines, such that they risk destroying the very raison d'être of planning and practitioners' capacity to propose appropriate planning schemes. Secondly, the parable reminds us that forms of knowledge and ways of working should respect the complexity of the phenomena with which practitioners plan.

Paraphrasing Tsoukas (2005: 2), how can researchers and practitioners avoid oversimplifying, reducing and/or even destroying the phenomena they wish to understand and to plan? How can researchers' and practitioners' thinking acknowledge the complexity of a phenomenon, such as a city, without being paralyzed by it? What forms might thinking and acting in complex situations take?

The terrain of conceptual challenges for planning theory appears to comprise a multiplicity of different interpretations and often-competing frameworks, often lacking ease of implementation in spatial planning practice. The authors in this Part argue that such apparent chaos could become more navigable through application of concepts related to pragmatism and to complexity. As Frame and Brown (2008: 227) suggest, the challenge for spatial planning practice is 'to develop capacities and technologies for turning complexity and uncertainty into strengths for securing progressive social and environmental change'.

Change is a fundamental process of the world about which we theorise and in which we plan. The future is open and often surprising. Practitioners are active agents who, whilst influenced by the socio-cultural-institutional practices in which they have grown up, live and work, undertake actions of which the consequences are relatively unknown. Their work will be interpreted by other human and non-human actants and incorporated into new networks and actions; of resistance and refusal, of adoption, of transformation and so on.

I believe that there can be no one meta-theory or universal practice 'best fitted' to spatial planning, faced as it is, with the many diverse conceptual challenges, that the authors in the volume indicate. We need to work with fluidity and change,

---

pragmatist thinking of C.W. Churchman, mentioned earlier.

rather than static patterns and stability. Change is inevitable. We need to transgress and traverse frontiers of thinking and doing. Too-rigid path dependency on outworn theoretical approaches and institutional structures will impede emergence of more spatio-temporally appropriate ways of thinking and acting. Pragmatic implementation of complexity thinking – Grabher's (2004) situative pragmatism – shifts the perspective in spatial planning from that of attempting to control change in (assumed relatively stable) social-, urban-, resource- and eco-systems, to that of plans becoming 'participants in a multi-agent planning game' (Portugali 2008: 260) in which practitioners live with contingency, adapt to uncertainty and seek ways to channel change in more desirable directions. (See the Introduction to Part 1.)

Linking back to the third volume of *Critical Essays*, I recall the closing words to the Introduction to Part 3 and suggest that the concepts discussed by the authors in this Companion offer 'the possibility of surprise ... and the delight and challenges of that' (Massey 2005: 105) for spatial planning in complexity.

References

Alfasi, N. and Portugali, J. (2007) 'Planning rules for a self-planned city' *Planning Theory* 6(2): 164–82.

Alhadeff-Jones, M. (2008) 'Three generations of complexity theories: nuances and ambiguities' *Educational Philosophy and Theory* 40(1): 66–82.

Allen, P. (1984) 'Towards a new synthesis in the modelling of evolving complex systems' *Environment and Planning B* 12: 65–84.

Allen, P. (2003) *Cities and Regions as Self-Organizing Systems: Models of Complexity*. Amsterdam: Gordon and Breach.

Ansell Pearson, K. (1999) *Germinal Life: The Difference and Repetition of Deleuze*. London: Routledge.

Antle, J., Stoorvodel, J. and Valdivia, R. (2006) 'Multiple equilibria, soil conservation investments, and the resilience of agricultural systems' *Environment and Development Economics* 11: 477–92.

Axelrod, R. (1984) *The Evolution of Cooperation*. New York: Basic Books.

Bateson, G. (1972) *Steps to an Ecology of Mind*. Northvale, NJ: Jason Aronson Inc.

Batty, M. (1969) 'A review of the theory pertaining to spatial organisation', in Masser I. (ed.) *The Use of Models in Planning*. Liverpool: Department of Civic Design, University of Liverpool, 1–27.

Batty, M. (2005) *Cities and Complexity: Understanding Cities with Cellular Automata, Agent-based Models, and Fractals*: Cambridge, MA: MIT Press.

Batty, M. and Longley, P. (1994) *Fractal Cities: A Geometry of Form and Function*. Oxford: Academic Press.

Bebbington, J., Brown, J., Frame, B. and Thomson, I. (2007) 'Theorising engagement: the potential of a critical dialogic approach' *Accounting, Auditing and Accountability Journal* 20(3): 356–81.

Benenson, I. and Torrens, P. (2004) *Geosimulation: Automata-based Modelling of Urban Phenomena*. London: Wiley.

Bergmann, L., Sheppard, E. and Plummer, P. (2009) 'Capitalism beyond harmonious equilibrium: mathematics as if human agency mattered' *Environment and Planning A* 41: 265–83.

Bergson, H. (1896) *Matière et Mémoire*. Paris: PUF.

Bergson, H. (1921) *Durée et Simultanéité à propos de la Théorie d'Einstein*. Paris: F. Alcan.

Bergson, H. (1975) [1921] *Creative Evolution* (trans. Mitchell, A.). Westport, CT: Greenwood Press.

Bergson, H. (1988) [1911] *Matter and Memory* (trans. Paul, N. and Palmer, W.). London: Allen and Unwin.

Blanco, H. (1994) *How to Think About Social Problems: American Pragmatism and the Idea of Planning*. Wesport, CT: Greenwood.

Booher, D. and Innes, J. (2006) 'Complexity and adaptive policy systems: CALFED as an emergent form of governance for sustainable management of contested resources', Proceedings of the 50th Annual Meeting of the ISSS, *<http://journals. isss.org/index.php/proceedings50th/article/viewfile/295/68>* [accessed 22/12/2008].

Brown, J., and Frame, B. (2007) 'Democracy, sustainability and accounting technologies: the potential of dialogic accounting', Landcare Research Working Paper. *<http://www.landcareresearch.co.nz/publications/researchpubs/Brown_frame_paper_dialogue_accounting.pdf#search=%22accounting%20technologies%22>* [accessed December 2009].

Brown, J. and Fraser, M. (2006) 'Approaches and perspectives in social and environmental accounting: an overview of the conceptual landscape' *Business Strategy and the Environment* 15(2): 103–17.

Bruner, J. (1986) *Actual Minds, Possible Worlds*. Cambridge, MA: Harvard University Press.

Byrne, D. (2003) 'Complexity theory and planning theory: a necessary encounter' *Planning Theory* 2(3): 171–8.

Byrne, D. (2005) 'Complexity, configurations and cases' *Theory, Culture and Society* 22(5): 95–111.

Campbell, H. and Marshall, R. (2000) 'Public involvement and planning: looking beyond the one to the many' *International Planning Studies* 5(3): 321–44.

Campbell, H. and Marshall, R. (2002) 'Utilitarianism's bad breath? A re-evaluation of the public interest justification for planning?' *Planning Theory* 1(2): 163–87.

Chettiparamb, A. (2006) 'Metaphors in complexity theory and planning' *Planning Theory* 5: 71–91.

Chettiparamb, A. (2007) 'Re-conceptualising public participation in planning: a view through autopoiesis' *Planning Theory* 6(3): 263–81.

Christensen K. (1985) 'Coping with uncertainty in planning' *Journal of the American Planning Association* 51: 63–73.

Christensen, K. (1999) *Cities and Complexity*. Thousand Oaks, CA: Sage.

Churchman, C.W. (1968) *The Systems Approach*. New York: Dell.

Cilliers, P. (2005a) 'Knowing complex systems', in Richardson, K. (ed.) *Managing Organizational Complexity: Philosophy, Theory and Application*. Greenwich, CT: Information Age Publishing, 7–19.

Cilliers, P. (2005b) 'Complexity, deconstruction and relativism' *Theory, Culture and Society* 22(5): 255–67.

Clark, N. (2005) 'Ex-orbitant globality' *Theory, Culture and Society* 22(5): 165–85.

Coaffee, J. and Murakami Wood, D. (2009) *The Everyday Resilience of the City*. Basingstoke: Palgrave Macmillan.

Cooper, M. (2006) 'Pre-empting emergence: the biological turn in the war on terror' *Theory, Culture and Society* 23(4): 113–35.

COSnet (2008) Comparison of Complex Systems Approaches and Applications. <*http://www.complexsystems.net.au/wiki/Comparison_of_Complex_Systems_Approaches_and_Applications*> [accessed 05/02/2009].

Davidson, D. (1984) 'What metaphors mean', in Davidson, D. *Inquiries into Truth and Interpretation*. Oxford: Oxford University Press.

de Roo, G. (2007a) 'Preface', in de Roo, G. and Porter, G. (eds) *Fuzzy Planning: The Role of Actors in a Fuzzy Governance Environment*. Aldershot: Ashgate, ix–xi.

de Roo, G. (2007b) 'Understanding fuzziness in planning', in de Roo G. and Porter G. (eds) *Fuzzy Planning: The Role of Actors in a Fuzzy Governance Environment*. Aldershot: Ashgate, 115–29.

DeLanda, M. (1997) *A Thousand Years of Nonlinear History*. New York: Swerve.

DeLanda, M. (2002) *Intensive Science and Virtual Philosophy*. London: Continuum.

Deleuze, G. (1994) [1968] *Difference and Repetition* (trans. Patton P.). London: Athlone.

Deleuze, G. 1986 [1983] *Cinema 1: the movement-image* (trans. Tomlinson, H. and Habberjam, B.). Minneapolis, MN: University of Minnesota Press.

Deleuze, G. and Guattari, F. (1987) [1980] *A Thousand Plateaus: Capitalism and Schizophrenia* (trans. Massumi, B.). London: Athlone Press.

Deleuze, G. and Parnet, C. (2002) [1977] *Dialogues II* (trans. Tomlinson, H. and Habberjam, B.). New York: Continuum.

Department of the Army (2006) *Counterinsurgency, Field Manual 3-24*. Marine Corps Warfighting Publication, 3–33.5, Washington DC: Marine Corps.

Derrida, J. (1982) [1972] *Margins of Philosophy* (trans. Bass, A.). Chicago, IL: University of Chicago Press.

Dewey, J. (1958) [1925] *Experience and Nature*. New York: Dover.

Dewey, J. (1980) [1934] *Art as Experience*. New York: Peregrine Books.

Dewey, J. (1988) 'Time and individuality', in Hickman L. and Alexander T. (eds) *The Essential Dewey, Vol. I*. Bloomington, IN: Indiana University Press, 217–26.

Dillon, M. and Neal, A. (eds) (2008) *Foucault on Politics, Security and War*. Basingstoke: Palgrave Macmillan.

Dillon, M. and Lobo-Guerrero, L. (2009) 'The biopolitical imaginary of species-being' *Theory, Culture and Society* 26(1): 1–23.

Dubois, R. (1959) *Mirage of Health: Utopias, Progress and Biological Change*. New Brunswick, NJ: Rutgers University Press.

Duffield, M. (2002) 'War as a network enterprise: the new security terrain and its implications' *Cultural Values* 6(1-2): 153–65.

Duit, A. and Galaz, V. (2008) 'Governance and complexity – emerging issues for governance theory', *Governance: an International Journal of Policy, Administration and Institutions*: 21(3): 311–35.

Einstein, A. (1905) 'On the electrodynamics of moving bodies' *Annalen der Physik* 17: 891–921 (in German).

Einstein, A. (1916) 'The foundation of the general theory of relativity' *Annalen der Physik* 49: 769–822 (in German).

Ellis, P. (1998) 'Chaos in the underground: spontaneous collapse in a tightly-coupled system' *Journal of Contingencies and Crisis Management* 6(3): 137–52.

Emison, G. (1997) 'The potential for unconventional progress: complex adaptive systems and environmental quality policy' *Duke Environmental Law and Policy Forum* 7(1), <http://www.dlc.dlib.indiana.edu> [accessed 27/07/2009].

Emison, G. (2004a) 'Pragmatism, adaptation and Total Quality Management: philosophy and science in the service of managing continuous improvement', *Journal of Management in Engineering* 20(2): 56–61.

Emison, G. (2004b) 'Analyzing and Managing Reflective Public Policy'. Paper presented to The MidWest Political Science Association conference, Chicago, IL, 15/04/2004, <http://www.allacademic.com/meta/p83839_index.html> [accessed 20/05/2009].

Filchakova, N., Robinson, D. and Scartezzini, J-L. (2007) 'Quo vadis thermodynamics and the city: a critical review of applications of thermodynamic methods to urban systems' *International Journal of Ecodynamics* 2(4): 222–30.

Fontan, J-M., Klein J-L., and Tremblay, D-G. (2004) 'Innovation and Society: broadening the analysis of the territorial effects of innovation', Research Note no. 2004–07A, Télé-université Université du Québec à Montréal.

Forester, J. (1989) *Planning in the Face of Power.* Berkeley, CA: University of California Press.

Forester, J. (1993) *Critical Theory, Public Policy and Planning Practice: Toward a Critical Pragmatism.* Albany, NY: SUNY Press, Albany, NY.

Foucault, M. (1977) [1975] *Discipline and Punish* (trans. Sheridan, A.). Harmondsworth: Penguin.

Foucault, M. (2003) [1997] *Society Must be Defended, Lectures at the Collège de France 1975–76* (trans. Macey, D.). London: Allen Lane.

Foucault, M. (2007) [2004] *Security, Territory, Population, Lectures at the Collège de France 1977–78,* (trans. Burchell, G.). Basingstoke: Palgrave Macmillan.

Frame, B. and Brown, J. (2008) 'Developing post-normal technologies for sustainability' *Ecological Economics* 65(2): 225–41.

Frenkel, A. and Ashkenazi, M. (2008) 'Measuring urban sprawl: how can we deal with it?' *Environment and Planning B, Planning and Design* 35(1): 56–79.

Friend, J. and Hickling, A. (1987) *Planning under Pressure: The Strategic Choice Approach.* Oxford: Pergamon Press.

Gandy, M. (2005) 'Cyborg urbanisation: complexity and monstrosity in the contemporary city' *International Journal of Urban and Regional Research* 29(1): 26–49.

Gleick, J. (1987) *Chaos.* New York: Viking.

Goodwin, B. (1997) 'Community, creativity and society' *Soundings* 5: 111–23.

Gould, S. and Eldredge, N. (1977) 'Punctuated equilibria: the tempo and mode of evolution reconsidered' *Paleobiology* 3: 115–51.

Grabher, G. (2004) 'Learning in projects, remembering in networks? Communality, sociality and connectivity in project ecologies' *European Urban and Regional Studies* 11(2): 103–23.

Guattari, F. (1995) [1992] *Chaosmosis* (trans. Bains, P., and Prefanis, J.). Bloomington, IN: Indiana University Press.

Guattari, F. (2000) [1989] *The Three Ecologies* (trans. Pindar, I. and Sutton, P.). London: Athlone Press.

Habermas, J. (1971) [1968] *Knowledge and Human Interests* (trans Shapiro, J.). Boston, MA: Beacon Press.

Habermas, J. (1976) [1973] *Legitimation Crisis* (trans. McCarthy, T.). Cambridge: Polity Press.

Habermas, J. (1979) [1976] *Communication and the Evolution of Society* (trans. McCarthy, T.). London: Heinemann.

Habermas, J. (1984) [1981] *The Theory of Communicative Action, Vol 1, Reason and the Rationalisation of Society* (trans. McCarthy, T.). Boston, MA: Beacon Press.

Habermas, J. (1987) *The Philosophical Discourse of Modernity: Twelve Lectures* (trans. Lawrence, F.). Cambridge: Polity.

Habermas, J. (1995) 'Peirce and communication', in Ketner, K. (ed.) *Peirce and Contemporary Thought*. New York: Fordham University Press, 243–66.

Habermas, J. and Luhmann, N. (1971) *Theorie der Gesellschaft oder Sozialtechnologie?* Frankfurt-am-Main: Suhrkamp Verlag.

Hanneman, R. and Riddle, M. (2005) *Introduction to Social Network Methods.* Riverside, CA: University of California <http://faculty.ucr.edu/~hanneman/> [accessed 27/02/2008].

Hansen, M. (2000) 'Becoming as creative involution? Contextualising Deleuze and Guattari's biophilosophy' *Postmodern Culture* 11(1). *<http://muse.jhu.edu/login?uri=/journals/pmc/v011/11.1hansen.html>* [accessed 06/02/2009].

Healey, P. (2008) 'Introduction to Part III', in Hillier, J. and Healey, P. (eds) (2008b) *Critical Essays in Planning Theory, Volume 2, Political Economy, Diversity and Pragmatism*. Aldershot: Ashgate, 355–63.

Healey, P. (2009) 'The pragmatic turn in planning thought' *Journal of Planning Education and Research* 28: 277–92.

Helbing, D., Molnár, P., Farkas, I. and Bolay, K. (2001) 'Self-organizing pedestrian movement' *Environment and Planning B, Planning and Design* 28(3): 361–83.

Heylighen, F. (2000) 'Foundations and methodology for an evolutionary world view' *Foundations of Science* 5: 457–90.

Hillier, J. (2007) *Stretching Beyond the Horizon: A Multiplanar Theory of Spatial Planning and Governance.* Aldershot: Ashgate.

Hillier, J. and Healey, P. (eds) (2008a) *Critical Essays in Planning Theory, Volume 1, Foundations of the Planning Enterprise*. Aldershot: Ashgate.

Hillier, J. and Healey, P. (eds) (2008b) *Critical Essays in Planning Theory, Volume 2, Political Economy, Diversity and Pragmatism*. Aldershot: Ashgate.

Hillier, J. and Healey, P. (eds) (2008c) *Critical Essays in Planning Theory, Volume 3, Contemporary Movements in Planning Theory*. Aldershot: Ashgate.

Hillier, J. and Van Wezemael, J. (2008) ' "Empty, swept and garnished": the Public Finance Initiative case of Throckley Middle School' *Space and Polity* 12 (2): 157–81.

Hoch, C. (1984) 'Pragmatism, planning and power' *Journal of Planning Education and Research* 4(2): 86–95.

Hoch, C. (2006) 'What can Rorty teach an old pragmatist doing public administration or planning?' *Administration and Society* 38(3): 389–98.

Hoch, C. (2007a) 'Pragmatic communicative action theory' *Journal of Planning Education and Research* 26(3): 272–83.

Hoch, C. (2007b) 'Making plans: representation and intention' *Planning Theory* 6(1): 15–35.

Holland, J. (1995) *Hidden Order: How Adaptation Builds Complexity*. Redwood City, CA: Addison-Wesley.

Holland, J. (1998) *Emergence: From Chaos to Order*. Redwood City, CA: Addison-Wesley.

Holman, N. (2008) 'Community participation: using social network analysis to improve developmental benefits' *Environment and Planning C, Government and Policy* 26(3): 525–43.

Ingold, T. (1990) 'An anthropologist looks at biology' *Man (NS)* 25: 208–29.

Jones, W. (2003) Complex Adaptive Systems. <http://crinfo.beyondintractability.org/essay/complex_adaptive_systems/> [accessed 05/02/2009].

King, M. (1993) 'The "truth" about autopoiesis' *Journal of Law and Society* 20(2): 218–36.

Koenig, R. and Bauriedel, C. (2009) 'Generating settlement structures: a method for urban planning and analysis supported by cellular automata' *Environment and Planning B, Planning and Design* 36(4): 602–24.

Koro-Ljungberg, M. (2004) 'Displacing metaphorical analysis: reading with and against metaphors' *Qualitative Research* 4: 339–60.

Kwa, C. (2002) 'Romantic and Baroque conceptions of complex wholes in the sciences', in Law, J. and Mol, A. (eds) *Complexities: Social Studies of Knowledge Practices*. Durham, NC: Duke University Press, 23–52.

Lafontaine, C. (2007) 'The cybernetic matrix of "French Theory"' *Theory, Culture and Society* 24(5): 27–46.

Lambooy, J. and Moulaert, F. (1996) 'The economic organisation of cities: an institutional perspective' *IJURR* 20(2): 217–37.

Latour, B. (1997) 'On actor-network theory: a few clarifications plus more than a few complications' *Soziale Welt* 47(4): 367–81.

Law, J. (2004) 'And if the global were small and noncoherent? Method, complexity and the baroque' *Environment and Planning D, Society and Space* 22: 13–26.

Law, J. and Urry, J. (2003) [2002] 'Enacting the social', Centre for Science Studies, Lancaster University. <*http://www.lancs.ac.uk/fass/sociology/papers/law-urry-enacting-the-social.pdf*> [accessed December 2009].

Law, J. and Urry, J. (2004) 'Enacting the social' *Economy and Society* 33(3): 390–410.

Lawson, T. (2003) *Reinventing Economics*. London: Routledge.

Leibniz, G. (1998) [1714] *Philosophical Texts* (trans. Francks R. and Woolhouse R.S.). New York: Oxford University Press.

Lewin, R. (1993) *Complexity: Life on the Edge of Chaos*. London: Dent.

Lorenz, E. (1996) *The Essence of Chaos*. Seattle, WA: University of Washington Press.

Luhmann, N. (1992) 'Operational closure and structural coupling' *Cardozo Law Review* 13: 1419–41.

Luhmann, N. (1995) [1984] *Social Systems* (trans. Bednarz Jnr., J. and Baecker, D.). Stanford, CA: Stanford University Press.

Mackenzie, A. (2005) 'The problem of the attractor' *Theory, Culture and Society* 22(5): 45–65.

Marks, J. (2006) 'Molecular biology in the work of Deleuze and Guattari' *Paragraph* 29(2): 81–97.

Marshall, S. (2008) *Cities, Design and Evolution*. London: Routledge.

Martin, R. and Sunley, P. (2007) 'Complexity thinking and evolutionary economic geography' *Journal of Economic Geography* 7: 573–601.

Massey, D. (2005) *For Space*. London: Sage.

Maturana, H. and Varela, F. (1980) [1972] *Autopoiesis and Cognition* (trans. unknown). Dordrecht: Reidel.

Maturana, H. and Varela, F. (1987) [1982] *The Tree of Knowledge* (trans. Paolucci R.). Boston, MA: Shambala.

McLoughlin, J.B. (1969) *Urban and Regional Planning: A Systems Approach*. London: Faber & Faber.

McWhinney, W. (2005) 'The white horse: a reformulation of Bateson's typology of learning' *Cybernetics and Human Knowing* 12(1-2): 22–35.

Medd, W. and Marvin, S. (2005) 'Complexity and spatiality: regions, networks and fluids in sustainable water management', in Richardson, K. (ed.) *Managing Organizational Complexity: philosophy, theory and application*. Greenwich, CT: Information Age Publishing, 493–504.

Mehmood, A. (2010) 'A preliminary texonomy of evolutionary metaphors in spatial planning', *Planning Theory* 9(1): 63–87.

Mingers, J. (2002) 'Can social systeme be autopoietic? Assessing Luhmann's social theory' *The Sociological Review* 50(2): 278–99.

Moobela, C. (2005) 'From worst slum to best example of regeneration: complexity in the regeneration of Hulme, Manchester' *Emergence* 7(1): 29–42.

Morgan, G. (1997) *Images of Organization*. Thousand Oaks, CA: Sage.

Morin, E. (1977) *La Méthode, Vol. 1: La Nature de la Nature*. Paris: Seuil.

Morin, E. (1980) *La Méthode, Vol. 2: La Vie de la Vie*. Paris: Seuil.

Morin, E. (1986) *La Méthode, Vol. 3: La Connaissance de la Connaissance*. Paris: Seuil.

Morin, E. (1991) *La Méthode, Vol. 4: Les Idées: Leur Habitat, leur Vie, leurs Mœurs, leur Organisation*. Paris: Seuil.

Morin, E. (2001) *La Méthode, Vol. 5: L'humanité de L'humanité, L'identité Humaine*. Paris: Seuil.

Morin, E. (2004*) La Méthode, Vol. 6 : Ethique*. Paris: Seuil.

Nicolis, G. and Prigogine, I. (1977) *Self-Organization in Nonequilibrium Systems*. New York: Wiley.

Nietzsche, F. (nd) [1873] 'On truth and lying in a non-moral sense' (trans. Kaufmann W. and Breazeale, D.), *The Nietzsche Channel* <http://www.geocities.com/thenietzschechannel/> [accessed 17/07/2009].

Novotny, H. (2005) 'The increase of complexity and its reduction' *Theory, Culture and Society* 22(5): 15–31.

O'Connor, M. (1999) 'Dialogue and debate in a post-normal practice of science: a reflexion' *Futures* 31: 671–87.

Plummer, P. and Sheppard, E. (2006) 'Geography matters: agency, structures and dynamics' *Journal of Economic Geography* 6: 619–37.

Plummer, P. and Sheppard, E. (2007) 'A methodology for evaluating regional political economy', in Fingelton, B. (ed.) *New Directions in Economic Geography*. Cheltenham: Edward Elgar, 250–76.

Poincaré, H. (1914) [1908] *Science and Method*. Paris: Flammarion.

Poincaré, H. (1993) *New Methods of Celestial Mechanics* [1982, vol. 1; 1892, vol 2; 1899, vol 3. Book 2: 1905, vol 1; 1907, vol 2. 1; 1909, vol 2. 2; 1911, vol 3]. New York: American Institute of Physics.

Portugali, J. (2000) *Self-Organisation and the City*. Heidelberg: Springer.

Portugali, J. (2008) 'Learning from paradoxes about prediction and planning in self-organizing cities' *Planning Theory* 7(3): 248–62.

Potts, J. (2000) *The New Evolutionary Micro-Economics: Complexity, Emergence and Adaptive Behaviour*. Cheltenham: Edward Elgar.

Potts, J. (2001) 'Knowledge and markets' *Journal of Evolutionary Economics* 11(4): 413–21.

Prigogine, I. (1955) *Introduction to Thermodynamics of Irreversible Processes*. Springfield, IL: Thomas.

Prigogine, I. (1980) *From Being to Becoming: Time and Complexity in the Physical Sciences*. San Francisco, CA: WH Freeman.

Prigogine, I. and Lefevre, R. (1968) 'Symmetry-breaking instabilities in dissipative systems, II' *Journal of Chemical Physics* 48: 1695–700.

Prigogine, I. and Stengers, I. (1984) [1979] *Order out of Chaos*. New York: Bantam.

Protevi, J. (1999) 'Some remarks on the philosophical significance of complexity theory', <http://www.protevi.com/john/DG/PDF/Remarks_on_Complexity_Theory> [accessed December 2009].

Pulselli, R., Ciampalini, F., Galli, A. and Pulselli, F. (2006) 'Non equilibrium thermodynamics and the city: a new approach to urban studies' *Annales de Chimie* 96(9–10): 543–52.

Rabeharisoa, V. and Callon, M. (2002) 'The involvement of patients' associations in research' *International Social Science Journal* 54(171): 57–63.

Richardson, K. and Cilliers, P. (2001) 'What is complexity science? A view from different directions' *Emergence* 3(1): 5–23.

Rigney, D. (2001) *The Metaphorical Society*. Lanham, MD: Rowman and Littlefield.

Rose, N. (2004) 'Governing the social', in Gane, N. (ed.) *The Future of Social Theory* London: Continuum, 167–85.

Semetsky, I. (2003) 'Deleuze's new image of thought, or Dewey revisited' *Educational Philosophy and Theory* 35(1): 17–29.

Semetsky, I. (2006) *Deleuze, Education and Becoming*. Rotterdam: Sense Publishers.

Semetsky, I. (2008) 'On the creative logic of education, or: re-reading Dewey through the lens of complexity science' *Educational Philosophy and* Theory 40(1): 83–95.

Sheppard, E. (2008) 'Geographic dialectics?' *Environment and Planning A* 40: 2603–12.

Simon, H. (1947) *Administrative Behaviour*. New York: Macmillan.

Simon, H. (1962) 'Architecture of complexity' *Proceedings of the American Philosophical Society* 106: 467–82.

Simon, H. and Newell, A. (1958) 'Heuristic problem solving: the next advance in operations research' *Operations Research* 6: 1–10.

Smith, J. and Jenks, C. (2005) 'Complexity, ecology and the materiality of information' *Theory, Culture and Society* 22(5): 141–63.

Stengers, I. (1997) *Power and Invention: Situating Science: Theory out of Bounds, Vol 10*. Minneapolis, MN: University of Minnesota Press.

Stengers, I. (2000) *The Invention of Modern Science: Theory Out of Bounds, Vol 19*. Minneapolis, MN: University of Minnesota Press.

Stengers, I. (2004) 'The challenge of complexity: unfolding the ethics of science. In memoriam Ilya Prigogine' *E:CO* 6(1–2): 92–9.

Styhre, A. (2006) 'Organization creativity and the empiricist image of novelty' *Creativity and Innovation Management* 15(2): 143–9.

Suteanu, C. (2005) 'Complexity, science and the public: the geography of a new interpretation' *Theory, Culture and Society* 22(5): 113–40.

Thrift, N. (1999) 'The place of complexity' *Theory, Culture and Society* 16(3): 31–69.

Tsoukas, H. (2005) *Complex Knowledge: Studies in Organizational Epistemology*. Oxford: Oxford University Press.

Urry, J. (2003) *Global Complexity*. Cambridge: Polity.

Urry, J. (2005) 'The complexity turn' *Theory, Culture and Society* 22(5): 1–14.

Veblen, T. (1919) *The Place of Science in Modern Civilisation and Other Essays*. New York: B.W. Huebsch.

Verma, N. (1998) *Similarities, Connections, Systems: The Search for a New Rationality for Planning and Management*. Lanham, MD: Lexington Books.

Von Bertalanffy, L. (1951) *General System Theory: A New Approach to Unity of Science*. Baltimore, MD: Johns Hopkins University Press.

Waddington, C. (1977) *Tools for Thought*. Frogmore: Paladin.

Waldrop, M. (1993) *Complexity: The Emerging Science at the Edge of Order and Chaos*. London: Viking.

Wallerstein, I. (1996) *Open the Social Sciences: Report of the Gulbenkian Commission on the Restructuring of the Social Sciences*. Stanford, CA: Stanford University Press.

Witt, U. (1999) 'Bioeconomics as economics from a Darwinian perspective' *Journal of Bioeconomics* 1: 19–34.

Witt, U. (2003) *The Evolving Economy: Essays on the Evolutionary Approach to Economics.* Cheltenham: Edward Elgar.

Zolo, N. (1992) 'The epistemological status of the theory of autopiesis and its application to the social sciences', in Febbrajo, A. and Teubner, G. (eds) *State, Law, and Economy as Autopoietic Systems: Regulation and Autonomy in a New Perspective.* Milan: Giuffré, 67–124.

Governance and Planning: A Pragmatic Approach[1]

Niraj Verma

Good governance has emerged from developing country contexts to become part of the Western policy lexicon. For developing countries it implied the rule of law, decentralization and the reduction of corruption, often at the behest of international donor agencies.[2] In the advanced capitalist contexts of the West, it has come to mean the sound and effective 'management of … rules and practices affecting policy making' (Kjaer 2004: 188). Given that the rules and practices can be formal or informal, restricted or widespread, within or outside government, a key task of good governance consists of furthering trust, community and accountability by vigorous and sustained interaction of state and civil society (Cohen 1989; Dryzek 2000; Elster 1998).

Such a broad construction of good governance raises questions about what exactly this discourse brings to urban planning. A concern for the relationship of citizens with each other and with government is hardly a novel idea for planners. Nor are issues of trust and accountability new to planning theory (Flyvbjerg 1998; Healey 2007; Raja and Verma 2009). There is, however, a difference between a planning orientation and that of related fields. Public policy and political science, for instance, emphasize the separation of authority at federal, state or local levels and this is a key context for their scholarship. Planning, on the other hand, is concerned with how all policies, programs and initiatives, come together and get enacted at the local level. This local orientation is not so much a preference for a geographical scale as it is a bias towards implementation and action.[3] Given this context, we might ask: is the idea of good

---

1 A previous version of this chapter was presented at the Conceptual Challenges for Planning Theory Mini-Conference, 9–11 January 2008, Newcastle University (UK). I am grateful to conference participants for their comments.

2 For an insightful and somewhat contrarian account, see Tendler (1997).

3 An American planner who deals with housing must simultaneously juggle HUD policies (federal) and property taxes (state) even as she is engaged in sorting issues in city hall (local). This sentiment is similar to the pithy 'all politics is local' attributed to former US House Speaker, Tip O'Neil.

governance simply a restatement of the best traditions of planning? Or, given the much greater connectivity and convergence of geographical scales – the network society and the flat world are examples – does the demand of good governance pose fundamental challenges for planning?

There is no handy answer to either question. Although planning's shared responsibility to create and protect 'deliberating enclaves' (Sunstein 2001) is hardly arguable, there is concern that geographical and other changes make such a goal problematic. Can we have genuine interaction over disparate networks? Is communicative action a realistic agenda in an interspersed world? Allow me to make it a bit more concrete with an example.

Suburbanization, for instance, has separated communities of work from communities of home, often drawing wedges between them. Similarly, globalization has separated actions and their consequences over multiple time zones making local planning as we know it virtually impossible. But, while this is happening the power of technological resources at our command, particularly the internet, has increased dramatically. Recent surveys by the Pew Charitable Trusts (Estabrook et al. 2007) found, for example, that 77 per cent of Americans have internet access. Similar numbers are found in Europe. The paradox of growing separation of communities and growing connectivity through technology behooves us to inquire into the meaning and significance of genuine discourse, community and trust between people and to assess its potential and its vulnerabilities.

In a stance that may seem different from how governance is typically seen, I will argue that good governance represents a softening of attitudes towards key planning tasks. It is a difference in emphasis, not a new agenda. This softening can be understood by its contrast to a command and control form of government and administration. If certitude of knowledge, clarity and decisiveness characterized the command and control paradigm, good governance espouses a deliberate precariousness and a willingness to entertain competing perspectives. A key point of this chapter is to defend this interpretation of good governance for urban planning.

At the same time I will explore the challenges that this context of good governance raises for the very idea of local planning. How does a planner – and hence planning – maintain their identity and independence in the technologically networked world? And in such a world how does planning foster genuine discussion over salient issues?

My exploration of these issues will be in the form of a dialectical interplay of two ideas, both of which position new technologies, such as the internet, in relation to civil society. The burgeoning writings on e-governance constitute one of these ideas while the sociology of the 'network society' is the other. Although still intellectually sparse, the e-governance literature is driven by a general optimism that the spatial divide can be overcome by e-technologies, such as internet and communication technologies or ICT (Docter and Dutton 1998; O'Looney 2002). The optimism implies, for instance, that city hall in the age of information can go electronic and presumably with suitable technological help it might even make up for the lost conviviality of spatial connectedness.

The second idea, the network society, can also be read as privileging ICT but it does so in a different way. In *The Power of Identity* (1997), one of three volumes in his trilogy, Castells (1997) shows that marginalized groups use ICT to maintain links between themselves and to coalesce around questions of identity. As a result ICT becomes a way for these groups to preserve their insularity leading to what Castells calls 'new social movements'.

Using 'sentiments' and 'reasons', two ideas at the cornerstone of the philosophy of William James, I will argue that the possibility of good governance in an age of internet and the network society rests on the ability to usefully combine reasons and sentiments. That is to say, can we successfully integrate the rational mind with the passionate one? In my assessment, while e-governance is concerned with rationality and instrumentality, it is not particularly about sentiment and so, left to itself, it is unlikely to build the kinds of enclaves that deliberative democracy demands. New social movements, on the other hand, promote enclaves, even over dispersed networks, by imbuing passion in new and unusual ways. So, what is one to do? My conclusions are decidedly open-ended in that I will argue that we require a more sophisticated understanding of public participation where sentiments and reasons act in concert. At the same time I will also suggest that the philosophy of William James provides a useful way of thinking about these issues.

Good Governance and Urban Planning

Compared to public administration and political science the field of urban planning is a late entrant to discussions on governance. Yet, many core ideas in contemporary urban planning, including some of long standing, are better understood as part of the discourse of governance than of any other previous category of planning or planning theory. The list of these ideas is fairly extensive and includes the ideas of collaboration, negotiation, civil society, communicative action, gendering, truth, participation and others. As a result, unlike public administration or public policy, where 'governance' derives its meaning by contrast to a single dominant idea of 'government' (Kettl 2000), in planning the term is best understood by contrast to a variety of concepts, giving it richer and more varied meaning.

In other words, while political scientists and other social scientists see governance as primarily a departure from government, for planners this is only one aspect of its meaning. This is because despite Tugwell's characterization of planning (Friedman 1987: 106) as a '*superpolitical* activity' or as 'The Fourth Power of Government', planning is not the monolith agent of the state in the way that public administrators or public policy scholars view their professional domain.[4] In general the discourse on governance within planning implies a paradigm rather than a single idea. It implies a softening of approach in recognition of the special

---

4   On this see Richard Peiser's 'Who plans America? Planners or Developers?' *Journal of the American Planning Association* Autumn 1990: 496–503.

nature of planning problems, what Rittel and Webber (1973) characterized early in the planning literature as 'wicked problems'.

We see this softening in a variety of ways. Social concerns are more likely to be approached in studies of social capital than through the more hard-line social movements. Similarly, command and control in all sectors – not just government – have given way to collaboration and negotiation. Advocacy, while still a key concern for planners, is less a stand-alone conversation than it is a concern for wider civil society. Table 14.1 summarizes some of these examples to show that governance in planning has meant a softer, gentler and more realistic notion of planning than before. The contrast is shown as between command and control and governance paradigms.

Table 14.1   Governance and its contrasting paradigm

COMMAND AND CONTROL	GOVERNANCE
Advocacy	Civil society
Conservation	Sustainable development
Regulation	Collaboration
Competition	Cooperation
Carrying capacity/ limits to growth	Growth management/smart growth
Ghetto and slums	Enclaves and informal sector
Hierarchies	Networks
Client	Citizen planner

This move is particularly relevant because even the dominant conversations in planning and the practice of planning can no longer be organized around the tension between government and market (Verma 1995). Of particular note is the emergence of what we might call the 'citizen planner' replacing the notion of public and clients. In other words the planning challenge in a governance paradigm is not just to deal with multiple constituencies or multiple publics each with a different set of preferences. It is not just to have a customer service attitude towards its clients or to increase efficiency of service delivery for its constituents. Rather, there is an epistemic need to see our constituents as citizen planners that deserve respect for their individual expertise.

Horst Rittel (1984) anticipated this kind of planning several years ago when he argued for the 'symmetry of ignorance' as the true relation between planners and planned. The symmetry of ignorance recognizes that each stakeholder of the planning enterprise commands some knowledge (expertise) and confesses lack of knowledge (ignorance) about some aspects of the planning enterprise. This distribution of knowledge and ignorance among stakeholders is, however, distributed in relatively unknown and sometimes unknowable ways. From this perspective, the idea of the citizen planner reinforces the sentiment behind the symmetry of ignorance and implies a learning model of planning.

Clearly the meaning of good governance changes under such a paradigm. In the public administration and related literatures several lists compete for what exactly constitutes good governance. One example from the Commission of the European Communities (2001: 10) lists five principles: openness, participation, accountability, effectiveness and coherence. Another example comes from Rod Rhodes (2000) who identifies seven meanings of governance but all seven take the contrast for governance to be government. The contrast illustrates that in planning instead of simply being a move away from government, a governance paradigm in planning represents a softer approach that recognizes the difficulties of its subject-matter. Seen thus, such a paradigm is an ethos rather than a set of attributes and the ethos demands greater sensitivity and engagement with the context of planning.

Urban Planning Challenges to Good Governance

The more fine grained and nuanced the demand on governance the less likely that stock solutions will have currency. In a regulatory or command and control approach it is possible to rely on law-like statements that demarcate what is permissible from what is not. Even when the regulations are complex, clever arrangement or brute force can reduce this complexity to a larger number of simple rules.[5] But, when the charge is to further an ethos that results in trust, community and genuine engagement, the resulting complexities are not reducible.[6] Ideas such as trust and engagement are purposeful categories and are cheapened or destroyed once we equate them with strategies and rules. In Habermasian terms they are of the *lifeworld* whereas strategies and rules derive from the *system*. In the context of public participation or civic engagement, we might say that tokenism results when the *lifeworld* colonizes the system.

Urban planning's response to increasing trust, furthering conviviality, and cultivating community is to invest in 'place', milieu, or other versions of the modern agora. The sentiment takes many forms. Ed Blakely's study of gated communities with its thesis that social contract cannot sustain without social contact (Blakely and Snyder 1997) is one example. Other examples come from urban designers. Stephen Carr and Kevin Lynch presaged a similar sentiment almost 50 years ago in arguing that barriers in the city prevent genuine learning:

---

5   Elsewhere (Verma 1998: 21–22) I have called this structural complexity or complexity of arrangement and contrasted it with teleological complexity.

6   Contrast, for instance, Hillier's (2009) sophisticated treatment of complexity in this volume with the simplicities of a command and control perspective.

> *Too often the city fences us away from other kinds of people. By the scale, impersonality and even hostility of its places and institutions, the city tends to discourage independence of action and to encourage fear and feelings of powerlessness. The white mother and child in the suburb are kept from new experiences about as effectively as their black counterparts in a ghetto housing project. (Carr and Lynch 1968: 1278)*

Indeed, Carr and Lynch (p. 1279) connected this to identity: 'the urban environment ... is a medium for transmitting the form and content of contemporary society, a territory to be explored, and a setting for the testing of identity'.

In other words if environmental determinism represents the pathology of urban design scholarship it does not follow that trust and community are fully volitional categories either. Robert Putnam's (2000) charge that civic engagement needs both 'bonding' and 'bridging' social capital is incomplete without including the vibrant urban communities described by Jane Jacobs (1961) or without factoring in the inter-generational tensions documented by Myers (2007) or the identity politics described by Castells (1997).

This helps to further clarify the differences between good governance in public administration or political science from that in planning. In the former, the good governance demand of greater trust, transparency and accountability is largely a matter of an agent's volition, i.e., an agent can make right or wrong choices in the face of incentives. So, part of the focus in this literature is in the structuring of incentives so that an agent can overcome 'moral hazard' and choose the right option. The idea of ethical behaviour embedded within this scenario is morally demanding but only weakly linked to cognition. The role of the mind in these cases is to simply understand that given the alignment of incentives it is not rational to give in to the temptation of deception, graft, corruption or cover-up. But, this is problematic: a smarter mind than one presumed in the design of incentives might figure out how to play the incentives and game the system. Or, a risk-taking mind might deliberately disregard the penalties and bias on the side of temptation.

While this notion of good governance is relevant, urban planning's accent on milieu and community addresses a different problem. Rather than the corrective behaviour associated with the design of incentives, good governance in planning implies a learning model whereby the attempts to change perception and preference are more fundamental and the links between the moral and cognitive are intertwined at every level, visible only at the micro-structure of planning and not as grand sequential separations between incentive, cognition, and moral choice.

Planning Theory, Deliberation and Spatial Transformation

Although deliberation is a staple of planning theory, with few exceptions (Healey 1999, 2005; Gualini 2005), its recent theorizing has glossed over the context of spatial transformation and is not connected with place. At the same time although there are general calls for integration of the city within planning, e.g., Fainstein

2005, there is only modest link to bringing about 'spatial consciousness' (Healey 2005: 148) through discourse and deliberation. A curious anomaly in this is Mel Webber's theorizing (1963), where he wrote about the non-place urban realm that ultimately would lead to 'community without propinquity'. Whether contemporary technological innovations are equipped to do this is the continuing question of the rest of the paper.

E-Governance and Interest without Passion

In a book that became a classic, Albert Hirschman (1977) revisited a question already made famous by Max Weber: how did the once disdained pursuit of self-interest, including money-making and even greed, that is associated with market capitalism, transform to a virtue? Although the origin of modern capitalism is not relevant to my argument, Hirschman's overall idea is helpful. First, is the suggestion that money-making offered a 'countervailing passion' to replace other more destructive passions, such as those arising from honour, ambition and the lust for power and sex. Second, the insight that countervailing passion becomes 'interest' which starts appearing reasonable and rational as action becomes more predictable.

In other words, it takes passion – not reason – to counter a more destructive passion and what later might appear as reason is a countervailing passion that is institutionalized into interest. Indeed, this shows the continuity of reason and passion and poses a challenge to any theory that strongly separates them.

Suppose we replace 'economic interests' with 'technology' in Hirschmann's thesis? This is the strategy adopted by the distinguished socialist, Robert Wuthnow, who presages the importance of Hirschman's work to the study of the impact of technology:

> ... technology and the new class of experts and technicians it creates are now championed as a check on the arbitrary power of the bourgeoisie ... The manner in which scientific and technological discoveries are made is often proclaimed to be sufficiently complex to preclude arbitrary manipulation by terrorists, demagogues, and other men of passion. Technology, engineering, systems analysis, data processing – are all advanced in the name of predictability and planning, and are frequently depicted as genuine improvements over the haphazard conditions of the open market. (Wuthnow 1979: 430)

Can technology as embodied in e-governance succeed in containing the power of bureaucracy? If the lessons from Hirschmann are any indication, without first serving as a 'countervailing passion' the prospects for such a result seem dim and actual developments in e-governance bear this out. As illustration, and with some risk for oversimplification of an involved literature, consider three geographically distributed examples of e-governance. The North American – and primarily US based – discourse is influenced by then Vice President Al Gore's *National*

Table 14.2   Major issues in e-governance

Countries/ Regions	Context	Major Issue/ Concern	Authors/ Agencies (examples)
1. North America	National performance review	Contracting out 'Hollow State'	Milward and Provan; Kettl, OMB, others
2. Developing Countries	Democratization, devolution	Constitution writing, polling systems, corruption	World Bank
3. Europe	Expansion of the European Union[a]	Coordination, bureaucracy, efficiency of government	European Commission

Note: [a]In other contexts, the EU discussion is more like the North American in its efforts to increase efficiency.

Performance Review (NPR), with its focus on making government look and operate more like business. This leads to an image of government that is more client-based (with subsequent concerns about the meaning of citizenship). But ultimately this gets morphed into cross-sectoral collaboration and resultant 'contracting out' of some core activities of government to the private sector. In turn this raises concerns about the hollow state (Milward and Provan 2000), a significant but unsurprising conclusion given that the firm in the corporate world has also been described as a 'nexus of treaties' (Aoki et al. 1990).

In international development and particularly in developing countries, e-governance focuses on property rights, the rule of law and reduction of corruption as the major concerns. Here good governance takes the form of capacity building, signifying a shift in World Bank and other donor aid from project support to investment in people. Of course, the political-economy of this is problematic. To take one argument, in a globalizing world built capacity rarely stays in place without system-wide improvements to retain it. This is the traditional brain-drain of talent and skill from developing to developed countries.

While NPR evoked much interest in streamlining government, assisted no doubt by the market-based reforms of the Thatcher and then Blair governments in the UK, in the past decade the European agenda of e-governance has reflected the European Union's preoccupation with expansion. This has given e-governance a dual image. At times it resembles the North American and UK-based discourse on productivity and efficiency but at other times like it moves towards the discourse on institutional reforms, such as concerns of the rule of law and reduction in corruption.

By seeing its agenda as going beyond government, e-governance has unwittingly privileged government in its discourse. This has the effect of restricting e-governance to doing more efficiently the tasks customarily handled by government. So, electronic polling replaces paper ballots; web-based Government to Business contracting (G to B) brings efficiency in procurement, and quick and easy connections between city hall and citizens (clients or customers) become possible. While these may bring greater efficiency in terms of faster responses, multi-way rather than only two-way communication, and far greater production volumes than ever previously possible, they lack the passion that genuine discourse in civil society demands.

Passion and the Network Society

Contrast the discussion on e-governance to that of 'deliberative democracy' (Elster 1998), multiculturalism (Taylor 1994), and calls for a sustained commitment to reason-giving (Sunstein 2001), and we see the missing passion in e-governance. The 'network society' (Castells 1996) comes much closer to capturing the passions of an ICT revolution. It does so by coalescing around issues of identity. Elsewhere (Verma and Shin 2004), I have shown the connections between Castells' formulation of the network society and Habermasian communication action. Here I want to briefly revisit some key points regarding the network society, taking into account Hirschman's distinction of passion and interest.

A key aspect of the network society is in how it derives its legitimacy. Castells tells us that the interconnected nature of the network society brings about a tension between the Self and the Net. If we do a bicameral division of self as inward and net as external, a key lesson from Castells' work is that the external forces – the net – threaten to take over control of the Self by taking away its ability to be self-reflexive. This is best explained by the aid of an example. Take the case of globalization, a key manifestation of the network society.

As a result of globalization, or at the least influenced by it, we see relative homogenization of preferences. I-pods and cell phones are just as popular in India, Africa and Europe as they are in the United States. At some level, however, these preferences can almost be seen as creations of technology. The technologies not only influence availability, clever marketing and advertising, including images on television and the internet, create demand where none existed. In such cases, philosophers of technology tell us, it is no longer useful to see technology as a means; it is an end.

The transformation is fundamental and takes place at the level of meaning and affects the identity of the user of the technology. For example, cell phones issued to corporate employees likely create expectations of access beyond office-hours. Facebook and social networking sites redefine the meaning of privacy.

Castells' focus is on the process of this change. Drawing on Giddens (1991), Castells identifies three identities that both influence the process and become its ingredients. Legitimizing identity is traditionally the preserve of the nation-state. Resistance identity counters the dominant identity and assists in the self-identification of members. Finally, project identity ushers in a phase when dissent is visible, proactive and even accepted. While the categories and arguments are much more involved than can be explained here, suffice it to say that a major contribution of Castells' work is to show that in the network society the transformation of

407

resistance to project identity does not go through the traditional legitimating stage of engagement with the nation-state. Rather, legitimacy comes from an expansion of the resistance until it becomes a project.

This characteristic of the network society is what makes it different from anything that preceded it. In the civil rights movement or the labour movement, for instance, to gain acceptability the movements first gained political legitimacy by conducting marches in the public domain. Such public displays were essential in the transformation of these movements from outlying resistance to mainstream project. By contrast, the 'new social movements' seek no such public approbation. Their 'method' is to retain internal connectivity within the network society while growing the resistance. The sheer size of the resistance finally converts it to project. Castells' examples are the gay and lesbian movement or the environmental movement. The passion that drives these movements is evident in their use of ICT and the network society. Their insularity from the mainstream is their strength because of their connectedness on a widespread global scale. This 'countervailing passion' finally transforms a limited resistance to a major political force. Its sheer size and importance transform it to a project and an interest.

Combining Passions and Reasons

The American philosopher, William James, was unlike most of his contemporaries. A professor of psychology at Harvard, James was a practising medical doctor with a specialization in psychiatry. Along with the mathematician, Charles Peirce, James was a leader of the movement that we now know as American pragmatism. Perhaps because of his background, James' pragmatism was directed against analytic philosophy's penchant to engage in seemingly endless puzzles that were intellectually interesting but practically worthless.

In planning we know this tension as that between 'rigor and relevance' (Schön 1963; Verma 1998). Unlike some discussions in planning that castigate theory for its inaccessibility, James and his colleagues took analytic philosophy to task for its philosophical and theoretical simple-mindedness. Philosophy wasn't simply abstruse or inaccessible; it was dilettantish and impoverished. James was no 'midwife' who sought to apply philosophical knowledge to concrete problems.[7] Nor was he constructing a dumbed-down 'philosophy for dummies', to use a metaphor from a popular series of how-to books. Rather he saw analytic philosophy's aloofness as a consequence of its preference to solve easy, make-believe puzzles rather than difficult but real problems, and he wanted to challenge this and to suggest an alternate way of thinking about practical problems.

I am making this sojourn into Jamesian philosophy not just to emphasize James' unusual position but to show how James' integration of sentiment and reason is

---

7   Planning theorists will recognize the 'midwife' reference from William Baer's (1977) paper with the term in its title.

unusual among philosophers of his time. The sentiment of rationality is powerful because it turns conventional meanings of rationality on its head. Unlike many others who took to heart the Weberian description of rationality as the absence of 'drives, impulses, wishes and feelings', James thought that such a rationality, even if possible, would be blind. As Gerald Myers, no admirer of James, writes in his commentary of James, whom he calls 'one of the last major introspective psychologists prior to the behaviorist take-over':

> James' statement is significant for revealing how he, like countless others, worried about introspections' leading to morbidity, to self-preoccupation resulting in depression ... The problem with heeding your despair is not that you will change it but that you will prolong it and to your distress. (Myers 1997: 11)

Like other elements of James' philosophy 'blindness' is fundamental in that it influences the truth in each of us. the way And in *The Will to Believe*, one of his best known collection of essays (and where *The Sentiment of Rationality* was reprinted), James carries this further in describing rationality as something that we should 'sense', just as we do other emotions and even objects. There has been considerable debate in the philosophical literature surrounding James' essay.[8] While we will not go into this here, suffice it to say that while James' ideas of rationality changed as his empiricism became more developed in all cases the essential integration between logic and psychology, preparedness and truth, and sentiment and reason is fundamental to his theorizing.

One way of thinking of the integration of passion and reason from the perspective of our discussion on governance is to go to James' description of two impulses in each of us. On one hand, we have a passion for parsimony and simplification of our concepts whereby we take away all aspects that we regard as non-essential. On the other, we have a passion to get acquainted with the particulars. Elsewhere I have argued (Verma 1998) that James' strategy to deal with this was one of abstract classification along with a parallel strategy that admits uncertainty and precariousness in our tasks. While we might consider the first to be a rational sentiment we must also recognize that every such action leaves unsaid many other sentiments. This latter arises out of the admission of precariousness. James' philosophy becomes relevant for governance because what is said and what is unsaid is systematic, not random and not capricious. When the passions that prove so essential to the network society are discounted in favour of the machines of e-governance, a sanitized discourse results where governance has only an instrumental face.

For governance to be inclusive and to have a commitment to reason-giving demands not just a fair and balanced discourse but one which brings in those systematically marginalized sentiments and passions into deliberate play. There are

---

8   See, for example, essays by David Lamberth, Hilary Putnam and James Conant in Putnam (1997) for a flavour of how James' work differed even from the other pragmatists.

several examples when planners have done this. Advocacy planning is premised on the knowledge of systematic inequalities and attempts to right wrongs. Ideas like story-telling try to bring in sentiments that are systematically excluded. I have called this approach of righting wrongs as the new comprehensiveness (Verma 1998: 45). The dialectic between e-governance and the network society suggests that just by becoming electronic and using ICT city hall is unlikely to be able to overcome the loss of intimacy and conviviality that contemporary cities need and demand. Public participation using ICT may already have a 'project identity'. But, it should first step outside this comfort-zone of a project identity if it is to meaningfully engage the passions of its citizen planners. Without it, I suspect we will have more and newer forms of tokenism, except that this time the tokenism will be over electronic and distributed networks.

References

Baer, W.C. (1977) 'Urban planners: doctors or midwives?' *Public Administration Review* 37(6): 671–78.

Blakely, E. and Snyder, M. (1997) *Fortress America: Gated Communities in the United States*. Washington, DC: Brookings Institution Press.

Carr, S. and Lynch, K. (1968) 'Where learning happens' *Daedalus* 97(4): 1277–291.

Castells, M. (1996) *The Rise of the Network Society*. Oxford: Blackwell.

Castells, M. (1997) *The Power of Identity*. Oxford: Blackwell.

Cohen, J. (1989) 'Deliberative democracy and democratic legitimacy', in Hamlin, A. and Pettit, P. (eds) *The Good Polity*. Oxford: Blackwell, 17–34.

Commission of the European Communities (2001) 'European Governance: A White Paper' Brussels, 25 July.

Docter, S. and Dutton, W.H. (1998) 'The first amendment online: Santa Monica's public electronic network', in Tsagarousianou, R., Tambini, D., and Bryan, C. (eds) *Cyberdemocracy: Technology, Cities, and Civic Networks*. London: Routledge, 125–51.

Dryzek, J. (2000) *Deliberative Democracy and Beyond: Liberals, Critics, and Contestations*. Oxford: Oxford University Press.

Elster, Jon (ed.) (1998) *Deliberative Democracy*. Cambridge: Cambridge University Press.

Estabrook, L., Witt, E., and Rainie, L. (2007) 'Information searches that solve problems' Pew Internet and Life Project, 20 December.

Fainstein, S. (2005) 'Planning theory and the city' *Journal of Planning Education and Research* 25: 121–30.

Feigenbaum, H., Hening J., and Hammett, C. (1998) *Shrinking the State: The Political Underpinnings of Privatization*. Cambridge, MA: Cambridge University Press.

Flyvbjerg, B. (1998) *Rationality and Power: Democracy in Practice, Morality and Society*. Chicago, IL and London: University of Chicago Press.

Friedmann, J. (1987) *Planning in the Public Domain: From Knowledge to Action.* Princeton, NJ: Princeton University Press.

Giddens, A. (1991) *Modernity and Self-Identity: Self and Society in the Late Modern Age.* Cambridge: Polity Press.

Gualini, E. (2005) 'Reconnecting space, place, and institutions: inquiring into local governance capacity in urban and regional research', in Albrechts, L. and Mandelbaum, S. (eds) *The Network Society: A New Context for Planning.* London: Routledge, 284–306.

Healey, P. (1999) 'Institutional analysis, communicative planning, and shaping places', *Journal of Planning Education and Research* 19(2): 111–21.

Healey, P. (2005) 'Network complexity and the imaginative power of strategic spatial planning' in Albrechts, L. and Mandelbaum, S. (eds) *The Network Society: A New Context for Planning.* London: Routledge, 146–60.

Healey, P. (2007) 'The new institutionalism and the transformative goals of planning', in Verma, N. (ed.) *Institutions and Planning.* Oxford: Elsevier, 61–87.

Hillier, J. (2009) 'Poststructural Complexity: an ocean of theoretical and practice stories', in this volume.

Hirschman, A. (1997) *The Passion and the Interest.* Princeton: Princeton University Press.

Jacobs, J. (1961) *The Death and Life of Great American Cities.* New York: Random House.

Kelman, S. (2002) 'Strategic contracting management' in Donahue, J.D. and Nye Jr., J.S. (eds) *Market-Based Governance.* Washington, DC: Brookings Institution, 88–102.

Kettl, D.F. (2000) 'The transformation of governance: globalization, devolution, and the role of government' *Public Administration Review* 60 (6): 488–97.

Kjaer, A.M. (2004) *Governance.* Cambridge and Malden MA: Polity, introduction.

Milward, H.B. and Provan, K.G. (2000) 'Governing the Hollow State', *Journal of Public Administration Research and Theory* 10(2): 359–79.

Myers, D. (2007) *Immigrants and Boomers: Forging a New Social Contract for the Future of America.* New York: Russell Sage.

Myers, G. (1997) 'Pragmatism and introspective psychology' in Putnam, R.A. (ed.) *The Cambridge Companion to William James.* Cambridge: Cambridge University Press.

O'Looney, J.A. (2002) *Wiring Governments: Challenges and Possibilities for Public Managers.* Westport, CT: Quorum Books.

Peiser, R. (1996) 'Who plans America: planners or developers?' *Journal of the American Planning Association*, Autumn 1990: 496–503; reprinted in Stein, J. (ed.) *Classic Readings in Real Estate and Development.* Washington, DC: ULI.

Pew Internet and American Life Project (2007) 'Home broadband adoption 2007' (John Horrigan and Aaron Smith data memo June 2007). http://www.pewinternet. org/pdfs/PIP_Broadband%202007.pdf (Accessed October–December 2007).

Putnam, R.D. 2000. *Bowling Alone: The Collapse and Revival of American Community.* New York: Simon & Schuster.

Raja, S. and Verma, N. (2009) 'Got perspective? A theoretical view of fiscal impact analysis', working paper, University at Buffalo, New York.

Rhodes, R.A.W. (2000) 'Governance and Public Administration', in Pierre, J. (ed.) *Debating Governance: Authority, Steering, and Democracy*. Oxford: Oxford University Press, 54–90.

Rittel, H. and Webber, M.M. (1973) 'Dilemmas in a general theory of planning' *Policy Sciences* 4: 155–69.

Rittel, H. (1984) 'Second-generation design methods', in Cross, N. (ed.) *Developments in Design Methodology*. New York: John Wiley, 317–27.

Schön, D. (1963) *Displacement of Concepts*. London: Tavistock.

Sunstein, C. (2001) *Designing Democracy: What Constitutions Do*. Oxford: Oxford University Press.

Taylor, C. (1994) *Multiculturalism* (edited and introduced by Amy Gutman). Princeton, NJ: Princeton University Press.

Tendler, J. (1997) *Good Government in the Tropics*. Baltimore: Johns Hopkins University Press.

Verma, N. (1995) 'What is planning practice? The search for suitable categories' *Journal of Planning Education and Research* 14: 178–82.

Verma, N. (1998) *Similarities, Connections, and Systems: The Search for a New Rationality for Management and Planning*. Lanham, MD: Lexington Books.

Verma, N. (2007) 'Institutions and planning: an analogical inquiry', in Verma, N. (ed.) *Institutions and Planning*. Oxford: Elsevier.

Verma, N. and Shin, H. (2004) 'Communicative action and the network society: a pragmatic marriage?' *Journal of Planning Education and Research* 24: 131–40. Reprinted in Albrechts, L. and Mandelbaum, S (eds) *The Network Society: A New Context for Planning*. London: Routledge, 9–23.

Webber, M.M. (1963) 'Order in diversity: community without propinquity' in Wingo, L. (ed.) *Cities and Space*. Baltimore: Johns Hopkins University Press, 25–54.

Wuthnow, R. (1979) Review: Legitimating the Capitalist World Order' *The American Journal of Sociology* 85(3): 424–30.

Coping with the Irreducible Uncertainties of Planning: An Evolutionary Approach

Luca Bertolini

The Challenges of Irreducible Uncertainty

The question of how to shape the future is perhaps the one that most distinguishes planning as an activity. Myers (2001: 366) remarks for instance that, '[t]he future is the only topic that other professions have ceded to planners as relatively uncontested turf'. However, the ground of identification which the future provides to planners is not, and cannot be a firm one, as the future is by definition uncertain. Myers (2001: 365) also observes that, '[t]wo difficulties constrain planners' role in shaping the future. First, the future consequences of planning actions are not knowable with much certainty … Second, … decisions about the future require agreement among a great many stakeholders'. Finding ways of dealing with such fundamental uncertainty and disagreement is a, if not *the*, central task facing planners.

In a classic contribution to planning theory, Christensen (1985) characterized the challenge as that of coping with disagreement on planning goals (what?) and means, or what she terms 'technologies'[1] (how?). When we agree on both goals and means planning is essentially a matter of 'programming'. When we agree on the means but not the goals, it is a matter of 'bargaining'; when we agree on the goals but not the means, one of 'experimentation'. When we disagree on both means and goals there is 'chaos', and we need to find ways of somehow structuring the problem in order to move towards or into one of the other, more tractable situations (see Figure 15.1).

This last case is especially intriguing. Such 'chaos' seems increasingly common in contemporary, deeply contested governance settings (see Hillier's Introduction to Part 3 of this volume). At the same time, it seems increasingly less clear how, if at

---

1   The term 'technology' is used here in the broad sense of 'means to achieve goals'. In this respect a transportation system is a technology, as are also a parking regime, or a marketing campaign. In the rest of the chapter I will use the two terms interchangeably.

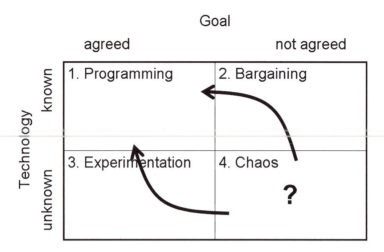

Figure 15.1 Coping with uncertainty in planning

Source: Christensen 1985.

all, we could 'move out' of chaos. For example – all sustainable urban development rhetoric notwithstanding – will 'bargaining' ever make us finally agree on whether the environment, society or the economy should take priority in urban development? Will 'experimentation' ever make us finally agree on how to best preserve the environment, strengthen society or enhance the economy in a city? And if agreement is possible, should we also pursue it, or should we rather cultivate a pluralistic variety of views on what goals to pursue and what means to employ? How then to cope with the all too common situations, where uncertainty and disagreement about planning goals and means appear irreducible, or even desirable?

In another, earlier, classic contribution to planning theory, Rittel and Webber (1973) had already made their point in this respect. For them, all but the most trivial planning problems were 'wicked' (Christensen would say 'chaotic'), 'for they defy efforts to delineate their boundaries and to identify their causes, and thus to expose their problematic nature' (p. 167). While most of their paper is devoted to discussing why uncertainty and disagreement about planning goals and means are irreducible, Rittel and Webber also suggest a possible approach for coping with this. Such an approach 'should be based on a model of planning as an argumentative process in the course of which an image of the problem and of the solutions emerges gradually among participants, as a product of incessant judgment, subjected to critical argument' (p. 162).

The idea of planning as a participatory, argumentative process has since, of course, become a dominant paradigm in at least planning theory (see the chapters by Sager and Versteeg and Hajer, this volume). In Rittel and Webber's suggestion there is, however, more than just a plea for more participation (as in advocacy planning) or a more communicative rationality (as in collaborative planning). They also indicate what the *purpose* of participation and communication should be ('letting an image of the problem and of the solutions gradually emerge among participants'), and *how* this could be achieved ('through incessant judgment, subjected to critical argument'). Rittel and Weber did not go much further than evocative statements. However, I believe that further exploring such thoughts could help us better understand how we could cope with the ever more 'chaotic' and 'wicked' nature of contemporary planning problems, and provide more articulation to the notion that planning should be participatory and communicative. In order to do this, in this chapter I will identify the approach sketched by Rittel and Webber as evolutionary and akin to emerging characterizations of design processes. I will then articulate this idea by means of a reformulation of Christensen's typology of planning challenges, and illustrate its workings through one concrete example. Finally, I will point at some implications of the argument for future efforts in planning theory development.

The Planning Process as a Design Process; the Design Process as an Evolutionary Process

While Rittel and Webber evoke, rather than fully articulate, their model of planning, their views strongly resonate with emerging insights into how designers go about with their work (Cross 2007). Designers of new products are, by definition, confronted with elusive problems and solutions. While there might be agreement about what are less or more successful design products, at least in term of their appreciation by users, it is much less clear how designers achieve such results. To address this issue, detailed empirical studies of real-world design processes have been carried out in recent years and some of the defining features of these processes have been pinpointed. Crucially, and similarly to what Rittel and Webber (1973) hypothesized, design problems and solutions are identified *jointly* rather than *sequentially* in the design process. Design processes are aimed at finding internally and context consistent *problem-solution combinations*, not solutions for previously defined problems. The definition of problems and solutions is kept fluid until such combinations have been found. 'Creative leaps' are all about finding 'bridges' between problems and solutions that allow such combinations. In the words of Cross:

> *During the design process, partial models of the problem and solution are constructed side-by-side, as it were. But the crucial factor, the 'creative leap', is the bridging of these two partial models by the articulation of a concept … which enables the partial models to be mapped onto each other. (Cross 2007: 78)*

415

Valkenburg and Dorst (1998) have studied this dynamic in the work of industrial design teams. Their framework of analysis is inspired by Schön's (1983) characterization of design as reflection-in-action and applied to detailed visual and audio records of design processes. According to Valkenburg and Dorst designer teams appear to be engaged in a 'reflective conversation with the situation', which iteratively entails '*naming* the relevant factors in the situation, *framing* a problem in a certain way, *making moves* toward a solution and [*reflecting* on] these moves' (1998: 251, emphasis added). Different rounds and levels of feedback spurred by continuous reflection are at the essence of the process. Reflection can lead to new moves towards a solution, but also to new framing of the problem or naming. In particular, Valkenburg and Dorst find evidence that breakthroughs in the design process tend to occur when design teams change frames, that is, when problems are defined in new ways (analogous to the 'bridges' mentioned by Cross).

The above characterization of design seems also a fruitful characterization of planning. There is however, an important difference between the two. Problems in industrial design, but also in architecture or engineering, tend to be more limited in terms of the numbers and diversity of those involved, the magnitude of potential repercussions on society, and their spatial and temporal horizons. In planning, 'reflection in action', needs to engage many more and more diverse actors, and address many more levels of impacts and scales. However, and this is the essence of the argument here, in order to successfully tackle its 'chaotic' and 'wicked' problems planning should also be a process of 'reflection in action', and thus one iteratively linking naming situations, framing problems, moving towards solutions and reflecting on each of these, in order to identify consistent problem-solutions combinations amenable to collective action. However, even implementing these will not lead the process to a termination, as the repercussions of action in a changing societal context will inevitably and continuously generate the need for new rounds of naming, framing, moving and reflecting.

The design process, as described by Valkenburg and Dorst, closely resembles an evolutionary process of *variation* (of moves, frames and names) and *selection* (through reflection). The crucial difference with biological evolution is that the process engages not so much, and certainly not only, material entities, but rather immaterial concepts and ideas. It is as much an evolution in the understanding of the situation as it is an evolution in the situation itself, both generating the other (it is thus *co*-evolution). The development pattern is reminiscent of that of autopoiesis, an essential characteristic of living organisms: 'autopoiesis, or self-making, is a network pattern in which the function of each component is to participate in the production or transformation of other components in the network. In this way, the network continually makes itself. It is produced by its components and in turn produces those components' (Capra 1996: 158; see also 163–4).

How to further articulate this evolutionary process in a way that accounts for the more unbounded nature of planning activities relative to design activities? An attempt is made in the following section, by means of a reformulation of Christensen's (1985) characterization of how to cope with uncertainty in planning discussed in the introduction.

Coping with Irreducible Uncertainty in Planning

According to Christensen, planning problems can be characterized in terms of the uncertainty about goals and the means of achieving them. The existence of both disagreement about goals and uncertainty about means results in 'chaos', and 'order' must somehow 'be discovered'. This last, 'chaotic' situation is particularly relevant here. Situations of this type seem by no means atypical in planning. They are, on the contrary, characteristic, as contended above. But what is 'chaos' exactly? And, more importantly, what does 'discovering order' mean exactly? Figure 15.2 sketches a possible, evolutionary interpretation.

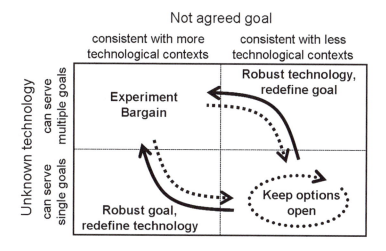

Figure 15.2 Coping with irreducible uncertainty in planning

In the figure, the bottom right quadrant – disagreement about goals and uncertainty about means, or 'chaos' – of Christensen's typology is highlighted: goals are *always* not agreed, technologies are *always* unknown. The starting point is the observation that even when there is no agreement on the goals, a distinction can be made between goals that are not agreed but that are consistent with different future technological contexts[2] and goals that are not. For instance, a goal as 'accommodating change in the urban economy' might not be shared by all participants but will remain meaningful irrespective of how the technological context will develop. On the contrary, a goal

---

2   The term 'technological context' is used here to synthetically identify aspects of the context (technical, economic, social and cultural) that together determine the effectiveness of certain means in achieving certain goals. They might include such things as the availability of previously unknown intervention options, improved knowledge on the effects of interventions, but also broader changes in the economic, social and cultural sphere affecting the desirability or feasibility of interventions.

as 'accommodating the growth of a specific economic sector in a specific location' is not only a goal that not everybody might share but is also one that is much more dependent on a specific technological context (for example, a location which is central in a railway dominated urban transportation context will not necessarily be so in a car dominated urban transportation context). Similarly, even when not enough is known about the effectiveness of technologies, a distinction can be made between technologies that only have the potential to serve limited goals (as for instance an urban transportation system connecting a limited number of places in a limited number of ways) and technologies that have the potential to serve more goals (as a more articulated urban transportation network connecting more places in more ways).

If goals are not agreed and only relevant in a limited range of future technological contexts, and technologies are unknown and can only serve limited goals, options should be kept open. With reference to the illustrations above, an irreversible choice for 'accommodating the growth of a specific economic sector in a specific location' should not be made, acknowledging the fact that other sectors and other locations could later emerge. The same would apply, on the technologies side, to 'a transportation system connecting a limited number of places in a limited number of ways': other goals could later emerge, requiring a system connecting other places in other ways. By contrast, when goals are not agreed but are consistent with more technological contexts, and when technologies are unknown but can serve many goals they are, at least potentially, robust goals and technologies and should be further 'bargained' and 'experimented' with. With reference to the illustrations above, even if not everybody agrees, a goal as 'accommodating change in the urban economy' should be acknowledged, as it is likely to continue to play a role in whatever future technological context. The same applies to the technology 'a transportation network connecting more places in more ways', because it is likely to be able to serve more goals (including emerging, yet unknown, ones). In both cases, if the test of bargaining and experimenting is passed, decisions should be taken and actions implemented. If not, options should be re-opened.[3]

Paraphrasing Rittel and Webber (1973), the purpose of the process is thus letting an image of goals and means gradually emerge among participants, as a product of incessant judgment, subjected to critical argument. Paraphrasing

---

3   The term 'robust' is used here in the sense of 'compatible with different goals and means'. It thus identifies decisions and actions that shape conditions for a *variety* of futures to unfold, as opposed to decisions and actions that are only aimed at one particular future. The term is complementary to the notion of 'leaving options open'. The latter are decisions and actions that, because they are compatible with a too limited range of goals and means, should not be implemented (or not yet). This interpretation of robustness is close to that suggested in policy and decision analysis approaches exploring ways of dealing with irreducible or 'deep' uncertainty (Lempert et al. 2003). It is also related to the notion of 'resilience' ecologists are beginning to use in order to identify the ability of natural, social or economic systems to respond and adapt to shocks and external changes (Capra, 1996; ICSU, 2002).

Cross (2007), it entails constructing side-by-side partial models of goals and means. The crucial factor, the 'creative leap', is the bridging of these two partial models by the articulation of a concept which enables the partial models to be mapped onto each other; that is, to identify combinations of goals and means that acknowledge and reflect the participants' knowledge (or ignorance) and agreement (or disagreement) and which in that sense are 'robust'. Paraphrasing Valkenburg and Dorst (1998), such combinations can be identified by an iterative process of naming the relevant factors in the situation, framing a problem in a certain way (identifying potential goals and means), making moves toward a provisional synthesis (a potential combination of goals and means) and reflecting on these moves. The process can be characterized as an evolutionary process of variation (of names, frames and moves) and selection (through reflection). Planning is about setting up and governing the process. In the following section, an example will be used to illustrate these notions.

An Illustration: Planning the HSL in the Randstad

Fundamentally different and constantly changing views on the project goals and means characterized the planning of the High Speed Line (HSL) South in the Netherlands, linking Amsterdam to Rotterdam, Antwerp and Brussels. The case is extreme in its complexity, and as such helps show the sort of planning approach that coping with irreducible uncertainties might require. It also documents the possibilities of, but also the limits to, such an approach in the present institutional context. I will focus on just one representative phase and aspect of this still unfolding development: the selection of the HSL route in the Randstad, the highly urbanized West of the Netherlands, between the cities of Rotterdam and Amsterdam. My main source of information is the extensive reconstruction of the case made by the commission installed by the Dutch parliament to enquire into mega transport projects decision making (Tweede Kamer der Staten-Generaal 2004b; see also Priemus 2007)

Alternative routes between Rotterdam and Amsterdam have been at the centre of the political and technical debate around the HSL South in the 1990s. Figure 15.3 shows some of these alternative routes. Different interpretations of the project goals and means emerged during the debate. Three main ones can be distinguished. A first interpretation centred on the development of a competitive transport product for the international traveller. A second interpretation focused, alternately, on mitigating local impacts in general and on the preservation of the landscape of the Green Heart (the central open area in the Randstad) in particular. A third interpretation aimed predominantly at reinforcing the urban structure of the Randstad, improving connections both among the main cities and also between the main cities and metropolitan areas both inside and outside of the Netherlands.

This multiplicity of interpretations of goals and means translated in a number of irreducible uncertainties and practical dilemmas. From within the transport

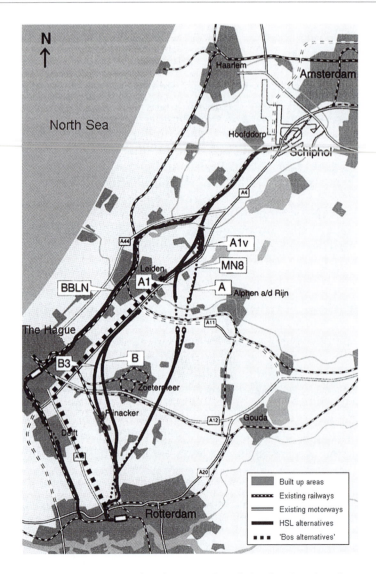

Figure 15.3   Alternative routes for the HSL-South in the Randstad
Source: Adapted from Tweede Kamer der Staten-Generaal 2004b.

development interpretation achieving the shortest travel times between the main traffic generators seemed crucial. This led to a preference for routes directly linking Amsterdam, Schiphol airport and Rotterdam right across the Green Heart (such as the A routes in Figure 15.3). The local impact mitigation and landscape preservation interpretation argued instead for routes staying out of the Green Heart and using already existing infrastructure corridors (the BBLN route in Figure 15.3). From within the interpretation aiming at reinforcing the structure and position of the

Randstad, most important was the connection of all the main urban centres to the HSL South; thus not just Amsterdam, Schiphol and Rotterdam, but importantly also The Hague, the seat of the national government and of many international institutions. This interpretation preferred the BBLN route too.

Not all interpretations were equally strong. The first, transport interpretation was for long the only interpretation, and the one to which central government always gave priority. The second, environmental interpretation, acquired strength during the consultation phase to become an effective counterpart. These two interpretations eventually dominated the debate around alternative routes in the Randstad. They each had a clear champion in the national government: the Ministry of Transport and Public Works (V&W) and the Ministry of Housing, Spatial Planning and the Environment (VROM) respectively. VROM was also supportive of the third interpretation (the Randstad and the Green Heart are after all the main pillars of the Dutch spatial planning doctrine). However, in the debate this interpretation tended to be associated with a local lobby (most notably, the municipality of The Hague) rather than with a national interest. The different interpretations of the goals and means of the project seemed irreconcilable: the most desirable route for the one was the least desirable for the other two, and the other way round. More than once a total stalemate loomed. After a long and turbulent process, compromise between the first two interpretations was reached. The HSL would cut straight across the Green Heart, but a tunnel would be dug under its most valuable section. The only concession to the third interpretation was a High Speed Train (HST) 'shuttle' to The Hague: a HST service on conventional tracks branching out from the main line in Rotterdam a few times a day.

The process leading to this compromise, which I lack space to describe in more detail, provides fascinating insights into how relatively robust combinations of goals and means emerge through incessant re-naming, re-framing, and re-moving, fuelled by reflection. However, it also, and crucially, shows how opportunities for identifying *more* robust combinations are missed, because the 're-' does not go far enough. The final solution was, as we have seen, above all a combination (Cross would say 'bridge') between the first two interpretations, transport and the environment, and which largely frustrated the third, the Randstad. It was thus only partially robust. However, during the debate combinations of goals and means also emerged that held the promise of bridging *all* three interpretations. The most apparent of these ultimately unfulfilled 'creative leaps' were the so-called 'Bos alternatives', named after a civil servant who developed the initial idea on his own initiative. The common denominator of the 'Bos-alternatives' was the aligning of the HSL with the A4 and A13 existing motorways (running South of Leiden and The Hague and East of Delft in Figure 15.3), thus achieving *both* competitive travel times, avoidance of the Green Heart, *and* a fully-fledged station in The Hague.

As a governmental commission recognized, the 'Bos alernatives' were a good second best option in *all* the three interpretations (Tweede Kamer der Staten-Generaal 2004b: 82). Because they were new ideas, developed as a reaction to previously unrecognized dilemmas, they had not been included in the official route selection procedures thus far. Their evident potential, and the very large societal support they enjoyed almost instantly (at one point a majority of parliament members was in their favour), forced their later inclusion in the procedure. However, this inclusion was not in a way that allowed full exploration of their potential. It was not so much substance matters, but rather the fear of delays in the decision-making process, that was the decisive argument for discarding them. The same procedural argument would later also be evoked 'not to learn' from other crucial, emerging insights. For instance, the international travel market would show as much less important than initially thought, to the advantage of a burgeoning demand for fast travel within the Netherlands, thus further questioning the choice not to stop in The Hague. Furthermore, a substantial, unexpected lengthening of the travel time in the Belgian section of around 20 minutes – due to decisions beyond the control of the Dutch government – would put the couple of extra minutes that the 'Bos-alternatives' would have cost in even greater perspective. Finally, the tunnel under the Green Heart would demonstrate a much more symbolic, than an effective, solution to the landscape preservation issues there; certainly if related to the very high costs involved. All these new insights were not accounted for. In retrospect, the initial route choice (and 'frame') does not seem to have ever been seriously questioned. Mitigation measures have been accepted as a necessary price to pay on the way to its implementation, but re-consideration of the original choice ('re-framing') has never been a real option, whatever its potential: it was always 'too late'. As a consequence, variation in naming, framing and moving was limited, and even when present, reflection was not fully allowed to select among the different options.

Altogether, the compromise route appears a sub-optimal choice in many respects, and one that could not adapt to emerging insights, whatever the breadth of consensus. Was it also an inevitable choice? Or could perhaps a planning approach be adopted that was more receptive to the multiple *and* emergent interpretations of the project's goals and means? There is no easy answer. It is intrinsic for mega infrastructure projects (as for other planning issues) to be, to a large degree, irreversible, and this characteristic necessarily affects the planning process. During the Dutch parliamentary enquiry the dilemma was poignantly summarized by W. Korf, project director of the HSL: 'The apparently logical sequence: first demonstrate the usefulness and necessity [of a project] and then articulate and implement the decision, does not hold. The usefulness and necessity of a project continue to remain a matter of discussion. But at some point a decision must be taken whether to sign the contracts or stop altogether' (Tweede Kamer der Staten-Generaal 2004a: 140).

While there are no easy answers, posing the question may still provide a focus for the analysis of the planning process and help direct the search for improvements. As far as mega infrastructure projects are concerned, the Dutch parliamentary enquiry advocates a more thorough, divergent and transparent exploration of alternatives in the initial phases of the process (Tweede Kamer der Staten-Generaal 2004a). This amounts to providing for *more variation* in interpretations in a phase of the process where *selection by reflection* can be allowed to work more freely and thoroughly and would thus guarantee that more informed choices are made in the first place. Also, Flyvbjerg et al. (2003) complement their appraisal of dismal past experiences in the planning of mega infrastructure projects by pointing at a possible, and – in some instances – even better emerging approach. This would be, above all, directed at increasing stakeholder accountability and public awareness of the risks. It would seek that risks are distributed more evenly and that more effective ways of managing them are adopted. These are also suggestions that point in the direction of *increasing sources of variation* and *improving mechanisms of selection*. All this is important, but it should be also acknowledged that it will not eliminate uncertainty. Accordingly, both the exploration of alternatives and the assessment of risks cannot be carried out once and for all, because views on goals and means will keep changing, soliciting new definitions of problems and solutions and putting existing ones in a different light. A complementary direction of improvement would thus have to assess the scope for allowing evolutionary mechanisms to operate throughout the planning process (not just at the beginning), thus increasing opportunities to translate lessons in action as they are learned. It would, however, also have to acknowledge the fact of the inevitable irreversibility of certain decisions and actions (not all options can be indefinitely kept open). The crucial question is: which planning institutions and strategies can foster this?

Speculations

In this chapter, recognition of the ever-more-irreducible uncertainties surrounding planning issues has been the point of departure in a search for a conceptualization of planning that is rooted in such recognition. Inspiration has been found in suggestions of how to tackle 'wicked' problems made by Rittel and Webber and Schön in the past and their more recent articulations in analyses of design processes. The core notion they together provide is that the planning process is one where situations, problems and solutions are defined jointly and interactively, in the course of what Schön would call a 'reflective conversation with the situation'. This 'conversation' is a quintessentially evolutionary process, where variation concerns both the situation and its interpretations, both problems and solutions, and selection operates through multiple reflections. Building upon these ideas, a reformulation of Christensen's characterization of how to cope with uncertainty in planning has been proposed. It moved from the contention that uncertainty on both planning goals and means is irreducible, and that planning processes should be geared at identifying 'robust' combinations of goals and means. Robust combinations are also uncertain, but, crucially allow *more* futures to coexist (and what could be a better ambition for planning in a diverse society?). In order to identify these combinations planners need to engage stakeholders in processes of variation in interpretations and selection by reflection, analogous to those recorded in design processes. The case of planning the HSL in the Randstad illustrated these concepts, but also showed some of the formidable challenges that gearing the planning process towards a 'reflective conversation with the situation' poses. I believe that a main focus of future efforts in planning theory should be on better understanding and defining these challenges, as well as on promising ways of addressing them. The task is urgent, because increasing diversification *within* societies and increasing linkages *between* societies all mean that the irreducibility of the uncertainties surrounding planning goals and means is bound to grow.

References

Capra, F. (1996) *The Web of Life*. London: HarperCollins.

Christensen, K.S. (1985) 'Coping with uncertainty in planning' *APA Journal* Winter: 63–73.

Cross, N. (2007) *Designerly Ways of Knowing*. Basel: Birkhäuser.

Flyvbjerg, B., Bruzelius, N. and Rothengatter, W. (2003) *Megaprojects and Risk: An Anatomy of Ambition*. New York: Cambridge University Press.

ICSU (2002) *Resilience and Sustainable Development*. Paris: International Council for Science.

Lempert, R.J., Popper, S.W.and Banks, S.C. (2003) *Shaping the Next One Hundred Years: New Methods for Quantitative, Long-Term Policy Analysis*. Santa Monica: RAND.

Myers, D. (2001) 'Introduction' *APA Journal* 67(4): 365–7.

Priemus, H. (2007). 'Development and design of large infrastructure projects: disregarded alternatives and issues of spatial planning' *Environment and Planning B: Planning and Design* 34: 626–44.

Rittel, W.J., and Webber, M. (1973) 'Dilemmas in a general theory of planning' *Policy Sciences* 4(2): 155–69.

Schön, D.A. (1983) *The Reflective Practitioner: How Professionals Think in Action*. New York: Basic Books, New York.

Tweede Kamer der Staten-Generaal (2004a) *Grote Projecten Uitvergroot: Een Infrastructuur voor Besluitvorming*. Den Haag: Sdu Uitgevers.

Tweede Kamer der Staten-Generaal (2004b) *Reconstructie HSL-Zuid: De besluitvorming Uitvergroot*. Den Haag: Sdu Uitgevers.

Valkenburg, R., and Dorst, K. (1998) 'The reflective practice of design teams', in *Design Studies* 19(3): 249–72.

Cybernetic Spatial Planning: Steering, Managing or Just Letting Go?

Nikos Karadimitriou

Introduction

Understanding spatial phenomena as expressions of complex processes is a concept that has been utilized extensively in studies of cities and the built environment. Similarly, the quintessentially modernist notion that socio-spatial phenomena are amenable to some form of monitoring and control has been, and still is, one of the cornerstones of spatial planning and planning practice, in spite of the postmodernist critique. The growing recognition that the social sciences are dealing with '… complex adaptive systems, self organising, self referential, autopoietic, and thus with their own strategies and expectations, with intertwining processes of emergence and adaptation …' (Geyer and van der Zouven 2001: 11) poses the ultimate challenge for spatial planning: if nothing else, totally accurate prediction in such systems is impossible in principle and thus it is next to unfeasible to foresee the effects of spatial planning interventions.

At first glance this conclusion seems to concur with the critique launched at the modernist backbone of spatial planning (even after its recent communicative turn) that (a) one *could not* practise spatial planning since it is generically doomed to fail even by its own standards due to a lack of adequate theoretical and/or practical tools or (b) one *should not* practise spatial planning either because it is serving the interests of capitalism/elites or because it is stifling creativity and spontaneity and is ignoring difference. What I argue in this chapter is that, although total control of complex sociospatial systems is indeed both impossible and undesirable, it is, however, possible (and can also be desirable) to influence, but not determine, the trajectory and evolution of such systems. In many ways this is what planning and planners have been doing by definition, although this theoretical understanding of their predicament is relatively recent.

From this schism between the theoretical understanding of cities and urban processes and its embodiment in spatial planning practices emerges, in my view, the key challenge for complexity theory and planning. This challenge lies not so much in the relevance of complexity theory's concepts nor in the value it adds in terms of explanatory power but, crucially, in suggesting approaches/attitudes and subsequently institutions, practices and tools that would increase the effectiveness of the actors engaged with planning. Notwithstanding the difficulties in making the distinction between the two following categories, it could be argued that so far complexity has provided powerful 'theories in planning' but has been less effective in suggesting workable 'planning theory(-ies)'/'theories of planning' (Faludi 1973a, 1973b). The chapters in this volume advance both aspects and I believe that insights from cybernetics can usefully contribute in that effort.

To the extent that structure and function can be analytically separated, systems theory emerged with a predominant concern for the structure of systems whereas cybernetics' predominant initial concern was with system function (control, communication). Although systems theory and cybernetics emerged in the 1940s and 1950s (von Bertalanffy 1968; Ashby 1956) they informed planning theory and practice in the 1960s when strategic spatial planning took the form of 'Comprehensive Planning' (Albrechts 2004). This relatively short-lived effort to integrate '... nearly everything – at different administrative levels (Albrechts, this volume, Chapter 7) was to prove an elusive and costly endeavour that in many ways discredited systems thinking in the eyes of many built environment academics and professionals for decades; quite the opposite of what Chadwick would have hoped for.

'Closed system' thinking permeates the system-based rational approaches that even today lie at the heart of much of the practice of planning; indeed many planning systems in existence are organized along such principles. Furthermore, the ambiguous social, economic and physical heritage that rational comprehensive planning has left behind (see, for example, Healey 1993) is present in cities all over the world. Yet at the same time that the application of General (Closed) Systems Theory to planning was planting the seeds of its own demise, the application of open systems thinking in other domains was forging new pathways in our understanding of socio-spatial configurations.

Following the footsteps of Jane Jacobs (1961: 433), who described cities and urban problems as 'problems in organised complexity', Nicolis and Prigogine used a town as the perfect illustration of a dissipative structure[1] (Nicolis and Prigogine 1977) – an idea that was explored in greater depth by Allen (Allen 1981; Allen and Sanglier 1981), who revisited classical location theory. At the same time Haken's theory[2] of synergetics, was also quickly taken up by Weidlich (1987) in his study of social systems (see also Weidlich and Haag 1988). More recently, Bak's work on 'self-organized criticality' (Bak 1996; Bak et al. 1988; 1991) also lent itself to applications explaining socio-economic phenomena. These approaches, enriched with ideas borrowed from Mandelbrot's, Turing's and von Neumann's work

---

1   Dissipative structures are open systems using inflows from their environment to increase their level of organization, while at the same time by extension they dissipate entropy back to their environment.

2   See the following section of this chapter.

(amongst others), generated a wide variety of applications of the concept of self-organization in the study of the built environment leading to Portugali's work on self-organizing urban environments (Portugali 1997, 1999), Allen's work on cities and regions as self-organizing systems (Allen 1997) and Batty's work on fractals, agent based models and cellular automata (Batty and Longley 1994; Batty 1997, 2005) to name but a few.

This is, of course, not a comprehensive list of authors nor a complete mapping of the theoretical influences underpinning present day applications of complexity theory to cities. Indeed depending on which aspects of urbanity one is exploring, the list could expand[3] to include inputs from the application of complexity to a wide and diverse variety of disciplines like biology, law, economics, management, etc. This variety serves to show, however, that work on this paradigm meshes together ideas from a diverse range of disciplines, from physics and chemistry to sociology, architecture and politics, true to von Bertalaffny's vision of a less compartmentalized scientific endeavour. Still, the key concept underlying this systems-based understanding of the world is that irrespective of domain or scale and irrespective of the complexity of the interactions and the diversity of the actors involved in those interactions, the objects under examination will organize themselves in systems in a way that obeys a uniform set of fundamental but abstract principles which try to explain why those systems operate in the way they do. There is no claim, however, that the application of these principles should allow one to accurately predict and describe in detail the systems and their future state.

Why should we employ such approaches whilst exploring socio-spatial phenomena in twenty-first century capitalist societies? Why should we strive to base planning practice on an understanding of cities founded on complex systems? One good reason has to do with the rise of the 'mediated society' (Lachs 1976) and the challenges it poses for governance. Lachs argued that one of the fundamental processes underlying our highly urbanized capitalist societies is the disjunction between planning and action; executing and facing the consequences. This process, combined with (and caused in part by) the ever increasing complexification of the world we live in, creates a gap in responsibility and accountability and increases alienation. It also reduces the capacity of the individual, be it policy maker or layperson to fully understand his or her environment. A similar argument was taken much further in the postmodernity discussion (for example, see Harvey 1990). In an increasingly fragmented, unintelligible environment where moral hazards abound, theoretical approaches and practical tools are needed that could potentially cope with the vastly increased degrees of freedom available to human action.

If we assume that the relationship between individuals and societies follows a structuration process (Giddens 1984) then any individual or collective action does influence spatial evolution by definition (and the reverse applies, of course). Socio-spatial phenomena, the expressions of humanity's spatial existence, will not vanish if planning disappears. In the absence of any form of collectively sanctioned

---

3   For a more detailed mapping of the influences on and varieties of systems approaches, see Ison et al. 2007: 1343.

attempt to influence them, the spatial expressions of society will still evolve, most likely in a direction serving elites. The Victorians were the first to discover that in a capitalist world largely structured around power relations it is not a matter of whether we need planning, but a matter of what sort of planning we need.

It is worth considering here the argument that planners should leave things to take their course unhindered and not stifle spontaneous expression of the diverse constituents of society. After all, if societies are self-organizing then order of some form will emerge out of the interactions of their constituents. This is indeed an idea worth exploring further. Spontaneity and diversity are inherent attributes of any complex system and as will be discussed below, any effort to totally control such systems does not only pose grave ethical issues, but can have extremely adverse outcomes in terms of system stability. Complex dynamic socio-spatial systems stabilize around attractors, but stabilization in such systems is dynamic and it emerges together with the emergence of social norms that bound individual action. We are all embedded in societies; our actions help in creating new norms as well as reinforce and reproduce existing ones. Perturbations will occur and de-stabilization will take place as part of this process of structuration (Giddens 1984). To ignore the instability inherent in complex systems, is to ignore the potentially catastrophic ramifications for the welfare of society as a whole (and thus for individuals) that unhindered 'spontaneous' and 'creative' actions may have, especially when driven by social norms forged within a capitalist mode of production. It is also to ignore the evolutionary advantages that social norms have as a means of coordinating action, thereby allowing humankind to cope with the task of survival. Thus any idealization of bound-less individual expression as a purely creative force is as dystopian as is the notion that we can detach ourselves from society in order to totally control it. This is something that early political theorists like Alexis de Tocqueville vigorously argued.

Examples of the catastrophic outcomes of boundless individual action are plentiful: tragedies of the commons, the credit crunch, financial scams. The list can be equally long as the list of disbenefits from totally regulated action. Based on the undesirable outcomes of both total regulation and no regulation at all, I would say that capitalist societies do indeed need to explore the benefits of exerting influence on their socio-spatial evolution through some form of collective, organized, interest-mediating endeavour which provides boundaries to the actions of individual actors. However, the question remains open as to the scope, the expectations from and the way they should go about this effort. The question also remains open as to whether a set of values and behavioural norms exists whereby individual behaviour based on it would be able to overcome the externalities and coordination problems inherent in both market capitalism and socialism.

These issues become even more interesting when considering the implications of circular causality and our difficulty to completely detach ourselves from the systems we want to intervene in as planners. This difficulty makes the outcomes of goal-oriented behaviour very uncertain, since actors cannot accurately (if at all) distinguish goals and purposes of systems they are immersed into. As Healey

(2007: 31) argues, 'steering' the trajectory of a city is an 'impossible task' therefore '… all conscious interventions to shape urban dynamics need to be evaluated not as steps towards given ends, or movements along defined trajectories. Instead, they are risky experiments, taken within a particular hypothesis about what is important about urban dynamics end directed by particular values about what cities should be like'.

The recent work of Portugali (1999, 2006) and Alfasi and Portugali (2007), building on Haken's theory of synergetics, provide some first ground-breaking ideas on the form a planning system should take given the nature of socio-spatial systems. In their view this new form of spatial planning should be focusing on an 'urban code' that arranges the way the three key 'built elements' (singular, linear and district) 'relate to each other and to the structure of the city' (Alfasi and Portugali 2007: 170–71). The authors have also argued that a planning system should be organized on 'Just-in-Time' instead of 'Just-in-Case' principles in order to be able to manage the complexity embedded in the production of the built environment (Alfasi and Portugali 2004). In a similar fashion de Roo (2007) revisits 'Actor Consulting' in search of a decision support system aimed at dealing with the 'fuzziness' of the spatial planning process. I will argue below that a Cybernetic variety-based approach, which recognizes this ever-increasing complexity and offers tools to understand it and harness it, would also be valuable to planning; albeit not without its own limitations.

The scope of the chapter is to build bridges and provide insights more than to provide prescriptive answers. Similar to self-organization, cybernetics is one of the few fields whose language can be used to describe phenomena across many different disciplines. It 'provides concepts and terminology to build bridges between different knowledge domains' where 'models, metaphors are shared' but any such effort also requires 'logical coherence and pragmatic usefulness' (Scott 2004: 1367). The chapter therefore aims at contributing to this process of 'compilation' of cybernetics for spatial planning by providing a framework of appropriate metaphors and by suggesting principles based on which practical tools could be developed; something that has only sparsely been done until today and from a very specific managerial angle (see, for example, Beer 1979, 2004; Schwaninger and Kroener 2004).

Following the introduction which looked into some of the principles of self-organization and some of the challenges that the complexity turn poses for planning, in the following section, I revisit cybernetics, synergetics and self-organized criticality in order to provide a variety-based explanation for the unmanageability of complex socio-spatial systems. In the subsequent section, I outline different existing approaches which aim at assisting planners or even more boldly, aim at reconfiguring spatial planning and I propose some fundamental principles that could underlie the implementation of spatial planning in the future. I conclude with a summary of the key ideas referred to in this chapter and pose a set of questions and challenges for spatial planning in an increasingly complex and uncertain world.

Key Elements of Cybernetics and Self-Organization for Spatial Planning

Cybernetics, a discipline studying 'all possible machines' (Ashby 1956) engaging with issues of 'control and communication in the animal and the machine' (Wiener 1948) started off with what was later called first-order cybernetics. First-order cybernetics, the 'cybernetics of observed systems', promised order and certainty to a world of uncertainty and chaos by providing the conceptual tools to systematically examine in abstract terms any durable system, rather unemotively termed a 'machine'. Cities, humans, animals, regions and airconditioning installations could therefore be 'steered' through the use of cybernetic principles. First-order systems thinking, a dearest child of modernism, and its scientific rationality provided the basis for the systems approach to urban planning (see McLoughlin 1969) in the 1950s and 1960s. Unsurprisingly, given our present day understanding of cities, the outcomes of the application of first-order cybernetic principles in urban planning fell far short of expectations.

If systems thinking in Urban planning has been tried and thoroughly tested in the 1960s and 1970s, what is the point of revisiting it in 2009? In my view, despite the limitations of first-order cybernetics, some of the fundamental ideas behind cybernetics as such have not lost their appeal. In terms of theory, second-order cybernetics emerged just as Comprehensive Planning was waning, but crucially that was the same period when approaches based on complexity also began to appear. By definition, spatial planning is about intervention, about engagement with the actors and systems whose interactions give rise to the immense complexity and dynamism of socio-spatial formations. It borders on the tautological to say that cybernetics could be a useful theoretical tool in a spatial planner's efforts to understand and exert influence in complex socio-spatial systems. I am assuming, of course, that some form of effort to influence is desirable, as I argued earlier.

In this section, therefore, I attempt to articulate a plausible answer to the questions posed above. Firstly, I explore some recent and not so recent developments in cybernetics, mainly to highlight the significant conceptual advances that cybernetics has made ever since the focus of planning theory and practice turned elsewhere. Secondly, I will examine how approaches based on second-order cybernetics could be relevant to spatial planning, focusing in particular on the role of communication. Thirdly, I will focus on the importance of system variety and will argue that transcomputability renders many, if not most, socio-spatial systems unmanageable. Fourthly, I will briefly engage with ideas from synergetics (Haken) and self-organized criticality (Bak) in order to argue that, given the unmanageability of socio-spatial systems and their self-organization at a critical state, it may be time to rethink what we expect, or believe we should expect, of spatial planning.

First-order Cybernetics

The key idea behind first-order cybernetics is that any system that is open with regard to flows of energy, but organizationally closed, could be analyzed in terms of 'processes' and 'products'. Thus, planners operating according to first-order cybernetic principles would, as a matter of course, be perfectly capable of detaching themselves from the socio-spatial systems under consideration in order to observe, define, analyze and intervene with a view to controlling the system at hand *in its totality*. The word 'control' is used in cybernetics in a different way than in everyday language; it is rather about steering a system towards an intended state – it is *enabling*. Control in cybernetics is therefore teleological. It also requires communication, a crucial aspect of cybernetic systems on which I elaborate further below. In the case of first-order cybernetics applied in spatial planning, the controller is an observer/planner capable of detaching themselves from the urban environment *on* which they are operating (see Table 16.1 below).

This ability of the observer to detach his or herself is, however, the assumption that posed the greatest difficulty in the application of first-order cybernetics to social systems. If nothing else, one could argue that detachment is impossible to achieve as circularity in the form of feedback lies at the heart of cybernetics. The difficulties that first-order cybernetics faced in their application to psycho-social systems prompted von Foerster to introduce second-order cybernetics, the 'cybernetics of observing systems' (von Foerster 1974, 1981) by analyzing cybernetics itself on cybernetic principles. He thus contributed to the rise and growth of constructivist epistemologies, most notably expressed in von Glasersfeld's radical constructivism (von Glasersfeld 1987, 1991).

Second-order Cybernetics

Second-order cybernetics introduces the reflexive aspects of any actor (see Table 16.1) that engages with a system. It thus emphasizes the impossibility of distinguishing sharply between controlled and controller, between system, goal and observer. Second-order cybernetics, therefore, places the observer inside the system – an active part of it – and the control that this observer exerts becomes explicitly shared amongst the components of the system itself. The distinction between controller and controlled therefore becomes arbitrary and circular causality emerges. Assuming no other influences (for the sake of this argument), is a city's trajectory controlled by its Municipal Administration, or is the Municipal Administration controlled by the city? Second-order cybernetics recognizes that control is shared and has thereby led to the understanding that self-organizing systems exercise self-steering.

A crucial element as far as steering or 'enabling control' is concerned, is communication. In every cybernetic system both intent and feedback have to be transmitted. This means, therefore, that cybernetic systems comprise actors (subsystems) actively engaging with each other in exchanges of information. Yet from a cybernetic point of view '... an organism does not receive "information" as

Table 16.1   Definitions of first- and second-order cybernetics

Author	First-order cybernetics	Second-order cybernetics
Von Foerster	the cybernetics of observed systems	the cybernetics of observing systems
Pask	the purpose of a model	the purpose of a modeller
Varela	controlled systems	autonomous systems
Umpleby	interaction among the variables in a system	interaction between observer and observed

Source: Adapted from Umpleby 2001.

something transmitted to it, rather, as a circularly organised system it interprets perturbations as being informative' (Scott 2004: 1369). Thus, given the enormous diversity between humans, Glanville argues that '… there is no effective unambiguous "coded" communication … to do this to humans we must provide a reprogramming course, and even then we only succeed in very limited areas' (Glanville 2004: 1382). In the words of von Foerster (quoted in Scott 2004: 1370): 'systems that are truly self organising will always expand beyond the frames of reference adopted by observers to model their behaviour; they are in principle unpredictable unless training, conditioning or other constraints make them become so, in which case they become "trivial machines" rather than interesting "non trivial" machines they were formerly'.

Glanville argues, therefore, that in second-order cybernetics we should drop the notion of 'coded' communication and instead focus on Pask's 'Conversation Theory' (Pask 1975) which approaches the exchange of communication in a cybernetic system as a cybernetic system in itself. To quote Glanville's constructivist argument (2004: 1382): 'Communication takes place between entities that build understandings (meanings) out of their interpretations of what they sense their conversational partner (or partners) offer them. This understanding is fed back to their partner(s) in new offerings that the partner(s) in turn interpret and compare to their original intention. This dual generation of what might have been called messages constitutes feedback and allows errors to be detected and new offerings/ messages to be tendered that attempt to correct such errors'.

This understanding of communication is echoed in ideas that have hugely influenced spatial planning in the form of communicative planning theory (CPT). Yet, viewed through a second-order cybernetic approach, the emergence of collectively shared meaning, which is key for CPT, would only be considered relevant and important to the extent that it would influence the self-organizing processes driving the creation of meaning by the actors involved. The emergence of a collectively shared meaning is a possibility, but not the only one. Nor do the incessant feedback loops inherent in complex systems guarantee the stability of a common understanding, should it emerge. Crucially, second-order cybernetics embeds spatial planners firmly within the systems they are otherwise trying to influence through their actions, deliberatively or otherwise.

What Allmendinger and Tewdwr-Jones (2002) point out is that planners have a value system and are bound by social norms. According to that value system and those norms, they favour certain ideas, promote some agendas over others, favour certain opinions and interests instead of others. This is inevitable. Even by choosing to promote dialogue and collaboration they opt for one of many alternatives to participation and planning and their effort will be bounded by their limitations. What CPT does, then, is to provide a moral justification behind a specific set of behavioural norms which are somehow considered morally superior. At the same time, however, CPT undermines the professionalization of planning by replacing expert planning knowledge with facilitation skills as the necessarily required and relevant body of knowledge (Allmendinger and Tewdwr-Jones 2002).

A second-order cybernetics approach to planning would also indicate that planners are not that special after all: they are just another influencing factor and as such they will inevitably influence the system they get involved with in one way or another. Their knowledge is not invalidated and may actually be crucial in expanding the variety of a 'controlling system', but the first-order expectations of the effectiveness of their action in terms of control are severely diminished. The examination of the concept of variety in the next section will make this much more evident.

The Laws of Requisite Variety and Multi-scale Variety

A fundamental contribution to understanding control in the cybernetic sense is Ashby's Law of Requisite Variety (Ashby 1956) and the emanating Conant-Ashby theorem. In the Law of Requisite Variety, Ashby formalized the condition which allows one system to control another: the controlling system must have at least as much variety as the system it seeks to exert control over; variety here meaning the number of different states a system could take. The Conant-Ashby theorem claims that 'every good regulator of a system must be a model of that system' (Conant and Ashby 1981), which Schwaninger (2000: 212) re-iterated in the following way: 'the result of an organizational process cannot be better than the model on which the management of that process is based, except by chance'.

In the case of spatial planning, Ashby's Law and the Conant-Ashby theorem throw up an intriguing perspective: the socio-spatial formations which planners deal with have potentially enormous variety (i.e., an enormous number of potential future states), so large that in some cases most of them may well be 'transcomputable' (Ashby 1956). This would effectively also mean that anything but the most trivial of socio-spatial systems can be essentially unmanageable. The lack of computational power is probably the most frequently quoted explanation for the problems faced by the application of first-order cybernetics, or any type of modelling, in spatial planning.

Given both the ease with which variety within a system can increase and the existing material limits to computational capacity, it is highly doubtful that there

433

will ever be enough computational capacity to tackle the complexity of anything but the most trivial of socio-spatial systems at least in first-order cybernetic terms. Having said that, in the last 20 years there have been dramatic developments in the efforts to manage chaotic systems in the physical sciences. The introduction of 'chaos control algorithms' (Huebler 1989) is a good example of how 'controlled chaos' could be achieved through predictive algorithms.The recent work of Kiss et al. (2007) is the culmination of decades of work on the effectiveness of feedback control on chaotic systems. Kiss and his collaborators were able to direct a chaotic chemical system towards different states of synchronization through the application of weak feedback signals.

There are two main issues with feedback control in socio-spatial systems. Firstly, the question whether it is possible to ever provide the computational power that would allow the operation of feedback or predictive algorithms in complex socio-spatial systems. Secondly, the question whether it would ever be possible to find an 'objective' programmer or a 'non-reflexive' set of actors. This inability to be perfectly detached from the system under examination, as argued above, combined with the reflexive nature of the actors comprising social systems poses grave difficulties in the effort to implement first-order goal-oriented 'steering' in socio-spatial systems. This does not mean, however, that the trajectory of socio-spatial systems cannot be influenced. Indeed, this trajectory is actively created by the interactions of actors, so by definition any individual action and, even more so, any action trying to align at least a subset of those interactions towards a specific direction will have an effect on the system as a whole.

It is worth mentioning here the recent generalization of the Law of Requisite Variety to take scale into account (Bar-Yam 2004). With the Law of Multiscale Variety, Bar-Yam argues that '... the effectiveness of a system organisation can be evaluated by its variety at each scale of tasks to be performed' and therefore '...organizational structures, i.e. coordination mechanisms, always have a tradeoff in behaviors ... large scale behaviors must come at the expense of high variety at a fine scale'. (p. 44). What this means is that for large scale efforts of narrow focus which require highly coordinated actions of many individuals, there is a tradeoff between effectiveness and variety. This can be performed most effectively through hierarchical organization. Inversely, tasks that require high variety control systems need to be small-scale and unhierarchical (market based or egalitarian) in order to be effective. I will discuss the implications of multi-scale variety further below.

Interestingly, although the effort of spatial planning may be to lead a socio-spatial system towards a desirable 'optimal' commonly agreed state, the outcome of an effort to reach that state may be destabilizing to the system as a whole. The issue then is not whether spatial planning will have an effect, but that the exact nature and extent of that effect are unpredictable. In the next section I examine why that is by utilizing metaphors from the theories of synergetics and self-organized criticality.

Synergetics and Self-organized Criticality

Haken's Theory of Synergetics (Haken 1983a, 1983b) was originally developed in an effort to understand physical phenomena of self-organization such as the laser, but it was through Haken's collaboration with Portugali that synergetic principles were applied to planning. Haken observed that where self-organization occurs, phenomena are characterized by periods of relative stability followed by periods of increased volatility. Although the appearance of an instability incident is certain – due to the system reaching its boundaries or due to external perturbations – the sequence of appearance of such incidents is not. It is precisely because of this instability that '… a collective state is formed, but it acquires its meaning only with respect to the surroundings and, in a way, with respect to its value for the survival of the whole system' (Haken 2006). Haken therefore asserted that complex multi-component systems could be described at the macro level by only a few 'order parameters' which largely govern (or 'enslave') the majority of micro-variables that characterize a particular system's components. An order parameter 'informs the atoms how to behave' and 'enslaves' the atoms but 'is itself generated by the joint action of the atoms' (Haken 2006: 25). Consequently, instead of the wealth of information required to describe all possible states that atoms can take, only one piece of information is required resulting in 'enormous compression of information' (p. 25), i.e. in variety attenuation.

Domanski and Judge (1994: 12, quoted in Nijkamp and Reggiani 1998: 9) argue that this approach is 'especially useful in the examination of the dynamics and system transformations of social and economic systems. It makes possible a reconstruction of changes and macroscopic processes which give rise to the emergence of new temporal, spatial and spatio-temporal structures'.

According to Portugali (2000), change in socio-spatial self-organizing systems can be categorized in three variants: (i) change from one stable state to another through bifurcations whereby previous states disappear ('stratigraphic'); (ii) change from one steady state to another whereby remnants of previous states remain 'enslaved' by the new 'order parameters' ('furcative'); (iii) change from one steady state to another whereby the existing order parameter re-interprets and engulfs other parameters thus increasing its internal complexity ('hermeneutic'). The spatial expressions of each variation would be quite distinct: an example of stratigraphic change would be the total demolition of the built stock and its replacement by new forms (like the post-war UK slum clearance programme); an example of furcative change would be the gradual replacement of the built stock in a neighbourhood; hermeneutic change would be the re-use of the existing stock of buildings (old warehouses and factories as loft apartments, for example).

Interestingly, furcative change can operate either in a cooperative mode or by enslaving the fast-moving variables in 'captivity areas' (Portugali 1997, 2000), 'local regions of instability' where residual fast-moving variables oscillate locally. In those areas the socio-spatial configuration can take alternative forms and quickly interchange between them or allow for many coexisting forms. For example, areas like Christiania in Copenhagen, the Silicon Valley a few decades ago or Kreuzberg in Berlin are all quite different, with some more mixed and varied than others. All these areas can be viewed as spatial expressions of slaved parameters (fast-moving variables) from the more widely accepted social values, property rights and tenure norms, the Fordist mode of production, etc. (order parameters). These fluctuations are both institutional and spatial differences in norms and values that are then both reflected on space and reinforced by space and, quite interestingly, demonstrate segregation and clustering on many occasions. Portugali's argument (Portugali 2000) is that such areas are necessary in order to ensure the stability of the overall system and also to provide alternatives for the set of 'order parameters' around which the system will be stabilized after the next round of destabilization. During periods of instability the system would 'test' many different alternatives, or new potential slow-moving macro-variables that would emerge out of the existing pool of fast-moving ones. Eventually, the system would begin to be 'slaved' by a new set of variables, thus entering a new period of dynamic stability.

Bak (1996) approached fluctuations from a different angle. He observed that dissipative self-organizing systems tend to reach a critical state where the stability of their form (at the critical threshold) is maintained by a series of dissipation events. The distribution of such events in a system operating in a self-organized critical state follows a power law and thus events are unpredictable in their frequency but predictable in their distribution. Batty and Xie (1999) suggest that city evolution follows self-organized criticality principles. Indeed their case study (Buffalo, New York) has remained at the critical threshold for several decades. Bak observed as well that whenever such a system was influenced in a way that did not allow energy to be dissipated by a series of many small events, it dissipated its energy in a major and usually catastrophic event. He gives the collapse of the USSR as a pertinent example of this observation. On the contrary, an equilibrium system (not critically self-organized) ' ... driven by many independent minor shocks would show much smaller fluctuations' (Bak 1996: 191) that would be ' ... given by a Gaussian curve, better known as the "bell curve" which has negligible tails', and therefore no major fluctuations (Bak 1996: 192).

The conclusion is that the only effective way to avoid reaching otherwise inevitable major dissipative events (catastrophes) in an open dissipative self-organizing complex system is to promote dissipation through a series of minor dissipation events. This keeps the system in an 'unnatural state' of dynamic equilibrium, away from self-organized criticality. Any attempt to eliminate dissipation events in an effort to eliminate fluctuations in the system will inevitably lead in to system breakdown. The assumption that a city is a complex system, or actually a web of complex systems which, unless consciously driven to equilibrium, will operate according to the principles of self-organized criticality also provides a useful insight into the scope of planning. According to the principles of self-organized criticality, the consequences of any effort to totally control a city's socio-spatial form by eliminating any form of spontaneous actor behaviour or any crisis in its economy will inevitably lead to major and probably catastrophic dissipation events.

These two approaches by Bak and Haken/Portugali leave open the prospect of intervention in complex socio-spatial systems, although they highlight the potential pitfalls. On the one hand, self-organized criticality makes clear that any effort to control the fluctuations/dissipation in a socio-spatial system with a view to reaching an optimal state that contradicts its inherent fluctuations or dissipation processes, will lead to breakdown. On the other hand, both self-organized criticality and synergetics leave open the possibility to attract the system around slow-moving variables that allow fluctuations in captivity areas, or to avert catastrophic instability by facilitating several small-scale dissipation events which would maintain a dynamic equilibrium.

Seen through this lens, spatial planning could, in principle, be contributing to the extremely difficult task of managing major fluctuations either by assisting society in the creation of 'order parameters' or by enhancing the rate of minor dissipation events. Alfasi and Portugali (2007) argue in favour of a planning system that operates based on a set of basic rules. Other authors in this volume also argue for a reshaping of spatial planning into a 'transformative practice' which would: 'involve constructing "desired" answers – images/visions and strategies for action – to the structural problems of our society' (Albrechts, Chapter 7); 'be concerned with trajectories rather than specified end-points' (Hillier, Chapter 17); and move 'towards an understanding of planning as the modulation of singularities' (Van Wezemael, Chapter 9, based on DeLanda 2003). If this scope is to be accepted as the scope for planning then there is one more notion that needs to be dropped: the need/tendency to evaluate in teleological terms the process and the outcome of creating the 'order parameters'. Since it is very hard to know whether what we are doing is a step towards the 'right' direction and the sociospatial system is in constant evolution, it seems very likely that policy makers, regulators and spatial planners, could only attempt to achieve periods of stability long enough to give the impression of order. As Vickers (1972) insightfully realized, order is just an illusion that can endure for a certain period of time. I discuss the limits to interventions further in the following section.

Steering, Managing or Just Letting Go?

A system does not have to be extraordinarily complex in order to become unmanageable. The necessary condition for unmanageability is that the variety of the controlled system is greater than that of the controlling system. The direct consequence of applying Ashby's law from what Bruner (1986) coined a 'logico-scientific' point of view is that if socio-spatial systems were to be controlled, then either the variety of the controlled system would have to be decreased or that of the controlling system would have to be increased. It has been suggested that if one goes down that route then attenuation and amplification should happen simultaneously in a process called 'variety engineering' (Beer 1979, 1994). Variety, by the way, is inextricably linked to fluctuation. Variety is an expression of the possible states that a system can achieve: the less variety in a system, the fewer possible states exist between which it can fluctuate. Since as I have already argued, socio-spatial systems are mostly transcomputable and any attempt to 'freeze' them leads to breakdown. The attempt to reach an 'optimal state' and to preserve this state in the long run through the reduction or elimination of fluctuations is doomed to fail and if too restrictive it will lead to system breakdown. This does not mean, however, that such attempts are not taking place.

An attempt to influence the self-steering of socio-spatial systems by just reducing the variety in the (notionally) controlled system (thus reducing the potential for fluctuations) could involve measures like the removal/exclusion of actors or the institutional elimination of possible future socio-spatial configurations through regulation. This in essence would be to reverse-engineer the three forms of change described by Portugali (stratigraphic, furcative and hermeneutic). There are plenty of examples and practices in the history of planning that could be seen as efforts to solve problems through variety reduction. The Urban Development Corporations (UDCs) in the 1980s were set up to tackle a problem that remained intractable for decades: the return of economic activity into vast inner-city sites on previously-developed land. These spaces were embedded in the daily lives of local communities, were under the jurisdiction of well established systems of governance, had various owners and posed a series of risks to potential investors. The UDCs operated in a specially created institutional context where public accountability was limited. They were endowed with significant powers completely circumventing the existing governance structures, had a specific and limited vision to pursue and had substantial amounts of direct or indirect finance at their disposal. Yet, although this approach significantly reduced the possible future states of the Docklands, UDC success still depended on amenable conditions in systems beyond UDC's reach, such as the property markets. Interestingly, the early problems and the eventual derailment of the scheme due to the collapse of Olympia and York can also be attributed, in cybernetic terminology, to the difference in variety between the group of actors running the Canary Wharf project and the external environment (i.e. the market). This discrepancy did not allow them to develop risk management options that would help them cope with an adverse property market situation, and they thus found themselves unable to adapt and survive during a downturn.

Given the importance of communication in controlling cybernetic systems, another way to reduce variety would be to restrict communication between the elements of a system to that which is desirable. Jails are the example par excellence of applying such a methodology in order to control a population. This may sound impossible to do in a western democracy during an era of informational overload, yet this is what the citizens of several states are facing every time they try to websearch using 'inappropriate' terms. Significantly for planning, many of the new measures that have been or are about to be introduced to the UK planning system follow a similar logic. For example, the procedures concerning the location of nuclear reactors or the procedures concerning big infrastructure projects reduce the potential communication exchanges that would otherwise have to take place if the standard UK planning system path was to be followed. This restriction of the number of stakeholders and of the scope and intensity of communication thus restricts the possible future outcomes of the process.

It appears, therefore, that it is not so much a question of whether this type of variety-reducing interventions are taking place: they clearly are in many cases and have been throughout the history of planning. In my view it is a matter of whether this approach is desirable on ethical grounds as well as of whether the outcome of such a process is desirable even by those who implement it in the first place. Von Foerster (1992) discusses the ethical issues surrounding the application of cybernetic principles on social systems and argues that the key principle underlying such applications should be not to impose restrictions on choice. Restricting choice essentially amounts to variety attenuation since it restricts the possible futures that can be pursued (see Van Wezemael, Chapter 9 this volume). The challenge, therefore, is to put in place mechanisms that allow for the widest possible representation and that permit for a flexible examination of the widest possible range of available choices without compromising its effectiveness and without becoming too complex and thus unmanageable. The importance of choice is paramount in another respect too. In an environment where the consequences of individual actions for the system are largely unpredictable, the individual cannot be held responsible for the systemic results of his or her actions. Individuals, however, can be held accountable for the criteria they use to guide their choices (i.e. the ethics of their choices). Needless to say that an effort to control systems just through variety reduction without any ethical considerations runs against the pluralist principles of democracy and is best suited to autocratic regimes.

In addition, reducing the variety of a sociospatial system to an extent that matches the variety of just a handful of actors, runs the risk of leading to a built environment that suits a limited range of needs, wishes and aspirations. History is littered with grand architectural designs which architects find stunning and which the users find completely dysfunctional. Britain's urban motorways were promoted, to put it crudely, with the interests of car users, car producers and the construction companies in mind, under the influence of a technocratic regime very much enthralled by the motor car. As a result, Birmingham is still struggling with its motorway inheritance which now has to be partially dismantled in order to make the city centre more inclusive and welcoming to a variety of users. It is not unexpected, however, that 'grand projects' or other major interventions require an approach based on variety attenuation which is the most effective approach for the delivery of such projects, according to the Law of Multi-scale Variety.

A further option in an effort to control systems through controlling variety (and one which has been argued for by several authors in the past), is to increase the variety of the controlling system to match that of the socio-spatial system which it strives to control or 'enact' (Weick 1979). This option bears the risk that eventually the controlling system builds up so much complexity that it itself becomes unmanageable. Although participatory practices emerging out of CPT may not specifically refer to, or aim at, variety engineering, their practical applications could be described as variety attenuation in cybernetic terms: the inclusion of as many views as possible and the reiteration of those views to promote understanding can be seen as a principle promoting variety attenuation.

A combination of the two approaches involves variety engineering focusing the controlling system on managing the residual variety with which the otherwise self-steering subsystems cannot cope (Beer 1979, 1994). The dictum that a good manager is the one that lets his or her employees get on with their jobs uninterrupted is well known. The 'Subsidiarity Principle' that structures the relations between the different levels of governance in the EU is another demonstration of how this idea has been implemented. In that respect it would be interesting to explore the usefulness of applying tried and tested models of communicative interaction like Team Syntegrity, introduced by Beer in 1994 (see Schwaninger 2000). Although Team Syntegrity is a sophisticated management method feeding into variety engineering processes, it does address issues of participant centrality and peripherality and assures adequate knowledge diffusion amongst large groups of participants. Still, as Team Syntegrity takes the pragmatic step of engulfing processes of variety attenuation and amplification it may, in its current form, be incompatible with the Habermasian foundations of CPT. Team Syntegrity is affected by 'communicative distortion' thus obstructing the whole process from reaching the 'ideal speech situation'. It is quite effective, however, in stabilizing systems of actors around key ideas, strategies and so on.

There is yet another set of options emanating out of an alternative interpretation of Ashby's Law and the Conant-Ashby theorem. If socio-spatial systems are inherently unmanageable, then planners could, in true second-order cybernetic fashion, frame their understanding of the process and the outcomes of their steering efforts within a new context. Elsewhere in this volume (Chapter 2), Roy argues for a recognition of 'urban informality' in planning as a valid analytical tool despite ostracism of the concept from what she called 'EuroAmerican planning theory'. Glanville (1997, 2007) is also a proponent of such an approach. He argues that there are certain advantages to unmanageability, mainly the possibility for new, previously unthought of, ideas, proposals and realities to emerge and thrive. Unmanageability leaves room for creativity and innovation as well as for solutions to emerge that are good enough but not necessarily 'optimal' or 'best', as Glanville continues.

In that respect, such an approach bears interesting resemblances to the description of planning Allmendinger gave when he paraphrased Healey: '… it is future pointing, not future defining' (Allmendinger 2002: 206). This is complementary to Friedmann's argument that planning should take the form of a locally based 'way of probing the future in order to make more intelligent and informed decisions in the present' (Friedmann et al. 2004). A key function for planners in this approach would be to put in place the 'pointing' or 'probing' devices. It requires people who are able to design, implement and operate the management systems that would foster the communication process supporting the reflexive conversation amongst the different actors participating in influencing the socio-spatial system at hand. The process would have to be characterized by a lack of 'steering' in a certain direction from planners by virtue of their access to a body of professional knowledge to which only they can lay claim. Actors should be left to create and enrich their own understandings of the 'Others'. Within such a context a planner becomes just another actor whose knowledge and arguments can and should be heard during the process of variety attenuation. This effort would not be directed towards reaching an 'optimal state' but (a) towards facilitating the emergence of the 'slow-moving variables' around which the socio-spatial system could be attracted or (b) towards creating a regulatory framework that would allow frequent minor dissipation events in order to avert a major catastrophic breakdown. In my view, option (b) above is both untenable because it presupposes first-order interventions/ total knowledge and also undesirable because it would limit any creative influence that would threaten to shift the status quo.

With that in mind, and based on Dahl's insights on autonomy and control in democratic regimes (Dahl 1982) it is important to set out some general principles that in my view should characterize a planning system trying to negotiate the conflicting objectives and aspirations laid out in the previous sections:

- It should be based on democratic decision-making: its foundations should be those of direct democracy.
- It should be decentralized, individual units (i.e. planning jurisdictions), which at the lowest level should be small enough to allow for direct participation.
- It should be layered in a way that mirrors the 'emergent' nature of the issues that it is called to deal with.
- It should be operating on the basis of subsidiarity, higher levels should not intervene in matters that the lower levels have the competency to deal with.
- It should be scale-free: each level should have complete responsibility for all matters arising within that level, including strategic considerations.
- It should be custom made for the specific social, geographical and temporal context it would be called to operate in.
- The planning bureaucracy at each level should be independent from other bureaucracies, to allow for mutual control.

A planning system organized around such principles would be structured in small units that would give rise to larger units: a model of the form of the socio-spatial system it would be trying to affect. It would be a system embracing variety and choice as notionally it would take into account each and every one of the individual actors constituting the socio-spatial system in question. It would be efficient, since the quantity of communication moving between levels would be smaller compared to other, more centralized systems.

What would the outcome of such a planning system be? Nobody knows, nobody has ever done it. Notwithstanding the substantial differences, in some ways such a planning system resembles the logic of the UK planning system as it was envisaged in 1947. Combined with nationalized development rights the simulation of such a system demonstrated superior social efficiency (Webster and Wu 2001). This would facilitate evolution as 'structured adaptive response' whereby macrostructure would affect individuals and the response of individuals would affect macrostructure in return.

Conclusions

This chapter began by posing specific questions regarding the usefulness of re-engaging with cybernetics and the fundamental question of whether steering socio-spatial phenomena is actually necessary. I set about answering these questions by positioning spatial planning within a social context of ever-increasing complexification and alienation, which increase the need of individuals to find tools that would help them understand their environment. I then selectively explored the developments that have taken place in cybernetics since the 1960s, and I highlighted especially the emergence of second-order cybernetics and their focus on the reflexive aspects of planners who, as a result, become embedded within the socio-spatial systems they are notionally trying to steer: spatial planning becomes an effort to influence the self-steering of self-organizing socio-spatial systems.

The two most important aspects in any effort to influence such systems are communication and variety. The laws of cybernetics leave only certain pathways open when considering ways to intervene in complex adaptive socio-spatial systems. Steering necessitates communication, yet communication between subsystems of different variety is never a perfect mapping. It involves the creation within each actor/subsystem of an image of what the 'Other' means. It is this image that is reciprocally communicated through feedback loops spiralling through time. In this way the communicating systems increase their internal complexity (variety), thus enhancing their ability to adapt and co-evolve.

This increased adaptability emanates from the Law of Requisite Variety and the Conant-Ashby theorem which state that variety is the crucial parameter defining control. No system can be controlled by another, less complex, system unless that control becomes restrictive, thus reducing the complexity of the controlled system. The outcomes of failed attempts to control complex socio-spatial systems through much less complex controlling systems plague societies all over the world. Roy's chapter in the current volume is full of stories demonstrating how authoritarian or failed states are unsuccessful in creating effective interest-negotiation mechanisms. In her examples, interests are negotiated through informal channels, where power relations are much more prevalent, to the point of overt physical violence. Crucially, however, the negotiation does indeed take place and innovative adaptive societal responses do emerge. The question is not whether individuals and societies will find ways to survive in the absence of (state) mediation – and thus in a formal-institutional vacuum – but whether that response is more efficient, effective or equitable than the formal democratic alternative.

I suggested that the most intriguing perspective in the future application of second-order cybernetics in spatial planning would be to learn how to deal with and accept the outcomes of unmanageability. Inevitably, given the difficulties of managing complex socio-spatial systems, planners or regulators generically, are doomed to 'fail'. Such 'failure', however, refers to a first-order teleological understanding of socio-spatial systems. It means that the original set of goals was not achieved in its totality. In a second-order understanding, it is to be expected that our lives will not necessarily pan out exactly as we wish, yet we still make plans and strive to achieve them: we influence the way our life goes as active participants in its course. In a societal context there would be an additional concern about how to decide which direction to take. To use a phrase from Van Wezemael (Chapter 9, this volume): which modulation of singularities do we actualize and how do we reach that decision? Since restrictive control is ethically undesirable, largely ineffective and potentially catastrophic, spatial planners are in essence left with trying to invent forms of variety engineering that respect choice. This may well entail a planning system which would assist the efforts of society to exert influence on the self-steering processes guiding any socio-spatial system by rooting itself in direct democracy. That could well be the most effective mechanism to manage variety in an ethically acceptable way. In the words of Glanville (2007, p. 1173), such a planning system would also amount to experimenting with different ways to 'try again, fail again, fail better'. Therefore eventually, a variety-based second-order view of spatial planning can only help societies let go of the teleological understanding of planning.

References

Albrechts, L. (2004) 'Strategic (spatial) planning reexamined' *Environment and Planning B: Planning and Design* 31(5): 743–58.

Alfasi N., and Portugali J. (2004) 'Planning just-in-time versus planning just-in-case' *Cities* 21(1): 29–39.

Alfasi, N., and Portugali, J. (2007) 'Planning rules for a self-planned city' *Planning Theory* 6(2): 164–82.

Allen, P. (1981) 'The evolutionary paradigm of dissipative structures', in Jantsch, E. (ed.) *The Evolutionary Vision*. Boulder, CO: Westview Press, 25-71.

Allen, P. (1997) *Cities and Regions as Self-organising Systems: Models of Complexity*. London: Taylor and Francis.

Allen, P., and Sanglier, M. (1981) 'Urban evolution, self organisation and decision making' *Environment and Planning A* 13: 169–83.

Allmendinger, P. (2002) *Planning Theory*. Basingstoke: Palgrave Macmillan.

Allmendinger, P., and Tewdwr-Jones, M. (2002) 'The communicative turn in urban planning: unravelling paradigmatic, imperialistic and moralistic dimensions' *Space and Polity* 6(1): 5–24.

Ashby, W.R. (1956) *Introduction to Cybernetics*. New York: Wiley.

Bak, P. (1996) *How Nature Works: The Science of Self-organised Criticality*. New York: Springer-Verlag.

Bak, P., and Chen, K. (1991) 'Self organized criticality' *Scientific American* 264: 46–53.

Bak, P., Chen, K., and Wiesenfeld, K. (1988) 'Self organized criticality' *Physical Review A* 38: 364–74.

Bar-Yam, Y. (2004) 'Multiscale variety in complex systems' *Complexity* 9(4): 37–45.

Batty, M. (1997) 'Cellular automata and urban form: a primer' *JAPA* 63(2): 266–74.

Batty, M. (2005) *Cities and Complexity*. Cambridge, MA: MIT Press.

Batty, M., and Longley, P. (1994) *Fractal Cities*. London: Academic Press.

Batty, M., and Xie, Y. (1999) 'Self organized criticality and urban development' *Discrete Dynamics in Nature and Society* 3(2–3): 109–24.

Beer, S. (1979) *The Heart of Enterprise*. Chichester: John Wiley and Sons.

Beer, S. (1994) *Beyond Dispute: The Invention of Team Syntegrity*. Chichester: John Wiley and Sons.

Beer, S. (2004) 'Reflections of a cybernetician on the practice of planning' *Kybernetes* 33(3/4): 767–73.

Bruner, J. (1986) *Actual Minds, Possible Worlds*. Cambridge, MA: Harvard University Press.

Conant, R.C., and Ashby, W.R. (1981) 'Every good regulator of a system must be a model of that system', in Conant, R. (ed.) *Mechanisms of Intelligence: Ashby's Writings on Cybernetics*. Seaside, CA: Intersystems Publications, 205–14.

Dahl, R. (1982) *Dilemmas of Pluralist Democracies: Autonomy vs. Control*. New Haven: Yale University Press.

DeLanda, M. (2003) *War in the Age of Intelligent Machines* 5th edition. New York: Zone Books.

de Roo, G. (2007) 'Actor consulting: a model to handle fuzziness in planning', in de Roo, G., and Porter, G. (2007) *Fuzzy Planning: The Role of Actors in a Fuzzy Governance Environment*. Aldershot: Ashgate, 131–50.

de Roo, G., and Porter, G. (2007) *Fuzzy Planning: The Role of Actors in a Fuzzy Governance Environment*. Aldershot: Ashgate.

Domanski, R. and Judge, E. (1994) *Changes in the Regional Economy in the Period of System Transition*. Polish Academy of Sciences: Warsaw.

Faludi, A. (1973a) *Planning Theory*. Oxford: Pergamon Press.

Faludi, A. (1973b) *A Reader in Planning Theory*. Oxford: Pergamon Press.

Friedmann, J. et al. (2004) 'Strategic spatial planning and the longer range' *Planning Theory and Practice* 5(1): 49–67.

Geyer, F., and van der Zouwen, J. (2001) 'Introduction to the main themes in sociocybernetics', in Geyer, F., and van der Zouwen, J. (eds) (2001) *Sociocybernetics: Complexity, Autopoiesis and Observation of Social Systems*. London: Greenwood Press.

Giddens, A. (1984) *The Constitution of Society: Outline of the Theory of Structuration*. Berkeley, CA: University of California Press.

Glanville, R. (1997) 'The value of being unmanageable: value and creativity in cyberspace', in Eichman, H., Hochgerner, J. and Nahrada, J. (eds) (2000) *Netzwerke: Kooperation in Arbeit*. Vienna: Falter Verlag.

Glanville, R. (2004) 'The purpose of second order second-order cybernetics' *Kybernetes* 33(9/10): 1379–86.

Glanville, R. (2007) 'Try again. Fail again. Fail better: the cybernetics in design and the design in cybernetics' *Kybernetes* 36(9/10): 1173–206.

Haken, H. (1983a) *Synergetics: An Introduction*. Berlin: Springer-Verlag.

Haken, H. (1983b) *Advanced Synergetics*. Berlin: Springer-Verlag.

Haken, H. (2006) *Information and Self-organisation* 3rd edition. Berlin: Springer.

Harvey, D. (1990) *The Condition of Postmodernity: An Inquiry into the Origins of Cultural Change.* Cambridge, MA: Blackwell.

Healey, P. (1993) 'Planning through debate: the communicative turn in planning theory', in Fisher, F. and Forester, J. (eds) *The Argumentative Turn in Policy Analysis and Planning.* London: UCL Press, 233–53.

Healey, P. (2006) *Collaborative Planning* 2nd edition. Basingstoke: Palgrave Macmillan.

Healey, P. (2007) 'Re-thinking key dimensions of strategic spatial planning: sustainability and complexity', in de Roo, G., and Porter, G. (2007) *Fuzzy Planning: The Role of Actors in a Fuzzy Governance Environment.* Aldershot: Ashgate, 21–41.

Huebler, A. (1989) 'Adaptive control of chaotic systems' *Helv Phys Acta* 62: 343–6.

Huebler, A. et al. (2007) 'Managing chaos' *Complexity* 12(3): 10–13.

Ison, R.L. et al. (2007) 'Systemic environmental decision making: designing learning systems' *Kybernetes* 36(9–10): 1340–61.

Jacobs, J. (1961) *The Death and Life of Great American Cities.* New York: Random House.

Kiss, I.Z. et al. (2007) 'Engineering complex dynamical structures: Sequential patterns and desynchronisation' *Science* 316: 1886–9.

Lachs, J. (1976) 'Mediation and psychic distance', in Geyer R., and Schweitzer D. (eds) *Theories of Alienation.* The Hague: Martinus Nijhoff.

McLoughlin, B. (1969) *Urban and Regional Planning: A Systems Approach.* London: Faber & Faber.

Nicolis, G., and Prigogine, I. (1977) *Self Organisation on Non-equilibrium Systems: From Dissipative Structures to Order Through Fluctuations.* New York: Wiley.

Nijkamp, P., and Reggiani, A. (1998) *The Economics of Complex Spatial Systems.* Amsterdam: Elsevier.

Pask, G. (1975) *Conversation Theory.* London: Hutchinson.

Portugali, J. (1997) 'Self organising cities' *Futures* 29(4–5): 353–80.

Portugali, J. (1999) *Self Organisation and the City.* Berlin: Springer-Verlag.

Portugali, J. (2006) 'Complexity theory as a link between space and place' *Environment and Planning A* 38: 647–64.

Repenning, N., and Sterman J (2001) 'Nobody ever gets credit for fixing problems that never happened' *California Management Review* 43(4).

Schwaninger, M. (2000) 'Managing complexity – the path toward intelligent organizations' *Systemic Practice and Action Research* 13(2): 207–41.

Schwaninger, M., and Kroener, M. (2004) 'City planning: dissolving urban problems insights from an application of management cybernetics' *Kybernetes* 33(3/4): 557–76.

Scott, B. (2004) 'Second-order cybernetics: an historical introduction' *Kybernetes* 33(9/10): 1365–78.

Taylor, N. (1998) *Urban Planning Theory Since 1945.* London: Sage.

Tsoukas, H., and Hatch, M.J. (2001) 'Complex thinking, complex practice: the case for a narrative approach to organisational complexity' *Human Relations* 54(8): 979–1013.

Umpleby, S.A. (2001) 'What comes after second order second-order cybernetics?' <http://www.gwu.edu/~umpleby/recent_papers/2001_what_comes_after_second_order_cybernetics.htm> (accessed 20 November 2008).

Vickers, G. (1972) *Freedom in a Rocking Boat: Changing Values in an Unstable Society*. London: Penguin.

von Bertalanffy, L. (1968) *General System Theory: Foundations, Development, Applications*. New York: George Braziller.

von Foerster, H. (1960) 'On self organising systems and their environments', in Yovits, F.C. and Cameron, S. (eds) *Self-Organising Systems*. London: Pergamon Press, 30–50.

von Foerster, H. (1974) *Cybernetics of Cybernetics*. Urbana, IL: University of Illinois Press.

von Foerster, H. (1981) *Observing Systems (Systems Inquiry Series)*. Salinas: Intersystems Publications.

von Foerster, H. (1992) 'Ethics and second order second-ordercybernetics' in *Cybernetics and Human Knowing* 1(1) available at <www.fleck.kvl.dk/sbr/Cyber/cybernetics>

von Glasersfeld, E. (1987) *The Construction of Knowledge*. Salinas, CA: InterSystems Publications.

von Glasersfeld, E. (1991) (ed.) *Radical Constructivism in Mathematics Education*. Dordrecht: Kluwer.

Webster, C., and Wu, F. (2001) 'Coase, spatial pricing and self-organising cities' *Urban Studies* 38(11): 2037–54.

Weick, K.E. (1979) *The Social Psychology of Organizing*. Reading, MA: Addison-Wesley.

Weidlich, W. (1987) 'Synergetics and social science', in Graham, R., and Wunderlin, A. (eds) *Lasers and Synergetics*. Berlin: Springer-Verlag, 238–56.

Weidlich, W., and Haag, G. (1984) *Concepts and Methods of Quantitative Sociology*. Berlin: Springer-Verlag.

Weidlich W., and Haag, G. (1988) (eds) *Interregional Migration: Dynamic Theory and Comparative Analysis*. Berlin: Springer-Verlag.

Wiener, N. (1948) *Cybernetics: Control and Communication in the Animal and Machine*. Cambridge, MA: MIT Press.

Strategic Navigation in an Ocean of Theoretical and Practice Complexity

Jean Hillier

Introduction

As my embarkation point for the voyage that is this chapter, I take a quotation from Salman Rushdie's *Haroun and the Sea of Stories*. When the boy, Haroun, looked into the sea of stories:

> [h]e looked into the water and saw that it was made up of a thousand thousand and one different currents, each one a different colour, weaving in and out of one another like a liquid tapestry of breathtaking complexity; and Iff explained that those were the Streams of Story … And because the stories were held here in fluid form, they retained the ability to change, to become new versions of themselves, to join up with other stories and so become yet other stories. (Rushdie 1990: 72)

In the Ocean of Stories that is planning theory and practice we see human and non-human stories, flowing, interconnecting, congealing and transforming the molecular and molar lines of trajectories. It is increasingly accepted by academics and practitioners that a city is an 'endless kaleidoscope of possible viewpoints' or landmarks; a 'mobile panorama of interacting events' (Cooper 2005: 1693). We are beginning to regard cities, human and non-human actants not as 'things-in-themselves' but as complex, multiple and mutable elements of connections and disconnections, relations and transitions. The recent introduction of a range of concepts, including complexity, multiplicity, emergence, becoming, assemblage and so on represents a relatively new and important shift in thinking of theorization and, by extension, of methodology (Venn 2006) in planning.

I offer a multiple, relational approach of dynamic complexity to understanding contingencies of place and actant behaviours, based predominantly on the work of Gilles Deleuze and Félix Guattari. If spatial planning is concerned with 'discovering the options people have as to how to live' (Thrift 1996: 8), then it is concerned with understanding the world in terms of practical effectivity rather than of classificatory representation – not the what, but the pragmatic Deleuzean how: not so much 'what does it mean?' but 'how does it work?' (Deleuze and Guattari 1984: 109, 129). The relevance of pragmatism for spatial planning theory and practice is being increasingly recognized (see Healey 2009; Verma, this volume), as indicated in the Introduction to Part 3.

Rather than seeing the flux of movements in societies as sets of things with stable qualities, and thinking of themselves as people who might act upon these things, planning theorists and practitioners might instead view movement as productive; a Deleuzoguattarian open whole traversing and connecting across space and time. This is a problem of understanding the 'place' of the folding of intensive and extensive and the Deleuzoguattarian virtual-actual within an open whole.

I am drawn to Foucault's ideas of immanence and to Deleuze and Guattari's ideas of becoming or moving beyond. These notions allow unexpected elements to come into play and things not to quite work out as expected. They allow us to see planning and governance as experiments or speculations entangled in a series of modulating networked relationships in circumstances at the same time both rigid and flexible, where outcomes are volatile: where problems are not 'solved' once and for all but are rather constantly recast, reformulated in new perspectives. Questions become issues of problematization rather than of neat solutions. This is to view speculation as creation rather than as scientistic proof-discovery. I regard experimentation as a violation of prescribed conventions; a transgression of boundaries, in which genres are blurred and jumbled. Speculation is a tentative method of knowing, working within an ideology of doubt and uncertainty: of what might become.

The material in this chapter is a temporary fixity of my ongoing 'gropings in the dark, experimentation, modes of intuition' (Deleuze and Guattari 1987: 461), entangled in the oceans of complex poststructuralism or poststructuralist complexity. My small part in the rhizome of Conceptual Challenges reflects my theoretical genealogy through work by Habermas, Foucault, Laclau and Mouffe and Lacan and its recent rupture with my discovery of the potential for creative transformation offered by Gilles Deleuze's generative ontology of difference.

Like the volume as a whole, this chapter is itself a rhizomic 'little machine' (Deleuze and Guattari 1987: 4) attempting to establish connections between ideas and issues raised in other chapters. I regard it as a particular 'direction in motion' (Deleuze and Guattari 1987: 21); a multiplicity connected to other multiplicities, yet possessing a kind of stability and stockpiling or coding of information. I offer a brief understanding of complexity and an introduction to the notions of cities, planning authorities and planning processes as complex assemblages. I adopt a poststructuralist standpoint and, after outlining a Deleuzoguattarian-inspired approach to planning as speculation and experimentation, I present a multiplanar theory of planning as strategic navigation. I then develop some initial methodological thoughts on how the theory might translate into strategic spatial planning practice.

I conclude that spatial planning theory and practice will inevitably be anexact stories where the unexpected and the aleatory lurk.

A Poststructuralist Perspective on Complexity, Complex Adaptive Systems and Complex Meshworks

folding relational continua into and out of each other to selective, productive effect … a way of placing relation against relation. (Massumi 2002: 204)

Although there is a multiplicity of published material available on complexity across a wide range of disciplines, there appears to be little agreement on what complexity theories actually entail. There is no all-embracing complexity theory, but a number of different theories coming from different research traditions (ranging from systems theory to cybernetics) and utilizing different methodologies including computer modelling and ethnographic case studies. It appears that several, very different, schools of thought have developed, variously described as logico-scientific or narrative (Bruner 1986), hard or soft (Richardson and Cilliers 2001), romantic or baroque (Law 2004), computational, scientific, mathematical or critical (Cilliers 2005) and ecological (Smith and Jenks 2005) as outlined in more detail in the Introduction to Part 3.

Definitions of complexity are context-dependent. Social theorists have adopted/adapted the language of complexity from the natural sciences. As John Urry (2005: 1) indicates, complexity thinking 'derives from developments over the past two decades or so within physics, biology, mathematics, ecology, chemistry and economics, from the revival of neo-vitalism in social thought (Fraser et al. 2005; [and Pløger, this volume]) and from the emergence of a more "complex structure of feeling" that challenges some everyday notions of social order (Maasen and Weingart 2000; Thrift 1999)'. Complexity thinking is thus multidisciplinary; concerned with relationships and processes of unpredictable movement or emergence where there is a tension between structure/order and a lack of structure/chaos. As Clark (2005: 166) suggests, complexity theory enables acknowledgement of 'the unmanageability of the contemporary world whilst also holding open the possibility that novel forms of organisation or structuring might emerge spontaneously out of a sea of dense and disorderly interaction'. (See also Karadimitriou, this volume.)

Key 'properties' of many complexity theories include: distributed connectivity (functions and relations are multi-scalar), openness, non-linearity, emergence and self-organizing adaptive behaviour which may display elements of path dependence, but which are fundamentally non-deterministic (Martin and Sunley 2007). Cilliers summarizes 'the view from complexity' as follows:

- 'Complex systems are open systems.
- They operate under conditions not at equilibrium.

- Complex systems consist of many components. The components themselves are often simple (or can be treated as such).
- The output of components is a function of their inputs. At least some of these functions must be non-linear.
- The state of the system is determined by the values of the inputs and outputs.
- Interactions are defined by actual input–output relations and they are dynamic (the strength of the interactions change over time).
- Components on average interact with many others. There are often multiple routes possible between components, mediated in different ways.
- Some sequences of interaction will provide feedback routes, whether long or short.
- Complex systems display behaviour that results from the interaction between components and not from characteristics inherent to the components themselves. This is sometimes called emergence.
- Asymmetrical structure (temporal, spatial and functional organization) is developed, maintained and adapted in complex systems through internal dynamic processes. Structure is maintained even though the components themselves are exchanged or renewed.
- Complex systems display behaviour over a divergent range of timescales. This is necessary in order for the system to cope with its environment. It must adapt to changes in the environment quickly, but it can only sustain itself if at least part of the system changes at a slower rate than changes in the environment. This part can be seen as the 'memory' of the system.
- More than one description of a complex system is possible. Different descriptions will decompose the system in different ways. Different descriptions may also have different degrees of complexity.' (Cilliers 2005: 257, in Hillier 2007: 43)

Cilliers (2005: 257) indicates, in particular, differences between 'a more strictly mathematical and computational view' derived largely from cybernetics, systems and chaos theory which may see 'an underlying unity in a world of heterogeneous objects and phenomena' (Kwa 2002: 24) and 'a more critical understanding of complexity' (Cilliers 2005: 257). This latter is a qualitative, Leibnizian-inspired view of connected entities, folds and infinitely varied patterns, not an essence, but an operative function (Deleuze 1993: 3) which argues that complexity theory does not provide us with exact tools to solve our complex problems (Cilliers 2005: 257) but confronts us with the limits of our understanding and shows us why complex problems are so wicked.

Differences across this apparent divide are increasingly being bridged (explained in the Introduction to Part 3 and exemplified by Karadimitriou, this volume) as authors such as Plummer and Sheppard (2006; 2007), Martin and Sunley (2007) and Bergmann et al (2009) demonstrate. Dialogues are taking place and resonances emerging as scholars on both sides of the divide recognize that mathematical modelling methodologies alone cannot explain complex socio-economic behaviours (Martin and Sunley 2007) and that qualitative relational approaches to socio-spatial dynamics may benefit from mathematics-based understandings, for instance of autopoiesis or neurosystemic activities (Connolly 2002; Mingers 2002; Chettiparamb 2007).

For instance, Ilya Prigogine's (1968, 1980; Prigogine and Stengers 1984) work on complex systems, including issues of far-from equilibrium conditions, autopoiesis, path dependency and energized interaction, has had a significant influence on theorizing complexity both quantitatively and qualitatively. Prigogine (2004) suggests that in unstable, dynamic, 'chaotic' systems, more than one choice of future path or 'solution' will appear, or emerge. 'There is no certainty' (2004: 7–8).

In 1995 John Holland described what he termed complex adaptive systems (CAS) in which networks of agents (individuals, organizations) act and adapt to changes taking place both within the network and in its external environment. From its development in the natural sciences, CAS-based analyses have migrated to the fields of organization management and recently to strategic planning, notably via Axelrod and Cohen (1999) in the work of Judith Innes and David Booher (1999; Booher and Innes 2002, 2006; Connick and Innes 2003).

Several authors argue that we can view cities as CAS (Portugali 2000, 2008; DeLanda 2006, this volume), planning authorities as CAS (Booher and Innes op. cit.) and strategic spatial planning processes as CAS (Booher and Innes op. cit.; Moobela 2005). Whilst I disagree with the CAS criterion of autopoiesis, I do agree with Portugali (2008) who indicates that emergence is a key characteristic of such complex systems. If we regard emergence as 'the mutual constitution of local-to-global or "upward" causality that produces focused systematic behaviour and the global-to-local or "downward" causality that constrains the local interaction of components' as Bonta and Protevi (2004: 32) suggest (see also Van Wezemael, this volume), then we can begin to identify a topology of interrelated processes and spatial relations of inclusion and exclusion, connections and disjunctions: a 'space without edges' (Serres 2000: 51) where boundaries of meaning, space and time, are blurred and in flux.

Gilles Deleuze's work resonates strongly with that of Michel Serres, his 'best friend' (Serres 1996), employing metaphors of folding, lines and perspectives, as he attempts to map the dynamism of emergence. For Deleuze, relations are vital to the active construction of existence. It is the contingent 'circumstances, actions, and passions' (Deleuze and Parnet 2002: 56) of life which provide for the specific forms of relations between different terms. Relations are endowed with a positive reality as they are not derived from the terms or entities themselves. Relations are not subordinated to the essence of things. Rather, they come into being via practice. Relations are thus 'effects of the activities and practices of individuals who are different yet nevertheless interacting' (Hayden 1995: 286), as Van Wezemael illustrates (this volume).

Based on Deleuzoguattarian ideas and recent work in fluid dynamics, authors such as Sheller (2004) and Law (2004) challenge the traditional concept of networks (popularized by authors such as Castells 1996) as being representations of flows or lines between fixed points or nodes, which thereby reify presence and absence, while DeLanda (1998; 2006, this volume) prefers the term 'meshwork' to network, as meshwork emphasizes interconnections between heterogeneous entities in a fluid, open-ended future. A space of flows is thus a topological space of lines rather than of points. Moreover, points are not fixed (Cartesian-style) but lie on the intersections of many lines. 'We looked for foci of unification, nodes of totalisation, and processes of subjectification in arrangements, and they were always relative' (Deleuze 1995: 86). Organizations, then, may be recognized as complex systems of relations (Deleuzoguattarian assemblages) in complex open environments.

Different complexities thus relate to different ontologies. They all call for different strategies of complexity reduction. We have to have complexity reduction in order to cope – to be able to 'go on'. There is a niche for computer modelling as well as micropolitical ethnography. They require both sound theoretical foundation and methodology.

Strategic Spatial Planning as Strategic Navigation: Multiplanar Speculation and Experimentation

a productive encounter with chaos. (O'Sullivan 2006: 62)

Imagine ...

It is the middle of the ocean. Several people are paddling a raft. They are not shipwrecked, but have come together for some reason (it could be a race or a dare). It is a makeshift raft, with makeshift paddles. The people do not know where they are very precisely and they are out of sight of land, trying to make headway in an ocean of varying currents, with varying waves, wind speeds and directions. Their overall objective – or trajectory – is to reach land.

How might they go about getting there? I argue that they would probably attempt this through a series of short-term projects, such as:

- trying to work out where they are. They might think through questions such as: where do they think they came from? How might they have got here from there? What can they remember? What landmarks did they pass?
- trying to work out future potentialities. Questions might include: what are the elements involved and what are the relations or connections (and disjunctions) between them? Which relations are likely to be more powerful? With what implications? For example:
  - the condition of the raft and the paddle – these are very makeshift and need constant repair/patching up; elements fall off; chemicals in a plastic container are leaking and eating away the rope binding the raft together;
  - the ocean and its currents – the people may anticipate the general direction of the currents but they cannot predict them;
  - the weather – what might the effects be of sun? Storms? Seeing stars and

the position of constellations? Or is it too cloudy to see the night sky?

– the strength of the people on board the raft – this relates to availability of food, water, heat, body mass, physical and mental strength, and so on;

– desires of the people on board – to survive? To be a hero? To remain adrift just long enough to attract sponsorship for a book deal with potential film rights?

– chance (the aleatory), including hazards such as icebergs, huge containers lost from ships;

– hope – of seeing a ship which stops; that the blur on the horizon turns out to be land.

Having worked out the relations between these (and other) elements, can the people on board tweak any of them so that the outcomes might be more favourable? There is a need to negotiate between philosophical or ethical ideals and the practical necessity of getting things done. What experimentation might be productive? For instance, ditching a sick person to save food and water for the others? Dumping the chemicals container to save the rope, although the container gives the raft extra buoyancy? Making the raft look aesthetically attractive?

The people will need to 'live' together, with flexibility and adaptability; a situation of creative experimentation. Depending on circumstances and what seems to work (or not), they will probably change their means (perhaps making a sail, ditching a container), the direction they go in (possibly someone thinks they see land far off to the left), and perhaps even their goals. Of course, with several people on the raft, they probably will not agree on the direction in which they want to go or the actions they should take to get there.

I refer to the above as 'strategic navigation'.[1] I believe that it resonates with practices of strategic (spatial) planning. It also resonates with the work of French theorists, Gilles Deleuze and Félix Guattari.

Deleuze and Guattari's theorizing promotes pragmatic, speculative experimentation. Deleuze, in particular, focuses on the potentialities of the multiplicity of forces which could be activated rather than on transcendent questions of the 'good' or on a negativity of what is absent. Trajectories, movement and transformation are vital. 'Becoming' is a movement between things, disrupting meanings, understandings and ways of being. Concepts are fluid, folding across and into each other, not always harmoniously and often in agonistic dissonance where differences come into contact. Becoming, then, is 'supremely pragmatic' (Massumi 1992: 100). Deleuze actually calls his philosophy a 'pragmatics', as he aims to lever open new spaces and make new connections of lines between elements.[2]

---

1   I am indebted to Catherine Wilkinson for introducing me to the work of Richard Hames (2007) who uses the term 'strategic navigation'. Hames is clearly thinking along similar lines to myself. He also puts theory into practice in the field of organizational management. (See <http://www.richardhames.com>)

2   Several scholars identify connections between Deleuze and Guattari and early

To me, strategic spatial planning represents a form of practice of strategically navigated becoming. It evolves, it functions, it adapts, somewhat chaotically, always pragmatically, concerned with what can be done, how new things, new foldings and connections can be made experimentally, yet still in contact with reality (Hillier 2007). As practised, strategic spatial planning attempts to embrace a future that is not characterized by the continuity of the present, nor by the repetition of the past, but by a difference that can never be fully grasped (May 2005). On this point, see Luca Bertolini's exploration of planning as evolutionary governance in this volume.

I argue that spatial planning should accommodate fluidity and immanence and have some form of temporary fixity (Hillier 2007). I propose that strategic spatial planning be concerned with trajectories rather than specified end-points. In regarding strategic spatial planning as an experimental practice working with doubt and uncertainty, engaged with speculation as adaptation and creation rather than as scientistic proof-discovery – a speculative exercise, a sort of creative agonistic – I suggest a new definition of spatial planning as strategic navigation along the lines of the investigation of 'virtualities' unseen in the present; the speculation about what may yet happen; the temporary inquiry into what at a given time and place we might yet think or do and how this might influence socially and environmentally just spatial form (Hillier 2007).

In theorizing strategic spatial planning as a form of strategic navigation, I adopt the ontological conceptualization of planes used by Deleuze and Guattari (1987: 265): 'perhaps there are two planes, or two ways of conceptualising the plane'. Deleuze and Guattari also refer to planes as plans. In French the word plan refers to both a plane (or plateau) and a plan, scheme or project. Deleuze and Guattari typically use the plane for a type of thinking which mediates between 'the chaos of chance happenings ... on the one hand, and structured, orderly thinking on the other' (Stagoll 2005: 204). As such, I find their ideas to be extremely relevant to the praxis of spatial planning.

The first type of Deleuzoguattarian ontological plane is a plane of immanence (1994). The second type is a plane of organisation (1987). I argue for the broad trajectories/visions of strategic spatial planning to be background plan(e)s of immanence and for more specific local/short-term plans and projects as foregrounded plan(e)s of organization (see schematic descriptors, Table 17.1). For simplicity, I use the term plane, rather than plan.

---

twentieth century American pragmatists. For instance, Semetsky (2003; 2006) traces a Deweyan legacy through Deleuze's work; Massumi (2002) and Lazzarato (2005) trace William James' radical empiricism and Deleuze (1986; 1989) himself acknowledges C.S. Peirce's influence on the development of the concept of the diagram. As Rorty (1982: xviii) wrote: '[o]n my view, James and Dewey were not only waiting at the end of the dialectical road which analytical philosophy travelled, but are waiting at the end of the road which, for example, Foucault and Deleuze are currently travelling'.

Table 17.1   Schematic descriptors of the planes of immanence and organization

Plane of Immanence	Plane of Organization
becomings/emergence	transcendence
open-ended trajectories	closed goals
multiplicities of meshworks	hierarchical relations of power
chance/aleatory	planned development
smooth space (with some striation)	striated space (with some smoothing)
unstructured	structured
dynamism of unformed elements	stability of judgement and identity
flux and fluidity	inertia or sluggish movement
power to	power over

Source: Hillier 2007: 243.

Planes of Immanence

This broad plane is defined not by what it contains, but 'rather by the forces that intersect it and the things it can do' (Kaufman 1998: 6). It is the temporary product of a mapping of forces (see below). As Kaufman (1998: 6) continues, such mapping 'is at once the act of charting out a pathway and the opening of that pathway to the event of the chance encounter'.

The plane is an object of construction; a practice (Bonta and Protevi 2004: 62) which maps and records performance of actants' desires: 'a disorganised flux that allows itself to be coded' (Colebrook 2002: 114). The plane is open to 'new connections, creative and novel becomings that will give it new patterns and triggers of behaviour' (Bonta and Protevi, 2004: 62–3). It is the 'virtual realm of potentials'. The 'key move' is to construct a plane by collaborative experimentation – to work experimentally together on my metaphorical raft in order to reach land.

The plane of immanence is a praxis that leaves the ends of each line or path of knowledge open to extension (Skott-Myhre 2005); not something closed or the end of a process. A plane (long-term strategic plan or trajectory) of foresight; of creative transformation, of what might be. Chance is important, however. We should not forget the potential for unforeseen challenges and opportunities to emerge. The plane is not a definitive method, state of knowledge nor a set of opinions. Rather it 'functions like a sieve over chaos' (Boundas 2005: 273), implying a sort of 'groping experimentation' (Deleuze and Guattari 1994: 41) of multiplicities of concepts, many of which never come to be as originally intended.

Planes of Organization

Deleuzoguattarian planes of organization (1987) support the day-to-day 'rigid, dichotomous segmentarities of personal and social life' (Patton 1986: np). These planes contain hierarchical power relations which regulate or stratify our worlds (into zones of land uses, for example) and fix identities (such as female, male; resident of suburb x or town y). This is a teleological plane concerned with the development of forms and the formation of subjects supported by stability of judgement and identity. It is a plane of transcendence.

The plane of organization is a transcendent plan or blueprint with certain goals for development. These goals are predetermined standards (such as land use regulations or a design guide) to which things are submitted in judgement and ordered by the forms of representation (whether applications meet the standard criteria, etc.). Local area action plans, design briefs, detailed projects are typical planes of organization. They tend to be relatively local or micro-scale, short-term and content specific. They facilitate small movements or changes along the dynamic, open trajectories of planes of immanence.

The planes of immanence and organization exist simultaneously and are interleaved; a multitude of layers that are sometimes fairly closely knit together and sometimes more separate. The two planes become coexistent such that blocks of space-time and segments of one plane run up against, through and over those of the other. We, as actants, inhabit both planes at the same time. In the words of Deleuze and Guattari (1987: 213), 'every politics is simultaneously a macropolitics and a micropolitics'.

The theory offers the potential for multiple plans:

- several (or perhaps one collectively preferred) 'macropolitical' trajectories or 'visions' of the longer-term future, including concepts towards which actants desire to move, such as sustainability (planes of immanence);
- shorter-term, location-specific, 'micropolitical', detailed plans and projects with collaboratively determined tangible goals, for example, for main street regeneration, provision of affordable housing and so on (planes of organization).

Multiplanar theory comprises macro, molar lines of broad trajectories or 'visions' of master signifiers such as sustainability, a good place to live, accessibility and so on – a plane of immanence – which enable becomings, and molecular lines proceeding by thresholds (Deleuze and Parnet 2002) – a plane of organization – of stratified segments marking small movements or changes; shorter-term decisions and projects. There is no dualism between the different kinds of planes and lines, rather circuits of connection along a frontier of multiplicity, of folding together, of connection and juxtaposition. Strategic spatial planning practices operate on the frontier of both planes. There is a need for both longer-term visions and shorter-term decisions.[3]

It might be suggested that these ideas are merely another form of incrementalism, particularly as Lindblom (1975) works with an example of a burning ship (raft?) and the objective of its evacuation. However, I argue that through thinking incrementally, without some sort of plan, the passengers would be likely to die on Lindblom's burning ship before any form of solution was invented.

In addition, the limited number of alternatives considered by what have been termed reactive or neo-liberal incremental approaches, is regarded as leading to excessive narrowness (Tarter and Hoy 1998) especially in its conceptualization of communication (Sager 1994), a lack of vision (Amdam 2004; Sager 2002) and innovation (Etzioni 1968) in which the future largely resembles the past. It is thus inherently conservative in contrast to Deleuzean poststructuralist thinking which emphasizes foresighting, resistant breaking away (lines of flight) and deterritorialization/destabilization strategies, which are highly innovative and often radical.

Incrementalism also eschews ends-thinking (Faludi 1973), 'leading nowhere' (Etzioni 1967: 387), in 'organisational drift', aimlessly 'meandering to avoid negative reaction' (Tarter and Hoy 1998: 224), proceeding 'without knowing where we are going' (Forester 1984: 23). Multiplanar theory, however, offers broad trajectories towards ends, such as environmental sustainability, 'a good place to live' and so on: leading somewhere.

Multiplanar Cartographies for Strategic Navigation

It's always about going from one place to another and how you get there.
(Lepage 2003 in Dundjerovic 2003: 153)

In this section I attempt to translate the broad picture of multiplanar theory into a practice of strategic navigation. I explore ideas of change/transformation as powerful and strategic (generated through Deleuzoguattarian *agencement*) and ask how, why, when, with what costs and what implications, do relations between actants gather sufficient instruments, devices, force etc. to generate *agencement* and eventuate change rather than simply remain assemblages. Assemblages possess the resources for transformation but it is the strategic relations of *agencement* (as outlined below) that make change real/actualization of the virtual. How might planners create 'beneficial' *agencements* and obstruct non-beneficial ones, or is this too much interference?

---

3   The idea of two planes resonates with Tsoukas and Chia's (2002) synoptic and performative accounts of organizational change, Latour's (2004) two 'houses', Albrechts' (2006; Albrechts and van den Broeck 2004) multi-track approach to strategic spatial planning and UN-HABITAT's (2009) call for a 'two-pronged' flexible, 'forward' long-range spatial plan consisting of broad frameworks and principles, with which detailed local plans and mega-projects should mesh.

The challenge for strategic navigation is to think methodologically, following the relationalities and intensities which cut across objects, events and us as theorists and researchers. Deleuze and Guattari (1987: 146) describe their cartography or 'pragmatics' as comprising four circular components:

- the generative component – the tracing of concrete mixed semiotics and pointing towards the potentiality of what might emerge;
- the transformational component – making a transformational map of the regimes and their possibilities for translation and creation;
- the diagrammatic component of the relational forces that are in play 'either as potentialities or as effective emergences';
- the machinic component[4] – the study of assemblages/*agencements* and outline of programmes of what might emerge.

This is a topological investigation concerned with evolution and transgression, similar to Foucauldian genealogy, in which research avoids including 'ready-made entities' such as a political action or a social class (Due 2007: 144) as explanatory principles. Rather, it concentrates on critical points 'in the spaces of coexistence between systems' (Due 2007: 144), exploring how entities and processes respond to both their own logics and to external pressures and stimuli. It is an exploration of relations between entities, events and structures: a generative analysis of 'how forces of different types come to inhabit the same field of stratification and of the sorts of events and processes which take place between the subsystems of this field' (Due 2007: 145) – 'where', 'when' and 'how'.

Analysis not only traces relational connections, conjunctions and disjunctions (Deleuze 1990; Deleuze and Guattari 1984) between elements in an assemblage or *agencement*, but maps their potential transformations. What events might transpire from the relations between discourses, texts, practices, laws, affects, silences? Deleuze and Guattari (1987: 146 above) suggest a pragmatic method of making a tracing; then making a transformational map of possibilities for translation and creation; then, making diagrams of the perceived positive and negative forces that could play in each case and deciding if, when and how to intervene in attempts to 'tweak' assemblages and *agencements* beneficially. Inclusive, democratic discussion could develop negotiated trajectories and Deleuzean fabulations (strategic spatial plans on the plane of immanence) and major project plans or local action plans (on the plane of organization) in a form of strategic spatial planning as strategic navigation.

In order to explore what strategic navigation might entail in strategic planning practice, I now turn to the practical role of topological analysis of the relational forces between elements in a Deleuzoguattarian assemblage or *agencement*. I then introduce how, through tracing, mapping and diagramming, we might better understand how things came to be and begin to anticipate or foresee what could eventuate or actualize in the future.

---

4   A 'machine' might be broadly understood as a durable system.

Assemblage/*Agencement*

John Phillips (2006) points out that the traditional translation of Deleuze and Guattari's term *agencement* by the English term 'assemblage' is 'not a good approximation' (Phillips 2006: 108). As Phillips indicates, there is a world of difference between the terms. Deleuze and Guattari only rarely use the French term *assemblage*, for which 'assemblage' would be the literal translation. Assemblage would be used to refer to, for example, disparate elements in a bicycle, which are assembled, combined or joined together. Deleuze and Guattari tend to use the words *ensemble* or *association* rather than *assemblage* to indicate non-directional groups of actors.

The term *agencement* implies agency and strategy. Deleuze (1988a [1970]) appears to have developed the notion of *agencement* from his work on Spinoza's idea of the common notion; the 'having in common' becoming a 'third body' in an event. *Agencement* thus implies an agency and immanence which assemblage does not. An *agencement*, therefore, is more than simply an assemblage. It is a process of 'agencing' (Bogue 2007: 145–6) – an active bringing-into-existence of its own agency. In the concept of *agencement* the constituent elements intersect, fold together and transform themselves and each other. They create and unmake territories, opening up and/or closing off possible lines of flight.

In asking 'what makes an assemblage into an *agencement*', one would investigate the relations between the entities or elements in the collective: 'in a multiplicity, what counts are not the terms or the elements, but what there is "between", the between, a set of relations which are not separable from each other' (Deleuze and Parnet 1987: viii). Moreover, *agencements* are 'passional' compositions of desire (Deleuze and Guattari 1987: 399). The rationality of an *agencement* does not exist without the desires which constitute it and the passions (affects) which it brings into play (Deleuze and Guattari 1987: 399).

An *agencement* achieves vitality through its relations, but as Buchanan (2000: 120) notes, 'it also has its illnesses'. The most potent 'illness' is that of stratification. Deleuzean strata are the actualized 'striated' regulations or orderings of elements which result from processes of organizing, sorting and consolidation (Deleuze and Guattari 1987). Over-stratification or regulation stultifies and inhibits transformation, as illustrated by Hillier and Van Wezemael's (2010) empirical example from North East England. 'When positioning of any kind comes a determining first, movement comes a problematic second' (Massumi 2002: 3).

Tracing

To trace, or understand, entails looking back, often from above, in a systematic manner.[5] Tracing involves discovering relations between elements in assemblages/

---

5   The French term *quadrillage* implies gridding both for detailed inspection and to maintain control (as in a town in insurrection).

agencements. To trace is to describe and to analyze the diversity of relations, the modalities of coordination, the discourses, the emotions, affects, etc. – in other words, the conditions of possibility – and how they were mobilized to shape actants' frames, representations and behaviours. Deleuze and Guattari's pragmatism is agonistic, referring to the role of relational difference and conflict in creative transformation (see also Pløger, this volume). Special attention should, therefore, be paid to tensions or strife between different ways of connecting, controlling and framing issues through connection, conjunction and disjunction. Assemblages and *agencements* are continuously subject to change as relationships fold and unfold, compose and decompose in the play of internal antagonisms and agonisms. Conflicts tend to arise over the relations which control framing and also about which entities and issues are included in the connections (presence) and which are excluded (absence). The assemblage is thus not independent of and does not precede the traced relationships: 'it is nothing other than the occurrence of these relationships' (Eriksson 2005: 601).

In order to trace relationships, I introduce three main sets of 'variables': Michel Foucault's notion of the *dispositif* and its elements of power, knowledge and subjectivity, analyzed, in particular, through discourse, but also through materiality; together with Deleuze and Guattari's two axes of materiality/expressivity and territorialization. I develop a method of tracing in more detail elsewhere (Hillier 2008; 2009). In this chapter I have space only to outline briefly what I regard as the main elements.

As John Pløger (2008) demonstrates, the French term *dispositif* has typically been mistranslated as 'apparatus' in English. This has led to it having technical, functionalist connotations which, as Pløger points out, completely miss the moral aspects of politicization and subjectivization, and the generative aspects which Deleuze describes. Foucault (1980: 194–5) described a *dispositif* as 'a thoroughly heterogeneous ensemble consisting of discourses, institutions, architectural forms, regulatory decisions, laws, administrative measures, scientific statements, philosophical, moral and philanthropic propositions – in short, the said as much as the unsaid. Such are the elements of a *dispositif*. The *dispositif* itself is a network of relations that can be established between these elements. Secondly, what I'm trying to identify in this *dispositif* is precisely the nature of the connection that can exist between these heterogeneous elements'. The key points here are that the *dispositif* is an ensemble of elements; that Foucault is specifically interested in the connections and relations between elements; that he is interested in discursivities and materialities, the present and the absent, and that the *dispositif* has a strategic function and tends to perform in response to something; perhaps a threat or disorder (Huxley 2007).

Foucault (1984) suggested that the *dispositif* implicates three fundamental elements of experience: relations of power, games of truth or knowledge, and forms of relation to oneself and to others (subjectivization and subjectification).[6] Pløger

---

6   I distinguish between subjectivization as self-actualization, or taking on a subject-position, and subjectification as the subjective identification of others, or accordance of a subject-position.

(2008) indicates that a *dispositif* comprises both discursive and material forces, which, in certain relational configurations develop the capacity to regulate, govern and/or empower specific entities: 'an *agencement* of desire will include *dispositifs* of power' (Deleuze 1997: 186). Foucault (1978: 92–3) stated that power 'must be understood in the first instance as the multiplicity of *force relations* immanent in the sphere in which they operate and which constitute their own organization; as the *process* which, through ceaseless struggles and confrontations, transforms, strengthens, or reverses them; as the *support* which these force relations find in one another, thus forming a chain or system, or on the contrary, the *disjunctions* and contradictions which isolate them from one another; and lastly, as the *strategies* in which they take effect, whose general design or institutional crystallisation is embodied in the state apparatus, in the formulation of the law, in the various social hegemonies' (emphasis added). I have quoted from Foucault at length as he gives a very clear understanding of where and how power performs. Foucault stresses that power performs in the 'moving substrate of force relations' (1978: 93). It is, therefore, not a structure, nor an institution, but a 'complex strategical situation' (1978: 93). Power is a striated or 'stratified dimension of the assemblage' (Deleuze and Guattari 1987: 531).

Power is intrinsically and extrinsically linked to knowledge. Foucault and Deleuze would agree that knowledge is discursive. Demonstrated knowledge articulates and actualizes the relationship between forces (i.e. power) (Deleuze 1988b: 70). There is a need to distinguish between knowledge as a 'thing' or noun, as the object of analysis and knowledge in terms of the power relationships which inhabit various knowledge practices (May 1993). Knowledge is 'a matter of giving reasons' (May 1993: 93). It is justified, not by truth per se, but by claims that are accepted as being true. In turn, these claims are justified by other claims. Knowledge rests on justification. Knowledge is a series of contingent networks of mutually reinforcing justifying claims. Tracing involves unfolding the claims which have had important inferential roles in particular discourses and the generation of knowledge.

Power operates through stratification in which social strata (defined by actants often as a classification of 'us' and 'them') are created by processes of subjectification/subjectivization and signification, underlain by a process of organization. Subjectification positions the subject through the way in which it organizes or positions its speakers and sets out their choices for them: 'they may enter into these forced, conjugated choices or be silent' (Thanem and Linstead 2006: 46). Deleuze and Guattari (1987: 75–85; 119–34) argue that subjectification occurs through language and discourse.

Whilst tracing Foucauldian *dispositifs* is clearly valuable, Deleuze reminds us that *agencements* are more than *dispositifs* which are 'situated among the different components of the *agencement*' (1997: 186). Deleuze and Guattari complement the *dispositif* by defining the concepts of assemblage/*agencement* along two axes. One axis defines the roles which components may play, from the purely material to the purely expressive (Deleuze and Guattari 1987: 503–4). Material components include elements such as bodies, time, energy, buildings, technology, laws, each of which can be enforced/stabilized or challenged/destabilized: 'of actions and passions, an intermingling of bodies reacting to one another' (Deleuze and Guattari 1987: 88). Expressive components include texts and nonlinguistic visibilities such as gestures, desires and charisma, each of which can also be enforced and/or challenged. Deleuze (1988b) suggests that one can trace relations of power and identify subjectifications/subjectivizations on the material/expressive axis.

The second axis concerns the reterritorialization/deterritorialization, coding/ decoding and stabilization/destabilization of assemblages/*agencements*. An assemblage/*agencement* can have components working to stabilize or territorialize and code it at the same time as other components work in the opposite direction. The axis of territorialization is concerned with process. One can trace the constitution of territories via striation/stratification and the lines of flight or deterritorialization along which an assemblage might either break down or transform into an *agencement*. What 'ideological commitments, assumptions, blockages, categories, oppositions have traced themselves into industry analysis and policy frameworks?' (Wise 2002: 229). How? What effects do they have?

Tracing overlays the product of something on to the process of its production. Tracing is an act often performed at the micropolitical site level,[7] analyzing 'the unfolding state of affairs within which situations or sites are constituted' (Woodward et al. 2007: 5) – how did we get here? How did things come to be like this? As the authors explain, the challenge is to think methodologically from the inside, to disentangle the mesh of intensities to discover 'what pressures and affects are working within and constituting them; test out all the relations', to explore the stratifications and blockages, and to comment on relationality, affects and 'conditions of dynamic relation' (2007: 6–7).

Mapping

Deleuze and Guattari (1987: 12) urge us to 'make a map, not a tracing'. There is a pivotal difference between tracing or unfolding something in retrospect and mapping trajectories through diagrams to anticipate whether relations 'can serve as indicators of new universes' (Guattari 1986: 102, cited in Bosteels 2001: 895). To map involves discovery and perception of indicators or landmarks as something to head towards. An analytic cartography thus involves both the deductive interpretation, especially of ruptures and discontinuities, of 'symptoms' (on a tracing) of an actual situation – 'a perspectival lattice or hermeneutic frame of reference' – and the invention of new heterogeneous, experimental assemblages and pragmatic diagrams (on a map) – 'a way of marking out the territory on the road' and 'a furtive glance sideways into an undecidable future of desire' (all quotations Bosteels 2001: 895).

I regard Deleuzean-inspired mapping as a form of creative experimentation in contact with the real. Creative mapping of connections and potentialities pays attention, therefore, not only to affect and the trajectories of future becomings, but

---

7   For a case example of tracing Antony Gormley's *Another Place*, see Hillier (2010).

also to the already-delineated tracings of *dispositifs*, roles and processes, the beliefs and habits which express actants' desires. Maps are complexities, in constant states of production; of variation, expansion, conquest and capture (Antonioli 2003: 100). Their surface comprises lines of flight, molar strata and molecular fluxes, often in tension. There is no predetermined logic or order; only immanent criteria which orientate encounters between, and transformations of, elements. The issue is not to attempt to define long-term detailed programmes of action, but to raise questions of potential agency and of socio-economic-political and institutional conditions of change. 'It is ... a question of mapping their trajectory to see whether they can serve as indicators of new universes of reference capable of acquiring enough consistency to turn around a situation' (Guattari 1986: 102, cited in Bosteels 2001: 895).

Deleuze was impressed by the generative aspects of Foucault's concept of *dispositif* (Deleuze 1988b) and there are distinct resonances between Deleuzoguattarian ideas of mapping and the notion of Foucauldian *dispositifs* as 'ensembles of becoming' (Pløger 2008). Both are concerned with gesturing towards the virtual and an 'as yet undreamed-of heterogenesis' (Bosteels 2001: 895). Methodologically, then, as in tracing, the Foucauldian *dispositif* is a useful starting point. With the addition of the two Deleuzoguattarian axes of materiality/ expressivity and territorialization as component roles and processes respectively, we have a potentially strong set of relational variables to map and from which to identify the main driving forces.

Might practitioners be able to facilitate mapping as an aid to strategic navigation? In his psychoanalytical group therapy practice Guattari (2000) used the concept of phantasy to help establish group identities which were not based in some form of subjugation to institutional power. One way of introducing phantasy to strategic spatial planning could be through the use of prospective or foresighting techniques (see Albrechts 2004; 2005; 2006; this volume). Foresighting might be described as thinking in action; mapping a 'geography of the unknown' (Albrechts 2006: 1491). Foresighting invites consideration of the future as immanent, something created dynamically. Forecasting, in contrast, tends to be built on transcendence, a future already decided by trend extrapolation, 'like a mystery that simply needs to be unravelled' (Hillier 2007). Foresighting involves an open exploration of the potential (and the impotential) of many futures through development of radically alternative exploratory scenarios, as practised by the French organisation, Futuribles (<www.futuribles.com>). It involves a 'conscious, purposive, contextual, creative and continuous action to represent values and meanings for the future' (Albrechts 2005: 254).

As an exploration of conjectures rather than of facts, foresighting 'modulates virtual potential to actualization in a conceptual system' (Massumi and Manning 2007: np). By mapping and diagramming speculations about the relations between elements, we may be able to develop new practices of thinking and working which focus on relations.

Diagramming

Mapping, as above, generates 'a set of various intersecting lines' (Deleuze 1995: 33) or diagram. Deleuze offers at least two[8] different understandings of the diagram during the evolution of his thinking. The first understanding is developed from Michel Foucault's (1977) work, indicating not only the relations between constitutive capacities of power, but also the *dispositif* of heterogeneous elements engaging deterritorialized systems of discursivities and materialities. In such a reading, the diagram comprises two states, of immanence and organization. It is a map of the discursive and material forces expressing the immanent relations of power. It also allows evaluation of the organizational potentiality of various *agencements* to actualize. As Braidotti (2000: 170) explains, a diagram is 'a cartographic device that enables the tracking of an intersecting network of power-effects that simultaneously enable and constrain the subjects'.

In his work on the artist, Francis Bacon, however, Deleuze appears to derive his conceptualization of diagram from the pragmatic semiotic theory of C.S. Peirce (1868). Deleuze describes the diagram as 'the operative set of asignifying and non-representative lines and zones, line-strokes and colour-patches' whose function is to be 'suggestive' of 'possibilities of facts' (Deleuze 2003: 101). Whilst diagrams are 'a chaos', they nevertheless contain 'a germ of order' of what might be (Deleuze 2003: 102). Deleuze (2003: 137–8) also suggests that in art, as in other activities which oscillate between the 'beforehand' and an 'afterward' (such as strategic spatial planning), there is a need for stopping or resting points. Diagrams are such resting points in a sea of immense agitation and flux. Deleuze adds that the diagram 'must remain localised' (2003: 138) rather than attempt to cover the entire artwork, and that 'something must *emerge* from the diagram' (emphasis in original).

Whatever one's preferred definition of diagram, it is concerned with the dynamic interrelation of relations (Massumi 1992) at the interface between the virtual and the actual: 'a topological hyperspace of transformation' (Massumi 2002: 184). Diagrams (or plans), then, lie in a zone of indiscernability between two forms, a form-that-is-no-longer and another form which does not yet exist (Bogue 2003: 156). They act as modulators or intercessors between ideas and what may become. Diagrams create possibilities; imaginary alternative worlds which promise something new; a hope of living otherwise (Bogue 2003: 177). Through the creative use of diagrams, strategic planners may be able to cast aside the habits or clichés of practice, to 'destroy the figurative coordinates of conventional representations and to release the possibilities of invention' (Ambrose 2006: 207): to resist universalizing abstractions (such as the good) and to think contingency, difference and relationality as a kind of creative agonistic. By mapping connections between different relations of force on to a diagram, one may be able to anticipate the potential distribution of 'the power to affect and the power to be affected' (Deleuze 1988b: 73, cited in McCormack 2005:

---

8   Latham and McCormack (2004: 707–8) and Batt (2004: 5) identify three and four understandings respectively.

124) – the power of force relations between the various elements associated with the metaphorical raft.

Strategic navigation as a process thus requests strategic planners to diagram and engage the virtual events immanent within their worlds. Such a process would involve 'teasing out the proliferating interconnections' between elements entering into 'the play of virtual differences' (Bogue 2007: 9–10), experimenting with them and anticipating potential tensions and conflicts. What new assemblages might eventuate; what *agencements*? As Bogue (2007: 10) describes, this is 'both a process of exploring and hence constructing connections among differences, and a process of undoing connections in an effort to form new ones'. A practical 'thinking otherwise' in an experimental activation of the potential of the virtual. A 'what might happen if …?' approach, not so much to predict, but to be alert to as-yet unknown potentialities (Deleuze, 1988c: 1–2). As such, Deleuze (1988b: 44) also emphasizes that, in addition to relational connections, diagrams also include virtual (unseen) free or non-connected points of 'creativity, change and resistance'; political points which often come from the outside to surprise us.

Diagrams, then, are useful tools for spatial planning practice as strategic navigation. 'Diagrammatic interventions are generative, creative gestures, not programmatic or prefiguring ones' (McCormack 2005: 144). They put the tracing on the map, 'mak[ing] history by disassembling previous realities and significations, and in their place constitute new points of emergence or creativity, unexpected conjunctions and improbable continuums'. They 'double history with a becoming' (both quotes Deleuze 1988b: 42–3) and yield clues as to which meshworks of elements might become strategically powerful *agencements* and which remain as non-strategic assemblages (see Hillier and Van Wezemael 2009).

Nevertheless, we must not forget that any diagram is always 'an incomplete abstraction' painted from a 'restricted point of view' (Massumi 1992: 68) constrained by the ideology of the artist actant. Diagrams are always a form of representation of the artist's desire, inevitably haunted by the excluded and the unknown outside and the endless potential for politics and resistance.

Deleuze and Guattari's (1987) fourth pragmatic (or machinic) component concerns the evaluative study of assemblages/*agencements* and their potentialities, with a view to intervening strategically. This component would entail attempting to select and to facilitate, or strategically navigate towards, potentially 'good' encounters and to avoid 'bad' ones. This is a pragmatic exercise in which strategic planners would attempt to intervene and manipulate relational forces and their potential connections, conjunctions and disjunctions, their possible trajectories, bifurcations, mutations. In other words, to diagnose becomings (Bergen 2006: 109). Massumi and Manning (2007) ask: what conditions should be in place for a relation to be induced? How might the conditions be modulated so that they can generate unfoldings and new foldings, whilst being open-ended and welcoming of chance?

Cartography (strategic navigation) would not be a process of standing back and describing, but of entering the relations between elements and 'tweaking' (Massumi 2002: 207) as many as possible in order to get a sense of what may emerge: 'pragmatic tweaking: a hands-on experimentation in contextual connectivity'

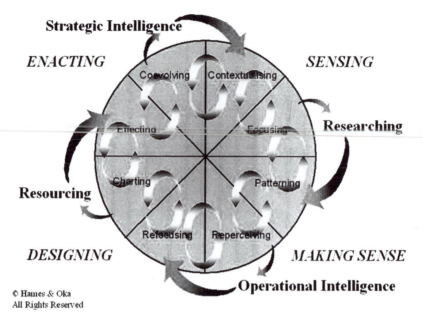

Figure 17.1 **The spiral of strategic learning**

Source: Hames (2007b: 6). Reproduced with permission.

(Massumi 2002: 243).[9] Nothing, however, eventuates precisely as anticipated. 'Becoming is directional rather than intentional' (Massumi 1992: 95). The aleatory is often a powerful force. Strategic planning involves 'working with odds, guesses, predictions and judgements but not ever with certainty' (Rose 2007: 468).

Resonating with Deleuzean-inspired tracing and mapping, Hames (2007a: 228–9) defines strategic navigation as 'the art of confidently and ethically finding viable paths into the future, negotiating unknown terrain and unprecedented complexity while retaining integrity and relevance'. He advocates 'strategy-as-process' – 'a continuous braiding of intelligence creation with insightful action' (Hames 2007a: 81) – based on appreciation of a 'system's (e.g. a city or region) past, present and potential futures.

Strategic navigation is a conversation that weaves between the molecular of specific episodes and local or micro stories, the networks and coalitions, assemblages and *agencements* of governance processes, and the molarities of governance cultures (Hillier 2008). Hames (2007a: 253, 2007b: 6) depicts this conversation as a strategic-learning spiral of sensing (tracing), making sense and designing (mapping and diagramming) and enacting. (see Figure 17.1).

Reperceiving and refocusing would entail scenario or foresight-based mapping and diagramming of issues and implications, before 'leverage points' are identified

---

9   See Karadimitriou on restricting choice, this volume.

and pertinent responses are designed in a strategic 'plan' (chart) component. The spiral incorporates continuous reflexion, reperception and revision of information, ideas and intentions as new knowledges emerge, circumstances alter and decisions themselves change the context and issue focus. Some possible questions for practitioners to consider are suggested in Table 17.2, which should be read together with Figure 17.1.

Table 17.2   Thinking strategic navigation in practice: explanations and questions

Contextualizing performs understanding of the context in which strategic planning is to take place; a sensing of what is going on and how things came to be. Questions include:

- What are the key characteristics of the socio-economic-political environment?
- What are the critical relationships between these characteristics?
- What were their conditions of possibility?
- What were and are the dynamics of force relations between actants?
- What is changing?
- What are actants' general and specific wants and needs?

Focusing arrives at an initial, shared understanding of critical issues. Questions include:

- What are the most strategically significant issues requiring attention?
- What are the relationships between these and other issues?
- What relationships matter most?
- What most concerns key decision makers?
- What control or influence can planners exercise over these issues and their relationships?
- What assumptions lead us to these conclusions?
- Do other actants share these conclusions?
- What can we be certain about and what is uncertain?

Patterning integrates different perspectives and new knowledges into planners' understandings of what is happening and might happen in the future. Questions include:

- What patterns of change can we identify?
- How and why are these patterns changing?
- What are the gaps in our current thinking and knowing?
- Where can we get the information from?

- Are there other ways of perceiving the issues which raise different questions, problems, opportunities?

Reperceiving involves deepening awareness and understanding through finding new ways to view issues. Foresighting or prospective exercises can offer multiple perspectives on alternative futures. Outcomes can significantly change beliefs about what is important to actants. Questions include:

- What new insights can be gleaned from the various prospectives?
- What are the conditions of possibility of the various prospectives?
- What are the key relations between actants?
- How may force relations play out in the future?
- What changes might there be and why?
- What implications do these insights have for strategic planning?

Refocusing examines what, from the prospectives investigated, could be more or less likely to take place and could be more or less strategically important and why. Refocusing filters attention. Questions include:

- What are the most significant issues requiring attention?
- What specific factors make these issues critical and why?
- How might these issues be addressed?
- Does the planning system have the capacities to address these issues?
- What other actants should be involved?
- What should plans address in the short- and long-term and why?

Charting involves preparing appropriate plans. Questions include:

- What strategies are possible?
- What strategies might become possible in the short or longer-term future, how and why?
- What are the possible consequences, risks and opportunities of these strategies?
- How can strategic plans be prepared so that the local planning authority remains responsive and adaptive?
- How can the linkages between the components of the strategic plans be described?
- Do the strategies address key leverage points?

Effecting implements the plans. Questions to consider before implementation include:

- How will we know if the plans are effective in navigating towards our strategic intentions?
- What would be an appropriate monitoring system?

- How would we accommodate requirements for systemic change in the plans?
- What are we unaware of that may cause problems in the future?

Co-evolving enables adaptation of practice and plans in the light of changes caused by those practices and plans. Questions include:

- What signals will indicate that a fundamental change is occurring in the context from which we defined the strategic plans?
- What are the critical, unintended consequences of our plans?
- Do we need to think differently about our strategic intentions?
- Are we ignoring any force relations, connections or actants that might be critical?
- Do our plans need to change?

Source: Adapted from Hames (2007a, 2007b).

Hames (2007a: 256) analogizes a conversation to a 'sensory web' which monitors and analyses the structures, links, relationships and information flows which 'really matter to different people, in different geographies, over time' and to agree what is and may become significant, or less so, in collaborative creation of 'pathways into sustainable "preferred" futures' (both quotations, Hames 2007a: 121). Continuous monitoring is also required to ensure both that shorter-term plans and projects (on the plane of organization) do not 'veer off' the broader trajectory of the longer-term vision (the plane of immanence), 'seduced' either by conventional thinking and inertia or 'the latest flavour of the month' (Hames 2007a: 250), perhaps for yet another iconic building or retail centre. Monitoring should also ensure that the longer-term vision remains relevant.

Deleuzoguattarian cartography, therefore, looks both at coherent molar complexity and also at multiple, folded, micro- or molecular complexity. Both are necessary. But what is also necessary, is to think transversally across relations and networks, rather than hierarchically, in attempts to identify the 'compossibility' (being within the realm of possibility of the same actualization) of molecular or molar potentials (Deleuze 1990: 171–2).

Non-Conclusion

> *There is too much out there: nothing has to be there, so many things that can be. (May 2005: 62)*

The future is outside control, conceptually and behaviourally. 'There is no transcendence guiding the present, giving form to a particular future that has to happen this way and not others' (May 2005: 63). The past is yet to be determined as we overwrite or restructure it. It is a virtuality of the present and future, creating a union between the past (the place of memory) and the future (the place of prospective or foresighting). Strategic spatial planning is a kind of creative agonistic between presence and absence, manifest and latent, the general and the particular. It is about learning something new and providing the opportunities for the emergence of 'people-to-come' and the 'not-yet', not pre-determined or pre-identified by a 'rational space or an adequate place' (Rajchman 1998: 31). I regard planning as strategic navigation: speculative and creative, yet structured, experimentation in the spatial Deleuzoguattarian fabulation.

Massumi (2002: 242) describes fabulation as 'a conceptual groping towards potential-to-be' (Massumi 2002: 242). Fabulation is comprised of creation and prognosis. As Lambert (2002: 137) describes, it is 'the art of invention as well as a conceptual avatar of a "problem-solving" instinct that remedies an unbearable situation' – particularly with regard to the situation of 'the people who are missing'. The aim of fabulation as a 'genuinely creative process' (Bogue 2006: 209), is 'where the writer and the people go toward one another' (Deleuze 1989, in Lambert 2002: 137) in attempts to make new possibilities visible.

In fabulation the subject (geographical area, people or policy area) is constructed as a site of oscillation between reality and the virtual, which intersect in a state of transformation or a becoming. Deleuze (1989) suggests that becoming should be expressed as a collective will; 'a collaborative process of invention' (Bogue 2006: 212). Becoming and its fabulation belong 'to a people, to a community, ... whose expression they practice and set free' (Deleuze 1989: 153). Fabulation, then, is a collective but non-unifying articulation of differences which 'harmonizes difference through interpenetration' (Follet 1998: 34) to produce what Follet terms 'common thought' (1998: 34).[10] Common thought is the outcome of a process in which differences are neither suppressed nor superseded, but in which they are integrated into a 'whole'. Moreover, 'the strength of this whole lies precisely in the preservation and interrelation of difference' (Holland 2006: 197): a form of agonistic pragmatism.

Strategic spatial plans are inevitably fables, political fictions or 'visions' (Deleuze 1997) which 'speak the possibles' (after Boundas 2006: 24). To think or fabulate a field of possibility means 'arranging it according to some concept ... thereby constructing a temporary and virtual arrangement according to causal, logical and temporal relations. Such thinking is always a response to some particular set of circumstances' (Stagoll 2005: 205). For instance, Deleuze and Guattari (1987: 251) suggest that tentative criteria may be developed from practical experience and judgement[11] in order to anticipate potential becomings. However,

---

10 This concept of common thought includes more similarities with Chantal Mouffe's (2005) notion of 'conflictual consensus' than with a Habermasian consensus produced through communicative action: 'the essential feature of common thought is not that it is held in common, but that it has been produced in common' (Follet 1998: 34).

11 See Flyvbjerg (1993; 1998) and Hillier (2002) on the role of practical wisdom/phronesis, intuition and anticipation.

the range of potentialities that can become possibilities that can become actualized is constrained by 'an ordering and filtering system' (Due 2007; 9) which imposes a determinate structure on the socio-economic-political processes with which the performances of thinking, foresighting and fabulation are entangled. This 'ordering and filtering system' is that of strata and molarities (such as governance cultures, Interpol, the CIA, etc.) which may block creative transformation. Through mechanisms of organization, signification and subjectification, powerful entities with a desire for constancy and stability can dogmatically halt lines of flight, block fluidity (May 2005) and the generation of strategic *agencements* which they perceive as unfavourable.

In a world where many institutions regard 'emergence' as 'emergency', emergences are monitored, evaluated and regulated so that they do not become emergencies, threatening to governments, citizens and businesses (Dillon 2002; Ilachinski 2004; Krebs 2002a, 2002b; Roberts 2000a, 2000b), agencies, such as police, counter-terrorist organisations, MI6, the CIA and US Defense Force, attempt to anticipate 'bad' events-to-come in order to avoid them or to limit their 'surprise' by planning how to react (Anderson 2008; Dillon 2008). As White et al. (2007: 192) state, risk prediction strategy 'consists of reconfiguring relationships among and capacities of identities in order to anticipate and respond to perceived … threats'. Nevertheless, in attempts to manipulate, we must not forget that any diagram is always 'an incomplete abstraction' painted from a 'restricted point of view' (Massumi 1992: 68) constrained by the ideology of the artist-actant. Diagrams are always a form of representation of the 'artist's' desire, inevitably haunted by the excluded and the unknown outside and the endless potential for politics and resistance.

Cognisant of such constraints, I suggest that there is potential for strategic planning practitioners 'to respond to problems in new ways, to re-invigorate life and thought through the problems that give rise to them' (Williams 2003: 2). As such, long-term strategic planning – planning on the plane of immanence – could be a more inclusive, democratic, open and creative imagination of the past-present-future where there is foresighting of possible future scenarios and collaborative, critical discussion about their potential consequences for different actants. Planes of organization contain vertical power relations which temporarily both striate our worlds and fix identities as they support the everyday segmentarities of life.

Improvisation is important in forms of strategic planning practices which would be performative rather than strictly normative/prescriptive, concerned with navigating 'journeys rather than destinations' and with establishing the conditions for the development of alternatives. This would be a pragmatic approach in which 'policy plugs into production, and production into policy' (Wise 2006: 191, 2002: 230). It would be bureaucratically and politically unsettling and 'risky', for, as Wise (2006: 191) explains, 'it will not only apprehend the probability of "opportunities that are unforeseen", but simultaneously anticipate the movements of the city and accept that policy outcomes are experimental and unpredictable'.

Is it possible to extract a practical method from Deleuzoguattarian-inspired thinking without making that very thinking inoperative? Through representation of Deleuzoguattarian concepts, there is a danger that they may lose their disruptive, transgressive potential, especially if used as a 'template' for action. Nevertheless, for those 'who want to do something with respect to new uncommon forces, which we don't quite yet grasp' (Rajchman 2000: 6), I offer Deleuzoguattarian cartography as an 'anexact' practice 'open and connectable in all its dimensions' (Deleuze and Guattari 1987: 12); a topological approach concerned less with exact measurement than with spatial relations, with inclusion and exclusion, connections and disjunction, with communication and with agonism.

By investigating specific stories about specific situations (the micropolitical) and tracing relationalities (the connections, conjunctions and disjunctions between elements), by making visible the various *dispositifs*, de- and re-territorializations, the discursivities and materialities, the power-plays and subjectifications/subjectivizations, we can develop an understanding of the roles of actants (both human and non-human) in what took place and the processes which performed. Looking at the relations between elements (the Deleuzoguattarian lines) rather than at the elements themselves (the points), would be relatively new practice for most spatial planning practitioners, but by tracing the multiplicity of ways in which actants attempt to generate and express power through subjectivating others (e.g. through constraining their choices, their self-subjectifications, etc.), through organization (actions, laws, decisions) and through signification (discourses) we can begin to unfold the actualized, contingent systems which were constructed.

In this manner, tracing offers us a temporarily stabilized grid of reference for understanding what was actualized. If we then place the tracing on the map, by mapping the diagonals or transversals across molar and molecular lines and potential lines of flight, to expose potentialities and possibilities, we can generate a diagram. Plan contents would no longer be questions of land use per se, but of interrelationships between different actants (including land uses). Planners would 'map out a range of circumstances' (Deleuze 1995: 26), situations and relations or lines: 'lines are the basic components of things and events. So everything has its geography, its cartography, its diagram'. Mapping lines and diagrams of relations of power or forces enables construction of trajectories (strategic plans) representing navigation towards desired virtualities of future development of the place or territory. Then comes experimentation – Deleuze's (1983) dice throw. But, how to be a 'good' player? Deleuze (1983: 26–7) explains that good players experiment. They affirm chance and 'explore the virtual rather than … cling to the actual' (May 2005: 65). I noted the potential of prospective or foresighting in this respect. Creativity is experimentation, recognizing the limitations of particular constraints.

Creative experimentation is often a by-product of conflict. As such, I believe that planning practitioners should work with difference, conflict and the political rather than seek to eradicate or evacuate it. Deleuzoguattarian-inspired practice would accept conflict and agonism as integral aspects of governance, in performing 'an art of inhabiting the intervals, where new foldings arise to take our forms of inhabitation in new and uncharted directions' (Rajchman 1998: 32). I advocate fabulation, potentially an inclusive, democratic 'what might happen if …?' approach which allows disparate points of view to co-exist; which has a concern for indeterminate essences rather than ordered ones; for emergent properties rather than fixed ones; and for intuition and uncertainty, multiplicity and complexity rather than systematic predictabilities. Strategic spatial planning as strategic navigation is a performance of risk-taking, of not being in total control, of transcending the technicalities of planning practice to create an 'open reading frame for the emergence of unprecedented events' (Rheinberger 1997: 31). Welcome on board!

Acknowledgements

My thanks to John Forester, Patsy Healey, Andrew Law and participants at the Newcastle mini-conference in January 2008 for comments on an earlier draft of this chapter and to Sandro Balducci, John Pløger and Cathy Wilkinson for helping me work this current iteration of my thoughts on Strategic Navigation.

References

Albrechts, L. (2004) 'Strategic (spatial) planning re-examined' *Environment and Planning B, Planning and Design* 31: 743–58.

Albrechts, L. (2005) 'Creativity as a drive for change' *Planning Theory* 4(3): 247–69.

Albrechts, L. (2006) 'Bridge the gap: from spatial planning to strategic projects' *European Planning Studies* 14(10): 1487–500.

Albrechts, L. and van den Broeck, J. (2004) 'From discourse to facts: the case of the ROM project in Ghent, Belgium' *Town Planning Review* 75(2): 127–50.

Ambrose, D. (2006) 'Deleuze, philosophy, and the materiality of painting' *Symposium* 10(1): 191–211.

Amdam, R. (2004) 'Institutional leadership in regional planning and development', paper presented to AESOP congress, Grenoble, 10–14 July. Copy available from author: <roar.amdam@hivolda.no>.

Anderson, B. (2008) 'No bad surprises: anticipating the event', paper presented to RGS-IBG Annual Conference, 26–9 August, London.

Antonioli, M. (2003) *Géophilosophie de Deleuze et Guattari*. Paris: L'Harmattan.

Axelrod, R. and Cohen, M. (1999) *Harnessing Complexity*. New York: Free Press.

Batt, N. (2004) 'L'expérience diagrammatique: un nouveau régime de pensée', in Batt, N. (ed.) *Penser par le diagramme de Gilles Deleuze à Gilles Châtelet*. Paris: Presses Universitaire de Vincennes, 5–28.

Bergen, V. (2006) 'La politique comme posture de tout agencement', in Antonioli, M., Chardel, P-A. and Regnauld, H. (eds) *Gilles Deleuze, Félix Guattari et le Politique*. Paris: Éditions du Sandre, 103–14.

Bergmann, L., Sheppard, E. and Plummer, P. (2009) 'Capitalism beyond harmonious equilibrium: mathematics as if human agency mattered' *Environment and Planning A* 41: 265–83.

Bogue, R. (2003) *Deleuze on Music, Painting and the Arts*. New York: Routledge.

Bogue, R. (2006) 'Fabulation, narration and the people to come', in Boundas, C. (ed.) *Deleuze and Philosophy*. Edinburgh: Edinburgh University Press, 202–23.

Bogue, R. (2007) *Deleuze's Way: Essays in Transverse Ethics and Aesthetics*. Aldershot: Ashgate.

Bonta, M and Protevi, J. (2004) *Deleuze and Geophilosophy: A Guide and Glossary*. Edinburgh: Edinburgh University Press.

Booher, D. and Innes, J. (2002) 'Network power in collaborative planning' *Journal of Planning Education and Research* 21(3): 221–36.

Booher, D. and Innes, J. (2006) 'Complexity and adaptive policy systems: CALFED as an emergent form of governance for sustainable management of contested resources', *Proceedings of the 50th Annual Meeting of the ISSS*, <http://journals.isss.org/index.php/proceedings50th/index> [accessed 22/12/2008].

Bosteels, B. (2001) 'From text to territory: Félix Guattari's cartographies of the unconscious', in Genosko, G. (ed.) *Deleuze and Guattari: Critical Assessments of Leading Philosophers*, Vol. II. New York: Routledge, 881–910.

Boundas, C. (2005) 'The art of begetting monsters: the unnatural nuptials of Deleuze and Kant', in Daniel, S. (ed.) *Current Continental Theory and Modern Philosophy*. Evanston, IL: Northwestern University Press, 254–79.

Boundas, C. (2006) 'What difference does Deleuze's difference make?' in Boundas, C. (ed.) *Deleuze and Philosophy*. Edinburgh: Edinburgh University Press, 3–28.

Braidotti, R. (2000) 'Terratologies', in Buchanan, I., and Colebrook, C. (eds) *Deleuze and Feminist Theory*. Edinburgh: Edinburgh University Press, 156–72.

Bruner, J. (1986) *Actual Minds, Possible Worlds*. Cambridge, MA: Harvard University Press.

Buchanan, I. (2000) *Deleuzism: A Metacommentary*. Durham, NC: Duke University Press.

Castells, M. (1996) *The Rise of the Network Society*. Oxford: Blackwell.

Chettiparamb, A. (2007) 'Re-conceptualising public participation in planning: a view through autopoiesis' *Planning Theory* 6(3): 263–81.

Cilliers, P. (2005) 'Complexity, deconstruction and relativism' *Theory, Culture and Society* 22(5): 255–67.

Clark, N. (2005) 'Ex-orbitant globality' *Theory, Culture and Society* 22(5): 165–85.

Colebrook, C. (2002) *Understanding Deleuze*. Sydney: Allen and Unwin.

Connick, S. and Innes, J. (2003) 'Outcomes of collaborative water policy making: applying complexity thinking to evaluation' *Journal of Environmental Planning and Management* 46(2): 177–97.

Connolly, W. (2002) *Neuropolitics: Thinking, Culture, Speed*. Minneapolis, MN: University of Minnesota Press.

Cooper, R. (2005) 'Relationality' *Organization Studies* 26(11): 1689–710.

DeLanda, M. (1998) 'Deleuze and the open-ended becoming of the world', <http://www.diss.sense.uni-konstanz.de/virtualitaet/delanda.htm [accessed December 2009]

DeLanda, M. (2006) *A New Philosophy of Society*. New York: Continuum.

Deleuze, G. (1986) [1983] *Cinema 1: The Movement-image* (trans. Tomlinson, H.). Minneapolis, MN: University of Minnesota Press.

Deleuze, G. (1988a) [1970] *Spinoza: Practical Philosophy* (trans. Hurley, R.). San Francisco, CA: City Light Books.

Deleuze, G. (1988b) [1986] *Foucault* (trans. Hand, S.). Minneapolis, MN: University of Minnesota Press.

Deleuze, G. (1988c) 'Nouveau millénaire' *Défis littéraire* 257, <http://www.france-mail-forum.de/index2b.html#Deleuze> [accessed 29/11/2006].

Deleuze, G. (1989) [1985] *Cinema 2: The Time-image* (trans. Tomlinson, H. and Galeta, R.). Minneapolis, MN: University of Minnesota Press.

Deleuze, G. (1990) [1969] *The Logic of Sense* (trans. Lester, M. and Stivale, C.). London: Athlone.

Deleuze, G. (1993) [1988] *The Fold: Leibniz and the Baroque* (trans. Conley, T.). London: Athlone.

Deleuze, G. (1994) [1968] *Difference and Repetition* (trans. Patton, P.), London: Athlone.

Deleuze, G. (1995) [1990] *Negotiations 1972–1990* (trans. Joughin, M.). New York: Columbia University Press.

Deleuze, G. (1997) 'Desire and pleasure' (trans. Smith, D.W.), in Davidson, A. (ed.) *Foucault and his Interlocutors*. Chicago, IL: University of Chicago Press, 183–92.

Deleuze, G. (2003) [1981] *Francis Bacon: The Logic of Sensation* (trans. Smith, D.W.) London: Continuum.

Deleuze, G. and Guattari, F. (1984) [1972] *Anti-Oedipus: Capitalism and Schizophrenia* (trans. Hurley, R., Seem, M. and Lane, H.). London: Athlone.

Deleuze, G. and Guattari, F. (1987) [1980] *A Thousand Plateaus: Capitalism and Schizophrenia* (trans. Massumi, B.). London: Athlone.

Deleuze, G. and Guattari, F. (1994) [1991] *What is Philosophy?* (trans. Tomlinson, H. and Burchill, G.). London: Verso.

Deleuze, G. and Parnet, C. (1987) [1977] *Dialogues* (trans. Tomlinson, H. and Habberjam, B.). London: Athlone.

Deleuze, G. and Parnet, C. (2002) [1977] *Dialogues II* (trans. Tomlinson, H. and Habberjam, B.). New York: Continuum.

Dillon, M. (2002) 'Network society, network-centric warfare and the state of emergency' *Theory, Culture and Society* 19(4): 71–9.

Dillon, M. (2008) 'Space, species, event', paper presented to RGS-IBG Annual Conference, 26–9 August, London.

Due, R. (2007) *Deleuze*. Cambridge: Polity Press.

Dundjerovic, A. (2003) *The Cinema of Robert Lepage: The Poetics of Memory*. London: Wallflower Press.

Eriksson, K. (2005) 'Foucault, Deleuze, and the ontology of networks' *The European Legacy* 10(6): 595–610.

Etzioni, A. (1967) 'Mixed scanning: a third approach to decision making' *Public Administration Review* 27: 387–92.

Etzioni, A. (1968) *The Active Society*. New York: The Free Press.

Faludi, A. (1973) *Planning Theory*. Oxford: Pergamon.

Flyvbjerg, B. (1993) 'Aristotle, Foucault and progressive phronesis: outline of an applied ethics for sustainable development', in Winkler, E. and Coombs, J. (eds) *Applied Ethics: A Reader*. New York: Blackwell, 11–27.

Flyvbjerg, B. (1998) *Rationality and Power*. Chicago, IL: University of Chicago Press.

Follet, M. (1998) *The New State: Group Organization and the Solution of Popular Government*. Philadelphia, PA: University of Pennsylvania Press.

Forester, J. (1984) 'Bounded rationality and the politics of muddling through' *Public Administration Review* 44: 22–31.

Foucault, M. (1977) [1975] *Discipline and Punish* (trans. Sheridan, A.). Harmondsworth: Penguin.

Foucault, M. (1978) [1976] *The Will to Knowledge: The History of Sexuality*, Vol. 1 (trans. Hurley, R.). Harmondsworth: Penguin.

Foucault, M. (1980) *Power/Knowledge: Selected Interviews and Other Writings 1972–1977* (ed. Gordon, C.). New York: Pantheon.

Foucault, M. (1984) 'Polemics, politics and problematizations', interview with Paul Rabinow (trans. Davis, L.), <http://foucault.info/foucault/interview.html> [accessed 02/02/2007].

Fraser, M., Kember, S. and Lury, C. (2005) 'Inventive life: approaches to the new vitalism' *Theory, Culture and Society* 22(1): 1–14.

Guattari, F. (1986) *Les années d'hiver 1980–1985*. Paris: Bernard Barrault.

Guattari, F. (2000) [1989] *The Three Ecologies* (trans. Pindar, I. and Sutton, P.). London: Athlone Press.

Hames, R. (2007a) *The Five Literacies of Global Leadership*. San Francisco, CA: Jossey-Bass.

Hames, R. (2007b) *The Five Literacies of Global Leadership: The Code Book. 3: Strategic Inquiry Memory Jogger*, <http://www.thefiveliteracies.com> [accessed 12/02/2008].

Hayden, P. (1995) 'From relations to practice in the empiricism of Gilles Deleuze' *Man and World* 28: 283–302.

Healey, P. (2009) 'The pragmatic tradition in planning thought' *Journal of Planning Education and Research* 28(3): 277–92.

Hillier, J. (2002) *Shadows of Power: An Allegory of Prudence in Land Use Planning*. London: Routledge.

Hillier, J. (2007) *Stretching Beyond the Horizon: A Multiplanar Theory of Spatial Planning and Governance*. Aldershot: Ashgate.

Hillier, J. (2008) 'Interplanary practice: towards a Deleuzean-inspired methodology for creative experimentation in strategic spatial planning' in van den Broeck,

J. and Moulaert, F. (eds) *Empowering the Planning Fields: Ethics, Creativity and Action*. Leuven: Acco, 43–77.

Hillier, J. (2010) 'Encountering Deleuze in Another Place', paper submitted to *European Planning Studies*.

Hillier, J. and Van Wezemael, J. (2010) 'The construction of agency in participatory strategic planning', in de Roo, G., Hillier, J. and Van Wezemael, J. (eds) *Complexity and the Planning of the Built Environment*. Aldershot: Ashgate.

Holland, E. (2006) 'Nomad citizenship and global democracy', in Fuglsang, M. and Sørensen, B.M. (eds) *Deleuze and the Social*. Edinburgh: Edinburgh University Press, 191–206.

Holland, J. (1995) *Hidden Order: How Adaptation Builds Complexity*. Reading, MA: Helix Books.

Huxley, M. (2007) 'Geographies of governmentality', in Crampton, J. and Elden, S. (eds) *Space, Knowledge and Power: Foucault and Geography*. Aldershot: Ashgate, 185–204.

Ilachinski, A. (2004) *Terrorism, Nonlinearity and Complex Adaptive Systems*, <www.cna.org/isaac/terrorism_and_cas.htm> [accessed 12/11/2007].

Innes, J. and Booher, D. (1999) 'Consensus building and complex adaptive systems – a framework for evaluating collaborative planning' *APA Journal* 65(4): 412–23.

Kaufman, E. (1998) 'Introduction', in Kaufman, E. and Heller, K.J. (eds) *Deleuze and Guattari: New Mappings in Politics, Philosophy and Culture*. Minneapolis, MN: University of Minnesota Press, 3–19.

Krebs, V. (2002a) 'Mapping networks of terrorist cells' *Connections* 24(3): 31–4.

Krebs, V. (2002b) 'Uncloaking terrorist networks' *First Monday* 7(4) <http://firstmonday.org/htbin/cgiwrap/bin/ojs/index.php/fm/article/view/941/863> [accessed December 2009].

Kwa, C. (2002) 'Romantic and Baroque conceptions of complex wholes in the sciences', in Law, J. and Mol, A. (eds) *Complexities: Social Studies of Knowledge Practices*. Durham, NC: Duke University Press, 23–52.

Lafontaine, C. (2007) 'The cybernetic matrix of "French Theory"' *Theory, Culture and Society* 24(5): 27–46.

Lambert, G. (2002) *The Non-Philosophy of Gilles Deleuze*. New York: Continuum.

Latham, A. and McCormack, D. (2004) 'Moving cities: rethinking the materialities of urban geographies' *Progress in Human Geography* 28(6): 701–24.

Latour, B. (2004) *Politics of Nature*. Cambridge, MA: Harvard University Press.

Law, J. (2004) 'And if the global were small and noncoherent? Method, complexity and the baroque' *Environment and Planning D, Society and Space* 22: 13–26. [2003] <http://www.lancs.ac.uk/fass/sociology/papers/law-and-if-the-global-were-small.pdf> [accessed December 2009].

Lazzarato, M. (2005) 'Multiplicité, totalité et politique' *Revue Multitudes* 23 <http://www.generation-online.org/p/fplazzarato3.htm> [accessed 23/06/07].

Leibniz, G.W. (1998) [1714] *Monadologie*. Ditzingen: Reclam.

Lepage, R. (2003) 'Interview with Aleksandar Dundjerovic', in Dundjerovic, A. (2003) *The Cinema of Robert Lepage: The Poetics of Memory*. London: Wallflower Press, 147–57.

Lindblom, C. (1975) 'Ths sociology of planning: thought and social interaction', in Bornstein, M. (ed.) *Economic Planning, East and West*. Cambridge, MA: Bellinger, 23–60.

Maasen, S. and Weingart, P. (2000) *Metaphors and the Dynamics of Knowledge*. London: Routledge.

Martin, R. and Sunley, P. (2007) 'Complexity thinking and evolutionary economic geography' *Journal of Economic Geography* 7: 573–601.

Massumi, B. (1992) *A User's Guide to 'Capitalism and Schizophrenia': Deviations from Deleuze and Guattari*. Cambridge, MA: MIT Press.

Massumi, B. (2002) *Parables for the Virtual*. Durham, NC: Duke University Press.

Massumi, B. and Manning, E. (2007) Plenary paper presented at Architecture in the Space of Flows Conference, Newcastle University, Newcastle-upon-Tyne.

May, T. (1993) *Between Genealogy and Epistemology*. Philadelphia, PA: Pennsylvania State University Press.

May, T. (2005) *Gilles Deleuze: An Introduction*. Cambridge: Cambridge University Press.

McCormack, D. (2005) 'Diagramming practice and performance' *Environment and Planning D, Society and Space* 23: 119–47.

Mingers, J. (2002) 'Can social systems be autopoietic? Assessing Luhmann's theory' *The Sociological Review* 50: 278–99.

Moobela, C. (2005) 'From worst slum to best example of regeneration: complexity in the regeneration of Hulme, Manchester' *E:CO* 7(1), <http://connection/ebscohost.com/content/article/1038791138.html;jsessionid=100ACE27A2DF7F6844C1F9C4EA2ECDF6.ehctc1>.

Mouffe, C. (2005) *On the Political*. London: Routledge.

O'Sullivan, S. (2006) *Art Encounters Deleuze and Guattari*. Basingstoke: Palgrave Macmillan.

Patton, P. (1986) 'Godard/Deleuze: sauve qui peut (La Vie)', *Frogger* 20 [copy available from the author on request, via email at <prp@unsw.edu.au>].

Peirce, C.S. (1868) 'On a new list of categories' *Proceedings of the American Academy of Arts and Sciences*, 7: 287–98.

Phillips, J. (2006) 'Agencement/assemblage' *Theory, Culture and Society* 23(2–3): 108–9.

Pløger, J. (2008) 'Foucault's dispositif and the city' *Planning Theory* 7(1): 51–70.

Plummer, P. and Sheppard, E. (2006) 'Geography matters: agency, structures and dynamics' *Journal of Economic Geography* 6: 619–37.

Plummer, P. and Sheppard, E. (2007) 'A methodology for evaluating regional political economy', in Fingelton, B. (ed.) *New Directions in Economic Geography*. Cheltenham: Edward Elgar, 250–76.

Portugali, J. (2000) *Self-Organisation and the City*. Berlin: Springer-Verlag.

Portugali, J. (2008) 'Learning from paradoxes about prediction and planning in self-organising cities' *Planning Theory* 7(3): 248–62.

Prigogine, I. (1968) *Introduction à la Théorie des Processus Irréversibles*. Paris: Dunod.

Prigogine, I. (1980) *From Being to Becoming: Time and Complexity in the Physical Sciences*. San Francisco, CA: W.H. Freeman and Co.

Prigogine, I. (2004) 'Beyond being and becoming' *NPQ*, Fall: 5–12.

Prigogine, I. and Stengers, I. (1984) [1979] *Order out of Chaos*. New York: Bantam.

Rajchman, J. (1998) *Constructions*. Cambridge, MA: MIT Press.

Rajchman, J. (2000) *The Deleuze Connections*. Cambridge, MA: MIT Press.

Rheinberger, H-J. (1997) *Towards a History of Epistemic Things: Synthesising Proteins in the Test Tube*. Stanford, CA: Stanford University Press.

Richardson, K. and Cilliers, P. (2001) 'What is complexity science? A view from different directions' *Emergence* 3(1): 5–23.

Roberts, N. (2000a) 'Coping with wicked problems', paper presented at International Public Management Network Research Conference, Sydney, 4–6th March. <http://www.psmprogram.sa.gov.au/wp-content/uploads/2008/02/roberts-n-2000-wicked-problems.pdf>

Roberts, N. (2000b) 'Wicked problems and network approaches to resolution' *International Public Management Review* 1(1) <http://www.ipmr.net> [accessed 06/07 2006].

Rorty, R. (1982) *The Consequences of Pragmatism*. Brighton: Harvester.

Rose, M. (2007) 'The problem of power and the politics of landscape: stopping the Greater Cairo ring road' *Transactions of the Institute of British Geographers* NS 32: 460–76.

Rushdie, S. (1990) *Haroun and the Sea of Stories*. London: Granta.

Sager, T. (1994) *Communicative Planning Theory*. Aldershot: Avebury.

Sager, T. (2002) *Democratic Planning and Social Choice Dilemmas*. Aldershot: Ashgate.

Semetsky, I. (2003) 'Deleuze's new image of thought, or Dewey revisited' *Educational Philosophy and Theory* 35(1): 17–29.

Semetsky, I. (2006) *Deleuze, Education and Becoming*. Rotterdam: Sense Publishers.

Serres, M. (1996) 'Interview with Hari Kunzru' *Mute* 4(Winter/Spring), <http://www.jbf.dial.pipex.com/art_tech_ec_files/serres.htm> [accessed March 2006].

Serres, M. (2000) [1977] *The Birth of Physics* (trans. Hawkes, J.). Manchester: University of Manchester Press.

Sheller, M. (2004) 'Mobile publics: beyond the network perspective' *Environment and Planning D, Society and Space* 22: 39–52.

Skott-Myhre, H. (2005) 'Towards a minoritarian psychology of immanence and a psychotherapy of flight: political meditations on the society of control' *parallax* 11(2): 44–59.

Smith, J. and Jenks, C. (2005) 'Complexity, ecology and the materiality of information' *Theory, Culture and Society* 22(5): 141–63.

Stagoll, C. (2005) 'Event', in Parr, A. (ed.) *The Deleuze Dictionary*. Edinburgh: Edinburgh University Press, 87–9.

Tarter, C.J. and Hoy, W. (1998) 'Toward a contingency theory of decision making' *Journal of Educational Administration* 36(3): 212–28.

Thanem, T. and Linstead, S. (2006) 'The trembling organisation: order, change and the philosophy of the virtual', in Fuglsang, M. and Sørensen, B. (eds) *Deleuze and the Social*, Edinburgh: Edinburgh University Press, 39–57.

Thrift, N. (1996) *Spatial Formations*. London: Sage.

Thrift, N. (1999) 'The place of complexity' *Theory, Culture and Society* 16(3): 31–70.

Tsoukas, H. and Chia, R. (2002) 'On organisational becoming: rethinking organisational change' *Organization Science* 13(5); 567–82.

UN-HABITAT (2009) *Global Report on Human Settlements: Revisiting Urban Planning.* *Nairobi:* UN-HABITAT.

Urry, J. (2005) 'The complexity turn' *Theory, Culture and Society* 22(5): 1–14.

Venn, C. (2006) 'Cultural theory, biopolitics, and the question of power' *Theory, Culture and Society* 24(3): 111–24.

White, H., Godart, F. and Corona, V. (2007) 'Mobilizing identities: uncertainty and control in strategy' *Theory, Culture and Society* 24: 181–202.

Williams, J. (2003) *Gilles Deleuze's 'Difference and Repetition': A Critical Introduction and Guide.* Edinburgh: Edinburgh University Press.

Wise, P. (2002) 'Cultural policy and multiplicities' *International Journal of Cultural Policy* 8(2): 221–31.

Wise, P. (2006) 'Australia's Gold Coast: a city producing itself', in Lindner, C. (ed.) *Urban Space and Cityscapes.* London: Routledge, 177–91.

Woodward, K., Jones, J.P. III and Marston, S. (2007) 'The eagle and the flies, a fable for the micro', SECONS Discussion Forum, Contribution No. 12, SECONS, Bonn <www.giub.uni-bonn.de/grabher> [accessed 01/09/2007].

Index